The Minor Prophets

The Minor Prophets

An Exegetical and Expository Commentary

Volume 3
Zephaniah, Haggai, Zechariah, and Malachi

Edited by

Thomas Edward McComiskey

Baker Books
A Division of Baker Book House Co
Grand Rapids, Michigan 49516

Library of Congress Cataloging-in-Publication Data

(Revised for vol. 3)

The Minor Prophets.

Includes bibliographical references and index.
Contents: v. 1. Hosea, Joel, and Amos—vol. 2. Obadiah, Jonah, Micah, Nahum, and Habakkuk—vol. 3. Zephaniah, Haggai, Zechariah, and Malachi.
1. Bible.—O.T.—Minor Prophets—Commentaries. I. McComiskey, Thomas Edward. II. Bible. O.T. Minor Prophets. English. New Revised Standard. 1992.
BS 1560.M47 1992   224′.907   91-38388
  ISBN 0-8010-6285-3 (v. 1)
  ISBN 0-8010-6307-8 (v. 2)
  ISBN 0-8010-2055-7 (v. 3)

For information about academic books, resources for Christian leaders, and all new releases available from Baker Book House, visit our web site:
                    http://www.bakerbooks.com

Contents

Abbreviations

Bibliographical

ANEP James B. Pritchard (ed.), *The Ancient Near East in Pictures Relating to the Old Testament* (2d ed., Princeton: Princeton University Press, 1969)

BDB Francis Brown, Samuel R. Driver, and Charles A. Briggs, *A Hebrew and English Lexicon of the Old Testament* (Oxford: Clarendon, 1907; corrected printing in 1953)

BHS Karl Elliger and Wilhelm Rudolph (eds.), *Biblia Hebraica Stuttgartensia* (Stuttgart: Deutsche Bibelgesellschaft, 1977)

GKC Emil Kautzsch (ed.), *Gesenius' Hebrew Grammar* (trans. A. E. Cowley; 2d ed.; Oxford: Clarendon, 1910)

IBHS Bruce K. Waltke and Michael O'Connor, *An Introduction to Biblical Hebrew Syntax* (Winona Lake, Ind.: Eisenbrauns, 1990)

ISBE Geoffrey W. Bromiley et al. (eds.), *The International Standard Bible Encyclopedia* (4 vols.; Grand Rapids: Eerdmans, 1979–88)

KB Ludwig Koehler and Walter Baumgartner, *Lexicon in Veteris Testamenti Libros* (Leiden: Brill/Grand Rapids: Eerdmans, 1953)

TDOT G. Johannes Botterweck and Helmer Ringgren (eds.), *Theological Dictionary of the Old Testament* (trans. David E. Green et al.; 8 vols. to date; Grand Rapids: Eerdmans, 1974–)

TWOT R. Laird Harris, Gleason L. Archer Jr., and Bruce K. Waltke (eds.), *Theological Wordbook of the Old Testament* (2 vols.; Chicago: Moody, 1980)

Bible Versions

AV Authorized (King James) Version
JB Jerusalem Bible
NAB New American Bible
NASB New American Standard Bible
NEB New English Bible
NIV New International Version
NRSV New Revised Standard Version
RSV Revised Standard Version

General

LXX Septuagint
MT Masoretic Text

Hebrew Transliteration Scheme

Consonants		Vowels		
א	ʾ	בָ	ā	*qāmeṣ*
ב	b	בַ	a	*pataḥ*
ג	g	בֶ	e	*sĕgôl*
ד	d	בֵ	ē	*ṣērê*
ה	h	בִ	i	short *ḥîreq*
ו	w	בִ	ī	long *ḥîreq* written defectively
ז	z	בָ	o	*qāmeṣ ḥāṭûp*
ח	ḥ	בוֹ	ô	*ḥōlem* written fully
ט	ṭ	בֹ	ō	*ḥōlem* written defectively
י	y	בוּ	û	*šûreq*
כ ך	k	בֻ	u	short *qibbûṣ*
ל	l	בֻ	ū	long *qibbûṣ* written defectively
מ ם	m	חַ	a	furtive *pataḥ*
נ ן	n	בָה	â	final *qāmeṣ hēʾ*
ס	s	בֶי	ê	*sĕgôl yôd* (בֶי = êy)
ע	ʿ	בֵי	ê	*ṣērê yôd* (בֵי = êy)
פ ף	p	בִי	î	*ḥîreq yôd* (בִי = îy)
צ ץ	ṣ	בָיו	āyw	
ק	q	בֲ	ă	*ḥāṭēp pataḥ*
ר	r	בֱ	ĕ	*ḥāṭēp sĕgôl*
שׂ	ś	בֳ	ŏ	*ḥāṭēp qāmeṣ*
שׁ	š	בְ	ĕ	vocal *šĕwāʾ*
ת	t	בְ	–	silent *šĕwāʾ*

Introduction

The corpus of biblical books we call the Minor Prophets has not enjoyed great prominence in the history of biblical interpretation. It is not difficult to understand why this is so. Where is the edification for a modern Christian in a dirge celebrating the downfall of an ancient city? How can the gloomy forecasts of captivity for Israel and Judah lift the heart today? The Minor Prophets seem to have been preoccupied with nations and events that have little relevance to today's world. How unlike the New Testament they are!

A careful study of these prophets reveals, however, that many of the themes they expound transit the Testaments. They speak of the love of God as well as his justice. Their prophecies are not all doom, but are often rich with hope. Hosea based his hope on God's compassion. Joel envisioned a new era for the people of God. Amos spoke of the restoration of David's collapsing monarchy. And Micah foresaw the coming Ruler whose birthplace would be the insignificant town of Bethlehem. That these prophets often expressed themselves in culturally and historically conditioned forms that seem foreign to us should not diminish the force of their messages. This should challenge us to discover how the prophets faced the foreboding circumstances of their times and how their words illumined the dark night of human rebellion and divine justice. Anyone who reads the Minor Prophets and hears only words of recrimination and judgment has not read them fairly. Within the dismal events these prophets describe lurks the hand of God, and beyond these events is the bright prospect of a kingdom inaugurated by one whom Zechariah portrays as suffering betrayal, piercing, and eventual death. The Minor Prophets are not as time bound as we may think.

The purpose of this commentary is to clarify the messages of these spokesmen for God by bringing the reader into the structures of language in which these messages found expression. While readers who do not know Hebrew may find the Exegesis (at the top of each page) imposing, the authors have translated the constructions so that these readers may comprehend the discussion and have access to the Hebrew text. The readers may thus observe more deeply how the author has grappled with the problems of the text. Readers of English commentaries do not always have access to this level of interpretation.

The translations in parentheses following each Hebrew construction are keyed to the author's translation. This translation, which appears in the left column of each translation page, is a literal rendition of the Hebrew. The column on the right of each translation page is the New Revised Standard Version (NRSV). The reader thus has at hand two perspectives on the sense of the text. Where the Masoretic versification differs from the NRSV, the Hebrew verse number is given first, with the English verse number in square brackets.

The Exposition (at the bottom of each page) is designed to amplify the conclusions reached in the Exegesis. The authors frequently discuss related theological and hermeneutical issues in the Exposition. The Hebrew appears in transliteration here. This alerts the reader who knows Hebrew to the construction that the author is discussing without encumbering the reader who does not know Hebrew with unfamiliar characters. It also aids the reader by facilitating pronunciation of the Hebrew constructions. The preacher will find in this section observations on the text that will stimulate ideas for using the Minor Prophets in contemporary preaching.

The Hebrew scholar, as well as the student of Hebrew, will appreciate the depth of interaction with the Hebrew text that characterizes the Exegesis. The authors have made every effort to utilize the highest standards of scholarly exegesis and to interact with the current literature throughout their commentaries. The introductions to the commentaries cover various issues relating to the individual prophecies.

The editor and authors present this work to the world of biblical scholarship with the hope that it will contribute to a deeper understanding of the messages of the Minor Prophets and their relevance for us today. If this commentary causes the voices of these ancient men of God to ring with greater clarity in a world that sorely needs spiritual and moral strength, the effort will have been worthwhile.

I wish to express my appreciation to the authors for their scholarly contributions, cooperation, and patience throughout the years in which this work has been in preparation. I owe a debt of gratitude to Allan Fisher of Baker Book House for his encouragement.

Thomas Edward McComiskey
Hawthorn Woods, Illinois

In Memoriam

Thomas Edward McComiskey
(1928–1996)

Husband, father, leading scholar, master teacher—Thomas E. McComiskey was at all times a model of the balanced Christian leader.

The commentary on Zechariah and the edition of this volume on the Minor Prophets were the last scholarly contributions of Tom McComiskey, professor of Old Testament at Trinity Evangelical Divinity School. This volume is a fitting memorial, since his great love and gift was an exegetically meticulous and theologically deep exposition of the Old Testament.

Tom McComiskey was one of a group of scholars who, from the 1960s to the 1990s, led a generation of Old Testament scholars to the place of eminence that evangelical scholarship enjoys today in the larger world of academia. We are all indebted to his leadership and vision. His great passion in his later years was biblical theology. He singlehandedly launched the American College of Biblical Theologians. His impact will be felt in evangelical scholarship for years to come.

Grant R. Osborne
Professor of New Testament
Trinity Evangelical Divinity School

Zephaniah

Introduction

There is a compelling simplicity about Zephaniah's message: he has only one topic, and he never digresses from it. His book opens with a vision of world disaster, embracing both the outside world (1:2–3) and the professing people of God (1:4–6). He identifies this disaster as "the day of the LORD" (1:7–18) and calls for preparation (2:1–3). His next concern is to show this day in action, shattering the nations (2:4–15) but merited equally by Jerusalem (3:1–5). Unexpectedly—as if forcing itself into the prophet's consciousness—the day also has a spark of hope (2:6–7, 9d, 11), and the remainder of the prophecy (2:8–3:20) is concerned with how this comes about. Zephaniah has handed down this message of doom and hope in a shapely, stylish form. It is a coherent, compelling eschatological vision.

Theology

Theologically, Zephaniah is not innovative, standing for mainstream Yahwism. Remarkably, many commentators find him to be without a "gospel" of the mercy of God and with only the most meager of hopes that anything can be done to escape the rigors of that day. Some even refuse him any message of hope at all, deferring passages of hope to a later date and another hand. This dubious approach arises from two main causes: first, from an inadequate grasp of how the Lord defined his name at the time of the exodus. It is a two-sided name, including both salvation (for Israel) and judgment (for Egypt). He is by nature the God of holy wrath and the God of holy hope—inseparable components of his deity. Second, a gospel of mercy is denied to Zephaniah through a failure to contextualize what he actually said (see the Exegesis and Exposition of 2:3). There was no need for him to

Contributor:
J. Alec Motyer
B.A., M.A., B.D.
Principal and Dean
of Trinity College,
Bristol (Retired)

897

spell out a gospel message to those who already knew that the Lord had provided the way whereby they might return to him in penitence and faith.

Author

Nothing is known about Zephaniah save what little his book reveals. Alone of the prophets he traces his ancestry back four generations, but he gives no sure explanation why. Craigie (*Twelve Prophets*, p. 106) may be correct in observing that it simply reflects his appreciation of his family roots, but why stop at four generations? It seems more persuasive to surmise that the Hezekiah whom he names as his great-great-grandfather was none other than King Hezekiah (2 Kings 18–20; 2 Chron. 29–32; Isa. 36–39; J. Smith, *Zephaniah*, pp. 182–83; G. Smith, *Twelve Prophets*, p. 46; Baker, *Zephaniah*, p. 91). The absence of the title *king* with Hezekiah's name can be explained by Zephaniah's contemporaries knowing that he was of royal blood. Zephaniah's awareness of the royal lifestyle (1:8) may be a small straw in the wind. More significant is that he concerns himself only with the upper echelons of society—princes, judges, prophets, priests (1:8–9; 3:3–4)—and not directly with the average Israelite. In this regard he is a "city prophet," like Isaiah and Micah. Unlike them he does not allude to the lot of the poor, only to the misconduct of the religious and civil leaders. His book does not include a call-narrative or an indication of how he came to be a prophet. It does reveal, however, a man with impeccable prophetic credentials (see the Exegesis and Exposition of 1:1).

Date

The date given for Zephaniah's ministry, the days of Josiah (2 Kings 22–23; 2 Chron. 34–35), suits the contents of the book. Josiah came to the throne of Judah following the religiously disastrous reigns of Manasseh and Amon (2 Kings 21; 2 Chron. 33). The land was in desperate need of religious reform and spiritual awakening, and in the purposes of God, Josiah was the reformer. The narrative in 2 Kings leaps to Josiah's eighteenth year, when he initiated the repair of the house of the Lord (22:3–7). Second Chronicles reveals some background to this by recording that "in the eighth year of his reign, while he was still a boy, he began to seek the God of his ancestor David" (34:3). It is interesting to speculate (see the Exposition of 1:1) that Zephaniah may have been the godly influence within the palace, turning the young king's mind to the Lord. This, of course, would account for his tracing his pedigree back to Hezekiah, the earlier reforming king.

Circumstances were favorable to Josiah's acting with a free hand in Judah (and Israel—see 2 Kings 23:15–20), for he came to the throne in 640 B.C. when the Assyrian Empire, within which Judah was a vassal state, was in terminal decline. In the east, Babylon was rising in importance; in the west, there was no effective imperial rule. Under Psamtik I (664–610 B.C.), Egypt withheld tribute from 655 onward. "As Assyria lost her grip on her empire, Judah found herself . . . by default . . . a free country" (Bright, *History of Israel*, p. 316).

The part played by the Scythians in this period is somewhat uncertain. A nomadic people from southern Russia, they penetrated the ancient Near East in the early eighth century, lived in an uneasy alliance with Assyria, and (according to Herodotus 1.103–5) ran wild over the whole region, reaching as far as Egypt. It used to be assumed that Zephaniah discerned in this Scythian threat the onset of the day of the Lord. All this must be viewed with caution, although Oppenheim ("Scythians") believes Scythians raided along the Palestine coast, were bought off by Psamtik, and sacked Ashdod and Ashkelon. Rice (*Scythians*, p. 45) dates a Scythian invasion as late as 611 B.C., but discerns no particular menace to Judah.

It has to be asked at what point in Josiah's reign Zephaniah ministered, though little hangs on reaching a firm conclusion. As is pointed out in the Exegesis of 1:4, the reference to a "remnant" of Baal does not necessarily require a date after the reforms of Josiah had swept the main Baal shrines out of the land. The reference to Baalism, the astral cults, and the worship of Molech (1:4–5) sounds like an evil inheritance from Manasseh and Amon, and the reference to the compromising behavior of princes and priests (1:8–9) suggests a time in the king's earlier days before he began to implement reform. Since Josiah reigned 640–609 B.C. (Thiele, *Mysterious Numbers*, p. 180), Zephaniah's ministry may be placed in the second half of the seventh century.

In a sense, the history of the times has nothing to say about Zephaniah's message. Throughout the book there is a sense of distance from historical events. For example, the predictions regarding the day of the Lord are full of military motifs—but without reference to any particular enemy and thus resistant to any attempt to define the enemy. Zephaniah, says G. Smith (*Twelve Prophets*, p. 48), "tears himself loose from history altogether. . . . The Day of the Lord assumes what we call 'the supernatural.'" Zephaniah is rooted in the flow of history (see the Exposition of 2:4–15), but his concern is only with the goal—the eschaton—the day when calamitous human efforts to run the world will coincide in an awesome climax with the Lord's purposes of judgment and hope.

Unity

Since J. G. Eichhorn's commentary in 1824, the Book of Zephaniah has experienced much the same specialist treatment as the rest of the prophets, ranging from F. Schwally (see G. Smith, *Twelve Prophets*, pp. 41, 43), who denied all of chapters 2–3 to Zephaniah, save for 2:12–15, to P. R. House (*Zephaniah*), who sees the whole book as a dramatic unity. One cannot but be impressed alike by the self-assurance and the subjectivism of those early literary commentators, much of whose approach sadly remains in BHS.

Many have sought to give objectivity to their literary judgments by searching for a metrical arrangement in Zephaniah and then passing judgment on lines and passages that seem not to conform. J. Smith (*Zephaniah*, p. 175) urges that "the science of Hebrew metre is as yet [in 1911] in an inchoate state. . . . Conclusions as to the integrity of a text which are based solely or primarily upon metrical considerations are inevitably open to grave suspicion." Unfortunately, Smith did not remember his own caveat! More recently, literary criticism has taken a more hopeful line in searching not for a linear metrical schema but for poetic patterns and shapes to whole poems. In the case of Zephaniah, as the present commentary seeks to show, this approach calls into question allegations of intrusive or disruptive passages and later insertions. Not only the book as a whole but each separate item within it displays a remarkable and often beautiful cohesion, setting at a discount also the tendency to devalue the literary quality and competence of Zephaniah and revealing him as a literary master on the pattern of Isaiah.

The book consists of carefully honed oracles accurately built into a coherent message. While a date long after the time of Zephaniah is sometimes suggested (Smith and Lacheman, "Authorship of the Book of Zephaniah," p. 137; see House, *Zephaniah*, p. 13), the contents of the book suit the date it proposes for itself. It would presuppose a curious mentality to think that Zephaniah should be certain that he is the vehicle of the very words of God and then leave these words to the uncertain chances of an indefinite transmission process and the editorial hands of some future unknown. There is no difficulty in assuming that the prophet was also the poet and the editor.

Text

It is often alleged that the Masoretic Text of Zephaniah is in a sorry state of preservation. Close examination, however, reveals that this opinion may have arisen through failure to recognize the special needs of poetic diction, especially the way poetry delights in brevity, aphorism, and allusion. When judged according to Hebrew prose, some verses that might otherwise be dismissed as impossible, even grammatically monstrous, are rather found to conform to poetic norms—and usually to exemplify usages known elsewhere in the Hebrew Bible. Verhoef (*Haggai and Malachi*, p. 18) observes that "my fifteen year experience in Bible translation has strengthened my conviction that the majority of the proposed alterations to the text [of the Old Testament] . . . are really unnecessary." This is very true of Zephaniah.

The Septuagint is uniformly unhelpful. One soon comes to realize that every least obscurity in the Hebrew text baffled the Septuagint translator(s) and led them to produce a piece of Greek often without clear meaning of its own and shedding no light on its Hebrew original.

Analysis

It is usually presumed that all the prophets originally delivered their messages by preaching. This may indeed be the case, provided we note that in every case the "books" of the prophets contain the carefully crafted essence of that preaching, the essential word of the Lord preserved for posterity and maybe also publicized at the time along the lines of Isaiah 8:1 and 30:8. We actually see this recording work in progress in Jeremiah 36. If all this is true of Zephaniah, it is also true that, as he has bequeathed his work to us, the original preaching (if there was such) has disappeared into a coherent book presentation, a structured treatise on the theme of "the day of the Lord." As the following outline of contents shows, following the superscription, the book falls into three parts:

Superscription (1:1)
I. **The End of the World: Is There Any Hope? (1:2–2:3)**
  A. The End Announced—for the World (1:2–3a) and for Judah (1:3b–6)
  B. The End Described—for Judah (1:7–14a) and for the World (1:14b–18)
  C. An Appeal to Readiness—to Judah (2:1–2) and to the World (2:3)
II. **Judgment and Hope: An Enigma (2:4–3:8)**
  A. World Overthrow, Hope for Israel (2:4–15)
  B. The Failure of Judah (3:1–5)
  C. Hope in a Day of Wrath (3:6–8)
III. **The End of the World: Hope in All Its Glory (3:9–20)**
  A. The Enigma Solved (3:9–13)
  B. Oneness of Joy (3:14–17)
  C. The Lord's People, the Praise of All the Earth (3:18–20)

Further exploration shows how carefully this book has been crafted. The entire book represents a complex chiastic format:

I. **The End of the World: Is There Any Hope? (1:2–2:3)**
  A the end (1:2–6)
    a¹ the world (1:2–3a)
    b¹ Judah (1:3b–6)
  B the day (1:7–18)
    b² Judah: the imminent day (1:7–14a)
    a² the world: the bitter day (1:14b–18)
  A′ the end: a probation time (2:1–3)
    b³ Judah (2:1)
    c¹ the critical time (2:2)
    a³ the world (2:3)

II. **Judgment and Hope: An Enigma (2:4–3:8)**
  A the surrounding world: its overthrow, Israel's possession (2:4–15)
    • west: Philistia—its disappearance (2:4–6) and Judah's possession (2:7)
    • east: Moab/Ammon—judgment by the God of Israel (2:8–9c), Israel's possession (2:9d–10), and the world's worship (2:11)
    • south: Cush—slain by the Lord's sword (2:12)
    • north: Assyria—its disappearance (2:13–15)
  B the failure of Judah (3:1–5)
  C hopeful waiting for the day of wrath! (3:6–8)
    a⁴ the world (3:6)
    b⁴ Judah (3:7–8a)
    a⁵ the world (3:8b)

III. **The End of the World: Hope in All Its Glory (3:9–20)**
  A the enigma solved (3:9–13)
    a⁶ the uniting of the world: Babel reversed (3:9–10)
    b⁵ the purging of the people: Jerusalem purified (3:11–13c)
    c² the time of peace: Eden restored (3:13d)
  B oneness of joy: the people and the Lord (3:14–17)
  C the Lord's people, the praise of all the earth (3:18–20)
    b⁶ the perfected people (3:18–19)
    a⁷ the attracted world (3:20)

Section I is demarcated by an *inclusio*: the opening poem (1:2–6) climaxes on the charge of failure to seek (*biqqēš*) the Lord; the concluding poem three times commands to put this fault right (2:3). This is the major section on the day of the Lord: *yôm* (day) occurs at 1:7, 8, 9, 10, 14, 15 (five times), 16, 18; 2:3. The parallel *ʿēt* (time) occurs at 1:12. Both words recur near the end of the book: *yôm* in 3:8, 11, 16, and *ʿēt* in 3:19, 20 (twice).

Section II opens with *kî* (for), introducing an explanation of the foregoing proclamation of judgment. It also includes the enigmas that amid judgment on the world (2:4–6, 8–9c, 12, 13–15; 3:6, 8b) there is also hope (2:11b) and that Judah is promised an inheritance (2:7, 9d) while at the same time meriting judgment with the world (3:6–8). The section is bracketed by an *inclusio* involving *mēʾên yôšēb* (without inhabitant; 2:5; 3:6) and—typical of Zephaniah—the same word, *pāqad* (2:7; 3:7), with two shades of meaning.

Sections I and II belong together thematically with their concentration on judgment and wrath. The Lord's "cutting" (*kārat*) of humankind and Judah (1:3–4) and of the world and Judah (3:6–7) forms an *inclusio*. The "outstretched hand" of God, portending judgment, overshadows both Judah (1:4) and Assyria (2:13). Common to both sections are the following terms and phrases: "in the fire of his jealousy all the earth will be eaten up" (1:18; 3:8), *pinâ* (corner tower; 1:16; 3:6), *šāpak* (to pour out; 1:17; 3:8), *šāmam* and cognate words (to be desolate or ruined; 1:13; 2:4, 9, 13, 15; 3:6), and *nĕʾum* (this is the word of . . . ; which acts as a further *inclusio* in 1:2, 3, 10; 3:8). The balance between the two concluding poems of each section, 2:1–3 and 3:6–8, creates a rounded formation:

a   Judah (2:1–2)
b   the world with Judah (2:3)
b′   the world (3:6)
a′   Judah with the world (3:7–8)

Section III moves between the reference to world devotion to the name of the Lord (3:9) and world acknowledgment of the name of Israel (3:19–20). Like section II, it opens with *kî*, introducing an explanation of the preceding enigma of a judgment into which the note of hope intrudes: the same Lord who justly judges also plans a glorious reversal whereby the divisiveness of sin will be canceled worldwide (3:9–10), Jerusalem will be renewed (3:11–13c), and Eden will be restored (3:13d). Following this the book ends on a rhapsodic note with the Lord and his people wrapped in mutual joy (3:14–17), with the Lord's people restored and central to the whole world (3:18–20).

Sections II and III are bound together by an *inclusio* formed by the words *šāb šĕbût* (restore captivity; 2:7; 3:20). Note also the words *šĕʾērît* (remnant; 2:7, 9; 3:13), *rāʿâ* (to pasture; 2:7; 3:13), *yārāʾ* (to fear; 3:7, 15, 16), and *ʿālaz* (to exult; 3:14) or *ʿallîz* (exultant; 2:15; 3:11). The effect of these links is to bind the messages of judgment and hope together: the latter is not alien to the former but intrinsic and inseparable.

Sections I and III contain matching expressions of universality that form an *inclusio* for the whole book: *pĕnê hāʾădāmâ* (the face of the earth; 1:2–3) and *kol-hāʾāreṣ* (all the earth; 3:19–20).

Note also "the word of the LORD" (1:2) and "says the LORD" (3:20). Significant contrasts include the false king (*malcām*; 1:5) and the true king (*melek yiśrāʾēl yhwh*; 3:15), the baffled warrior and the saving warrior (*gibbôr*; 1:14; 3:17), the name to be obliterated (1:4) and the admired name (3:19–20), Jerusalem under judgment (1:4, 12) and Jerusalem restored to divine favor (3:14, 16), the call to humility (*ʿănāwâ*; 2:3) and the humble people (*ʿānî*; 3:12), the prevalence of deceit (*mirmâ*; 1:9) and the city free of deceit (*tarmît*; 3:13). The book also begins and ends with oracles based on the formulas *in that day* and *at that time*:

a   visitation upon those who act with deceit (1:8)
b   voices of terror (1:10)
c   the complacent assumption of an inactive God (1:12)
a′ past rebellious doings and no more deceit (3:11)
b′   voices of joy; no more fear (3:16)
c′   the active Lord restoring his people (3:19–20)

Thus the divine justice that must be expressed in wrath (section I) is exactly balanced by divine love (section III; 3:17), which works renewal and brings restoration for the Lord's people and for the whole world.

All three sections begin and end with oracles combining the world and the people of God. The opening oracles of each section (1:2–6; 2:4–7; 3:9–13) reflect the theme of the book: unrelieved judgment becomes judgment mingled with hope and then total hope. The concluding oracles of the first two sections (2:1–3; 3:6–8) are thematically linked (note the same thematic linkage of 3:18–20). The people whose shame was in all the earth (3:19) become the people whose praise is in all the earth (3:20).

Select Bibliography

Baker, David W. *Nahum, Habakkuk, and Zephaniah: An Introduction and Commentary*. Tyndale Old Testament Commentaries. Downers Grove, Ill.: InterVarsity/Leicester: InterVarsity, 1988.

Bright, John. *A History of Israel*. 3d ed. Philadelphia: Westminster, 1981.

Craigie, Peter C. *Twelve Prophets*. Vol. 2. Daily Study Bible. Philadelphia: Westminster/Edinburgh: Saint Andrew, 1985.

Cross, Frank M. "The Divine Warrior in Israel's Early Cult." Pp. 11–30 in *Biblical Motifs: Origins and Transformations*. Edited by Alexander Altmann. Cambridge, Mass.: Harvard University Press, 1966.

Davidson, Andrew B. *Hebrew Syntax*. 3d ed. Edinburgh: T. & T. Clark, 1901.

Dennett, Edward. *Zechariah the Prophet*. London: Broom & Rouse, 1888.

Dhorme, Édouard. *A Commentary on the Book of Job*. Translated by Harold Knight. London: Nelson, 1967.

Driver, Samuel R. *A Treatise on the Use of the Tenses in Hebrew*. 3d ed. Oxford: Clarendon, 1892.

Eaton, J. H. *Obadiah, Nahum, Habakkuk, and Zephaniah: Introduction and Commentary*. Torch Bible Commentaries. London: SCM, 1961.

House, Paul R. *Zephaniah: A Prophetic Drama*. Journal for the Study of the Old Testament Supplement 69/Bible and Literature Series 16. Sheffield: Almond, 1988.

Johnson, Aubrey R. *The Cultic Prophet in Ancient Israel*. 2d ed. Cardiff: University of Wales Press, 1962.

Kapelrud, Arvid S. *The Message of the Prophet Zephaniah*. Oslo: Universitetsforlaget, 1975.

Kleinert, Paul. *Zephaniah*. Translated and enlarged by Charles Elliott in *Commentary on the Holy Scriptures* by John P. Lange. English translation edited by Philip Schaff. Reprinted Grand Rapids: Zondervan, n.d.

McKay, John W. *Religion in Judah under the Assyrians, 732–609 BC*. Studies in Biblical Theology 2/26. London: SCM/Naperville: Allenson, 1973.

Mowinckel, Sigmund. *He That Cometh*. Translated by George W. Anderson. Oxford: Blackwell, 1956.

Oppenheim, A. Leo. "Scythians." P. 252 in *The Interpreter's Dictionary of the Bible*. Vol. 4. Edited by George A. Buttrick. Nashville: Abingdon, 1962.

Pusey, Edward B. *The Minor Prophets: A Commentary*. Vol. 2. Reprinted Grand Rapids: Baker, 1950.

Rad, Gerhard von. *Old Testament Theology*. 2 vols. Translated by David M. G. Stalker. Edinburgh: Oliver & Boyd/New York: Harper & Row, 1962–65.

Rice, Tamara T. *The Scythians*. Ancient Peoples and Places 2. London: Thames & Hudson/New York: Praeger, 1957.

Smith, George A. *The Book of the Twelve Prophets, Commonly Called the Minor*. Vol. 2. Rev. ed. New York: Harper, 1928.

Smith, John M. P. *A Critical and Exegetical Commentary on Micah, Zephaniah, and Nahum*. International Critical Commentary. Edinburgh: T. & T. Clark, 1911.

Smith, Louise P., and Ernest R. Lacheman. "The Authorship of the Book of Zephaniah." *Journal of Near Eastern Studies* 9 (1950): 137–42.

Smith, Ralph L. *Micah–Malachi*. Word Biblical Commentary 32. Waco: Word, 1984.

Thiele, Edwin R. *The Mysterious Numbers of the Hebrew Kings*. 2d ed. Grand Rapids: Zondervan, 1983.

Tidwell, N. L. A. "*Wā'ōmar* (Zech 3:5) and the Genre of Zechariah's Fourth Vision." *Journal of Biblical Literature* 94 (1975): 343–55.

Verhoef, Pieter A. *The Books of Haggai and Malachi.* New International Commentary on the Old Testament. Grand Rapids: Eerdmans, 1987.

Wenham, Gordon J. *Genesis 1–15.* Word Biblical Commentary 1. Waco: Word, 1987.

Superscription (1:1)

MOTYER

1 The word of the LORD that came to Zephaniah son of Cushi, son of Gedaliah, son of Amariah, son of Hezekiah, in the days of Josiah son of Amon, king of Judah.

NRSV

1 The word of the LORD that came to Zephaniah son of Cushi son of Gedaliah son of Amariah son of Hezekiah, in the days of King Josiah son of Amon of Judah.

1:1. הָיָה . . . דְּבַר־יְהוָה (the word of the LORD . . . came): In translation, this formula requires a verb of motion, but Hebrew uses the verb הָיָה (to be). The sense of this formula is that the word of the Lord became a living reality to Zephaniah. The verb הָיָה goes beyond "being or existing" to include the sense of active presence (Hag. 1:1). The translation "came" usefully expresses one side of the truth by pointing to the origin of this revelation in the Lord, while its sense of becoming an active, present reality emphasizes another side: that is, Zephaniah was inspired to receive, understand, and then express the divine word without tarnishing its divine reality and truth. The first words of Zephaniah's book thus express the reception of the divine word; the last words, אָמַר יְהוָה (says the LORD; 3:20), complete the picture. What came from God has been spoken on earth by a man without ceasing to be what the Lord says.

1:1. Part I of the Book of Zephaniah contains three sections: 1:2–6 announces judgment on the world, 1:7–18 relates the day of the Lord to the themes of nearness and bitterness, and 2:1–3 urges preparation while there is time. The first section may be subdivided into 1:2–3b and 1:3c–6, with each subsection beginning with the phrases *this is the word of* and *from the face of the earth*. The movement is from the general (earth, human, beast; 1:2–3) to the specific (Judah, priests, those who bow; 1:4–6). The thought is expressed in the following symmetrical arrangement:

A the world under judgment (2–3b)
  a comprehensive: everything (2)
  b specific: the human and animal creation (3a)
  c the moral factor (3b)
B humankind under judgment (3c–6)
  a' comprehensive: humankind (3c)
  b' specific: Judah (4a)
  c' the religious factor (4b–6)

Beginning the record of his ministry with the wonder of coming to possess "the word of the LORD," Zephaniah brings the record to a conclusion in 3:20 with the affirmation "says the LORD." He was a faithful steward of the divine word (compare Acts 6:2, 4; 20:20, 27; 2 Tim. 1:13; 2:15; 3:14–17; 4:2; Titus 1:9). As in all the prophets, we find in Zephaniah, first, the objective fact of divine revelation: "The word of the LORD came" (see the Exegesis). This "coming" (*hāyâ*) of the word is, more literally, its *becoming a reality* in the mind of the prophet. We know nothing of the processes involved. This is a work of God. We do know, however, that it was the experience of specially prepared people (Jer. 1:4) who were brought into divine fellowship (Isa. 6:5–8; Ezek. 1:28–2:2) and within that fellowship made privy to divine secrets (Jer. 23:18, 22; Amos 3:7). There was no crushing of human personality or overriding of human mental processes; rather, the prophetic state lifted the individual into the presence of God. This experience made the prophets more truly human than they were before, so that they were enabled to receive his revelation. Second, there was a sense of the authority of the words of God. Five times (1:2, 3, 10; 2:9; 3:8) Zephaniah asserts, "This is the word of the LORD [*nĕ'um yhwh*]." This formula stamps the seal of divine authority on what has been proclaimed. Could people accept a message of total world destruction (1:2–3)? Was the destruction of Jerusalem believable (1:10)? Will the destruction represented by Sodom be repeated (2:9)? Is there a straw of hope in the flood tide of judgment (3:8)? The prophet's response to each of these questions is buttressed by the affirmation: "This is the word of the LORD." If the prophet is to say something that appalls (1:2–3), shocks (1:10), horrifies (2:9), or seems too good to be true (3:8), he needs to be sure of his ground; he needs the authority of the divine word. Third, Zephaniah believed that his words were God's words (3:20). The word that "came" (*hāyâ*) to him from the Lord and was then passed on from him in human speech did not cease in any way to be the very speech of God himself. This was true both fully and in detail, in substance as well as in the words that conveyed it. All this constitutes the uniqueness of the ministry of the prophets, as well as of the apostles (1 Cor. 2:10–13). The values of revelation, authority, and verbal inspiration reside, however, in the whole Bible as God's word. The word that came pure from God was received, without detriment to it, by chosen individuals, and it was then transmitted and inscripturated in unsullied purity (2 Tim. 3:16; 2 Peter 1:21). It is to this word that we are called to be faithful stewards, and it is the acknowledged authority of this word that activates an authoritative ministry.

There may be another facet of Zephaniah's stewardship in the superscription. That he traced his pedigree back four generations is best explained if he was a descendant of King Hezekiah (see the Introduction). If so, he himself was the bearer of the godly tradition exemplified in Hezekiah, which was about to flower again in Josiah. Was Zephaniah the hidden influence within the palace from which the reform movement sprang? To link the best of the past with the needs of the present is the essence of stewardship (2 Tim. 2:2).

I. The End of the World: Is There Any Hope? (1:2–2:3)

A. The End Announced—for the World (1:2–3a) and for Judah
(1:3b–6)

MOTYER

2 I will put an end to everything, taking it
away
from the face of the earth.
This is the word of the LORD.
3 I will put an end to human and beast,
I will put an end to birds from the sky
and fish from the sea,
and to the ruins along with the wicked.
Yes, I will cut humankind
from the face of the earth.
This is the word of the LORD.
4 And I will stretch out my hand against
Judah
and against all those who live in Jerusalem,
and I will cut from this place whatever remains of Baalism:
the name of the incense burners along
with the priests,
5 and those who bow in worship on the
rooftops to the host of heaven,
and those who bow in worship—who
swear loyalty to the LORD but who
swear by their "king,"
6 and those who backslide from following
the LORD,
who have ceased to seek the LORD or
look to him.

NRSV

2 I will utterly sweep away everything
from the face of the earth, says the
LORD.
3 I will sweep away humans and animals;
I will sweep away the birds of the air
and the fish of the sea.
I will make the wicked stumble.
I will cut off humanity
from the face of the earth, says the
LORD.
4 I will stretch out my hand against Judah,
and against all the inhabitants of Jerusalem;
and I will cut off from this place every
remnant of Baal
and the name of the idolatrous priests;
5 those who bow down on the roofs to the
host of the heavens;
those who bow down and swear to the
LORD,
but who also swear by Milcom;
6 those who have turned back from following the LORD,
who have not sought the LORD or inquired of him.

2. The construction אָסֹף אָסֵף (I will put an end to) involves several linguistic problems. The first term (אָסֹף), the infinitive absolute of אָסַף (to gather [up], take away), emphasizes the following verb, which is usually the indicative of the same root (but see Isa. 28:28; Jer. 8:13). The second term (אָסֵף) in this construction is the apocopated first-person singular imperfect hiphil of סוּף (to come to an end; hiphil: to bring to an end). This use of a shortened (or jussive) form cannot be explained, but the occurrence of the same form twice in 1:3 suggests that it is a Hebrew idiom that we do not currently understand. This should caution against BHS's alteration of אָסֹף אָסֵף to אֹסֵף (I will take away), the first-person singular imperfect qal of אָסַף. The Septuagint offers little help, but it does confirm the infinitive-absolute construction. A similar construction in Jeremiah 8:13 involves the same two verbs, suggesting that this construction may be a colloquial usage involving anomalies similar to the familiar שָׁב שְׁבוּת (bring back captivity), arising perhaps from assonance (2:7; 3:20). As far as we can make a literal rendering (though it ignores the apocopation) the construction states, "By taking away I will put an end to." נְאֻם־יְהוָה (this is the word of the LORD; lit., the word of the LORD) often appears abruptly and even intrusively, as if it were a seal suddenly stamped down to validate the divine authenticity of what is being said (see the Exegesis of Hag. 1:1).

3. אָסֵף (I will put an end to) occurs twice in this verse, both times being the same jussive form as in 1:2. The Septuagint reflects this form in its use of ἐκλιπέτω (let be cut off). אָדָם וּבְהֵמָה (human and beast) and עוֹף־הַשָּׁמַיִם וּדְגֵי הַיָּם (birds from the sky and fish from the sea) amplify and extend the meaning of כֹּל in 1:2. The contrast of terrestrial groups (human and beast) and nonterrestrial creatures (birds and fish) expresses totality. וְהַמַּכְשֵׁלוֹת (and to the ruins): The only other instance of מַכְשֵׁלָה is in Isaiah 3:6, where it occurs in a context having to do with the collapse of society due to sin. So also here: Zephaniah traces judgment to its root cause and forecasts that the works of the wicked, as well as the wicked themselves, will be swept away. אֶת cannot function here as the sign of the direct object since no verbal idea, either explicit or implicit, occurs in connection with it. When used as a preposition, a suitable translation is "together with" (BDB, p. 85; Gen. 6:13; 11:31), which fits the context by associating the ruins with the wicked. J. Smith (*Zephaniah*, p. 186), BHS, and the New Revised Standard Version suspect that this final line is a later addition; Smith argues that a reference to the wicked is premature (but does not say why). The poem as it stands is balanced (see the outline at the Exposition of 1:1), and in both sections the threat of judgment (1:2–3a, 3c–4a) is justified by specifying what it is that merits divine anger (1:3b, 4b–6). House (*Zephaniah*, p. 127) concurs with BHS in emending וְהַמַּכְשֵׁלוֹת to וְהִכְשַׁלְתִּי (and I will make [the wicked] to stumble) on the ground that this emendation offers a better parallel to the next phrase,

---

2. The suggestion that Zephaniah was the force behind the reform movement cannot be proved. What is certain is that Zephaniah lived to see the corrupt kings Manasseh and Amon replaced by a good king, Josiah. Yet he knew that things had already gone beyond the point where a change of government would change the destiny of the world. And even though he lived to see Josiah's reform sweep the country, he did not revise his message. Hindsight tells us that divine mercy continued to postpone the end that Zephaniah forecast, and we still face the certainty of it. Human nature remains impervious to the beneficial effects of good rulers and further reformations; it remains unchanged even by additional centuries of divine grace so that life in every aspect (1:3)—and indeed the planet itself (1:18; 3:8)—remains under divine judgment.

3. The reason why everything is under judgment remains constant throughout time: the wicked (*hārĕšā'îm*). This word, even more commonplace in Hebrew than in English, indicates humankind's ordinary "badness," which constitutes the greatest environmental threat of all. Even now the earth is in ruins. Everything of beauty and joy (including the whole animal creation) is diseased by contagion from sinful humans (Gen. 3:16–19). And if we should grumble that the cause is too slight to merit the threatened effect—that the end of the world is too massive a penalty for the pettiness of our sin—we need only recall that sin has also infected our moral perceptions: we are not—nor can we be—trustworthy judges of what is fitting. The Judge of all the earth (Gen. 18:25) does right and "this is the word of the LORD" (Zeph. 1:2).

Zephaniah 1:3 indicates that the fifth and sixth days of creation (Gen. 1:20–31) are undone. By including "fish," the coming judgment exceeds even the flood (Gen. 7:21–23). Zephaniah (like Genesis) sees the creation caught up in

וְהִכְרַתִּי (I will cut). This, however, presupposes a rigidity in the use of parallelism unsupported by Old Testament evidence. וְהִכְרַתִּי (yes, I will cut): וּ (yes) is used resumptively. כָּרַת (to cut; Lev. 17:10; 20:1–3) is "a strong word indicating annihilation. . . . It is used at times in the technical sense of carrying out the death penalty" (Baker, Zephaniah, p. 92). פְּנֵי הָאֲדָמָה (the face of the earth): Coupled with נְאֻם־יְהוָה (this is the word of the LORD), these words give the second movement of the poem a parallelism with the first (1:2). נְאֻם (word): See the Exegesis of 1:2.

4. וְנָטִיתִי יָדִי (I will stretch out my hand): The outstretched hand of judgment is one of many linguistic links between Zephaniah and Isaiah (Isa. 5:25; 9:11 [12], 16 [17]; 10:5; 14:26–27), but at its foundation the outstretching of the Lord's hand is an exodus motif for salvation (Exod. 7:5, 19; 9:22; 14:16, 26). The reversal of a symbol is typical of Zephaniah: the gesture of salvation is now one of judgment. וְהִכְרַתִּי (and I will cut) is the same word (כָּרַת) as in 1:3, where it refers to the judgment of the world. מָקוֹם (place) is a semitechnical term for a sanctuary or shrine (Deut. 12:5; 1 Kings 8:29–30). The reference here could be to Jerusalem or the temple. שְׁאָר הַבַּעַל (whatever remains of Baalism) may mean all that is left of Baal (after the rest has been destroyed). This would suggest a date for Zephaniah (see the Introduction) after Josiah's purges had left only pockets of Baalism (2 Chron. 36:13–14; Jer. 9:13 [14]; 19:4–9). But the words do not necessarily involve such a connotation, and it is better to be less specific. The Lord will not be endlessly patient with usurping gods, and when the time comes he will deal finally with "whatever remains"—that is, all that is then found (note the same word in Isa. 14:22). הַבַּעַל (Baal) could possibly be the Assyrian Bel, since Zephaniah belongs within the Assyrian period, but it is much more likely to be the Palestinian Baal, a constant snare to the people of God from the time of the conquest. McKay (Religion in Judah, p. 67) concludes: "The various deities worshipped in Judah during the period of Assyrian domination lack the definitive aspects of the Assyrian gods and generally exhibit the characteristics of popular Palestinian paganism." אֶת־שֵׁם (the name): To cut off the name signifies erasing even from memory. There is no certainty about what הַכְּמָרִים (the incense-burners; also in 2 Kings 23:5 and Hos. 10:5) refers to. It may be related to the Assyrian kumru (priest), supposedly adopted in the Assyrian period, but McKay (p. 37) says that Old Assyrian kumru had dropped out of use before the Assyrian domination of Judah. It may be related to כָּמַר (to be hot or excited; Gen. 43:30; 1 Kings 3:26; Lam. 5:10), meaning one practicing a frenzied or ecstatic religion. Burning incense is the only function Scripture assigns to this order (2 Kings 23:5). עִם־הַכֹּהֲנִים (along with the priests) distinguishes the כְּמָרִים as a distinct order, but more than that we cannot say. The context requires that הַכֹּהֲנִים be those who served Baal (2 Kings 11:18); it is not until 1:5b that Zephaniah alludes to syncretistic worship.

---

human sin (Gen. 3:14–19; see Rom. 8:19–22) and condemnation.

4. Judgment falls on false religion ("whatever remains of Baalism"), the functionaries of error ("the incense-burners along with the priests"), and the devotees of other gods ("those who bow in worship . . . to the host of heaven"). Judgment begins at the house of God (1 Peter 4:17). Much will be required from those to whom much has been given (Luke 12:48). When the Lord says, "You only have I known" (Amos 3:2), he also says, "Therefore I will punish you for all your iniquities." The progenitor of the tribe of Judah had a history of privilege and grace: he was not the firstborn by right but by appointment (Gen. 29:32–35; 49:8–10); his family became the bearer of kingship (Ps. 78:68–69), but history, privilege, and position offer no security from divine scrutiny. Those who "live in Jerusalem" were in the very presence of the Lord (Deut. 12:5) and within arm's length of the means of grace and of the knowledge of God (compare Luke 13:25–27). But their loyalty lay elsewhere (Zeph. 1:4–5) and their heart was cold toward him (1:6).

Baal was the god of productivity: his function in Canaanite religion was to make land, animals, and humans fertile. Baal was another name for the gross national product, and wherever people see bank balances, prosperity, a sound economy, productivity, and mounting exports as the essence of their security, Baal is still worshiped. Baal was also the god of religious excitement (1 Kings 18:26b) and sexual free-for-all (Num. 25:1–3). Human sexual acts were publicly offered to him to prompt him to perform his work of fertilization. No wonder his officiants were called the "frenzied ones" (see the Exegesis). Wherever excitement in religion becomes an end in itself and wherever the cult of "what helps" replaces joy in "what's true," Baal is worshiped.

5. וְאֵת (and) continues the sequence of direct objects in 1:4–5, each one relating to the verb וְהִכְרַתִּי (and I will cut). הַמִּשְׁתַּחֲוִים (those who bow in worship) appears twice in this verse, the second time, immediately before הַנִּשְׁבָּעִים (who swear loyalty). This troubles some textual critics, but R. Smith (*Micah–Malachi*, p. 126) rightly sees it as done for deliberate effect. The contrast here is between positive devotion to the stars and pretended devotion to the Lord: they swear to (לְ) Yahweh and swear by (בְּ) their "king." In Genesis 21:23, לְ is used of the one to whom an oath is made and בְּ of the basis on which the oath rests. By this neat turn of phrase Zephaniah exposes an expressed loyalty to the Lord, while the actual basis of life is מַלְכָּם (their king). One recension of the Septuagint and the Vulgate reads "Milcom," the Ammonite god (1 Kings 11:5, 33; 2 Kings 23:13) also known as Molech (Lev. 18:21; 20:5; 1 Kings 11:7; 2 Kings 23:10). There can be little doubt that the word is based on מֶלֶךְ (king), to which perhaps, in the Old Testament, the vowels of the noun בֹּשֶׁת (shame) were introduced as a mark of reprobation. Solomon sanctioned the worship of Molech (1 Kings 11:7), which contin-

ued until Josiah destroyed it (2 Kings 23:13–14). Since מֶלֶךְ is one of the titles of the Lord (Isa. 6:1, 5), the point is aptly made that they swear by one king, yet live by another. In deliberate contrast, Zephaniah notes it as a mark of the coming glorious day that "the King of Israel, the LORD, is within you" (3:15).

6. הַנְּסוֹגִים (those who backslide): For סוּג with the sense of backslide, see Psalm 44:19 [18] and 53:4 [3] (contrast Isa. 50:5). This slipping away from the Lord is elaborated in the synonymous verbs בִּקֵּשׁ (to seek) and דָּרַשׁ (to look to). The secular example of בִּקֵּשׁ, as yearning or active devotion (Song of Sol. 3:1–2; 5:6), captures the heart of both verbs (in the following pairs, the first reference exemplifies בִּקֵּשׁ and the second דָּרַשׁ): they express a serious turning to the Lord (2 Chron. 11:16; Ps. 119:10), a commitment to devotion (Pss. 27:8; 119:45), praying for help (2 Sam. 12:16; Ps. 34:5 [4]), and seeking guidance in perplexity (Gen. 25:22; 2 Sam. 21:1). So Zephaniah exposes "the apostasy of their hearts" (Kleinert, *Zephaniah*, p. 14), the practical atheism that treats God as an irrelevancy.

---

5. The prophet now denounces astral cults (compare Deut. 4:19; 17:3; Jer. 7:18; 8:2; 44:17–25), prevalent throughout the period of Manasseh and Amon (2 Kings 21:3, 5, 21) and into the time of Josiah (2 Kings 23:5, 12). These cults may have been stimulated by Assyrian influence, but they were primarily rooted in preconquest Canaan (note place-names like Beth-shemesh, "House of the Sun"; Josh. 15:10). The words *on the rooftops* indicate that worship was offered directly to the heavenly bodies without using idols.

Nowadays, not many of the Lord's professing people bow on the rooftops, but in a world awash with astrologers the reality of astral devotion is still present. Wherever occultism is practiced and children made the victims of satanic rituals, people still worship the king of the underworld to whom, of old, they made their children pass through the fire as living sacrifices (2 Kings 21:6). On these things divine judgment must fall. How the Lord must hurt when such gods are preferred to him and he is marginalized in the lives of his people, whose creed may be impeccable (Zeph. 1:5b) but whose lives rest on other foundations (1:5c).

6. The second half of the poem (1:3c–6) is more specific than the first half. The general accusation of wickedness (3a) becomes the precise accusation

of religious error (4b–5a), disloyalty (5b), apostasy (6a), and practical atheism (6b). Such charges are only justifiable on the basis of divine revelation. This is the difference between the world (2–3a) and the Lord's people (4), between judgment on the basis of conscience and judgment on the basis of the word of God (note Amos 1:3–2:3 and contrast Amos 2:4–5).

The much briefer allusions to worldwide judgment (Zeph. 1:2–3b) have been leading up to these specific charges against the Lord's people: by giving a universal context to the specific condemnation of Israel, Zephaniah follows standard prophetic practice. Doctrinally, the point is that Judah and Jerusalem were supposed to be the magnet drawing the world to the Lord (Isa. 2:2–4); instead, they were at one with the world in condemnation. There could be no sharper exposure of their failure to live up to the divine intention. Six groups are singled out: Baalists, false priests, astral devotees (Zeph. 1:4b–5a), syncretists (5b), backsliders (6a), and practical atheists (6b). The first three are actively committed to other gods; the Lord has no place in their religion. The second three pretend a devotion that is actually unreal (5b), have departed from a devotion they once professed (6a), or have now reached the ultimate irreligion where the Lord is not a living reality to them at all (6b). The double reference to "those who bow in worship" (5) forms a domino link between the two triads. The overall movement from external idolatry (4b–5a) to the apostasy of the heart (5b–6) may be expressed symmetrically:

a   positive: Baal religion (4b)
b   double description (positive): Baal served (4c)
c   actual worship: the astral cults (5a)
c′   pretended worship: ostensibly the Lord, really the "king" (5b)
a′   negative: the Lord deserted (6a)
b′   double description (negative): the Lord ignored (6b)

Zephaniah 1:6 adds another dimension to the grief the Lord must feel when his own people marginalize him in their lives. Zephaniah refers here to those who do not follow the Lord, do not seek his fellowship and guidance, and do not look for his help. Deep as the hurt is over public apostasy (4–5), the deeper wound is inflicted when personal devotion and the daily walk with God (6) are abandoned.

I. The End of the World: Is There Any Hope? (1:2–2:3)

B. The End Described—for Judah (1:7–14a) and for the World (1:14b–18)

MOTYER	NRSV
7 Silence in the presence of the sovereign LORD! For the day of the LORD is near: for the LORD has prepared a sacrifice; he has consecrated his invited guests. 8 And it shall be, in the day of the LORD's sacrifice, I will visit punishment upon the princes and upon the king's sons and upon all who dress themselves in foreign dress. 9 And I will visit punishment, that day, upon everyone who skips over the threshold: those who fill their Lord's house with violence and deceit. 10 And it shall be in that day— this is the word of the LORD— Listen! A scream from the Fish Gate, and a wail from the Mishneh, and a great crashing from the Hills! 11 Wail, you who live in the Mortar, for all tradespeople have been brought to silence, all who weigh out money have been cut down. 12 And it shall be, at that time, I will search through Jerusalem with lamps, and I will visit [punishment] on the men who are settled on their lees, who say in their heart, "The LORD does no good and he does no harm."	7 Be silent before the Lord GOD! For the day of the LORD is at hand; the LORD has prepared a sacrifice, he has consecrated his guests. 8 And on the day of the LORD's sacrifice I will punish the officials and the king's sons and all who dress themselves in foreign attire. 9 On that day I will punish all who leap over the threshold, who fill their master's house with violence and fraud. 10 On that day, says the LORD, a cry will be heard from the Fish Gate, a wail from the Second Quarter, a loud crash from the hills. 11 The inhabitants of the Mortar wail, for all the traders have perished; all who weigh out silver are cut off. 12 At that time I will search Jerusalem with lamps, and I will punish the people who rest complacently on their dregs, those who say in their hearts, "The LORD will not do good, nor will he do harm."

MOTYER	NRSV

MOTYER

¹³ But their wealth shall become loot
   and their houses desolation;
they will build houses but not live [in
      them],
   and plant vineyards but not drink their
      wine.
¹⁴ The great day of the LORD is near,
   near and speeding on apace!
Listen! The day of the LORD!
   Bitterly there the Warrior cries out!
¹⁵ A day of rage is that day:
   a day of distress and constraint,
   a day of ruin and ruination,
   a day of darkness and blackness,
   a day of cloud and mist,
¹⁶   a day of trumpet sound and battle cry,
against the fortified cities
   and against the lofty corner towers.
¹⁷ For I will bring distress to humankind
   and they will walk like the blind
   for it is against the LORD that they have
      sinned.
And their blood will be poured out like
      dust
   and their flesh like refuse.
¹⁸ Neither their silver nor their gold
   will be able to deliver them.
On the day of the LORD's rage
   for in the fire of his jealousy
   all the earth will be eaten up:
for a complete work—yes, and suddenly
      accomplished—
   he will do with all those who live on
      earth.

NRSV

¹³ Their wealth shall be plundered,
   and their houses laid waste.
Though they build houses,
   they shall not inhabit them;
though they plant vineyards,
   they shall not drink wine from them.
¹⁴ The great day of the LORD is near,
   near and hastening fast;
the sound of the day of the LORD is bitter,
   the warrior cries aloud there.
¹⁵ That day will be a day of wrath,
   a day of distress and anguish,
   a day of ruin and devastation,
   a day of darkness and gloom,
   a day of clouds and thick darkness,
¹⁶   a day of trumpet blast and battle cry
against the fortified cities
   and against the lofty battlements.
¹⁷ I will bring such distress upon people
   that they shall walk like the blind;
   because they have sinned against the
      LORD,
their blood shall be poured out like dust,
   and their flesh like dung.
¹⁸ Neither their silver nor their gold
   will be able to save them
   on the day of the LORD's wrath;
in the fire of his passion
   the whole earth shall be consumed;
for a full, a terrible end
   he will make of all the inhabitants of
      the earth.

7. The interjection הַס (silence) looks as if it developed from הָסָה (so KB, p. 239; Num. 13:30; Neh. 8:11). It has the general sense of awe in Judges 3:19 (also Amos 6:10; 8:3). Habakkuk 2:20, Zechariah 2:17 [13], and Zephaniah 1:7 form an interesting series. For Habakkuk the mere presence of the Lord calls for reverential silence; in Zechariah, the Lord is stirred into action to accomplish a worldwide blessing centered on Jerusalem; and Zephaniah sees the dark underside of this worldwide objective, the Lord's *dies irae*. Only silence befits the anticipation, not of the awesome events as such, but of the advent of the sovereign Lord (אֲדֹנָי יְהוִה, only here in Zephaniah). יוֹם יְהוָה (the day of the LORD): From now on, this concept dominates Zephaniah's message, occurring eighteen more times and comprising a true summation of prophetic thinking about the day of the Lord (see the Exposition). כִּי (for) introduces the reason why there is to be silence in the Lord's presence: because of the impending day of the Lord. קָרוֹב (near) occurs in Zephaniah only here and in 1:14a (twice) as a deliberate *inclusio*. Imminence is part of the prophetic definition of the day of the Lord (Ezek. 7:2, 10; 30:2–3; Joel 1:15; Hag. 2:6), as it is in the New Testament, which expects the imminent return of the Lord Jesus Christ. The second occurrence of כִּי seems not to relate to the first clause of this verse, but to the immediately preceding clause (כִּי קָרוֹב יוֹם יְהוָה), which states

---

7. Zephaniah now introduces two oracles on the day of the Lord. Dealing respectively with Judah (1:7–14a) and the world (1:14b–18), he reverses the order of 1:2–3a and 1:3b–6, resulting in an abb'a' arrangement. The keynote of the section is sounded in the *inclusio* "the day is near" in 1:7 and 1:14a. Internal divisions are marked by "in that day/time" (1:8, 10, 12). First, the higher echelons of society are brought under judgment (1:8–9); then disaster strikes the city and the business community (1:10–11); finally, those under judgment are described, not by status or function, but as the spiritual and theological (1:12–13) equivalents of the practical atheists in 1:6. The Lord's judgment (1:10–13) appears to be executed by an invader bringing in terror (1:10) and plundering (1:13). As is typical of Zephaniah's historical allusions, this is too general to pinpoint. He, like Isaiah, uses historical imagery in the service of theology. He sees people devoted to acquisition: the frivolous luxury of alien dress (1:8), trading and bartering (1:11), wealth and real estate (1:13). The picture of the invader exposes the evanescence and insecurity of a temporal and terrestrial life in which God is marginalized. Thus the social orientation of judgment in 1:7–14a balances the religious orientation of 1:3b–6, in each case the root of the matter being the denial of the living reality of the Lord (1:6, 12).

> a   the imminent day (7)
> b   on princes and priests (8–9)
> c   on the city and its citizens (10–11)
> d   on practical atheism (12–13)
> a'   the imminent day (14a)

The dramatic words with which 1:7 opens prepare the way for the announcement of the day of the Lord. The wickedness of humans (1:3) and the compromise and apostasy of the Lord's people (1:4–6) would be of infinitely less consequence were it not for the wrath of God. With this verse Zephaniah's diagnosis goes deeper. He has probed the character of humankind; now he probes the character of God and finds there an opposition to sin that issues in death. To speak of the day of the Lord as a day of sacrifice (1:7–8) places it within the long biblical tradition that where there is sin there must also be death—and this because Yahweh is the Holy One. The revelation that sin brings death began in Genesis (2:17); Exodus brought the revelation of the sinner endangered by the holiness of God (3:5; 19:12, 20–24); and Leviticus (17:11) enshrined at the heart of the sacrificial system the principle that the wages of sin is death. Zephaniah takes the word of divine grace (the provision of a sacrifice for sin) and makes it the vehicle of the message of wrath: those who have long despised the sacrifice that God provides become the sacrifice their sin merits.

Zephaniah 1:7 provides the first encounter in his book with the prophetic concept of the day of the Lord. The Hebrew word *day* (yôm) is used idiomatically for a decisive event or series of events, a moment or period in which destiny is settled (Isa. 9:3 [4]). Amos (5:18–20) inherited a tradition expecting a determinative divine action aimed at least at the well-being of the Lord's people. Mowinckel (*He That Cometh*) argued that this originated in cultic ceremonies wherein darkness and distress were banished and peace secured by the divine advent. Von Rad's view (*Old Testament Theology*, vol. 2, pp. 119–25) that this expectation arose from holy war concepts has on its

that the day of the Lord is imminent. It is imminent because (כִּי) the Lord has already prepared the sacrificial meal and invited his guests. Everything is ready for the portentous events that the day of the Lord presages. הֵכִין . . . זֶבַח (has prepared a sacrifice): Several passages (Isa. 34:6; Jer. 46:10; Ezek. 39:17–20) illuminate this concept (also Rev. 19:17–21), and in all of them the objects of the Lord's wrath are the material for sacrifice (demonstrating, incidentally, the theology of wrath that is central to the idea of sacrifice). הִקְדִּישׁ קְרֻאָיו (he has consecrated his invited guests): See 1 Samuel 16:5 (contrast 20:26). The Lord's guests are not here identified, but identification is unnecessary since this is not allegory. They are mentioned only to give verisimilitude to the picture of the sacrifice and the feast: everything is indeed ready; there

will be a sacrifice and meat to eat! קְרֻאִים (invited guests; lit., the called ones; 1 Sam. 9:13; 2 Sam. 15:11): קָרָא (call) reappears in Zephaniah only in the matching third section (3:9). The Lord calls to his sacrifice; the restored world calls on his name.

8. וְהָיָה בְּיוֹם (and it shall be in the day): House (*Zephaniah*, pp. 127–28) rightly criticizes BHS, J. Smith (*Zephaniah*, p. 208), and Kapelrud (*Zephaniah*, p. 28), who "apparently . . . believe most formulaic sayings of this nature are additions. No textual or contextual evidence supports this claim, and it must be rejected." וּפָקַדְתִּי עַל (I will visit punishment upon): ו (untranslated) contributes to the flow of thought in this section by introducing a clause that states the circumstances attendant on the day of the Lord's sacrifice. פָּקַד must always be interpreted contextually. The

---

side the pervasive military motifs used of the day (e.g., Isa. 13:4–22). But this is not an either/or situation (Cross, "Divine Warrior"). The cultic traditions of Israel (e.g., Pss. 2, 48) included the gathering of the kings against Zion and against the Lord's king; in this way warrior terminology and cult terminology are complementary, not mutually exclusive. Prior to our first contact with the term in Amos, we know little regarding what was actually expected. The people of Amos's time (5:18), absorbed by their privileged position, were happily expecting the Lord to come on their behalf. Amos countered by declaring that their privilege rather brought them greater certainty of divine judgment (3:2) and that the day would be darkness, not light (5:18). Amos was not necessarily the first to grasp this aspect of the divine day: we know only de facto that this is the situation recorded in his book and that for him as for all the prophets the darkness of judgment and the light of hope (9:11, 13) are mingled. In addition, in some sense the prophets saw significant historical events as the day of the Lord. Isaiah (13:1–6) looked forward to the fall of Babylon; Amos (5:18–27) thought of the captivity of northern Israel. In each case, however, neither in prospect nor in retrospect was the day of the Lord fully realized. The prophets simply had in mind that these were events of such a dire nature that they exemplified a reality that would be fully demonstrated when the day finally came. But it is this ultimate day that preoccupies Zephaniah. His thinking is insistently universal (1:17a, 18b; 2:11; 3:6, 8b, 9, 20). He seems uninterested in identifying specific historical events: it might be possible, for example,

to offer a date for the abandonment of Gaza and the destruction of Philistia (2:4–7), but not if we view Zephaniah's whole picture, including Judah's peaceful occupation of Philistia. Zephaniah is using, rather, the north-south-east-west motif as a picture of universality and of the centrality of the Lord's people to his world purposes. Likewise, when 1:10–11 suggests the fall of Jerusalem to an enemy attack, there is no clue as to the identity of the enemy. Zephaniah, whether under historical or theological prompting, has left us a tract on the day of the Lord—the climax alike of history, sin, and the purposes of God.

8. In the three stanzas of this poem, Zephaniah specifies those who are the objects of divine displeasure (1:8, 9, 12) and interleaves the consequences of life apart from the Lord (1:10, 11, 13). Considering the latter first, he teaches (1:10–11) that life without God is life without a future. People scream in terror, buildings crash down, business and banking come to an end. As on another occasion, they were eating and drinking, marrying and giving in marriage (Matt. 24:38–39), but the flood came and took them all away. Zephaniah also teaches (1:13) that life without God is life without satisfaction. The cup of wealth, property, and business is raised to the lips—only to be dashed away. When we see it happening otherwise, as we often do, it is due to the sheer unmerited mercy and goodwill of our sovereign God and his longing that sinners come to repentance (Rom. 2:4; 2 Peter 3:9). But imminence is part of the definition of the day of the Lord—it is always near (Zeph. 1:7). There is no security in anything earthly, for all is under sentence. But here

basic meaning, "to visit, inspect" (Dhorme, *Job*, p. 514), develops a number of nuances: "to give care and attention to" (Exod. 3:16), "to visit with benefit" (Gen. 21:1; Exod. 4:31), "to visit with punishment" (Exod. 32:34; Jer. 6:15), "to number" (Num. 4:27; 26:63), "to find absent" (1 Sam. 25:15), "to number off for a duty" or "to appoint" (Deut. 20:9), and "to lay a responsibility on" (2 Chron. 36:23). This wide diversity of meaning is accompanied by inconsistency in syntax: with a direct object, the verb can have either beneficial (Ruth 1:6) or hostile (Isa. 26:14) intent; and פָּקַד plus עַל (on) means "to punish" (as here) or "to give a charge or responsibility to" (Zeph. 3:7; Num. 4:27; see the Exegesis of Hos. 1:4). בְּנֵי הַמֶּלֶךְ . . . הַשָּׂרִים (the princes . . . the king's sons) refers to the royal family in general, rather than specifically to Josiah's family. If Zephaniah was of royal blood he would be in a position to observe royal manners (note the reference to שָׂרִים, princes, in the matching section, 3:3). כָּל־הַלֹּבְשִׁים (all who dress): The flow of thought does not suggest priests in the garb of alien religion (so Baker, *Zephaniah*, p. 95), but the princely households frivolously dazzled by supposed foreign sophistication. Since Israel had its own national regulations of dress (Num. 15:38; Deut. 22:12), which were not arbitrary but linked with religious loyalties (Num. 15:39–40), Zephaniah's charge is not as unimportant as might seem at first sight. The issue at stake was the distinctiveness of the people of God. The leaders of fashion chose rather to be like the nations: "The strange apparel shows the estranged heart" (Kleinert, *Zephaniah*, p. 15).

9. וּפָקַדְתִּי (and I will visit punishment): The repetition of this form (see the Exegesis of 1:8) signals another object of punishment and shifts our attention away from the frivolous nobles to another class of people in Zephaniah's society. ו (and) on וּפָקַדְתִּי is a coordinating conjunction creating another element in the sequence of divine activities. הַדּוֹלֵג (who skips): Zephaniah replaces the sober "do not step on the threshold" (1 Sam. 5:5) with a deliberately trivializing word in order to caricature the antics introduced into the Lord's worship. The piel participle of דָּלַג (to leap, skip) plus עַל (upon, over) is used in Song of Solomon 2:8 of the lover springing (דִּלֵּג) over the mountains and leaping (קָפַץ) over the hills to reach his beloved. In 2 Samuel 22:30 (par. Ps. 18:30 [29]), it occurs with a direct object: "jumping over a wall" (note its absolute use in Isa. 35:6). הַמִּפְתָּן (the threshold) remains imperfectly understood (1 Sam. 5:4–5; Ezek. 9:3; 10:4, 18; 47:1), but the example in Ezekiel 46:2, where the prince worships "at the threshold [מִפְתָּן] of the gate," shows that some such translation as "threshold" cannot be wildly astray. בַּיּוֹם הַהוּא (that day) refers back to the day cited in the first line of 1:8. אֲדֹנֵיהֶם (their Lord): On the divine title אֲדֹנִי plus suffix, compare "their Lord" (Neh. 3:5), "our Lord" (Neh. 10:30 [29]; Pss. 8:2, 10 [1, 9]; 135:5), and "his Lord" (Hos.

Zephaniah singles out the leaders (1:8–9) as the objects of divine wrath. Leaders carry a burden of responsibility inseparable from their position. It matters how they live, what they do, how they legislate. Maybe people cannot be made good by an act of Congress but they certainly can be helped to be bad. The line between the legally permissible and the morally right is easily erased. Did the leaders of Zephaniah's day say, "How I dress is my business. It is part of my private life and has nothing to do with my position or work"? But by their dress (see the Exegesis) they were eroding the distinction between the Lord's people and the world around and exemplifying a failure of loyalty to him and a carefree attitude toward his law. The life of the leader matters. David's immorality brought his family and ultimately his dynasty crashing about his ears. There is no distinction between the private and public for those in the public eye. And this applies equally to leaders in the church: Why else is it that the qualifications are overwhelmingly moral and spiritual (1 Tim. 3:1–13; Titus 1:5–9)? It matters what sort of marriage is exemplified in the rectory or manse; it matters what family life is like there. Ministers' habits matter, as well as their temperament and reputation.

9. The clue to the meaning of this much disputed verse is the accusation of violence (*hāmās*) leveled against the priests in the parallel passage, 3:4, with its use of the verb *hāmĕsû* (see analysis in the Introduction). Zephaniah opened (1:8) with an attack on state leaders. A matching attack on religious leaders is appropriate. There is a balance between princes and judges on the one hand and prophets and priests on the other in 3:3–4. The link between "skips over the threshold" and 1 Samuel 5:4–5 can therefore stand. Just as the princes affected foreign dress, so the priests imported alien religious fetishes. "Their Lord" is, consequently, a reference to Yahweh. In relation to the religious leaders of his day, then, Zephaniah lays a specific charge: they practice ritual and give teaching and direction at variance with the word

12:15 [14]). חָמָס (violence) is used mostly of social disruption (Gen. 6:11, 13; Ps. 55:10 [9]). It also has wider significance: in Deuteronomy 19:16, a "malicious witness" (lit., "witness of violence") connotes someone under oath who does violence to the truth. The "man of violence" (Prov. 16:29 NASB) abuses the norms of neighborliness. So here, as in 3:4, the priests violently mishandle the law of the Lord. וּמִרְמָה (and deceit): Not only do the priests mishandle the law, but they also practice deceit against those who trustfully come for guidance (Mal. 2:7). In contrast to this deceit, note the purging of the "deceitful [תַּרְמִית] tongue" from the renewed Zion (3:13).

10. בַּיּוֹם הַהוּא (in that day): See the Exegesis of 1:8. נְאֻם־יְהוָה (this is the word of the LORD): See the Exegesis of 1:2. קוֹל (listen!; lit., a voice) is often used as an exclamation (1:14; 2:14; Isa. 40:6). שַׁעַר הַדָּגִים (the Fish Gate) was a main gate on the northern side of the city of Jerusalem between the Old Gate and the Sheep Gate (2 Chron. 33:14; Neh. 3:3; 12:39). Jerusalem was most vulnerable from the north, and from there came its greatest enemies. This gate is chosen for its suitability to picture the final onslaught. הַמִּשְׁנֶה (the Mishneh) was "the 'Second' ... or *New Quarter* ..., a more recent addition ... to the north of the Temple and the main part of the city" (Baker, *Zephaniah*, p. 97). It would be the first area to fall before the invader once the Fish Gate had been breached. Second Chronicles 33:14 may refer to the enclosing of the Mishneh. הַגְּבָעוֹת (the Hills): The context suggests a reference to an area inside the city perimeter, not to the surrounding hills. Perhaps

some higher areas were known as "the Hills" (J. Smith, *Zephaniah*, p. 199; Baker, *Zephaniah*, p. 97).

11. הֵילִילוּ (wail) recalls the noun יְלָלָה (a wail) in 1:10. It tellingly personalizes the sound into suffering people. מַכְתֵּשׁ (the Mortar) occurs as "the hollow place" in Judges 15:19 and in its technical sense as "a mortar" in Proverbs 27:22. The verb כָּתַשׁ (only in Prov. 27:22) means "to pound or grind to dust." Possibly a business area situated in a hollow, such a place-name in Jerusalem is not otherwise known. Zephaniah uses this word to make a contrast with the Hills. The niphal of דָּמָה (to be silent) is used elsewhere of the silence that follows disaster (Isa. 15:1) and death (Ps. 49:13, 21 [12, 20]). עַם כְּנַעַן (tradespeople; lit., people of Canaan): See the Exegesis of Hosea 12:8 [7]. Dhorme (*Job*, p. 628) says that כְּנַעֲנִים (Canaanites) has "lost its character as an ethnic designation to become no more than a simple appellative for 'traders' " (Job 40:30 [41:6]; Prov. 31:24). There is possibly a double meaning here: they were people of the Lord, but in business they had become Canaanites! נִכְרְתוּ (have been cut down): See the Exegesis of 1:3. נְטִילֵי כָסֶף (who weigh out money): Note נָטַל (to weigh) in Isaiah 40:15. The word does not refer to moneychangers, but to those engaged in buying and selling. Zephaniah is not showing an animus against trade or money-making. Rather, he chooses a place normally alive with the buzz of conversation and humming with activity as a foil for the silence that will follow the devastation.

of God (see the Exegesis). The priests of the day no doubt found it helpful to adopt Philistine ritual but, as Calvin remarks, worship must conform to the will of God as its unerring standard. Jesus said that worship resting only on human tradition is vain—empty of spiritual reality, failing to reach God (Matt. 15:6–9).

10. The second segment of the oracle of the imminent day turns from state and church leaders (1:8–9) to the city itself and the common person in the street. The contrasts between a place (the Fish Gate) and an area (the Mishnah), between the Hills and the Mortar, indicate totality of devastation. These verses contain no accusations, no sin to justify the judgment (contrast 1:12–13), simply total devastation. Such is the day of the Lord.

11. The contrast between the words *wail* and *silence* (1:10) also indicates totality of devastation. The wailing, however, soon becomes a deathly

hush as the resulting devastation stands mutely before us. The devastation the prophet describes finds its focus in "all who weigh out money." The rich, oppressing classes have had much to do with the day of the Lord and its devastating effects on the nation. In the Bible, wealth is not a vice any more than poverty is a virtue, but the Bible asks three questions concerning wealth: How was it acquired? How is it being used? What is the attitude of the possessor to the possessions? It is the last that concerns Zephaniah. He found Jerusalem full of rich fools (compare Luke 12:15–21). They had much goods laid up for many years and could sit back without a care; this was what life is all about!

Amos also emphasizes the destructive nature of the day of the Lord (5:18–20). He counters the popular view that the day of the Lord would be to the advantage of the people. Evidently the people

12. בָּעֵת הַהִיא (at that time): See the Exegesis of 1:8. While יוֹם (day) in 1:8, 10 points to the definiteness and decisiveness of the coming event, עֵת (time) points to the suitability of the event, indicating (like the New Testament καιρός) a moment or period marked by characteristic and suitable events, not by date. For example, April is a date, but spring is a time (עֵת or καιρός). So the day of the Lord is not an arbitrary time, but an exact time that is appropriate and merited. אֲחַפֵּשׂ (I will search through): qal חָפַשׂ means "to search" (Ps. 64:7 [6]; Prov. 2:4); the piel (as here) is a true intensive: "I will busy myself searching through" (GKC §52f). בַּנֵּרוֹת (with lamps) further intensifies the picture. No dark corner will be overlooked, no hiding place undetected. וּפָקַדְתִּי (and I will visit [punishment]): See the Exegesis of 1:8. הָאֲנָשִׁים (the men): The alteration of הָאֲנָשִׁים to הַשַּׁאֲנַנִּים (the complacent ones) by BHS and the New International Version only proves that emendation can be insidious. The idea is suitable (though sufficiently present without being labored), but the change lacks manuscript evidence (Baker, *Zephaniah*, p. 98 n. 1; House, *Zephaniah*, p. 128). הַקֹּפְאִים (who are settled): קָפָא occurs elsewhere only in Exodus 15:8 and Job 10:10 (and possibly Zech. 14:6) with the sense of congeal or coagulate. עַל־שִׁמְרֵיהֶם (on their lees): In the refining process, wine needs stillness. At the right point, however, the liquid must be racked or drawn off from the impurities that have sunk to the bottom. If this is not done, these impurities (שֶׁמֶר) infect the wine, making it bitter and unpalatable. Zephaniah implies that the lees have repossessed the wine, making the whole a sour, jellylike mass. בִּלְבָבָם (in their heart): לֵבָב (heart) has strong psychological connotations. It frequently occurs in contexts that inform the word with the idea of the center of cogitation—the deep recesses of the mind in which the cognitive and emotional values that control the will are formed (Deut. 4:29; 8:2; 1 Sam. 13:14).

13. וְהָיָה (but ... shall become) in association with לְ is the regular way of expressing "to become." The verb הָיָה (to be, become) also governs the parallel clause וּבָתֵּיהֶם לִשְׁמָמָה (their houses [shall become] desolation), indicated by the repeti-

---

thought that Yahweh's destruction of the nations on that day would result in their vindication. Amos points out, however, that the destructive effect of the day of the Lord is against all sin, whether it is the sin of the nations or the sin of Israel itself.

12. The anthropological depiction of Yahweh in this verse is a somber one. He searches through the darkness of Jerusalem's night with lamps. The review of contrasting groups in his society (1:8–9 and 1:10–11) indicates that in the Lord's imminent judgment none will escape. Hence, 1:12a emphasizes the thoroughness of the search, 1:12b underscores the ground of judgment (i.e., complacent practical atheism), and 1:13 points to loss and nonfulfillment.

The word *visit* (*pāqad*) occurs here without a direct object (see Isa. 10:12; Jer. 44:13). We are not told what Yahweh "visits" upon (ʿal) "the men settled on [ʿal] their lees." The unusual expression *settled on their lees* describes them as impure wine. It is typical of Zephaniah that he develops the wine metaphor theologically, not socially as Isaiah does (1:22–26; 5:7). Not as an outward, professed creed but as a conviction of the heart, the Lord is irrelevant. The contrast between "good" (*yāṭab*) and "harm" (*rāʿaʿ*) again expresses totality by means of contrast: he does nothing at all (Gen. 31:24). This is not atheism as a dogma but practical atheism; it does not say, "God is not there," but, "God is not here"—not that God does not exist but that he does not matter.

In relation to this philosophy of life, the prophet reveals both the mind of God and the mind of humans: the Lord (1:12a–c) is determined to root out every vestige of evil, searching it out with lamps. But behind the errant lifestyle is a theology (1:12e–f) that the Lord is there (in heaven) but not here (in daily life), that the Lord is alive but not active. If it is permissible to understand "good" and "harm" as more than a conventional expression like "good, bad, or indifferent," then their attitude was that there is no reason to expect his help ("the LORD will not do good") nor to fear his disapproval ("nor will he do harm"). This is, as Craigie (*Twelve Prophets*, p. 114) puts it, "the comfortable conviction that God is otiose."

13. The practical atheist (1:12) is typically the person of property with a bank balance (wealth), real estate (house), and business (vineyard). The day of the Lord will expose the transience of ownership ("their wealth shall become loot"), the insubstantiality of property ("their houses desolation"), and the uncertainty that materialism will bring its promised fulfillments ("build houses but not live [in them], / and plant vineyards but not drink their wine"). All this is clearly reminiscent of the "vengeance of the covenant" (Lev. 26:25) with its futility curses (Deut. 28:30)—a more

tion of לְ on לִשְׁמָמָה. חֵילָם (their wealth): In a significant number of contexts, this word, which denotes strength, has the sense of possessions or resources (Gen. 34:29; Deut. 8:17). וְלֹא יֵשֵׁבוּ (but not live [in them]): יֵשֵׁב (live) is not accompanied by an object or preposition, but it is clear that we must supply the idea of live "in them."

14a. קָרוֹב (is near) expresses the idea of indefinite proximity. Context determines the degree of proximity. Here, the companion clause informs the first קָרוֹב with a greater degree of specificity. קָרוֹב וּמַהֵר (near and speeding on): The association of מַהֵר (speeding on) with קָרוֹב indicates that the day of the Lord is not simply lurking at a distance, but is moving quickly to its destined role. It is imminent (Joel 1:15). מַהֵר may be a piel participle without preformative *mem* (GKC §52s; BHS), but it occurs on seventeen other occasions (e.g., Exod. 32:8; Deut. 4:26) as an adverb (i.e., as an infinitive absolute used adverbially; on the form, see GKC §52o; for a parallel construction of the infinitive absolute, see 1 Sam. 3:12 and Davidson, *Hebrew Syntax* §87).

14b. קוֹל (listen!; lit., a voice): See the Exegesis of 1:10. This dramatic opening links the two oracles, the first with its insistence on the nearness of the day; now the call to listen, because it is

within earshot. יוֹם יְהוָה (the day of the LORD): See the Exegesis of 1:7. מַר (bitterly) is an adjective used adverbially (as in Isa. 33:7). I have chosen to construe מַר with the second clause, but it is possible that it belongs to the first (as in the NRSV), where it would describe the bitter portents that Yahweh's voice announces. The second clause would thus complement the first by asserting that, in view of the bitter portents that Yahweh announces, even the warrior will cry out in fear. This view does not seem as likely as the one adopted here, however, because it inexplicably anticipates the thought of 1:16b and 1:18a and is contrary to the little we know about צָרַח (cries out). The only other occurrence of this verb is in Isaiah 42:13 (hiphil), where it occurs in apposition with רוּעַ (shout). צרח may connote the sense of wailing, but we lack evidence on this point. For the most part, the adverb שָׁם (there) functions in a local sense. However, it also connotes "in those circumstances." Dhorme (*Job*, p. 534) rightly observes that "the connotation of time" may be attributed to שָׁם in Job 35:12 (compare its use in Ps. 14:5 and Prov. 8:27). The גִּבּוֹר (warrior) could be the enemy, but throughout the oracle, it is Yahweh himself who is the assailant. It is he who

---

potent and probable background to the darker side of the day of the Lord than either the cult or holy war.

14a. With a final reference to the imminent day, Zephaniah rounds off his masterly poem. He adds now the adjective *great*, for it is no interim day he has in mind but the day itself (see the Exegesis of 1:7). He also amplifies the idea of imminence with the words *speeding on apace*.

14b–18. This second oracle, the first of Zephaniah's marvelous seven-part poems (the others are 2:13–15 and 3:14–17) on the day of the Lord (1:14b–18; see the Exegesis of 1:7), turns to its worldwide range. Two sections on the theme of divine rage (1:14b–16a, 18b–c) form an *inclusio* within which the matching themes of defenselessness (1:16b, 18a) and helplessness before judgment (1:17a, c) lead inward to a central exposure (1:17b) of the root cause of this universal calamity:

a   the day of rage in full expression
    (14b–16a)
b   human defenses unavailing (16b)
c   humankind helpless (17a)
d   explanation: sin (17b)

c'   humankind destroyed (17c)
b'   human wealth unavailing (18a)
a' the day of rage in full execution (18b–c)

Thematically, in this poem, Zephaniah continues from the point reached at 1:13. Contrary to the assumption that God is transcendent but not imminent in history, there is a God to whom the human race will one day have to give an account, however marginal they may seek to make him in the present.

On the one hand Zephaniah widens his perspective in this section to encompass all who live on earth (1:18), but on the other hand the ferocity of the day is brought home to the individual—in disorientation (1:17a), accusation (1:17b), and death (1:17c). In the beginning, the Creator looked on creation and found it "very good" (Gen. 1:31), but now the seven days are recapitulated (in the sevenfold description of Zeph. 1:14b–16a) as days of wrath: a day of divine rage (14b–15a), trouble on humankind and ruin on the world (15b–c), and holiness (15d–e) brought to bear as in a battle (16a). The total impact of the poem is the awesomeness of the day, spelled out by Zephaniah,

is offended by sin (Zeph. 1:17b), and it is he with whom sinners have to deal (1:18b).

15. עֶבְרָה (rage) is assigned "its etymological sense of 'overflowings' " by Dhorme (*Job*, p. 617; so also BDB, p. 720; contra KB, p. 677). The Lord has long contained his anger (Isa. 42:14), but on the day of the Lord it will burst like a flood. צָרָה (distress) expresses the idea of pressure or straitening. It has here the sense of people hemmed in with no escape. מְצוּקָה (constraint) has a similar sense. The two nouns שֹׁאָה וּמְשׁוֹאָה (ruin and ruination) are formed from the same root. Basic to the verbal form of שֹׁאָה is the sense of a din or crash (BDB, p. 980); by extension, the verb can mean to crash in ruin (Isa. 6:11; Dhorme, *Job*, p. 432). Occurring together also in Job 30:3 and 38:27, the two nouns create the assonance characteristic of Zephaniah and, because they comprise a double formation from the same root (similar to the use of שָׁעֵן in Isa. 3:1), signify everything that שֹׁאָה (ruin) can possibly mean. חֹשֶׁךְ (darkness): The desolation touches the cosmos, making it what it was before the ordering hand of God transformed it—the light of sun and moon are gone. Human-

kind set out to rule without God, but this rule has brought back the primeval meaninglessness of Genesis 1:2. עָנָן וַעֲרָפֶל (cloud and mist) are reminiscent of Sinai (Exod. 19:16; 20:21; Deut. 4:11; 5:19 [22]; also 1 Kings 8:12; Ps. 97:2; Joel 2:2), pointing to the presence of God in holiness.

16. שׁוֹפָר (trumpet sound) is a ram's horn, frequently used to sound an alarm in battle (2 Sam. 2:28; Job 39:25). In Exodus 19:16, the trumpet was a summons of grace to enter the divine presence. Typically Zephaniah reverses the symbolism. It is now the mustering of the Lord's host to battle (Jer. 4:19; Amos 2:2). "They had not listened to the voice of the trumpet as it called them . . . ; now they shall hear 'the voice of the Archangel and the trump of God'" (Pusey, *Minor Prophets*). תְּרוּעָה (battle cry) is basically a "shout," here contextualized to mean "a shout of alarm." The meaning "corner towers" for הַפִּנּוֹת is an extended definition of פִּנָּה (a corner; Exod. 38:2; 2 Chron. 26:15; Prov. 7:2; Zeph. 3:6). The military motif, typical of day of the Lord passages, now changes focus and moves from the attackers to the defenders. Humankind has built up defenses—fortified cities

---

succinctly stated by Paul (2 Thess. 1:8–9) and Peter (2 Peter 3:7, 10, 12). It is well to remember that Zephaniah is not a bygone, but the voice of repeated biblical eschatological warning—against which there is no defense (1:16b, 18a), before which people are helpless (1:17a, c), and the cause of which is moral and spiritual culpability (1:17b). The day of the Lord is not arbitrary; it is the logical outgrowth of what humankind is (1:17b), it will bring what humankind deserves (1:17a, c), and it will expose the uselessness of what humans trust (1:16b, 18a). The onset of this ever-imminent day is determined by the innermost divine counsels (Mark 13:32; Acts 1:7) but "in the last resort, it is human beings who precipitate the dreadful Day of the Lord by working out in the world the corruption that festers within them" (Craigie, *Twelve Prophets*, p. 117).

14b. The Warrior here is best understood as the Lord himself (see the Exegesis). Verses like Isaiah 33:7 and Amos 5:16 indicate that one aspect of the awesomeness of the day of the Lord will be the way it incapacitates and reduces to tears the unlikeliest of people. To that extent a reference to a human warrior here would not as such be strange. But in the development of the poem human reactions are not noted until verse 17; up to that point Zephaniah is wholly preoccupied with the divine Assailant. Knowing the Lord as

Scripture reveals him, the bitterness of his cry is both that of outraged holiness and that of an anguished heart.

15–16. Baker (*Zephaniah*, p. 101) observes that *day* occurs six times, a sort of reversal of the six days of creation: "Creation [coming] full-circle to where it was before God actively formed the universe. . . . Sovereign benevolence . . . replaced by judgment." Note how the single idea of light (day 1) is matched by the single word *rage* (v. 15a), the vast expanses of water and sky (day 2) suffer distress and constraint, the ordering of sea and land (day 3) become ruin and ruination, sun and moon (day 4) are replaced by darkness and blackness, the open expanse of the sky (day 5) is shrouded in cloud and mist, and humankind (day 6) faces its distinctive termination in trumpet and battle cry. Once there was a time when darkness overwhelmed Israel's enemies (Exod. 10:22–23) while they enjoyed the light of divine favor; there was another time when they experienced a darkness indicative of divine holiness (Exod. 20:21), yet that holy darkness signified the presence of a God near at hand, intending to live among his people. It was a very different darkness Zephaniah sensed! Against this darkness of the holy God, acting in rage, no defenses avail, whether the strength of a city wall or the height of a tower.

and raised corners—but they, as the following context shows, are of no avail.

17. וְהֲצֵרֹתִי (for I will bring distress): ו (for) functions here as a simple clause-coordinating conjunction connecting this clause to the preceding litany of portents that will characterize the day of the Lord. Since the statement that ו summarizes the preceding portents within the general category of "distress," I translate the particle "for." The verb צָרַר (to distress) links to the first description of the fearful day—צָרָה (distress) in 1:15. כַּעִוְרִים (like the blind) has the sense here of helpless bewilderment and lostness (Isa. 59:10), which is one of the curses of the covenant (Deut. 28:29). כִּי (for) introduces the reason why they will suffer distress—because of their sin. לַיהוָה (against the LORD): Sin is ultimately serious—not because it damages personality or disrupts society, but because it offends the Lord. חָטָאוּ (they have sinned) has the literal sense of "miss the mark" in Judges 20:16. The word came to denote the general concept of sin, especially in passages where it balances other words for sin and is informed by them. וְשֻׁפַּךְ . . . כֶּעָפָר (will be poured out like dust): The only other reference to dust being poured out is Leviticus 14:41, where the plaster is removed from an infected house and its dust "poured out" in an unclean place. The lives of Zephaniah's audience, infected by sin, are unclean and will be treated as the unclean is treated. This would explain a most unusual simile, but possibly the picture is that of helplessness before the onslaught (2 Kings 13:7; Isa. 41:2). עָפָר (dust) does not seem to be used simply as metaphorical of what is worthless. לְחֻמָם (flesh) occurs elsewhere only in Job 20:23. KB (p. 478) refuses to recognize the word and emends the text in both places (as does BHS), but Dhorme (Job, p. 302) notes an Arabic cognate laḥm (flesh, meat) and approves the rare word. גְּלָלִים (refuse), with the meaning "dung," expresses something that is fit only to be taken out and burned (1 Kings 14:10).

18. גַּם (neither) denotes basically the concept of complementation or addition. The construction גַּם . . . גַּם has the sense of "both . . . and." Since this construction appears here in a negative sentence, "neither . . . nor" is an appropriate translation (GKC §154a n. 1c). The scansion of the lines in BHS does not reflect the sense of the clausal relationships: וּבְאֵשׁ (for in the fire of) does not adequately balance בְּיוֹם עֶבְרַת (on the day of rage). בְּיוֹם עֶבְרַת complements the preceding clause, rather than the following (see the Exposition of 1:16–18). עֶבְרָה (rage) forms an inclusio with its use in 1:15; while 1:14b–16a concentrates on the full expression of divine rage, 1:18b concentrates on the full effect it achieves. אֵשׁ (fire), the symbol of active holiness (Exod. 3:2–5), is God's holy outrage expressed in applied anger. קִנְאָה (jealousy) depicts the passionate determination of the Lord to have the full devotion of his people for himself (Exod. 20:5; 34:14). This concept includes his burning zeal to defend his cause and achieve his purposes (Isa. 9:6 [7]) and to leap to the aid of his people (Isa. 59:17; Zech. 1:14; 8:2). כָּלָה (a complete work; lit., a completion) is used adverbially (meaning "wholly") in Genesis 18:21 and Exodus 11:1. The idea of completion later came to be linked with consumption or annihilation, that is, a full end (Isa. 10:23; Jer. 4:27; 5:10; Ezek. 11:13; 20:17). נִבְהָלָה (suddenly accomplished): The niphal of בָּהַל means either "to be in haste" (Prov. 28:22) or "to be terrified" (Gen. 45:3). Here, the participle, qualifying a completion, and emphasized by the particle אַךְ, has the sense of both "yes, and suddenly accomplished" and "yes, and one to be dreaded." כָּל־יֹשְׁבֵי הָאָרֶץ (all those who live on earth): This sudden, fearful end is to fall on the earth as well as on its inhabitants: place and people alike, the sinner as well as the infected environment.

17–18. Humans may categorize their sins into the serious, the mediocre, and the insignificant. To Zephaniah (see James 2:10–11) the mere fact of sin excited and merited the whole weight of divine rage. The simple statement "they have sinned" is sufficient. Sin, of course, would be no more than a pity (in that it blights life) were it not that God is what he is. Were he complacent or, like the gods of Canaan, morally neutral, no harm would threaten the sinner. But he is the God of fiery (actively holy) jealousy, and therein lies our problem. Salvation is not, in the first instance, doing something for the sinner (i.e., expiation) but satisfying the holiness of God (propitiation). It is from Zephaniah as much as from any other biblical writer that Peter learned that the present cosmic order is reserved for fire in the day of the Lord (2 Peter 3:7, 10–12).

I. The End of the World: Is There Any Hope? (1:2–2:3)

C. An Appeal to Readiness—to Judah (2:1–2) and to the World (2:3)

MOTYER

2 Gather yourselves together! Gather,
nation devoid of feeling.
2 Before the decree takes effect,
like chaff clear gone all at once;
before there has yet come upon you
the flaming anger of the LORD;
before there has yet come upon you
the day of the anger of the LORD.
3 Seek the LORD, all you humble ones of the
earth
who are determined to do as he decides;
seek righteousness,
seek humility.
Perhaps you may be covered in the day of
the LORD's anger.

NRSV

2 Gather together, gather,
O shameless nation,
2 before you are driven away
like the drifting chaff,
before there comes upon you
the fierce anger of the LORD,
before there comes upon you
the day of the LORD's wrath.
3 Seek the LORD, all you humble of the land,
who do his commands;
seek righteousness, seek humility;
perhaps you may be hidden
on the day of the LORD's wrath.

2:1. הִתְקוֹשְׁשׁוּ וָקוֹשׁוּ (gather yourselves together! gather): The first term is a reflexive hithpoel, the second an intransitive qal. KB (pp. 860–61) questions the meaning "to gather," but it seems incontestable in the light of the poel examples in Exodus 5:7, 12; Numbers 15:32; and 1 Kings 17:10, 12. גּוֹי (nation) is not always used of Israel in a derogatory sense, as here (contrast Exod. 19:6). The thrust of Zephaniah's message has been the loss of national and religious identity by conforming to the world. Israel is now addressed as such (the definite article expresses the vocative case). לֹא נִכְסָף (devoid of feeling): The verb כָּסַף is difficult to understand. Normally meaning "to long (for)" (Job 14:15), in certain contexts it requires the sense "to grow pale" (the noun כֶּסֶף [silver, money] probably denotes "the pale metal"; BDB, p. 494). The meaning "to grow pale" may have emotional overtones depicting color draining away. When כָּסַף has the meaning "to long for" it is accompanied by the preposition לְ (Gen. 31:30; Job 14:15; Ps. 84:3 [2]). Since it is not accompanied by לְ here, the meaning is not "longed for [by God]." No object is expressed, and the verb has an absolute sense: insensitive, devoid of feeling: "unresponsive to the Lord."

2. לֶדֶת (takes effect) is an infinitive absolute of יָלַד (to bear, bring forth). This clause literally states "before the bringing forth of the decree." The New International Version's "arrives" is an elastic understanding of לֶדֶת. The compressed nature of the Masoretic Text has led to widespread emendation. The New Revised Standard Version follows a widely emended text only vaguely prompted by the Septuagint. חֹק (decree) may be the subject or object. Since, however, all that has preceded is the Lord's "decree" regarding his day, the meaning must be, "What now remains is for the decree, already issued, to bring forth, that is, to take effect." Derived from חָקַק (to engrave [Ezek. 4:1] or to inscribe [Isa. 30:8]), חֹק expresses the will of God in its most unchangeable form (as if carved in stone). The New International Version's "the appointed time" is justifiable in the light of Job 14:13 (Dhorme, *Job*, p. 201). כְּמֹץ (like chaff) is never used in the Old Testament simply as a simile of speed but always of swift-acting divine judgment before which the guilty are helpless (Job 21:18; Pss. 1:4; 35:5; Isa. 17:13; 29:5; Hos. 13:3). Hence the New International Version's translation ("that day sweeps on like chaff") is inadmissible. עָבַר is used attribu-

---

2:1. The poem in 2:1–3 concludes §I of Zephaniah's prophecy. The call to "seek (*biqqēš*) the LORD" (2:3) forms an *inclusio* with the charge in 1:6 that they have not sought the Lord. There is also a link between this concluding section of §I and the balancing conclusion to §§II–III. The structure of this poem involves a difficult decision. On the one hand the imperative plus the vocative in 2:1 is matched by the imperative plus the vocative in 2:3, suggesting that these verbs begin the two divisions of the poem. On the other hand the threefold *bĕṭerem* (before) of 2:2 and the threefold *biqqēš* (seek) of 2:3 balance each other. This latter yields the following arrangement:

a   summons to assemble (1)
b   threefold ground of urgency (2)
    the Lord's decree has gone forth
    the Lord's anger is coming
    the Lord's day is coming
b' threefold command to seek (3a–c)
    spiritual: the Lord
    moral: righteousness
    personal: humility
a' motivation: shelter from divine anger
    (3d)

The nation is to gather itself. This gathering represents the concerted effort of the nation to heed the prophet's warning. Zephaniah is concerned more with national repentance than with the repentance of only a small sector within the nation.

2. Like other prophets, Zephaniah may be taking advantage here of one of the recurring festival gatherings of Israel to present his call (2:3). Amos (5:4–6) appears to use the verb *seek* (*dāraš*) of such an occasion. Into the religious gaiety of the feast (Amos 5:23), the prophetic voice urges a different level of reality: not the backward look to what the Lord did in the past (Lev. 23:39–43), not joy in his contemporary goodness (Deut. 16:15), but trembling before what is to come. The threefold *bĕṭerem* (before; Zeph. 2:2) underlines the urgency of the call: time is not on our side! Once judgment comes, it will speed through the land like flying chaff; it will be as terrible as fire; it will be the coming of the Lord himself. G. Smith (*Twelve Prophets*, pp. 70–71) is quite wrong to say that Zephaniah has only a "sternly ethical" message. What would a contemporary have made of the call to "seek the Lord" (the point where Zephaniah's remedial action begins)? The way into the personal relationship that this call implies was well known,

tively: the chaff that has passed away. The suggested translation "clear gone" reflects the force of the perfect tense. יוֹם (all at once; lit., a day) is an ellipsis for יוֹם אֶחָד ([in] one day; i.e., suddenly) and is similar to its use in Ezekiel 48:35 (also 1 Sam. 2:34; Isa. 9:13 [14]; Zech. 3:9). See also the reference to speed or suddenness in Zephaniah 1:18. בְּטֶרֶם (before) is used three times in this verse, the last two times in the phrase בְּטֶרֶם לֹא (before . . . yet). The negative particle לֹא merely serves to strengthen בְּטֶרֶם (GKC §152y), hence "before yet," "before ever," or "when . . . not yet." חֲרוֹן אַף (the heat of anger) links the conclusions of §I and §II to Zephaniah 3:6–8. אַף (anger) is related to אָנַף (to breathe heavily, snort; hence, to be angry); the dual אַפַּיִם means "nostrils." It refers to the sudden explosion of anger (see the Exegesis of 1:18). יוֹם . . . יְהוָה (the day . . . of the LORD) adds the final note of urgency. The imminent judgment (2:2a) that is expressed in divine anger (2:2b) is not a passing chastisement but the day itself, the final settling of accounts.

3. עַנְוֵי (humble ones of) is related to עָנָה (to be low). The עֲנָוִים are those at the bottom of life's heap, those who can be pushed around and exploited by the influential, by vested interests (Ps. 9:13–14 [12–13]). Spiritually they are ready to see themselves at the bottom of the heap in God's eyes, those who have no power to help themselves nor any influence to bring pressure on God (Pss. 25:9; 149:4). Characteristically the humble cry out to the Lord (Ps. 10:17) and seek him (Ps. 69:33 [32]). In this spirit of self-understanding they are now called to act. But part of true lowliness is taking the servant's place, being at the Lord's disposal; hence the following determination. מִשְׁפָּטוֹ (as he decides; lit., his judgment or decision) is related to שָׁפַט (to judge, give an authoritative decision). The noun is the statement of such a decision. It is therefore part of the legal vocabulary of the Old Testament: the Lord's law is what he has decided is the right course of action for his people (Ps. 119:7). The translation "determined to do" for פָּעֲלוּ reflects the perfect tense. Driver (*Tenses in*

readily available, divinely guaranteed. The whole tabernacle–temple concept was governed by Exodus 29:43–46: the Lord was there, ready and willing to meet his people and speak with them; the appointed sacrifices were the way to draw near (see the Exegesis and Exposition of 3:2). The purpose of the sacrificial system was that the Lord in all his glory might come among his people (Lev. 9:2–6) and that they might hear the words of peace (Num. 6:22–27). Far from having "no gospel," Zephaniah knew that "there is a way for man to rise to that sublime abode: an offering and a sacrifice" (from "Eternal Light" by Thomas Binney)—the same good news that has reached fulfillment in the one sacrifice for sins forever (Heb. 10:12). Though he could not speak of Calvary's cross, Zephaniah knew the same way to God:

There's a way back to God from the dark
  paths of sin;
There's a door that is open, and you may go
  in;
At Calvary's Cross is where you begin
When you come as a sinner to Jesus.
(E. H. Swinstead)

Regarding the compressed Hebrew of the opening line of 2:2, House (*Zephaniah*, p. 129) is right that "the sense of the verse is intelligible and does not require emendation." When he describes the Masoretic Text as "obscure," we must insist that

it is the acceptable obscurity of aphoristic and allusive poetry.

3. The threefold note of urgency in 2:2 is matched by a threefold imperative in 2:3: "seek [*biqqēš*] the Lord" (see the Exegesis of 1:6). Typical of Scripture, the first move is to go directly to the Lord. Every other religion says, Become righteous, become humble; then perhaps God will accept you. But in the Bible the only way to flee *from* God is to flee *to* him. Absence of this earnest relationship invites condemnation, and this must now be put right. It must be done in a spirit of humility ("humble ones") with the intention of obedience ("determined to do as he decides").

For Zephaniah's hearers, as for us, the subjective enjoyment of the objective divine work of redemption depends on the spirit in which it is sought: the humility that is ready to take the beggar's place (Matt. 5:3) and, once mercy has been received, to live in obedience (Zeph. 2:3a; see also Exod. 24:7–8). It also depends on the changed life to which it leads: the evidence of reality provided in the works that follow: righteousness (*sedeq*) in life and humility (*ʿănāwâ*) in heart. So far, then, we find that in principle Zephaniah shares with us in the gospel of salvation.

But when he says "perhaps" (*ʾûlay*), do we conclude that he lacks a gospel of assurance? By no means! The "perhaps" of Zephaniah matches the "if by any means" of Paul (Phil. 3:11 AV). A trembling humility accompanies a true sense of sin

Hebrew §13) states: "The perfect is employed to indicate actions the accomplishment of which lies indeed in the future, but is regarded as dependent upon . . . an unalterable determination of the will." צֶדֶק (righteousness) is, first, the character of God—those principles of right that encapsulate his holiness and are in turn expressed in his judgments or decisions (Isa. 5:16). Derivatively, צֶדֶק expresses principles and practices of right that the Lord expects in his people (Isa. 1:21; 51:1; the feminine צְדָקָה in Job 27:6; Isa. 5:7). Since "the righteous LORD love[s] righteousness" (Ps. 11:7 AV), Zephaniah's call is equivalent to the fundamental principle of the law, "You shall be holy, for I the LORD your God am holy" (Lev. 19:2). The noun עֲנָוָה (humility) is cognate with the adjective עָנִי (humble) and is used in Proverbs 15:33, 18:12, and 22:4 to connote a humble demeanor before people

and humility before God. אוּלַי (perhaps): Baker (*Zephaniah*, p. 104) offers a theologically precise comment: "'Perhaps' safeguards God's sovereign freedom, but the fulness of who he is relieves this 'perhaps' of any anxiety or uncertainty. . . . From the side of man, God's forgiveness should not be misused as 'cheap grace'" (1 Peter 1:17–19). תִּסָּתְרוּ (you may be covered): Unerringly, Zephaniah puts his finger on the heart of the matter: the ultimate danger to the sinner is God's holy nature. The way of salvation must provide satisfaction (Exod. 12:12–13) and shelter (Exod. 12:22–23). The theological equivalent of the verb סָתַר (to cover) is the atonement vocabulary of the verb כִּפֶּר, illustrated in a secular meaning in Genesis 6:14 ("to coat," i.e., "to cover") and theologically in Leviticus 17:11 ("to make atonement," i.e., "to cover by an equivalent payment").

---

and a true appreciation of what is involved in seeking divine forgiveness and reconciliation. It is in relation to this that Paul says "if" and Zephaniah says "perhaps." Neither word evidences any uncertainty that the Lord will "pardon, cleanse, relieve"; rather they yield a proper sense of the enormity of what is being asked and of the sinner's temerity in asking it. They do not reflect hesitation in coming and resting upon the

God of all grace, but an urgent nervousness lest we should fail, whether in the humility of our approach, in the credibility of our determination to obey, or in the consequent evidence of a changed life. Since we call on him as Father, we, too, pass the time of our sojourning in fear (1 Peter 1:17–19); since we possess salvation, we work it out in fear and trembling (Phil. 2:12–13).

II. Judgment and Hope: An Enigma (2:4–3:8)
A. World Overthrow, Hope for Israel (2:4–15)

MOTYER

4 For Gaza will be abandoned,
    and Ashkelon become a desolation.
Ashdod? by noon they will drive it away!
    And Ekron will be uprooted.
5 Ho, inhabitants of the seacoast,
    nation of the Cherethites.
The word of the LORD is against you,
    Canaan, land of the Philistines:
I will so destroy you that there will be no
    inhabitant.
6 And it, the seacoast, will become pastures
        with wells for shepherds
    and enclosures for flocks.
7 And the coast will belong to the remnant
        of the house of Judah.
    Upon them they will find pasture;
in the houses of Ashkelon, in the evening,
    they will lie down.
    For the LORD their God will visit them
        and bring back their captivity.
8 I have heard the insults of Moab
    and the abuse of the sons of Ammon,
with which they have insulted my people
    and acted grandly against their territory.
9 Therefore, as I myself live—
        this is the word of the LORD of hosts,
        the God of Israel—
surely Moab will be like Sodom
    and the sons of Ammon like Gomorrah:
a place for mallow to claim,
    and a salt pit,
    and a desolation forever.
The remnant of my people will despoil
        them,
    and the remainder of my nation will
        possess them.

NRSV

4 For Gaza shall be deserted,
    and Ashkelon shall become a desola-
        tion;
Ashdod's people shall be driven out at
        noon,
    and Ekron shall be uprooted.
5 Ah, inhabitants of the seacoast,
    you nation of the Cherethites!
The word of the LORD is against you,
    O Canaan, land of the Philistines;
and I will destroy you until no inhabi-
        tant is left.
6 And you, O seacoast, shall be pastures,
    meadows for shepherds
    and folds for flocks.
7 The seacoast shall become the possession
        of the remnant of the house of Judah,
    on which they shall pasture,
and in the houses of Ashkelon
    they shall lie down at evening.
For the LORD their God will be mindful of
        them
    and restore their fortunes.
8 I have heard the taunts of Moab
    and the revilings of the Ammonites,
how they have taunted my people
    and made boasts against their territory.
9 Therefore, as I live, says the LORD of hosts,
    the God of Israel,
Moab shall become like Sodom
    and the Ammonites like Gomorrah,
a land possessed by nettles and salt pits,
    and a waste forever.
The remnant of my people shall plunder
        them,
    and the survivors of my nation shall
        possess them.

MOTYER

¹⁰This they will have in exact return for their
pride,
for they insulted and acted grandly
against the people of the LORD of
hosts.
¹¹ That awesome one, the LORD, is against
them,
for he has determined to starve out all
the gods of the earth,
and all the coastlands of the nations, each
in its own place,
will bow in worship to him.
¹² Even you, Cushites, are they who will be
slain by my sword.
¹³ And, oh, may he stretch out his hand
against the north
and destroy Assyria
and make Nineveh a desolation,
dry as the desert.
¹⁴ And flocks will lie down in the middle of
it,
every animal in swarms:
both pelican and owl will lodge on top
of its pillars.
Listen, there is singing at the window,
ruin on the threshold:
for he has exposed the cedar work.
¹⁵ This is the exultant city
that lived in complacency,
that said in its heart,
"I—and none beside!"
How it has become a desolation!
a den for the beasts!
Everyone passing by it will whistle,
will motion with the hand.

NRSV

¹⁰ This shall be their lot in return for their
pride,
because they scoffed and boasted
against the people of the LORD of hosts.
¹¹ The LORD will be terrible against them;
he will shrivel all the gods of the earth,
and to him shall bow down,
each in its place,
all the coasts and islands of the nations.
¹² You also, O Ethiopians,
shall be killed by my sword.
¹³ And he will stretch out his hand against
the north,
and destroy Assyria;
and he will make Nineveh a desolation,
a dry waste like the desert.
¹⁴ Herds shall lie down in it,
every wild animal;
the desert owl and the screech owl
shall lodge on its capitals;
the owl shall hoot at the window,
the raven croak on the threshold;
for its cedar work will be laid bare.
¹⁵ Is this the exultant city
that lived secure,
that said to itself,
"I am, and there is no one else"?
What a desolation it has become,
a lair for wild animals!
Everyone who passes by it
hisses and shakes the fist.

4. כִּי (for): See the Exposition. עֲזוּבָה (abandoned) is a passive participle construed with הָיָה (to be). When the participle occurs with the imperfect of הָיָה, as here (תִּהְיֶה), it emphasizes a continuing action or state (GKC §116r). Note the similar construction in Isaiah 2:2: נָכוֹן יִהְיֶה ([the mountain of the LORD's house] shall be established): The abandonment of Gaza will thus be a continuing state.

לִשְׁמָמָה (become a desolation): לְ frequently accompanies הָיָה (to be) with the meaning "become." In this line הָיָה . . . לְ governs both clauses: Gaza will become abandoned, and Ashkelon will become a desolation. אַשְׁדּוֹד . . . יְגָרְשׁוּהָ (Ashdod? . . . they will drive it away): אַשְׁדּוֹד is a *casus pendens* or, to use a modern linguistic term, the topic portion of a topic-and-comment structure in which a writer

---

2:4–3:8. The second section of Zephaniah's book begins at 2:4, where "for" introduces it as an explanatory comment on the worldwide judgment threatened in the first section. As an explanation it describes how judgment will cover all the earth, justifies this divine action by making specific accusations, and qualifies judgment by an unexpected and unexplained note of hope (2:11; 3:8). From the vantage point of Judah, the prophet looks west to Philistia (2:4–7), east to Moab/Ammon (2:8–11), south to Cush (2:12), and north to Assyria (2:13–15), finally bringing the dire message home to Judah (3:1–5). The number *four*, linked with the four cardinal points of the compass, is a motif for coverage of the whole earth. Here is a typical world: the militarily tough Philistines, the vaguely related (Gen. 19:36–38) but unpredictable Moab and Ammon, the distant and hardly known Cush, and the superpower Assyria. Here is the world in its political diversity: the city-states of Philistia, the minor sovereignties of Moab and Ammon, and the monolithic imperialist Assyria. From all this Zephaniah stands back and sees that it is the Lord only who is sovereign, who decrees the destinies of all alike. His is a calm kingship, unswayed by worldly power, religious affiliation, proximity or remoteness on the face of the earth.

The "Poem of the Nations" (vv. 4–15) is Zephaniah at his literary best. We should note how balanced is his arrangement of his material: the first and third oracles (Philistia, Cush) do not explain the coming judgment. Philistia is opposed by "the word of the LORD" (v. 5), Cush by his sword (v. 12); the second and fourth (Moab, Assyria) explain the judgment: Moab denigrated the Lord's people (vv. 8, 10), Assyria was incarnate pride (v. 15); the first two oracles (Philistia, Moab) look forward to the Lord's people taking possession (vv. 6–7, 9); the third and fourth (Cush, Assyria) make judgment the final act (vv. 12–13, 15). In addition to this balanced treatment, there is the rhythmical arrangement of individual topics observable in verses 4–11. This would suggest that these verses form an originally self-contained

poem to which Zephaniah added the Cush and Assyria oracles in order to achieve a universal motif.

The first "stanza" of this poem, on Philistia, may be structured like this:

A Philistia emptied and destroyed (4)
  a Gaza: people gone
  b   Ashkelon: place destroyed
  a' Ashdod: people driven away
  b'   Ekron: place uprooted
B divine action in destruction (5)
  a woe pronounced: target indicated
  b   the people named: Cherethites
  c   the power behind the destruction: word of the Lord
  b'   the place named: land of the Philistines
  a' woe implemented: agent and extent
B' divine action in restoration (6–7b)
  a new use (6)
    1 shepherds: water supplied
    2 flocks secure
  b   new owners (7a)
  a' new use (7b)
    1 shepherds: pasturage supplied
    2 flocks in security
A' Philistia repopulated (7c)
  a divine visitation
  b   human restoration

Both A and A' commence with explanatory *kî* (for), and "Ashdod . . . noon," three lines from the beginning, is matched by "Ashkelon . . . evening," three lines from the end.

4. Like Jeremiah (25:20) and Zechariah (9:4–7), Zephaniah does not mention Gath among the five cities of the Philistines (1 Sam. 6:16–18). Maybe as a result of Uzziah's military campaign (2 Chron. 26:6), Gath was already in decline. Zephaniah presents a stylized picture of Philistia, tracing the cities from north to south, for he is not thinking of Philistia as the historical entity of his own day but using it as an eschatological picture. It is as if he were saying, Here is a principle that will govern

states a topic and then makes a comment on the topic (see the Exegesis of Hos. 9:13). The question mark following Ashdod in my translation tries to reflect this emphasis. בַּֽצָּהֳרַיִם (by noon): See the Exposition.

5. חֶבֶל הַיָּם (seacoast): חֶבֶל means "cord" or "rope" (Josh. 2:15), then by extension "measuring line" (Zech. 2:5 [1]), hence "measured portion or region" (Josh. 17:5; Zeph. 2:7). Here it has the sense of "region of the sea." The word כְּרֵתִים (the Cherethites) may owe its origin to Philistine links with Crete (Baker, *Zephaniah*, p. 105), but continued in use as a synonym for Philistine (1 Sam. 20:14, 16; Ezek. 25:16). דְּבַר־יְהוָה עֲלֵיכֶם (the word of the LORD is against you) is regarded by BHS as an addition. But to do so leaves, as House shows (*Zephaniah*, p. 129), the direct speech, וְהַאֲבַדְתִּיךְ (I will so destroy), with no introduction, and the balanced structure of the poem is thereby destroyed (contrary to J. Smith's view [*Zephaniah*, p. 217] that the presence of this phrase "mars the metrical form"). Rather, the reference to the word of the Lord makes this the very heart of the oracle. The verbal expression of his mind and will partakes of his irresistibility. עֲלֵיכֶם (against you): The preposition עַל (against) is often no more than a

synonym for אֶל (to, unto) but here merits its full force. כְּנַעַן (O Canaan): Why Canaan? It cannot be a gloss (so BHS), for nothing requires explanation. The use of "Canaanite" to connote a trader in 1:11 (Baker, *Zephaniah*, p. 105; J. Smith, *Zephaniah*, p. 217) has no bearing on the context. The name *Canaan*, however, would bring the Philistines within the scope of the ancient curse (Gen. 9:25) and in that way enhance the word of the Lord that was against them. Also, Canaan is specifically the promised land (Gen. 12:5; 13:12–15; Ps. 105:11) that the people of God had never fully possessed. To link Philistia with Canaan in this way and then to predict that it would become Judah's possession (Zeph. 2:7) aptly alludes to the fulfillment of the promise. Whatever the Lord's people deserve, he will never go back on his word.

6. וְהָיְתָה חֶבֶל הַיָּם (and it, the seacoast, will become): The verb וְהָיְתָה (and . . . will become) is feminine. Since חֶבֶל (coast) is always masculine, the implied subject must therefore be אֶרֶץ (land) from the previous line, with חֶבֶל הַיָּם (seacoast) in amplificatory apposition. נְוֹת כְּרֹת רֹעִים (pastures with wells for shepherds) offers a typical assonance, and the rush to emend the text, based on the supposed difficulty of כְּרֹת (wells), is extraordi-

---

the final settlement of world affairs in the day of the Lord. When they entered Canaan, the Lord's people made many compromises. The whole land was included in the divine promise (Gen. 13:14–15; Deut. 34:1–4), yet the Philistines, though sometimes subdued (1 Sam. 7:13; 2 Sam. 5:17–25), were never possessed. In the day when the Lord sets all things to rights, there will be no such adjustment of his promises and purposes: his people will possess their possessions (see Obad. 17–21 with its recurring use of the idea of "possessing"). But Zephaniah preserves a certain detachment or "distance" from historical events. With the possible exception of Assyria (2:13–15), we cannot really say that his forecasts met with this or that historical fulfillment. Nevertheless his preview of the day of the Lord is firmly bedded in historical processes. The implication of "deserted . . . desolation . . . uprooted" is of military assault and overthrow. Thus the day of the Lord is not an arbitrary infliction but coincides with and works through the horrific climax of human mismanagement of world affairs. The eternally laid plans of heaven are in the hand that controls and directs the historical processes of earth. Suddenness is the order of that day: "by noon" it will be all over, and "in the evening" occupation will be complete (v. 7)!

J. Smith (*Zephaniah*, p. 216) notes Herodtus's story (2.157) that Pharaoh Psammetichus I (664–610 B.C.) besieged Ashdod for twenty-nine years. This would have happened in Zephaniah's lifetime. Is the prophet making a wry contrast between this, the height of human military endeavor, and the ease and speed of the Lord's victory?

5. The poetic shape of this verse tells a theological story. The verse is bracketed by its opening ("inhabitants") and closing ("inhabitant") words. The second and fourth lines have the complementary ideas of "nation" and "land." The central line traces all to the agency of "the word of the LORD." The divine agent in creation (Ps. 33:6; see also Gen. 1:3; Heb. 11:3; 2 Peter 3:5) is the overmastering agent in history; in both arenas alike he "spoke and it came to be" (Ps. 33:9; Isa. 13:3).

6–7. The word of the Lord is the central, determinative factor in the course of history (v. 5); the people of the Lord are the central concern that determines all his actions. The whole course of history is for their final welfare and their secure inheriting of his promises. In contrast to the war-imagery of verses 4–5, pastoral peace now provides the motifs: "pastures . . . shepherds . . . flocks . . . pasture . . . lie down" (specifically of animals at rest). As so often in the Old Testament, and not

narily insensitive. There is no reason why the verb כָּרָה, which has the sense of dig (Gen. 50:5), should not give rise to a noun כָּרָה (pit, cistern, well; BDB, p. 500). Nor is there any reason to refuse Zephaniah the right to coin an assonantal word for his own purposes. It subtly recapitulates the reference to the Philistines as כְּרֵתִים (Cherethites) in 2:5. House (*Zephaniah*, p. 121), indeed, finds a reference to them here: "The land by the sea, / where the Cherethites dwell." The picture of pastoral peace is probably an intentional contrast with the warlike reputation of the Philistine states. גְּדֵרוֹת (enclosures): See Numbers 32:16; 1 Samuel 24:4 [3]; Psalm 89:41 [40].

7. חֶבֶל (the coast) stands as an elliptical expression for חֶבֶל הַיָּם (the region of the sea); see the Exegesis of 2:5. שְׁאֵרִית (the remnant) basically describes something left over. Isaiah 44:17 speaks of the remainder of a piece of wood from which an idol has been fashioned. More frequently שְׁאֵרִית refers to people who have survived a catastrophe (1 Chron. 4:43; Isa. 37:4; Jer. 25:20). Theologically, the word describes the people through whom God carries on his redemptive activity (Gen. 45:7; Isa. 37:32; Mic. 2:12; 4:7). עֲלֵיהֶם יִרְעוּן (upon them they will find pasture): When רָעָה (to feed) occurs with the preposition עַל (upon), it regularly indicates the place of pasturing (Isa. 49:9). The suffix הֶם (them) is masculine while its obvious antecedents in 2:6, whether נְוֺת (pastures) or גְּדֵרוֹת (enclosures), are feminine. Hence BHS and GKC §135p adjust to עַל־הַיָּם (by the sea). This is an easy and suitable solution, but it is perhaps better to appeal to the

usage whereby "masculine suffixes (especially in the plural) are not infrequently used to refer to feminine substantives" (GKC §135o; also §122g). On the other hand, the plural suffix could refer back to חֶבֶל (coast) considered as a collective singular (GKC §135p), as happens in Genesis 15:13 and Numbers 16:3. כִּי (for) introduces a clause stating the cause of Judah's restoration—Yahweh's visit. פָּקַד (to visit) occurs without עַל (on) and has a favorable sense: God attends his people to act on their behalf (see the Exegesis of 1:8). שָׁב שְׁבוּתָם: Uncertainty besets the traditional rendering "bring back their captivity." If the translation "captivity" (שְׁבָה means to take captive) is correct (Dhorme, *Job*, p. 650), any necessary reference to the Babylonian captivity should be excluded (R. Smith, *Micah–Malachi*, p. 136; Eaton, *Zephaniah*, p. 141). The use of this expression in Job 42:10, Psalm 85, Psalm 126, and Ezekiel 16:53 indicates a general rather than a specific reference. Johnson (*Cultic Prophet*, p. 67 n. 4) prefers the root שׁבת (to be firm), which yields the meaning "to restore well-being."

8. שָׁמַעְתִּי (I have heard): The first-person inflection refers to Yahweh. The verb שָׁמַע denotes hearing, but frequently connotes appropriate action, which may include obedience by people (1 Sam. 8:7; Isa. 1:19; Mic. 5:14 [15]) or a favorable (Num. 20:16; Deut. 33:7) or judgmental (Ps. 78:59) response by God. Here, Yahweh responds with action appropriate to Moab's reproaches against his people (Zeph. 2:9). חֶרְפַּת (the insults of) has the basic sense of casting blame or scorn on someone

least in Isaiah and Zephaniah, the note of hope is sounded unexpectedly. Theologically, this is because hope comes solely from God and by divine action; it is against the grain alike of deservings and expectations. Yet the fact remains: in a world brought to ruin under divine judgment, the Lord is at work on behalf of his people, to preserve, enrich, and bring them into the possession of what he has promised. Note how "bring back" forms a contrasting *inclusio* with "drive away" (v. 4).

8–11. The words *my people* (v. 8), *my people . . . my nation* (v. 9), and *the people of the LORD* (v. 10) provide the story line of this subsection. At the same time the stress on the Lord's people provides a foil for the wider hope the poem expresses. As Baker (*Zephaniah*, p. 108) says, "The oracle closes with a step back from the narrow geographical . . . focus on Moab and Ammon . . . to encompass the rest of the world"

as a total worshiping community. The poem itself is beautifully balanced:

A insults heard (8)
  a the Lord listening
  b the mockers
  c the mocked
B divine response (9)
  a' the Lord's oath
  b' overthrow of the mockers
  c' vindication of the mocked
A' insults avenged (10–11)
  b'' exact requital on the mockers
  c'' because of whom they mocked
  a'' the Lord's triumph

8. As cousin-nations (Gen. 19:37–38), Moab and Ammon were treated with considerateness (Deut. 2:9, 19). The rule in Deuteronomy 23:4 [3] is neither racist nor nationalist, but a proper safe-

(Job 27:6; Ps. 74:10; Prov. 14:31). While other nuances may apply, the context here calls for scorn. מוֹאָב (Moab): See the Exposition. וְגִדּוּפֵי (and the abuse of) is part of a construct chain that literally states "the abuses of the sons of Ammon." The root גדף is synonymous with its companion word in this line (חֶרְפַּת) in that both convey a sense of reviling. Psalm 44:17 [16] also combines these words in parallel, laying emphasis on the shame that these verbal actions bring on their objects. The words convey the sense of scornful taunting and insult. While these two words do not always require verbal expression (Num. 15:30), that God has heard (שָׁמַעְתִּי) them implies that they were spoken. The expression וַיַּגְדִּילוּ (and acted grandly) may suggest invasion or land acquisition (elsewhere it means "to assume airs"). The hiphil of גדל (lit., to make great) should be transitive, but in the present construction it usually occurs without an object (see Pss. 35:26; 38:17 [16]; 55:13 [12], where it is parallel with חָרַף; also Jer. 48:26, 42 [of Moab]; Lam. 1:9). Psalm 41:10 [9] uses גְּדַל to mean "to make the heel great against," that is, "to act with great treachery"; its meaning in Ezekiel 35:13 and Obadiah 12 is "to make the mouth great, to make large claims, or to mouth great insults." גְּבוּל is strictly "border" (Josh. 15:1–2), hence what a border contains, namely, territory (Amos 6:2).

9a–c. לָכֵן (therefore) introduces the logical result of Yahweh's awareness of the taunts against his people: divine punishment. חַי־אָנִי (as I myself live) is the second most common form of divine oath in the Old Testament (the first is niphal שבע, to swear). This oath is similar to Egyptian oaths using ʿnḫ (life; H. Ringgren, *TDOT* 4:324–27). Divine oaths contain various agents by which God swears; for example, בְּקָדְשׁוֹ (by his holiness; Amos 4:2) and בֶּאֱמוּנָתֶךָ (by your faithfulness; Ps. 89:50 [49]). The reference to the life of Yahweh is similar to those oath formulas where Yahweh swears by himself (Gen. 22:16; also Heb. 6:13). When God swears by his life, he swears by his own nature and character—by his own existence as a divine entity. The oath is as sure as the life of Yahweh who swore it (Deut. 32:40–41). נְאֻם (the word of): See the Exegesis of 1:2. צְבָאוֹת (of hosts) is strictly a noun in apposition to יְהוָה (the LORD): "The Lord, he is hosts"—that is, in his own person and nature he *is* (not that he simply possesses) every potentiality and power (Hag. 1:2). In Zephaniah the title occurs only here (2:9–10). In the matching portion of §I (1:2–6) the Lord's people are found worshiping "the host of heaven." How faithful is the God who nonetheless exercises omnipotence on their behalf! The particle כִּי (surely) functions as an asseverative in oath formulas (as does כִּי אִם), denoting the certainty of the result (GKC §159ee). מִמְשַׁק (a place . . . to claim): KB (p. 534) leaves this word unexplained. The hypothetical root משק appears as מֶשֶׁק in Genesis 15:2, where a connotation like acquisition or pos-

---

guard of the purity of the Lord's congregation. Hostility, however, soon emerged (Num. 22:1–6) and continued (Judg. 3:12–30; 11:4–11; 1 Sam. 11:1; 12:12; 14:47). David was threatened by Moab (Ps. 60); the Ammonites were deliberately provocative (2 Sam. 10); and the savage reprisal exacted in 2 Samuel 12:31 suggests (though is not justified by) a long history of animosity. Second Chronicles 20 indicates further prolongation of enmity. But in this as in everything else (Rom. 12:19–21) vengeance belongs to, should be left to, and will be seen to by the Lord. Prohibited from avenging themselves, the meek (Matt. 5:5) will nevertheless inherit the earth, for the principle of legal recompense enunciated in Deuteronomy 19:19, like every other precept of his law, reflects a holy reality within the divine nature that the Lord's people cannot be mistreated with impunity. Every earthly hurt is registered in heaven, for whoever touches his people touches the apple of the Lord's eye (Zech. 2:12 [8]). If Zephaniah 2:4–7 shows that

the promises of the Lord will be kept, 2:8–11 shows that his law is equally inviolable.

9. Only in the Moab/Ammon oracle does the Lord speak, in Zephaniah, of "my people" (also vv. 8, 10) and of himself as "the God of Israel." It is in relation to "cousins" that this exclusivist doctrine is thus quietly stressed, for not even near-kinship is the same as membership. The revelation of the Lord, admission to his fellowship, shelter beneath his care, confidence in his ultimate vindication—these are blessings only for the elect. Yet (see v. 11), true to Old Testament theology, it is in this exclusivist context that universal hope is proclaimed! But the Lord's people have a well-founded security. The oath-taker is their God, "the God of Israel"; they are his elect, "my people"; and the oath rests on the surest foundation, the being ("as I live") and the omnipotence ("the LORD of hosts") of God himself. Sodom and Gomorrah became a prophetic motif for divine overthrow (Isa. 1:9; 13:19; Jer. 49:18; 50:40; Lam. 4:6; Amos 4:11; see also Deut. 29:22 [23]).

934

session suits the context. The preformative *mem* often connotes place where. Thus, "place of possession" is as near as we can come to the sense here. If alteration is desired, Psalm 126:6 offers מֶשֶׁךְ (sowing). חָרוּל (mallow) is a weed that grows spontaneously on untended land (Prov. 24:31). It might be thistles (Dhorme, *Job*, p. 434), chickling (KB, p. 332), chickpea (BDB, p. 355), or nettles (Jewish tradition). Job 30:7 describes it as something under which outcasts and homeless gather, which makes "thistles" and "nettles" a bit un-likely. Pusey (*Minor Prophets*, p. 138) cites a nineteenth-century traveler who saw mallow growing in rank luxuriance in Moab, especially in deserted Arab camps. מִכְרֵה (pit) occurs only here (see the Exegesis of 2:6 for כָּרַת, to dig). The phrase מִכְרֵה־מֶלַח means a place of digging for salt. The combination of מֶלַח (salt) and חָרוּל shows that we are dealing with ideas and motifs, not factual prediction, for salt precludes further growth (Deut. 29:22 [23]; Ps. 107:34; Jer. 17:6). The thought is this: "If anything were to grow (which, of course, it will not!), it would be mallow."

9d. שְׁאֵרִית (the remnant of): See the Exegesis of 2:7. עַמִּי (my people) is parallel to גּוֹי (my nation) and thus informs it with favorable intent (2:1). Generally speaking, עַם specifies Israel in relation to its history with God, while גּוֹי (nation) depicts the people as a national entity among other nations. On the form גּוֹי, see Ezra 6:21 and Jeremiah 26:6 (GKC §8k).

10. זֹאת (this) is construed in the feminine (or neuter) because of the impossibility of assigning a gender to the concepts to which it relates. This particle generally introduces a new person or concept into the discussion (2:15), rather than referring to a person, object, or concept already mentioned (GKC §136a). Here, however, it appears to refer to the preceding judgment saying (2:9) because of the lack of a specific statement of judg-

ment in 2:11 to which it may refer. Also, the reference in 2:10 to the mistreatment of the Lord's people complements the pronouncement of the victory of the Lord's people (עַמִּי) in 2:9. תַּחַת (in exact return) functions as a preposition of precise equivalence or substitution (Gen. 22:13; Exod. 21:23–24; Isa. 53:12). גְּאוֹנָם (their pride), related to גָּאָה (to be high), expresses haughtiness or arrogance. On חֵרְפוּ (insulted) and וַיַּגְדִּלוּ (and acted grandly), see the Exegesis of 2:8. יְהוָה צְבָאוֹת (the Lord of hosts) links the concluding verses of this section (2:10–11) with 2:9, which is its centerpiece (see the Exegesis of 2:9a–c for the meaning of צְבָאוֹת).

11. נוֹרָא (that awesome one; lit., one worthy to be feared), a niphal participle, is related to יָרֵא (to be afraid). The Septuagint reads ἐπιφανήσεται, understanding the Hebrew as נִרְאָה ([the Lord] will reveal himself [against them]). BHS follows the Septuagint. נוֹרָא is an appositional adjective (GKC §132b) and is emphatic (a similar construction is found in Isa. 10:30; 53:11). כִּי (for) does not introduce direct causation, for that would necessitate a statement giving the reason for Yahweh's negative attitude. Rather, כִּי introduces proximate causation. That is, it explicates the preceding statement by fleshing out its particulars (2 Sam. 23:5; Isa. 1:30). The required meaning of רָזָה (he has determined to starve out) is clear, but does the Masoretic Text express it? The adjective רָזֶה has the sense of lean or emaciated (Num. 13:20), and the noun רָזוֹן connotes emaciation (Isa. 10:16). Both nouns are related to רָזָה (to become lean), which in the niphal occurs only in Isaiah 17:4. Since the qal, which occurs only here, normally has an intransitive sense (to be lean) rather than the transitive sense this context seems to require, BHS alters the Masoretic Text's qal to a piel and its perfect tense to the imperfect: יְרַזֶּה (he will make lean). The piel does not occur elsewhere in

---

10. The great principle that "the Lord knows those who are his" (2 Tim. 2:19) has earthly as well as eternal implications. We do not always take the Lord's side but he never fails to take ours, for we are "the people of the Lord of hosts." The accusation of pride against Moab (see also Isa. 16:6; 25:10–11) sums up all that is implied in the attitude of taunting, reviling, and boasting of verse 8. Moab's attitude of superior scorn and careless dismissal speaks of a dominance certain of one's own unchallengeable rightness and primacy. On this deadly sin of pride, see the summary following verse 15.

11. Zephaniah offers his own comment on verse 11 in 3:9–11. As it stands, "to bow in worship" might be no more than enforced and unwilling acknowledgment of a God mightier than those they have known. It could be an admission devoid of "wonder, love, and praise." Far from being so, Zephaniah begins here the doctrine of the coming worldwide Israel, which he will presently teach more plainly and which other places in the Old Testament make explicit. See the extended note following verse 15.

12. The demonstrations above and below of the self-contained poetic nature of verses 4–11 and

the Old Testament but analogy suggests that it would be transitive. Comparison, however, with a parallel formation like רָצוֹן (acceptance), where qal רָצָה is transitive (to accept; Hos. 8:13), suggests that until further knowledge arises the Masoretic Text is best left alone. If we regard the perfect tense as a perfect of determination it is very forceful. כָּל־אֱלֹהֵי הָאָרֶץ (all the gods of the earth): For an equally abrupt reference to the overthrow of the gods, see Exodus 12:12. A similar reference is appropriate in Zephaniah in the light of 1:4. The phrase אִיֵּי הַגּוֹיִם (the coastlands of the nations) occurs elsewhere only in Genesis 10:5. Wenham (Genesis, p. 219) remarks that the reference seems to be to "nations furthest removed from Israel geographically. Some of them are described in Ezek 38:6 as coming 'from the uttermost parts of the north.' Others reflect Israel's western horizon." Zephaniah uses כָּל (all) both to emphasize universality and to balance כָּל־אֱלֹהֵי הָאָרֶץ in the previous line: all false worship will be starved out and all true worship offered. אִיֵּי (the coastlands of; lit., islands, regions) came to refer to distant lands, especially those reached only by water (Esth. 10:1; Ps. 72:10; Isa. 11:11; 24:15; 66:19; Jer. 25:22; 31:10; Ezek. 26:18).

12. With only a brief allusion, Zephaniah moves from neighboring lands, through the universal reference in 2:11, to the remote south. Cush is frequently linked with Egypt (Gen. 10:6; Isa. 20:3; 45:14; Nah. 3:9), and it is usually suggested that it lies to the south (Wenham, Genesis, p. 221). There is no need to make its mention in Zephaniah refer to Egypt under the Ethiopian dynasty (780–664 B.C.) or to find significance in

Cambyses II's campaigning in Upper Egypt in 525 B.C. (Baker, Zephaniah, p. 109). No narrowly local events or fulfillments cater to the picture Zephaniah is painting of the day of the Lord. His concern is the universal scope of the day and so he reaches out to the far south: hence, he says גַּם־אַתֶּם (even you!). הֵמָּה (they who): The vocative כּוּשִׁים (O Cushites) modulates into the third-person plural "they who," a construction called an emphatic vocative (found also in Isa. 22:16; 47:8; 48:1; 54:1, 11; GKC §144p).

13. וְיֵט (and, oh, may he stretch) along with וִיאַבֵּד (and destroy) and וְיָשֵׂם (and make [a desolation]) are jussive in form and are often classed with unexplained jussives that replace the imperfect on rhythmic grounds (so GKC §109k; Driver, Tenses in Hebrew §§170–75, rejects this explanation). Driver (§172) sensibly urges that a jussive meaning was intended. It is as if Zephaniah were himself caught up in the divine program and was urging it on to completion. Note the same excited prophetic involvement in Zechariah 3:5, where Tidwell ("Wā'ōmar," p. 352) thinks of the "heavenly council" in session with Zechariah contributing to the discussion (see also Isa. 6:8). Dennett (Zechariah the Prophet, p. 31) puts it well: "It would seem as if the prophet had been so brought into communion with the mind of God . . . that he is used to become its expression. . . . He intercedes . . . that it might at once be done." נָטָה יָד (to stretch out the hand) reflects a gesture of intent to act (Exod. 7:5; Isa. 23:11; Jer. 51:25). צָפוֹן (the north): Assyria lies to the east, but the northern Arabian desert intervenes. When Mesopotamian powers interfered in Palestinian affairs, therefore, they

---

13–15 respectively suggest that this tiny oracle on Cush has been edited into its present position by Zephaniah in order to complete the north-south-east-west presentation of his worldview. Yet, brief though it is, it covers three characteristic aspects of day of the Lord theology: no part of the world will escape, not even remote Cush; the day will bring about a final settlement with the Lord's foes, a judgment unto death ("slain"); and the great Agent himself is at work ("my sword"). There is a threefold "no-escape": no escape for any people, no escape from the wages of sin, no escape from divine confrontation.

13–15. Verses 13–15 comprise another of Zephaniah's marvelous seven-part poems (see 1:14b–18 and 3:14–17). Like the others it has a balanced trajectory, moving progressively to and then from a central point:

a	judgment threatened, bringing desolation (13)
b	Nineveh occupied by "nations" (14a)
c	Nineveh a place of bird-song (14b)
d	explanation: "he has exposed" (14c)
c'	contrast: Nineveh exultant and complacent (15a)
b'	contrast: Nineveh's claim to uniqueness (15b)
a'	judgment inflicted: desolation a reality (15c–d)

The a-sections are thematically linked and provide inclusios: the hand of God and the hand of man, and two related words for "desolation." The b-sections form a contrast: Nineveh occupied by "nations" of beasts as against Nineveh's claim to

necessarily came from the north. צִיָּה כַּמִּדְבָּר (dry as the desert): Nineveh occupied a particularly well-watered site, with rivers skirting the city on the southwest and northwest and extensive irrigation canals. No greater transformation could be suggested, nor a more dramatic evidence of the power of the divine hand.

14. וְרָבְצוּ (and [flocks] will lie down): Occupation by animals is another way to indicate lack of human inhabitants (Isa. 13:20–22). כָל־חַיְתוֹ־גוֹי (every animal in swarms; lit., all animals of a nation): The ending וֹ on חַיְתוֹ (animal) is an emphatic construct state (GKC §90k; see Ps. 50:10). גוֹי (nation) is difficult. The Septuagint offers relief with τῆς γῆς (of the earth), which House (*Zephaniah*, p. 130) accepts as "a good change." BHS suggests that גוֹי arose through confusion with the following גַם, and that we should insert הַשָּׂדֶה (of the field), as in Psalm 104:11.

Baker (*Zephaniah*, p. 109) thinks that the Septuagint reading arose from an original Hebrew גֵּיא (beasts of the valley), an expression not found elsewhere. The only other instance where גוֹי is used with animal associations is Joel 1:6, where it refers to a locust swarm (note the use of עַם [people] in reference to the locusts in Joel 2:2, which is also applied to ants and coneys in Prov. 30:25–26). This still leaves Zephaniah's expression unusual and difficult, but hardly beyond poetic license. Zephaniah may have wanted a word like גוֹי to make a contrast with the isolationism of proud Nineveh (2:15b). KB (p. 819) says that the קָאַת (pelican) is perhaps a "species of owl" (House, *Zephaniah*, p. 130). In reality we know no more than that it is a forbidden species of bird (Deut. 14:17; also Ps. 102:7 [6]; Isa. 34:11). קִפֹּד (owl) is identified by KB (p. 845) as a "short-eared owl" (the word occurs elsewhere only in Isa. 14:23;

be uniquely alone; note also "in the middle" (v. 14a) and "in its heart" (v. 15b). The c-sections are another contrast: there is singing in Nineveh—that of undisturbed birds, very different from the exulting that once was there! So we are led to the central and explanatory d-section, the destroying work of God. Like the other seven-section poems the a-section is longer than the b-c-d sections, and the central d-section is a three-word explanation. But unlike the others, this is a prediction that was fulfilled within a century. Nineveh fell to the Babylonians in 612 B.C. and was utterly destroyed. An "interim fulfillment" like this guarantees all else that has been promised or threatened.

13. The charge against Assyria and Nineveh its capital is soulmate to the pride found in Moab (v. 10). In Moab pride looked outward and denigrated others; in Assyria pride looks inward and finds everything to delight: personal uniqueness, superiority, complacency, security. The unrecognized factor is the understated "he" of verses 13–14! As he records the consequences of self-sufficiency as a philosophy of life, Zephaniah begins with a grim transformation in the environment: the well-watered Nineveh (see the Exegesis) transformed into an arid desert! In Genesis 3:17–19, there was an environmental consequence of Adam's bid for self-sufficient freedom from God's law, and it is always so. The creation always sides with its Creator against the rebel. The holy life of God that makes "nature" fertile (Ps. 104:30) only grudgingly lends itself to the needs of sinful

humans and ultimately will cease to do so. God's world will not forever support God's enemy. Nineveh is part of Scripture's early-warning system.

14. Humans have ceased to be, and the beasts have taken over. When the Lord's vineyard refused to produce the fruit of righteousness, the beasts invaded (Isa. 5:5). It is in the same spirit that Isaiah envisages the day when the earth itself is polluted by its inhabitants because they have transgressed God's laws, and through this broken, barren waste the gathering remnant makes their way home to Zion (24:16). Humankind holds its tenure on the earth only by holy obedience. Zephaniah matches the earth-creatures of 2:14a with the air-creatures of 2:14b. Every sort of creature in every location underscores the awesome reality of the absence of humanity. Baker (*Zephaniah*, p. 110), calling attention to Leviticus 26:21–22, notes that this "sort of abandonment to nature is not uncommon for those who oppose God." Every sort of human craft in stonework or woodwork, whether at the top (pillar), in the middle (window), or at the bottom (threshold)—a whole series of contrasts—sketches total ruination. The environment was destroyed in verse 13, all human achievement follows in verse 14. Just as on demolition sites we see once lovingly papered walls exposed to the elements, so here costly carved cedar is laid bare in the ruined city. In the seven-line poem of 1:14b–18, three Hebrew words offered an explanation: "They have sinned against the LORD." Matching words offer the

34:11). Neither bird is ordinarily a city dweller, which enhances the unnaturalness of the situation. בְּכַפְתֹּרֶיהָ (on top of its pillars; lit., on its capitals): See כַּפְתּוֹר in Amos 9:1. קוֹל (listen; lit., a voice): See the Exegesis of 1:10. The Septuagint reads θηρία φωνήσει (wild beasts shall cry), hence BHS suggests כּוֹס (little owl; Ps. 102:7 [6]) for קוֹל, a clever but unnecessary suggestion. יְשׁוֹרֵר is imperfect and may be translated it "keeps singing" (quite undisturbed). חֹרֶב denotes dryness and, by extension, a desolate ruin (NIV: "rubble"). The Septuagint has κόρακες (ravens), reading עֹרֵב. Reference to a bird fits the context but is not so suited to a position on a threshold. BHS adopts the alteration; House (p. 131) thinks the confusion was created by the Septuagint. כִּי (for) presents the reason for the structural ruin: God has so destroyed the great buildings that the paneling of the interior walls is exposed.

15. זֹאת הָעִיר הָעַלִּיזָה (this is the exultant city): Apart from here and 3:11, the intensive adjective עַלִּיזָה (exultant) is used only in Isaiah (13:3; 22:2; 23:7; 24:8; 32:13). לָבֶטַח (in complacency) can possess a good sense, "in safety" (Isa. 14:30), but also a bad sense (here and in Judg. 18:7). For the whole phrase יוֹשֶׁבֶת לָבֶטַח (lived in complacency), see Isaiah 47:8. Throughout Zephaniah there are many such reminders of Isaiah: Zephaniah is nearest of all the prophets to Isaiah's style and skill with words. יִשְׁרֹק (will whistle): See 1 Kings 9:8 and Jeremiah 19:8. This verse couples clapping hands and whistling as gestures of derision (see Job 27:23). יָנִיעַ (will motion): This verb (נוּעַ) is not found elsewhere with יָד (hand; in Isa. 37:22 it occurs with רֹאשׁ, head). Zephaniah must have changed the picture in order to provide the *inclusio* with the outstretched hand of 2:13.

explanation here: human sin has met its Judge and "he has exposed the cedar work."

15. The city which once weighed all others in its balances and found them wanting finally becomes derided ("whistle") and nonchalantly dismissed by every casual observer. Along with environment (v. 13) and achievement (v. 14), repute (v. 15) has disappeared. Such is the end of vaunting self-satisfaction.

Great principles relating to God's governance of the human arena are set forth by Zephaniah. The first is that the Lord is God of all the earth. By naming four nations, Zephaniah presents a typical worldview: militarily tough Philistia, volatile Moab and Ammon, distant and vaguely known Cush, and overshadowing superpower Assyria. We would find it easy to name modern equivalents. But Zephaniah stands back from all this and sees only the Lord sovereignly decreeing the destiny of all alike. Nothing interferes with his calm sway, neither worldly power nor spiritual claim.

The second principle is that the Lord plans for the spiritual needs of the world. Verses 8–10 express an exclusivist theology: one people on earth knowing and belonging to the Lord, favored with his care. True to the biblical doctrine of election as well as to Zephaniah's message of hope, this oracle also makes the promise of a universal people of the Lord (2:11). Zephaniah was not enabled to tell how God will win the nations "but all the coastlands . . . will bow in worship" (2:11). Here, in the Old Testament, is the innumerable company of Revelation 7:9–12. For he will not give his glory to another nor his praise to graven images (Isa. 42:8); he has sworn that to himself every knee shall bow (Isa. 45:23)—not as second-class citizens (note Isa. 19:24), for "in the LORD all the offspring of Israel will be justified" (Isa. 45:25 NASB).

The third principle is that the Lord is in charge of the whole historical process. Zephaniah preserves a certain detachment from history. He does not seem to have been moved by historical circumstances to minister as he did; nor can we say (except possibly regarding Assyria) that what he forecast had this or that historical fulfillment. But though he lacks historical connection in this sense, his perception of the day of the Lord is firmly bedded in historical processes. When Gaza is abandoned (2:4), it will be through a swift military attack. The Cushites will fall by the sword (2:12). And the ruin of Assyria (2:13–15) suggests enemy activity (2:10–11, 13, 16b). When Isaiah (13:19–22) speaks similarly of Babylon, it is as the result of the onslaught of a mighty host inflicting the Lord's anger. And this is the very point Zephaniah implies. The day of the Lord is not an arbitrary infliction but coincides with the horrific climax of human mismanagement of world affairs. The eternally laid plans of heaven are in the hand that molds and rules the historical processes of earth.

The fourth principle is that the Lord's people are central to his world purposes. The purpose behind the divine hostility against Philistia is that the coast will belong to the remnant of the house of Judah (2:7a). Moab and Ammon will become like Sodom, and "my nation will possess them"

(2:9). Philistia, Moab, and Ammon, of course, are addressed here not only as historical entities but as aspects of Zephaniah's worldview. Two ideas govern this action of the Lord. One is his faithfulness to his promises. The whole land, pledged to Abram (Gen. 13:14–15) and shown to Moses (Deut. 34:1–4), included Philistia (Josh. 13:2), which the people never did possess (see the Exegesis of 2:5 regarding Canaan). The Lord's people may settle for a compromise, but he will never go back on his promises (Num. 23:19). The other idea governing the Lord's action is that the Lord's people cannot be mistreated with impunity, and he to whom vengeance belongs will see to its just requital (Zeph. 2:8, 10). Whatever the outworking will be, it is to this that Jesus refers in Matthew 5:5; this is the kingship of the blood-bought people (Rev. 5:10); this is the obverse side of their comfort in the day when God wipes away every tear (Rev. 7:17).

The fifth principle is that the Lord is the fierce enemy of pride. The pride of Moab (Zeph. 2:10; see also Isa. 16:6; 25:10–11) and of Nineveh (Zeph. 2:15) brought about their downfall. The one sin specified as provoking final judgment on the world is the sin of self-sufficiency (Zeph. 2:15a–b; see Isa. 47:8–9), the all-destroying sin (Zeph. 2:13, 15). In expectation of the day, Zephaniah rightly calls people to humility (2:3). Following the example of Jesus, who testified that he is lowly (Matt. 11:29; see Acts 8:33; Phil. 2:3), the New Testament insists on the virtue "humble-mindedness"

II. Judgment and Hope: An Enigma (2:4–3:8)
B. The Failure of Judah (3:1–5)

MOTYER

3 Ho, rebellious and defiled,
 oppressive city!
² It has not listened to the voice,
  it has not accepted discipline;
 in the LORD it has not put its trust,
  to its God it has not drawn near.
³ Its princes within it are roaring lions;
  its judges, wolves of the evening who
   did not eat at morning;
⁴ its prophets are unprincipled, men of utter
  treachery;
  its priests profane every holy thing,
   wreak havoc on the law.
⁵ The LORD, that righteous one, is within it.
  He does nothing wrong;
 morning by morning he gives his decisions;
   at first light, he is not missing.
 The committed wrongdoer has no notion
  of shame.

NRSV

3 Ah, soiled, defiled,
 oppressing city!
² It has listened to no voice;
  it has accepted no correction.
 It has not trusted in the LORD;
  it has not drawn near to its God.
³ The officials within it
  are roaring lions;
 its judges are evening wolves
  that leave nothing until the morning.
⁴ Its prophets are reckless,
  faithless persons;
 its priests have profaned what is sacred,
  they have done violence to the law.
⁵ The LORD within it is righteous;
  he does no wrong.
 Every morning he renders his judgment,
  each dawn without fail;
  but the unjust knows no shame.

3:1. הוֹי (ho): This initial summons matches the opening oracle of this series (2:5). The people of God are summoned to judgment exactly as are the people of the world. מֹרְאָה (rebellious) exemplifies a final-*he* verb that adopts a final-*aleph* form (GKC §75rr). In thirty-six out of forty cases מָרָה denotes rebellion against God. Within the vocabulary of rebellion, it is the rebel's obstinacy (Deut. 21:18; Ps. 78:8). נִגְאָלָה (defiled): Seven of the ten

occurrences of this verb refer to personal defilement (e.g., Neh. 7:64; Isa. 59:3). יָנָה (to oppress) always indicates oppression of people (Deut. 23:17 [16]; Ps. 74:8). Thus the opening charge is comprehensive, addressing their relationship to God, to self, and to other people.

2. שָׁמְעָה בְקוֹל (listen to the voice) is made up of two components. First there is the verb שָׁמַע (to hear), followed by the preposition בְּ. This combi-

---

(Luke 14:11; Acts 20:19; Rom. 12:16; Eph. 4:2; James 4:10; 1 Peter 3:8).

3:1–5. Zephaniah again (see 1:4–6, 8–13) turns to appraise Jerusalem. Like Isaiah and Micah, he is a prophet of the city, open-eyed to its faults; unlike them, his focus is almost wholly civic and religious. But he draws the fundamental dividing line in the same place: whatever the basis on which the world is judged, the people of God are judged for turning from revealed truth (Amos 2:4) and for neglecting proffered spiritual privileges (Isa. 65:2).

Like Amos, Zephaniah uses the rhetorical device of condemning surrounding nations, but all the while—unannounced to his hearers—bringing their own condemnation ever closer. Their sense of security increased by observing that judgment was moving ever farther away—first Philistia (3:4–7) and then Cush (3:12) and Assyria (3:13–15)—and by the assumption that when the prophet accuses a "city" (ʿîr; 3:1) he must still be speaking about Nineveh. But the city Zephaniah accuses has heard divine revelation (3:2a), has known the divine law (3:2b), and has been invited to trust (3:2c) and approach God (3:2d). It has a familiar civil and religious structure: princes, judges, prophets, priests (3:3–4). It is the city that the Lord indwells (3:5)—their own Zion! The poem consists of three four-line stanzas, flanked by an initial summons and a concluding comment:

a   a summons: the offending city (1)
b   a charge: the Lord refused (2)
c   leaders under condemnation (3–4)
b'   without excuse: the Lord available (5a–d)
a'   a comment: incorrigible sinfulness (5e)

The thrust of the poem is that the offenses of the city (3:2) and leaders (3:3–4) are inexcusable because of the indwelling God (3:5a–d). Each line of

the first two stanzas stands in contrast to the third stanza in an abcdd'c'b'a' relationship:

The City	God
a has not listened (2a)	**a'** was speaking and never absent (5d)
b would not accept discipline (2b)	**b'** constantly made his decisions known (5c)
c would not trust (2c)	**c'** is totally trustworthy (5b)
d did not draw near (2d)	**d'** was always available (5a)

A similar relationship exists between the actions of the leaders when contrasted to those of the Lord:

The Leaders	God
a princes failed their duty (3a)	**a'** was never away from his post (5d)
b judges thought only how to satisfy themselves (3b)	**b'** was constantly making his judgments known (5c)
c prophets were treacherous (4a)	**c'** was free from deviancy (5b)
d priests defile the holy (4b)	**d'** set the standard (5a)

This stunning indictment is finally nailed down by the comment that there is no sense of repentance or need (3:5e). The charge (3:1) has been more than proved.

1. For the meaning and implications of the three keywords, "rebellious," "defiled," and "oppressive," see the Exegesis, but note also how Zephaniah exposes another facet of Old Testament thinking. In 2:13 he drew out the relationship between obedient living and a true environmentalism; here he makes precisely the same connection between obedience to God and true society, with personal holiness as the middle

nation means "to give heed to" and is a standard expression for "to obey." Second, there is the noun קוֹל (voice). Here, without the definite article, it exemplifies the construction known as indefiniteness for the sake of emphasis (see GKC 125c; Isa. 28:2; 31:8). It is as though to say "a voice (you know whose!)." See the Exegesis of 1:10. מוּסָר (discipline) combines in its sphere of meaning the ideas of instruction, direction, and correction (note the four elements in 2 Tim. 3:16). קָרְבָה (drawn near): The secular example of a man approaching a woman sexually (Isa. 8:3) illustrates the personal nearness this word can imply. No sooner was Moses excluded from the tabernacle by the glory of holiness (Exod. 40:35) than the Lord told him to tell the people תַּקְרִיבוּ אֶת־קָרְבַּנְכֶם (you shall bring your offering; lit., you shall bring near [hiphil קָרַב] a "bringing-near" offering [קָרְבָּן];

Lev. 1:2). This is the heart of biblical religion: peaceful enjoyment in the presence of the Holy God.

3. שָׂרֶיהָ (its princes) refers to the executive arm of government. The metaphorical שֹׁאֲגִים (roaring) communicates a sense of dread. The use of this word, which signifies the pouncing roar of the lion (Judg. 14:5), underscores the cruel, oppressive, and self-seeking power of the leaders. שֹׁפְטֶיהָ (its judges): See Deuteronomy 1:16–18 and 16:18–20. זְאֵבֵי עֶרֶב (wolves of the evening) were notoriously fierce (Hab. 1:8). The Septuagint reads λύκοι τῆς Ἀραβίας (wolves of Arabia), but understanding these as desert wolves destroys the contrast between "evening" and "morning" (J. Smith, *Zephaniah*, p. 239; House, *Zephaniah*, p. 131). לֹא גָרְמוּ (who did not eat): גָּרַם (to eat) occurs elsewhere only in Numbers 24:8 and Ezekiel 23:34

term. Old Testament history bears this out. The law that the Lord gave to his redeemed people at Sinai put first our dutiful obedience to him and out of that developed in orderly sequence the safeguarding of society by due observance of his laws, with the family as the middle term. All throughout the historical period, social integrity went hand in hand with Yahwism, the worship and following of the Lord; lapse into Baalism—or whatever such "god" was in vogue—brought social oppressiveness and disintegration. Zephaniah's perceptive ordering of his words establishes that true society arises from committed obedience (not rebellion) and from personal holiness (not defilement). Putting the matter another way: social reformation arises from a return to God and to individual moral integrity. To seek to reform society in the hope that this will produce high standards and good people is to put the cart before the horse; it is converted and godly individuals that make good society.

2. The charge against the city is failure to conform to the word of God (3:2a–b) and failure to live in the fellowship of God (3:2c–d)—favored by revelation but neither heeding nor obeying, and favored by relationship but not responding in trust and love. The basic essentials were missing: attention (3:2a), submission (3:2b), reliance (3:2c), and fellowship (3:2d). The voice (*qôl*) is the Lord addressing his people (see the Exegesis) by whatever means he has appointed for that purpose. The hallmark of the people of God has always been their possession of the word of God: Adam (Gen. 1:28; 2:16), Abraham (Gen. 17:1), Israel (Exod. 19:9; Deut. 4:32–34). As centuries passed, the

knowledge of the person and law of God accumulated until in due course the New Testament was added to the Old (2 Tim. 3:14–16). Although the form and quantity of revealed truth changed, the basic requirement never altered: the Lord's people live by the Lord's word (2 Tim. 1:13; 2:15; 3:14–16; 4:2). Furthermore, possession of the divine word was to be matched by an attitude to it well expressed in the quadrilateral of Deuteronomy 5:1: "Hear, learn, keep, do"—listening, understanding, retaining, acting. But Zephaniah's people were not listening, nor did they bend their wills and their ways to the discipline (see the Exegesis) of submissive obedience.

The life to which God calls his people, however, is not one of outward conformity but of obedience resting on trust and fellowship. Trust responds to divine sufficiency and leans on divine strength; drawing near responds to divine invitation and rejoices in the divine presence. The purpose of the appointed sacrifices was to "bring near" into the presence of the Lord one whose sin would automatically disqualify and exclude.

The word, however, is not an end in itself but a means to the greater end of the knowledge of God whereby he is discovered to be trustworthy (3:2c) and whereby he is discovered to be loving and desirable and is sought for himself alone (3:2d). Zephaniah does not define the current lack of trust, but would he have meant other than Isaiah 30:15? In the often-threatening circumstances of life, the people of God turn to worldly reliances or, in the case of Isaiah's audience, to worldly alliances. To put it another way, we rejoice in justification by faith and find that this simplicity of

(piel). Here it is in the qal and therefore reckoned dubious by some (KB, p. 193). The verb is denominative from גֶּרֶם (bone), with the suggested meaning "to gnaw, chew," which suits all the references. BDB (p. 175) proposes a verb גָּרַם meaning "to leave," thus, "leave nothing [until morning]" (Baker, *Zephaniah*, p. 112; House, p. 131). לַבֹּקֶר, however, is not the most obvious way of expressing "until morning" (see עַד־[הַ]בֹּקֶר, which occurs in Exod. 12:10 and about twenty other times). On the other hand, לְ on לַבֹּקֶר could readily mean "time when," thus, "at morning" (Pss. 30:6 [5]; 49:15 [14]). A wolf that did not eat at morning would be a wolf indeed by evening!

4. פֹּחֲזִים (unprincipled) is a qal participle of פָּחַז (to gush over [of water]), hence to be insolent, uncontrolled, undisciplined (note the related nouns in Gen. 49:4; Jer. 23:32 [of prophets imparting baseless teaching]). The verb occurs elsewhere only in Judges 9:4 of people ready for anything, that is, volatile people. בֹּגְדוֹת is either a distribu-

tive plural (every sort of treachery) or a plural of amplitude (the deepest treachery). בָּגַד occurs with various nuances: to disobey known truth (1 Sam. 14:33), to let down (Job 6:15), to go back on one's word (Exod. 21:8), to be (maritally) unfaithful (Jer. 3:20), to refuse the Lord's word (Jer. 5:11), and to apostatize from the Lord (Hos. 5:7). For the expression חִלְּלוּ־קֹדֶשׁ (profane every holy thing), see Leviticus 19:8. In Leviticus 20:3, it connotes defiance of the Lord's ruling regarding sacrifice to Molech. חָמְסוּ (wreak havoc): The verb חָמַס (to pervert) may refer to violating the Lord's law (Ezek. 22:26) or doing violence to persons (Jer. 13:22; 22:23). The cognate noun חָמָס refers to violent conduct (Gen. 6:11, 13), wrong done to persons (Gen. 16:5), and violence to the truth (Exod. 23:1; Ps. 35:11). Hence, here it means to do violence to the true meaning and intent of the law (contrast Mal. 2:5–7) and thereby to wrong and hurt people.

5. The absence of the definite article with the adjective makes צַדִּיק (that righteous one) apposi-

---

trust in Christ deals with the offense of sin and secures peace with God and our place in heaven—but then in the face of life's demands we turn from the way of faith and trust human efforts and expedients. The great experience of the power of faith somehow does not carry over into areas of intrinsically lesser demand: we trust him for salvation (Acts 16:31) but not in storms (Matt. 8:26).

The idea of drawing near to God is rooted in the cult (see the Exegesis), but it also has a wider use: coming into the divine presence (Deut. 5:24 [27]; 1 Sam. 14:36; Isa. 48:16), standing before him (Lev. 9:5), praying to him (Ps. 119:169). In a word, then, it speaks to us of coming to the Father, in the Son, by the Spirit (Eph. 2:18) for the enjoyment of his presence, prayer, correction, and direction—all the things that are encompassed by the notion of walking with God, especially those set-apart times of worship (corporate and private), the blessedness of the Lord's Table, and the hallowed simplicity of the private room and the open Bible. It is the delight of the Lord's people in the Lord himself.

3–4. The leadership is now condemned. The civil leaders are accused under animal metaphors: Nineveh was occupied by beasts (2:14a) to signify the absence of human occupants; in Jerusalem the beasts have already taken over! The leaders of the people of God were *mis*leaders (3:3–4). Princes and judges together formed the administrative and judicial arms of Israelite society, and they (Exod. 18:21–22; Deut. 16:18–20), just as much as proph-

ets (Deut. 18:18; Jer. 23:16–29) and priests (Mal. 2:5–7), were ministers of God's word. They were to be governed by the word of revelation on the one hand and the welfare of people on the other. The reference to morning and evening may even go back to the foundational example of Moses, who sat from morning to evening hearing cases, ministering the directive word of God (Exod. 18:13–16). But Zephaniah saw the princes and judges as leaders with a wrong concern: eager for gain, out for themselves, using the power of office for self-advantage. And he saw the prophets and priests as leaders without concern: not avaricious but just unconcerned for the things of God and the good of fellow humans. There are thus three basic principles of leadership: (1) it should be exercised in accordance with what God has revealed; (2) it should be characterized by a readiness (like Moses) to subordinate self-advantage to people's welfare and by a freedom from self-seeking; and (3) it should be known by its character (the most important quality in leadership), that is, the quality and integrity of the person.

5. The purpose of this concluding stanza (see the Exposition of 3:1–5) is to show that it is not through any change or failure in its God that the city and its leaders are what they are. Setting forth the needlessness and seriousness of spiritual declension, the lines are alternately positive and negative: a and b combine to say that the Lord is righteous in character and perfect in action; c and d reveal him as assiduous in kingly oversight and

tional and therefore emphatic (see the Exegesis of 3:3). The Lord's righteousness is his consistency of character (Ps. 11:7), reliability in relation to his stated purposes (Neh. 9:8), and correctness in all his actions (Ps. 145:17). עַוְלָה (wrong): The root עול expresses the idea of deviancy (Ps. 71:4; Isa. 26:10). The noun is used widely for the general idea of wrong (2 Chron. 19:7; Pss. 92:16 [15]; 119:3). בַּבֹּקֶר בַּבֹּקֶר (morning by morning) is distributive (with this meaning elsewhere in Exod. 16:21 and Lev. 6:5 [12]). מִשְׁפָּטוֹ (his decisions): See the Exegesis of 3:3. The word מִשְׁפָּט is related to שֹׁפְטֶיהָ (its judges) in 3:3b. For this royal duty, see Jeremiah 21:12 and Psalm 101:8. Zephaniah brings his accusation full circle (compare 3:2a–b with 3:5c–d): they would not listen to the divine voice but it was always there, always speaking. לָאוֹר (at first light): House (Zephaniah, p. 124) links this structure with the foregoing and translates it as "He brings His justice to light" (see the

RV), but the parallelism between בַּבֹּקֶר בַּבֹּקֶר and לָאוֹר is more effective. For אוֹר as daylight or dawn, see Judges 19:26, Nehemiah 8:3, and Job 24:14. לְ expresses time when (see the Exegesis of 3:3). נֶעְדָּר (missing): For the contextual sense of this verb, see 1 Samuel 30:19, 2 Samuel 17:22, Isaiah 34:16, and Isaiah 40:26. בֹּשֶׁת . . . לֹא־יוֹדֵעַ (has no notion of shame; lit., unknowing of shame): Following the idiom of the negative participle, this almost means "cannot know" or "has no way of knowing"—that is, constant attention to deviancy sears the conscience. עַוָּל (the committed wrongdoer) is related to עַוְלָה (does nothing wrong) in 3:5b, reiterating the contrast between the Lord and his city that is so deeply embedded in the foregoing stanzas (see the Exposition). The adjective עַוָּל is intensive in form and "distinguishes the individual who makes a profession of unrighteousness" (Dhorme, Job, p. 235).

---

ever faithful to his responsibilities; and a and d stress his presence with his people: he is within the city, never absent.

The substance of the relationship is that whatever they needed was available in the Lord. Indeed, it is his presence that ultimately seals their culpability, for it made their declension needless. Just to take note of the ever-present Lord in his character (3:5a), conduct (3:5b), wisdom (3:5c), and constancy (3:5d) would have provided them with a searching standard and a motive and model to amend their lives.

Zephaniah speaks first of God's character. Yahweh is described as "that righteous one." "Righteous" (saddîq) has two facets. The first concerns his nature: every principle and practice of holiness is part and parcel of what he is. This sweetest reassurance implies the full sufficiency of the saving grace that he extends to sinners and the full efficacy of the means he has provided so we can approach him and live with him. He comes among his unworthy ones not by adjusting his nature down, but by providing a salvation that lifts us up and makes us free in his righteous presence (Heb. 10:19–22). The second facet of God's righteousness is his reliability in relation to his pledged word: because he is what he is, every promise is made sure. He is the all-sufficient God for our needs.

Verse 5 also cites Yahweh's conduct: "He does nothing wrong." This brings us the assurance we need that no mistakes are being made—despite our being baffled at the turn of events; the experi-

ences that come to us, our family, and our friends; the blows of life; its strange mixture of joy and sorrow; its inequalities. We need constantly to recall that his thoughts are not our thoughts nor our ways his ways (Isa. 55:8) and, even more, to say to ourselves over and over again: "He has done everything well" (Mark 7:37).

Yahweh's wisdom is the subject of line c (see the Exposition of 3:1 for the relation of the third stanza of this poem to the first two stanzas). The first wish of the saving God is to reveal to his people how he wisely rules for the ordering of their lives: having redeemed his own from Egypt, he brought them directly to Sinai to make known his law (Exod. 20:1–20). And it should be the first wish of the redeemed to live so as to please God their Savior. The words morning by morning (babbōqer babbōqer) recall the fellowship into which the Lord daily brought his servant and within which he made his will known (Isa. 50:4). This becomes the model (Isa. 50:10) for all who would fear the Lord.

Finally, 3:5 speaks of the Lord's constancy. The last line of the stanza reiterates what was implicit in the first and affirmed in the third. Here is a truth about the Lord so important that it must be said yet again: he is always here; he is never absent. He is neither like Baal (1 Kings 18:27) nor the disappointing waters of Job 6:15–20. Rather, as with Psalm 123:1, we look up to him only to find that all the time he has been looking down to us.

Spiritual decline, however, is an ever-present possibility, no matter how needless the nature of our God makes it. While we long for true spirituality, we know that the pressure to go the other way is constant and that every thought, word, or deed without or against the Lord hardens the heart, making us just a little bit more like what we choose. This is why rebellion comes: when the will refuses the rule of the Lord, inner defilement and then outward wrong follow until, busy with wrongdoing (see the Exegesis of 3:5), the conscience goes blank. We live our lives in tension between the opportunity of life with the Lord and the downward pull of temptation and sin.

II. Judgment and Hope: An Enigma (2:4–3:8)
C. Hope in a Day of Wrath (3:6–8)

MOTYER

6 I have determined to cut down the nations:
  their corner towers are doomed to desolation.
I have determined to bring ruin to their
streets,
  so that there is no passerby.
Their cities are doomed to be laid waste,
  so that there is not a single person, not
  an inhabitant.
7 I said, "Surely you will fear me; you will
accept discipline"—
and its habitation would not be cut off:
everything I had entrusted to it.
  They, however, spared no effort to act
  corruptly in all their doings.
8 Therefore wait confidently for me—
  this is the word of the LORD—
  for the day I rise to the prey.
For it is my decision to gather the nations,
  to assemble the kingdoms,
to pour out on them my indignation,
  all my flaming anger,
for in the fire of my jealousy all the earth
  will be eaten up.

NRSV

6 I have cut off nations;
  their battlements are in ruins;
I have laid waste their streets
  so that no one walks in them;
their cities have been made desolate,
  without people, without inhabitants.
7 I said, "Surely the city will fear me,
  it will accept correction;
it will not lose sight
  of all that I have brought upon it."
But they were the more eager
  to make all their deeds corrupt.
8 Therefore wait for me, says the LORD,
  for the day when I arise as a witness.
For my decision is to gather nations,
  to assemble kingdoms,
to pour out upon them my indignation,
  all the heat of my anger;
for in the fire of my passion
  all the earth shall be consumed.

6. הִכְרַתִּי (I have determined to cut down) is a perfect of certainty, hence determination. גּוֹיִם (the nations): The matching oracle (2:1–3) addresses the Lord's people as a גּוֹי (nation); now, along with all the nations, their doom is sealed. נָשַׁמּוּ (are doomed), like its companion verb in the parallel structure (הִכְרַתִּי), is a perfect reflecting determination. פִּנּוֹתָם (their corner towers): See the Exegesis of 1:16. The last four lines have a place-person-place-person theme: that is, totality by means of contrast. Basic to הֶחֱרַבְתִּי (I have determined to bring ruin), a hiphil of חָרֵב (note the noun חֹרֶב in 2:14), is the sense to be dry, hence to be in ruins. חוּצוֹתָם includes streets, town squares, and so on. נִצַּדּוּ (are doomed to be laid waste), a niphal of צָדָה, is not used elsewhere.

7. אָמַרְתִּי (I said) brings us right into the divine mind and heart. אַךְ (surely) is a particle, emphasizing the idea it introduces (BDB, p. 36). House (*Zephaniah*, pp. 131–32; see BHS) alters תִּירְאִי (you will fear) and תִּקְחִי (you will accept), both second-person singular verbs, to תִּירָא and תִּקַּח (third-person singular feminine) in the interest of leading into מְעוֹנָה (its habitation), but the quotation marks should be placed around the direct discourse (as in my translation; see the NIV). The words אַךְ־תִּירְאִי are reflected in אַל־תִּירְאִי of 3:16.

The fear expected is not craven fear but godly reverence that bears the fruit of obedience (1 Peter 1:17–19)—a fear that itself is the response to supremely loving goodness. מוּסָר (discipline): See the Exegesis of 3:2. The two references interlock: 3:2 is the fact of Zion's obduracy; 3:7 expresses the Lord's blighted hopes. מְעוֹנָה (its habitation) can refer to God's heavenly habitation (Deut. 26:15), his earthly house (1 Sam. 2:29; Ps. 26:8), God himself as the habitation of his people (Ps. 90:1), and a variety of animal dens (Jer. 10:22). Isaiah 64:10 [11] speaks of "our holy . . . house [בַּיִת]," meaning the house of the holy God entrusted to our keeping. A sense similar to this suits the passage here, as indeed the qualifying words (everything I had entrusted to it) explain. For מְעוֹנָה, the Septuagint has ἐξ ὀφθαλμῶν αὐτῆς (from its eyes), apparently reading מֵעֵינֶיהָ, which is adopted by BHS. פָּקַדְתִּי (I had entrusted to it): See the Exegesis of 1:8. The literal meaning of הִשְׁכִּימוּ (they . . . spared no effort; lit., they rose early), a hiphil of שָׁכַם, may be seen in Genesis 22:3. Metaphorically, it indicates zealousness or enthusiasm (Jer. 7:13, 25). In an idiomatic expression of two verbs without a connective (הִשְׁכִּימוּ הִשְׁחִיתוּ, they rose early, they acted corruptly; GKC §120g), the second verb carries the main meaning and the

---

3:6–8. This section ends §II of Zephaniah. Throughout, the message of doom—the only possible consequence of §I—has been enforced, while at the same time we have been teased with intimations of hope (2:6–7, 9, 11). These concluding verses maintain the suspense. In the midst of their announcement of unrelieved disaster comes the call (3:8a) to wait confidently for the Lord—yet the hope seems to be taken away as soon as it is given. On the relationship between these verses and 2:1–3 (the concluding section of §I), see the Introduction.

A divine devastation (6)
  a comprehensive: nations executed
  b detailed: fortifications, habitations, inhabitants
B divine disappointment over Zion (7–8a)
  a expectation of response, bringing escape from execution (7a–b)
  b disappointment and its result (7c–8a)
    ongoing corruption (7c)
    is there still hope? (8a)
    the day of prey (8c)

A' divine wrath (8b)
  a nations gathered
  b purpose
    divine anger in its entirety
    over all the earth

This subsection begins with an affirmation of divine devastation of the world. This grim picture covers groups ("nations"), individuals ("passers-by," "inhabitant"), military installations ("corner towers"), thoroughfares ("streets"), and domestic dwellings ("cities"). Yet even when hope is gone, hope stirs!

6. Zephaniah observes his people continuing to live in complacent unresponsiveness even though they are aware of the Lord's commitment to future judgment. The divine determination in this regard is known: no defense can avail ("towers"), no city community ("streets . . . cities") make secure.

7–8a. The blank conscience of 3:5 reappears in 3:7d: "They . . . spared no effort to act corruptly." Note the link between "morning by morning" (3:5c) and "they got up early, they corrupted." What a tragedy! Yet one so often lived out—the Lord up and about, ready to meet with us (Isa.

first qualifies it: they acted corruptly, enthusiastically. כָּל עֲלִילוֹתָם (all their doings) prepares the way for the same expression in 3:11. A total commitment to sin is met here with a total coverage of mercy—but not yet: Zephaniah is still preoccupied with essential judgment and all we have at this moment is the enigmatic hint that follows in 3:8 (wait confidently).

8a. In the prophets the particle לָכֵן (therefore) frequently introduces a pronouncement of divine punishment based on a preceding accusation of wrong (Ezek. 5:10–11; Zeph. 2:9). Here, the following encouragement from God seems to violate the consistent use of לָכֵן in judgment sayings. It is possible, however, that לָכֵן refers back to 3:6, which expresses Yahweh's determination to destroy the nations. The statement following לָכֵן affirms that Yahweh will rise to the prey, but the prey is the nations according to the following line. Since the destruction of the nations is the context in which he will vindicate his people (3:11–13c; compare 3:8b–10), Yahweh's encouragement to the people to wait for him does not seem out of place. We may paraphrase this section (3:6–13c): "I will utterly destroy the nations. I thought you, my people, would fear me, and avoid punishment, but you did not. Therefore [לָכֵן] you must wait for me to rise against the nations. Then I will effect your vindication and deliverance." The use of the particle לָכֵן with the following verb thus creates an enigma. Zephaniah must use חַכּוּ (wait confi-

dently) if his message is not to be totally one of judgment. חָכָה (to wait), the very verb to use if Zephaniah wishes to be enigmatic (Eaton, *Zephaniah*, p. 149), is used in a neutral sense of waiting (2 Kings 7:9) and in a bad sense of robbers lying in wait (Hos. 6:9). It refers to Yahweh waiting to have mercy (Isa. 30:18a) and to people waiting for blessing (Isa. 30:18b; 64:3 [4]; Hab. 2:3). It never means waiting for the blow of judgment to fall. Hence, it should be translated "wait confidently, expectantly, or hopefully." In case the tension between waiting in hope and looking forward to judgment seems too contradictory, the message is authenticated with נְאֻם־יְהוָה (this is the word of the LORD; see the Exegesis of 1:2). עַד (the prey): See Genesis 49:27 and Isaiah 33:23 for the sense of this word. The Septuagint reads εἰς μαρτύριον (for testimony), reflecting לְעֵד, which is adopted by House (*Zephaniah*, p. 132), BHS, and the New International Version. Eaton (*Zephaniah*, p. 149) prefers the translation "the day that I rise up once for all," but there is no instance of עַד with the meaning "once for all." The word עֵד (testimony) suggests a court in session, with Yahweh witnessing for the prosecution. This is apt enough, but עַד (prey) suits the prevailing sense of destructive judgment and provides a dark foil to the light of hope in the call to wait.

8b. מִשְׁפָּטִי (my decision): For this sense of מִשְׁפָּט, see the Exegesis of 2:3. לֶאֱסֹף (to gather; see the Exegesis of 1:2) forms an *inclusio* between

50:4); we, eagerly out of bed to pursue, at best, our own way or, at worst, to corrupt all our doings. The Lord, awaiting our fellowship and left disappointed! Yet it is to such, to those too busy to meet him, that the Lord says, "Wait in confident, hopeful expectation for me" (see the Exegesis of 3:8a). The confirmatory words *this is the word of the LORD* (see the Exposition of 1:1) in 3:8 separate this command from the ensuing reference to the day, asserting as a truth in its own right that there is always hope in God. We never go so far away, fall so deeply down, get so irretrievably lost that we are beyond his love, care, and remedial action. Remember Jonah (2:4, 6 [5, 7]): "Then I said, 'I am driven away from your sight; how shall I look again upon your holy temple?' . . . I went down to the land whose bars closed upon me forever; yet you brought my life up from the Pit.'" We cannot, however, ignore that the call to "wait" lies alongside the Lord's determination to take his prey on that day. But even so there is hope—for "the builder will be saved, but only as through fire"

(1 Cor. 3:15). This is not to trivialize the awesomeness of that day—with this passage before us, how could we?—but it is to remind ourselves that the Lord will never abandon us. Once we are of his flock, nothing can pluck us out of his hand (John 10:28). Zephaniah seems determined at this point to stress the enigmatic side of the Lord's ways (see the Exegesis). Somehow judgment and hope are both true. As in Isaiah 30:18, the Lord imposes a waiting period on himself until he can have mercy, so here he imposes a waiting period on his people until his wrath is justly satisfied. Isaiah said, "Blessed are all those who wait for him." Zephaniah would approve.

8b. Matching 3:6 in its stress on universality, the ending of the poem adds that all the claims of wrath will be satisfied: all the provocation he has endured ("indignation"; see the Exegesis), all the "anger" he would express, all that his holiness ("fire") demands, all that his determination that no other shall usurp his honor ("jealousy")—and this over "all the earth."

the end of §II and the beginning of §I. גּוֹיִם . . . מַמְלָכוֹת (nations . . . kingdoms): If a distinction is intended, the former is the political entity and the latter the political system. The use of the two words together implies that nothing will be overlooked. The same is true of the doublet זַעְמִי . . . אַפִּי (indignation . . . anger), where the pairing expresses every manifestation of divine wrath. זַעַם expresses indignation. If we can press the meaning further, it is indignation felt, that is, anger as a response to provocation (Prov. 25:23). חָרוֹן (see the Exegesis of 2:2) has the sense of heat or fierceness (of anger). כִּי בְּאֵשׁ (for in the fire): See the Exegesis of 1:18.

III. The End of the World: Hope in All Its Glory (3:9–20)
A. The Enigma Solved (3:9–13)

MOTYER

9 For then I will turn over to the peoples a
    clarified speech,
  so that they, all of them, will call on
    the name of the LORD,
  so that they will serve him shoulder to
    shoulder.
10 From the regions of the rivers of Cush, my
    suppliants,
  the daughter of my scattered ones, will
    bring my offering.
11 In that day,
  you will not be ashamed because of all
    your doings
    in which you rebelled against me,
  for then I will remove from within you
    your proudly exulting ones,
    and you will never again be haughty in
    my holy mountain.
12 And I will leave a remnant within you,
    a people humble and dependent,
    and they will take refuge in the name of
    the LORD.
13 As the remnant of Israel, they will not do
    wrong,
    and will not speak a lie,
    nor will there be found in their mouth
    a deceitful tongue.
  For it is they who will find pasture
    and lie down,
    and there will be nothing to make them
    tremble.

NRSV

9 At that time I will change the speech of
    the peoples
    to a pure speech,
  that all of them may call on the name of
    the LORD
    and serve him with one accord.
10 From beyond the rivers of Ethiopia
    my suppliants, my scattered ones,
    shall bring my offering.
11 On that day you shall not be put to shame
    because of all the deeds by which you
    have rebelled against me;
  for then I will remove from your midst
    your proudly exultant ones,
  and you shall no longer be haughty
    in my holy mountain.
12 For I will leave in the midst of you
    a people humble and lowly.
  They shall seek refuge in the name of the
    LORD—
13   the remnant of Israel;
  they shall do no wrong
    and utter no lies,
  nor shall a deceitful tongue
    be found in their mouths.
  Then they will pasture and lie down,
    and no one shall make them afraid.

9. כִּי־אָז (for then): The element of surprise in the message of hope is maintained. Logic would expect כִּי (for) to introduce further elaborations of judgment but instead it reaches back to the hint of blessing in 3:8a. אָז (then) is important, referring to the time when the divine anger will have been fully spent (3:8b). The holy wrath of God must be satisfied but, being satisfied, there is a channel in which mercy can flow. אֶהְפֹּךְ (I will turn over), a characteristic verb of judgment,

became almost a technical verb for what the Lord did at Sodom (Gen. 19:25, 29; Deut. 29:22 [23]; Jer. 20:16; Amos 4:11). The usage here, however, is unique, for there is no other example where the verb is used to express "to bring x back to y" (the closest example is 1 Sam. 10:9). Zephaniah must therefore have chosen the verb deliberately because of its overtones of wrath: when more and more anger is to be expected, suddenly hope is shining, for light has dawned. שָׂפָה בְרוּרָה (a clari-

---

9–20. There is a justly lyrical quality in Zephaniah's three concluding oracles. With the furiousness of the day of the Lord over, he looks at the other side of the coin, where we find his subtle use of the motifs of Babel, Jerusalem, and Eden (3:9–13); the high emotion of his third and final seven-part poem (3:14–17); and the final sigh of contentment over a world put to rights (3:18–20).

The first oracle records the Lord's intention to set the whole world to rights. This covers the peoples (3:9) and the remnant (3:12–13). The following two oracles deal with the same divisions of humanity in reverse order: the Lord's people are found at one with him in fullness of joy (3:14–17), and this people becomes central to the whole world (3:20). Just as §II is linked to §I by an explanatory *kî* (for; 2:4), so §III is linked to §II (3:9). Thus, §II explains the universal judgment announced in §I, while §III explains the enigma of hope in §II and, more immediately, answers the question raised by the call (3:8) to "wait in confident expectation." In one sense, of course, there is no solution to the enigma at all, no structured explanation. Hope does not, in that sense, "stand to reason"; it does, however, "stand to theology." Part III of Zephaniah is still a study of the day of the Lord. We do not come to the end of §II, as it were, saying, "The day of the Lord is over; what now?" Zephaniah's messages continue to describe what will happen in that day (3:11, 16, 19–20), and it is important to recall the balance between these descriptions and those of §I (see 1:8, 10, 12). The same Lord is in action and the same day is being fulfilled, but, because the Lord so wills, the day is double-sided—and hope has the last word. (For a general introduction to §III and its integration with §§I–II, see the Introduction.)

9–13. The three sections of this poetic meditation announce themselves: third-person plural (3:9–10) changes to second-person singular feminine (which means Jerusalem; 3:11–13c). Verse 13d returns to a third-person plural form. The "purified speech" of 3:9 identifies 3:9–10 as the

reversal of Babel (Gen. 11:1–9); the fearless security of 3:13c is the return of Eden (see also Isa. 11:6–9).

a   Babel reversed: the uniting of the peoples (9–10)
    one speech (9a)
    one Lord (9b–c)
    one religion (10)
a' Jerusalem renewed: the purging of the people (11–13c)
    general: all shame over rebellion removed (11a–b)
    because of (1) divine action removing pride (11c–d)
    because of (2) divine action securing a remnant (12a)
    humble (12b)
    trustful (12c)
    undeviating (13a)
    pure in speech (13b–c)
a" Eden restored: sufficiency and security (13d)
    pasture
    rest
    fearlessness

This whole promissory oracle rests on three first-person singular verbs of divine action: "I will turn" (3:9), "I will remove" (3:11), and "I will leave" (3:12)—with no explanation of how or why the Lord will so act.

9. This verse begins with the word *for* (*kî*), and each section of this poem contains the word (3:9, 11d, 13d; for its logical function, see the Exegesis). It introduces here a statement that describes the canceling of the confusion of Babel. Zephaniah does not dwell on the wonder of a united humanity as such, but shows it as a functioning reality; just as the central motivation of Babel was to organize life without God, so now the unified

fied speech): שָׂפָה (lip) also connotes speech (Isa. 29:13, where שָׂפָה in parallel with פִּי [mouth] describes speech devoid of sincerity). בְּרוּרָה (clarified) is a qal passive participle of בָּרַר (to be pure, clean, clear). Both the verb (Isa. 52:11) and its adjective בַּר (Ps. 24:4) are used mainly of purity. Originally it "signifie[s] what shines ([Song of Sol.] 6:10), and by derivation what is clean and pure" (Dhorme, *Job*, p. 158); see also Job 33:3: "My lips will speak clearly" (Dhorme, p. 486). The Babel-syndrome has been reversed. לִקְרֹא . . . בְּשֵׁם יְהוָה (so that they . . . will call on the name of the LORD) is a general description of worship (Gen. 4:26; 12:8). שְׁכֶם אֶחָד (shoulder to shoulder; lit., with one shoulder): שְׁכֶם (shoulder) is used metaphorically (Gen. 49:15; 1 Sam. 10:9) but never elsewhere with this meaning.

10. מֵעֵבֶר (from the regions of): The construction מֵעֵבֶר plus לְ possesses the sense of beyond (1 Chron. 6:63 [78]), here meaning beyond the rivers of Cush (כּוּשׁ), located at the extremities of the politically significant nations. The expression

here extends the prophet's perspective to regions that may have been unfamiliar to his hearers. It appears to be an expression signifying "the uttermost reaches" and thus possesses a degree of universality. עֲתָרַי (my suppliants): The root עתר III appears elsewhere only in Ezekiel 8:11, with the sense of perfume. If this is the sense here, we must translate it as a *casus pendens* in apposition to מִנְחָתִי (my offering). On "offering" as a perfume, compare Genesis 8:21 and Leviticus 1:9. The "perfume" is metaphorical of the full acceptability of the offering to the Lord. The translation "suppliants" assumes derivation from עָתַר I (to entreat; Gen. 25:21; Exod. 10:18). Either translation is suitable: "perfumes" offers good parallelism with "offering," but the link of "suppliants" with 3:9 is slightly preferred. פּוּצַי (my scattered ones) is related to פּוּץ (to be scattered), as in Genesis 11:4, 8–9. On the basis of this link with the Babel account, the reference is not to a distant dispersion of Israel but to the gathering of a people for the Lord from Cush and, by implication, from the

---

world centralizes the Lord, using its newfound speech to call on the name of the Lord.

The Genesis process, in fact, has gone into reverse, and humanity, which in sin moved ever farther and farther from Eden, is brought back (3:13d) into its perfect provision, rest, and security. This vision of the incoming Gentiles is completed in 3:20, where they are seen to be at one with the people of the Lord. Zephaniah does not quite express the "fellow heirs, members of the same body" like Paul does in Ephesians 3:6 (Isa. 19:25), but he approximates the "sharers in the promise" as he sees the earth praising the name that the people of God bear: the promise to Abraham that in his seed (the believing family of Rom. 4:16–25 and Gal. 3:7) all families of the earth would find the blessing they need (Gen. 22:18).

10. The theme of unity (3:9) now gives way to that of universality, and Cush is singled out as an instance of the whole world worshiping the Lord. Once under judgment (2:12) but now within the sphere of grace, this is a vision of unity. At Babel (Gen. 11:1–9), people thought that by the invention of bricks and mortar they could be the authors of their own security. They spoke only to each other. God was not in their reckoning, and they suffered what they feared: scattering and dislocation. When the Lord restores a clarified speech (3:9a), he not only remedies the symptom but deals with a cause. Speech is now directed to the Lord (3:9b); he is their court of appeal and

their union is hallowed in commitment (3:9c), supplication, and worship (3:10). Zephaniah tells nothing of the means whereby this will be done, only that divine action ("I will change") has remedied the cause and the effect of Babel. There is great emotional intensity in the threefold "my." It emphasizes not only the reality of their acceptance but the satisfaction of the Lord in their homecoming. They come with a sense of their need ("suppliants"); they are those who have always belonged to the Lord though until now they neither knew nor responded to him ("scattered"; John 11:52); and the Lord has provided the way by which they may enter his presence ("offering").

11. Not only will the world experience unity as a result of the reversal of Babel's confusion of language (v. 10), but there will be changes for the Lord's people as well. God will deal with causes and effects. The Lord promises that he will end the accusations of conscience where they hurt most—in the matter of rebellion against God (3:11b–c). He will also remove pride from the community (3:11d) and from the heart (3:11e). In this way he leaves nothing undone of all that needs to be done for sinners. The purging of conscience (Heb. 9:14; 10:2) is the spiritual side of the divine work of salvation, making us acceptable to God but by that same transaction we are set within a pure community (Eph. 2:4–6; Heb. 12:22–24) and belong to it as personally delivered from

whole world (compare John 11:52). מִנְחָתִי is whatever offering Yahweh commanded and will accept. The Gentiles are accepted on the same ground as Israel.

11. בַּיּוֹם הַהוּא (in that day) refers to the time the prophet has just described, that is, the day when Yahweh gathers Gentiles to himself from among the nations. In that day God will preserve and transform his remnant people. Divine action will remove both the proud (11d) and pride (11e) and will preserve a remnant, humble and trustful (12), holy and pure in speech (13a–c). Zephaniah does not say how this will be done. לֹא תֵבוֹשִׁי (you will not be ashamed) provides a link with 3:5, where the lack of shame (בֹּשֶׁת) speaks of deadness of conscience; now, however, there is a clear conscience. עֲלִילֹתַיִךְ (your doings) is the same word that Zephaniah used to describe the ground of condemnation in 3:7. Every divine cause of complaint is gone, as well as every accusation of conscience. פָּשַׁעַתְּ (you rebelled): The verb פָּשַׁע connotes in its secular occurrences the willful rebellion of a subject against an overlord (2 Kings 3:7); in its theological sense it means spiritual rebellion (Isa. 1:2). The same is true of the noun פֶּשַׁע (secularly: Gen. 50:17; theologically: Ps. 51:3 [1]). כִּי־אָז (for then): The removal of the accusing conscience (Zeph. 3:11b) arises from divine removal of the heart of human sinfulness—the sin of pride. עַלִּיזֵי גַאֲוָתֵךְ (your proudly exulting ones): The adjective עַלִּיז (exulting) matches the charge against Assyria in 2:15. גַאֲוָתֵךְ is related to גָּאָה (to be high), yielding the sense of loftiness, haughtiness, arrogance, or a high opinion of oneself. The removal of arrogant

people is followed by the removal of the offense of pride. גָּבְהָה (be haughty) is a qal infinitive construct (GKC §45d). The verb גָּבַהּ (to be high) is synonymous to גָּאָה, hence the sense to be haughty. הַר קָדְשִׁי (my holy mountain): Only here does Zephaniah describe Zion as the Lord's mountain. According to 3:4, the only other verse where Zephaniah uses the word קֹדֶשׁ (holiness), the Lord's holiness was constantly in jeopardy in the condemned city. Here, the divine nature is at rest among a transformed people.

12. וְהִשְׁאַרְתִּי (and I will leave a remnant): ו connects this positive statement to the preceding "negative" side of Yahweh's work in removing the haughty and their haughtiness. The clause introduced by ו answers to the fear that may have arisen at the affirmation that God will effect such a removal: Is the removal absolute? Does it portend the end of the nation? The assurance that God will leave a remnant affirms his commitment to his promise to give Abraham a posterity (Gen. 15:1–6). Thus, the negative work of removing pride (Zeph. 3:11) is accompanied by the positive creation of the remnant. This is a definitive passage on the idea of the remnant (see the Exposition of 3:12–13c). עָנִי (humble): See the Exegesis of 2:3. Though עָנִי can express the sense of low estate in worldly goods (Deut. 15:11) or without worldly resource or influence (Ps. 35:10), here it describes those who are poor in spirit, knowing their beggarly need before God (Ps. 34:7 [6]). דַּל (dependent) can express the opposite idea to rich (Ruth 3:10), but its first meaning is "weakness," here "knowing one's need of divine strength" (Isa. 25:4). וְחָסוּ:

the infection of pride. On the keywords expressive of these great truths, see the Exegesis.

12–13c. Zephaniah continues his description of how the Lord will deal with his people: he will preserve a remnant (wĕhišʾartî). The earlier references to Jerusalem's total degeneracy (v. 1), refusal of the divine word and way (v. 2), failure to trust (v. 2), and all this in contrast with the determination of the righteous Lord (v. 5) to bring in worldwide judgment (v. 6), cannot but raise the question whether God's patience has run out to the extent that his great promises (e.g., Gen. 12:7; 15:5, 13–21; 22:17–18) no longer stand. Zephaniah refuses to let us believe such a thing. Rather he joins other prophets in foreseeing a preserved remnant (Isa. 8:9–22; Mic. 2:12; 5:7 [8]; 7:18). It is not that in this way the Lord will perpetuate a national entity but that he will create a people such as he has always wished to possess as his

very own (Exod. 19:5–6; Deut. 7:6). Zephaniah marks out five characteristics of this true people of the Lord: as *humble*, they know their own beggarliness, that in them dwells no good thing (Matt. 5:3; Rom. 7:18); as *dependent*, they seek all that they need in God; they fly to him constantly for *refuge*, for they have received and believe the revelation of his nature that his name encapsulates; they are the only *Israel*, the preserved, redeemed *remnant*; their lives, doing *no wrong*, are free of deviation from the Lord's law; and what they say contains no lie because their mouth and tongue are *not deceitful* (see Pss. 12:3–5 [2–4]; 17:1; 31:19 [18]; 34:14 [13]; 141:3; James 3:1–5).

13d. Zephaniah now moves to metaphorical language and pictures the remnant as a flock of sheep (see Mic. 2:12–13), a pastoral motif that abounds throughout the Bible: Psalms 23:1; 74:1; 77:21 [20]; 80:2 [1]; 95:7; Isaiah 40:11; 63:11; Ezekiel 34:12–23;

"Take refuge" is the literal meaning of חָסָה. While often translated "trust," it is primarily active trust, that is, running to the Lord for shelter. שֵׁם (the name) indicates how a person is known. In the case of the Lord, it means those aspects of his character that he has made known by revelation (Prov. 18:10).

13a–c. שְׁאֵרִית (as the remnant of): See the Exegesis of 2:7. עַוְלָה (wrong): See the Exegesis of 3:5. The perfected remnant becomes like their God. כָּזָב (a lie) is something that pretends, not merely contrary to truth (שֶׁקֶר) nor the insubstantiality of falsity (שָׁוְא), but the lie masquerading for truth. לְשׁוֹן תַּרְמִית (a deceitful tongue): The accusation of

deceit (using מִרְמָה) is leveled against Jerusalem in 1:9. In the Jerusalem to come, deceit (תַּרְמִית) will have been eradicated.

13d. כִּי (for) introduces a causal clause that gives the reason why the people will humbly seek the Lord—because they will no longer be guilty of moral wrong or deceptive speech. הֵמָּה (they): The separate third-person pronoun attached to the third-person verb makes the word extremely emphatic: "It is they who . . ." The pronoun includes the gathered Gentiles of 3:9–10 and the transformed remnant of 3:11–13c. To all alike is promised provision (pasture; compare 2:6–7), rest (lie down; as in 2:7), and security (tremble).

36:37; Matthew 25:33; John 10:14–16; 21:16; Hebrews 13:20; 1 Peter 2:25. Zephaniah follows his great model, Isaiah (11:6–9), in using the pastoral motif for the return to Edenic bliss—and yet Eden was a place of horticulture, not pasturage, though possibly the latter may be implied in Adam's caring dominion over the beasts. Maybe the prophets saw pastoral peace as the renewal of Davidic blessings

(1 Sam. 16:11; Ps. 78:70–72); maybe, more subtly, they looked back to Abel (Gen. 4:2), in whose post-Edenic flock was found an offering acceptable to the Lord, and saw this as a model for the people bound to the Lord by the blood of sacrifice. In any case, Zephaniah painted in terms of simplicity itself a picture of provision ("pasture"), restfulness ("lie"), and security ("tremble").

III. The End of the World: Hope in All Its Glory (3:9–20)
B. Oneness of Joy (3:14–17)

MOTYER

14 Sing out, daughter Zion,
shout aloud, Israel,
    rejoice and exult wholeheartedly,
      daughter Jerusalem.
15 The LORD has set aside the judgments
      against you;
    he has made your enemy turn tail.
The King of Israel, the LORD, is within
    you.
    You will never fear evil.
16 In that day it will be said to Jerusalem:
Do not fear, Zion;
    do not let your hands hang listless.
17 The LORD your God is within you.
    He is a warrior who saves.
He will be glad over you with rejoicing;
    he will be silent in his love;
    he will be elated over you with songs.

NRSV

14 Sing aloud, O daughter Zion;
    shout, O Israel!
Rejoice and exult with all your heart,
    O daughter Jerusalem!
15 The LORD has taken away the judgments
      against you,
    he has turned away your enemies.
The king of Israel, the LORD, is in your
    midst;
    you shall fear disaster no more.
16 On that day it shall be said to Jerusalem:
Do not fear, O Zion;
    do not let your hands grow weak.
17 The LORD, your God, is in your midst,
    a warrior who gives victory;
he will rejoice over you with gladness,
    he will renew you in his love;
    he will exult over you with loud singing

14. רָנַן ;רָנִּי means "to utter a ringing cry." The cry may be one of lamentation (Lam. 2:19), awe (Lev. 9:24), or joy (Ps. 96:12). This context informs the word with the sense of a cry of exultant joy (note שִׂמְחִי in line 2). בַּת־צִיּוֹן (O daughter Zion) is a frequent synonym for Jerusalem and its inhabitants (2 Kings 19:21; Isa. 3:17; Jer. 4:31). The companion word יִשְׂרָאֵל (O Israel) in the parallel structure calls for this sense here. בַּת יְרוּשָׁלַם (O daughter Jerusalem) is also a synonym for Jerusalem (Lam. 2:13; Mic. 4:8). When the word בַּת (daughter) occurs in construct with a political or geographical entity, it generally means the aggregate of the people of that entity. Zephaniah uses the word in this fashion in 3:10 (also Jer. 4:11, 31). Sometimes, however, this construction may refer to the entity itself (Isa. 1:8). The reference to joyful shouting envisions בַּת יְרוּשָׁלַם as the inhabitants of the city.

15. הֵסִיר (has set aside): Basic to the sense of hiphil סוּר is the idea of removal. In some cases the legal meaning "to set aside" is appropriate (Josh. 11:15; Job 27:2; 34:5; see Dhorme, *Job*). If this is the sense here, we may understand the statement to affirm that the legal claims ("judgments") against Zion have been annulled. The plural מִשְׁפָּטַיִךְ (the judgments against you) is distributive (see the Exegesis of 2:3), that is, "every possible judgment." פִּנָּה אֹיְבֵךְ (he has made your enemy turn tail): For this meaning of the piel (here transitive of hiphil), see Jeremiah 46:21 and 47:3. The Lord thus pursues his purpose of not only bringing his

---

14–17. The previous oracle ends on a note of fearlessness (3:13d); this one centers on a double encouragement not to fear (3:15d, 16). The Jerusalem section of the last poem describes what would be removed "from within you" (3:11) and what would be left "within you" (3:12); here is a greater wonder, the Lord himself "within" them (3:15, 17). Thus, Zephaniah picks up the promised reality of the new Jerusalem and describes it further. This oracle is another of Zephaniah's marvelous seven-part poems (the others are 1:14b–18 and 2:13–15):

a   the joy of Zion over the Lord (14)
b   the Lord's action in deliverance (15a–b)
c   the Lord, the indwelling king (15c)
d   the city without fear (15d–16)
c'   the Lord, the indwelling God (17a)
b'   the Lord's action in salvation (17b)
a'   the joy of the Lord over Zion (17c–e)

J. Smith (*Zephaniah*, p. 261) reports that few defend Zephaniah's authorship of this passage, mainly because threat gives way to promise. In House's view (*Zephaniah*, p. 133), since the ending (3:14–20) "caps the entire drama, and . . . is foreshadowed throughout the book, to remove these verses would destroy the purpose of every part of Zephaniah." One does not have to accept House's view of Zephaniah as a dramatic dialogue to agree with what he says. Smith, however, is right that "the whole spirit . . . of the section is that of . . . the so-called Deutero-Isaiah" and that "the fulfilment of the promises here made" is severed "from all historical agencies." Zephaniah is nearer in literary spirit and talent to Isaiah than is any other prophet. Throughout his prophecy he suggests but never specifies historical links: his purpose is to present a tract on the day of the Lord, whenever it might happen, and this is as true of its promissory as of its threatening aspects.

14. The address is to Zion, Israel, and Jerusalem, that is, respectively, the city of David (2 Sam. 5:7) where the messianic promises (Isa. 28:16) were set, the people whom the Lord redeemed (Exod. 4:22), and the capital of the united kingdom (Ps. 122). Zephaniah envisages the fulfillment of these great streams of promise. The phrase *O daughter Zion (bat-ṣîyôn)* is an appositional genitive. Zion is the Lord's daughter, and the people of Zion his family.

15. Throughout the concluding poems in Zephaniah, the Lord is the sole agent of all the blessing that is to come, whether the prophet is viewing the world and its united people or, more narrowly, Jerusalem as the specific focus of the Lord's work. Everything depends on first-person singular verbs: restoring (v. 9a); purging (v. 11d); regenerating (v. 12a); vindicating, healing, gathering, transforming (v. 19); gathering, exalting, fulfilling (v. 20). In the present verse he is, in particular, the satisfied God who found a way to "set aside the judgments" that stood against his people. Isaiah (45:21) expressed the same thought by describing him as "a righteous God and a Savior," and Paul echoed it by writing of one who is "just and the justifier" (Rom. 3:26 AV). It is one thing to deal with sin within the sinner so that conscience no longer accuses (Zeph. 3:11): this is the guiltiness of sin. It is a different thing to deal with sin as it outrages the holy character of God: this is the

people to himself but providing a secure place to live (Exod. 6:7–8); 2 Sam. 7:10, 23). The "setting aside" of legal charges speaks of their peace with God; the banishing of their foes, of their secure tenure of the blessings of their salvation. מֶלֶךְ יִשְׂרָאֵל יְהוָה (the King of Israel, the LORD): Both title and name are exegetically and theologically exact: the King guarantees their safety and security; the Lord, dwelling among them, evidences the setting aside of every legal accusation and the ensuing peace with God their Savior. Hence the fearlessness, which is the theme of 3:16. רַע has the sense of trouble or calamity (Isa. 45:7), not moral wrong, since the flow of the context (Zeph. 3:15–19) affirms Yahweh's determination to eliminate external threats and dangers from his people.

16. בַּיּוֹם הַהוּא (in that day): Each occurrence of this formula refers to the previously described event or period of time (see the Exegesis of 1:7). In this context it refers to the time when Yahweh will dwell in the midst of his people (3:14–15). יֵאָמֵר (it will be said) is more characteristic of Isaiah (4:3; 19:18; 32:5; 61:6; 62:4 [twice]) than of any other prophet. In the prophetic books, it occurs otherwise three times in Jeremiah, twice in Hosea, once in Ezekiel, and here. אַל־תִּירָאִי (do not fear) is construed in the feminine, as are the previous verbs that address the people as בַּת־צִיּוֹן (3:14). Here, however, the address is to צִיּוֹן (O Zion) without בַּת (daughter). There seems to be no distinction when these terms are applied to the people whom God delivers. The absence of fear (3:7) was one of the Lord's complaints against his people. A

distinction should be drawn between the fear of the unforgiven sinner and the reverential fear that motivates obedience (1 Peter 1:17–19). אַל־יִרְפּוּ יָדָיִךְ (do not let your hands hang listless): In its secular occurrences the verb רָפָה describes the act of sinking, for example, burning grass collapsing to the scorched earth (Isa. 5:24) and the waning light of day (Judg. 19:9). Here it refers to hands that hang useless in fear (see 2 Sam. 4:1; Neh. 6:9). In the parallelism of these two lines, fear is the inward state and listless hands the external evidence and consequence. The Lord's salvation is comprehensive: fear is banished as to its objective causes (3:15: "evil"), its subjective reality (3:16: "not fear"), and its immobilizing effect (listlessness).

17. גִּבּוֹר occurs frequently, always with the sense of a military hero or champion. It is used of Yahweh (Ps. 24:8; Isa. 10:21; Jer. 14:9; 32:18), as well as of the Messiah (Pss. 45:4 [3]; 89:20 [19]; Isa. 9:5 [6]). The reference to the Lord's delivering power looks back to the parallel words *making your enemy turn tail* in 3:15, but it also amplifies the assurance of 3:17 by noting the Lord's ability to deal with every cause of fear (3:15). יוֹשִׁיעַ (who saves) forms a relative clause with the relative pronoun (אֲשֶׁר) unexpressed. This גִּבּוֹר is capable of delivering his people. The word יָשַׁע connotes deliverance by divine action (Isa. 30:15; 45:17) from human enemies (Num. 10:9; 2 Sam. 22:4), sin (Isa. 64:4 [5]; Jer. 4:14), and distress (Ps. 34:7 [6]; Ezek. 34:22). שִׂמְחָה (rejoicing) forms an *inclusio* with שִׂמְחִי (rejoice) in 3:14. יַחֲרִישׁ (he will be silent) is the hiphil of חָרַשׁ (to be silent). On two occa-

offense of sin, and it constitutes a deeper and more necessary work, for there can be no salvation until God is satisfied. He is, however, also the indwelling God, a king, securing them from fear (v. 15c), outward and inward (vv. 15d–16c; see the Exegesis). This indwelling is the objective verification of his inward satisfaction over his people. There is nothing now to alienate the Holy One; at-one-ment has been achieved. This indwelling is also the central divine objective in the work of redemption (Exod. 29:46).

16. In 3:15d, reference is made to the end of objective cause of fear ("never fear evil"), but now there is something different and deeper. "Do not fear" proclaims the end of the subjective emotion of fear. (On the contrast between fear that is gone and fear that must abide, see the Exegesis.) Delivered from both fear and fearfulness, however, the Lord's peole are renewed for action, freed for activity, saved to serve: "Do not let your hands hang

listless." What activity is this? Prayer, praise, and worship (3:9, 20), holiness in life and speech (3:13), trusting and resting (3:12–13), rejoicing (3:14).

17. Verse 17a bears the same relation to 3:15d–16 as its parallel 3:15c bears to 3:15a–b: it confirms the reliability of what is promised—untroubled circumstances and an untroubled mind secured by the presence of the Lord. The common element in the parallel is "the LORD," the God whose nature was defined in Egypt when he saved his people and overthrew his enemies. Commentators who deny a message of hope to preexilic prophets simply fail to grasp the theology of the name of Yahweh on which the prophetic ministry rested: his name forbids him to be only judge or redeemer; he must be both. It is the fullness of his divine nature as the Judge and Redeemer of the exodus revelation (Exod. 3:15; 20:2) that he now comes to indwell his people. He is the Judge who has wondrously "set aside the judgments against

sions the hiphil has a transitive meaning "to silence." To this extent the New International Version's translation ("he will quiet you") has substance. But lines 17c and 17e both refer to the Lord's feelings toward Zion (the pronouns *you* are singular feminine; see 3:14) and a change from feelings to ministry would be intrusive and destroy the balance between 3:17c–e and 3:14. Such is the Lord's love that it goes beyond even divine words. The same argument applies against

the readiness of BHS, J. Smith (*Zephaniah*, p. 257), and House (*Zephaniah*, p. 133) to follow the Septuagint's καινιεῖ (he will renew or refresh), which reads יְחַדֵּשׁ (renew) for יַחֲרִישׁ. The Masoretic Text shows a natural progression from the feeling of joy (3:17c) to the silence of adoration (3:17d) to vocal exultation (3:17e). יָגִיל (he will be elated) is widely used in the vocabulary of joy. It is rather stronger in meaning than the other words for joy used in this oracle.

---

you" (Zeph. 3:15); the Redeemer who lives among his redeemed. But he is also the intensely loving God (v. 17c–e). Most often the Lord's love is expressed by the Hebrew word *ḥesed*. This is the love that issues in commitment, the "ever-unfailing" fidelity of love, love that lives in the will as much as in the heart. Here, however, the word is *ʾahăbâ*, the passionate love of Jacob for Rachel (Gen. 29:20) and of Michal for David (1 Sam.

18:28), the fond love of Jacob for Joseph (Gen. 37:3), Uzziah's devotion to gardening (2 Chron. 26:10), Jonathan's deep friendship with David (1 Sam. 18:3), the devotee's delight in the Lord's law (Ps. 119:97). This too is the Lord's love for his people (Hos. 3:1), a love that delights him (Zeph. 3:17c), makes him contemplate his beloved with wordless adoration (v. 17d), a love that cannot be contained but bursts into elated singing (v. 17e).

III. The End of the World: Hope in All Its Glory (3:9–20)
C. The Lord's People, the Praise of All the Earth (3:18–20)

MOTYER

18 Those who are grieved because of the ap-
      pointed feasts
   I will remove;
they will be far from you,
      the one on whom the imposition was a
      reproach.
19 Look, I am going to deal with all who hu-
      miliated you.
At that time,
   I will save the lame,
      and the outcast I will gather,
and I will make into a praise and a name
      those whose shame was in all the earth.
20 At that time,
   I will bring you—
      the time when I gather you—
yes, I will appoint you to be a name and a
      praise
      among all the peoples of the earth:
when I bring back your captivity before
      your very eyes,
      says the LORD.

NRSV

18   as on a day of festival.
   I will remove disaster from you,
      so that you will not bear reproach for it.
19 I will deal with all your oppressors
      at that time.
And I will save the lame
      and gather the outcast,
and I will change their shame into praise
      and renown in all the earth.
20 At that time I will bring you home,
      at that time when I gather you;
for I will make you renowned and praised
      among all the peoples of the earth,
when I restore your fortunes
      before your eyes, says the LORD.

18. נוּגֵי would appear to derive from the verb נכה, but KB (p. 600), refusing to recognize this verb, prefers to emend to כִּימֵי (as in the days of) BHS prefers כְּיוֹם, which (with the following word, מוֹעֵד) it would add to 3:17: "As in the day of a solemn assembly." This agrees with the Septuagint's καὶ εὐφρανθήσεται ἐπὶ σὲ ἐν τέρψει ὡς ἐν ἡμέρᾳ ἑορτῆς (and he will enthuse over you with delight as in the day of the feast). House (Zephaniah, p. 133) follows this as the best sense of a verse whose meaning must be an open question. BDB (p. 387), however, understands נוּגֵי as a niphal participle of יָגָה (to be grieved). The piel form of יָגָה occurs in Lamentations 1:4 with the transitive meaning "to grieve," while in Lamentations 3:33 the hiphil form means "to afflict." The present formation could be the niphal participle (see GKC §69t and §27n). While this form cannot pass without notice, neither is it inadmissible. In the present case the verb is followed by מִן (מִמּוֹעֵד). This usage is not exemplified in other instances of יָגָה but would allow this sense: "Those who are grieved because of the appointed feasts." אָסַפְתִּי (I will remove): See the Exegesis of 1:2. While אָסַף generally means "to gather to," it also admits the meaning "to remove," even when not construed with מִן (from; Gen. 30:23; Ps. 85:4 [3]; Isa. 4:1). The sense of "removal from" is underscored by the following clause: מִמֵּךְ הָיוּ (they will be [far] from you). For this meaning of the prefixed preposition מִן, see Psalm 49:14 [15], Proverbs 20:3, and Isaiah 14:19. "You" is singular feminine, that is,

---

18–20. While the linguistic and syntactical conundrums in 3:18 can at best be handled tentatively (see the Exegesis), the overall theme is plain. The Lord is on the side of his people and will deal with all who have humiliated them (3:19a). He will save and gather them and transform their reputation in the world (3:19b–f), and he will excite worldwide admiration for those whose captivity he has restored (3:20). At first sight this seems a less glorious hope for the world than we may have expected, but Zephaniah was deeply sensitive to the old traditions and they were the natural vehicle for his thought. From the start it had been the Lord's purpose to bless the world in his people (Gen. 12:3; 22:18; Isa. 2:2–4). Sometimes this was expressed in subordinationist terms (Isa. 45:14–25), emphasizing the truth that there is no way into the knowledge of the Lord except by submission to those who know him already. Zephaniah crystallizes this divine world plan into a vision of all the peoples—even those who once despised (3:19f)—acknowledging the name and praise of the people of the Lord (3:20):

A the people purified and vindicated (18–19a)
  a false members removed (18)
  b the end of humiliation (19a)
A′ the people recovered and transformed (19b–f)
  a′ disadvantages remedied (19b–d)
  b′ the end of disrepute (19e–f)
A″ the people regathered and acknowledged (20)
  a″ universal repute (20a–d)
  b″ the end of captivity (20e–f)

As my translation indicates, the Hebrew of this oracle is far from smooth; this may be deliberate, reflecting the excitement with which Zephaniah contemplated the day when a pure (3:18–19a) and whole (3:19b–f) people would at last be what at the first they were called to be—the magnetic and admired center of the world.

18. The Hebrew of this verse is terse and allusive (see the Exegesis), as indeed it is the nature of poetry to be. Zephaniah was not writing a doctoral dissertation, and we must not judge his Hebrew as if he were. Judged as poetry, his lines offer a plain meaning. The substance of the verse is that in every religious society there are those whose membership is a pretense. They are mere conformists. When the *appointed feasts* come round, they will "of course" keep them—but at the same time resent the intrusion into their regular programs. Amos finds them in his day keeping the festivals but longing for them to be over quicker or sooner in order that they may open up shop once more (Amos 8:4–6). He further provides us with a comment on this verse in Zephaniah by observing that their rush back to business is motivated by a commercial dishonesty that takes advantage of the poor and defenseless. This is the best understanding of "the imposition," for Amos uses this very word *maśʾēt* in 5:11 of the exactions the unscrupulous rich made upon the helpless poor. The movement of thought in Zephaniah is precisely the same. False religion is the soil from which springs social inequality and wrongful use of power. In the Lord's day, when all wrongs are righted, there will neither be the religious pretended (v. 18a) nor the injustices, inequalities, and oppressions that such a person promotes, and with his disappearance the

addressing Zion. If this understanding of the words in this line is valid, this clause complements the sense of אָסַף just suggested. That הָיוּ (they will be) is in the perfect tense underscores the certainty of what Yahweh has affirmed he will do (i.e., the perfect of confidence). מַשְׂאֵת עָלֶיהָ (the one whose obligations): מַשְׂאֵת, a noun form of the verb נָשָׂא (to lift, bear, carry), has several meanings, but the sense that best fits this context is "obligation" (see 2 Chron. 24:6, 9; Amos 5:11). The shift from the second-person singular (מִמֵּךְ) to the third-person singular (עָלֶיהָ) is typical of the prophets and is an idiom of emphasis. עָלֶיהָ (lit., upon her a reproach): The feminine suffix הָ is in apposition with נוּגֵי מִמּוֹעֵד (those who are grieved), creating this assertion: "I will remove those who are grieved by the appointed feasts—they shall be far from you—the one upon whom [עָלֶיהָ] the imposition is a reproach." The Masoretic Text throughout this verse presents difficulties, but it is neither unexemplified nor impossible. It promises a purified people, free at last of all those who insincerely conformed to Zion's religious observances (see the Exposition).

19. הִנְנִי (look, I . . .) adds a note of emphasis to the following assertion. עֹשֶׂה אֶת־ (am going to deal with) is the participle *futurum instans* (GKC §116p) of עָשָׂה (to do), used here (without a stated object) with the sense of acting (against) or dealing with (as in Gen. 34:31 and Exod. 21:9). מְעַנַּיִךְ (who humiliated you): This piel participle has the transitive sense of humbling or afflicting, treating as an underdog (Gen. 15:13). This goes beyond what was mentioned in 3:18, pointing to Zion's outside oppressors. This internal/external pattern is common to the three sections of this oracle. בָּעֵת הַהִיא

(at that time) reminds us that we are still hearing what God will do for his people at the time of their purification. It is the logical connection of בַּיּוֹם הַהוּא (in that day) in 3:16 (see the Exegesis of 1:12). Behind the reference to הַצֹּלֵעָה (the lame) lies the motif of the final pilgrimage to Zion (Isa. 35), when no personal inability will be allowed to prevent the Lord's pilgrims from coming safely home. Rather, the Lord will provide everything necessary for them (Isa. 42:16; Jer. 31:7–9). צָלַע (to limp) is used elsewhere only in Genesis 32:32 [31] and (metaphorically) Micah 4:6–7. וְהַנִּדָּחָה (and the outcast): For a similar assertion, see Psalm 147:2 (compare 2 Sam. 14:13–14; Isa. 16:3–4; Mic. 4:6). וְשַׂמְתִּים לִתְהִלָּה (and I will make into a praise): For the construction שִׂים לְ, see Micah 1:6 and 4:7. The gathered outcasts will be transformed from despised objects of shame to a people who are worthy of praise. וּלְשֵׁם (and a name): By extension שֵׁם (name) signifies reputation (Abraham was promised a great reputation [שֵׁם] according to Gen. 12:2). The restored people will be "made a reputation [שִׂים לְ]," that is, Yahweh will make them into a people who reflect the glory of their status as a people whose fortunes God has restored. בְּכָל־הָאָרֶץ בָּשְׁתָּם (those whose shame was in all the earth) is an attributive clause (a relative clause without relative pronoun). For the idea, see 2 Thessalonians 1:10.

20. בְּעֵת הַהִיא (at that time) ends the series of time indicators that began in 3:11—all referring to the time when God will judge the nations and vindicate his people. For עֵת (time), see the Exegesis of 1:12. וּבְעֵת קַבְּצִי אֶתְכֶם (the time when I gather you): The conjunction ו is explanatory, with the sense of "that is" (indicated in my translation with a

---

"reproach" that such behavior brought on the Lord's people will be gone.

19. Verse 18 deals with the communal transformation of the Lord's people, among whom there will be no false or socially domineering member. The transformation is now both widened and deepened. There is a new universal status and a new individual transformation:

a no more oppressors (19ab)
   b the personally helpless saved (19c)
   b' the personally banished gathered (19d)
a' no more shame, only praise universally (19ef)

We may take it that "all you oppressors" (v. 19a) develops the thought of the internal

oppressors of verse 18, taking into account the oppressive powers of the earth. Thus the oppressing earth (v. 19ab) becomes the praising earth (v. 19ef). The "lame" is the one whose internal weakness makes him helpless; the "outcast" is the one whose external circumstances separate him from the community of the blessed. But by divine action all such limitations are overcome. Nothing will be allowed to militate against the salvation and gathering together of the Lord's intended community nor against the outshining of their new society to the admiration of the whole world.

20. As 3:19 continues and develops verse 18, so verse 20 enlarges on verse 19. The great series of first-person verbs continues: all is of God (2 Cor. 5:18). It is he who creates the purged society (v. 18), deals with the oppressors (v. 19a),

dash). This insertional explanation identifies the time in question as the gathering time of 3:19, linking the two verses. The שֵׁם (name) and תְהִלָּה (praise) are now seen in their impact on the watching world. The reversal of these two nouns is a stylistic variation from 3:19. שֵׁם signifies "repute": there will be about them something that excites praise. בְּשׁוּבִי אֶת־שְׁבוּתֵיכֶם (bring back your captivity): See the Exegesis of 2:7. The plural suffix כֶם־ indicates that the Lord addresses all his people. The day will be marked by the liberation of the people of God from everything that ever bound them or injured their well-being. לְעֵינֵיכֶם (before your very eyes) indicates a personal, direct experience. אָמַר (says) is a perfect tense. In English this would look to the past, whereas the purpose of the Hebrew structure is to stress definiteness, something the Lord has decided upon. Zephaniah's vision of the eschatological future is not wishful thinking: it is a divine commitment.

---

saves those whose natural state made them helpless (v. 19cd), transforms the repute of his people (v. 19ef). Now he gathers his whole people (Mark 13:27), secures their glory before the watching world, and allows them actually to experience the reversal of all that had ever limited or constricted them. There are two points where something fresh is asserted, not going beyond what 3:18–19 said or implied by offering a special emphasis: "Before your very eyes" assures the Lord's people that they will actually and certainly enter into and enjoy this promise for themselves; "and says the LORD" underwrites the promise with a specified pledge. It is something to which the Lord has made his personal commitment.

Haggai

Introduction

The assumption that we can enjoy Christian standards and benefits without Christian commitment is prevalent today. On the moral front, leaders in church and state and ordinary folk alike are baffled by the disappearance of norms of conduct that until recently were accepted as axiomatic. Many causes are suggested, but the truth is that these disappearing values have only a fragile rootage in fallen human nature; they are values taught by revelation, written in Scripture, embodied in the Lord Jesus Christ—and where there is no knowledge of him and commitment to him they die by starvation. The same is true of the benefits of an ordered, prosperous society.

Governments work on the assumption that a healthy gross national product is the consequence of a proper industrial base, efficient management, skilled workers, and the due operation of market forces—in other words, that economic health depends on an effective economic system. Haggai, however, rose to challenge the view that economics can be left to the economists. Here, too, we live in God's world and unless he is given the central place and honor, the laws he created will work not for our blessing but for our bane. Thus Haggai speaks to our concern that world resources should meet world need and to our longing that not only will needs be satisfied but also that life will be satisfying. He addresses the problem of inflation more explicitly than any other prophet; his book is a tract for our times.

The Lord's Messenger with the Lord's Commission

We know nothing of Haggai except what his book and Ezra 5:1–2 and 6:14 suggest. He was a prophet of the Lord; his recorded

*In Memoriam
Joyce Baldwin
(Caine) and Tom
McComiskey—
masters and
lovers of the
Word of God*

*Contributor:
J. Alec Motyer
B.A., M.A., B.D.
Principal and Dean
of Trinity College,
Bristol (Retired)*

public ministry occupied fifteen weeks during 520 B.C.; with Zechariah, he promoted the movement that led to building the Second Temple. Beyond this lies legend or surmise, all equally profitless. Was he himself old enough to have seen the First Temple (2:3)? If so, surely he would have asked, "Who is left among us?" not "among you?" Was he a priest because he knew the laws of holiness, or was he not because he needed to ask (2:11–13)? But the levitical commonplace involved was surely something everyone knew. We do not know if he returned with the exiles from Babylon or was born in Judah among the survivors of the great captivity. Haggai left for us all he felt we needed to know—that he enjoyed the highest honor known to humankind: he was the Lord's prophet (1:1), the Lord's messenger with the Lord's commission (1:13).

Theologically, Haggai was thoroughly orthodox. Though he alluded only once to the covenant (2:5), he taught in the direct line of the Mosaic exodus–Sinaitic tradition and its Davidic development. The divine name *Yahweh* (the LORD) occurs thirty-four times in the thirty-eight verses of his book, and fourteen of these stress divine omnicompetence with the ancient epithet *LORD of hosts* (see on 1:2). Within this accepted theological and religious framework, Haggai had three dominant interests.

Messianism

Haggai's book begins and ends with references to Zerubbabel (1:1; 2:20). Though Haggai began his ministry at a public festival, he did not look to the assembled people but to the Davidic Zerubbabel (1 Chron. 3:1, 19) for the impetus to build the house, and he returns to him with the promise that in Zerubbabel the Lord will rebuild the house of David. The parallel with David is striking, for David wanted to build the Lord's house, and in response the Lord vowed to build the king's house. This recapitulation of 2 Samuel 7:1–11 shows that the messianic element is not an afterthought but the framing context of the whole message and that it was his messianic urgency that made Haggai the prophet who encouraged the builders. To see this more fully we must turn to the subject for which he is most famous.

The House of the Lord

So central is the building of the house of the Lord to Haggai that many concur with Knight (*New Israel*, p. 61) that the book implies that Haggai "took the superstitious view that God had not blessed his people merely because they had not begun to rebuild the temple." Pfeiffer (*Introduction to the Old Testament*, p. 603) contrasts Haggai with previous prophets in that his "concern was not the moral and religious wickedness of his people, but adherence to the rules of Levitical purity and the fulfillment of ritual acts." More moderately, Coggins (*Haggai*, p. 19) says that Haggai charged the community with "failure to reestablish the regular cultic round in the temple," sharing Petersen's view (*Haggai*, p. 49) that without the house the cult lacks normative wholeness. Closer examination of 2:14 shows, however, that it is the people who render the offerings "defiled," not defective offerings that defile the people. For Haggai as for earlier prophets, the offerer was a key factor in the acceptability of the offerings before God. To Isaiah (1:10–15), Jeremiah (7:9–11), and Amos (5:21–24), people who were set on wrong abused the ordinances of God and brought divine condemnation upon themselves through what God intended for their blessing. Hosea (6:6) and Micah (6:6–8) emphasized rather that people whose lives were not positively set upon right abused the divine ordinances, and it is with these prophets that Haggai is to be associated, especially with Micah.

The commands in Exodus 25:8 and 29:44–46 legitimizing the tabernacle say, "Make me a sanctuary and I will dwell among them" (my translation). The same concept prompted the first house (1 Kings 8:27; see 2 Sam. 7:5), and was Haggai's motivation in pressing for the second. Had Israel refused to provide the tent in the wilderness, would not the Lord have replied, "Then you do not want me among you"? The order of events in Exodus through Leviticus shows that the tent comes first as a means of the grace of the indwelling God and that the cultic, levitical round of sacrifices is necessary because the Holy One dwells there. The normative heart of the Israelite community is not the cultus but the indwelling holy God in whose presence his people are made secure only by the shedding of blood. Haggai stood firmly within this tradition. The refusal to build the house was the rejection of the offer of grace, the grace of divine indwelling. But one further clarification is important. Canaanite religion dealt in techniques—earthly acts supposed to exert pressure on the gods—but biblical religion deals with obedience. The building of the house is not a cultic technique whereby humans pressure or even seek to please God; it is an act of obedience performed in the faith that God will keep his promise. The Lord's case against Haggai's people was simple: "You did not want me" (see the Exegesis and Exposition at 2:17).

Second Samuel 7 binds the Davidic kingship and the Lord's house inextricably together. It originated the long tradition whereby the prophets linked the messianic day to the house concept. In Isaiah the cleansed people and the newly created city are centered on the Lord's "booth" (4:2–6), and the reestablished people rejoice in the courts of his sanctuary (62:9). Jeremiah looks forward to the day when the Branch shall reign on David's throne and the levitical priests minister before the Lord (33:14–26). Ezekiel envisages the temple community and the indwelling Prince (40–48). Malachi predicts the day when the Lord shall suddenly come to his temple (3:1–4). Haggai also lived within this tradition. The presence of the Lord in his house among his people was a pledge of the great day and the greater coming and presence.

Historical Background

After the decree of the Persian emperor Cyrus in 538 B.C., exiles led by Zerubbabel returned to the land of Judah (Ezra 1). At the site of Solomon's temple they built an altar and reinstituted the sacrifices called for by the Mosaic law (Ezra 3). They also prepared to rebuild the temple, but work stopped in response to opposition from neighboring enemies. In the sixteen years that followed, the people built themselves houses, but no work was done on the Lord's house until the prophets Haggai and Zechariah rebuked and challenged the people (Ezra 4:24–5:2).

Darius I Hystaspes, in whose second year Haggai ministered (1:1), came to the throne of the Persian Empire in confusing circumstances. His predecessor, Cambyses, returning through Palestine from an Egyptian campaign, learned of serious rebellion at home and died somewhat mysteriously. His relative Darius, supported by the army, returned to Media and overthrew the usurping Gaumata. It took Darius two years to restore calm to the empire. Jerusalem was in the large satrapy of "Babylon and Babylon beyond the River" with one superintendent governor and district governors in, for example, Samaria and Jerusalem. It is by no means clear what sort of liberty of action this gave Zerubbabel, and probably not until Nehemiah's governorship and later did Judah enjoy any sort of provincial autonomy. The substantial point, however, is that by 520 B.C. the empire was secure in Darius's hands and there was no unrest, actual or envisaged. Haggai and Zechariah were not political opportunists seizing on the empire's difficulties and using ostensibly religious movements as a cloak for nationalist ambitions. They were true to their prophetic calling and theology, summoning people back to God and leaving the future in his hands.

Date

Haggai mentions four dates on which he ministered. Babylonian texts and new moon astronomical tables allow these to be fixed accurately to within one day (Baldwin, *Haggai*, p. 29):

Reference	Darius's Year	Month	Day	Calendar Date
1:1	2	6	1	29 August 520 B.C.
1:15	2	6	24	21 September 520 B.C.
2:1	2	7	21	17 October 520 B.C.
2:10	2	9	24	18 December 520 B.C.

Only the first date is fully stated. Subsequent dates follow Hebrew idiom in not necessarily naming units of measurement where the context makes it obvious what is intended (see the Exegesis of 1:15).

Where historical problems are alleged in Haggai it is because a theoretical reconstruction is attempted. Cases in point are Rothstein's attempt (*Juden und Samaritaner*, pp. 5–41) to identify "the people of the land" as Samaritans, Hanson's search (*Dawn of Apocalyptic*, pp. 172–78) in Haggai for the conflicting parties alleged to be found in Isaiah 56–66, or Petersen's view (*Haggai*, p. 63) that Haggai 2 and Ezra 3 refer to the same events (see the Exegesis for interaction with these views).

Text

Our primary witness, the Masoretic Text , is in a good state of preservation. Where scholars propose emendations it is possible to justify the Masoretic Text on the ground of usage exemplified elsewhere in the Hebrew Bible. (The alleged interpolation in the text at 2:5 is explained in the Exegesis.)

The Septuagint is a loose and expansionist translation. It is in broad agreement with the Masoretic Text, and where it adds (2:9, 14, 21–22) or exhibits minor differences, it would be hazardous to say that it represents a distinct Hebrew tradition. It is an extremely unsafe guide. A scroll from Wadi Murabbaʿat contains much of Haggai (289 out of a possible 600 words; Verhoef, *Haggai*, p. 18). It is unfortunately fragmentary at 2:5. Minute differences from the Masoretic Text occur at 2:1, 3, but otherwise the scroll supports the Masoretic Text (including the order of verses), as do also the Peshitta (with allowances for the influence of the Septuagint) and the Targum.

Editorial Work

The Book of Haggai has been carefully presented as both a chronological and a rounded theological statement of the prophet's message (see the Exegesis). Coggins (*Haggai*, p. 25) speaks for the majority when he says that in the prophets the "editorial process remains very elusive." Specialists seem extraordinarily hesitant regarding the prima facie likelihood that the prophets were their own editors. A man conscious of being the vehicle of the word of God will not, in a literary age, leave those words to the uncertainties of oral transmission or to the less informed care of other hands. There is no compelling argument against the view that Haggai—and who better?—was his own editor. Beuken (*Haggai*, pp. 27–48) attempts to set Haggai in a "Chronistic milieu," but his case has been seriously challenged (see Mason, "Editorial Framework"). It is just as likely that Haggai provided a model for the Chronicler's style of presentation (Baldwin, *Haggai*, p. 30). Ackroyd ("Studies in the Book of Haggai," pp. 163–76) thinks a century or two of oral transmission intervened before the work was committed to writing. It is, however, intrinsically unlikely that after a hundred or more years either "Darius" or "the prophet Haggai" would have been considered sufficient identification, and it seems almost perverse to deny Haggai such an obvious task as committing his oracles to writing.

Analysis

The content of Haggai has been carefully edited—we may presume by Haggai himself—and consists of a series of six oracles in a balanced pattern. The chronological framework guarantees that this deeper pattern is not artificially imposed but runs with the grain of the message. To see this pattern is the first step in exegesis. The book has an A-B-B-A formation:

A a pair of oracles on the same date (1:1, 3): the negative consequences of the unbuilt house (1:1–11)
   a Zerubbabel and Joshua addressed: popular refusal to build the house (1:1–2)
   b the people addressed: the neglected house the cause of bane (1:3–11)
    * a double call to "take it to heart" (1:5, 7)
B "I am with you" (1:13): the Lord's presence energizing the present work (1:12–15a)
   • the leaders respond in obedience (1:12)
   • the word of divine assurance (1:13)
   • making a start (1:14–15a)
B' "I am with you" (2:4): the Lord's presence guaranteeing coming glory (1:15b–2:9)
   • former glory (1:15b–2:3)
   • the word of divine assurance (2:4–5)
   • the coming glory (2:6–9)
A' a pair of oracles on the same date (2:10, 20): the blessed consequences of the restored house (2:10–23)
   b' the people addressed: the restored house the cause of blessing (2:10–19)
    * a double call to "take it to heart" (2:15, 18)
   a' Zerubbabel addressed: the Lord will restore David's house (2:20–23)

Examination shows that this is a carefully structured presentation. Haggai's book opens (1:1–2, 3–11) and ends (2:10–19, 20–23) with pairs of oracle dates, with each oracle in the pair being on the same day. The addresses to leaders and people at the beginning is balanced by addresses to people and leaders at the end. In addition, the addresses to the people each consist of a double call to "take it to heart" (1:5, 7; 2:15, 18). Within this "bracket" lie two oracles (1:12–15a; 1:15b–2:9) linked by the common words "I am with you" (1:13; 2:4). These are words of encouragement regarding the Lord's delight in the present work of building and his purposes for the future of the house. This arrangement displays Haggai's essential message: the significance of the Lord's house in the setting of Israel's messianic hope.

While both the Exegesis and Exposition will proceed on the basis of this expanded chiastic analysis, the following simplified analysis of the six oracles will provide the outline for this commentary:

I. **Oracle to Zerubbabel and Joshua: The Lord's House Unbuilt (1:1–2)**

II. **Oracle to the People: The Neglected House the Cause of Bane (1:3–11)**

III. **Oracle to the Workers: The Lord's Presence in the Present (1:12–15a)**

IV. **Oracle to the Leaders and People: The Lord's Presence for the Future (1:15b–2:9)**

V. **Oracle to the Priests and People: The Restored House the Cause of Blessing (2:10–19)**

VI. **Oracle to Zerubbabel: David's House to Be Built (2:20–23)**

Select Bibliography

Ackroyd, Peter R. "Some Interpretive Glosses in the Book of Haggai." *Journal of Jewish Studies* 7 (1956): 163–67.

———. "Studies in the Book of Haggai." *Journal of Semitic Studies* 2 (1951): 163–76; 3 (1952): 1–13.

Baldwin, Joyce G. *Haggai, Zechariah, Malachi: An Introduction and Commentary.* Tyndale Old Testament Commentary. Downers Grove: InterVarsity, 1972.

Beuken, W. A. M. *Haggai–Sacharja 1–8: Studien zur Überlieferungsgeschichte der frühnachexilischen Prophetie.* Studia Semitica Neerlandica 10. Assen: Van Gorcum, 1967.

Cody, Aelred. "When Is the Chosen People Called a Goy?" *Vetus Testamentum* 14 (1964): 1–6.

Coggins, Richard J. *Haggai, Zechariah, Malachi.* Old Testament Guides. Sheffield: JSOT, 1987.

Davidson, Andrew B. *Hebrew Syntax*. 3d ed. Edinburgh: T. & T. Clark, 1901.

Dhorme, Édouard. *A Commentary on the Book of Job*. Translated by Harold Knight. London: Nelson, 1967.

Ellison, Henry L. *Men Spake from God: Studies in the Hebrew Prophets*. London: Paternoster, 1952.

Gelston, A. "The Foundations of the Second Temple." *Vetus Testamentum* 16 (1966): 232–35.

Hanson, Paul D. *The Dawn of Apocalyptic*. Philadelphia: Fortress, 1975.

Hillers, Delbert R. *Treaty-Curses and the Old Testament Prophets*. Biblica et Orientalia 16. Rome: Pontifical Biblical Institute, 1964.

Jones, Douglas R. *Haggai, Zechariah, and Malachi: Introduction and Commentary*. London: SCM, 1962.

Knight, George A. F. *A Biblical Approach to the Doctrine of the Trinity*. Scottish Journal of Theology, Occasional Papers 1. Edinburgh: Oliver & Boyd, 1953.

———. *The New Israel: A Commentary on the Book of Isaiah 56–66*. International Theological Commentary. Grand Rapids: Eerdmans, 1985.

Macdonald, John. "The Particle את in Classical Hebrew: Some New Data on Its Use with the Nominative." *Vetus Testamentum* 14 (1964): 264–75.

McIlmoyle, J. "Haggai." Pp. 743–47 in *The New Bible Commentary*. Edited by F. Davidson. Grand Rapids: Eerdmans, 1953.

Mason, Rex A. "The Purpose of the 'Editorial Framework' of the Book of Haggai." *Vetus Testamentum* 27 (1977): 413–21.

May, Herbert G. " 'This People' and 'This Nation' in Haggai." *Vetus Testamentum* 18 (1968): 190–97.

Moore, Thomas V. *The Prophets of the Restoration*. New York: Carter, 1856. Reprinted as *A Commentary on Haggai, Zechariah, and Malachi*. Geneva Series Commentary. London: Banner of Truth, 1960.

Perowne, Thomas T. *Haggai and Zechariah*. Cambridge Bible for Schools and Colleges. Cambridge: Cambridge University Press, 1897.

Petersen, David L. *Haggai, Zechariah 1–8*. Old Testament Library. Philadelphia: Westminster/London: SCM, 1984.

Pfeiffer, Robert H. *Introduction to the Old Testament*. Rev. ed. New York: Harper, 1948

Pusey, Edward B. *The Minor Prophets: A Commentary, Explanatory and Practical*. Vol. 2. 2d ed. Grand Rapids: Baker, 1950.

Ridderbos, Jan. *De kleine Propheten*. Vol. 3. Korte Verklaring der heilige Schrift. Kampen: Kok, 1952.

Rothstein, Johann W. *Juden und Samaritaner—Die grundlegende Scheidung von Judentum and Heidentum: Eine kritische*

Studie zum Buche Haggai und zur jüdische Geschichte in ersten nachexilischen Jahrhundert. Beiträge zur Wissenschaft vom Alten Testament 3. Leipzig: Hinrichs, 1908.

Rudolph, Wilhelm. *Haggai, Sacharja 1–8, 9–14, Maleachi*. Kommentar zum Alten Testament 13/4. Gütersloh: Mohn, 1976.

Saydon, P. P. "Meanings and Uses of the Particle אֶת." *Vetus Testamentum* 14 (1964): 192–210.

Smith, George A. *The Book of the Twelve Prophets*. 2 vols. Expositor's Bible. Reprinted Grand Rapids: Baker, 1943.

Sperry, Willard L. "The Book of Haggai: Exposition." Vol. 6 / pp. 1040–49 in *The Interpreter's Bible*. Edited by George A. Buttrick. Nashville: Abingdon, 1956.

Thomas, David W. "The Book of Haggai: Introduction and Exegesis." Vol. 6 / pp. 1037–49 in *The Interpreter's Bible*. Edited by George A. Buttrick. Nashville: Abingdon, 1956.

Verhoef, Pieter A. *The Books of Haggai and Malachi*. New International Commentary on the Old Testament. Grand Rapids: Eerdmans, 1987.

Wenham, Gordon J. *The Book of Leviticus*. New International Commentary on the Old Testament. Grand Rapids: Eerdmans, 1979.

Wiseman, Donald J. "Haggai." Pp. 781–85 in *The New Bible Commentary*. 3d ed. Edited by Donald Guthrie and J. Alec Motyer. Grand Rapids: Eerdmans, 1970.

I. Oracle to Zerubbabel and Joshua: The Lord's House Unbuilt (1:1–2)

MOTYER

1 In the second year of King Darius, in the sixth month, on the first day of the month, the word of the LORD came through the prophet Haggai to Zerubbabel the son of Shealtiel, governor of Judah, and to Joshua the son of Jehozadak, the high priest:

2 Thus the LORD of hosts says:
This people says:
The right time has not come,
the right time for the LORD's house to be
built.

NRSV

1 In the second year of King Darius, in the sixth month, on the first day of the month, the word of the LORD came by the prophet Haggai to Zerubbabel son of Shealtiel, governor of Judah, and to Joshua son of Jehozadak, the high priest: 2Thus says the LORD of hosts: These people say the time has not yet come to rebuild the LORD's house.

1:1. לְדָרְיָוֶשׁ (of Darius): Darius was the king of Persia in the time of Haggai's ministry (see the Introduction). The first day of the month (יוֹם אֶחָד לַחֹדֶשׁ) was marked by special offerings (Num. 28:11–15), so that each month began in commitment to the Lord. It was also a time of trumpet sounding (Num. 10:10), summoning the Lord to the aid of his people. While there is no plain reason why Haggai first spoke in "the sixth month," dereliction surrounding the altar would put a question mark over the meaningfulness of this plethora of offerings and over the likelihood of divine response to a spiritually careless people.

הָיָה דְבַר־יְהוָה (the word of the LORD came): הָיָה (came) in this conventional messenger formula is the verb "to be"; it does not express motion; it is much more an expression of active presence than of bare existence. The divine name, for example, is a pledge that "I will be actively present" (see אֶהְיֶה in Exod. 3:14). So in this instance, nothing is divulged regarding the processes of revelation but simply the miraculous: "The word of the Lord became an active reality." בְּיַד (through) is literally "by the hand of." יָד (hand), besides its literal sense, has several broad senses. When it occurs with prepositions it may connote possession

---

1:1–11. The heart of Haggai's message is encapsulated in these verses. We learn the sort of society he lived in, the forces shaping its experiences, and what its central problem was. It is a stylishly shaped presentation of truth:

a   divine word exposing failure (2)
b   a false priority: the fact (3–4)
c   the first call to thoughtfulness: the situation appraised (5–6)
c'   the second call to thoughtfulness: the remedy prescribed (7–8)
b'   a fasle priority: the consequences (9)
a'   divine action chastening failure (10–11)

1:1. Like the prophecies of Ezekiel, Jonah, and Zechariah, Haggai's book has no formal title. Coupling this with Haggai's simple description as "the prophet" suggests that the book as we have it was "published" near enough to the events to make further description needless. The date (see the Introduction) has been fixed as 29 August 520 B.C. By this time Darius was master of his empire and Haggai's ministry took place in a time of political stability.

The words ḥāyâ dĕbar yhwh (the word of the LORD came) introduce us to the prophetic experience. On the divine side, there is the objective gift of "the word of the LORD" (see 1:3; 2:1, 10, 20), that is, the word that originated in God. The familiar "thus the LORD says" (1:2, 7; 2:6, 11) or "the LORD says" (1:8; 2:7, 9) goes on to assert that what originated in God is then voiced by him on earth as though speaking in his own person; see "the voice of the LORD their God" (1:12). Haggai's favorite formula, "this is the word of the LORD" (1:9, 13; 2:4 [thrice], 8, 9, 14, 17, 23 [thrice]), sums up the whole matter—the identity of the earthly message with its heavenly original. This formula is actually a noun in the construct state preceding the divine name, nĕʾum yhwh (word [or declaration] of the LORD), and its function is to act as a seal, stamping the prophet's word as the authentic divine word. On the human side, prophecy is the accurate transmission by the chosen agent of what the Lord has spoken; in 1:12, "the voice of the LORD" and "the words of Haggai" are identical. The same is implied when Haggai is simply commanded to "say" (2:2, 21); what he speaks is what the Lord would speak. This identity of human and divine words rests on verbal inspiration. Thrice we are told that the word came "through" (bĕyad; lit., by the hand of) Haggai (1:1, 3; 2:1) and twice "to" (ʾel) him (2:10, 20). "To" (ʾel) stresses God's activity, originating and sending his word, watching over its accurate reception, that is, the work of revelation; "through" (bĕyad) signifies his inspiration of his messenger to be the bearer of the word and to transmit it unchanged. "Through" (bĕyad) occurs over forty times in the Old Testament, typically, of Moses (e.g., 1 Kings 8:53, 56) or the prophets in general (e.g., 1 Sam. 28:15). Note its "secular" use in Jeremiah 27:3. This foregoing discussion of revelation and inspiration defines what is meant by calling Haggai hannābî (the prophet).

How did Haggai describe the society in which he lived? It is quite usual to understand Haggai to imply hardship and poverty, but a more careful consideration of what he actually says shows that this was not quite the case. We have rather the general impression of some level of affluence, for according to 1:4, people were able to do in their private homes what Solomon had done in the temple and the palace (1 Kings 6:9; 7:3, 7). Yesterday's luxury was today's necessity, and the people as a whole were expecting and able to secure their comforts.

So, what was wrong? Haggai answers on two levels: the outward evidence of the eyes and the

973

(Exod. 10:25; Josh. 6:2) as well as agency (Exod. 9:35; Num. 4:37), and it frequently refers to God's speaking "by the agency of prophets" (BDB, p. 391). זְרֻבָּבֶל (Zerubbabel): See the Introduction. פֶּחָה (governor) is an Aramaic word probably borrowed from Assyrian (see the Introduction). יְהוֹשֻׁעַ (Joshua): See the Introduction.

2. כֹּה אָמַר (thus says): כֹּה usually points to what follows; here it directs our attention to the content of the prophetic speech that follows. אָמַר (says) in the perfect tense expresses definiteness or decisiveness. It is not that the Lord spoke thus at some time in the past but that this is his definitive present utterance. David used the same tense in a decisive royal pronouncement in 2 Samuel 19:30 (GKC §106i). יְהוָה צְבָאוֹת (the Lord of hosts): Examples like Psalm 80:5 [4], יְהוָה אֱלֹהִים צְבָאוֹת (LORD, God of hosts), in which אֱלֹהִים (God) is in its absolute rather than construct form, show that יְהוָה is a noun in apposition with צְבָאוֹת and that the whole title means "Yahweh [who is] hosts," that is, the one who in himself *is* (not simply possesses) every potentiality and power (see Knight, *Doctrine of the Trinity*). צְבָאוֹת is an "intensive plural denoting the comprehensive scope of God's might" (Verhoef, *Haggai*, p. 52). הָעָם הַזֶּה (this people): Rudolph (*Haggai*, p. 74) restricts this description to those who returned from exile, but Petersen (*Haggai*, p. 47) rightly replies that "there is little reason to think that 'the people' refers to an entity different from 'the remnant of the people' in any of these texts." Others (Pusey, *Minor Prophets*, p. 300; Baldwin, *Haggai*,

p. 39) make it a title of rebuke in its own right, and Verhoef (p. 56) urges that it is peculiar to preexilic prophecies of doom. None of these claims is accurate. Of its eighty-five occurrences, extending from Exodus to Zechariah, over fifty are favorable. The description itself is noncommittal; only the context decides, and here the context is one of rebuke. The emphatic place given to the subject, הָעָם הַזֶּה אָמְרוּ (this people says), suggests that as Haggai speaks to the leaders, he gestures toward the assembled people. אָמְרוּ (says) is a perfect tense verb; its sense of completed action connotes the idea *have made up their mind*. לֹא עֶת־בֹּא עֶת־בֵּית יְהוָה לְהִבָּנוֹת (the right time has not come, the right time for the LORD's house to be built): The wording of this statement appears unusual and terse, but we know little of colloquial Hebrew, and to reconstruct the text on the uncertain basis of the Septuagint comes close to folly (see BHS, RSV, NIV). עֶת־בֹּא (time . . . come): עֵת plus an infinitive occurs in Genesis 24:11, and with לֹא (not) plus an infinitive in Genesis 29:7. These examples establish the translation offered above. עֵת (the right time) has the same sense as Greek καιρός, not a date so much as an opportunity, not a moment so much as "the right moment." So when the people said, "Not an opportune time of coming," they were recognizing a duty toward the Lord's house, but were (and for fifteen years had been) putting it off in favor of other demands on their time (the house of the LORD): The emphatic position of בֵּית יְהוָה cannot well be reflected, but it highlights Haggai's sense of outrage.

---

deeper level of a biblical worldview. We shall encounter his answers below.

2. When the people objected that it was not the right time to build, they betrayed the conviction that they had an obligation to restore the temple. The traditions they received recognized that behind the decree of Cyrus (Ezra 1:2–4) lay the directive of God (Ezra 1:1), but when they met with opposition and legal barriers were apparently put in their way (Ezra 4:4–5), the initial impulse to build withered and soon the claims of God ceased to receive priority. There followed "a sort of truce between conscience and covetousness" (Moore, *Prophets of the Restoration*, p. 58) until there was "no suitable time to men who are uninterested" (McIlmoyle, "Haggai," p. 745).

In Old Testament thought, the house was not desired for itself, as a sort of lucky charm (see Jer. 7:4), nor is there any suggestion that without the house any rituals performed must be defective (Petersen, *Haggai*, pp. 79–85). The house was the outward form of the real presence of the Lord among his people. To refuse to build the house was at best saying that it did not matter whether the Lord was present with them. At worst it was presuming on divine grace, that the Lord would live with his people even though they willfully refused to fulfill the condition of his indwelling that he had laid down. It amounted to seeking grace but refusing the means of grace. Not to build the house was not to want the Lord as and for himself.

II. Oracle to the People: The Neglected House the Cause of Bane (1:3–11)

MOTYER

³And the word of the LORD came through the prophet Haggai, saying:

4 Is it the right time for you yourselves to live in your houses—
paneled ones at that!—
and this house in ruins?

5 Now then, thus the LORD of hosts says:
Take to heart how things are going for you.

6 You have sown abundantly, but brought in little;
eaten, but without satisfaction;
drunk, but without stimulation;
dressed, but none keeps warm;
and the wage earner keeps his wages in a bag with holes!

7 Thus the LORD of hosts says:
Take to heart how things are going for you.

8 Go up to the hill country and bring wood and build the house,
and I will accept it with favor and bring glory to myself, the LORD says.

9 Expecting an abundance,
but look! How very little!
For you brought it home,
and I blew it away.
Why?—this is the word of the LORD of hosts—
Because of my house, which is in ruins,
and you are still running off, each one, to his own house.

10 Therefore on your account the heavens keep back some dew,
and the earth keeps back its produce;

11 and I have summoned dryness on the earth and on the mountains
and on the grain and on the wine and on the oil
and on that which the ground brings forth
and on humankind and on beast—
on all the labor of your hands.

NRSV

³Then the word of the LORD came by the prophet Haggai, saying: 4Is it a time for you yourselves to live in your paneled houses, while this house lies in ruins? 5Now therefore thus says the LORD of hosts: Consider how you have fared. 6You have sown much, and harvested little; you eat, but you never have enough; you drink, but you never have your fill; you clothe yourselves, but no one is warm; and you that earn wages earn wages to put them into a bag with holes.

7Thus says the LORD of hosts: Consider how you have fared. 8Go up to the hills and bring wood and build the house, so that I may take pleasure in it and be honored, says the LORD. 9You have looked for much, and, lo, it came to little; and when you brought it home, I blew it away. Why? says the LORD of hosts. Because my house lies in ruins, while all of you hurry off to your own houses. 10Therefore the heavens above you have withheld the dew, and the earth has withheld its produce. 11And I have called for a drought on the land and the hills, on the grain, the new wine, the oil, on what the soil produces, on human beings and animals, and on all their labors.

3. וַיְהִי דְבַר־יְהוָה (and the word of the LORD came) repeats the somewhat similar form in 1:1, thus adding emphasis to the affirmation that Yahweh has spoken. בְּיַד (through): See the Exegesis of 1:1. לֵאמֹר (saying) frequently introduces direct speech (see Gen. 1:22; Amos 2:12).

4. לָכֶם אַתֶּם (for you yourselves): The nominative אַתֶּם (yourselves) emphasizes the dative לָכֶם. It is idiomatically correct (see Deut. 5:3; 1 Sam. 19:23; 25:24; GKC §135g). סְפוּנִים (paneled) is a passive qal participle of סָפַן (to cover over), used in 1 Kings 6:9 of "cladding" the house with cedar, in 7:3 of paneling, and possibly in Jeremiah 22:14 of roofing. "Paneling" is most suitable here (Wiseman, "Haggai," p. 783; Petersen, *Haggai*, p. 48). The absence of the definite article makes the word an appositional adjective meriting the emphatic translation above (see also GKC §126z). חָרֵב (in ruins): See Jeremiah 33:10; Ezekiel 36:35, 38; Nehemiah 2:3, 17 for the same adjective in connection with the sacking of the temple in 587 B.C. וְהַבַּיִת הַזֶּה (and this house): וְ connects הַבַּיִת to the preceding words and thus creates a circumstantial clause: *seeing* this house is in ruins (see BDB, p. 253).

5. וְעַתָּה (now then) expresses resolution and describes the immediacy of Yahweh's determination to call the people to recognize their fault. שִׂימוּ לְבַבְכֶם עַל (take to heart; lit., set your heart upon) is not to be understood in the modern sense of a fixed longing, even though in Hebrew the heart is also the organ of desire, but in the sense of the heart as the locus of prudent thoughtfulness. לֵב (heart) occurs with the same verb and preposition in Job 1:8 (see also Hag. 1:7; 2:15, 18). דַּרְכֵיכֶם (how things are going for you; lit., your ways): The Hebrew noun דֶּרֶךְ (way, road) comes as easily as its English counterpart to express characteristic action (it is someone's way, that is, lifestyle or habitual behavior; 1 Sam. 18:14). This common meaning (consider where your chosen lifestyle is leading you) is preferred to that in Deuteronomy 28:29 (consider the experiences life is bringing you).

6. זְרַעְתֶּם (you have sown) is followed by four infinitives absolute: הָבֵא (brought in), אָכוֹל (eaten), שָׁתוֹ (drunk), לָבוֹשׁ (dressed). This construction stresses the verbal action rather than the agent and is therefore a particularly vivid way of bringing home what life has been like (GKC §113z). שָׂבְעָה (satisfaction) occurs as a noun (e.g., Isa. 23:18; 55:2). שָׁכְרָה (stimulation) is usually classed as an infinitive construct used as a verbal noun (see parallel forms in Exod. 30:18; 36:2; GKC §45d). But there is no reason, other than that it is not found elsewhere, why it should not be a noun here. The basic sense of this word is to be or become drunk (see Gen. 9:21). It also refers to social drinking or drink-

---

3. Verses 3–9 form the heart of Haggai's opening ministry and are a self-contained unit in their own right. The messenger formulas (1:3, 9) enclose two balanced statements (1:5–6, 7–8), each with the same introduction (1:5, 7) and a five-verb elaboration (1:6, 8), the first descriptive, the second prescriptive. The double use of *bayît* (house) in 1:4 and 1:9b and the repetition of *ḥārēb* (in ruins) form an *inclusio* that highlights the people's interest in their own houses and lack of interest in God's house.

The repetition of the messenger formula (1:1, 3) strengthens the prophet's assertion that Yahweh is speaking through him. The addition of *lᵉmōr* (saying) prepares us for the content of Yahweh's word. That word is in the form of a question.

4. The question Haggai asks cuts to the heart of the people's protestation in 1:2. The emphatic use of pronouns in this verse is instructive. We may paraphrase the question: Should *you* be living in paneled houses while *this* house lies in ruins? They put themselves ("you yourselves") and their comforts ("paneled houses") before the sacred task of obeying the Lord, whose house was in ruins.

Haggai may still be addressing the rulers. Baldwin (*Haggai*, p. 40) suggests that the governor's palace may have been under construction at the time. But the parallel in 1:9 ("still running off") is a comment on the whole people and determines the reference here. There was a national failure in priorities.

5. The prophet now calls the people to consider their ways. To this point their experience (*derek*, ways) has been negative. The prophet goes on to explain how difficult their ways have been. They have found no fulfillment in their hard efforts.

6. Haggai refers to three basic necessities of life: food, drink, and clothing. In typical prophetic fashion, he sees the hand of God in this lack of material necessities. In Moore's vivid words (*Prophets of the Restoration*, p. 66): "The events of life are the hieroglyphics in which God records his feelings towards us." The customary view (see Jones, *Haggai*, pp. 40–42)—that Haggai's people were passing through hard times—needs to be questioned. What the prophet exposes here is not

ing with enjoyment (Gen. 43:34; Song of Sol. 5:1). וְאֵין־לְחֹם לוֹ (but none keeps warm): The second-person plural pattern set by זְרַעְתֶּם (you have sown) is here broken by an individualizing singular pronoun לוֹ (for him). The entire phrase literally states, "And nonexistence of getting warm for him." For אֵין with a following infinitive, see 2 Chronicles 20:6 and 22:9 (it is not possible to).

7. יְהוָה צְבָאוֹת (LORD of hosts): See the Exegesis of 1:2. שִׂימוּ . . . דַּרְכֵּיכֶם (take . . . things going for you): See the Exegesis of 1:5.

8. עֲלוּ (go up): The plural imperative continues the address to the people sustained throughout this section. Haggai does not alternate between singular and plural modes of address as do Hosea and Amos. וְאֶרְצֶה־בּוֹ (and I will accept it with favor): Basic to this verb is the sense of favorable acceptance (see Pss. 44:4 [3]; 119:108; Isa. 42:1). Note also the cognate noun רָצוֹן (favor) in Leviticus 1:3. Verhoef (*Haggai*, p. 67) says, "In this semantic scope . . . the rebuilt temple will achieve the status of an acceptable offering in which the Lord again will take pleasure." וְאֶכָּבֵד (bring glory

to myself) is the niphal of כָּבֵד. For the connotation "to display one's glory, show oneself in all one's glory," see 2 Samuel 6:20. For its use with יְהוָה (LORD), see Exodus 14:4, 17–18. The niphal here could be considered tolerative: "I will let myself be glorified." The form of the word in the *Kethiv* is a simple imperfect: וְאֶכָּבֵד. The recommended reading (*Qere*) is a cohortative (וְאֶכָּבְדָה) used in its affirmative sense: "And I *will* bring glory to myself."

9. פָּנֹה (expecting) is an infinitive absolute that could be translated contextually as "you expected," but it is best to preserve the abruptness of the Hebrew. וְהִנֵּה (but look!): BHS inexplicably follows the Targum in altering וְהִנֵּה to וְהָיָה (and it became). לִמְעָט (how very little!): The noun מְעָט (a little [thing]) occurs here with the prefixed לְ of emphasis. וַהֲבֵאתֶם (for you brought) is understood here as carrying a *waw-explicativum* (GKC §154a n. b). הַבָּיִת could mean "the House," that is, the temple, in which case the reference would be to an offering of firstfruits. If הַבָּיִת is the temple, this would presumably be the divine refusal of the

---

hardship but nonfulfillment. They had seed to sow, food to eat, wine to drink, clothes to wear, gainful employment—but no true satisfaction. Their problem was not lack of goods but of good. In Haggai's time the futility curse was already at work (Deut. 28:38; see Hillers, *Treaty-Curses*, p. 28). Since they were an agrarian society, he describes their gross national product in agricultural terms. It was unimpressive. The harvest was not commensurate with the outlay (see Isa. 5:10). Haggai does not say that the crops failed but that they did not live up to expectation.

Demand was great (1:6). The people always wanted more to eat, more to drink, more to wear. Haggai does not say any went hungry, thirsty, or naked but that they had fallen short of what they wanted. In my translation the words *satisfaction* and *stimulation* reflect both the Hebrew and the times. This was the problem: they had goods but the good life eluded them; they were not hungry but neither were they satisfied; they were dressed but they were not comfortable.

According to the last phrase of 1:6, inflation was high. One can almost hear them say, "Money goes nowhere," or, "You wouldn't believe what I had to pay for this!" As Haggai put it, "You would think there was hole in my purse." It was not that they had no money; it was that the money did not go far.

7. Once again we hear the prophet appeal to the Lord of hosts and encourage the people to direct their attention to the way they have fared. The insistence of his words strikingly reflects the prophet's firm belief in God's immanence in history (a similar conviction is found in Amos 4:6–11).

8. There was plenty of stone from the destruction of the First Temple; the necessary heavy timbers had been imported (Ezra 3:7), and other timber could be found in the wooded hills of Judah (see Neh. 8:15). The emphasis, however, is on using what lies at hand. The important thing is not the size or magnificence of the house, but the *existence* of it—that they want the indwelling God among them.

9. Haggai bluntly lays the blame for the lack of fulfillment on the temple's lying in ruins. Commentators wonder if today's "science-conscious generation" (Jones, *Haggai*, p. 42) can share the "simple attribution" (Sperry, "Haggai," p. 1045) of life's adversities to the direct action of God. Jones (p. 42) is happy to accept that Scripture reveals "this connection [as] paramount." The Old Testament is not unaware of the existence of second causes, but constantly forces us to face that it is the First Cause with whom we have to deal. We live in this world—not as those clever enough to "work the system," to manipulate second causes (the manifold forces of nature) to our advantage—

offering—a possible meaning in light of Malachi 1:13. The run of the sentences, however, favors the idea of bringing the harvest to one's own house, only to be disappointed with it. וְנָפַחְתִּי (and I blew it away): The verb נָפַח is not used of winnowing, but that is the picture here. The winnowed crop is brought in only to be winnowed a second time by divine opposition. יַעַן מֶה (why?): On the pointing of מֶה, see GKC §37f. נְאֻם יְהוָה צְבָאוֹת (this is the word of the LORD of hosts): See the Exposition of 1:1. יַעַן בֵּיתִי (because of my house): See the Exposition. רָצִים (still running off) is a participle expressing continuing action.

10. עַל־כֵּן עֲלֵיכֶם (therefore on your account): עֲלֵיכֶם is doubly emphasized, first by being placed before the verb instead of in its customary place after it; second, by the striking assonance with עַל־כֵּן (therefore). This emphasis is doctrinally correct, for the root of their economic ills is not farming methods nor market forces nor world conditions but themselves. Since the Septuagint lacks any equivalent for עֲלֵיכֶם, some unwisely recommend its excision (see BHS). כָּלְאוּ (keep back): The verb כָּלָא in the qal is always transitive (see Gen. 23:6). Hence מִטָּל (some dew), the noun טַל with prefixed מִן, must be מִטָּל partitive. Since the people were still bringing in crops that they expected to

be good (1:9), they were not living in drought conditions. "Some of" is therefore an appropriate idea. Those, however, who wish to emend here prefer to elide מ as dittographic with the preceding שָׁמַיִם (heavens; Smith, *Twelve Prophets*, p. 235) or to follow the Targum in reading מְטָר (rain; Thomas, "Haggai," p. 1042). Baldwin (*Haggai*, p. 42) notes that "dew was important, especially in August and September, to prevent the ripening grain from wilting in the heat." וְהָאָרֶץ (and the earth): Since the earth is the Lord's and the life of the soil is his life (Ps. 104:30; contrast Isa. 40:7), the environment reflects the mind of the Lord and exhibits a moral vitality in both producing and withholding its fruits (Lev. 26:4, 20).

11. וָאֶקְרָא (and I have summoned): See 2 Kings 9:1; Psalm 105:16; also Ezekiel 36:29; 38:21. The first-person construction forcefully draws us back to the realization that Yahweh is speaking here. חֹרֶב (dryness): See Genesis 31:40 and Judges 6:37. The word is related to חָרֵב (in ruins), which appears in Haggai 1:9 and helps link the two sections together. Verhoef (*Haggai*, p. 76) refers to הַיִּצְהָר (corn), הַתִּירוֹשׁ (wine), and הַדָּגָן (oil) as "the three most important agricultural products of Palestine" (Deut. 11:14; 18:4). וְעַל כָּל־יְגִיעַ כַּפָּיִם (on all the labor of your hands): The initial וְ is best under-

---

but as those looking in faith and obedience to the God who rules and decides all. Haggai exists to challenge the story science tells, not of the way the universe works, but of the way life is to be lived in God's world.

10. In a way typical of the prophetic philosophy of history, Haggai looks to God as the cause of the nation's lack. Both prophet and people knew something was wrong. The system was not working. Theirs was an agricultural economy, and the forces supportive of it were misfiring. The fertilizing forces of heaven—the rainfall (see the Exegesis of 2:10, 19)—was less than guaranteed full fertility. They were not living in drought conditions but rainfall was sparse and crops were less than abundant.

11. Noting that God "summoned" (*wā'eqrā'*) the drought, Moore (*Prophets of the Restoration*, pp. 66–67) states, "God has not abandoned the universe to the sightless action of general laws but is so related to that universe as to be able to direct its laws to the fulfillment of his purposes [of] rewarding the good, punishing the evil, or answering prayer, without deranging or destroying the . . . action of those laws themselves."

Haggai's scriptural worldview taught him that the forces of nature are but agents in the hands of God. He is the power to be reckoned with in the practical affairs of life and the organizing power behind the scenes. Since we see today what Haggai saw in his day, the vital question for us is whether we share his worldview. Do we believe that economic facts are divine appointments? We who live in an affluent society plagued with dissatisfaction and preoccupation with inflation, do we share Haggai's insistence on an immediacy of the presence and action of the living God, who gave the crop a second winnowing (1:9) and who summoned (1:11) the agents of prosperity and adversity? In any event, Haggai was not an innovator, but reflected what all of Scripture teaches. The system we live in—whether seen in terms of economic laws and market forces or natural laws and weather conditions—is sovereignly managed by a holy God and serves his moral purposes.

There are two reactions to this basic situation. Human intuition says, "If this is God's world, and he is good, surely things should not be so." Some even proceed to use the adversities of life as an argument *against* the existence of God. The intuition is correct, the deduction is false. For if there

stood as *waw-explicativum* (equivalent to "that is"). It sums up the comprehensive nature of the divine opposition (for a similar expression, see 2:14). Both occurrences refer to human agricultural activities, the basis of the economy of the day. יְגִיעַ (labor) is from יָגַע (to grow tired, be weary). The thought is that however unsparing in effort

humans may be, it is not this that guarantees prosperity. The work ethic must ever be subject to Deuteronomy 8:18. כַּפַּיִם (hands) is the dual of כַּף, which strictly is the palm of the hand or the cupped hand, but in general use is synonymous with יָדַיִם, the dual of יַד (hand). See the Exegesis of 2:14.

---

is no good God, no one would feel pain and suffering to be a problem. If the world is simply chance, then pain, too, is one of the changes and chances of life and our intuition would tell us so. If the world belongs to humankind, then suffering is one aspect of our mismanagement and we should say, "It stands to reason." Pain is a *problem* only if our intuition is correct that the world is directly in the hands of a good, loving, all-wise, all-powerful God. The other reaction is to set out to "work the system," to find ways to offset possible failure of the water supply (see Isa. 22:9–14), to "manage" the economy so that market forces work for us and not against us. And this is not without truth, for we are called to be good stewards of the environment and its bounties, but it is not the central truth. For us, as for Haggai, the only proper reaction to a world run by a sovereign and holy God is to determine to be properly related to him in whose hand is our breath and in whose hand are all our ways (Dan. 5:23).

It was in these terms that Haggai explained the people's circumstance. God was in the system, but he was not their priority. It was not "an opportune moment," they said (1:2, 4, 9). There were far more important things to do. The house of the Lord could wait, and they could afford to let it wait.

In the Lord's eyes, however, there was more to it than that (1:2, 8–9). He was in the system all right, but he was not in their midst. This was the significance of the house—not the stone and timber, not even the ritual of which the house was the center, but that the Lord had commanded his people to provide for him a dwelling so that he might dwell among them (see Exod. 25:8; 29:43–46). Solomon rightly marveled that God should dwell in the house he had built (1 Kings 8:27) but God did—and in all his glory (1 Kings 8:10–11)! The sacrificial system with which the house was surrounded was not an end in itself; it was a derivative from the Holy One's dwelling there. To leave the house unbuilt was just another way of saying, "It matters not whether God is with us. When we get living conditions (1:4) and the economy right (1:6a) and develop a decent standard of living (1:6b–d) and negotiate proper wage rates (1:6e)—then we will have time for religion and for God." The Lord does not tolerate a society run on these lines. He is not a complacent onlooker; he will be central or he will be at odds.

III. Oracle to the Workers: The Lord's Presence in the Present (1:12–15a)

MOTYER

¹²And Zerubbabel the son of Shealtiel, and Joshua the son of Jehozadak, the high priest, and all the remnant of the people paid heed to the voice of the LORD their God and to the words of the prophet Haggai, recognizing that the LORD their God had sent him; and the people were afraid of the LORD.

¹³And Haggai, the LORD's messenger with the LORD's commission, said to the people:

I am with you.

This is the word of the LORD.

¹⁴And the LORD roused the spirit of Zerubbabel the son of Shealtiel, governor of Judah, and the spirit of Joshua the son of Jehozadak, the high priest, and the spirit of all the remnant of the people, and they came and undertook work in the house of the LORD of hosts their God ¹⁵on the twenty-fourth day of the month, in the sixth [month].

NRSV

¹²Then Zerubbabel son of Shealtiel, and Joshua son of Jehozadak, the high priest, with all the remnant of the people, obeyed the voice of the LORD their God, and the words of the prophet Haggai, as the LORD their God had sent him; and the people feared the LORD. ¹³Then Haggai, the messenger of the LORD, spoke to the people with the LORD's message, saying, I am with you, says the LORD. ¹⁴And the LORD stirred up the spirit of Zerubbabel son of Shealtiel, governor of Judah, and the spirit of Joshua son of Jehozadak, the high priest, and the spirit of all the remnant of the people; and they came and worked on the house of the LORD of hosts, their God, ¹⁵on the twenty-fourth day of the month, in the sixth month.

12. וַיִּשְׁמַע (and . . . paid heed to): שָׁמַע is literally "to hear." When this verb takes an indirect object, the meaning becomes "to listen to," hence "to pay heed" and "to obey." קוֹל (voice) is governed by בְּ and is an indirect object of שָׁמַע (see 1 Sam. 8:7), as דִּבְרֵי (words) is also connected to the verb by עַל (see Jer. 23:16; 26:5). We find in קוֹל and דִּבְרֵי the reality conventionally expressed by the prophetic "thus says the LORD." Like his fellow prophets, Haggai did not understand himself (nor did his hearers understand him) to be expressing the general purport of divine truth. Rather, in the words of the man was heard the voice of God (this is what verbal inspiration means). כַּאֲשֶׁר שְׁלָחוֹ יְהוָה

---

12. Three responses follow the prophetic call of 1:5–8, and the section is strung out along the line, "And Zerubbabel . . . paid heed" (1:12), "and Haggai said" (1:13), "and the Lord roused" (1:14). These are the three responses:

A. national response (12)
  1. listening: those who listened (12a); what they listened to (12b): a divine voice through a human agent
  2. fearing
B. prophetic response (13)
  1. the prophet's credentials: function and status
  2. the message of assurance: content and nature
C. divine response (14)
  1. the energizing of the national spirit
  2. the consequent work of obedience

Throughout 1:1–11, the divine epithets are "the LORD of hosts" (1:2, 5, 7, 9) or "the LORD" (1:3, 8); but after the "paid heed" of 1:12 it is "the LORD their God" (twice in 1:12) and "the LORD of hosts their God" (1:14) as well as the continuing covenant name, "the LORD" (1:12, 13 [thrice], 14). The curt "this people" of 1:2 becomes the theologically emotive description "the remnant of the people" (1:12, 14). Once they respond to the Lord's word, they show themselves to be truly the returned community—not just those who have come back to the land but (in the deeper sense of returning [šûb]; see Isa. 1:27) those who have come back to the Lord in repentance.

The movement of thought in these verses thus begins with a people who are different (1:12) and ends with a people who are renewed (1:14). The difference shows in their responsive attitude to the word of God. When Haggai leveled his accusation in 1:2 that the people were disinterested in temple building, the implication was that they had been invited to build and had refused. Now, however, things are different. The call to fetch timber (1:8) and build the house has met with a positive response. The disinterested people have become the listening, obedient people. It is to

such that the Lord came with quickening power (1:14)—a quickening that promoted active obedience to the word they had begun to heed.

Thus a new pattern emerges:

a responding to the Word (12)
b encouraged by the Word (13)
a' quickened by the Word (14–15)

This sequence is deeply important, for it contains the whole truth about the crucial matter of renewal, the revitalization of God's people.

When we begin to respond to the word of God (1:12), he immediately uses his word for our further encouragement (1:13) and follows with a renewing, inward work in our spirits to mobilize us for obedience (1:14). The word of God is his chosen instrument of renewal, in which the key human factor is obedience and the key divine factor an energizing work of God making that obedience possible.

What they had previously heard (1:2) as a piece of human exhortation that they could take or leave, they now know to be the voice of the Lord their God. The vocabulary and the human accent in which the words come are the same—the words of the prophet Haggai—but the people now know and acknowledge an inner reality. The articulation is human, the voice divine. The Lord is spoken of as "their God." This change of terminology must reflect some change in what they, too, were saying. Just as an unconverted person tends to speak of "God," but on conversion begins to say "the Lord" and "the Lord Jesus," so here it seems that they are beginning to say "our God" and "my God." The expression *the Lord their God* is not only his returning to them, but their returning to him in obedience. And they did so with a reverence so deep that it merited description as their being afraid of the Lord. Even to this extent were their hearts new.

This priority of the mind is true to the whole Scripture; it is through the mind that the heart is reached (Luke 24:27, 32); the mind is the focal point of transformation (Rom. 12:2); and just as the mind makes unconverted people what they

(recognizing that [lit., in accordance with] the LORD sent him): That is, in a manner appropriate to Haggai's divine commission (see Exod. 4:28). וַיִּירְאוּ (and . . . were afraid): יָרֵא in its simplest use governs a direct object. But here we have the much stronger idiom יָרֵא מִפְּנֵי (to be in fear because of, to be afraid of; lit., to fear from before). This is "the spirit of true religion . . . not the unwilling obedience of terror, but the hearty sense of godly fear" (Perowne, Haggai, p. 31). When the people spoke as in 1:2, there was no fear of God before their eyes (Ps. 36:1 [2]).

13. מַלְאַךְ יְהוָה (the LORD's messenger) introduces an immediately encouraging response. Baldwin (Haggai, p. 43) states, "God endorses and strengthens our good resolves." It is debated where exactly Haggai's message begins. For example, Ellison (Men Spake from God, pp. 120–21) translates, "Then spake Haggai, the Angel of the Lord is here with a message"; but מַלְאַךְ יְהוָה

may be an epithet of Haggai (Petersen, Haggai, p. 55). Either way the usage is unique: just as it would be unprecedented for Haggai to speak in the fashion of Zechariah of an angelic visitant, so it is unprecedented for him to be described in this way. Without argument and without explaining the words מַלְאַךְ יְהוָה, Thomas ("Haggai," p. 1043) calls the verse "probably a late addition," but Jones (Haggai, p. 43) urges that the words are deliberately used of Haggai: "As an angel is a heavenly visitant who comes from the court of heaven on the errands of God, so the prophet is one who is entrusted with God's secrets (Amos 3.7) and is sent to tell them to men." בְּמַלְאֲכוּת יְהוָה tips the balance in favor of the latter view, since it does not mean "the LORD's message" but "the LORD's business" (Wiseman, "Haggai," p. 783). The lovely assonance of the Hebrew (מַלְאַךְ יְהוָה בְּמַלְאֲכוּת יְהוָה) defies English representation: "messenger . . .

---

are (Eph. 4:17–19), so it is the new mind that is the hallmark of those who are Christ's (Eph. 4:20–24).

13. Why is Haggai here called "the LORD's messenger with the LORD's commission" unless to reflect the new popular awareness of him and his message that began to emerge in 1:12? True turning to God is ever marked by a fresh discernment of his word. In their terms this discernment was focused on the prophet and his divinely accorded status among them; for us the focus of attention is the whole of Holy Scripture and its God-intended status in the church. Haggai is the microcosm; the Scriptures, the macrocosm. When 1:12 says that they heeded "the words of the prophet Haggai," it implies that what they heard was truly human and that there was no suppression of the human personality of the prophet. The words were exactly such as he would characteristically have chosen to use. Yet this truly human word, colored by that human personality, was "the voice of the Lord." This miracle of revelation and inspiration expressed in verbal communication is not something we can explain, but in measure we can see what is involved. To do so, we must start with Jesus. Since the true nature of humankind is to be in the image of God (Gen. 1:26–27), it is true of Jesus also that he is the perfect human because he is the perfect image of God (Col. 1:15). This means that total identification with God does not diminish or suppress human personality, but rather brings it to perfection and causes it to flower in all its personal distinctiveness. Such was the case, in due measure, with the prophets and all the Bible

writers. Jeremiah speaks for all when he says that the true prophet was brought into a special intimacy with the Lord—admitted to the counsel of the Lord (Jer. 23:18; see Amos 3:7). Brought into this closeness with God, they were enabled to speak with his words (Ezek. 2:7–3:4; 1 Cor. 2:12–13). This did not suppress their personalities, for the closeness of God brings the personality to full flower. Rather, their depth of identification with God and his word is the reason why the Bible writers are larger and more colorful personalities than we find elsewhere. It is in this way that we can take up the whole volume of Holy Scripture and share the apostolic confession that all is "God breathed" (2 Tim. 3:16). But where this recognition of the word of God is backed by a determination (Hag. 1:12) to hear and heed it, two things follow in turn. The first is that the Lord delights to say, "I am with you." While in Haggai's Old Testament terms the presence of the Lord was conditioned upon setting apart a house for the Lord to dwell in, the Lord is here swift to teach that it is not the house per se that concerns him, but the house as symbolic of hearts that long for him to be central to life and to dwell in the midst of wills set to obey him. Where these realities are present, he rushes to assure of his real and living presence. In such a context the word of God is no dead letter but a living communication of vital truth.

14. The second thing that follows recognition of the word of God is the Lord's coming to his people with renewing power. The verb roused often means "to rouse from sleep." The leaders and peo-

commission." Haggai's status and function may be as near as we can get. For this use of prefixed בְ, see Exodus 25:40; 30:32. אֲנִי אִתְּכֶם (I am with you): See Exodus 3:12; Joshua 1:5; Jeremiah 1:8; Psalm 46:7, 11. Without making specific promises, these words promise everything. נְאֻם־יְהוָה (this is the word): See the Exposition of 1:1.

14. וַיָּעַר יְהוָה (and the LORD roused): ו could be understood as *waw-explicativum*: "For the LORD." It would thus be explanatory of the prompt reaction of 1:12 (see Baldwin, *Haggai*, p. 43: "Behind the willing response . . . was the silent working of the Lord"). This concurs with the use of the same verb in Ezra 1:1, 5. As Jones (*Haggai*, p. 43) remarks, it is the mystery of grace that the Lord "produces the willing mind." On the other hand, however, the series of *waws* in Haggai 1:12–14 more readily suggests sequence, and in this case Acts 5:32 is a scriptural commentary on these verses: the Lord gives his Spirit to those who obey him. רוּחַ: The Spirit of the Lord is not mentioned here (compare 2:5) but only the action of the divine upon the human spirit. A human as נֶפֶשׁ (soul) has individual distinctiveness; a human as רוּחַ (spirit) is conative, purposeful, girded for action. This divine stimulation was a common experience of all sections of the community, but it came about by a divine working in each—Zerubbabel, Joshua, and the remnant. The Lord blesses individually. וַיָּבֹאוּ (and they came) is a deliberate reversal of 1:2: it was, after all, "a time of coming" (עֶת־בֹּא, 1:2), and the change was wrought by the word of God. וַיַּעֲשׂוּ מְלָאכָה (and undertook work): See Exodus 35:21 and 36:1, where מְלָאכָה refers to the work on the tabernacle. This is surely the reason for the circumlocution involving "did" and "work" instead of a simple verb "worked." The people were back at the heart of covenant operation, setting in motion what effectuated the central purpose of redemption (Exod. 29:43–46).

15a. בְּיוֹם . . . בַּשִּׁשִּׁי (on . . . sixth [month]): See the Exposition.

---

ple were newly wakened. Haggai is about to express this experience in terms of the presence of the Holy Spirit (2:5) and 1:12–15 assures us that here, as in every other way, there is no fundamental difference between the doctrine of the Holy Spirit in the Old Testament and in the New. Then as now he is given to those who obey (Acts 5:32)—and, as Haggai reminds us, he is given in order that obedience to God may be real and effective, for in consequence of this renewing work of God "they came and undertook work in the house."

The Lord is the central blessing his people need—that he should be in the midst, the indwelling God. The context in which this indwelling becomes real is the word of God received and heeded (1:12), recognized for what it is (1:13), and obeyed in practical commitment of life (1:14).

15a. The existing arrangement of the book fits perfectly with the general consensus that 15a belongs with the preceding narrative and the date formula in 15b ("in the second year of King Darius") with the date given in 2:1. Rothstein (*Juden und Samaritaner*, pp. 53–73), however, suggests that 1:15 should be followed by 2:15–19. (For an even more far-reaching rearrangement of the text, see the NEB.) Thomas ("Haggai," pp. 1043–47) adopts Rothstein's position, and Jones (*Haggai*, pp. 50–51) provides a clear statement of it and offers cogent comment. The main arguments in support of it are the following:

1. In Haggai, dates otherwise precede the material to which they apply, but this date comes at the end.
2. If the date is correctly placed, there was a gap of twenty-three days before the work started.
3. The expression *laḥōdeš baššiššî* (belonging to the month, in the sixth) is odd.
4. The date, following the gap of twenty-three days, probably refers to the laying of the foundation stone, and since 2:15–19 reiterates the thought of 1:1–11, it should follow immediately.
5. The connection between 2:10–14 and 2:15–19 is tenuous.

It cannot honestly be said that these arguments are impressive—singly or cumulatively:

1. It is true that other dates in Haggai precede their material, but all the other material consists of prophetic oracles, whereas this section is primarily a narrative of fact. In the case of his oracles, Haggai could choose his time; here he records a date determined by the action of others.
2. It may seem odd to Rothstein that twenty-three days elapsed between the decision to build and the start of work. Anyone with experience of building work would be sur-

prised, however, that the commencement was so prompt. The gathering of materials (1:8), enlisting and organizing of workers, drawing up of building specifications, and planning the work—all must be undertaken before even clearance of the site begins, and, besides, the sixth month was harvesting month (Baldwin, *Haggai*, p. 43), so that many essential jobs would already preoccupy the potential workforce.

3. There is nothing odd about the words *belonging to the month, in the sixth. Laḥōdeš* (of the month) goes with the preceding day-number (see the Exposition of 1:1), as translated above, while *baššiššî* (in the sixth [month]) exemplifies the Hebrew idiom that units of measurement are customarily omitted where it is plain what unit is intended (see the Exposition of 2:16; GKC §134n). It is not necessary to follow Jones (*Haggai*, pp. 43–44) in seeing "in the sixth" as an explanatory gloss. It was obviously sensible for Haggai to express such a significant date unequivocally. Verhoef (*Haggai*, p. 89) notes A. S. Van Der Woude's comment that the date, placed finally like this, forms an *inclusio* with the date in 1:1.

4. Nothing whatever suggests that this date refers to the laying of the foundation stone. It fulfills a coherent function where it stands, and it is not permissible to move it to meet the needs of an unproven theory.

5. It is not true (see below) that 2:10–14 and 2:15–19 are only tenuously linked. Together they form a mutually supporting whole. The analysis in the Introduction begins to show this, as well as indicating the integrity of the book as it stands. Wholesale reordering is in any case without manuscript support.

IV. Oracle to the Leaders and People: The Lord's Presence for the Future (1:15b–2:9)

MOTYER

In the second year of King Darius, **2** In the seventh [month], in the twenty-first of the month, the word of the LORD came through the prophet Haggai:
2 Please say to Zerubbabel the son of
    Shealtiel, governor of Judah,
and to Joshua the son of Jehozadak, the
    high priest,
and to the remnant of the people:
3 What one among you is left who saw this
    house in its former glory?
And now how do you see it?
Is it not absolutely nothing in your eyes?
4 But now be strong, Zerubbabel—
this is the word of the LORD—
and be strong, Joshua son of Jehozadak,
    the high priest,
and be strong, all people of the land—
this is the word of the LORD—
and act,
for I am with you—
this is the word of the LORD of hosts,
5 the very thing that I covenanted with you
    when you came out of Egypt—
and my Spirit remains among you.
Do not be afraid!
6 For thus the LORD of hosts says:
Again—once—a little while—
I am going to shake the heavens and the
    earth,
and the sea and the dry land.
7 I will shake all the nations,
and the treasures of all the nations will
    come in,
and I will fill this house with glory,
    the LORD of hosts says.
8 Mine is the silver and mine the gold—
this is the word of the LORD of hosts.
9 Greater will be the glory of this latter
    house than that of the former,
says the LORD of hosts,
and in this place I will give peace—
this is the word of the LORD of hosts.

NRSV

In the second year of King Darius, **2** in the seventh month, on the twenty-first day of the month, the word of the LORD came by the prophet Haggai, saying: 2Speak now to Zerubbabel son of Shealtiel, governor of Judah, and to Joshua son of Jehozadak, the high priest, and to the remnant of the people, and say, 3Who is left among you that saw this house in its former glory? How does it look to you now? Is it not in your sight as nothing? 4Yet now take courage, O Zerubbabel, says the LORD; take courage, O Joshua, son of Jehozadak, the high priest; take courage, all you people of the land, says the LORD; work, for I am with you, says the LORD of hosts, 5according to the promise that I made you when you came out of Egypt. My spirit abides among you; do not fear. 6For thus says the LORD of hosts: Once again, in a little while, I will shake the heavens and the earth and the sea and the dry land; 7and I will shake all the nations, so that the treasure of all nations shall come, and I will fill this house with splendor, says the LORD of hosts. 8The silver is mine, and the gold is mine, says the LORD of hosts. 9The latter splendor of this house shall be greater than the former, says the LORD of hosts; and in this place I will give prosperity, says the LORD of hosts.

15b. For discussion of the best way to understand the date given in verse 15a–b, see the Exposition. בִּשְׁנַת שְׁתַּיִם לְדָרְיָוֶשׁ (in the second year of Darius) is the year 520 B.C. See the Introduction.

2:1. בַּשְּׁבִיעִי (in the seventh [month]): Haggai received this second oracle about seven weeks after the first. The twenty-first day of the seventh month was the last day of the Feast of Tabernacles (see Lev. 23:34–36). הָיָה דְבַר יְהוָה (the word of the LORD came): See the Exegesis of 1:1. בְּיַד (through): See the Exegesis of 1:1. The scroll from Wadi Murabbaʿat (see the Introduction) reads "to" instead of "through," but there is no reason to alter the Masoretic Text on this ground (Petersen, *Haggai*, p. 61). See further on 2:10.

2. אֱמָר־נָא (please say): The precative particle נָא attached to the imperative slightly softens the abruptness of the command. אֶל־שְׁאֵרִית (to the rem-

---

1:15b–2:9. Following the introduction (1:15b–2:2), verse 3 asks a question, answered in verses 6–9. Verses 3 and 9 form an *inclusio* expressed by "house," "glory," and "former." The emphatic "now" (ʿattâ) of verse 3 is picked up by the initial "but now" (wěʿattâ) of verse 4. This binds verse 3 and verses 4–5 together; and verses 4–5 share with verses 6–9 the common theme of divine promise. The section is thus a true unity.

- **A** introduction (1:15b–2:2)
  - the date: the last full day of Tabernacles
  - the divine word and its agent
  - the addressees: royal, priestly, and elect
- **B** past glory, a question raised (3)
  - the glory then
  - the discouraging now
- **C** another now (4–5)
  - **a** a summons to resolute activity (4a)
  - **b** divine promise (4b–5e)
  - **a′** a summons to fearlessness (5f)
- **B′** coming glory, a promise made (6–9)
  - **a** imminent cosmic turmoil (6)
  - **b** spoiling the nations: the Tabernacle parallel (7)
  - **c** divine sufficiency (8)
  - **b′** contrast: a greater glory than the past (9a)
  - **a′** contrast: the gift of peace (9b)

15b. In accordance with the foregoing discussion, we understand this half-verse to belong to chapter 2 and not chapter 1. As pointed out in the Introduction, Haggai's recorded prophecies were delivered within a very short period of time. Did he then return to whatever work had occupied him before his call to be a prophet (Amos 7:14–15)? Did he have any sense of disappointment over such a short ministry? But the word of God, however briefly spoken, cannot return void (Isa. 55:8–11), and out of his three months of prophetic activity, Haggai is still speaking two-and-a-half

millenniums later. We return, then, to listen to what the Lord said through him on 17 October, 520 years before Christ.

2:1. By the time the message that begins in 2:1 came to the people, they had done some weeks' work on the temple site—enough, perhaps, to impress on them the greatness of the undertaking and their own inadequacy. A message of encouragement was thus in order. Even on this ground the dating is significant, but more significant is the link with the Feast of Tabernacles and the fact that Solomon's temple was dedicated in the seventh month (1 Kings 8:2). This knowledge would have intensified the depressing comparisons of Haggai 2:3.

The Feast of Tabernacles memorialized Israel's coming out of Egypt (Lev. 23:43), providing a contemporary context for the reference to Egypt in Haggai 2:5. For the duration of the feast people left their houses and lived in makeshift "booths," reminding them that the Lord made them live in booths when he brought them out of Egypt. Wenham (*Leviticus*, p. 305) suggests that this annual act of discomfort would make the people appreciate the good homes into which the Lord finally brought them—and no doubt it would, as any but the most dedicated camper discovers on returning home! But the Bible does not actually offer this—or any—explanation. A *sukkâ* (booth) sometimes stands for something unstable and vulnerable (see Isa. 1:8), and it could be that the feast was meant to remind the people that when they were at their most vulnerable, in "the great and terrible wilderness" (Deut. 8:15), the Lord proved himself to be their sufficiency. Likewise, *sukkâ* is used of the tabernacle, the tent-dwelling of the Lord among his people (2 Sam. 11:11) and of the shelter provided by the Lord in the messianic day (Isa. 4:6). These thoughts are germane to Haggai's message here. The people are rightly aware of their deficiencies, but the Lord is ever among them as at the time of the exodus. The feasts of the seventh month involved many obligatory work-free days.

nant): The Septuagint and Syriac translations read "to all the remnant," presumably an accidental recollection of 1:12, 14. שְׁאֵרִית (remnant): See the Exposition of 1:12.

3. מִי בָכֶם is literally "who among you?" but with following singular verbs it must be translated "what one among you?" Few now had direct experience of the building destroyed sixty-seven years earlier. But childhood memories grow in size and doubtless the elderly were making exaggerated comparisons. In addition, the feast would have brought in from surrounding areas those who saw for the first time what was being undertaken and perhaps registered disappointment at what they saw. With עַתָּה (now), Haggai admits the obvious; he defers the word עַתָּה to the end of its clause (וּמָה אַתֶּם רֹאִים אֹתוֹ עַתָּה), throwing it into emphasis and admitting that it is all absolutely nothing (הֲלוֹא כָמֹהוּ כְּאַיִן, lit., is not the like of it like nothing?). For this idiom of the double כ emphasizing identity, see Isaiah 24:2 and Hosea 4:9. We do not know whether they were attempting to replicate the dimensions of Solomon's temple (1 Kings 6:2) or the larger building Cyrus permitted (Ezra 6:3). In any case the whole thing was drab and utilitarian compared with the glory of the past.

4. וְעַתָּה (but now): The עַתָּה that human eyes see (2:3) is not God's עַתָּה. The עַתָּה of human depression and defeatism becomes a different עַתָּה when it is embraced by the word of divine promise. חֲזַק (be strong) is a word of new beginnings (Josh. 1:6). Linked with וַעֲשׂוּ (and act), it relates the new beginnings to the act of temple building (1 Chron. 28:10, 20; see 2 Chron. 19:11). נְאֻם־יְהוָה (this is the word of the Lord): See the Exposition of 1:1. עַם הָאָרֶץ (people of the land) always takes its meaning from its context. In pre-exilic texts it is the "free, landowning . . . citizens . . . with full . . . political rights" (Verhoef, *Haggai*, p. 98). See 2 Kings 21:24. In Ezra (4:4) and Nehemiah (10:29) it is the syncretistic population of Palestine. In Haggai 1:2 it is a synonym for הָעָם הַזֶּה (this people) and in 1:12 for שְׁאֵרִית הָעָם (the remnant of the people). אֲנִי אִתְּכֶם (I am with you): As he had promised before, the Lord still dwells among his people (see 1:13; Exod. 25:8; 29:46). Haggai's controversy with his people was that by leaving the temple unbuilt they implied that it did not matter to them whether the Lord was among them (see 1:2, 8). But divine grace does not wait as though the Lord needed a house to live in: the token of their obedience is enough.

This, coupled with a sense of defeat, gave urgency to a recall to the work.

2. Two persistent roots of despondency were growing vigorously among Haggai's people: the past seemed incomparably better than the present, and the present seemed much less than worthwhile. Work had been started on the temple site, and the people were beginning to sense the huge task they had undertaken and how little they might expect to achieve. It was all very depressing. They could not match the greatness of the past nor even achieve much in the present. But the Lord knows the needs of his people and through the prophet Haggai tackles the problem of depression and despondency head on. Believers today need the same word of encouragement because of the often shattered state of the church, the seeming fruitlessness of effort, and the slow progress in building the temple of the Holy Spirit in fellowship and in personal life (1 Cor. 3:16; 6:19).

3. Solomon's temple was destroyed in 586 B.C., that is, sixty-six years before the date on which Haggai was speaking. No wonder, then, that he says, "Which one of you?" for his question would refer to people in their seventies and eighties, and we can readily imagine how their childhood or teenage memories had become exaggerated over the years. But this would make their despondency and consequent depression all the more real. Haggai was a sound psychologist: the first step in ministry to the despondent is to admit with them the reality of what is causing the despondency. The new house was indeed "absolutely nothing" by comparison! But, having identified with them, he can now turn to the positive steps necessary as a corrective.

4. The Lord's rejoinder to his people's despondency is to turn their minds from what they think to be true of themselves (we cannot match the past, we cannot achieve in the present) to what is true about him. They say "we," the Lord says "I . . . my Spirit"; they are speaking and he is speaking—three times over he calls their attention to his speaking to them. To which word will they listen? The key to tackling despondency is found here: stop listening to ourselves and start listening to him and his word of promise. Here, the Lord spoke to them of his sufficiency: "I am with you." He offers them only his presence, for in him they have all they need (see Exod. 3:12; Isa. 41:10; 43:2; Jer. 1:8; Matt. 28:20; Acts 18:9–10).

5. אֶת־הַדָּבָר אֲשֶׁר־כָּרַתִּי אִתְּכֶם בְּצֵאתְכֶם מִמִּצְרַיִם (the very thing that I covenanted with you when you came out of Egypt): Controversy surrounds this construction. Even to the careful Jones (*Haggai*, p. 46) these words are "an early gloss" because (a) they are syntactically awkward, (b) they are absent from the Septuagint, and (c) they intrude into the parallelism of אֲנִי אִתְּכֶם (I am with you) and וְרוּחִי עֹמֶדֶת בְּתוֹכְכֶם (and my Spirit remains among you). Baldwin (*Haggai*, p. 47) suggests that a marginal comment may have entered the text. Petersen (*Haggai*, pp. 61, 66) sees "a prosaic intrusion into the poetic discourse," the work of "a prophetic traditionist." Ridderbos (*De kleine Propheten*, p. 109), believing that אֶת־הַדָּבָר (the very thing) must be a definite object, obliges by arbitrarily adding "Remember." On the other hand, to remove these words deprives the oracle of overt reference to the exodus background (suggested by its date during Tabernacles) and leaves us without a clue to the relation between temple building and the promise "I am with you." But are the difficulties as intractable as is alleged? We can surely dismiss the Septu-

agint as evidence. The absence of the words is just as likely to have arisen from the inability of the translator(s) of the Septuagint to understand them. The charge of grammatical or syntactical awkwardness arises from the assumption that אֵת must always be the sign of the direct object. This is not so. Saydon ("Particle אֵת," p. 202) says that, rather than emend the text, "it is preferable to give the particle אֵת an emphatic, demonstrative meaning, 'this indeed is the word.'" Macdonald also ("Particle אֵת," p. 274) shows that אֵת can introduce an implied demonstrative (this is . . .) or a stressed antecedent (the very . . . which). Taken this way the words fit into a clever parallelism (see the Exposition). אֲשֶׁר־כָּרַתִּי (which I covenanted; lit., which I cut): The verb כָּרַת (to cut) is used for the solemn inauguration of a covenant relationship, derived from the practice of sealing a covenant-making ceremony with sacrifice (see Gen. 15:9–18; Exod. 24:4–8). כָּרַת is here used absolutely for "to covenant" (see esp. 1 Chron. 16:15–16 and Ps. 105:8–9, where דָּבָר and כָּרַת are used much as here). In the parallelism of this immediate context

---

5. Not only did the Lord speak to them of his sufficiency, but of his changeless faithfulness as well. At the Feast of Tabernacles (2:1–2) they had been looking back to Egypt and the exodus. Maybe, like Gideon (Judg. 6:13), the great acts of God in the past only exacerbated their present gloom—not even God is what he used to be! But he is the same, and "the very thing I covenanted with you when you came out of Egypt" remains the same today. By Haggai's day, centuries had passed since that great covenanting, and in that passage of time Israel had been guilty of every known sin, unfaithfulness, distrust, disloyalty, neglect, and betrayal of their God. But human sin and frailty cannot overthrow God's faithfulness (Rom. 3:3). The promise still stood. The Lord also spoke to the people of his active power at work among them: "My Spirit remains among you." The Lord's presence with his people is his live and dynamic power, not a mere observer or bystander, but the living God. In this Haggai joins with Zechariah (4:6) in affirming that it is not a matter of might (resources) nor of power (abilities) but of "my Spirit."

Such, then, are the promises of God; but 2:4–5 also brings us his requirements, one implicit, one explicit. The implicit requirement is faith. He has made promises; he expects his people to believe them, to trust that what he has promised he will most surely do. Faith believes that the Lord's

assessment of the situation is truer than the human assessment. Humans see an unattainable past and a hopeless present; the Lord sees his own presence, his covenanted word of blessing, his Spirit. Faith affirms God's view. It is of the first importance that in our despondency we must beware of spending more time listening to ourselves than talking to ourselves—listening to the tale of our hopelessness rather than telling ourselves the tale of God's promises. Alongside this obvious implication of faith is the requirement to be strong and work. In a word, because God is present and active, we must be vigorous and active. The presence and the promises of God are meant to mobilize his people; the Spirit of God is not a replacement therapy but a recruiting sergeant. Again, as Zechariah teaches, the basic truth that all is done by "my Spirit" (4:6) means that "the *hands* of Zerubbabel have laid the foundation . . . his *hands* shall also complete it" (4:9). The immediate duty (for them, house building; for us, the command of Col. 3:17) approached in faith, resting on the promises of God, and tackled with active commitment is the road through despondency to effectiveness. Despondency says, "I can't, therefore I won't"; obedience of faith says, "*I* can't, but *he* can, so *I* will."

The words *ʾet haddābār ʾăšer kārʾattî ʾittĕkem bĕṣē(ʾ)tĕkem mimmiṣrayim* (the very thing that I

(see the Exposition), "the very thing that I covenanted" adds weight to "this is the word of the LORD." It is not a fresh thought devised for the occasion but part and parcel of the solemn exodus–Sinai divine pledge sealed with covenant blood, a fundamental divine commitment. וְרוּחִי (and my Spirit): See the Exposition. עֹמֶדֶת (remains; lit., is standing, continues standing): While the participial form expresses what abides unchanging, the verb עָמַד (to stand) underlines the objective reality and permanence of God's presence (see Exod. 33:9; Ps. 119:90–91). אַל־תִּירָאוּ (do not be afraid): In the matching passage (Hag. 1:12–14) we were told that the people were afraid of the Lord; here they are told not to be afraid (see also Exod. 20:18–20). There is a right fear—the fear that is the beginning of wisdom—that should remain characteristic of the child of God (see 1 Peter 1:17). This fear lives

alongside an enjoyment of the divine presence and a facing of the future, both without fear.

6. כִּי (for): Verhoef (*Haggai*, p. 101) understands this particle to connote "in what the Lord is about to accomplish [they] will observe the reason . . . for God's assurance and encouragement that he will be with them" (2:4–5). עוֹד אַחַת מְעַט הִיא (again—once—a little while): For עוֹד (again) as a prefix of emphasis to a future act, see Exodus 11:1 and Isaiah 49:20. אַחַת (once): For the temporal use of this word, see Exodus 30:10 and Psalm 89:36 [35]. מְעַט הִיא: The literal sense of this expression is "it is a little." In the light of the two previous expressions of time, it must be understood temporally. The imminence of the eschatological day assumed in texts like Psalm 96:13 and 98:9 is made explicit. But (as in the second coming passages in the New Testament), it is imminent in God's timetable and therefore the object of con-

covenanted with you when you came out of Egypt) leaves in place a striking pattern:

a and act
b   for I am with you
c   for this is the word of the Lord of hosts
c′   the very thing I covenanted with you when you came out of Egypt
b′   and my Spirit remains among you
a′ do not be afraid

It is hard to see why such a lucid text needs questioning or emending. This verse affirms that God's Spirit continues to abide with the people. In the exodus texts the Spirit of God endows Bezalel (Exod. 31:3; 35:31), is "on" Moses, comes to "rest on" the elders (Num. 11:17, 25–29), came on Balaam (Num. 24:2), and was "in" Joshua (Num. 27:18), who was "full of" the Spirit (Deut. 34:9). Indeed Isaiah 63:10–14 teaches that the Spirit is the mode of divine presence and action in the whole exodus experience: grieved by rebellion (Hag. 2:10), "set among" (*śim*, not *ʿamad* as in Haggai) the people by the Lord (2:11), giving them rest (2:14). It is this truth that Haggai now reflects—and suitably so, for thus he stresses that the Lord's presence by his Spirit is not static or ornamental but dynamic, energizing, since the Spirit is the outgoing, personal divine agent of the will of God. Note the balance between the two "I am with you" oracles (1:12–15; 2:1–9; see the Introduction). In the former the divine presence

leads to an energizing of the human spirit; in this oracle, to the continuing presence of the Lord's Spirit.

6. The present obedience of the people of God (2:4), under the blessing of God (2:4b–5), will, through signal and cosmic divine action (2:6–7), be crowned with surpassing glory (2:9a), in which the original purpose of the temple as a work of peace will be realized (2:9b).

The tiny word *for (kî)* with which this verse begins is as important as any in the section. It looks back specially to the commands in 2:4–5. The people of God in their present situation can commit themselves confidently (2:4, "be strong") to active involvement in the work of God ("and act") and can do so without fear that all will come to nothing (2:5, "do not be afraid") "because" (2:6) the future is in the hand of God (2:6, "I am going to . . ."; 2:7, "I will . . . I will"; 2:9, "I will"), and it will be splendid with richness (2:7–8, "treasures . . . silver . . . gold"), full of the presence of the Lord in all his glory (2:7, 9) and bringing the blessing of peace (2:9). This future is wholly his doing. All the verbs in 2:6–9 describe the Lord's acts or consequences of what he has done. It is not, therefore, that the present commitment and obedience of his people (2:4–5) bring that future to pass (note how the coming glory is promised to this house; 2:7), but rather that present commitment in faith and obedience is the guarantee of entrance upon future blessings (see 2 Peter 1:5–11). Alerting us to the future that awaits, the Lord draws us forward as by a magnetic hope and thus girds us for present faithfulness, for our labor is not in vain in

stant, watchful expectation no matter how many years or centuries pass on our calendars (2 Peter 3:3–11). וַאֲנִי מַרְעִישׁ (I am going to shake) is a participle *futurum instans* (GKC §116p). The verb רָעַשׁ (to shake) is part of the theophany vocabulary in the Old Testament and is used both historically and eschatologically (see the Exposition).

7. וְהִרְעַשְׁתִּי (I will shake all nations): Only here is the verb רָעַשׁ (to shake) used directly of what the Lord will do to people (compare Nah. 1:5). The intention is not to forecast worldwide unrest but the Lord's real presence among the nations bringing about a particular result. There is no contradiction, therefore, between what Haggai says here

and Isaiah's picture in 60:4–7 of a willing pilgrimage of the nations bringing their gifts. וּבָאוּ חֶמְדַּת כָּל־הַגּוֹיִם (and the treasures of all the nations will come in): The result of the shaking is that the nations will yield their treasures. The word חֶמְדַּת (treasures) has received a traditional messianic interpretation: "what all the nations desire" becoming "he whom all the nations long for" (see Pusey, *Minor Prophets*, p. 311). As far as the word חֶמְדָּה is concerned, there is nothing intrinsically wrong with this. The word expresses the abstract idea of longing (1 Sam. 9:20; Dan. 11:37), as well as the concrete idea of what excites desire, what is held to be precious and desirable (2 Chron. 32:27;

---

the Lord (1 Cor. 15:58). In this way the promises of God in the present (2:4–5) are supported by his promises for the future (2:6–9). Like other eschatological promises of God, these are undated but imminent (2:6). The passage of over two thousand years since Haggai spoke does not invalidate what was promised or make him a false prophet. Hikers often see the summit of a mountain looming over the immediate crest and are kept toiling on by the sense of being almost there—only to find, on mounting the crest, that a valley and intermediate crests come between them and the summit. The Lord's promise of "a little while" was not false, for it was related to his plan, not our timetable; neither was it purposeless, for the prospect of attainment (as in the case of the hiker) is the stimulus we need. So also with the second coming of Christ. Many commentators note the promise of his imminent coming without always noting those places where the Lord warns also of a prolonged waiting time (e.g., Matt. 25:19; Luke 19:11!) and urge that the Lord and his apostles have been proved wrong. No, they envisaged an immediate return and in this they were right—and we, too, envisage an immediate return and we also are right. Immediacy is part of the definition of the event. Christ's return is actually immediate in the Father's scheme of things, and as for us, how often we are restrained from sin or held to the highest or strengthened to perseverance by hearing (as it were) the Lord's voice: "Hold the fort, for I am coming."

Haggai says that God will *shake* the heavens and the earth. We are not obligated to understand the word *shake (rāʿaš)* literally. The past helps us understand what is being said of the future. For example, in answer to David's cry for help, the earth shook (rāʿaš) and mountains trembled (Ps. 18:8 [7]), but in fact no such thing happened

within human experience at the time. The same is true when this conventional terminology is used of the exodus (Ps. 77:19 [18]; see Judg. 5:4; Ps. 68:9 [8]). We would be wrong therefore to think, simply on the basis of the shaking of heaven and earth, that Haggai foresees an actual, experienced turmoil of nations. This is not the purpose of the theophanic vocabulary. It points not to what is happening among peoples and nations but to the reality of the coming of God. The shaking is the reaction of the created to the Creator (Jer. 4:24–26; Nah. 1:5). The contrasting elements "heaven and earth" and "sea and dry land" express totality. The Lord is coming, in full divinity, to do a cosmic and worldwide thing.

7. Not only will the Lord shake the heavens and the earth, but the nations as well. This divine activity will yield up the nations' treasures, which will adorn Haggai's metaphorical temple. Like Zechariah (6:9–15), Haggai was reaching out to a greater hope that has begun to be realized in the universality of the church of Christ but that awaits its consummation when "from earth's wide bounds, from ocean's furthest coast, / through gates of pearl, streams in the countless host, / singing to Father, Son and Holy Ghost" (W. W. How, "For All the Saints Who from Their Labours Rest").

8. The thought is twofold: (1) to guarantee the foregoing promise (the Lord can bring the wealth of the nations into the house because it belongs to him) and (2) to focus attention especially (even exclusively) on the promise of the indwelling glory. People were depressed (2:3) by the poverty of what they were achieving, and the Lord would remind them that human wealth does not enrich God. What he seeks is not earthly splendor but a house to fill with his glory (see Ps. 50:10).

Jer. 12:10). The problem is, however, that the verb בָּאוּ (will come in) is plural and requires a plural subject. We must therefore either say (with GKC §145b, d—though not §145e) that the plural verb points to חֶמְדַּת כָּל־הַגּוֹיִם (treasures of all the nations) as a collective, or, more likely (with GKC §124r) that since the singular חֶמְדַּת is in construction with the plural גּוֹיִם (nations), the whole is reckoned a plural. In either event, emendation of חֶמְדַּת to חֲמֻדֹת (precious things), as BHS suggests, is needless. Haggai is making use of the exodus motif of taking spoil from the Egyptians (Exod. 11:2–3; 12:35–36), where the precious metals and other materials the Egyptians gave provided adornment for the tabernacle (Exod. 25:1–8; 35:21–29). In measure this prediction was fulfilled in Haggai's temple (Ezra 6:8–12; see Baldwin, *Haggai*, p. 48) and, of course, in the splendor of its successor, Herod's temple (Luke 21:5; John 2:20), but neither fulfilled the prediction of a movement among כָּל

הַגּוֹיִם (all the nations). וּמִלֵּאתִי . . . כָּבוֹד (fill . . . glory): Exodus 40:34–35 and 1 Kings 8:6–11 show that the glory Haggai has in mind is not the gold adornment but the Lord's presence (here and in 2:8). In this regard also the coming house will be in no way behind the former (rather, see 2:9). אָמַר (says): See the Exegesis of 1:2. יְהוָה צְבָאוֹת (LORD of hosts): See the Exegesis of 1:2.

8. לִי . . . וְלִי (mine . . . and mine): See the Introduction and Exposition.

9. מִן . . . גָּדוֹל (greater . . . than): The adjective with מִן (than, from) expresses comparison (GKC §133a). יִהְיֶה (will be): The imperfect tense expresses incomplete action and affirms that the glory yet awaits fulfillment. וּבַמָּקוֹם הַזֶּה (and in this place): The repetition of הַזֶּה (this) provides a conceptual and grammatical linkage between the "latter house" and "this place." שָׁלוֹם (peace): See the Exposition. נְאֻם (this is the word): See the Exposition of 1:1.

---

9. In context, Haggai is thinking of the latter house, which will come about by the shaking of the nations and toward which obedience in the present building is an essential factor (Malachi reached out to the same hope in 3:1–4). The thought moves on from what the temple is (a place of glory) to what it does (provide peace). David was forbidden to build the house. First Kings 5:3 explains David's function in the plan of God: to bring about the conditions of house building laid down in Deuteronomy 12:10–11; but 1 Chronicles 22:7–10 and 28:3 teach that this function disqualified him from house building, for how can a man of war build a house of peace? Such a task needs a Solomon, the man whose name means peace. Part of the greater glory of the latter house will be peace in its many-sided reality—peace with God, harmonious society, personal fulfillment—and all as a divine gift.

Haggai thus voiced three promises: rich adornment (2:7a, 8), the real presence of divine glory (2:7b, 9a), and the blessing of peace (2:9b), which comes as a great climax at the end:

a   richness (7a)
b   glory (7b)
a'   richness (8)
b'   glory (9a)
c   peace (9b)

The Lord's coming blessings are, first, compensatory. The inadequacies of the present (2:3) give way to the total splendor of the future (2:7a, 8). Second, the coming blessings are greater. Whatever is now known of the real presence of the Lord among his people (2:4–5), the coming glory will be greater (2:9a). But when? The Lord's promises achieved an interim fulfillment in Herod's temple (Mark 13:1–2; Luke 21:5; John 2:20). But Jesus lifted the fulfillment to a new plane when he spoke of the temple that is his body (John 2:21). Herod's Temple knew no cosmic shaking, no worldwide ingathering of the nations, no great divine glory. Yet even then the great shaking began: heaven was rent (Mark 1:10), earth was shaken (Matt. 27:51; 28:2), the rending entered the house itself (Mark 15:38), peace was proclaimed by the risen Lord of Peace (John 20:19–21; Eph. 2:14–17), and the worldwide ingathering was set in train (Acts 15:13–19). It is nothing compared to what will happen when 2 Peter 3:10 is fulfilled, when the innumerable blood-cleansed company surround the throne (Rev. 7:9–14), when the city is lit by the light of the glory of God and the Lamb is its lamp (Rev. 21:23), and when there is no temple because the Lord God Almighty and the Lamb are its temple (Rev. 21:22).

V. Oracle to the Priests and People: The Restored House the Cause of Blessing (2:10–19)

MOTYER

[10]On the twenty-fourth of the ninth [month] in the second year of King Darius, the word of the LORD came to the prophet Haggai:

[11] Thus the LORD of hosts says:

Do ask the priests for a ruling and say,

[12]Suppose a man is carrying holy flesh in a fold of his garment and with his garment he touches bread or stew or wine or oil—any foodstuff—does it become holy? In response the priests said, "No."

[13]And Haggai said, If someone defiled by a dead body touches any of these, does it become defiled? In response the priests said, "Yes, it becomes defiled."

[14] And Haggai responded and said,

So is this people and so is this nation before me—

this is the word of the LORD—

and so is every work of their hands,

and what they offer there—that is defiled.

[15] But now do take it to heart from this day onward.

Before stone was laid on stone in the temple of the LORD—

[16] when things were so—

one came to a heap of twenty measures and there were ten;

one came to the press to skim off fifty measures from the vat and there were twenty.

[17] I struck you with scorching and with mildew and with hail—

all the work of your hands—

but you never gave me your devotion!

This is the word of the LORD.

NRSV

[10]On the twenty-fourth day of the ninth month, in the second year of Darius, the word of the LORD came by the prophet Haggai, saying: [11]Thus says the LORD of hosts: Ask the priests for a ruling: [12]If one carries consecrated meat in the fold of one's garment, and with the fold touches bread, or stew, or wine, or oil, or any kind of food, does it become holy? The priests answered, "No." [13]Then Haggai said, "If one who is unclean by contact with a dead body touches any of these, does it become unclean?" The priests answered, "Yes, it becomes unclean." [14]Haggai then said, So is it with this people, and with this nation before me, says the LORD; and so with every work of their hands; and what they offer there is unclean. [15]But now, consider what will come to pass from this day on. Before a stone was placed upon a stone in the LORD's temple, [16]how did you fare? When one came to a heap of twenty measures, there were but ten; when one came to the winevat to draw fifty measures, there were but twenty. [17]I struck you and all the products of your toil with blight and mildew and hail; yet you did not return to me, says the LORD. [18]Consider from this day on, from the twenty-fourth day of the ninth month. Since the day that the foundation of the LORD's temple was laid, consider: [19]Is there any seed left in the barn? Do the vine, the fig tree, the pomegranate, and the olive tree still yield nothing? From this day on I will bless you.

MOTYER

18 Do take it to heart
   from this day onward,
   from the twenty-fourth day of the ninth
        [month],
   from the day the temple of the LORD was
        founded:
   take it to heart.
19 Is the seed again in store?
   Why, not even the vine or the fig or the
        pomegranate or the olive have borne!
   From this day I will bless you!

10. בְּעֶשְׂרִים וְאַרְבָּעָה (on the twenty-fourth) is December 18, two months after the date in 2:1 (see the Introduction). By this time the early rains would have begun and the work of sowing ended. This will prove an important consideration in the interpretation of 2:19. הָיָה דְבַר יְהוָה אֶל־ (the word of the LORD came to): See the Exegesis of 1:1. Why does the formula change here from בְּיַד (through; 1:1, 3; 2:1) to אֶל (to; see also 2:20)? They represent different sides of the miracle of prophecy, and the change possibly intends no more than that both sides were true of Haggai: he was a genuine prophet. But if Haggai was seeking a word from the Lord in anticipation of the announced date of laying the foundation (see the Exposition), it would be natural to say that, in response to his desire, the word came "to" him. This would apply equally to 2:20. הַנָּבִיא (the prophet): See the Exposition of 1:1.

11. כֹּה אָמַר (thus . . . says): See the Exegesis of 1:2. שְׁאַל־נָא (do ask) is the imperative softened by נָא (see the Exegesis of 2:2). תּוֹרָה is usually translated "law," though its fundamental meaning is "teaching." It was the priests' duty to teach the Lord's law, not least in ritual matters, applying divine truth to human life (see Lev. 10:10–11; Ezek. 22:26; Mal. 2:7).

10–11. In essence Haggai returns here to the foundational message of 1:1–11. The difference is not one of content but of emphasis. In 1:1–11 he concerned himself mainly with diagnosis of the malady and how it could be cured; here he repeats himself but goes on to the promise of the healthy and fulfilled life that awaits the cured patient.

As the analysis of Haggai in the Introduction shows, Coggins (*Haggai*, p. 36) is incorrect in treating 2:10–14 without close relation to the rest of Haggai. On the other hand, he is correct that these verses must not be denied to Haggai simply because in form they are a priestly ruling: "We should beware of supposing that prophets could never use forms of speech which originated from milieux different from their own" (p. 37). But who is being addressed? Rothstein promotes the idea that "this people" (2:14) is the immigrant community of 2 Kings 17:24–28 who became unorthodox Yahwists (Ezra 4:1–4) and Samaritan opponents of the Judahites. According to this view, Haggai is here calling for separation from an unclean people. But it is totally arbitrary to make a chronological shift from 536 B.C. to 520 B.C. As Verhoef (*Haggai*, p. 114) comments, "The historicity of the events described in Ezra 3:8–4:3 as having occurred in 536 B.C. need not be denied." To this Baldwin (*Haggai*, p. 51) adds that if Haggai had intended the Samaritans, why did he not say so? The burden of proof still lies, says May ("This People," p. 192), with those who propose this theory. The expressions *this people* (see the Exposition of 1:2) and *this nation* (2:14) do not necessarily have a bad meaning. Neither word requires that the address is other than to the temple builders.

There is also the question of the relation of 2:15–19 to 2:10–14. To Coggins (*Haggai*, p. 36), the link is "tenuous" and the suggestion of bringing 2:15–19 in connection with 1:15a is widely canvassed. Once, however, the attempt is made to shift 2:15–19, it appears that there is no simple procedure. Verse 15 opens with *but now (wĕʿattâ)*. In Haggai's usage (1:5; 2:4) this always records a movement of thought within an oracle. To make it refer simply to the date in 1:15a would be contrary to his linguistic practice. Do we then delete it or assume that at some stage an opening to the oracle was lost? In addition, there is no textual evidence for any order other than the present. But is the link between 2:10–14 and 2:15–19 really so tenuous? As the book has come to us, the two sections belong within an editorial unity; the date in 2:10 reappears (with considerable emphasis) in 2:18. The occurrence in 2:12 and 2:19 of the verb *to bear (nāśāʾ)* is an additional element of *inclusio*. The phrase *work of their/your hands* (2:14, 17) is a "domino" link between the sections. The date in 2:10 is not self-explanatory (see further below); it has no special meaning in the ecclesiastical calendar and does not of itself offer a reason why Haggai should have approached the priests for a ruling. No doubt the laying of the foundation of the temple was announced ahead of time and was a public occasion of importance on which Haggai, as the prophet of temple building, would have longed to speak a "word" from the Lord. To bring his message home by means of a priestly ruling would be directly appropriate to the founding of a priestly house. The search for a priestly ruling on holiness and uncleanness is not self-explanatory but in context it flows into and finds its adequate explanation in the verses that follow.

As remarked in the Exposition of 2:6 and 2:9, if Haggai's people thought that undated eschatological reassurances were not the present help they needed, the oracle at the temple founding meets this objection with its resounding and climactic "from this day I will bless" (2:19).

In the light of all this it is all the more essential to see the integrated unity of verses 10–19:

12. הֵן (suppose): GKC §159w doubts that this word has any connection with the word הִנֵּה (behold). It appears throughout the Old Testament with a conditional sense (Exod. 8:22; Lev. 25:20). בְּשַׂר־קֹדֶשׁ (holy flesh) occurs elsewhere only in Jeremiah 11:15, where the meaning is by no means plain. But here it is clear enough. Certain portions of the sacrifices were reckoned holy (see Lev. 6:11 [18]; Num. 6:20). Imagine, therefore, a priest carrying away what is due to him. Haggai is not, of course, interested in the bearer but only in the inability of a holy burden to convey its holiness by contact. Nor does he apply this truth to the contemporary situation, for the principle that holiness is not communicable by touch is not stated for its own sake but only as a preface to the negative case to follow. נָזִיד (stew): See Genesis 25:29 and 2 Kings 4:38. וְאֶל־כָּל־מַאֲכָל (any foodstuff) has *waw-explicativum*, similar in sense to the English "that is" (GKC §154a n. b).

13. טְמֵא־נֶפֶשׁ (defiled by the dead) is explained by Numbers 19:11: הַנֹּגֵעַ בְּמֵת לְכָל־נֶפֶשׁ אָדָם (those who touch the dead body of any human being; NRSV) and was recognized shorthand (see Lev. 22:4; Num. 5:2; 9:6–7). Such defilement is communicable by contact.

14. וַיַּעַן (and . . . responded): עָנָה does not always connote "to reply to a query." Here, the priests had not asked Haggai a question, but rather made an affirmation. The verb עָנָה has a broad connota-

---

A. The unclean people (10–14)
   1. Date (10)
   2. The priestly rulings (11–13)
      a. The first ruling: holiness is not contagious (11–12)
      b. The second ruling: uncleaness is contagious (13)
   3. Conclusion (14)
      a. Concerning the people
      b. Concerning their work and their religion
B. The blessed people (15–19)
   1. The first call to thoughtfulness: the past (15–17)
      a. Divine chastening (15–17a)
      b. Human unresponsiveness (17b)
   2. The second call to thoughtfulness: the future (18–19)
      a. The decisive date (18)
      b. The absoluteness of the divine word (19ab)
      c. The promise (19c)

12–13. Certain portions of the sacrifices (Lev. 6:18–22 [25–29]; Num. 6:20) were reckoned holy. We can imagine, therefore, a priest carrying away what was due to him. Haggai, however, is not interested in the bearer but only in the holy burden's being unable to convey its holiness by contact. Neither does he attempt to apply this truth to the contemporary situation, for the positive case that holiness is not communicable is not stated for its own sake but only to lead to the negative case to follow.

Haggai's approach to his ministry on this occasion may well have puzzled his hearers, familiar though they were with the ritual concepts to which he referred. If he said to us, "If you touch something with a dirty hand you will leave a dirty mark but if you touch something with a clean hand you will not leave a clean mark," we could only agree, but surely we would wonder what the relevance was. He couched the same message in the religious language of his day. As the Exegesis shows, things like sacrificial meats could become holy. In essence this word connotes separated, that is, set apart for God or belonging to the divine sphere of reality. But, like the clean hand that does not leave a clean mark, this holy status was not communicable. The priests had no difficulty in making their ruling; all this was commonplace. The hearers may well have replied, "So?"

14. The application of Haggai's observation is that a people defiled in the Lord's sight (2:14a) spreads its contagion both to its secular (agricultural and wage earning) activity (every work of their hands) and to its religion (what they offer there). The national economy and the religious exercises of the people were "defiled." Just as "holy" has the sense of belonging to the divine sphere or acceptable to God, so "defiled" connotes outside the divine sphere, abhorrent, or unacceptable to God. We do not know how they replied to this—or if they replied at all. But we can well imagine someone saying, "Here, wait a minute! What do you mean by calling my daily work defiled? I run a tidy farm, plan my business, pay my bills. What has religion to do with that?" And we can hardly fail to hear someone saying, "But this can't be right. I bring sacrifices to the altar to deal with my defilement before God. How can the sacrifice God has commanded be a defiled thing, unacceptable to him?" Haggai is challenging both the concept of a purely secular society and the

tion that permits its use in contexts like this one. BDB defines this function of the verb as "respond to an occasion, speak in view of circumstances" (p. 773). כֵּן (so) frequently has the function of signaling an analogy or comparison with a preceding affirmation, command, or description (Judg. 5:31). כֵּן occurs three times in this verse, extending the concept of defilement to the people and to the work of their hands. הָעָם־הַזֶּה (this people) is essentially parallel to הַגּוֹי הַזֶּה (this nation). כָּל־מַעֲשֵׂה יְדֵיהֶם (every work of their hands) finds its ultimate consequence in the parallel clause: וַאֲשֶׁר יַקְרִיבוּ (and what they offer; lit., bring near), a regular idiom. See Leviticus 1:2 especially in the light of Exodus 40:34–35; though the glory excludes, they are able to come near. After "work of their hands," the Septuagint reads, "and whoever approaches there will be defiled because of their early gains. They will be pained by reason of their labors. And you hated the one who reproves in the gates." Ackroyd ("Glosses in the Book of Haggai," p. 165) charitably sees this as some sort of interpretation, introducing factors of personal morality into the discussion. But apart from noting a relationship with Amos 5:10, it is hard to find meaning or relevance. שָׁם (there): See the Exposition.

15. וְעַתָּה (but now): This form is structurally significant in Haggai (see the Exegesis of 1:5 and 2:4), marking temporal and logical sequence within an oracle. נָא (do): See the Exegesis of 2:2. שִׂימוּ־נָא לְבַבְכֶם (take to heart [how things are going]): See the Exegesis of 1:5. וָמָעְלָה (onward): Notwithstanding the entry in BDB (p. 751) and Jones' note (*Haggai*, p. 51) that "the Hebrew can mean 'backwards' or 'forwards,'" there is no example in the Bible where the word refers to past time (Petersen, *Haggai*, p. 86; Verhoef, *Haggai*, p. 121; Beuken, *Haggai*, p. 209). This being so, 2:15b–17 is a paren-

---

notion that religious activity is self-validating. If people are not right with God, their society will be warped and ineffective, and their religion will reflect their character, not change it. The springs of life need to be clean if the outflow is to be clean.

The words *people* (ʿam) and *nation* (gōy) are parallel (see the Exegesis; Cody, "Chosen People"; May, "This People"). The former, ʿam, is more specifically the people with a history with God and a particular way of life; the latter, gōy, is the political entity, a nation among the nations, but still unique and special to the Lord. To call them hagōy (the nation) here is even a note of hope, considering that they were far from such, being but part of a Persian satrap. But with the Lord, nothing had changed.

The founding of the house marks a turning point in the people's spiritual and temporal fortunes. With this act they pass from divine hostility (2:17, "I struck") to divine blessing (2:19, "I will bless"). The unbuilt temple was a source of spiritual contagion. In Baldwin's vivid phrase (*Haggai*, p. 33), "the skeleton of the ruined Temple was like a dead body decaying . . . and making everything contaminated." But in what sense was the unbuilt house a contaminating agent? The house was important as the mode of the divine indwelling among the people (1:2); the unbuilt house was a statement that it was a matter of indifference whether the Lord was among his people. Hence his complaint was that, notwithstanding chastening, "you never gave me your devo-

tion" (2:17). Committing themselves to building was a testimony that the Lord mattered. Altar ceremonies without the house was religion without God, seeking benefits but shunning a relationship with the Lord from whom the benefits were sought. Such a religion is itself defiled and offers no cure for defilement.

15–17. Haggai vividly describes the desperate times through which they had lived. The yield of their produce was only half of what they expected. Resources were not going as far as they needed; life was harder than they wished. The prophets (with the rest of the Bible) share the view that created processes remain under the control of the Creator (Amos 4:9; see the Exposition of 1:9). The blessings and curses of Deuteronomy 28 rest on this assumption. That today we are often in a position to trace the course by which some natural event happens does not invalidate biblical thinking. The weather forecaster predicts weather, but it is still God who sends it.

To the unaided human mind, the situation demanded procedural reform. The gross national product was insufficient, and even what was produced did not seem to go as far as the producer envisaged. Then, as now, these are problems for the farmer, the economist, and the business owner. But to Haggai the problem was spiritual. The missing factor was not efficiency and know-how but the blessing of God. By now we know how to interpret references to the building of the temple. It is the divinely required precondition of the indwelling of God among his people; the

thetic backward glance before the forward look is resumed in 2:18. מִטֶּרֶם (before): The adverb טֶרֶם, which has the sense of "not yet, before" (see Gen. 2:5), is used mostly with prefixed בְּ (see Gen. 27:4) and only here with prefixed מִן (from). This is the מִן of "time when." Note that מֵאָז does not connote "from then" but "at that time, then," and מִקֶּדֶם does not connote "from beforehand" but "beforehand, earlier on"; so here מִטֶּרֶם simply has the sense of "before." אֶבֶן אֶל־אָבֶן (stone . . . on stone): See the Exegesis of 2:18.

16. מִהְיוֹתָם (when things were so): The unparalleled usage of this infinitive construct with prefixed מִן and third-person plural masculine suffix is a magnet for emenders. BHS and Petersen (*Haggai*, p. 86) emend to מַה־הֱיִיתֶם (how was it with you?; see also Thomas, "Haggai," p. 1047). Taking, however, prefixed מִן as expressing "time when" and the following infinitive construct with suffix as connoting "their being," "at the time of their being" expresses the idea "when things were so." We must not approach the text as if we were conversant with the flexibility of colloquial Hebrew. A further calling of attention to the past is not out of place in this context. יֶקֶב (press): In Isaiah 5:2 this word most likely describes a storage vat, but in Job 24:11 it is the vat where the grapes are pressed. פּוּרָה (vat) occurs elsewhere only in Isaiah 63:3, where it refers to the pressing vat. In the present case it comes rather unexpectedly at the end of the sentence. It cannot with any common sense be called an explanatory gloss on the first word (but see BHS!), for who would feel that יֶקֶב

needed explanation or who would explain a well-known word by a rare word? Possibly both words were in versatile use for either the upper, treading vat or the lower, storage vat, yielding a translation as above.

17. בַּשִּׁדָּפוֹן וּבַיֵּרָקוֹן (with scorching and mildew): See Deuteronomy 28:22; 1 Kings 8:37; and Amos 4:9. The first word describes the results of undue heat; the latter probably refers to a fungus caused by overly damp conditions: heat to wither, damp to rot. These opposites indicate that the Lord has a complete armory of chastisement at his disposal. בָּרָד (hail) is not a theophanic symbol here as it is in Psalm 18:14 [13] but a plague especially threatening to vines (Ps. 105:32–33). All this was related to a moral and spiritual purpose which, however, failed (see Amos 4:6–11). וְאֵין־אֶתְכֶם אֵלַי (you never gave me your devotion): Petersen (*Haggai*, p. 86) remarks that the Masoretic Text is "barbaric." The reason for this is, presumably, the occurrence of the accusative אֶתְכֶם after אֵין (there is not; lit., nothingness of). But see Genesis 23:8; 2 Kings 10:15; and the accusative after הֲלוֹא in Zechariah 7:7. See also Saydon ("Particle אֵת") and Macdonald ("Particle אֵת"), who insist on a more versatile use of אֵת than a restrictive definition as "the sign of the definite object" would allow (see also Davidson, *Hebrew Syntax* §72.4). אֵלַי (to me): See 2 Kings 6:11; Jeremiah 15:1; Ezekiel 36:9, where אֶל has the idiomatic sense of "giving allegiance to" or "siding with." As nearly therefore as we can follow the order and emphasis of the Hebrew, it states literally, "But nothingness of—

---

unbuilt house speaks of the unwanted resident. This is explained in 2:17, where failure in crops and failure in devotion belong together. The heart of their problem was that they acted as if life could be run without reference to God and as if grace would be theirs even though they neglected the means of grace. It would hardly be stretching the meaning of 2:17b to paraphrase: "But you did not want me!" At this point the coldness of the human heart and the hurt in the divine heart meet.

18–19. Verse 10 informs us that this oracle was given in the ninth month, that is, the month of December. In ancient Palestine summer (May–September) was hot, with little rain. Corn crops were harvested in May and June and fruits in August and September. The early rains of October and November permitted plowing and sowing for the following year. Cold weather, with intermittent rain and some snow, prevailed during

December through February, and in March through April the late rains fell, maturing the growing crops. Since this present oracle is dated mid-December, unless something exceptional had happened, sowing would have already taken place. This must determine our approach to the question with which the verse opens. One's interpretation depends on the meaning given to *zera*ᶜ and ᶜôd: Does *zera*ᶜ mean "seed for sowing" or "seed reaped and stored"? Does ᶜôd mean "still" or "again"?

Out of this three possibilities arise: (1) The seed is last year's crop ("is there seed still in the store?") with the implication that it has already run out and the barns are empty, and the promise is that this will not happen again. This does not, however, fit the circumstances of Haggai's day, for there is no reason to believe that the people ever lived in starvation conditions such as would happen if by mid-December the barns were empty.

as far as you are concerned—[loyalty] to me." There was nothing that the people gave to God in the midst of their economic woes. This is unexceptionable in both Hebrew usage and contextual suitability. נְאֻם יְהוָה (this is the word): See the Exposition of 1:1.

18. שִׂימוּ־נָא לְבַבְכֶם (do take it to heart): See the Exegesis of 1:5. יֻסַּד (was founded): In the majority of its occurrences יֻסַּד has the sense of "to found." It is used most often of the Lord founding the earth (but see 2 Chron. 24:27). In a wider sense it refers to the act of commencing a restoration work (Baldwin, *Haggai*, pp. 52–53; Gelston, "Foundations of the Second Temple"). Wiseman ("Haggai," p. 784) reports that more than one foundation ritual was common in building temples. We can, therefore, accept the word here in reference to the resumption of work. The evidence of 2:15 suggests that by this time stone had been laid on stone and that therefore the founding to which Haggai refers was not the placing of the first stone but some formal act officially inaugurating the work.

19. הַזֶּרַע can refer to either seed for sowing or seed reaped and stored (see the Exposition). עוֹד (again): See Genesis 4:25; 9:11; 1 Samuel 10:22; and the Exposition. מְגוּרָה (store) is found only here, with its meaning deduced contextually and

from Arabic cognates (KB, p. 544). וְעַד (why, . . . even; lit., and up to, as far as) exemplifies a common use of עַד as a particle of emphasis (e.g., Exod. 9:7; Num. 8:4; and Job 25:5, where Dhorme [*Job*, p. 369] notes, "The preposition עַד . . . in a negative sentence means 'not even' "). To translate וְ as "Why!" tries to catch the conscious exaggeration by which Haggai underscores that the promise of God antedates any evidence open to humans (for the fruit harvest was even later than the cereal harvest). הַגֶּפֶן . . . הַזַּיִת (the vine . . . the olive): See Deuteronomy 8:8; compare with Numbers 13:23. These are the fruits of the promised land. They are no doubt mentioned deliberately to call attention to good times ahead. מִן־הַיּוֹם (from this day): Pusey (*Minor Prophets*, p. 318) says, "All the Old and New Testament . . . bear witness to the Providence of God Who makes His natural laws serve to the moral discipline of His creature, man . . . [Who] framed the laws of His physical creation, so that plenty or famine . . . should coincide with the good or evil conduct of man, with his prayers or his neglect of prayer." What Pusey generalizes Haggai particularizes. The heart of the matter is whether the Lord's people want the Lord himself, whether it is vital to them that the Lord dwells in peace at the heart of their community.

---

(2) The seed is what has just been sown ("is the seed still in the store?"). It lies germinating in the ground, giving as yet no sign of what the harvest will be, but God promises a bumper crop. (3) The seed is the crop yet to be ("is the seed back again in the store?"). Long before the day of reaping comes, the Lord pledges the result. Either of the last two options are contextually apt (see Baldwin, *Haggai*, p. 52). The reason for choosing the third is that it fits marginally better with the words that follow and refers not to sowing or storing but to the coming crop.

When personal devotion to the Lord was absent, nothing went right (2:15–17), but when devotion is renewed, when by their action in temple building, they declare that it matters to them to have the Lord in their midst, when they return to a God-centered lifestyle, the Lord responds by marking the date off on his calendar as the begin-

ning of the blessing. Haggai's application of his teaching is solely to the national economy; he does not make a religious application even though he saw their religion as vitiated by defilement (2:14). Had he done so, the message would be the same. In their agriculture, they sought creation's blessings without loving the Creator; in religion, with their offerings, they sought redemption's blessings without loving the Redeemer. In promising blessing, Haggai is not making a shrewd calculation based on reading "economic indicators." The quantity and quality of next year's harvest are still far beyond the human eye (see the Exegesis of 2:19). He is asserting a matter of pure spiritual essence: the first call to the people of God is to love the Lord their God with all their heart and to do all that he requires, whereby he will live at peace in their midst. This is the key to blessing.

VI. Oracle to Zerubbabel: David's House to Be Built (2:20–23)

MOTYER

²⁰The word of the LORD came a second time to Haggai on the twenty-fourth of the month:
²¹ Say to Zerubbabel, governor of Judah:
I am going to shake the heavens and the earth,
²² and I will overturn the thrones of the kingdoms,
and I will destroy the strength of the kingdoms of the nations,
and I will overturn chariots and their riders,
and horses and their riders will go down, each by his brother's sword.
²³ In that day—
this is the word of the LORD of hosts—
I will take you, Zerubbabel son of Shealtiel, my servant—
this is the word of the LORD—
and I will make you like a signet ring,
for it is you I have chosen—
this is the word of the LORD of hosts.

NRSV

²⁰The word of the LORD came a second time to Haggai on the twenty-fourth day of the month: ²¹Speak to Zerubbabel, governor of Judah, saying, I am about to shake the heavens and the earth, ²²and to overthrow the throne of kingdoms; I am about to destroy the strength of the kingdoms of the nations, and overthrow the chariots and their riders; and the horses and their riders shall fall, every one by the sword of a comrade. ²³On that day, says the LORD of hosts, I will take you, O Zerubbabel my servant, son of Shealtiel, says the LORD, and make you like a signet ring; for I have chosen you, says the LORD of hosts.

20. שֵׁנִית (a second time): There are more blessings and wider issues than those associated in 2:10–19 with the building of the house. There the Lord responded to his people's devotion with a pledge of material well-being; now the vistas widen. The "promised land" hinted at in 2:19 is clarified: the kingdom of David will return and its worldwide aspects will come to fruition. בְּעֶשְׂרִים וְאַרְבָּעָה לַחֹדֶשׁ (on the twenty-fourth of the month): On the dates in Haggai, see the Introduction.

---

20. The final verses of his book reveal Haggai as the literary equivalent of an impressionist painter—he gives general tone and effect without elaborate detail. His colors are the thunderstorm and the earthquake (2:21), revolution (2:22a), clashing armies (2:22b–c), and civil conflict (2:22d). As in a carefully composed picture, where every stroke is designed to lead the eye to what is central, so here too the focus is like a shaft of sunlight illuminating one item—a ring shining on a finger (2:23).

Verhoef (*Haggai*, p. 142) is correct that "the content of 2:20–23 cannot adequately be explained from the contemporary history." The truth of the matter is that the attempt should never have been made. Jones (*Haggai*, p. 53) acutely remarks: "The whole spirit of Haggai and Zechariah is not that of political agitators, but of men of faith waiting upon God." To this Petersen (*Haggai*, p. 101) adds that "what has appeared to most commentators as hopelessly general language is, in fact, highly affective and effective discourse." We have here a wealth of traditional symbols bearing on the multifaceted day of the Lord, the ever-imminent eschaton. Seen in this light, these verses bring the Book of Haggai full circle. First, the opening address to Zerubbabel (1:1–2) is matched by this final address. Having started by addressing both Zerubbabel and Joshua (1:1), Haggai ends by addressing Zerubbabel alone. It was not his task (see Zech. 3:1–10; 6:12–13) to envisage the coming messianic Priest. But the link with 1:1–2 is deeper than an address to the same person. In 1:1, Zerubbabel, the Davidic descendant is, by implication, called to be prime mover in building the Lord's house. In 2:20–22, Zerubbabel is told that the Lord will build him a house. The Book of Haggai thus recaptures, in its own terms, the sequence of 2 Samuel 7:1–6, 11, where David, who wanted to build a house for the Lord, learns that the Lord plans to build a house for him. Haggai uses a series of six symbols of the day of the Lord:

- **a** shaking: David comes to the throne (21)
- **b** overturning: divine judgment on a sinful world (22a)
- **c** victory: opposing kingdoms destroyed (22b)
- **c'** final deliverance: all alien threat ended (22c)
- **b'** self-destruction of the world: secure inheritance (22d)
- **a'** Lord's king: David's house restored to divine favor (23)

The a-theme is the restoration of David; the b-theme, judgment on the opposing world; the c-theme, the full deliverance of the people of God.

21–22. How magnificent is the Lord in judgment! On the grandest scale, as befits the Creator, he reorders heaven and earth; he disposes of political structures and military might—and even if we alter the horse and chariot of ancient warfare to the horrifying weapons of today, it is still nothing to him. One day the heavens will pass away with a loud noise, the elements will be dissolved with fire, and the earth will be burned up (2 Peter 3:10); one day the lightning will shine from east to west, from one end of heaven to the other (Matt. 24:27; Luke 17:24), the day of the Son of Man will come, and the kings of the earth will look for rocks to fall on them and mountains to hide them from the mere face of him who sits on the throne (Rev. 6:15–16). At one and the same time, that day will be the punishment of Sodom ("overturn"), the conquering "strength" of the exodus, the settling of final issues as at the Red Sea ("horses and riders"), and the boomerang of self-destructive energies of sin let loose. This is another of the Lord's great interventions, as when Gideon's three hundred faced the Midianite confederation (Judg. 6:1–6, 33; 7:7–8, 22). The theme of the Gideon pericope (as indeed of the Book of Judges) is that of the security and well-being of the people of God and their enjoyment of what the Lord has given them. Under threat of the nations (as in Gideon's day and throughout Judg. 1–16) and equally under threat of religious, social, and moral declension (Judg. 17–21), the author of Judges sees that only a king will suffice (17:6; 18:1; 19:1; 21:25). Haggai picks up this theme. Within the embrace of the perfect king (2:21, 23) the self-destruction of sin will have its way with the world and the people of God will possess their possessions in peace. What

21. אֲנִי מַרְעִישׁ (I am going to shake): See the Exegesis of 2:6–7. Of the two historical events that are "earthshaking"—the exodus (Ps. 77:19 [18]; see also 68:9 [8]) and David's coming to the throne (Ps. 18:8 [7] par. 2 Sam. 22:8)—the latter is the more apt here, for it is the bracketing theme of the whole series in 2:21–23, and the exodus provides the motifs in the central c sections (see the Exposition). הַשָּׁמַיִם וְאֶת־הָאָרֶץ (the heavens and the earth) reflects cosmic and worldwide divine action. The Lord will bring in the rule of David—not just on the promised earthly scale (Isa. 9:7) but as truly cosmic.

22. וְהָפַכְתִּי (and I will overturn) has as its basic sense to turn (Josh. 7:8; 2 Kings 21:13). Certain contexts call for the English sense of "overturn," as does this context. Baldwin (*Haggai*, p. 54) comments: "That Judah is small and defenceless makes no difference when God says *I will overthrow*." This theme never lost its reference back to divine action against Sodom (Deut. 29:22 [23]; Isa. 1:7–9; Jer. 20:16; Amos 4:11; Lam. 4:6), and it became "a Leitmotif in prophecies of doom" (Verhoef, *Haggai*, p. 143). Thus, when the Lord restores David according to promise, it will be in the context of a worldwide judgment on sin and the just punishment of sinners. כִּסֵּא (the thrones) signifies the world organized without reference to God and yielding submission to other kings than his king (Ps. 2). In the Masoretic Text the word כִּסֵּא is singular but can be translated as a plural according to the rule that the plural of the *nomen rectum* מַמְלָכוֹת (kingdoms) can make the whole construct plural (see 2:7; GKC §124r). Haggai may have intended the singular. If he did, the sense would be that behind the kingdoms of the world there is a single organizing power opposed to the Lord, as in Revelation 17:10–14. The two central sections in Haggai 2:21–23 belong together with their associated themes of victory and deliverance

(see the Exposition). וְהִשְׁמַדְתִּי (and I will destroy): The verb שָׁמַד has exodus affinities, though it is not a technical or semitechnical term (see Deut. 9:3; Amos 2:9). חֹזֶק (strength), apart from Amos 6:13, is used only of the Lord's power manifested at the exodus (Exod. 13:3, 14, 16). It is used here ironically. What is the combined strength of earthly kingdoms compared with the strength of the God of the exodus? The verb יָרַד (to go down) is not a synonym for "collapse" or "fall" and must be explained here by Exodus 15, where Pharaoh's horses and riders (15:1) and chariots (15:4) "went down into the depths like a stone" (15:5). The meaning of the Red Sea episode was that "the Egyptians whom you see today you shall never see again" (Exod. 14:13); that is, it was the finalizing of the exodus victory, the moment of the assured deliverance of the people and the end of the alien power that enslaved them. אִישׁ בְּחֶרֶב אָחִיו (each by his brother's sword): אִישׁ frequently functions in texts as an individualizing element (GKC §139b). The combination אָח (brother) and אִישׁ (man) corresponds to English "one . . . another" (BDB, p. 26). For the significance of the motif of internecine strife among the enemies of the Lord's people, see, for example, Judges 7:22; 1 Samuel 14:20; 2 Chronicles 20:23. Haggai picks up this aspect of the past and projects it into the future: like all sin, the sin of hating, oppressing, and opposing God's people is ultimately self-destructive.

23. בַּיּוֹם הַהוּא (in that day) is a solemn eschatological introduction that gives weighty emphasis to this verse. As Petersen (*Haggai*, p. 102) observes, this expression does "much more than provide a simple connective between vs. 22 and 23. It provides a conceptual transition from the general future to a specific moment at which Yahweh will act decisively." נְאֻם יְהוָה (this is the word of the LORD) appears three times in this verse, also adding emphasis to it (see the Exposition of 1:1). Each ele-

---

a great and awesome day! But over it all, in calm and sovereign holiness presides the God who promises to overturn and destroy and whose word effectuates the judgment of which it speaks (Rev. 19:20–21).

And equally how magnificent in salvation the Lord is! Overturning Sodom, he saved Lot (Gen. 19); destroying the strength of Egypt, he saved his people (Exod. 10:7; 12:33); when the waters returned over the pursuing armies, it was in order that Israel might stand still and see the salvation of the Lord and be assured that their bondage was over once and for all (Exod. 14:13–14). So it will be

in the day of the Lord. As those who do not obey the gospel suffer punishment and eternal destruction, he himself shall come to be glorified in his saints and marveled at among all those who believe (2 Thess. 1:9–10).

23. Finally, how faithful to his messianic promises the Lord is! Zerubbabel, the Davidic descendant, was in reality the heir to nothing. There was no throne for him to mount or crown to wear, no empire to rule or royal acclaim to enjoy. It is not even certain that his title of governor was anything more than honorific. The whole Davidic enterprise had long since run into the sand. But to

ment of the promise—the certainty of the coming day and the divine election and status of Zerubbabel—is thus signed, sealed, and settled. אֶקָּחֲךָ (I will take you) is used to designate election (Exod. 6:7; Deut. 4:20, 34) and David (2 Sam. 7:8; Pss. 18:17 [16]; 78:70; see also Jer. 33:26). It affirms another element of the promise, namely, Zerubbabel's sta-

tus, as does the following title: עַבְדִּי (my servant). While the title *servant* is given to Moses more often than to any other, David is the one who is most often called עַבְדִּי (*my* servant; twenty-one times; e.g., 2 Sam. 3:18). כַּחוֹתָם (like a signet ring): For background on this, see Jeremiah 22:24, and, for its meaning, see the Exposition.

---

write off the Davidic promises would be to forget the faithfulness of God, who does not lie or change his mind (Num. 23:19). When the time of fulfillment came, the ground from which the messianic root sprang (Isa. 53:2) seemed if anything drier—but out of it came the glory! From Zerubbabel, Matthew (1:13–16) traced through a series of unknowns to a man named Joseph, who in due time bequeathed Davidic descent to his supposed firstborn, Jesus. In him the servant status of David (Ps. 89:4 [3]) was linked with the servant of Isaiah 52:13. The intimacy and dignity of the signet came to one who from all eternity was in the bosom of the Father and who was the effulgence of his glory and the express image of his substance (Heb. 1:3). Though on the cross he was mocked as "the *chosen* of God" (Luke 23:35), he was in truth the chief cornerstone, chosen and precious, the foundation of security to the believer and the ground of condemnation to those who stumble at his word (1 Peter 2:6–8). The Lord himself had suddenly come to his temple (Mal. 3:1).

Pusey (*Minor Prophets*, p. 320) states: "God reverses to Zerubbabel the sentence on Jeconiah." Whether the signet was worn as a neck pendant (Gen. 38:18, 25), a finger ring (Jer. 22:24), or a bracelet (Song of Sol. 8:6), it bore the owner's name or mark so that it could be used as a personal identification (Gen. 38:18; 1 Kings 21:8). Nearest in wording to Haggai is Song of Solomon 8:6, where the beloved desires her name to be engraved on her lover's heart and arm, making her central to his affections and the first call on his strength. In Haggai, as in the Song of Solomon, it is the wearing, not the using of the signet that is mentioned. It symbolizes the possession and enjoyment of a close and precious relationship. The king will be the identity by which the Lord will be known. Thus the blessings promised to Zerubbabel rise to a climax: election ("I will take")

leads to function ("my servant") and to a choice relationship of uniqueness and love ("signet").

In what sense are these great promises made to and expected to be fulfilled in Zerubbabel? Many commentators hold that Haggai believed Zerubbabel to be the Messiah and that the turn of events proved him to be mistaken. But to interpret the passage in this way is to forget the way in which the kings of David's line were addressed. Jones (*Haggai*, p. 53) reminds us that in principle this sort of identification of king with Messiah was made in relation to every king: "In so far as the king does not realize the high conception of kingship . . . the hope is thrown more and more into the future."

We have seen in the foregoing context how key events of the past (David's coming to power, Sodom, the exodus, Gideon) became symbols of the coming day, and the same is true of key people. David became so identified with what the Lord would yet do that not only was every successive king compared with him but the Messiah was even called David (Ezek. 34:23). Many psalms are royal anthems, designed to hold up before the actual king the mirror of the true. Psalm 2 (a coronation anthem), 45 (a wedding anthem), and 72 each delineate a personage larger than life and more than human. Identification with an actual king seems direct, but ongoing experience made the Lord's people look further and wait longer. The day of the Lord is always intended to be the imminent expectation of the Lord's people, just as the New Testament expects a soon-coming Lord Jesus and rightly so, and just as we ourselves continue to say, "Maybe today." In Zerubbabel the Lord's eschatological, Davidic purposes are renewed and reinvigorated and stamped with the supreme validation: "The word of the LORD of hosts."

Zechariah

Introduction

In the commentary on Hosea in volume 1 of this series, I attempted a fresh approach to the text. Using mainly the primary tools of exegesis, I made an effort to let the text speak for itself, appealing to other scholars' works only when they aided the exegetical process. The experience was a rich one because I felt I was hearing Hosea as I had not heard him before. The reader will judge the value of that effort.

In this commentary I take somewhat the same approach, but I also borrow from the methodology of biblical theology. In my opinion, biblical theology is a distinct discipline, not simply a way of doing Old or New Testament theology. It is based on solid principles of exegesis and is historical in nature. By "historical" I mean that the interpreter will, where possible, exegete a text against its historical background and will observe the development of the text's theology across the Testaments, observing the rich faceting it receives in its progress through redemptive history.

I have tried to understand what the message of the Book of Zechariah would mean to the ancients who first heard it, especially those laboring at the temple site, but I have also followed its theological concepts as they transit the Testaments to become an integral part of the early Christians' proclamation that the messianic age has dawned. Lamarche (*Zacharie*, pp. 8–9) shows that the passion narratives of the Gospels quote from Zechariah 9–14 more than from any other portion of the Old Testament.

*To my son
Douglas
for his love
and companionship
for his devotion
to scholarship
in study and teaching
God's Word,
following in
my footsteps*

*Contributor:
Thomas Edward
McComiskey
Ph.D., Brandeis
University*

Especially important to the proclamation of the early church are Zechariah 9:9–10, 11:12, 12:10, and 13:7–9.

Historical Background

As we turn to the prophecy of Zechariah, we leave behind the long years of exile to enter the postexilic period. The history of this period begins with the brilliant military successes of King Cyrus, who ruled the Persian Empire from 538 B.C. to 530 B.C. By 550, Cyrus had defeated the Median Empire, and in 538 his armies conquered Babylon. The events surrounding his accession of Syria–Palestine are unclear, but by 538 "all western Asia to the Egyptian frontier was his" (Bright, *History of Israel*, p. 361).

In the same year, Cyrus issued a decree ordering the restoration of the Jewish cultus in Jerusalem (2 Chron. 36:22–23; Ezra 1:1–4; 6:3–5). Attesting to the faith that enabled many Jews to spiritually survive the captivity, the first wave of exiles returned to Jerusalem under the leadership of Sheshbazzar (Ezra 1:8, 11), whom Cyrus appointed as governor (Ezra 5:14). Ezra 5:16 credits Sheshbazzar with laying the temple's foundation, while Ezra 3:8 and Zechariah 4:9 give that honor to Zerubbabel. Perhaps Zerubbabel took up the work after a faltering start by Sheshbazzar. In addition, Ezra 3:8 places the initial efforts of Zerubbabel two years after the return from the captivity (536 B.C.), creating the possibility that Sheshbazzar began the work immediately upon his return but could not continue, perhaps because of his advanced age (see Bright, *History of Israel*, p. 366 n. 59).

If the returned exiles expected the dawn of Yahweh's universal reign, with Jews and Gentiles flocking to Jerusalem, their hopes soon faded. Jews did not leave the population centers of the empire in vast numbers, and interference from the longtime inhabitants of the land frustrated the building efforts (Ezra 4:1–24), bringing the work on the temple to a halt (Ezra 4:24). Ezra 4:4 tells us that this interference in the affairs of the Jews "discouraged the people of Judah, and made them afraid to build." Because the people completed the foundation in 536 and did not begin the construction of the temple structure until 520 (Ezra 4:24), the foundation lay neglected for over a decade and a half.

After the death of Cyrus, his son Cambyses acceded to the Persian throne (529–522 B.C.), adding Egypt to the already extensive empire. Returning from the Egyptian campaign, Cambyses learned that Gautama had usurped the throne, claiming to be his murdered brother. For reasons unknown to us, Cambyses took his own life, whereupon Darius, an officer in the Persian army who belonged to the royal Hystaspes family, laid claim to the throne and then secured it by executing Gautama. Darius I (the Great) Hystaspes ruled the Persian Empire from 521 B.C. to 486 B.C.

The accession of Darius to the throne did not immediately stabilize the empire. There was widespread revolt among various ethnic groups within the far-flung realm, which the events surrounding his accession may have fueled. From Media to Egypt, fiercely independent peoples created serious instability in the empire, which required swift action on the part of the new emperor. The most serious threat to Darius's authority seems to have been an insurrection in Babylon, where Nindintu-bel declared himself king and reigned until Darius deposed him. Another rebellion in Babylon followed soon after, only to meet a similar fate. We cannot be sure of the length of time it took Darius to secure his empire, but it was probably close to two years. The oracle in Zechariah 1:7–17 is dated toward the end of that year (1:7) and reflects a time of peace throughout the empire.

The messianic hope that had motivated many Jews to return to Jerusalem seemed to be fading by 520 B.C. (for a detailed study of the dating of events in this period, see Ackroyd, "Historical Problems," pp. 13–22). Zechariah's second dated oracle (1:7–17), which its superscription (1:7) places in 520 B.C., Darius's second year (for the most part I follow Thiele, *Mysterious Numbers*, for biblical dates), reflects the popular belief that Yahweh had forsaken his people to look with favor on the surrounding nations. The prophet represents the Lord as countering this belief: "I am very jealous for Jerusalem and for Zion. And I am extremely angry with the nations that are at ease" (vv. 14–15). It is not difficult to understand why the people felt as they did, for galling frustrations faced them at every turn. Ezra 5:3–17 tells of the period of inaction that Tattenai (governor of the province) and Shethar-bozenai caused, prompting a decree from Darius (Ezra 6:1–12). We do not know if their investigation of the work on the temple was a sincere effort to determine if the Jews were engaging in sedition, or if it was prompted by ulterior motives. While the section of the decree that addresses Tattenai is couched in strong language ("Now you, Tattenai, . . . keep away"; Ezra 6:6), possibly suggesting that Darius suspected Tattenai's motives, the fact that Tattenai did not order an immediate halt to the work (Ezra 5:5) may indicate that he was acting only as a loyal government official with the good of the empire at heart. Whatever his intentions, Tattenai's intrusion into the Jews' internal affairs must have impeded the progress of the construction for a considerable time.

Outside interference was not the only factor contributing to the people's inaction, for many of them faced serious hardship. The prophet Haggai says of these times, "You have sown much, and harvested little; you eat, but you never have enough; . . . you that earn wages earn wages to put them into a bag with holes" (1:6). Struggling to keep food on the table and faced with the formidable task of building their temple, these dispirited people let the work fall into neglect. One can understand how this discouraging situation would raise nagging questions about Yahweh's commitment to the community, dulling the people's motivation to build. Had the sins of the fathers terminated forever Yahweh's relationship with his people? If so, why build a temple?

The prophet Zechariah would not hear of this. His first words to the people acknowledged Yahweh's anger against the fathers, but held out the hope of a restoration to divine favor if the people should turn to their God (1:2–3). He affirmed that Yahweh had chosen Jerusalem as the seat of his dominion and that the people would be successful in their efforts to build the temple (1:16–17).

From the perspective of the ordinary citizens of Jerusalem, the most pressing problem they faced was severe economic depression. For the prophet Haggai, however, bleak times were not the primary concern, for he looked beyond the economic depression, seeing the root cause as the people's neglect of the temple: "You have looked for much, and, lo, it came to little. . . . Why? . . . Because my house lies in ruins" (1:9). Zechariah took a different approach to the hard times, for he perceived them as fading before the bright prospects that God had in store for his people (see the Exposition of 8:10–12).

Without a temple the community lacked spiritual cohesion. The house of the Lord was the seat of Yahweh's presence, but instead of witnessing to the presence of their God, the rubble-strewn temple site was a mute testimony of their neglect. Zerubbabel, the civil leader in the postexilic community, would have been most affected by the community's lack of incentive to build, for it was his responsibility to lead them in the project. It is thus not surprising that an important prophetic oracle relates directly to him (Zech. 4:1–14). Clearly, if the community was to survive, it needed leaders who could not only rally the people to the task, but who could overcome their spiritual lethargy by authoritatively assuring them of divine assistance. The situation called for a prophetic voice, and both Haggai and Zechariah met the challenge (Ezra 5:1; see also 6:14). It must have been difficult for these prophets to claim that Yahweh was still loyal to his people when the hard economic times seemed to belie their words, but they succeeded. With the opposition of Tattenai behind them, the laborers took up the work with the full support of Darius, whose decree ordered: "Let the governor of the Jews and the elders of the Jews rebuild this house of God on its site. ... Let it be done with all diligence" (Ezra 6:7, 12). Not only did Darius's decree approve the building enterprise; it also provided the funds for rebuilding the temple from the royal revenues (Ezra 6:8). The completed temple was not only a witness to the renewed spirit of the people, but also to the dedication of Haggai and Zechariah to their Yahwistic faith and their firm conviction that Yahweh would not forsake his promises.

As Jews returned to their homeland in increasing numbers, they began to inhabit the outlying areas. Zechariah 7:2 indicates that Bethel was a settled community in 518, the fourth year of Darius's reign. Construction work on the temple would have been well along at this time, and the delegation that came to Zechariah from Bethel (7:2–3) probably saw its rising walls even as they approached Jerusalem. The theological question the disputants at Bethel raised (see the Exposition of 7:3ff.) alarmed Zechariah, eliciting from him a lengthy answer (7:4–8:23). The urgent spirit of his response betrays his view that their question reflected a flagging loyalty to their Yahwistic heritage. The spiritual sickness that caused the preexilic community to perish was eating away at the vitals of the new community.

The work prospered (Ezra 6:14), however, and the laborers finished the temple in 516 B.C., Darius's sixth regnal year (Ezra 6:15). Much of the success of the venture was due to the able leadership of Zerubbabel and Joshua the high priest (Ezra 2:2; 3:8; 4:2; 5:2). Ezra 6:16–22 records the account of the celebration that followed the completion of the temple.

It is sad to read that the leaders of the fledgling community, like those before the exile, proved faithless (Zech. 10:3), but such was the case (see the Exposition of 10:3; 11:1–3, 5). Because of their unwise leaders, the people would fall into the hands of a wicked leader (see the Exposition of 11:15–17). Beyond this dismal prospect, however, the prophet envisioned a future bright with hope (chaps. 12–14).

Author and Date

The name *Zechariah* is common in the Old Testament, as well as during the postexilic period, and probably means "Yahweh remembers." In spite of his prominence in early postexilic Judaism, we actually know very little about the prophet Zechariah. Besides the book that bears his name, he appears in the Book of Ezra and in the apocryphal books 1–2 Esdras. In 1 Esdras, Zechariah appears along with Haggai in an account of the building of the temple roughly similar to Ezra's account: "The holy work [on the temple] prospered, while the prophets Haggai and Zechariah prophesied" (1 Esdr. 7:3). First Esdras 6:1 also refers to the prophetic activity of these prophets, adding that Zechariah was "the son of Iddo" (as Zech. 1:1 states). In all probability Iddo was Zechariah's grandfather and Berechiah his father (see the Exposition of 1:1). In 2 Esdras, which is largely apocalyptic, Zechariah appears along with several other prophets as leaders of a people who will replace the disobedient people to whom Ezra allegedly prophesied (1:38–40; see also 1:1). The Book of Ezra adds little to our knowledge of Zechariah, observing that he and the prophet Haggai prophesied to the Jews before the temple construction began (5:1) and that the builders prospered under their prophetic ministry (6:14). If the Iddo in Zechariah 1:1 is the same one who appears in Nehemiah 12:4 as a priest who "came up with Zerubbabel" (12:1), then Zechariah belonged to a priestly family (see also Neh. 12:16), but of this we cannot be certain. (For a discussion of the age of Zechariah, see Smith, *Micah–Malachi*, p. 168.)

The several dated oracles (1:1, 7; 7:1) that appear in the first part of the book place chapters 1–8 within the first four years of the reign of Darius I (521–518 B.C.). The date of the second part of the book, however, is another matter. (For a further discussion of the date of the book, see the discussion of integrity below.)

Text

The Masoretic Text of Zechariah has come down to us in good condition (see Jansma, "Hebrew Text and the Ancient Versions"). Difficulties of a textual nature do confront us in this book, but before we attribute difficult readings to faulty transmission, we must satisfy ourselves that they are not valid components of the writer's language structures. That is not to denigrate critical methodologies; it is to say only that we must not judge a text from which we are separated by centuries on the basis of modern language conventions.

Zechariah 6:6, for example, is problematic (Smith, *Micah–Malachi*, p. 175) in that it appears to omit a word before the participle *yōṣ'îm* (are going). A literal rendering of line A of this verse is, "The one with the black horses are going to the land of the north." Obviously, the clause needs a reference to the chariot horses, which I have supplied in my translation: "The one with the black horses, [they] are going to the land of the north." It may seem more arbitrary to supply a word in a line of text than posit a textual corruption, but as I observe in the Exegesis of 6:6, it is grammatically permissible in ancient Hebrew to omit an appropriate pronoun before a participle, especially when the text makes the subject clear (*IBHS*, p. 624). A similar syntactical condition exists in 6:3: "[The horses were] powerful." Grammatical conventions thus make it uncertain that the text as it stands is textually corrupt.

The Masoretic Text of Zechariah differs from the Septuagint in a significant number of cases, but when one tests the readings of the Septuagint by Hebrew usage and the laws of context, the Masoretic Text often proves superior. For example, if we judge the Septuagint reading of 8:23 by Hebrew usage, we discover a grammatical anomaly. The Septuagint reads, "In those days if ten men of all the languages," which validly renders *'ăšer* as a conditional particle but creates the questionable syntactical structure of a conditional clause without an apodosis. On the other hand, grammatical usage allows *'ăšer* to answer to the sense of "that": "In those days [it will be] *that* ten men" (see the Exegesis of 8:20, 23). For another example of Hebrew usage rendering a Septuagint reading questionable, see the Exegesis of 12:10.

There are several passages where the context supports the Masoretic Text over the Septuagint. In 1:21 [2:4], the Septuagint witnesses to the presence of *lĕyaddôt* (to terrify), but reads it as the plural of *yād* (hand): "These have come forth to sharpen them [the horns] for their [the workers'] hands." Judged against the laws of context, this pericope lacks a satisfying conclusion. Why do the workers sharpen the horns (the nations that cast down Israel and Judah)? We are left with feelings of vague uncertainty. Each vision in 1:7–6:8 ends with a positive application of its content to the people of God, but if the intent of the Septuagint's reading of this verse is to imply that the nations are sharpened for future activity against Israel and Judah, it is not consonant with the consistent pattern of assurances for Israel that the broader context establishes.

Context also helps interpret 5:1. The Septuagint has a flying scythe (*drepanon*), not the Masoretic Text's scroll (*mĕgillâ*), reading the word as *maggāl* (a scythe or sickle) or as the unattested feminine *mgllh* (from the also unattested root *ngl*). While a scythe is appropriate to the destructive tone of the context, we do not expect the text to delineate the proportions of a scythe in area dimensions (length and width) as it does in verse 3 (see Gen. 13:17; Exod. 26:2; Deut. 3:11; 1 Kings. 6:3; Ezek. 40:20; 42:11; 45:5; and see the dimensions of the sword in Judg. 3:16). That curses of the law are written on this object influences our reading "scroll" instead of "scythe."

Some Septuagint readings witness to the Masoretic Text in spite of differences in translation. For example, the Masoretic Text of 6:10, 14 cites three names—Heldai, Tobijah, and Jedaiah—whose consonants the Septuagint construes as words forming a sentence, not as proper names (see the Exposition of 6:14). In 11:11, two words in the Masoretic Text (*kn ʿnyyy*, thus the afflicted of) are represented in the Septuagint as one word (*Chananaioi*, Canaanites).

Of a more general nature is the Septuagint's *ana meson tōn duo oreōn tōn kataskiōn* (between the shady mountains) in 1:8 for the Masoretic Text's *bên hahădassîm ʾăšer bammĕṣulâ* (among the myrtle trees that were in the valley), evidently reading the letter *reš* (ר) where the Masoretic tradition witnesses to *dalet* (ד) in the word *hădassîm* (myrtle trees). Because of the unlikelihood of two mountains standing in a hollow, the Septuagint translator(s) probably understood the Masoretic Text's *mṣlh* (hollow) to represent an unattested word for shadow based on the root *ṣll* (to grow dark; the noun *ṣl* is a shadow), thus rendering the Septuagint's reading suspicious. The word *mountains* in the Septuagint may have been induced by the similarly colored horses that appear between two mountains in 6:1–3.

The scope of this work does not permit a more detailed study, but these observations should at least support my conclusion that the Masoretic Text of the Book of Zechariah has suffered little in transmission. Many of the differences between the Masoretic and Greek texts indicate that the Septuagint translators struggled with the same problems and text structures as does the modern interpreter of Zechariah. The reader will find other textual problems discussed throughout the commentary, the most crucial of these being the textual problem in 11:13.

Literary Genre

One often finds the term *apocalyptic* applied to the Book of Zechariah. This term, however, is not well defined (Smith, *Micah–Malachi*, pp. 174–75), and we should use it with caution. While other prophetic books (e.g., Ezekiel, Daniel) also receive the designation *apocalyptic*, we may not define them by later Jewish apocalyptic works, but must take them on their own terms, remembering that Jewish apocalyptic is "recognizable as 'the child of prophecy' " (Russell, *Jewish Apocalyptic*, p. 104; but see von Rad, *Old Testament Theology*, p. 303).

To the degree that Zechariah shares certain interests with Jewish apocalyptic writings—such as angels and Satan, a cataclysmic end, the unity of history, judgment on Gentile nations, esoteric symbolism, the ultimate triumph of God—we may call it apocalyptic, understanding that we must not force other distinctives of Jewish apocalyptic into Zechariah without exegetical warrant. This book stands before us as a tapestry of literary types, extending from narrative prose to the depiction of religious experience in shimmering symbols. Whatever designation we give them, Zechariah's symbols represent the deep spiritual experience of a man who understood himself to stand squarely within Israelite prophetic tradition (1:2–6). Like others of his predecessors, Zechariah believed in the sovereignty of Yahweh over history, Davidic messianism, a suffering redemptive figure, the validity of the Abrahamic promise, and Yahweh's conquest of the nations— in short, apart from contemporary concerns, there is little in this book that we do not find in one form or another in the preexilic and exilic prophets. At the same time, we must recognize the uniqueness of the genre of this book, for its style and presentation of theological ideas give it a character that is distinct in Israel's prophetic heritage.

Zechariah 1:7–6:15 is primarily symbolic in nature, whether representing Zechariah's message in cosmic vision or prophetic activity (6:9–15). Viewed from the perspective of a literary type, symbolism has a unique force, impressing itself on the mind and touching the emotions with greater facility and power than prosaic literary types. The symbols in this section of Zechariah are peculiarly appropriate because they convey a perspective that reaches far beyond the immediate concerns of the temple builders. The cosmic symbols impress us with a profound sense of God's activity in history, moving human events to a monumental climax. It is as though we stand above time, observing in the prophet's symbolic language the awesome forces at work in the world that we cannot otherwise perceive.

It is easy to read too much into symbols, and we must be careful to base our conclusions only on text-intentions. If a text does not define a symbol, its significance may not lie within the text's interest. We should not neglect the impetus the symbol had for its immediate audience, for to do so is to uproot the symbol from the ground in which it found life. Using symbols as he did, the prophet weaves a tapestry of redemptive history, portraying in vivid imagery God's work in history.

Another major literary type in this book is the oracle (maśśāʾ) or "burden." In the Wisdom Literature, maśśāʾ can refer to a wise (Prov. 30:1; 31:1) or authoritative (2 Kings 9:25; Jer. 23:33) saying. According to 2 Kings 9:25–26, an oracle is a declaration of God, spoken by a prophet, expressing judgment on an individual (see also 1 Kings 21:19). Jeremiah 23:33 is definitive in this regard, for when anyone asks, "What is the oracle of the LORD?" Jeremiah is to reply, "As for [ʾet] what the oracle is—the LORD will abandon you" (my translation). Jeremiah's use of the term reflects the earlier affirmation of Judah's abandonment in 12:7. The subsequent verses (23:34–37) assert that only one to whom the Lord has entrusted his word can utter an oracle; all others must inquire only as to what the Lord said. The oracle in this context is thus a declaration of God through a prophet, expressing divine judgment. The various oracles in Isaiah 13–30 have the same function, pronouncing divine judgment on non-Israelite nations. In

Zechariah 12:1, the word *maśśāʾ* introduces an extensive prophetic statement that affirms hope for Israel, but in a context of judgment on the nations. (Depending on its extent, the oracle beginning at Zech. 9:1 is similar.)

The word *maśśāʾ* can introduce entire prophetic books. A typical oracle, the Book of Nahum is an extended judgment ode against Nineveh. On the other hand, Habakkuk interweaves divine judgment on the wicked people of his day with ultimate judgment on the Chaldeans. The Book of Malachi also follows this pattern, beginning with judgment on Edom and condemning Malachi's contemporaries for neglecting their duties. There are two features common to the prophetic oracle: it is an authoritative utterance, and it contains pronouncements of judgment.

It is difficult to understand how the noun *maśśāʾ* (oracle) relates to its verbal affinity *nāśāʾ* (to lift, carry). Is it a burden God placed on a prophet, or an utterance that one pronounces (takes up) as one would take up a discourse (e.g., Num. 23:7, 18)? Some scholars perceive a wordplay in Jeremiah 23:33 in which the writer sets *maśśāʾ* over against *nātaš* (to abandon), ostensibly establishing an antithesis between these words that calls for the translation "burden" for *maśśāʾ*. It is not certain, however, that the writer intended such a pun. We observe Yahweh's resolve to abandon (*nātaš*) his people as early in Jeremiah as 12:7, and it is likely that 23:33 simply reflects that statement of divine resolve, referring to it as a *maśśāʾ*. If the writer intended such a pun, we wonder why he did not choose a verb more appropriate to "burden," such as *šālak* (to cast) or *sûr* (to remove). We also cannot be certain that Jeremiah's wordplay in verse 36 (the oracle will be a burden) is definitive or simply a pun. McKane ("משא," p. 40) does not attribute the sense of "burden" to the word *maśśāʾ* in Jeremiah 23:33–40, while de Boer ("משא," p. 214) opines that "in the headings of prophetic oracles *maśśāʾ* means 'burden imposed on. . . .' These headings show us that the term had acquired a technical sense." This technical sense is the argument, thesis, or title of the passage it introduces.

The flexibility in the use of the oracle in the prophets shows that it was not a bound literary form, and we must observe each occurrence of *maśśāʾ* on its own terms. The context of the Zecharian oracles determines what the prophet's burden was. The primary element these oracles share with other prophetic oracles is a preoccupation with judgment on the nations. This

and hope for God's people are the major contextual energies in the Zecharian oracles, and we should study their contents within this conceptual grid.

Integrity

Few books of the Old Testament have received as much critical attention as the Book of Zechariah. While chapters 1–4 and 7–8 have undergone extensive critical analysis (Fohrer, *Introduction*, p. 463), the problem that has received the most attention is the relationship of chapters 9–14 to the rest of the book. Giving them a preexilic provenance, Joseph Meade (1586–1638) assigned chapters 9–11 to Jeremiah on the basis of the free rendering of Zechariah 11:13 that Matthew 27:9 attributes to the prophet Jeremiah. In 1785, William Newcome argued for a preexilic date for chapters 9–11, noting that Ephraim (the northern kingdom) appears to have independent existence in those chapters and that the enemies of the people are Assyria and Egypt. Toward the end of the eighteenth century, scholarly opinion began to move in another direction. In 1797, Corrodi (*Versuch einer Beleuchtung*, p. 107) placed chapters 9–14 well after the time of Zechariah. Eichhorn (*Einleitung*, pp. 444ff.) profoundly influenced Zecharian studies with his contention that 9:1–10:12 is late, comprising an account of Alexander's conquest of Syria–Palestine. He also maintained that chapter 14 was Maccabean in origin, dating it to 161 B.C.

The view that holds the field today is that chapters 9–14 have their provenance in the Greek period. Strongly influencing this view is the striking similarity of the events of 9:1–8 to Alexander's advance through Syria–Palestine in 332 B.C. Egypt appears in this section, possibly pointing to the reign of the Ptolemies over Palestine following the death of Alexander. The Greek Empire, now faded into the past, may have become a prophetic motif for Israel's eschatological enemies (Thomas, *Zechariah*, p. 611).

The structure of Zechariah continues to undergo close scrutiny. Luria ("Seventh Vision") suggests revision of the order of 5:5–11 and 6:9–15, maintaining that the former pericope contains the thought of Joshua the high priest, not that of Zechariah. Following the categories established by Robert Polzin, Hill ("Dating Second Zechariah") analyzes the text of Zechariah 10–14 and concludes that it was written around 515–475 B.C., a span of time within which Zechariah could have lived. Portnoy and Petersen ("Biblical Texts") challenge Y. Radday's and D. Wickmann's application of statistical analysis to the unity of Zechariah and encourage the integration of other methodologies with statistical analysis.

Several scholars take a literary approach to the integrity of Zechariah. In 1961, Lamarche (*Zacharie*) observed a chiastic arrangement of apparently diverse literary units in chapters 9–14. He attributed the arrangement to an author writing around 500–480 B.C., whose intent was to combine the literary pieces into a unified whole, the theme of which is the triumph of the kingdom of God. Baldwin (*Zechariah*, pp. 74–81) presents a superb example of this approach, finding a chiastic structure in the first section of the book as well (pp. 80–81). Baldwin suggests that "Zechariah . . . was also the editor or that the editor was intimately aware of the prophet's style" (p. 81). (For a somewhat similar approach, see Kline, "Structure"; for a critique of Lamarche, see Harrelson's review.)

Childs (*Old Testament as Scripture*, p. 480) observes no "direct literary dependence of 9–14 on 1–8 such as a conscious patterning, midrashic expansion, or a prophecy–fulfillment relationship." He does, however, observe a congruity of subject matter between the two sections (pp. 482–83), concluding that the linking of chapters 9–14 with chapters 1–8 is "to expand, develop, and sharpen the theological pattern of the end time which had begun to emerge in Proto-Zechariah" (p. 483).

Anyone who carefully reads the Hebrew text of Zechariah becomes immediately aware of a change of atmosphere and language in chapters 9–14 (see Ladd, "Prophetic Apocalyptic"). It is as though we enter a different world. No longer do we hear assurances that the nations are at rest (1:11, 15; 2:4 [1:21]; 6:8); rather, we witness the nations in violent upheaval (9:15; 12:9; 14:1–3). Hope for the immediate future, so prominent in Zechariah 1–8, fades in the prophet's doleful portrayal of the nation's rejection (11:10–11). Cosmic visions give way to eschatological pronouncements. We find words in this section we have not encountered before, and the writing style sometimes seems more stilted than that in Zechariah 1–8, lacking, for example, discourse connectors like "this is what the LORD says," "utterance of the LORD," or "then I responded."

The major question facing us is not why Zechariah 9–14 confronts us with these difficulties, but whether its pronouncements are Zecharian. Can we observe enough conceptual discourse hinges to warrant some sort of conclusion regarding the book's structural cohesion? The lack of discourse connectors may be because the divine presence is not as immediate as it is in the previous night visions, where the angel of the Lord engages in dialogue with the prophet. We do not find many such stock phrases in the oracles against the nations in Isaiah 13–23. Since *maśśāᵓ* is primarily a judgment form, the preoccupation of Zechariah 9–14 with the nations may have governed its vocabulary and imagery.

There are two major lines of thought running throughout the book: the sovereignty of God and human responsibility. The book leaves no doubt about the former theme: God will see the temple through to completion and ultimately establish his kingdom. The latter line of thought, however, is a different matter. As the book develops the theme of human responsibility, it begins by reminding us of the earlier generations who failed in their obligation of obedience to the Lord (1:2–6). At the end of the first section, we find a conditional clause encouraging obedience: "This will happen if you diligently obey the voice of the LORD your God" (6:15). The balancing of these two passages creates an atmosphere of suspense as we enter the middle section of the book (chaps. 7–8), for we wonder if the people will again be disobedient, failing to see the bright promises of the kingdom of God that chapters 1–6 foreshadow.

The middle section does not greet us with hope. Rather, we observe a dismal picture of flagging obedience on the part of Bethel's leaders, which elicits an impassioned sermon from the prophet, interweaving divine sovereignty and human responsibility. In it he calls the people to obedience (7:8–10; 8:16–17), again reminding them of the earlier generations (7:11–14; 8:14).

The angel's question in 1:12 creates yet more suspense that carries throughout the book. This question reflects a longing for the upheaval among the nations that will herald the long-awaited kingdom of God. If Zechariah 1–8 was originally a separate work, it would have possessed an unsatisfying conclusion, for the reader would be left wondering when and how this upheaval will occur. A major theme of the first section, after all, is that the nations are at rest. While chapter 8 ends with a positive statement of divine sovereignty, the wavering obedience chapters 7–8 describe nevertheless leaves us wondering whether the people will fall into disobedience as did their forefathers.

It is in Zechariah 9–14 that we learn the answers to our questions. Yes, the people's disobedience will again lead to their dispersal among the nations (11:10). The gloomy clouds that were only on the horizon in chapters 7–8 now cover the sky. The national upheaval the angel of the Lord anticipated (1:12) appears dramatically in Zechariah 9–14, for the two oracles (maśśā') that comprise this section are preoccupied with the nations, and the second is especially concerned with the fact that their tumultuous uprising will herald the kingdom (14:1–9).

Several commonalities link the two major sections of the book, giving a distinctly Zecharian cast to chapters 9–14:

Theme	Zechariah 1–8	Zechariah 9–14
Yahweh's immanency in the sphere of the nations	1:15; 2:12 [8], 15 [11]; 6:8; 8:7	9:1–7, 13; 10:9–10; 11:10; 12:1–4, 9; 14:3, 13–15
inclusion of Gentiles among the people of God	2:15 [11]; 6:15; 8:22	9:7; 14:16
a coming king	6:11–12	9:9
questionable leadership	7:2–3	10:1–3; 11:4–5, 8
divine intervention on behalf of Jerusalem	1:14–17; 2:2–4 [1:19–21], 16 [12]; 8:3–4, 8	12:1–3, 8; 14:4–5, 10
ultimate cleansing from sin	3:4–5, 9	12:10–13:1
security for Jerusalem	2:9 [5]	14:11
upheaval among the nations	1:12 (see the Exposition)	14:2–3

If some themes, such as Yahweh as warrior (9:8, 15; 12:4, 7–9) and the universal reign of Yahweh (14:9), do not appear in Zechariah 1–8, it may be because they are more appropriate to the national interests of the maśśā'.

While these conceptual links do not prove Zecharian authorship of chapters 9–14, Mason ("Proto-Zechariah," p. 238) attributes these commonalities to a group or "related circle of tradition" reflecting "the same essential spirit and outlook of proto-Zechariah." Zechariah 9–14 certainly reflects the hopes and concerns of the prophet and brings Zechariah 1–8 to a satisfying conclusion.

The angel's question in 1:12 finds a startling answer in chapter 14, which pictures the nations rising in tumult. This distinctive postexilic concept of "shaking the nations," which also appears in Haggai (2:7, 22), is thus present in Zechariah 9–14 as well.

The non-Zecharian authorship of Zechariah 9–14 raises interesting questions, but the attention it has received seems to outweigh its importance. The book deals with theological issues prevailing in the time of Haggai and Zechariah and is structurally and conceptually cohesive. Coupled with recent linguistic studies, such as those of Hill, it is not out of the question to place the composition of the entire book within the time that Zechariah ministered to the postexilic community or within a reasonable time thereafter (see Jones, "Fresh Interpretation"). The reference to Greece is not historically anachronistic (Harrison, *Introduction*, pp. 952–53) and may be a motif representing all oppressing powers. What is of utmost importance in this regard is that the whole message of the book speaks to God's people today just as it did in the ancient past.

Theological Themes

Several theological themes transect both major sections of the book. We have already observed the complex theme of divine sovereignty and human responsibility. The latter line of thought encompasses the people's faltering efforts to build their temple and their failing obedience to their God. The prophet declares, however, that God will overcome the disobedience of his people through a pierced figure (12:10; see also 3:4, 9), whose wounding will effect sincere repentance on the part of the people (12:10) and lead to their cleansing from sin (13:1–6).

Another overarching theme is the symbolism of the temple. As we move through the first part of the book, we begin to feel strange stirrings that there is more going on than the building of a structure. If this were the book's only concern, why do we read pronouncements of a coming king and of Gentiles coming in great numbers to Yahweh? At 6:12 we begin to learn the answer, for it is the Branch who will build the temple. The sovereignty of God that brought the temple to completion has established on earth a temple far greater than the one on Mount Zion: the temple that the Branch builds—the kingdom of God—which is resident now in the church and which God will bring to eternal fruition.

Analysis

Select Bibliography

Abel, F. M. "Asal dans Zacharie xiv 5." *Revue Biblique* 45 (1936): 385–400.

Ackroyd, Peter R. "Two Old Testament Historical Problems of the Early Persian Period." *Journal of Near Eastern Studies* 17 (1958): 13–27.

———. "Zechariah." In *Peake's Commentary on the Bible.* Rev. ed. Edited by Matthew Black and H. H. Rowley. New York: Nelson, 1963.

Ap-Thomas, D. R. "Some Aspects of the Root *hnn* in the Old Testament." *Journal of Semitic Studies* 2 (1957): 128–48.

Baldwin, Joyce G. *Haggai, Zechariah, Malachi.* Tyndale Old Testament Commentary. Downers Grove, Ill.: InterVarsity, 1972.

———. "Ṣemaḥ as a Technical Term in the Prophets." *Vetus Testamentum* 14 (1964): 93–97.

Barker, Kenneth L. "Zechariah." Vol. 7 / pp. 595–697 in *Expositor's Bible Commentary.* Edited by Frank E. Gaebelein. Grand Rapids: Zondervan, 1985.

Brichto, Herbert C. *The Problem of "Curse" in the Hebrew Bible.* Society of Biblical Literature Monograph Series 13. Philadelphia: Society of Biblical Literature, 1963.

Bright, John. *A History of Israel.* 3d ed. Philadelphia: Westminster, 1981.

Brongers, H. A. "Some Remarks on the Biblical Particle Hᵃlōʾ." Pp. 177–89 in *Remembering All the Way . . . : A Collection of Old Testament Studies Published on the Occasion of the Fortieth Anniversary of the Oudtestamentisch Werkgezelschap in Nederland.* By B. Albrektson et al. Oudtestamentische Studiën 21. Leiden: Brill, 1981.

Carson, D. A. "Matthew." Vol. 8 / pp. 3–599 in *Expositor's Bible Commentary.* Edited by Frank E. Gaebelein. Grand Rapids: Zondervan, 1984.

Chary, T. *Agee, Zacharie, Malachi.* Sources Biblique. Paris: Gabalda, 1969.

Childs, Brevard S. *Introduction to the Old Testament as Scripture.* Philadelphia: Fortress, 1979.

Clark, D. J. "The Case of the Vanishing Angel." *Bible Translator* (1982): 213–18.

Clifford, Richard J. *The Cosmic Mountain in Canaan and in the Old Testament.* Cambridge, Mass.: Harvard University Press, 1972.

Comrie, Bernard. *Aspect: An Introduction to the Study of Verbal Aspect and Related Problems.* Cambridge: Cambridge University Press, 1976.

Corrodi, H. *Versuch einer Beleuchtung der Geschichte des jüdischen und christlichen Bibelcanons.* Vol. 1. 1792.

Dahood, Mitchell. "Zechariah 9:1: ʿEn ʾAdam." *Catholic Biblical Quarterly* 25 (1963): 123–24.

Davidson, A. B. *Hebrew Syntax.* Edinburgh: T. & T. Clark, 1964.

de Boer, P. A. H. "An Enquiry into the Meaning of the Term משא." *Oudtestamentische Studiën* 5 (1948): 197–214.

Delcor, M. "Les Allusions à Alexandre le Grand dans Zacharie 9:1–8." *Vetus Testamentum* 1 (1951): 110–24.

———. "Deux Passage Difficile: Zacharie 12:1 et 11:13." *Vetus Testamentum* 3 (1953): 67–73.

Eichhorn, J. G. *Einleitung in das Alte Testament.* 3 vols. Leipzig, 1780–83.

Finley, Thomas J. "The Sheep Merchants of Zechariah 11." *Grace Theological Journal* 3 (1982): 51–65.

Fohrer, Georg. *Introduction to the Old Testament.* Translated by David E. Green. Nashville: Abingdon, 1965.

Foulkes, Francis. *The Acts of God.* London: Tyndale, 1958.

Good, R. M. "Zechariah's Second Night Vision (Zech. 2:1–4)." *Biblica* (1982): 56–59.

Gordon, Cyrus H. "His Name Is One." *Journal of Near Eastern Studies* 29 (1970): 198–99.

———. *Ugaritic Textbook.* Rome: Pontifical Biblical Institute, 1965.

Greenfield, Jonas C. "The Aramean God Ramman/Rimmon." *Israel Exploration Journal* (1976): 195–98.

Harrelson, Walter. Review of *Zacharie ix–xiv: Structure Litteraire et Messianism* by Paul Lamarche. *Journal of Biblical Literature* 82 (1963): 116–17.

Harrison, Roland K. *Introduction to the Old Testament.* Grand Rapids: Eerdmans, 1969.

Hill, Andrew E. "Dating Second Zechariah: A Linguistic Reexamination." *Hebrew Annual Review* 6 (1982): 105–34.

Hoftijzer, J. "Remarks concerning the Use of the Particle ʾt in Classical Hebrew." Pp. 1–99 in כה: *1940–1965.* By P. A. H. de Boer et al. Oudtestamentische Studiën 14. Leiden: Brill, 1965.

Honeyman, A. M. "Hebrew סף 'Basin, Goblet.' " *Journal of Theological Studies* 37 (1936): 56–59.

Hyatt, J. Philip. "A Neo-Babylonian Parallel to Bethel-Sar-Ezer, Zech. 7:2." *Journal of Biblical Literature* 56 (1937): 387–94.

Jansma, T. "Inquiry into the Hebrew Text and the Ancient Versions of Zechariah ix–xiv." *Oudtestamentische Studiën* 7 (1950): 1–142.

Jones, D. R. "A Fresh Interpretation of Zechariah ix–xi." *Vetus Testamentum* 12 (1962): 241–59.

Keil, Carl F. *The Twelve Minor Prophets.* 2 vols. Translated by James Martin. Reprinted Grand Rapids: Eerdmans, 1969.

Kline, Meredith. "The Rider on the Red Horse (part I)." *Kerux* 5 (1990): 2–20.

———. "The Structure of the Book of Zechariah." *Journal of the Evangelical Theological Society* 34 (1991): 179–93.

Ladd, George Eldon. "Why Not Prophetic Apocalyptic?" *Journal of Biblical Literature* 76 (1957): 192–200.

Lamarche, P. *Zacharie i–xiv: Structure, Litteraire, et Messianisme.* Paris: Gabalda, 1961.

Lambdin, Thomas O. *Introduction to Biblical Hebrew.* New York: Scribner, 1971.

Lipinski, E. "Recherches sur le Livre de Zacharie." *Vetus Testamentum* 20 (1970): 25–29.

Luria, B. Z. "The Seventh Vision of Zechariah." *Beth Mikra* (1990): 237–41 [Hebrew].

McComiskey, Thomas E. *The Covenants of Promise.* Grand Rapids: Baker, 1985.

———. "Prophetic Irony in Hosea 1:4: A Study of the Hebrew Idiom *Pāqad ʿal* and Its Implications for the Fall of Jehu's Dynasty." *Journal for the Study of the Old Testament* 58 (1993): 93–101.

———. "The Seventy Weeks of Daniel against the Background of Ancient Near Eastern Literature." *Westminster Theological Journal* 47 (1958): 18–45.

McHardy, W. D. "The Horses in Zechariah." Pp. 174–79 in *In Memoriam Paul Kahle.* Edited by Matthew Black and Georg Fohrer. Beihefte zur Zeitschrift für die Alttestamentliche Wissenschaft 103. Berlin: de Gruyter, 1968.

McKane, W. "משׂא in Jeremiah 23:33–40." In *Prophecy: Essays Presented to Georg Fohrer on His Sixty-fifth Birthday.* Edited by J. A. Emerton. Berlin: de Gruyter, 1980.

Marenof, S. "Note concerning the Meaning of the Word Ephah, Zechariah 5:5–11." *American Journal of Semitic Languages* 48 (1931–32): 264–67.

Mason, Rex A. "The Relation of Zech. 9–14 to Proto-Zechariah." *Zeitschrift für die Alttestamentliche Wissenschaft* 88 (1976): 227–39.

May, Herbert G. "A Key to the Interpretation of Zechariah's Visions." *Journal of Biblical Literature* 57 (1938): 173–84.

Meyers, Carol L., and Eric M. Meyers. *Haggai, Zechariah 1–8.* Anchor Bible 25B. Garden City, N.Y.: Doubleday, 1987.

———. *Zechariah 9–14*. Anchor Bible 25C. Garden City, N.Y.: Doubleday, 1993.

Mitchell, H. G. *A Critical and Exegetical Commentary on Zechariah*. International Critical Commentary. Edinburgh: T. & T. Clark / New York: Scribner, 1912.

Naor, M. "Paired Passages in the Bible." *Beth Mikra* 35 (1990): 222–26 [Hebrew].

North, Robert. "Zechariah's Seven-Spout Lampstand." *Biblica* 51 (1970): 183–201.

Petersen, David L. *Haggai and Zechariah 1–8*. Old Testament Library. Philadelphia: Westminster, 1984.

Petitjean, A. *Les Oracles du Proto-Zacharie: Un Programme de Restauration pour la Communauté Juive après l'Exile*. Paris: Gabalda, 1969.

Porteous, N. W. "Jerusalem-Zion: The Growth of a Symbol." Pp. 93–111 in *Living the Mysteries*. Oxford, 1967.

Portnoy, Stephen L., and David L. Petersen. "Biblical Texts and Statistical Analysis: Zechariah and Beyond." *Journal of Biblical Literature* 103 (1984): 11–21.

Rad, Gerhard von. *Old Testament Theology*. Vol. 2. Translated by David M. G. Stalker. New York: Harper & Row, 1965.

Robertson, E. "The Apple of the Eye in the Masoretic Text." *Journal of Theological Studies* 38 (1937): 57–59.

Rubenstein, A. "A Finite Verb Followed by an Infinitive Absolute in Hebrew." *Vetus Testamentum* 2 (1952): 362–67.

Rudolph, W. *Haggai—Sacharja 1–8—Sacharja 9–14—Maleachai*. Kommentar zum Alten Testament. Gütersloh: Mohn, 1976.

Russell, D. S. *The Method and Message of Jewish Apocalyptic*. Old Testament Library. Philadelphia: Westminster, 1964.

Scott, R. B. Y. "Secondary Meanings of ʾaḥar." *Journal of Theological Studies* 50 (1949): 178–79.

Smith, Ralph L. *Micah–Malachi*. Word Biblical Commentary 32. Waco: Word, 1984.

Stuhlmueller, Carroll. *Haggai and Zechariah*. International Theological Commentary. Grand Rapids: Eerdmans, 1988.

Thiele, Edwin R. *The Mysterious Numbers of the Hebrew Kings*. 3d ed. Grand Rapids: Zondervan, 1983.

Thomas, D. Winton. *The Book of Zechariah, chapters 1–8: Introduction and Exegesis*. Vol. 6 / pp. 1053–88 in *The Interpret-*

er's Bible. Edited by George A. Buttrick. Nashville: Abingdon, 1956.

Torrey, Charles C. "The Foundry of the Second Temple at Jerusalem." *Journal of Biblical Literature* 55 (1936): 247–60.

Unger, Merrill F. *Zechariah: Prophet of Messiah's Glory.* Grand Rapids: Zondervan, 1970.

Vriezen, T. C. "Two Old Cruces." *Oudtestamentische Studiën* 5 (1948): 80–91.

Wiseman, D. J. *Illustrations from Biblical Archaeology.* Grand Rapids: Eerdmans, 1958.

Wright, G. Ernest. *Biblical Archaeology.* Philadelphia: Westminster, 1960.

I. An Oracle Urging the Postexilic Community to Turn to God (1:1–6)

McCOMISKEY

1 In the eighth month, in the second year of Darius, the word of the LORD came to the prophet Zechariah son of Berechiah son of Iddo, saying, ²The LORD was very angry with your fathers. ³Now, say to them, This is what the LORD of hosts says, Turn to me, utterance of the LORD of hosts, and I shall turn to you, says the LORD of hosts. ⁴Do not be like your forefathers, to whom the early prophets called, saying, "This is what the LORD of hosts says, Turn from your wicked ways and from your wicked deeds," but they did not listen, and they did not heed me, utterance of the LORD. ⁵Your forefathers—where are they? And those prophets—did they go on living indefinitely? ⁶But my words and my statutes that I commanded my servants the prophets, did they not overtake your forefathers? So they turned and acknowledged, "As the LORD of hosts purposed to do to us in accordance with our ways and in accordance with our deeds, so he has done to us."

NSRV

1 In the eighth month, in the second year of Darius, the word of the LORD came to the prophet Zechariah son of Berechiah son of Iddo, saying: ²The LORD was very angry with your ancestors. ³Therefore say to them, Thus says the LORD of hosts: Return to me, says the LORD of hosts, and I will return to you, says the LORD of hosts. ⁴Do not be like your ancestors, to whom the former prophets proclaimed, "Thus says the LORD of hosts, Return from your evil ways and from your evil deeds." But they did not hear or heed me, says the LORD. ⁵Your ancestors, where are they? And the prophets, do they live forever? ⁶But my words and my statutes, which I commanded my servants the prophets, did they not overtake your ancestors? So they repented and said, "The LORD of hosts has dealt with us according to our ways and deeds, just as he planned to do."

1:1. לְדָרְיָוֶשׁ (of Darius): לְ introduces the genitive (of) as it sometimes does with numerals (GKC §129f). It has a similar function in the superscription to Haggai (1:1). For a discussion of Darius and his reign, see the Introduction and Exposition. הָיָה ... אֶל (came to): See the Exegesis of Hosea 1:1. לֵאמֹר (saying) frequently follows forms of speech denoting communication introducing the content of what is said (Gen. 8:15; 41:16; 2 Sam. 3:18). In these instances, verbs such as דָּבַר (to speak), עָנָה (to answer), or אָמַר (to say) describe the action, and the content of that verbal action follows the

introductory לֵאמֹר. While the collocation הָיָה אֶל (came to) does not connote verbal communication in itself, its association with דָּבָר (word) gives it that function. Since it is the word of Yahweh that came to the prophet, לֵאמֹר (saying) appropriately introduces the content of that word. The qualifying phrase הַנָּבִיא (the prophet) is in apposition to זְכַרְיָה (Zechariah), not עִדּוֹ (Iddo), thus designating Zechariah as הַנָּבִיא. Placing the appellation at the end of such a sequence may create ambiguity with regard to the referent of the qualifying phrase, but since Zechariah was a prophet and Iddo is identi-

---

1:1. Zechariah received the first of his prophetic oracles in 520 B.C., the second year of Darius I Hystaspes. In all probability Darius had quelled the rebellion in his empire by this time (see the Introduction). If so, the year 520 marked a time of relative peace and security in the empire. The second oracle (1:7–17), which, like the first, is dated 520, supports this assessment of the political situation at this time when it declares that "the whole earth remains at peace" (1:11). Thus, Zechariah began his prophetic ministry at a time when the world had heard Babylonia's dying gasps and the nations were at rest—if only for a little while.

This verse draws our attention to an obscure corner of the Persian Empire. Security reigned throughout much of the far-flung dominion of Darius, but not in the little backwater province of Judea. Jerusalem still lay in ruins and its inhabitants, discouraged by the immensity of the task they faced and the apparent failure of cherished theological hopes to materialize, made little progress in their efforts to rebuild their country.

There was more at stake, however, than the failure of the returned exiles to restore their homeland, for the theological crisis that recent events had posed for the community had called into question nothing less than the integrity of Yahweh's word as the prophets had represented it. Haggai, a contemporary of Zechariah, predicted that the restoration of Yahweh's favor to his people would be preceded by an upheaval among the nations (Hag. 2:6–9, 21–23). Now, however, the nations were at rest, for the turmoil in the Persian Empire had quieted down, and even Babylonia, Israel's erstwhile enemy, was powerless. Evidently the recent unrest in the empire was not the "shaking" of which Haggai spoke, and it seemed unlikely that Yahweh was about to restore the nation to its former glory.

In the past, prophets had arisen in Israel to give direction to the nation in times of spiritual and national crisis. Now another prophet joins the ranks of these spokesmen for God. Zechariah felt a divine compulsion to address the plight of his compatriots, and within his prophetic consciousness the divine will began to become intelligible to him. As the desperate circumstances of his time and established prophetic traditions sparked that consciousness, he perceived Yahweh's will for the nation. The word of Yahweh "came to Zechariah." Now there would be direction for the people in a maze of lethargy and spiritual uncertainty.

The introduction calls Zechariah the "son of Berechiah son of Iddo," but the brief genealogies in Ezra 5:1 and 6:14 omit the reference to Berechiah, describing Zechariah only as the "son of Iddo." In all likelihood Iddo was the grandfather of Zechariah, and the genealogies in Ezra omit the name of Berechiah for reasons that are not now readily apparent. (We may observe a similar phenomenon in the references to Jehu's pedigree in 1 Kings 19:16 and 2 Kings 9:2, 14, where the name of Jehoshaphat appears as Jehu's father only in the references in 2 Kings.) We can only speculate why Berechiah's name appears here and not in Ezra (Mitchell, *Zechariah*, p. 82, regards it as a gloss). Perhaps Berechiah died at an early age or had not distinguished himself enough to warrant inclusion in the genealogies in Ezra. Neither do we find Haggai's descent listed in the superscription to his prophecy nor in Ezra 5:1, where he appears along with Zechariah whose ancestor Iddo is cited. Perhaps Haggai's parentage was of humble origin. If Iddo is the priest mentioned in Nehemiah 12:4, 16, the inclusion of his name in Ezra's genealogies would have sufficed to distinguish Zechariah's name. It would not have been necessary to include the name of his father Berechiah.

fied elsewhere only as a priest (Neh. 12:4), the sense here is clear.

2. קָצַף (to be angry) occurs here with a cognate accusative, קֶצֶף (anger). In this syntactical func-tion, a noun derived from the same root as the verb occurs in some position relative to the verb. This supplementation of the verbal action with a derived noun strengthens that action (GKC

---

2. The words of 1:2 encapsulate the first pro-phetic message that Zechariah felt impelled to communicate: "God was angry with your fore-fathers." The remainder of the oracle expands on this statement and may represent the prophet's own reworking of it. The statement recalls the Lord's anger with the disobedient ancestors of the nation's past. Lurking behind this statement is the implication that Yahweh's anger is not con-fined to the previous generations, but could lash out again if the people should follow the same path as their hapless predecessors.

The prophets' view of God's character and activity in the world is not a narrow projection of their own wish-fulfillment of God. They under-stood him to be capable of intense anger as well as of tenderness and mercy. If we fail to comprehend the rich faceting the Old Testament gives to the divine personality, we may end up constructing our own image of God. When that image fails us, we must not think it is God who failed us. If the early generations had acknowledged that Yahweh was capable of burning anger, they would have thought better of their propensity to violate the covenant.

We may wonder why this oracle begins on such a dismal note. Why did Zechariah not remind his discouraged listeners of God's grace instead of his intense anger? Their history con-tained numerous instances of God's gracious intervention on their behalf. In actuality, this reminder of Yahweh's wrath is a dark background against which the gracious invitation of verse 3 shines all the brighter. This oracle affirms that the people could escape the painful reality of divine judgment by turning to their God who, in conde-scending grace, would turn to them as well.

This verse appears to fit loosely into the con-text. The plural suffix on "your fathers" (ʾăbôtêkem) directs the words of this verse to the people without mentioning them previously, and the presence of Zechariah's name coupled with the word lēʾmōr (saying) in verse 1 leads us to expect verse 2 to contain a direct address, not to the people, but to the prophet (the word of the LORD came to Zechariah saying), as in many pro-phetic formulas of this type (e.g., Jer. 1:1–2; 2:1; Ezek. 6:1; 7:1; Jon. 1:1–2; Hag. 2:1–2, 10–11, 20–21; Zech. 6:9). Petersen (*Zechariah 1–8*, p. 129)

observes that the converted perfect wĕʾāmartā (now, say) in verse 3 contributes to the apparent looseness of verse 2 in its setting because this form "requires a preceding verb, something other than the qsp in v. 2." He concludes that "one senses something drawn out of its original context and placed in a new setting."

It is possible that there is a loose connection between verse 2 and its present context, but there are several factors that render the evidence for this possibility somewhat less compelling. In several passages in Jeremiah, the formula of address to the prophet is followed by a plural address to the peo-ple without a previous reference to them. For example, Jeremiah 11:1–2 says, "The word that came to Jeremiah from the LORD: Hear the words of this covenant," and there are similar structures in 18:5 and 27:12 as well. The singular mode of address here, followed by the plural, shows that Jeremiah had all the people in mind when he spoke to the king. In Zechariah 7:8–9, the pro-phetic formula precedes a plural address to the people. The plural form of address following the introductory lēʾmōr (saying) here in 1:2 thus fits comfortably in its setting (but see the discussion at 1:7–8). It is possible that the prophet himself, an amanuensis, or a later hand added the introduc-tory formula of verse 1, but there is no reason to hold that the process materially affected the form or content of the pericope.

Another consideration in this regard is that verse 2 may not comprise a direct statement to the prophet because its function in this text is to encapsulate the theme of the message the prophet received from God. In several prophetic introduc-tory formulas, lēʾmōr stands before a theme state-ment that the oracle goes on to develop, often pre-ceding the ensuing discussion with the formula "thus says the LORD" (as here in v. 3). This is true in Jeremiah 11:1–2, where the command to the people to hear the words of the covenant (v. 2) is the subject of the remainder of the pericope. It is true also in Haggai 1:1–6, where similar textual elements exist and the words of verse 2 referring to the people's lethargy comprise the theme of Haggai's response. The same structure exists in Zechariah 8:1–8, where the theme-statement appears in Yahweh's affirmation of jealousy for his people in verse 2 (see also Jer. 18:5–6 and

§117.9). The word *very* in my translation reflects this function. עַל (with) is commonly associated with this verb (Josh. 22:18), directing the verbal action to (or against) its object, אֲבוֹתֵיכֶם (your fathers). The plural suffix (כֶם‎-) indicates that the text directs these words to the people, not to Zechariah alone.

3. וְאָמַרְתָּ (now say): The translational equivalent one assigns to ו depends on the senses of the clauses it connects. Since the previous clause (v. 2) recalls God's anger with the generation that went into exile and the clause that ו introduces calls for the people to repent, the conceptual connection is "therefore" or "in the light of this." The succinct "now" in my translation is an effort to reflect this sense. The perfective וְאָמַרְתָּ with affixed ו does not appear to sustain a syntactical relationship with קָצַף (was angry), for it functions as an imperative here (GKC §112aa) and does not require a preceding verb (see the Exposition of v. 2). In 1 Kings 2:6, for example, a perfective with

functions in a similar fashion. After a description of Joab's treachery (v. 5), the context goes on to advise appropriate action (v. 6: וְעָשִׂיתָ [now act]). Its connection to the previous verse is to command an action in view of the preceding observation. The consecution required by ו here is similar. The command to speak to the people is a consequence of the previous affirmation of Yahweh's anger. יהוה צְבָאוֹת (the LORD of hosts) has a military connotation, depicting Yahweh as the commander of the hosts of heaven (Josh. 5:13–15; Isa. 13:4). This name depicts Yahweh's might, which may be displayed among the nations (Pss. 46:7–8 [6–7]; 59:6 [5]; Isa. 13:4) or in the life of an individual (Ps. 69:7 [6]). שׁוּבוּ (return): שׁוּב basically means "to change direction," but may be nuanced as to "return" or "turn back" (frequently with מִן, from) and to "turn away" or "restore." The prophets use this word to express the idea of turning to God or turning away from evil. נְאֻם (utterance) is a nominal form that frequently appears in the prophetic

---

27:12). Here in Zechariah 1:1–6 the words of verse 2 concerning the Lord's anger against the fathers is the subject of the subsequent plea extending through verse 6.

That *wĕʾāmartā* (now, say) lacks a preceding verb more appropriate in form or connotation than *qāsap* (was angry) does not necessarily indicate a loose connection with the context (see the Exegesis of v. 3). All in all, this introductory formula answers in form and content to other such prophetic formulas. Its function is to introduce the author of the collection of oracles (see Baldwin, *Zechariah*, p. 88, for the suggestion that "to Zechariah" was originally "to me").

3. The mode of address now moves from the plural "your" on "your fathers" (*ʾăbôtêkem*) in verse 2, to the singular "now, say" (*wĕʾāmartā*). This singular construction represents Yahweh addressing Zechariah and reflects the prophet's consciousness of the divine impulsion he felt to call the nation to repentance. *Waw* on *wĕʾāmartā* establishes a juxtaposition of clauses that is at once subtle and shocking. The apparently oblique reference in verse 2 to the Lord's anger with distant generations takes on a startling directness for Zechariah's community in this verse as it becomes the background for his plea to them to return to the Lord. Verse 2 is not a mere reference to the Lord's anger; it is a reminder of it. At the same time, it pictures Yahweh's anger as distant thunder rumbling in the past. There is still hope for the future, for the storm may be averted.

We are surprised that the prophet must call the people to return to the Lord, for his call implies that the wrath of God remains a threat to them. Could they so soon have fallen into disobedience? From the prophetic perspective, they had. They were not greatly different from their forebears. The temple foundation, standing unfinished, symbolized to both Zechariah and Haggai a deep-seated rebellion against Yahweh and the cultus that bound the people to him. Zechariah observed a growing lack of concern on the part of the people for their spiritual obligations (chaps. 7–8). Clearly, if the community was to survive, it needed to return to its Yahwistic heritage.

The prophet's plea to return to the Lord rings with divine authority. It is the "utterance of the LORD." The people were not to return to a weak tribal god, but to "Yahweh of hosts." Their God commanded the armies of heaven. The people had only to turn to Yahweh to experience his help on their behalf. "Turn to me" is Yahweh's gracious call to his people. Prophetic religion is not legalistic (Hos. 6:1–3; Mic. 6:6–8). The object of the people's spiritual renewal is Yahweh, who loves, remains faithful, eschews evil, and requires loyalty. In repentance they would find respite from their miserable condition.

One thing stood between them and destruction: a willingness to turn *from* the ways that had brought their fathers into exile and turn *to* a gracious God. The New Testament echoes the same

books to introduce divine declarations (see the comments at Joel 2:12 and Amos 2:11).

4. אַל־תִּהְיוּ (do not be): The negated jussive expresses a negative command. מִדַּרְכֵיכֶם (from your ways): דֶּרֶךְ (way) is a neutral term in the range of moral values. Depending on the context, the plural may connote either right or wrong, as do the two occurrences of רַע (wicked) here. For the second term in the clause, the *Qere* has וּמַעֲלְלֵיכֶם (i.e., וּמַעַלְלֵיכֶם, and your deeds), understanding the noun as מַעֲלָל (deed). The *Kethiv* has וּמַעֲלִילֵיכֶם, understanding the noun as עֲלִילָה (deed). The Masoretic Text points מ with *patah*, but, if pointed with *sere*, the resultant *Kethiv* (מֵעֲלִילֵיכֶם) becomes consonant with the repetition of מִן (from), which is common in compound clauses such as this (Gen. 12:1; Jer. 25:5; Jon. 3:8; the use in Isa. 58:13 appears to be an exception, but עֲשׂוֹת is a simple permutative). The masculine plural ending may seem anomalous on this feminine noun, but several feminine nouns (אַלְמָה, אֵימָה, שָׁנָה) take both feminine and masculine terminations (GKC §87m, n, q). Some Ugaritic nouns have a similar function (Gordon, *Ugaritic Textbook*, pp. 54–55). שָׁמְעוּ (lit., hear) is frequently translated "obey" (Gen. 3:17; Exod. 24:7; Josh. 1:18; Isa. 42:24). הִקְשִׁיבוּ (to heed): Qal קָשַׁב has the meaning "hear" (Isa. 32:3). Hiphil קָשַׁב frequently means "to give careful attention" (Prov. 2:2; Isa. 21:7). When this form occurs in connection with terms

for God's law or human response to God, it connotes obedience (1 Sam. 15:22; Neh. 9:34; Isa. 48:18; Jer. 6:19; Zech. 7:11). Here, the reference to the former prophets' call for repentance signals obedience to their plea.

5. אֲבוֹתֵיכֶם (your forefathers) resumes the previous reference to the forefathers. וְהַנְּבִאִים (and those prophets): I have translated the definite article on this form as "those" because it defines a substantive already cited in the immediate context, namely, הַנְּבִיאִים (the prophets) in verse 4. הַלְעוֹלָם (indefinitely): The word עוֹלָם denotes an indefinite expanse of time. The contexts in which it occurs invest it with various perspectives. It may connote antiquity (Deut. 32:7; Isa. 58:12), continuous existence (Jer. 18:16; Ezek. 25:15), or futurity (Lev. 25:32; Deut. 15:17). When the preposition לְ accompanies עוֹלָם, as here, its perspective is future from the standpoint of the entity the context describes—here, the early prophets. The interrogative ה expects a negative answer (GKC §150d). יִחְיוּ (did they go on living?) modifies the substantive הַנְּבִיאִים (prophets), which the context (v. 4) places in the past (הָרִאשֹׁנִים, the early [prophets]). Since it is a nonperfective verb, its aspect spans an entire period, viewing that period in its extension, not as an aspectual whole (perfective). The form הַלְעוֹלָם (indefinitely) creates an energy in this context that requires this nonperfective sense (see the discussion of the Hebrew conjuga-

message: Jesus said, "unless you repent, you will all perish" (Luke 13:5).

4. Once again, the text recalls the past generations who went into exile because of their disobedience. They serve as a warning as Zechariah recalls their stubborn refusal to heed the prophets of their day (see also 2 Chron. 36:15–16). This text summarizes the words of those prophets: "Turn from your wicked ways and your wicked deeds." These words resemble most closely Jeremiah's call to repentance (18:11; 25:5; 35:15). The plural "prophets" signals, however, that Zechariah had several prophets in mind. Perhaps he intended to summarize the pleas of all the prophets who ministered up to the fall of Judah, shaping those pleas in the framework of Jeremiah's language because he prophesied on the cusp of the exile. His prophetic word was the last the people heard before the initial wave of deportees went into exile.

This verse closes with the dismal observation that the early generations did not heed these prophets. As a result, they lost their inheritance, the land of ancient promise. Under the new cove-

nant, the inheritance of the believer is not a literal land, but according to Hebrews 3–4 it is the rest that the gospel offers (McComiskey, *Covenants of Promise*, pp. 199–209). As with the people of old, obedience to the gospel guarantees the continued enjoyment of our inheritance in Christ (John 12:26; 13:17; Col. 1:22–23; Heb. 3:6, 14; 6:11–12; 10:36; Rev. 2:10).

5. The force of the first rhetorical question in 1:5 is that their forefathers are no more. This is clear from the dynamic interplay of the clauses in this binary structure; we expect them to share a common concept. Since the second interrogative clause clearly asserts that the early prophets no longer exist, the thrust of the first question is similar. These questions imply that the generations that went into exile are no longer accessible and that the voices of the prophets who ministered to them are silent. These people and their spiritual leaders no longer belong to the world of reality. We must look to the next verse to learn the force these questions have in this section.

tions in *IBHS*, pp. 455–563). The translation above is an effort to reflect these functions of this verbal form. Imperfect (nonperfective) verbs frequently denote past action (GKC §107b).

6. אַךְ (but) frequently introduces restrictive clauses: the former generations passed away, but (אַךְ) Yahweh's word was an exception that continued to be effective. This particle may also function as an asseverative: "surely" (Smith, *Micah–Malachi*, p. 182; but see the Exposition). דְּבָרַי (my words): The combination of דָּבָר (word) with חֹק (statute) is Zecharian. Since צִוִּיתִי (I commanded) governs both דְּבָרַי and חֻקַּי (my statutes), they rep-

resent standards of obedience. There is little or no appreciable difference between these words in this context, functioning together as a word-pair that encompasses the whole of the prophetic message. הֲלוֹא (did not?) expects an affirmative answer (GKC §150e). הִשִּׂיגוּ (they overtake) has the basic sense of "overtake" in all its occurrences in the qal. וַיָּשׁוּבוּ (so they turned): The basic sense of "turn" (see v. 3) is evident here. In the qal this word always denotes the action of turning in relation to an entity stated or implied in the immediate context. Prepositions frequently enhance its function. When no preposition accompanies the

---

6. The sense one assigns to the particle *ʾak* that begins this verse depends on the thread of the discourse in verses 5–6 (see the Exegesis). One possibility is to regard the particle as an asseverative, giving it the meaning "surely." This may seem valid in view of the preceding rhetorical questions in verse 5 and may be paraphrased like this: "Your fathers and the early prophets, where are they? They no longer exist. *Surely* my word overtook your fathers in the exile, and they acknowledged the justice of their punishment." The implication is that the captivity brought the early generations and their prophets to an end.

This view, however, does not answer to all the elements of the discourse. It does not explain the function of the rhetorical question concerning the prophets. Why does the writer observe that they, too, no longer exist? And what complements the reference to the prophets in the symmetrical relationships of the subsequent context? The text-intention of this oracle is the validity of the prophetic word. The observation that the prophets no longer exist does not contribute measurably to this idea.

The translation "but" for *ʾak* fits the discourse more comfortably, a view that may be paraphrased, "The fathers and their prophets no longer exist in the world of reality, *but* there is a reality in this world where one generation rises and another falls—it is the 'words and statutes' that the prophets proclaimed."

The context underscores the reality of the prophetic word in two ways. One is that this word overtook (*nāśag*) the fathers (v. 6). That is, the prophets' warnings burst into sudden reality when the exile occurred. The second element is the fathers' admission of the reality of the divine word. They acknowledged that the prophetic warnings about their wicked ways and deeds (v. 4) were valid. The fathers and their prophets no

longer existed in Zechariah's time, but the exile witnessed to the validity of the prophets' words, and the reality of the exile lived on.

The use of *dābar* with reference to the prophets ("my words and my statutes") introduces us to the Old Testament theology of *word*. The word of Yahweh sometimes appears as a force active in the world and in the community of Israel: Yahweh's word can do good (Mic. 2:7); it can heal (Ps. 107:20) as well as fall upon a nation (Isa. 9:7 [8]); the word is a destructive fire (Jer. 5:14; 23:29); and it translates into events (Ezek. 12:28). Thus, personification and metaphor unveil an underlying theology of divine activity in this word. Here Yahweh's word is a force that can "overtake" (*nāśag*). It did this when the enemy swept in upon the people, taking them captive.

When the captivity occurred, the people had to admit the awful reality of the prophets' warnings ("so they turned"). Hosea also said that the people would acknowledge that their failure to fear the Lord had led to their demise as a nation (see the Exegesis of Hos. 10:3). The words ascribed to the people do not necessarily imply heartfelt repentance, for they do not state that the people returned to the Lord. They say no more than that the people acknowledged the error of their previous assessment of God's dealing with them and admitted that their behavior was the cause of their misfortune. (Petitjean, *Les Oracles*, pp. 50–51, understands verse 6b to be a confession used before the exile that continued in use in the postexilic period.) The purposes of God, which for centuries had found expression only in prophetic word, suddenly took shape in actual event. The prophets had been right after all. Even Moses, the greatest of the prophets, foresaw the exile: "The LORD will bring you . . . to a nation that neither you nor your ancestors have known" (Deut. 28:36). The people and their self-serving prophets had protested that God

verb (as here), the action of the verb is abstract: the people turned, that is, they changed their original assessment of the perceived facts. כַּאֲשֶׁר (as) occurs with כֵּן (so) in this context to introduce comparison. The measures God took in punishing his people were not arbitrary but completely in accord ("as . . . so") with what he had purposed for them. זָמַם (purposed) describes a process of cognition in which the thought focuses on some object. Context enhances the nuancing of this verb. In Proverbs 31:16, for example, the woman focuses her thought on a field, and in Psalm 31:14 [13], the parallel structure gives the word the sense of scheming. Here, the context gives the word the sense of God's purpose to punish the nation for its sin. כִּדְרָכֵינוּ וּכְמַעֲלָלֵינוּ (in accordance with our ways and in accordance with our deeds): The *kap* affixed to each of these substantives means "in accordance with," designating the factor that shaped the divine purpose. The intention of Yahweh to punish the nation was an action appropriate to the people's behavior.

would not allow his people to go into captivity (Jer. 26:6, 9, 11; Mic. 3:5–7), but the painful reality of the exile changed that assessment.

God's judgment on his people was not arbitrary, but measured and weighed in accordance with their "words and deeds." The Mosaic law set the standard for the people's obedience to God, but they forsook the law. One of the functions of the new covenant is to facilitate obedience (Jer. 31:33). Jesus, the mediator of the new covenant (Heb. 9:15), called for obedience on the part of his followers: "Blessed . . . are those who hear the word of God and obey it" (Luke 11:28); "If you love me, you will keep my commandments" (John 14:15).

This oracle is a gracious call to repentance. Zechariah's God is the God of the eighth-century prophets, who is at once just and loving and calls the people to all that his promises entail. The reality of the exile should have been enough to motivate the spiritual renewal to which Zechariah called the people. The builders learned that if God was to be actively present among them, they needed to turn to him.

II. First Vision: Riders among the Myrtle Trees (1:7–17)
A. Introduction of the Riders (1:7–10)

McCOMISKEY

[7]On the twenty-fourth day of the eleventh month, that is, the month of Shebat, the word of the LORD came to the prophet Zechariah son of Berechiah son of Iddo, saying, [8]I looked in the night, and there was a man mounted on a sorrel horse, and he was stationed among the myrtle trees that were in the hollow, and behind him were sorrel, spotted, and white horses. [9]And I asked, "What are these, my lord?" And the angel who spoke to me answered me, "I will show you what these are." [10]Then the man stationed among the myrtle trees continued, and he said, "These are [those] whom the LORD has sent to range throughout the earth."

NRSV

[7]On the twenty-fourth day of the eleventh month, the month of Shebat, in the second year of Darius, the word of the LORD came to the prophet Zechariah son of Berechiah son of Iddo: and Zechariah said, [8]In the night I saw a man riding on a red horse! He was standing among the myrtle trees in the glen; and behind him were red, sorrel, and white horses. [9]Then I said, "What are these, my lord?" The angel who talked with me said to me, "I will show you what they are." [10]So the man who was standing among the myrtle trees answered, "They are those whom the LORD has sent to patrol the earth."

7. See the Exegesis of verse 1 for several terms in this verse: לְדָרְיָוֶשׁ (of Darius), הָיָה . . . אֶל (came to), and הַנָּבִיא (the prophet).

8. הַלַּיְלָה (in the night) may connote several ideas. Petersen (*Zechariah 1–8*, p. 138) suggests that this construction refers to "this night just past, i.e., last night" (also Stuhlmueller, *Zechariah*, p. 63). Keil (*Minor Prophets*, p. 228), on the other hand, views it as an accusative of duration: "during the night of the day described in ver. 7." Only a slight nuance distinguishes these views. If, however, the oracle (vv. 9–17) existed independently of the prophetic formula (v. 8) until the process of compilation joined them, הַלַּיְלָה would not have had a previous reference, functioning only as an accusative of time or duration: "I saw by night" or "I saw during the night." The sense of progression that the discourse gives the narration of the visions (i.e., the *waw*-clauses and the sequence of references to the prophet lifting up his eyes; 2:1 [1:18]; 5:1, 5; 6:1) complements the view that הַלַּיְלָה is an accusative of time or duration (NIV: "during the night I had a vision"). The absence of a preposition with לַיְלָה (night) does not preclude the possibility that this construction is an accusative of duration (as it is in Neh. 4:16 [22];

for other accusatives of time with the article, see Jer. 28:16; Hos. 4:5 [הַיּוֹם]). וְהִנֵּה (and there was) draws our attention to the central character in this scene: אִישׁ (a man) receives fuller identification in verse 11, where we learn that this figure is an angel. Context determines whether רֹכֵב means "mount" (Gen. 24:61) or "ride" (1 Kings 1:44). Here, the figure was mounted or stationed (עֹמֵד) among the myrtle trees, not riding forth. אָדֹם (sorrel) connotes various shades of red (Gen. 25:30; 2 Kings 3:22). Here, it probably describes a reddish-brown (hence "sorrel"), as in the case of the "red [אָדֹם] heifer" in Numbers 19:2. הַהֲדַסִּים (the myrtle trees): The myrtle is common to Palestine and often reaches a height of thirty feet. בַּמְּצֻלָה (in the hollow): The several forms based on the root צוּל connote depth. While this form of the root occurs only here, it is clear that the context indicates a tree-grown depression, such as a valley floor or a hollow. The Masoretic tradition construes this noun as definite, "the hollow," but it is fruitless to attempt to identify it as some locale in the environs of Jerusalem familiar to the writer and his readers. In a consonantal text, the form could be indeterminate, and the context does not develop the identity of the location. Since this

---

7. The second oracle, like the first, begins with the date of its reception. Here, however, the date is more specific than the notation in 1:1, stating the day as well as the month. The reference to the twenty-fourth day is significant, for it was five months earlier to the day that the people had resumed work on the temple (Hag. 1:14–15). They had responded to Zechariah's call to turn to God (Zech. 1:3) and had demonstrated their commitment by five months of arduous labor. Now, in prophetic vision, divine sovereignty and human agency meet as God assures the people of the success of their work.

It is unusual to find *lēʾmōr* (saying) introducing the account of an event ("I saw in the night"), not verbal communication. That a similar prophetic formula lacking this word precedes such an account in 7:1–2 makes the presence of *lēʾmōr* here in 1:7 suspicious, and it is possible that *wayyōʾmer* (and he said) stood here originally. Since, however, no textual support exists for this emendation, we must consider another possibility. The formula here in 1:7 differs from the one in 7:1 in that the latter introduces a factual account (vv. 2–3), not divine revelation. Only when the prophet feels impelled to speak for God (v. 4) do we find *lēʾmōr* introducing God's words (v. 5).

Since *lēʾmōr* in 1:7 introduces the entire sequence of night visions, it creates an energy in this discourse that imparts to the visions the sense that they comprise verbal revelation from God. The representations of direct divine speech in these visions, as well as the numerous occurrences of the formula *nĕʾum yhwh* (utterance of the LORD) and the explanatory role of the angel of the Lord, are consonant with this function of *lēʾmōr*.

8. This verse introduces the "night visions" that dominate the first part of the book. The prophet tells us that during the dark hours, visions began to form in his mind (May, "Zechariah's Visions," p. 173). The opening words of this first vision create an atmosphere of foreboding. Powerful steeds stand shrouded in gloomy shadows. We do not feel that all is right. But we must wait until the vision unfolds.

It is fruitless to inquire what the myrtle trees may signify. Such speculation goes beyond the dimensions of the text. Perhaps their function is only to create atmosphere. It is also fruitless to give significance to the colors of the horses. The text has no interest in this (but Kline, "Red Horse," assigns identities to symbolic elements in this vision; see also Barker, "Zechariah," p. 611). Revelation 6:2–8 gives the colors of its horses

text is a description of a vision, it is unlikely that this hollow was a well known location. In all likelihood, the gloomy, tree-shrouded ravine contributes a sense of mystery and portent to the surreal picture of these sweating steeds that have just returned from their cosmic surveillance. שְׂרֻקִּים (spotted) is difficult to define. The root indicates red in several cognate languages, but this sense is unlikely in view of the preceding term. Arabic possesses a related root that connotes mixed colors. In Isaiah 16:8, this word indicates "grape clusters." If Zechariah's use of the word does not indicate red, it may describe a spotted or cluster-like formation on the coats of these horses. Since the horses in 6:1–8 are somewhat similar in their coloring to these, the horse here would correspond to the one called בְּרֻדִּים (spotted) in 6:3 (see the Exegesis of this verse).

9. וָאֹמַר (and I asked): Functioning as a clausal connector, ו appears at the beginning of each major clause in verses 9–15 and thus marks verses 8–15 as a logical unit. מָה־אֵלֶּה (what are these?): אֵלֶּה refers to the horses. It is the function of these figures that the text is concerned with. אֲדֹנִי (my lord) connotes a superior (Gen. 45:8; Neh. 3:5). The basic meaning of הַמַּלְאָךְ is "messenger"

(1 Sam. 6:21; 16:19; 2 Kings 1:2; Mal. 3:1). Since the messenger here interprets the vision for the prophet and since מַלְאָךְ is associated with the Lord in verse 11, I understand the word to designate a heavenly messenger. The construction הַדֹּבֵר בִּי (lit., the one speaking to me) differentiates the angel who mediates the vision from the figures in the background (see the Exposition). In all but one (5:1–4) of the visions in which this angel plays a role (1:14; 2:2 [1:19]; 2:7 [3]; 4:1, 4, 5; 5:5, 10; 6:4), this formula designates the mediating angel. The more common way to express "speak to" is דָּבַר plus אֶל (to) or עִם (with), but דָּבַר בְּ can convey that sense (Num. 12:6, 8; Hab. 2:1) and may be translated "speak by" (2 Sam. 23:2; 2 Chron. 18:27) or "speak in" (Jer. 20:9; 22:21; 26:15; Ezek. 36:6; Zech. 13:3). While the sense of speak by (or through) seems appropriate in this verse, which expresses prophetic activity (see the comments on Hos. 1:2), the context does not require it, for the prophet is not thinking of himself as a communicator but as an observer, for he must ask what it all means. The sense of "speak to" for the collocation thus adequately describes the dialogue between the angel and the prophet. מָה־הֵמָּה אֵלֶּה (what are these? lit., what are they—these [fig-

---

symbolic meaning, but there the significance of the colors is important to the text's intention. A text need not draw on all the symbolism of an apocalyptic motif. Here, Zechariah uses these figures only as cosmic observers. This verse does not acknowledge the presence of riders on the other horses, but there must have been such riders because verse 11 tells us that they spoke to the rider on the sorrel horse. Since this principal rider is an angel (v. 11), we may assume that the other riders are angels as well. That the text does not refer overtly to them imparts to these figures an ethereal quality that adds to the mystery of this night vision.

9. Since the text incorporates no other figure between the introduction of the man on the sorrel horse (v. 8) and the prophet's wondering question, "What are these, my lord?" (v. 9), it is natural to conclude that the question is addressed to this rider, not another angelic figure who stands apart mediating the vision. If we posit the existence of a separate informing angel, it is difficult to understand why the text forces our attention to the man on the sorrel horse. This figure draws the prophet's attention first, and the text distinguishes him from the other riders by placing them behind him (v. 8). This figure identifies the other

riders (v. 10) and receives their report (v. 11); his function is to explain the vision's symbolism (v. 10). He is not an integral part of the major symbol of this vision—the varicolored horses—for here in verse 9 he refers to these horses as "these." It is as though with a sweeping gesture he points to the horses, explaining their function, but he does not ride forth with them (v. 11). There is no compelling evidence for the presence of a separate informing angel in the sequence of visions in 1:7–2:5 and 3:1–6:8 (see the Exposition of 1:10, 13; but see Clark, "Vanishing Angel").

The question "what are they, these [figures]?" (NRSV: "what is the meaning of these seven ewe lambs?") inquires after the symbolic significance of the riders. We learn that they were a sign of good faith, and the question anticipates the function these figures have in the vision, which is why the words of verse 10 answer as they do.

The reference to "the angel who spoke to me" (*hammalʾāk haddōbēr bî*) may appear to be a studied effort to differentiate the rider on the sorrel horse from a mediating angel, but this is not necessarily the case. While the writer could have easily avoided ambiguity by omitting the words *the angel who spoke to me*, allowing only *wayyōʾmer* (and he said) to stand in the text, these

ures]?): אֵלֶּה (these) is the principal pronominal designator, carrying more force in the question than הֵמָּה (they). The formation is similar to הָאֵלֶּה מָה הֵנָּה שֶׁבַע כְּבָשֹׂת (lit., what are they—these seven sheep?) in Genesis 21:29 (see the Exposition).

10. וַיַּעַן (then continued; lit., and he responded) illustrates the broad function of עָנָה (to answer, respond) in that it follows a declarative statement, not a question. If one holds to the presence of a separate mediating angel in verse 9, וַיַּעַן will then indicate response to that angel's intent to explain the significance of the horses. If, however, the informing angel and the principal rider are one and the same, this construction linking two declarative statements nearly equals our use of "and [the speaker] continued," for it sustains a dual perspective by acknowledging the preceding statement while introducing the subsequent one. הָעֹמֵד (stationed): See verses 8 and 11. אֵלֶּה (these) picks up the preceding אֵלֶּה in the prophet's question in verse 9. לְהִתְהַלֵּךְ בָּאָרֶץ (to range throughout the earth): Hithpael הָלַךְ (to walk) has a sense often indistinguishable from the qal. If it possesses a distinct function in this context at all, it is to facilitate the expression of the verbal concept *range throughout* (although Ps. 73:9 gives a similar sense to qal with בְּ). בְּ (throughout) defines the sphere of the verbal action. That the earth is in view calls for a translation like "range throughout."

---

words may function as another element in this discourse that underscores the distinction of this rider from the others (see the Exposition of v. 10).

10. The identification of the figure in this verse as the one "standing among the myrtle trees" may also appear to differentiate him from the figure in verse 9, who is described as the angel who "spoke to" the prophet. It is not necessary to make this distinction, however, for both statements may just as easily refer to the same figure. In fact, the intention of the words *the man standing among the myrtle trees* may be to identify this figure with the mediating angel in the previous verse. The context delineates clearly only one speaker in the vision, namely, the rider on the sorrel horse (see below, v. 13).

Since *wayyaʿan* is not the primary verb for "saying" in this text but connects declarative statements (see the Exegesis), I understand it to mean "continue." If this is correct, it supports the suggestion that the figures of this and the preceding verse are the same, for this figure continues here the speech he began in verse 9.

The rider on the sorrel horse explains the mission of the other riders: the Lord has sent them to traverse the earth. We need not think that such figures exist or that this event ever took place in reality. It is an element in this vision that has as its primary purpose the communication of the prophetic word. This cosmic foray is the catalyst for the vision's message that the empire is enjoying relative peace.

II. First Vision: Riders among the Myrtle Trees (1:7–17)
B. Response of the Angel of the Lord to the Riders (1:11–12)

McCOMISKEY

[11] Then they addressed the angel of the LORD who was stationed among the myrtle trees and said, "We have ranged throughout the earth, and the whole earth is at rest and undisturbed!" [12] And the angel of the LORD responded and said, "O LORD of hosts, how long will you continue not to have compassion on Jerusalem and the cities of Judah with which you have been angry these seventy years?"

NRSV

[11] Then they spoke to the angel of the LORD who was standing among the myrtle trees, "We have patrolled the earth, and lo, the whole earth remains at peace." [12] Then the angel of the LORD said, "O LORD of hosts, how long will you withhold mercy from Jerusalem and the cities of Judah, with which you have been angry these seventy years?"

11. וַיַּעֲנוּ (then they addressed): וּ (then) functions simply as a clause connector, but because it introduces another element in the sequential development of this discourse, "then" answers nicely to that function. The context gives עָנָה the idea of responding in the broadest sense. Here, the riders respond not to a question, but to the sense of anticipation that the angel's description of their function (v. 10) creates. מַלְאַךְ יְהוָה (the angel of the LORD): See the Exposition. הָעֹמֵד (who was standing) recalls the same form in verses 8 and 10, where it also describes the man stationed among the myrtle trees. The use of the term here thus identifies the rider stationed among the myrtle trees as the מַלְאַךְ יְהוָה (the angel of the LORD; see the Exposition). הִתְהַלַּכְנוּ (we have ranged): See the Exegesis of verse 10. וְהִנֵּה is an untranslated mark of emphasis, which I attempt to reflect with a comma and an exclamation mark. יֹשֶׁבֶת connotes various ideas related to verbal action of settling, such as sit, dwell, or remain, but does not inherently mean "to dwell in peace." The text achieves this force by juxtaposing יֹשֶׁבֶת with the following participial construction: וְשֹׁקֶטֶת (and undisturbed). וּ then signals a syntactical connection between the verbal actions of these participles. Qal שָׁקַט always means "to be undisturbed": a land undisturbed by war (Josh. 11:23), a city undisturbed following the death of Athaliah (2 Kings 11:20), the world undisturbed when Yahweh uttered his voice (Ps. 76:9 [8]), and the unborn Job undisturbed by troubles (Job 3:11–13). The semantic ranges of the two participles overlap tangentially, each depicting the sense of quiet security that pervaded the empire in Zechariah's time.

12. וַיַּעַן (and responded): The use of עָנָה throughout verses 10–12 demonstrates its broad semantic range of responding to a condition or situation (Ps. 20:2, 7 [1, 6]; Isa. 41:17; Hos. 14:9 [8]), introducing an action appropriate to or corresponding with that condition or situation (see the commentary on Hos. 2:23–25 [21–23]). Here the angel's reaction is an appropriate response to the situation described in verse 11. תְּרַחֵם (will you continue to show mercy): In its secular uses, the verb רָחַם (to show mercy) indicates awareness of the misfor-

---

11. The angelic speaker is now described as "the angel of the LORD." In some Old Testament passages, this angel is identified with God (Gen. 16:11, 13; Judg. 6:11, 14; 13:21–22), but in others he is distinguished from God because God speaks to him (2 Sam. 24:16; 1 Chron. 21:18, 27) or because the angel of the Lord speaks to God (Zech. 1:12). These factors oppose the possibility that the angel of the Lord always represents a visible appearance of God. The view that this angel represents a preincarnate appearance of Christ lacks evidence and is largely analogical. The evidence best supports the view that the angel of the Lord is a representation of Yahweh in a way that actualizes his immanence, but not in direct theophany. Here, the angel symbolizes the divine presence, and the interplay between this angel and Yahweh (v. 12), between Yahweh and the angel (v. 13), and between the angel and the prophet (v. 14) enhances this vision by establishing the Lord's direct involvement in and understanding of the plight of his people.

The riders in this verse echo the principal rider's explanation of their mission. From their cosmic perspective, they observe that the earth is enjoying relative peace. The report of this condition would appear to be good news for the temple builders but, as we shall see in the next verse, the rider on the sorrel horse did not regard it so.

12. How ungrateful the angel's response sounds to us! The peace that reigned throughout the empire created a context in which the people could work unhindered by threat of attack or preoccupation with national unrest. The angel of the Lord, however, seems disappointed that the empire is now at peace and interprets this news as an indication of God's delay in coming to the aid of his people.

A belief distinctive to postexilic theology—that the kingdom would dawn only after an upheaval among the nations—justifies the angel's response (see the Exposition of v. 1). For many inhabitants of the empire, the report of the riders would have been good news, but to the returned exiles it signified that the prophetic word was yet to go unfulfilled. They had crossed miles of the Transjordanian wilderness with the voices of the prophets ringing in their ears—voices that described in stirring language the triumphant rule of Yahweh. The current peace in the empire dampened the hopes of the postexilic community and must have weakened their faith and resolve. The angel's disappointment thus reflects the community's disappointment. They, too, wondered, "How long?"

The angel's question implies that the delay of the kingdom was a delay of divine compassion. Jerusalem and the other cities of Judah seemed still the objects of God's wrath because there was

tune of others and a sympathetic response to their distress (1 Kings 8:50; Isa. 13:18; Jer. 42:12). The same holds true in its theological uses (Deut. 13:18 [17]; 2 Kings 13:23; Mic. 7:19). That רָחַם frequently occurs with object suffixes or the direct object marker (אֵת), as here, underscores its association with the display of kindness. Since the sympathetic response the angel desired is from a superior (God), I translate the word "show mercy." The use of "continue" in my translation reflects the sense of the imperfective form of this verb.

זָעַמְתָּה (you have been angry): It is difficult to distinguish זָעַם from other words connoting anger; its semantic range includes bringing divine anger into reality (a curse; Num. 23:7–8) and angry looks with no intention of overtly displaying that anger (Prov. 25:23). The context here calls for a tangible display of God's anger, for it refers to the calamity the nation had experienced in the captivity. זֶה (these) is singular, viewing the seventy years as a period of time (Gen. 31:38, 41).

---

no evidence that he was intervening to help the returnees. The rubble in the streets and the inescapable lethargy that plagued the people indicated to them that God continued to be angry at them for their disobedience. They could still fail in their efforts.

The seventy years to which 1:12 refers are those that spanned the time between the fall of Jerusalem (587 B.C.) and the year when Zechariah received this oracle (520 B.C.). Since this totals sixty-seven years, Zechariah evidently rounded off the figure. The seventy years cannot refer alone to the period of the exile, which ended with the decree of Cyrus in 538 B.C., because the angel's question, "How long will you continue not to show mercy . . . these seventy years?" shows that the span of time during which God withheld mercy from Israel extended to Zechariah's present. The circumstances that witnessed to the lack of divine mercy were contemporary with this oracle, namely, the unbuilt temple (v. 16) and the lack of national welfare (v. 17).

II. First Vision: Riders among the Myrtle Trees (1:7–17)
C. Response of the Lord to the Angel (1:13–17)

McCOMISKEY

¹³And the LORD answered the angel who spoke to me [with] good words—comforting words. ¹⁴And the angel who spoke with me said to me, Proclaim, saying: This is what the LORD of hosts says, I am jealous for Jerusalem and for Zion with great jealousy, ¹⁵and I am enraged at the nations that are secure. For I was angry only a little, but they intensified the disaster. ¹⁶Therefore, this is what the LORD says, I will turn to Jerusalem with compassion. My house shall be built in it, utterance of the LORD of hosts, and the measuring line shall be stretched over Jerusalem. ¹⁷Again proclaim, saying, This is what the LORD of hosts says, Again my cities will overflow with good, and the LORD shall again comfort Zion and again choose Jerusalem.

NRSV

¹³Then the LORD replied with gracious and comforting words to the angel who talked with me. ¹⁴So the angel who talked with me said to me, Proclaim this message: Thus says the LORD of hosts; I am very jealous for Jerusalem and for Zion. ¹⁵And I am extremely angry with the nations that are at ease; for while I was only a little angry, they made the disaster worse. ¹⁶Therefore, thus says the LORD, I have returned to Jerusalem with compassion; my house shall be built in it, says the LORD of hosts, and the measuring line shall be stretched out over Jerusalem. ¹⁷Proclaim further: Thus says the LORD of hosts: My cities shall again overflow with prosperity; the LORD will again comfort Zion and again choose Jerusalem.

13. The precise sense of טוֹבִים in this text is difficult to determine. We may conclude only that it signals a positive response from Yahweh. We must wait to learn more about its content. The substantive נְחֻמִים (comforting) underscores the positive nature of Yahweh's response and is in apposition with another substantive (דְּבָרִים), "words that are comforting." The appositive supplies further information about its companion word (*IBHS*, p. 230).

14. וַיֹּאמֶר (and said) introduces the direct speech initiated by וַיַּעַן (and answered) in verse 13. קְרָא (cry out) does not introduce the content of Zechariah's announcement, a function the text gives to לֵאמֹר (saying). קְרָא (cry out) initiates the act of verbal communication in which the prophet engaged. The semantic range of קָרָא is broad: name (Gen. 1:5; 16:11; 29:35), summon (Exod. 2:7), proclaim (Exod. 33:19; Lev. 23:21), cry out (1 Kings 13:4), read (Deut. 17:19), call for (Ezek. 38:21), and call upon (Gen. 4:26). In statements such as the one here, where it occurs without an object and preposition in an announcement-saying, the word connotes audible communication (Isa. 6:4; 40:3, 6; 58:9; Ezek. 9:1; Zech. 7:13), generally given in a loud voice (i.e., "cry out"). יְהוָה צְבָאוֹת (the LORD of hosts): See the Exegesis of verse 3. קִנֵּאתִי לְ (I am jealous for): The contexts in which קָנָא (to be jealous) occurs give it several nuances: lacking tolerance for a rival or competitor and vigilantly guarding a person or object. The context here does not favor one nuance over another, for it affirms that Yahweh is intent on guarding and caring for his people (v. 16), and the connecting antithetical clause (v. 15) establishes that the nations are not rivals for the affections of Yahweh. That the Lord is jealous for Zion indicates that his purposes for it remain intact and that he has not shared his loyalty with others. That קִנֵּאתִי (I am jealous) is a perfective, connoting a complete situation, implies that Yahweh's allegiance to his people is an established fact that did not have its inception only at the moment of the oracle. וְלִצִיּוֹן (and for Zion): לְ (for) channels the action of the verb קָנָא to צִיּוֹן

---

13. The answer to the angel's plaintive question is positive and comforting. It signals the fact that God will again have compassion on his people. The sovereign God is about to meet the feeble efforts of the builders and bring their work to completion. But this favorable response by God came only after the people themselves responded in a willing spirit and laid their hands to the task. God's people will accomplish nothing for his kingdom as long as they are inactive. God will use even the feeblest efforts as long as they stem from a spirit of willing obedience.

This verse virtually places beyond doubt the identification of the man on the sorrel horse as the mediating angel (see the Exposition of v. 10). The use of ʿānâ (answered) following the question of verse 12 guides us naturally to the conclusion that ʿānâ conveys the answer to that question. Verse 13 directs the answer to "the angel who spoke to me," identifying this mediating angel with the angel of the Lord in verse 12. Since verse 12 identifies the questioner as "the angel of the LORD," who in verse 11 is "the one who was stationed among the myrtle trees" (see also v. 8), the principal rider must be the angel who throughout the series of dramatic visions speaks to the prophet, mediating the visions and explaining their perplexing symbols to him.

14. The angel commands Zechariah to announce that the Lord is jealous for Jerusalem and Zion. There is no measurable distinction between Jerusalem and Zion in the syntactical structure in which these names occur. Zion has a more expansive sense in Zechariah (see 2:11 [7]), but at this point in the prophecy there is no indication that it means anything more than Jerusalem, as in 8:3 (see the Exposition of 1:17).

The people thought that the stability the Persian Empire was enjoying indicated that God had turned from them to look favorably on the nations. The community's miserable failures would have strengthened that conviction. That the angel's words address the question of Yahweh's fealty to his people shows that they doubted his loyalty. The affirmation that he was jealous for them was indeed comforting, for the nations were not, after all, a rival for Yahweh's promises and redemptive love, and he would continue to watch vigilantly over his people.

The text evinces a self-conscious effort to emphasize the intensity of Yahweh's jealousy for his people (see the Exegesis). The use of the cognate accusative along with the word *great* creates a sense of intense devotion and loyalty to the people on Yahweh's part. The response of the people to the prophet's plea in verse 3 did not create Yahweh's emotions of jealousy, for the perfect tense *qinneʾti* (I am jealous) indicates that it was already an established fact. The people's response of heart and hand enabled the Lord to demonstrate his positive feelings and translate them into palpable

(Zion) as well as to יְרוּשָׁלַ͏ם (Jerusalem), allowing for the possibility that these entities were in some way distinct in the mind of the writer (see Jer. 34:1, where לְחֵם עַל [to fight against] governs distinct entities). A compound prepositional structure in Zechariah 9:10 balances the distinct geographical entities Ephraim and Jerusalem (which have in common only their being metonymies for the people of God). In similar compound prepositional structures, however, it is impossible to determine if the writer posits a significant distinction between Mount Zion and Jerusalem (Isa. 10:12; 24:23; Joel 3:5 [2:32]). The context alone determines the sense of Zion here (see the Exposition). קִנְאָה (with jealousy) is a cognate accusative (see the Exegesis of v. 2). גְדוֹלָה (great) strengthens even further the intensity of the cognate accusative structure.

15. וְקֶצֶף (and with great anger): קֶצֶף (anger) is a noun (see v. 2 for its sense) functioning as a cognate accusative with קֹצֵף (enraged). My translation ("I am enraged") is an effort to reflect the intensity of the accusative (see GKC §117). גָדוֹל (great) balances גְדוֹלָה (great) in the previous verse and also contributes to the translation "I am enraged." The context gives the participle קֹצֵף a sense of contemporaneity with the events it describes. הַשַׁאֲנַנִּים (that are secure): שָׁאַן (secure) describes several concepts, all related to the idea of security (Ps. 123:4; Isa. 32:9, 18; 2 Kings 19:28 influences this word in the direction of security that leads to an improper attitude). Some clausal relationships governed by אֲשֶׁר require a causal

sense: "in that" or "for" (Gen. 30:18; Num. 20:13; Deut. 3:24). This context requires a similar causal sense because the reason for God's anger appears in the apodosis of this אֲשֶׁר clause. אֲנִי (I) occurring here with an inflected verb is intensive and establishes a contrast with the following pronoun הֵמָּה (they). ו (but) introduces a measure of contrast with the statement of the preceding clause and thus requires an adversative sense. הֵמָּה, like אֲנִי in the previous clause, accompanies an inflected verb (עָזְרוּ, they intensified) and is also intensive, rounding out the contrast between Yahweh and the nations. Basically meaning "to help" (Josh. 1:14; 1 Sam. 7:12; Ps. 118:13), עָזַר here forms a collocation in which לְ channels the action of the verb to its indirect object. In translation there is no appreciable difference in sense between the collocation and the verb construed with object suffixes. The collocation states literally, "[they] helped the evil." That is, they abetted the calamity. Since this statement occurs in a construction that contrasts Yahweh's role in the disaster with that of the nations, "intensified" is an appropriate translation of עָזְרוּ: The Lord was angry only a little, but the nations helped the disaster along—they furthered or intensified it. רָעָה (the disaster) may connote ethical evil (Deut. 31:18; Isa. 47:10) as well as distress or disaster (Isa. 47:11; Jer. 51:60, 62; Ezek. 7:5). The context clearly requires the latter sense because the captivity is in view; to assign even a small role to Yahweh in an event that the prophet judged to be morally evil would impugn Yahweh's character and belie the

---

progress in the work of building the temple and rebuilding the nation.

15. The angel meets the community's uncertainty about Yahweh's attitude toward the nations by assuring Zechariah that the Lord is angry with these nations. The security of the Persian Empire is not an indication that Yahweh has violated the trust of the community by transferring his loyalty to their former enemies. So far is he from looking favorably on these nations that he is enraged at them, not merely angry.

The angel describes these nations as secure. This reference to the stability of the empire does not imply that the security of the nations was the cause of Yahweh's anger; rather, it reveals the underlying doubts the community had about God's loyalty to them. The dismal situation in Jerusalem did not mirror the general progress of the rest of Darius's empire.

Zechariah's contemporaries might have questioned the words that the text puts on the lips of Yahweh: "I was angry only a little." The exiles had lost their homes; most never saw their country again; and they suffered humiliation at the hands of hostile powers. If this represents mild anger, what would the full display of Yahweh's wrath have wrought?

The answer to that question is apparent: it would have meant the extermination of God's people forever. That would have marked the limits of his anger. Such a display of divine wrath, however, would have violated Yahweh's fealty to his word. The community's traditions rang with affirmations of his ultimate loyalty to his people (e.g., Lev. 26:44–45). From the prophet's perspective, Yahweh's anger did not reach its full extent, but the nations that drove the people into exile exceeded acceptable bounds in the treatment of their captives. The captor nations were culpable

prophet's contention that the captivity was just recompense for the nation's wrong (1:3–6).

16. לָכֵן (therefore) introduces the result of Yahweh's anger against the nations. Because of the culpability their oppressors accrued (v. 15), the Lord will show compassion on his people. שַׁבְתִּי (I will return) is a perfective verb, likely connoting certainty. The collocation שׁוּב לְ- (turn to) may indicate "return to" as well as "turn to." Since this text does not allude to or develop the idea of Yahweh's past residence in Jerusalem but emphasizes the display of his compassion and mercy (v. 17), the translation *turn to* satisfies the linguistic demands of this text. The use of the two passive verbs—יִבָּנֶה (shall be built) and יִנָּטֶה (shall be stretched)—rather than first-person active verbs, which would represent God as building the temple, seems a studied attempt to avoid the idea of his actual presence in the city. The emphasis of this oracle is not on Yahweh's return to his once-forsaken people, but on the restoration of his love and pity toward them—emotions that his people had not experienced during the nearly seventy years that had elapsed since Yahweh had led them out of exile. בְּרַחֲמִים (with compassion): רַחֲמִים is always plural. This plurality, while difficult to understand, may represent the intensive plural or designate the several internal organs that the ancients regarded as the seat of the emotions. This latter possibility finds support in constructions where רַחֲמִים is the subject of the verb כָּמַר (to grow

warm; Gen. 43:30; 1 Kings 3:26). If this plurality designates the physical organs governing emotion, we can understand Proverbs 12:10, which says that the רַחֲמִים of the wicked are cruel (unless this is an oxymoron). The Septuagint translates רַחֲמִים in this verse by σπλάγχνα (internal organs). In all other texts, however, the word represents a positive emotion of concern, and the one occurrence of qal רָחַם (Ps. 18:2 [1]) yields "to love." Only when רַחֲמִים occurs with verbs such as עָשָׂה (to do; Zech. 7:9) and נָתַן (to give; Jer. 42:12) does it mean "acts of compassion." בֵּיתִי (my house) is the temple as the residence of deity (as in 2 Sam. 7:13; Zech. 4:9). נְאָם (utterance): The root נאם occurs as a finite verb only in Jeremiah 23:31, where it has the sense of speaking a prophetic oracle. In all other occurrences, this root has the nominal (or participial) form נְאֻם and always designates an utterance that the writer attributes to God (Gen. 22:16) or a prophetic oracle (Num. 24:3, 15; Jer. 23:31). This form adds a note of divine authority to the prophet's assuring words. יְהוָה צְבָאוֹת (the LORD of hosts): See the Exegesis of verse 3. וְקָוֶה (and the measuring line): *Qere* has קָו (measuring line), but the orthographic representation קוה in the consonantal text of 1 Kings 7:23 and Jeremiah 31:39 (*Qere* קָו) increases the likelihood that קוה is an alternate form of the word, not a textual corruption. There is no appreciable difference in meaning between the terms.

---

in the eyes of Yahweh, and he was enraged by the cruel excesses of the Assyrian and Babylonian armies. By their cruelty, the invaders intensified what was a just judgment on Yahweh's disobedient people. Isaiah refers to the intensity of the captors' treatment of the exiles when he addresses the Babylonians with these words: "I was angry with my people. . . . You showed them no mercy; on the aged you made your yoke exceedingly heavy" (47:6).

16. The spark that fired Yahweh's compassion for his people is the cruel treatment they suffered at the hands of their captors. This is the implication of *lākēn* (therefore) at the head of this verse (see the Exegesis). The Lord did not respond out of loyalty to his promise or to his people according to this verse; there is nothing theological here. The text speaks only of Yahweh's pity for his people, and this emotion is a sympathetic response to their suffering (Hos. 11:8). Theologically, he was loyal to his promise and through it to his people, but that is not the interest of this text. It is divine

compassion that the angel longed for (v. 12), and this verse assures the prophet that God's heart is not cold toward them but warm with compassion. It was not the exile that motivated the Lord to pity his people, for that was just; rather it was the inhumane treatment they received from their captors, for that was cruel.

As a result of Yahweh's compassion for his people, they will complete the temple and Jerusalem will continue to expand as the builders stretch their lines across rubble-strewn land, marking out plots and measuring walls. Thus God will accomplish what the people so desperately desire: a temple and a secure city in which they can build their homes. The people's frustrating inaction will come to an end, and divine enablement will bear them along. God's assistance, motivated by his sympathy for the plight of the people, was the sovereign act that removed the psychological and physical barriers that had hindered the work to this point. Now the labor of the

17. עוֹד (again): For the syntactical function of this particle, see the comments at Hosea 3:1. Here, עוֹד signals a sequencing that gives a measure of independence to the statement it introduces (see the Exposition). קְרָא (proclaim): See the Exegesis of verse 14. מִטּוֹב (with good): מִן denotes motion away from. The cities will flow *from* good in the sense that the overflowing streams this metaphor depicts have their source in divine goodness. וְנִחַם (shall ... have mercy): All piel occurrences of נחם indicate comforting (e.g., Gen. 37:35; Job 2:11; Isa. 40:1; Jer. 31:13; Zech. 10:2). The idea of God comforting the people as a political entity is solely prophetic (Isa. 12:1; 40:1; 52:9). וּבָחַר (choose): There is no appreciable difference between בָּחַר with (Num. 16:5; Deut 4:37; 12:11)

or without (Exod. 18:25; Num. 16:7; Deut. 12:14, 26) בְּ, both meaning "to choose." On occasion the use of בְּ with בָּחַר has the syntactical function of giving greater clarity and definition to the object in complex sentences (e.g., Num. 16:5; Deut. 12:11, 18). If בָּחַר appeared in this clause without בְּ, the clause could read, "And Jerusalem will again choose." The use of בְּ designates the direct object and avoids confusion on the part of the reader. The verb בָּחַר always describes the action of designating as one's own. צִיּוֹן (Zion): The companion word in the parallel structure is יְרוּשָׁלַם (Jerusalem), making it clear that צִיּוֹן refers to the city of Jerusalem, not the temple mount alone (see the Exegesis of 1:14).

---

people would result in success as they cooperated with a willing and all-powerful God.

17. The angel commanded Zechariah to make a second proclamation. The words *again proclaim* indicate that this verse states an assertion different in some way from the first proclamation. If there were no differentiation in the content of the two proclamations, there would be no need for the text to use the word *again (ʿôd)*. The force of this word signals another aspect of God's comforting words to his people.

One way the second proclamation differs from the first is its expanded scope. It turns from the temple and the city that housed it to the outlying areas, envisioning cities other than Jerusalem. From this the people learned that they would no longer struggle to maintain an insecure foothold in the land, but they would enjoy a restoration to full landedness. Another difference is the affirmation of "good" in the second proclamation (see below). This proclamation also depicts Yahweh's activity in a different light: he will comfort his people and again choose Jerusalem.

The expanded concept of the land has an underlying theological force, for the land was an important element in the promise that God made to the patriarchs and reiterated to David (McComiskey, *Covenants of Promise*, pp. 42–55). The affirmation that the people would inhabit the cities of the land affirmed God's loyalty to his covenanted oath (Gen. 15:17–21). The people probably would not have thought on this level. They were interested in building their homes and reestablishing their nation; apart from God's promised intent to establish his people in the land, however, they were doomed to fail even at these tasks.

The promise of landedness may seem irrelevant to the Christian, but it is a part of the everlasting promise, and the new covenant interprets landedness in a way that affirms its continuing validity to all who are under its jurisdiction. The new covenant defines the promise of landedness in both a territorial sense and a spiritual sense. In Romans 4:13, Paul states that landedness is a world conquered by Christ, and Hebrews 3–4 states that landedness is the rest those who are in Christ enjoy (see the Exposition of 1:4). That thousands upon thousands have found spiritual rest in the gospel of Christ affirms God's continued allegiance to his promise. The circumstances of landedness, defined as they are by a new and better covenant (Heb. 7:22; 9:15), have changed, but God's loyalty to his purposes has not veered in the slightest degree. He still promises rest and security to his people.

The cities will again overflow with good, a concept that appears several times in Deuteronomy, where it represents more than economic prosperity; it has to do with the thriving of families as well as of the nation (28:11; 30:9). Here it refers to economic prosperity because it is cities that overflow with good. There is nothing in this section that indicates that the writer had Deuteronomic concepts in mind. The abundance of good this text promises is national welfare.

Once again, the Lord will comfort Zion. The word *again (ʿôd)* points to an earlier time when Yahweh comforted his people, but the text does not specify this time. It is enough to know that the period of estrangement from his warm concern is at an end. The deep longing for Yahweh's consolation, which the angel reflects in verse 12, will be met with God's gracious activity on behalf of the struggling community.

The Lord will also choose Jerusalem again. The implications of this thought are shocking, for it forces the reader to the conclusion that, for a time, God had ceased to designate the nation as his own. We wonder about God's steadfastness and his loyalty to his promises, for God had in fact disowned his people if only for a time. (This is the force of the names of Hosea's children: Lo Ammi ["Not My People"] and Lo Runamah ["Not Pitied"].) God could let a generation fall from his grasp, but he was bound by his own word not to let them perish as a nation. And Gentiles were yet to enter the sphere of redemption, and one from this nation was to die on a lonely hill outside Jerusalem—God could not let his people perish. The theological concepts that find expression in this time are startling. The begrimed people lifting timbers into the wall and laying stone upon stone were symbols of God's sovereign love for his people throughout all generations.

Once again, the writer pairs Zion and Jerusalem with no apparent difference in meaning. It may seem that Zion is in parallel with "cities of Judah," thus designating the entire population, but this is not the case. The parallel structure consists of two conceptually united clauses:

And the Lord shall again comfort Zion,
and again choose Jerusalem.

The second clause corresponds only to the words *again have mercy on Zion* in the first clause, not to *my cities*. These companion clauses also share several common elements: each describes an act of the Lord, and each contains the particle ʿôd (again), as well as an object of divine activity (Zion and Jerusalem). They are thus conceptually and structurally parallel.

This vision contributes to the overarching theme of the book by encouraging the people in their building efforts. The world was at rest; they could work unhindered by political interference or threat of war. The vision spoke as well to their deep psychological needs. Their uncertainty about God's attitude toward them drained their resolve. Now they listened to the words of one whom they regarded as God's spokesman. He assured the people that God had not forsaken them and that their feeble efforts would meet with success. The knowledge that God was with them in their labors made the difference for the discouraged community. Jesus also assured his church of his continued presence (Matt. 28:20) and encouraged them to greater awareness of that presence (Matt. 18:20; John 15:4–5).

III. Second Vision: Four Horns and Four Workers (2:1–4 [1:18–21])

McCOMISKEY

2 And I lifted up my eyes and looked, and there were four horns, ²and I asked the angel who spoke to me, "What are these?" And he said to me, "These are the horns that scattered Judah, Israel, and Jerusalem." ³Then the Lord showed me four workers. ⁴And I asked, "What are these coming to do?" And he replied, saying, "These are the horns that scattered Judah to the extent that one could not lift one's head, but these have come to terrify them—to strike down the horns of the nations that lift up a horn against the land of Judah to scatter it."

NRSV

¹⁸And I looked up and saw four horns. ¹⁹I asked the angel who talked with me, "What are these?" And he answered me, "These are the horns that have scattered Judah, Israel, and Jerusalem." ²⁰Then the Lord showed me four blacksmiths. ²¹And I asked, "What are they coming to do?" He answered, "These are the horns that scattered Judah, so that no head could be raised; but these have come to terrify them, to strike down the horns of the nations that lifted up their horns against the land of Judah to scatter its people."

2:1 [1:18]. וָאֶשָּׂא (and I lifted up): ו (and) continues the unbroken sequence of light narrative particles beginning in 1:8 and ending at 2:9 [5]. This sequence indicates that the writer viewed the visions in this lengthy section sequentially, comprising a logically unbroken unit. וְהִנֵּה (and there was): See the Exegesis of 1:8. אַרְבַּע (four): See the Exposition. קְרָנוֹת (horns): קֶרֶן designates the focus of strength of a horned animal and occurs metaphorically on occasion to depict strength. In Hannah's prayer (1 Sam. 2:1–10), it occurs in its metaphorical sense, as it does in Jeremiah 48:25, where

the horn represents the power of Moab (see also Pss. 75:11 [10]; 92:11 [10]). The defensive power of a horn finds expression in 2 Samuel 22:3 (see also Ps. 18:3 [2]).

2 [1:19]. הַמַּלְאָךְ הַדֹּבֵר בִּי (the angel who spoke to me): See the Exegesis of 1:9. זָרָה (to scatter, winnow, fan): There is no need to posit a metaphorical sense for זֵרוּ because the context requires only a reference to the dispersing of the people into exile. אֶת־יְהוּדָה אֶת־יִשְׂרָאֵל וִירוּשָׁלָם (Judah, Israel, and Jerusalem): These entities all represent postexilic Judah (see the Exposition).

2:1 [1:18]. Zechariah becomes conscious of another vision forming before him. The mysterious riders and their varicolored horses fade away as four animal horns demand the prophet's attention. Perhaps they were in motion, thrusting about and creating a sense of foreboding in the prophet's mind. The horns represent the might of nations (see the Exegesis), and the number *four* has a sense that goes beyond its numerical value.

In the Old Testament, the association of the numeral *four* with the points of the compass gives it a sense of extensiveness or comprehensiveness. In Isaiah 11:12, this number designates the farthest reaches of the earth: "He will . . . assemble the outcasts of Israel . . . from the four corners of the earth," and Ezekiel 7:2 states that "the end has come upon the four corners of the land" (see also Rev. 20:8). In keeping with this are the several references to the four winds (Jer. 49:36; Ezek. 37:9; Dan. 7:2; 8:8; 11:4; Zech. 2:10 [6]). Four is sometimes the climactic number in expressions designating indefinite extent or comprehension. For example, it is for "three transgressions . . . and for four" that divine punishment will fall on the nations (Amos 1:3–2:6; see also Jer. 15:3). Multiples of four such as forty (Deut. 25:3; Ezek. 29:11–13; Jon. 3:4) and four hundred (Gen. 15:13) may also express the idea of comprehensiveness. In the Book of Revelation, the figure 144,000 comprehends the vast numbers of the redeemed (14:1)

Since the function of numbers in apocalyptic literature is not always to enumerate but to convey a symbolic concept appropriate to the extended sense of the numeral (McComiskey, "Seventy Weeks," pp. 35–45), the use of the number *four* in this vision does not require us to search for two countries besides Assyria and Babylon that were complicit in scattering Israel and Judah. As a matter of fact, the text studiously avoids identifying the horns with specific countries, omitting from its description the common

symbol for nations, namely, animals (note the use of various animals to designate nations in Dan. 7–8). The four horns appear in isolation from animal bodies as symbols sufficient to themselves, comprehending the totality of the power the nations of the world possess.

2 [1:19]. The perplexed prophet turns to the angel to inquire about the mysterious horns. Once again, he must ask what the figures represent, and the angel replies that these are the horns that "scattered Judah, Israel, and Jerusalem." It does not require a profound knowledge of apocalyptic symbolism to understand what this figure would have meant to the postexilic community. They would have understood the horns to represent the totality of forces that effected the tragedy of the exile, scattering the people to a far-off land. The text goes no farther; we know only that this vision confronts us with the inexorable events before which the nation fled helplessly into exile.

The Exegesis suggests that Judah and Israel were one in the mind of the writer, and thus "Israel" does not refer to the fallen northern kingdom. This view gains support from 2:4 [1:21], which cites only Judah as the object of the nations' destructive power, as well as from the postexilic prophecy of Malachi 2:11, where we encounter the same place-names: "Judah has been faithless, and abomination has been committed in Israel and in Jerusalem." Israel must refer only to postexilic Judah, because Malachi 2:11 addresses contemporary concerns and goes on to cite only Judah for wrongdoing. Thus, in Malachi the name *Israel* continues to reflect the sense of national identity and heritage it had in earlier times (1:1, 5; 2:16; 3:22 [4:4]), and it is clear that the exilic and postexilic communities continued to apply the name *Israel* to themselves (see Zech. 8:13; 9:1; 11:14; 12:1; and numerous examples in Ezekiel).

The use of "Israel" in this vision would remind the postexilic community of their patriarchal her-

3 [1:20]. וַיַּרְאֵנִי יְהוָה (and the LORD showed me): For the significance of this statement, see the Exposition (see also the commentary on Amos 7:1). אַרְבָּעָה (four): See the Exposition of verse 1. חָרָשִׁים (workers) connotes various types of artisans: engravers (Exod. 28:11), metalworkers (1 Sam. 13:19), and woodworkers and stoneworkers (2 Sam. 5:11). The emphasis here is not on their craftsmanship, but on their destructive force.

4 [1:21]. וַיֹּאמֶר (and he replied) has as its closest logical referent יְהוָה (the LORD) in verse 3; it is unlikely, however, that Yahweh is the subject of this verb (see the Exposition). אֲשֶׁר־זֵרוּ אֶת־יְהוּדָם (that scattered Judah) identifies the horns only with Judah; the northern kingdom is not in view. כְּפִי (to the extent that, in accordance with): Having the literal sense of "according to the mouth of," this construction connotes "in accordance with." The expression צֶל־פִּי in Genesis 43:7, for

example, has the sense of: "we answered *in accordance with* these questions." That is, the answers conformed to the questions. Here, כְּפִי introduces the extent of the reaction of the people to the devastation of the exile: one could not lift his head—a reaction in accordance with or in proportion to the fall of Judah at the hands of hostile forces. לֹא־נָשָׂא רֹאשׁוֹ (could not lift his head): The expression נָשָׂא רֹאשׁ may have the sense of lifting the head in honor (Ps. 24:7, 9) or in a menacing manner (Judg. 8:28; Job 10:15; Ps. 83:3 [2]). In negative clauses it connotes the opposite action of bowing in humiliation, and that is the sense here in Zechariah. לְהַחֲרִיד אֹתָם (to terrify them): Hiphil חָרַד (to make afraid; Lev. 26:6; Judg. 8:12; Job 11:19) is not coordinated by ו with its companion form לְיַדּוֹת (to strike down) and so creates an appositional structure in which the two infinitive clauses (to terrify, to strike down) overlap, thus showing that the action of terrifying is not a mere

---

itage and their history, which was rich with evidence of divine favor and assistance. Since this use of "Israel" in association with "Judah" in this vision does not encompass the exile of the northern kingdom (Israel), but only that of Judah, it renders even more tenuous efforts to find four nations that drove the former generations into exile (see the Exposition of 1:14).

3 [1:20]. Four workers now appear in the vision. We picture them with sinewy arms, and we imagine heavy hammers in their strong grasps. Perhaps they are smiths whose arms are blackened from working at the forge. It is clear that they represent powerful forces at work in the world, but we must wait for the explanation until the next verse. The numeral *four* again indicates that the forces they represent are comprehensive in nature.

We learn here that it is the Lord who initiated this vision ("the LORD showed me"), not the angel (3:1). The angel's function was to explain the visions to the often perplexed prophet (1:9–10; 2:1 [1:19]; 2:4 [1:21]; 2:8 [2:4]; 3:8–10; 4:6–7, 14; 5:3–4, 6–8, 11; 6:5–6, 8). That the Lord caused Zechariah to see these visions is consonant with 1:7, which tells us that "the word of the LORD came to Zechariah."

4 [1:21]. The prophet wonders what these workers will do, not what they are. The explanation he receives is introduced by *wayyōʾmer* (and he replied), the nearest logical referent of which is *yhwh* (the LORD) in verse 3. Since, however, it is the mediating angel who explains the visions throughout (see the Exegesis of 2:3 [1:20]), there is

no reason why we cannot understand the dialogue between the mediating angel and Zechariah to continue unbroken in this pericope.

We learn that the horns are the forces that dispersed Judah into captivity. Only Judah appears here, giving credence to the conclusion that "Israel" does not refer to the erstwhile northern kingdom. The text does not identify the historical forces that caused the exile, and we should not go further than the text permits. To this point in the vision, the four horns represent the full extent of human cruelty, military might, political machinations, lust for power—whatever else we can imagine—which destroyed preexilic Judah.

The sense of this vision, then, is that any military action against postexilic Judah is doomed to fail. It does not necessarily rule out future military or political interference in Judah's internal affairs, but affirms that any such intervention will not be successful. The restored nation was about to enjoy respite from another dispersion, but it is sad to observe that a later prophetic oracle in this book nullifies this guarantee (11:10). Like the previous oracle, this one encourages the builders in their work, for the strictures God had placed on the surrounding nations permitted the people to build unhindered by the threat of interference in their internal affairs.

We wonder why God places strictures on the nations of the world so that an obscure group of discouraged people could build a temple. Reading farther, however, we find that we cannot limit this text only to the exile of Judah, for if the horns

threat without consequence, but an actual intervention in time in which the terror the horns inspire is actualized in the destruction of the might of nations. The masculine suffix אֹתָם (them) referring to the feminine הַקְּרָנוֹת (horns) is not unusual (Davidson, *Hebrew Syntax*, p. 2). Piel יָדָה occurs only here and in Lamentations 3:53 (where the context supports "cast down"). The Septuagint understands לְיַדּוֹת as the plural of יָד (hand; see the Introduction). Good ("Zechariah's Second Night Vision") understands the word to designate a fold for animals. קַרְנוֹת הַגּוֹיִם (horns of the nations) establishes the horns as the might of foreign nations. הַנֹּשְׂאִים קֶרֶן (that lift up a horn): הַנֹּשְׂאִים (lift up) is a participle with no specific reference to time in this context. We expect a perfective, referring to the historic captivity of Judah by the Babylonians, but the use of a participle instead is significant, complementing the general application the text gives to this pericope (see the Exposition). The collocation נָשָׂא קֶרֶן (to lift a horn) occurs only here. קֶרֶן (horn), however, appears with רוּם (to raise, lift up) with various senses: to increase strength (1 Sam. 2:1, 10; Pss. 89:18 [17], 25 [24]; 92:11 [10]; 112:9; 148:14; Lam. 2:17; see also Luke 1:69), to exalt (1 Chron. 25:5), and to arrogantly boast (Ps. 75:5–6 [4–5]). While this collocation is not the one here, it is nevertheless instructive. In 1 Chronicles 25:5 and Psalm 148:14, for example, קֶרֶן appears as it does here, apart from construct relationships, unconstrued with suffixes. In these cases, the emphasis is solely on the verbal action—not on the subject, object, or possessor of קֶרֶן. Since the collocation נָשָׂא קֶרֶן occurs in isolation here in Zechariah, it emphasizes the verbal action (see the Exposition). אֶל (against) occurs frequently with נָשָׂא (to lift up) with the sense to or toward (e.g., Job 22:26; Pss. 25:1; 86:4; 121:1; Lam. 3:41), but in these instances the context gives it that sense. In Micah 4:3, on the other hand, we may just as easily translate אֶל as "against": "Nation shall not lift up sword against [נָשָׂא אֶל] nation." The hostile environment of Zechariah's vision of the horns also warrants translating אֶל as "against."

represent only Babylon's might, why are the workers coming only now to destroy a political power that is no longer a threat to postexilic Judah? This verse identifies the horns with "nations" (*haggôyim*), not one nation, and the verbal action of the participial clause "lift a horn" (see the Exegesis) allows for a timeless application of its intent. The timeless nature of this vision includes not only any nation that takes a threatening posture (lifts a horn) against postexilic Judah, but it assures God's people in every age that he is active in the world, opposing the forces that threaten his kingdom. It is for this reason that the visions are cosmic in scope.

IV. Third Vision: Man with the Measuring Line
(2:5–17 [1–13])
A. Introduction of the Man with the Measuring Line
(2:5–7 [1–3])

McCOMISKEY

⁵And I lifted up my eyes and looked and there was a man, and in his hand was a measuring line. ⁶And I asked, "Where are you going?" And he said to me, "To measure Jerusalem, to see what is its width and what is its length." ⁷And there was the angel who spoke to me coming forth—and another angel coming forth to meet him!

NRSV

2 I looked up and saw a man with a measuring line in his hand. ²Then I asked, "Where are you going?" He answered me, "To measure Jerusalem, to see what is its width and what is its length." ³Then the angel who talked with me came forward, and another angel came forward to meet him,

5 [1]. וָאֶשָּׂא (and I lifted up): See the Exegesis of 2:1. חֶבֶל מִדָּה (a measuring line): חֶבֶל has a broad range of meanings, including rope or cord. The combination מִדָּה and חֶבֶל indicates a measuring line.

6 [2]. הֹלֵךְ (going): This participle may indicate that the man was not standing still, but proceeding to accomplish his task. That he is moving swiftly is confirmed by the command of verse 8 [4] to run in pursuit of him. לָמֹד (to measure): This infinitive with affixed לְ expresses purpose, stating the reason for the man's taking up the measuring line. לִרְאוֹת (to see) balances the previous purpose clause (לָמֹד), stating in turn its purpose. כַּמָּה (what; lit., as what) expresses quantity (Gen. 47:8 ["how many are the years of your life?"]; 2 Sam. 19:35 [34]; Job 21:17; Ps. 119:84; Zech. 7:3).

7 [3]. וְהִנֵּה (and there was) draws our attention to the approach of the angel. It is difficult to express the strength of this particle apart from the archaic "behold!" (NRSV: "then"), but the use of the exclamation point in my translation is an effort to express the sense of an important moment in the sequence of events. הַמַּלְאָךְ הַדֹּבֵר בִּי (the angel who spoke to me): See the Exposition of 1:13. יֹצֵא (coming forth) is one of several participles in this pericope (the others in vv. 6–7 are הֹלֵךְ, הַדֹּבֵר, and יֹצֵא) that impart a sense of narrative flow. Like the previous infinitives in this verse, לִקְרָאתוֹ (to meet him) expresses purpose, but it is governed by יֹצֵא (to go, come forth) here, expressing the purpose for the "going forth" of the other angel.

---

5 [2:1]. The prophet lifts his eyes to observe another vision: a man holding a measuring line. We have already learned (1:16) that the measuring line (qāwh) will be stretched out over Jerusalem. We now have the feeling that events are moving in that direction, for here is someone prepared to measure the area of the city.

The text evinces no interest in who this man is. The man in 1:8 is an angel (see 1:11), but we do not learn that the man with the measuring line is anything more than a figure necessary to the intent of the vision (see the discussion of the identity of this figure in Meyers and Meyers, *Zechariah 1–8*, pp. 153–54). He and his measuring line are symbols of the rebuilding process that is about to begin.

6 [2]. The prophet feels a part of this vision, speaking to its central figure just as he did in the first vision. The young man walks speedily, for the principal angel must command the other angel to run after him (v. 8 [4]). Zechariah calls to the man, asking where he is going, and the answer is a heartening one: he is going to do the measur-

ing basic to the building enterprise. It is not individual plots of land that he will survey, but the city of Jerusalem itself. Not only does this symbol represent the reality of the construction that will soon begin in the city, but also the intention of God to aid the frustrated community in its task of rebuilding.

7 [3]. Suddenly the angel leaves the place where he was stationed and comes forward. Another angel leaves the ranks and meets him. If the angel who speaks to the prophet is the rider of 1:8 (see the Exposition of 1:13), we may understand the angel who comes forward to meet him to be one of the band of angelic riders who were standing among the myrtle trees behind the angel of the Lord. Zechariah must have felt a sense of foreboding as the majestic rider came forward. This mysterious activity and the text's use of the attention-drawing *hinnēh* (there was) peak our interest (as it must have Zechariah's) in what will now happen. Would the meeting of these two angels bode well for his people? The suspense that unfolds throughout the discourse is striking.

IV. Third Vision: Man with the Measuring Line (2:5–17 [1–13])

B. The Angel's Response to the Effort to Survey Jerusalem (2:8–9 [4–5])

McCOMISKEY

⁸And he said to him, "Run! Speak to that young man, saying, Jerusalem shall be inhabited like open villages because of the great number of people and animals in it, ⁹and I will be for it, utterance of the LORD, a wall of fire all around, and I will be glory in it."

NRSV

⁴and said to him, "Run, say to that young man: Jerusalem shall be inhabited like villages without walls, because of the multitude of people and animals in it. ⁵For I will be a wall of fire all around it, says the LORD, and I will be the glory within it."

8 [4]. The subject of וַיֹּאמֶר (and he said) is syntactically uncertain, but it must be the angel of the Lord, who has the principal role in the visions. The combination of the imperative רֻץ (run) with the following דַּבֵּר (speak) has no special conceptual significance. It is similar to the constructions קוּם . . . לֵךְ (rise . . . go) or שׁוּב . . . לֵךְ (go . . . return) found so frequently in the Old Testament, which are "equivalent to interjections, *come! up!*" (GKC, p. 325). The range of ages designated by הַנַּעַר (traditionally translated "young man") is broad, extending from infancy (Exod. 2:6; 1 Sam. 4:21) to an adult warrior (2 Sam. 18:5; 1 Chron. 12:29 [28]). הַלָּז (this) is a rare demonstrative that usually appears, as it does here, with a substantive determined by the article (הַנַּעַר). Not observably different in sense from זֶה (this), it draws our attention to its referent—the man of verse 5 [1]. Along with הִנֵּה (there was) in that verse, it underscores the importance of the young man in this vision. פְּרָזוֹת ([like] open villages) occurs only in the plural and designates unfortified towns (in Esth. 9:6–19, פְּרָזוֹת are differentiated from the fortified citadel of Susa; in Ezek. 38:11, פְּרָזוֹת refers to open towns unfortified by protective walls). The related noun פְּרָזִי designates someone dwelling in an unfortified

city (in Deut. 3:5, the noun מִבְצָר [fortification] stands in contrast to פְּרָזִי). פְּרָזוֹת is not construed with a comparative particle here; nevertheless, it functions as a formal comparison: "like open villages" (similar to פְּרָאִים בַּמִּדְבָּר, like wild asses in the desert; Job 24:5). תֵּשֵׁב (shall be inhabited): For "be inhabited," see Jeremiah 50:39, where יֵשֵׁב parallels שָׁכַן (to dwell). The reference to the great population of the city favors that sense in this context. יְרוּשָׁלַםִ (Jerusalem): Zechariah's hearers would surely equate this element of the text with their city (for its significance under the new covenant, see the Exposition). מֵרֹב (because of the great number): מִן connotes source (Deut. 7:7). The source of (or reason for) Jerusalem's unusual situation is the great increase in its population. אָדָם וּבְהֵמָה (people and animals) is a common expression indicating the totality of a population. It most frequently occurs in judgment sayings to depict the range of devastation resulting from divine judgment (Gen. 7:23; Exod. 9:25; 12:12; Ps. 135:8; Jer. 21:6; 32:43; 50:3; Ezek. 29:8; Hag. 1:11), but it also appears in affirmations of blessing (Jer. 31:27; Ezek. 36:11) as well as more prosaic passages (Lev. 27:28; Num. 3:13; 18:15; 31:26; Ps. 36:7

---

8 [4]. There is an urgency about the activity this text describes, for the mediating angel commands the other angel to run after the man with the measuring line. If I am correct in identifying the mediating angel as the man on the sorrel horse, the command he gives is appropriate to his position as the principal rider: the runner is to call out to the man that Jerusalem is to be inhabited like unwalled villages. Evidently he pursues the man to dissuade him from surveying the boundaries of the extant city because Jerusalem will exist without walls one day, and to measure it now would be premature and to measure it then would be impossible.

The text does not inform us as to why it underscores the youthfulness of the man with the measuring line. His youthful energy may have imparted a sense of the vigor with which God would work on the community's behalf, but it is useless to speculate. It is enough to know that the work is about to begin.

Jerusalem will need no walls because walls could not contain the vast numbers of people and cattle that will inhabit the city. The motif of great repopulation of humans and animals is a prophetic mode of expressing renewed national welfare and prosperity (Isa. 54:1; Jer. 31:27; Ezek.

36:10–11; 37–38; Hos. 2:1–2 [1:10–11]). From the perspective of the New Testament, this motif encompasses the church, recalling the promise to Abraham that he would be the father of a multitude (Gen. 15:5; 17:5–6; 22:17; see also Rom. 11:17–20). This is how the new covenant understands the Old Testament prospect of repopulation. The apostle Paul applies the promise of Isaiah 54:1 ("for the children of the desolate woman will be more than the children of her that is married, says the LORD") in this way. In Galatians 4:27, Paul quotes this verse to support the view that Jerusalem will one day give birth to vast numbers of children. These are the multitudes who belong to spiritual Jerusalem (v. 26), which symbolizes the place of citizenship of all who are governed by the new covenant (vv. 25–26). As Jerusalem transits the Testaments, it becomes a bold metaphor for the heavenly Jerusalem—the spiritual community of those who have found freedom in God's grace.

The promise of the previous vision (2:1–4 [1:18–21]), that God will protect the people of Judah from successful military intrusion, extends beyond Judah to include the people of God in every age. History bears record of the failed attacks of political forces and philosophical and

[6]). Here, it denotes blessing that spans both the old and new covenants (see the Exposition).

9 [5]. וְאֲנִי (and I will be): אֲנִי (I) refers to Yahweh, not the mediating angel, because of the immediately following נְאֻם־יְהוָה (utterance of the LORD), which always identifies the direct speech of Yahweh in Zechariah. The angel represents the word of Yahweh to the prophet. Meyers and Meyers (*Zechariah 1–8*, p. 156) suggest that אֶהְיֶה (I will be) represents the divine name that occurs in Exodus 3:14, not the verb *to be*. The resulting translation is "And I, I shall be to her I AM, oracle of the Lord" (Chary, *Zacharie*, p. 67) or "As for me, I am EHYEH for her" (D. N. Freedman, as quoted in Meyers and Meyers). The use of the pleonastic pronoun with an inflected verb is not infrequent (GKC §135a–b). The pleonastic pronoun אָנֹכִי/אֲנִי (I) appears with אֶהְיֶה (I am) in Deuteronomy 31:23; Judges 11:9; 2 Samuel 7:14; 1 Chronicles 17:13; Hosea 1:9; and in the frequent expression of the promise אֲנִי אֶהְיֶה לָהֶם לֵאלֹהִים (I shall be God to them): Jeremiah 11:4; 24:7; 30:22; 31:1; 32:38; Ezekiel 11:20; 14:11; 36:28; 37:23; Zechariah 8:8. In the expression of this promise in Zechariah 8:8 (וַאֲנִי אֶהְיֶה לָהֶם לֵאלֹהִים, and I shall be God to them), it is impossible to translate אֶהְיֶה as the divine name EHYEH because it

would break the familiar cadence of the promise that God will be God to his people. The use of the pleonastic pronoun may place emphasis on the pronoun (as in 1 Sam. 23:17 and 1 Kings 1:21) or provide poetic ballast (as in Jer. 31:33, where the pleonastic pronoun does not appear in the first clause [וְהָיִיתִי לָהֶם לֵאלֹהִים] but does in the second [וְהֵמָּה יִהְיוּ־לִי לְעָם, *they* shall be to me a people]). If the writer had wished to say "and I, I am EHYEH to it," he could have made this eminently clear by placing ו before חֹמַת (wall): "And I am EHYEH to her, utterance of the Lord, *and* a wall of fire." לָהּ (for her) relates the action of being a wall of fire directly to Jerusalem. Yahweh will be "Jerusalem's" wall of fire. חֹמַת אֵשׁ (a wall of fire) appears only here, but its significance is clear: a wall of fire is impenetrable. Yahweh is to become a protective barrier for his people against those who attempt to attack them. סָבִיב (all around), a substantive functioning adverbially, strengthens the force of חֹמַת אֵשׁ by emphasizing the extent to which Yahweh will be a protecting wall. וּלְכָבוֹד (and glory): Even though לְ (untranslated) appears in this clause before אֶהְיֶה (I will be), its separation from this verb does not necessarily give לְ independent force calling for the translation "for"

---

religious ideologies poised against the church. The forces at work in the world today, no matter how powerful, cannot destroy the quest of the human soul for God or obliterate the spiritual peace that comes to those who find the knowledge of God in Christ Jesus. It is for this reason that the prophet responds to the plight of these former exiles by recounting visions of angels, empires, and mysterious forces that control world events: the prophecy of Zechariah presents in bold panorama the history of redemption.

9 [5]. Heartening as the message that Jerusalem will exist without walls is, practical minds would eventually come around to another question: But what will protect the city if there are no walls? This leads to the metaphor of divine protection as a wall of fire surrounding God's people. Yahweh will become for his people a fiery barrier that not only shuts out the enemy, but consumes all who attempt to attack them. Once again, we encounter the theological principle observed in 2:4 [1:21]: God has placed strictures on the surrounding nations, preventing them from taking successful military action against Jerusalem.

The assurance of divine protection would encourage the people. They knew now that they could begin their labors untrammeled by threats

from without. But what about the internal situation? For years they had faced the shameful witness of the unfinished foundation that testified to their weakness. The community must have felt great shame because it had no rallying point, nothing to which it could point as a badge of honor. The people would be protected from without, but what about the humiliating situation within their community? What greater answer could they have received than that God will be the glory in their midst (v. 8)? They will complete the temple and God will dwell among them.

Yahweh does not become glory *for* Jerusalem, because *lamed* is not joined to the suffixal pronoun as it is in the previous clause ("I will be for *her* a wall of fire"). If it were, it would create the sense "I will be glory *for* her." Rather, the structure says that he will *be* glory among them. He is, and forever remains, glory among his people. The implications of this statement are profound. God will manifest his glory among his people by vindicating himself in the eyes of the nations and erasing the false images they had of him by proving himself to be the one who controls their destinies. He will manifest his glory to his own people in a similar way, controlling the course of events to fulfill his promises to them. In this way his peo-

(Keil, *Minor Prophets*, p. 242: "I shall be for glory"; see also Meyers and Meyers, *Zechariah 1–8*, p. 149: "as glory"). This collocation frequently means "to be, become" no matter where לְ occurs in the clause relative to הָיָה (Ps. 139:22; Jer. 22:5; 49:13; Joel 4:19 [3:19]). Since the parallel clause in this verse states simply what Yahweh will be (a wall of fire), there is no need to see the more purposive "for" here in this companion clause. The placement of לְ at the head of the clause may be for emphasis (e.g., Jer. 8:2; 22:5). By placing לְ with כָּבוֹד (glory) rather than ־ה (her) as in the first clause, the writer indicated that the emphasis of the second clause is on glory, not Jerusalem as in the first clause. The use of הָיָה without לְ in 2 Chronicles 10:7 (עֲבָדִים, servants) and with it in the somewhat similar context of 2 Chronicles 12:8 shows that no significant conceptual distinction exists between הָיָה and הָיָה plus לְ.

---

ple, as well as the nations, will know Yahweh in the sense that his activity in the arena of the nations will reveal aspects of his nature, which they failed to attribute to him.

The primary intention of this vision, universally applicable in its scope, is that God is present with his people to protect them. This principle would have meant much to the citizens of Jerusalem in Zechariah's time, but it has equal significance for the people of the heavenly Jerusalem (Gal. 4:27; Heb. 12:22). The new covenant also affirms the presence of the Lord with his people, for in the dark hours before the cross Jesus affirmed his continued spiritual presence among his followers (John 14:18–20; 16:12–15; 17:23) and stated that his presence is the glory of the church (17:22). His prayer that his people may be one (17:12) involves their divine protection. The vision of the man with the measuring line transcends time, incorporating in its scope the people of God in all ages.

The suggestion that *ʾehyeh* (I am) is the divine name has little to support it (see the Exegesis). It is true that it recalls the similar construction in Exodus 3:14 ("I AM has sent me to you"), and the reference to fire reminds us of the pillar of fire that accompanied the people after the exodus (Exod. 13:22), but we cannot be certain that the text intends this. The purpose of the pillar of fire was to lead, not protect—a concept different from the wall of fire here; as we observed in the Exegesis, the text could have expressed the divine name more clearly. We can be sure that the text declares that Yahweh will be a wall of fire round about and glory within, but we cannot be sure that it intends to say "I am EHYEH."

The emphasis on "I" in the words "I will be to her a wall of fire" is significant, for it emphasizes Yahweh's personal intervention on behalf of his people. The prophet Ezekiel had watched in dismay as the glory departed from Jerusalem, allowing the Babylonians to attack the city. Like Ezekiel, Zechariah assured his hearers that God's glorious presence will one day take up its abode with his people. This promise encompasses the people of God of all ages, not only postexilic Judah.

IV. Third Vision: Man with the Measuring Line (2:5–17 [1–13])

C. Call to Flee from the North (2:10–13 [6–9])

McCOMISKEY

¹⁰Up! up! and flee from the land of the north, utterance of the LORD, for like the four winds of the heavens I will spread you out, utterance of the LORD. ¹¹Up! Escape, O Zion, you who dwell with daughter Babylon, ¹²for thus says the LORD of hosts, In pursuit of glory has he sent me to the nations that plunder you, for whoever touches you touches the gate of his eye. ¹³For look, I brandish my fist against them, and they shall become plunder for their own slaves, and you shall understand that the LORD of hosts has sent me.

NRSV

⁶Up, up! Flee from the land of the north, says the LORD; for I have spread you abroad like the four winds of heaven, says the LORD. ⁷Up! Escape to Zion, you that live with daughter Babylon. ⁸For thus said the LORD of hosts (after his glory sent me) regarding the nations that plundered you: Truly, one who touches you touches the apple of my eye. ⁹See now, I am going to raise my hand against them, and they shall become plunder for their own slaves. Then you will know that the LORD of hosts has sent me.

10 [6]. הוֹי (up!) is an interjection occurring most frequently in judgment and lament sayings. In laments, it expresses pathos (1 Kings 13:30; Jer. 22:18; 30:7; 34:5), an emotion that probably exists, though not strongly, in divine judgment sayings, where pity mingles with the determination to punish (Isa. 1:4, 24; Amos 5:18; Mic. 2:1). We should not treat this interjection as a mere vocable devoid of conceptual content, for several of the contexts in which it occurs give it a semantic value. This is particularly evident in passages in which prepositions such as אֶל (Jer. 48:1), עַל (Jer. 50:26), or לְ (Ezek. 13:18) follow הוֹי. In these contexts, הוֹי betrays the sense of woe to or upon. The meaning of the word here is determined by the next construction (see the discussion of this interjection in the Exegesis of Mic. 2:1). וְנֻסוּ (and flee): ו (and) can begin a new clause, but most likely its function is to connect two verbal ideas—one implicit in הוֹי and the other the one to which it is affixed. The use of the verb נוּס (to flee) with ו points to the presence of an implicit verbal idea before וְנֻסוּ that is preliminary and appropriate to that construction. The presence of a verbal idea in an interjection may seem anomalous, but the interjection הַס (hush, be silent) is actually

inflected as a verb (הַסּוּ) in Nehemiah 8:11. Ellipsis of some unexpressed verbal idea such as "depart" before וְנֻסוּ is not likely here, since this literary device is not a mark of this book. נוּס does not always have the sense of fleeing from oppression or danger (Deut. 34:7; 2 Kings 9:3; Song 2:17; Isa. 35:10). The text gives no clear indication that those who are summoned are to flee for any reason other than what God will do for them, but the reference to the north, with its dark associations, may imply that the people were to flee from some form of oppression or captivity (see the discussion of "north" in the Exposition). מֵאֶרֶץ צָפוֹן (from the land of the north): צָפוֹן (north) was the direction from which Israel's Mesopotamian enemies entered the country (Jer. 1:14; 4:6; 6:1; Zeph. 2:13; see Zech. 6:8) and would recall to Zechariah's hearers the long years of exile. It has a broader significance here, however (see the Exposition). נְאֻם־יְהוָה (utterance of the LORD): See the Exegesis of 1:3. כִּי (for) introduces the reason for the call to return, which follows in the subsequent words of this clause. כְּאַרְבַּע רוּחוֹת הַשָּׁמַיִם (like the four winds of the heavens) establishes a comparison dependent on the verb פָּרַשׂ (to spread out). This expression denotes the four points of the compass (Jer.

---

10 [6]. In all likelihood, this section is a continuation of verses 5–9 [1–5], for it does not begin with the usual section headings and there is nothing that signals a change of subject. The presence of the same themes—population growth (v. 15 [11]) and divine protection (v. 12 [8])—makes it all but certain that we must view it as expanding on the assurances we find in the vision of the man with the measuring line.

The section begins with an urgent plea to flee from the north. This reference to the north would recall the nations that invaded Israel and Judah, sweeping down from the north to drive the people into exile. Why should the prophet make this plea? These captor nations were no more, and the Persian Empire held no apparent threat for the Jews remaining in Mesopotamia. From what should they flee?

We must recognize here a motif essential to the Old Testament's philosophy of history. Persons, places, institutions, and events often have future (sometimes eschatological) counterparts that share similarities but possess a larger significance appropriate to their function in the unfolding drama of redemption (Foulkes, *Acts of God*, pp. 23–33). For example, the old covenant precedes the more glorious new covenant, David pre-

figures the Davidic Messiah, another Elijah has appeared, and Hosea views the release of the people from captivity as another exodus.

In the same vein, Assyria and Babylon took on conceptual nuances that continued to have significance long after their demise as nations. Assyria, in particular, came to stand for any and all oppressing powers (Isa. 11:11; 19:23; Mic. 5:5–6; 7:12). Zechariah uses this motif in 10:10 when he says that—centuries after Assyria's collapse—God will gather his people "from Assyria." The use of "the north" in a similar fashion imparts to it a higher level of cognition, divorcing it from its original identity but preserving its historical significance and allowing that significance to have an application unlimited by time and historical particularity. In this way, apocalyptic literature gains a universal appeal, and therein lie its mystery and power. Since the north was no longer a threat to the postexilic community, we may understand this section to continue the broad appeal of the first part of this pericope (2:5–9 [1–5]), addressing the people of God in all ages.

The reason for the call to flee is stated in the *kî* (for) clause in the second line. It is because God will spread the people abroad (see the Exegesis). The verb *pēraśtî* (I will spread you out) may repre-

49:36; Ezek. 37:9; Dan. 11:4; see the Exposition of 2:1 [1:18]), thus indicating broad geographical extension. The collocation פָּרַשׂ כְּ means "to spread out as," not "to scatter to [the four winds]." The latter idea is expressed by פָּרַשׂ לְ (Ezek. 17:21: וְהַנִּשְׁאָרִים לְכָל־רוּחַ יִפָּרֵשׂוּ, and the survivors shall be scattered to every wind). Only in Jeremiah 18:17 does כְּ (as) function with a word for wind, but there the word is קָדִים (east wind): "Like the wind from the east, I will scatter them." When the numeral four occurs with רוּחַ (wind), it always connotes a comprehensive geographical expanse (see the Exposition of 2:1 [1:18]). Thus, to "spread out like the four winds" is to be like them, extending to the remote corners of the earth. פֵּרַשְׂתִּי (I will spread out): The contexts in which this verb occurs give it various nuances: to spread out a garment (Judg. 8:25), the hands (Ps. 44:21 [20]), or wings (Job 39:26). In the piel (the form here) it almost always means "to spread out." Only in Psalm 68:15 [14] does the piel form mean "to scatter." Context must determine its aspect (see the Exposition). אֶתְכֶם (you) addresses a plural subject. Since none is stated in this or the preceding pericope, we must assume that the unexpressed subject is implicit and that the text addresses all who live apart from the community of God's people.

11 [7]. הוֹי (up!): See the Exegesis of verse 10 [6]. צִיּוֹן (O Zion): It is possible to translate צִיּוֹן like the Septuagint as "to Zion" (εἰς Σιων), construing it as an accusative of direction (Meyers and Meyers, *Zechariah 1–8*, p. 161; NRSV) but this is not a likely translation (see below). הִמָּלְטִי (escape): While this verb can mean "to escape to/into" without an associated preposition (Gen. 19:19; 2 Kings 19:37), the absence of אֶל (to) before צִיּוֹן warrants consideration of the possibility that it is a vocative. The translation *to Zion* allows no explanation for the feminine singular construction of the participle יוֹשֶׁבֶת (you who dwell). Why should the mode of address suddenly change from the masculine אֶתְכֶם in verse 10 [6] to the feminine in verse 11 [7] and then revert again to the masculine אֶתְכֶם in verse 12 [8]? Only when the text addresses the people as בַּת־צִיּוֹן (daughter Zion) in verse 14 [10] does it depart from the masculine (vv. 13 [9], 14 [10]) to use the more appropriate feminine forms. If we posit צִיּוֹן (Zion) as the entity this clause addresses, we can understand the feminine constructions הִמָּלְטִי (escape) and יוֹשֶׁבֶת (you who dwell with), for in every instance where צִיּוֹן

---

sent a past or future perfective, and there is little in the immediate context to establish its aspect. When, however, we observe a conceptual connection between this section of the pericope and the previous one, the idea that God will spread out the people (future) responds to the previous section's affirmation that walls will not contain Jerusalem's vast population. God will spread his people abroad like the four winds that encompass the face of the earth.

If, on the other hand, one understands the verb as a preterite, observing that God had already scattered the people to the ends of the earth (Meyers and Meyers, *Zechariah 1–8*, pp. 163–64; Smith, *Micah–Malachi*, p. 194; Petersen, *Zechariah 1–8*, p. 172), it is difficult to understand why the call goes out only to the north and not to the extremities of the earth. If we regard the verb as future, it holds out the reason for the call to return—an element lacking in it if we regard the verb as a preterite. This call is to all people in every age to flee from the world to find a home with the "myriads and thousands of thousands" (Rev. 5:11–14) who will one day find community before God's throne.

The concept of territorial extension for God's people is present in other Old Testament prophets. Micah 7:11 looks forward to a day when "the boundary shall be far extended," and Isaiah 54:2 says, "Enlarge the site of your tent, . . . for you will spread out to the right and to the left, and your descendants will possess the nations, and will settle the desolate towns." We find this promise as early as Genesis 22:17, where Abraham learned that his offspring would "possess the gate of their enemies." The writer of Hebrews, like Zechariah, uses Jerusalem as a motif of community when he speaks of "the heavenly Jerusalem" to which we have come and "the assembly of the firstborn" (12:22–23).

11 [7]. Once again we hear the summons, "Up!" Like the previous occurrence of this interjection (v. 10 [6]), it precedes a verb commanding urgent departure. The reader may wonder at the labored discussion in the Exegesis regarding the syntactical function of ṣiyyôn (Zion), which concludes that the summons does not call the people *to* Zion but addresses them *as* Zion. That lengthy discussion was necessary because the conclusion has profound implications for our grasp of the prophet's theology, and we must make an effort to understand his words correctly.

The cry "Up! Escape, O Zion" gives Zion a sense it does not often possess. We are familiar with its use as the designation for the temple

is grammatically construed in Zechariah, it is feminine (2:14 [10]; 8:2; 9:9, 13; see the subsequent discussion). יוֹשֶׁבֶת (you who dwell with): If the text is calling the people to Zion rather than referring to them as Zion, we would expect this form to be יוֹשֵׁב (you who dwell with), in keeping with the preceding masculine plural אֶתְכֶם (you) in verse 10 [6]. The same is true of the imperative הִמָּלְטִי (escape), which would then be masculine plural as well. The sudden intrusion of the feminine must be because צִיּוֹן is feminine. בַּת־בָּבֶל (daughter of Babylon): There is no reason to believe that this designation means anything more than what its companion element אֶרֶץ צָפוֹן (land of the north) in the previous verse signifies (see the Exposition of v. 10 [6]). Since the people are warned to escape from בַּת־בָּבֶל because of God's impending judgment and because that judgment falls on the nations according to verses 12–13, בַּת־בָּבֶל must represent the nations.

12 [8]. כִּי (for) introduces the reason for the summons: God is going to pursue glory for himself among the nations. כֹּה אָמַר יְהוָה צְבָאוֹת (thus says the LORD of hosts): See the Exegesis of 1:3. אַחַר כָּבוֹד (in pursuit of glory): אַחַר (in pursuit of; lit., after) usually indicates position or time after. When linked with verbs, it takes on nuances appropriate to the verbal actions. In Hosea 2:7 [5], for example, אַחַר appears with הָלַךְ (go) to mean "to go after," and in Jeremiah 49:37 it occurs with שָׁלַח (send) to mean "to send after"—the same collocation that appears here. שְׁלָחַנִי (has he sent me): The formula "thus says the LORD of hosts" leads us to expect the following words to be a direct statement from Yahweh, requiring the suffix on שְׁלָחַנִי to refer to God, but this is problematical, for who can send God? Evidently it is Yahweh who sends the speaker (see the Exposition). הַגּוֹיִם הַשֹּׁלְלִים (the nations that plunder): שָׁלַל (to plunder) has the form of a participle, the action of which is contemporaneous with the current situation of Zion among the nations. These nations are oppressive in their treatment of God's people. כִּי (for) introduces the reason for Yahweh's coming

mount or as a surrogate for Jerusalem, but here, I suggest, it refers to God's people who are far removed from Jerusalem, dispersed throughout the world. We know these are God's people because verse 12 [8] expresses that concept. This function of "Zion" is not foreign to the Old Testament, for we find it in Isaiah 51:16. Particularly instructive in this regard is Isaiah 52:2, which addresses the oppression in Babylon and refers to the captive people as Zion. Like the call of Zechariah, this passage also summons the people to depart from Babylon (Isa. 52:11). Since Zion is a collective plural here, we may understand its companion element *yōšebet* (you who dwell with) to be so as well.

The major theological implication of this call to Zion is that God's people are not only those living in Jerusalem and its environs, but also those dispersed throughout the world. The people of Zechariah's day would have understood his call to summon Jews who were still living in the far reaches of the Persian Empire to return to their homeland. The scope of this pericope, however, is far broader than that, as the subsequent discussion will show. At this point we may observe that the reference to the nations as "daughter of Babylon"—long after Babylon's fall from power—detaches this exilic motif (Babylon) from its historical particularity and gives the pericope a more universal appeal, freeing it up for application to any age (see the Exposition of v. 10 [6]).

12 [8]. The reason for the summons to God's people to escape from the oppressing nations is that Yahweh has come to these nations in pursuit of glory. Coupled with the urgent command to escape, this statement becomes ominous. God is about to act in the arena of the nations, garnering glory for himself and warning his people to flee from the impending display of his wrath.

The phrase *in pursuit of glory has he sent we* is one of the most problematic in the book. Petersen (*Zechariah 1–8*, pp. 172–73) objects to the translation "after glory sent me" because it creates the unlikely notion that it is the prophet who was sent to foreign nations. He translates these words, "After (the) glory sent me." Chary (*Zacharie*, p. 70) understands ʾaḥar to mean "with" and kābôd "heaviness," resulting in the translation "with insistence he sent me." Baldwin (*Zechariah*, p. 109) lists several instances where ʾaḥar may mean "with" (Exod. 11:5; Ps. 73:24; Eccles. 12:2). Scott ("ʾaḥar") also translates ʾaḥar "with," and the New Revised Standard Version translates the phrase "after his glory sent me," which creates the sense that the speaker utters the words occurring at the end of verse 8 after "the divine glory" sent him. Thomas (*Zechariah*, p. 1066) emends ʾaḥar to ʾăšer and reads the phrase "whose glory sent me," while Vriezen ("Two Old Cruces") makes the interesting suggestion that ʾaḥar kābôd is an edi-

into the sphere of human history in pursuit of glory (אַחַר כָּבוֹד): the treatment his people are receiving at the hands of the nations. הַנֹּגֵעַ בְּ־ (whoever touches; lit., the one touching) here has the sense of hostile intent because of the previous reference to plundering. בְּבָבַת (the gate) is a difficult

expression. The absolute form בבה (construct בְּבַת) is unattested elsewhere. That Aramaic בבא and Akkadian babu both mean "gate" suggests that בְּבַת עֵינוֹ may be "the gate of the eye," connoting either the pupil or aperture of the eye (i.e., the opening of the eyelids), which the ancients may

---

tor's note indicating that verse 12 should follow kābôd at the end of verse 9 [5].

There is no need to identify the referent of the suffix on šĕlāḥanî (sent me) as Zechariah. It is the angel of the Lord who explains the visions and who speaks here in reference to himself. In 2:3 [1:20] and 2:4 [1:21] we observe a somewhat similar identification of the angel with Yahweh. We know now why this angel heads the host of cosmic riders that stand behind him (1:8): he has come not only to command them to traverse the earth, but also to pursue glory for Yahweh, whose words he represents.

The suggestion that ʾaḥar means "with" here is doubtful. In Ecclesiastes 12:2, the word may just as easily mean "after," describing the immediate return of sorrow. Exodus 11:5 may indicate that the servant girl stands behind (ʾaḥar) the handmill, and Psalm 73:24 may intend to say, "Afterward [ʾaḥar] you will receive me with honor." It is also not certain that kābôd (wealth, honor, and glory) ever indicates insistence. The interpretations of this verse that require emendation are speculative, lacking significant manuscript evidence.

The New Revised Standard Version translation ("after his glory sent me") presents several problems. Neither the Masoretic Text nor the Septuagint (opisō doxēs, after glory) allows for the reading "his." While the Old Testament (Pss. 16:9; 30:12; Isa. 58:8) does personify glory (kābôd), it never gives this concept the force of divine agency initiating human response. In Zechariah, the messenger formula always introduces immediate direct speech, making it likely that the words ʾaḥar kābôd (in pursuit of glory) are the words of the angel, not a parenthetic statement of the speaker. If the writer intended these words to be such a statement, we wonder why lēʾmôr (saying) does not appear after the word ʾetkem (you) instead of after kî (for).

The translation "in pursuit of glory" is not semantically objectionable and answers nicely to the syntactical demands of the immediate context as well as to the flow of discourse throughout the entire pericope. The kî that begins verse 12 leads us to expect a reason for the command to escape,

just as does the initial kî in verse 10b. The translation "with insistence he sent me" answers broadly to the contextual requirements of kî, but is semantically and philologically questionable (see above). The translation "in pursuit of glory has he sent me" is less oblique in its relation to kî, stating a reason for the command of verse 11. While kî does not always demand direct causation, the suggested translation "with insistence he sent me" does not give us a reason for the urgent call to escape; neither does it relate directly to the aspects of divine glory on which the remainder of this pericope expounds and which we may find elsewhere in prophetic theology. For example, verses 12–13 [8–9] state that Yahweh has sent the angel of the Lord to the nations because they have plundered his people. Yahweh will bring vengeance on these nations for what they have done. This act of retribution will confirm that he has sent this angelic messenger. In Ezekiel 39:21–24, we find a similar theme: God will display his glory among the nations by judging them, a divine activity that results in a correct knowledge of Yahweh's actions (v. 23) and brings glory to him by overcoming the false impressions that masked his glory. Thus, prophetic theology allows for the concept that Yahweh's judgment of the nations brings him glory.

In Zechariah 2:15 [11], we learn that Yahweh will call Gentiles to the benefits of his promise, for they will become his people (see Lev. 26:12) and he will dwell among his people. This association with his people will be a manifestation of his glory. Thus, the translation "in pursuit of glory has he sent me" complements the logical flow of the discourse.

The nations that plunder God's people are those in which the people are resident. These nations, like Assyria and Babylon, are motifs for all the nations, not simply those that sacked Jerusalem, carrying off its wealth. They provide a dark background against which the promise of geographical extension shines all the brighter.

The expression bābat ʿênô (the gate of his eye, or the daughter of his eye) is another perplexing problem in this pericope (see Robertson, "Apple of the Eye"). The traditional translation "the

have viewed as the entry (or gate) to the eye. The Septuagint reads κόρης for בָּבָה, which can indicate the pupil of the eye. It is also possible that this construction reflects dittography of ב (which is part of the collocation נֹגֵעַ בְּ־), in which case the original form would have been בַּת־עֵינוֹ (daughter of his eye), an expression that appears in Psalm 17:8 and Lamentations 2:18 to indicate the pupil of the eye. The masculine suffix on עֵינוֹ refers to Yahweh (see the Exposition of 2:14 [10]; see also 1:11).

13 [9]. הִנְנִי (look, I): This emphatic particle is construed with the first-person suffix. Since the suffix on שְׁלָחַנִי (vv. 12–13) refers to the angel of the Lord and since the suffix referring to God is third-person (עֵינוֹ, his eye; v. 12), the suffix on הִנְנִי must also refer to the angel. מֵנִיף (brandish) is a hiphil participle of נוּף that denotes undulating motion: the wielding of tools (Exod. 20:25; Deut. 27:5; Josh. 8:31), the waving of an object (the "wave offering"; Lev. 23:11), gesturing (2 Kings 5:11) or signaling (Isa. 13:2) with the hand, and sifting (Isa. 30:28). With עַל (as here) it indicates sweeping the

hand over (Isa. 11:15) or shaking the hand at (Isa. 19:16), not just menacingly, but effectively (see also Job 13:21). יָד typically indicates the hand, but fist is appropriate here; the modern expression *shake the fist at* captures the hostile sense of the Hebrew construction. עֲלֵיהֶם (over) receives its English sense from the function one assigns to its collocation. Here, "against" is appropriate, reflecting the hostile content of this statement. שָׁלָל denotes gain—generally gain from war (i.e., spoil or plunder)—but this sense is not found in every occurrence (see Prov. 1:13; 31:11). The context here gives this word the sense of plunder that others will gain from the destruction of the nations. וִידַעְתֶּם (and you shall understand): ו (and) introduces an action coordinate with that of the previous clause, both actions related to כִּי (for) at the beginning of the verse. The actions these clauses describe follow from the shaking of the angel's fist. Since יָדַע (to know) is experiential knowledge in this context, I translate it "understand." The verb is plural because it addresses exiled Zion (vv.

---

apple of my eye" (NRSV) may carry modern connotations that the Hebrew expression does not convey. If "gate" is the correct reading, the "gate of the eye" could be the conjunction of the eyelids. The sense is not that God's people are specially favored by him, as the translation "the apple of my eye" may imply, but that touching them is like touching the sensitive eyelashes, which react instantaneously to any object that brushes against them. If the better translation is "daughter of the eye," denoting the pupil of the eye (see the Exegesis), the sense is not greatly different, for the eyeball is also sensitive to touch. In this analogy, the eye is Yahweh's (ʿênô, his eye). As the eye is extremely sensitive to touch, so God is sensitive to what threatens his people. This statement develops further the important postexilic theme that God will protect his people and allow no hostile intervention. Petersen (*Zechariah 1–8*, p. 177) understands this figure to represent the eyeball: "Anyone who acts injuriously towards Israel is at the same time acting injuriously toward Yahweh."

13 [9]. It is the angel of the Lord, not Yahweh, to whom the first-person notations in verses 12–13 refer and who brandishes his fist at the nations, reducing them to plunder for their own slaves. The *waw*-clauses are coordinate, each stating a result of the angel's hostile action against the nations, and each is related to the *kî*-clause that

begins this verse, amplifying the reason for escape (v. 11) that *kî* introduces. This section may be paraphrased as follows:

> Escape! because (*kî*) God has sent me (the angel of the LORD) to get glory for himself among the nations who plunder you, for (*kî*) I shake my fist at these nations, and (*waw*) they are going to be reduced to plunder, and (*waw*) you will know that (*kî*) God has sent me (the angel of the LORD).

There is a philosophy of history in the first *waw*-clause. That the angel reduces the nations to plunder affirms that God is at work in time and history, causing nations to rise and fall (Isa. 40:23), but always reacting to threats against his people and preserving them as aliens in a hostile world. It is because of this divine protection that the church exists today in spite of efforts to silence its witness. Jesus prayed for the protection of his people (John 17:11–13, 21; and see 1 Peter 1:5).

The second *waw*-clause states that the result of the angel's activity among the nations is that God's people will understand that this angel is Yahweh's emissary. The people of Zechariah's time were aware of the angel's success. Imperial Assyria and mighty Babylon were no more, Cyrus had come on the scene of world history, and these events witnessed to God's activity in the world

11–12 [7–8]). כִּי (that) introduces an object clause. The object of their knowing is that (כִּי) Yahweh of hosts has sent the angel of the Lord. יְהוָה צְבָאוֹת (the LORD of hosts): See the Exegesis of 1:3. שְׁלָחָנִי (has sent me) recalls the previous occurrence of this verb in verse 12, sustaining the same suffixal referent—the angel of the Lord.

---

and his care for his people (see Isa. 40:2–4, 8–10; 44:28; 45:1). God was cognizant of the treatment his people had received among these nations (Zech. 1:15). The captor nations had touched the "gate" of Yahweh's eye, and he had brought them down. The events of history confirmed the angel's words, affirming that God is at work in the world garnering glory for himself as a mighty warrior. Today, the panorama of history witnesses to the rise and fall of nations (Isa. 40:23–24) while God continues to preserve a remnant in the world.

The protection from the nations that the angel provides God's people reflects the motif of protection that the fiery wall in the previous section symbolizes (2:5–9 [1–5]). This common theme between the account of the man with the measuring line and this section unites these two sections.

IV. Third Vision: Man with the Measuring Line (2:5–17 [1–13])

D. God's Dwelling in the Midst of Zion (2:14–17 [10–13])

McCOMISKEY

¹⁴Shout and rejoice, daughter Zion, for look, I am coming, and I will dwell among you, utterance of the LORD. ¹⁵And many nations will join themselves to the LORD in that day, and they will be to me a people, and I shall dwell among you, and you will know that the LORD of hosts has sent me to you. ¹⁶And the LORD will inherit Judah as his portion in the holy land and will again choose Jerusalem. ¹⁷Be silent, all flesh, before the LORD, for he has roused himself from his holy habitation.

NRSV

¹⁰Sing and rejoice, O daughter Zion! For lo, I will come and dwell in your midst, says the LORD. ¹¹Many nations shall join themselves to the LORD on that day, and shall be my people; and I will dwell in your midst. And you shall know that the LORD of hosts has sent me to you. ¹²The LORD will inherit Judah as his portion in the holy land, and will again choose Jerusalem.

¹³Be silent, all people, before the LORD; for he has roused himself from his holy dwelling.

14 [10]. רָנִּי (shout) denotes lifting the voice and frequently occurs in parallel structures to indicate shouting (Lev. 9:24; Ps. 78:65; Prov. 1:20–21; Isa. 52:8). In Psalm 59:17 it indicates singing, but the writer may have wished only to balance the two words to connote the vocal expression of joy: "shout" and "sing." By connecting וְשִׂמְחִי (and rejoice) to רָנִּי by ו (and), the context creates an atmosphere in which רָנִּי takes on the sense of exultant shouting. בַּת־צִיּוֹן (daughter of Zion) seems not to differ from Zion (the people of God) in Zechariah (see v. 15 [11]). כִּי (for) introduces the reason for the exultant shout: it is because God will take up his abode with his people. הִנְנִי (look, I): The first-person suffix refers to God, not the angel, because the phrase נְאֻם־יְהוָה (says the LORD) marks these words as Yahweh's. It is Yahweh—not the angel—who will take up residence among his people (v. 9 [5]). וְשָׁכַנְתִּי (and I will dwell): See the Exposition. נְאֻם־יְהוָה: See the Exegesis of 1:4.

15 [11]. וְנִלְווּ (and will join themselves): ו (and) indicates a conceptual unity between this clause and the preceding one. The union of Gentiles with Yahweh is related to the time when he will again dwell with his people. The presence of בַּיּוֹם הַהוּא (in that day) at the end of this clause, referring to that time, underscores this concept. לְוָה (join), occurring mainly in the niphal, means "join themselves" or "be joined." While this distinction is important in some contexts (e.g., Isa. 56:3, 6), the context here does not clearly call for one or the other. It is satisfied with the affirmation that Gentiles will be included among the people of God. This verb may convey the sense of physical union: be in league with (Esth. 9:27; Ps. 83:9 [8]; Dan. 11:34), be a covenant partner (Jer. 50:5), bond emotionally (Gen. 29:32, 34), or give allegiance to (Isa. 56:3, 6). Zechariah's context, however, does not require the sense of a literal influx of vast numbers of Gentiles into the land of Palestine (see the Exposition). Once again Abrahamic promise is in view, which is the earliest expression of Gentile (גּוֹיִם) inclusion in the benefits of the promise (Gen. 12:3). בַּיּוֹם הַהוּא (in that day) is the time

---

14 [10]. The people of God are to rejoice because Yahweh is coming to dwell among them. The first-person referents now revert from the angel to Yahweh ("utterance of the LORD"). The word šākan (dwell) recalls the account of the tabernacle and the theology of presence it represented. The purpose of this structure was that Yahweh might dwell among his people (Exod. 25:8). Exodus 29:45–46 links Yahweh's dwelling with his people to the promise that he will be God to them (Gen. 17:7); when the Lord takes up his abode with his people, they will understand that he is Yahweh, who brought them out of Egypt for the very purpose of dwelling among them. The tabernacle was the localization of the Lord's promise to be God to his people. First Kings 6:12–13 also relates the theology of presence to this promise, recalling God's reiteration of the Abrahamic promise to David (2 Sam. 7:11–13, 24). Zechariah 8:3 relates this concept to the promise as well (see also v. 8).

The theology of presence is not confined to the Old Testament, for the new covenant affirms the spiritual presence of Christ in his church. The new covenant views the church as a temple, both corporately (oikos: 1 Peter 2:5; naos: 2 Cor. 6:16; Eph. 2:21) and individually (naos: 1 Cor. 3:16–17), and affirms that Christ is resident in that temple (John 6:56; 14:20; 15:5; 17:23; 1 Cor. 6:19; 2 Cor. 13:5; Gal. 2:20; Col. 1:27; 1 John 3:24; 4:13).

15 [11]. There is a curious mixture of person referents in this verse. It is probably the angel who refers to "the LORD" in the first clause, but the words *they shall be to me a people* must echo the voice of God. Yet the angel certainly says, "You will know that the LORD of hosts has sent me to you." This blending of references to Yahweh and the angel attests to the angel's close association with God (see the Exposition of 1:11).

The promise that God will dwell with his people expands to include Gentiles (many nations) as well as Jews. The union of these peoples with Yahweh will occur when he takes up his abode with them (v. 14). The theology of God's presence relates to the promise that the Lord will be God to his people (Exod. 29:45–46; see the Exposition of v. 14 [10]). Now the words *they will be to me a people* echo that ancient promise. This expression of the promise is part of the fuller statement, "I will be your God, and you shall be my people," found in numerous places throughout the Old Testament. In Leviticus 26:12, this element of the promise is associated with the divine presence ("and I will walk among you"), as it is here.

This sweeping vitalization of Yahwism is another reason for rejoicing (v. 14). The people of Zechariah's day may have envisioned the transfer of Gentile allegiance to Yahweh as a massive influx of Gentiles into the postexilic community; the text does not, however, require this idea. History does not witness to such an event, and the

when Yahweh dwells among his people (v. 14 [10]). לִי (to me) sustains the first-person referents to Yahweh throughout this section (v. 14). לְעָם (a people): As with the second occurrence of the collocation הָיָה לְ in verse 9 [5], there is no need to view the same phrase here as "be *for* a people" (see the Exegesis of v. 9 [5]). "They shall be my people" is a suitable translation for this phrase. וְשָׁכַנְתִּי (and I shall dwell): See the Exegesis of verse

14 [10]. בְּתוֹכֵךְ (in your midst) has a feminine suffix referring to בַּת־צִיּוֹן (daughter of Zion) in verse 14 [10], which indicates that the union of Jews and Gentiles is בַּת־צִיּוֹן because Yahweh dwells in a community comprised of both peoples. שְׁלָחַנִי (has sent me) is the angel of the Lord.

16 [12]. וְנָחַל (and will inherit) continues the series of syndetic particles ו (and) that unites this section into a logical unit. נָחַל (inherit): As with

---

word *nilwû* (join themselves) does not necessarily connote a literal migration of Gentiles to post-exilic Judah (see the Exegesis). Yet the angel of the Lord said that when Yahweh dwells in this united community, "You will know that the LORD of hosts has sent me to you." Do the prophet's words represent an empty chauvinism designed to prod the lethargic community into action?

As we view the span of history from our vantage point, it is not easy to answer this question in the affirmative because of the church. It is a community of Jews and Gentiles (Eph. 2:11–16), and it claims the presence of God in its midst (1 Cor. 3:16; 2 Cor. 6:16; 1 Tim. 3:15; see the Exposition of v. 14). The existence of the church confirms the angel's words and attests to God's working in the world through his angelic forces, controlling the events of redemptive history. Since the formation of the church is removed from Zechariah's day by such a formidable span of time, we wonder how his community could know that God had sent the angel of the Lord. We must remember, however, that the prophet's words address the daughter of Zion—the people of God in every age—and the prophets frequently cast the final knowability of the divine will into the eschaton. It is the culmination of the processes of history that confirms the angel's mission. The Christian may understand "Zion" (v. 11 [7]) and "daughter of Zion" (v. 14 [10]) to transect the Testaments to embrace the church, bringing with them affirmations of divine promise.

The promise that the Lord will be God to his people is not forgotten in the new covenant, ringing as clearly there as it does in the old (2 Cor. 6:16; Heb. 8:10; Rev. 21:3). In 2 Corinthians 6:16, the apostle Paul links this promise to the theology of presence: "For we are the temple of the living God." The concept here in Zechariah 2:15 [11] of a multitude of people embracing Yahweh echoes the words of verse 8 [4] that "Jerusalem shall be inhabited as villages without walls, because of the multitude of people." This fact establishes a conceptual and literary connection to the account of the

man with the measuring line. This may seem a strange way to encourage the weary and discouraged builders on Mount Zion, for, after all, what relevance would this future event have for them? Even though they did not live to see Gentiles added to their numbers in the magnitude this passage describes, the prophet's assurances of a bright future for God's people would have affirmed God's faithfulness to them. If they had grown discouraged, forsaking Jerusalem and Judah to intermarry and thus losing their national identity, the church would not have become a reality. The people of Zechariah's day were an important link in the chain of redemptive events the Bible records. They might not have fully understood their awesome function in the divine plan, but Zechariah's words would have encouraged them to work on toward a distant goal, knowing that the future held the bright prospect of Yahweh dwelling in a kingdom of vast population and spiritual prosperity.

According to Exodus 29:45–46, Yahweh's manifestation of his presence in the tabernacle would have a cognitive value for the people, leading them to understand (*yādaʿ*) that he is Yahweh their God who led them from Egypt so that he might dwell among them. Yahweh's presence in the tabernacle confirmed that he was the God of their ancient heritage who, centuries before, had announced his purpose to be God to his people (Gen. 17:7). In the same way, Zechariah's theology of presence has a cognitive value ("you will *know* that the LORD of hosts has sent me to you"), leading the people to understand that Yahweh is active in history, operating through his angelic agencies. The union of Jews and Gentiles in the church attests to this divine activity in the world and confirms God's promise to Zechariah.

16 [12]. The reasons for rejoicing (v. 14 [10]) continue with the comforting assurance that God will inherit Judah, words reminiscent of the Song of Moses in Deuteronomy 32:8–10:

When the Most High apportioned the nations,
  when he divided humankind,

the English word *inherit*, the qal of this verb does not denote possession by right of succession, as Exodus 23:30; 34:9; Proverbs 3:35; 11:29; 28:10 show. Many contexts dealing with the apportionment of the land invest it with that connotation, however (e.g., Num. 18:23; Josh. 14:1, 17:6; Ezek. 47:14). Zechariah's use of חֵלֶק (portion) and אֲדָמָה (land) creates a metaphorical depiction of land-inheritance: the land of Judah will become the Lord's. חֵלֶק mainly designates a share of various materials, such as food (Deut. 18:8), booty (Num. 31:36), or land (Josh. 14:4). Less concretely, it refers to one's part in a dialog or dispute (Job 32:17) or to shared human experience (Eccles. 9:6). In each occurrence, there is a sense of ownership. Thus, Judah will become Yahweh's possession. אַדְמַת הַקֹּדֶשׁ (the holy land) occurs only here in the Old Testament. The root קדשׁ (holy) denotes the separation of the common and profane. The קֹדֶשׁ (holy place) of the tabernacle (Exod. 28:29) was holy because it localized the divine presence, and the ministrations of the tabernacle preserved the holiness of God in a profane world. וּבָחַר עוֹד בִּירוּשָׁלָם (and will again choose Jerusalem): ו (and) coordinates the two clauses in which we learn that the

Lord will inherit (נָחַל) Judah and again choose Jerusalem. The two actions these clauses describe are conceptually coordinate, depicting what will accompany the Lord's dwelling with his people (v. 15 [11]) and stating further reasons for God's people to be joyful (v. 14 [10]). בָּחַר (choose): See the Exegesis of 1:17. The collocation בָּחַר בְּ delineates the object יְרוּשָׁלַם (Jerusalem) more clearly than would simple בָּחַר; without בְּ the clause could also be translated "and Jerusalem will again choose," momentarily confusing the reader. עוֹד (again): We cannot be certain that this particle exerts an influence on the preceding clause, thus creating the sense that Yahweh will *again* inherit Judah. That concept is inappropriate because there are no earlier references in the Old Testament to Yahweh inheriting (נָחַל) Judah. The concept is, however, appropriate to the clause in which it appears because of the rich tradition affirming Yahweh's initial choice (בָּחַר) of Jerusalem (1 Kings 11:32, 36; 14:21; 2 Kings 21:7; 23:27; 2 Chron. 6:6, 34, 38; 12:13; Ps. 132:13). That God will again choose Jerusalem points to an earlier rejection of the city.

---

he fixed the boundaries of the peoples
    according to the number of the gods;
for the LORD's own portion was his people,
    Jacob his allotted share.
He sustained him in a desert land,
    in a howling wilderness waste;
he shielded him, cared for him,
    guarded him as the apple of his eye.

The terms *naḥălātô* (his inheritance), *ḥeleq* (portion), and *ʾîšôn ʿênô* (pupil of the eye) in the Song of Moses remind us of Zechariah's *nāḥal* (2:16 [12], *ḥeleq* (2:16 [12]), and *bābat ʿênô* (2:12 [8]). The Song of Moses states that the warm relationship to God that these terms describe would not continue because the disobedience of the people caused the severing of their relationship to him (Deut. 32:15–27). The allusion to Moses' song here in Zechariah, however, affirms that the Lord intends to give his people the status that Moses once envisioned for them.

The "holy land" cannot refer to the literal country of Palestine because the physical boundaries of that land would have been incapable of defining the limits of the vast numbers of Gentiles who will comprise the people of God. Even Jerusalem's boundaries will be obliterated by its great repopulation (v. 8 [4]). The holy land is the

locus of the divine presence that, according to the perspective of this text, includes Gentile nations spread abroad over the face of the whole earth (see Rom. 4:13).

Not only will God inherit his people, who are here called Judah, but he will again choose Jerusalem (see the Exposition of 1:17 [13]). The choice of this city by Yahweh is an important historical tradition. Because of Yahweh's choice of Jerusalem, Judah was preserved during the rift between the northern and southern kingdoms (1 Kings 11:13, 32, 36). It is the place where Yahweh chose to place his name (see the Exegesis) and establish his presence (Ps. 132:13). Because of the excesses of King Manasseh of Judah (2 Kings 21:11), however, prophetic voices announced the eventual destruction of Jerusalem (vv. 12–15). The city will lose its special privilege as God's chosen city. The prophet Zechariah takes up the threads of this Old Testament tradition and affirms that God will again choose Jerusalem. Zechariah is the last Old Testament writer to address the theme of the Lord's choice of Jerusalem, and he takes it to new heights. God forsook his people, but he will again choose them, taking up his abode in a Jerusalem that the prophet could scarcely envision (see the Exposition of v. 8 [4]).

17 [13]. הַס is an interjection calling for silence (Judg. 3:19; Hab. 2:20; Zeph. 1:7). See the Exegesis of 2:10 [6] for an allusion to this word in that verse. כָּל־בָּשָׂר (all flesh): The word בָּשָׂר has several connotations. Here the text requires the sense of living beings (as in Gen. 6:17, 19; 7:21; Lev. 17:14; Num. 18:15). כִּי (for) introduces the reason for all living beings to be silent before Yahweh: he is about to act. נֵעוֹר (roused himself) may mean "to awake" (as in Pss. 44:24 [23]; 57:9 [8]; 108:2; Song 5:2; Zech. 4:1), but this sense is not present in all its occurrences. The basic meaning of this word is "to arouse or stir up" (Judg. 5:12; Pss. 7:7 [6]; 59:5 [4]; Jer. 6:22; 25:32; 50:41). Here, the Lord, stirred to action, is about to effect what this pericope promises. מָעוֹן is a broad word for a place of habitation and may refer to the den of an animal (Jer. 9:10; Nah. 2:12) as well as to the locus of the divine presence in the tabernacle (2 Chron. 36:15). In Deuteronomy 26:15, it is in apposition to הַשָּׁמַיִם (heaven), and, in Jeremiah 25:30, it parallels מָרוֹם (on high) to designate the habitation of God. קָדְשׁוֹ (his holy): Yahweh's dwelling place is distinct from the world of the common and profane. The cosmic scope of this verse (all flesh) does not allow מָעוֹן to refer to an earthly dwelling of God, but refers to his habitation in heaven.

---

17 [13]. This terse closing statement calls the inhabitants of the earth to silent reverence in anticipation of the awesome events this pericope describes. God is to receive glory to himself as he enters the arena of the nations: mighty empires will become plunder for their erstwhile vassals; God will dwell with his people; Gentiles will own Yahweh as Lord and share in Israel's ancestral promises; his people will once again become his precious possession. No wonder the world is called to reverence in anticipation of these awesome events. This verse lifts our eyes to the abode of God, and we see him rousing himself to action. The mighty figure of Yahweh stands now before us. Ominously he prepares to step forth into the sphere of nations to bring about their downfall. But God comes to lend his people strength and to dwell among them as their God and their glory.

The vision of the man with the measuring line begins to fade as we prepare to observe the next vision. We have learned that this young man is preparing the way for the restored community to rebuild the city of Jerusalem. There is, however, a greater Jerusalem that this text envisions, and this young man—who symbolizes the forces and agencies of God that will effect the building of Jerusalem—symbolizes as well the divine agencies that control the course of history, determining the events that will culminate in the inception and continuation of the church in the world.

V. Fourth Vision: The High Priest Symbolizes the Branch (3:1–10)

A. The High Priest's Filthy Garments (3:1–4)

McCOMISKEY

3 Then he showed me Joshua the high priest standing before the angel of the LORD and the adversary standing at his right to accuse him. ²And the LORD said to the adversary, "The LORD rebuke you, O adversary! The LORD who chooses Jerusalem rebuke you. Is this not a stick snatched from the fire?" ³Now Joshua was clothed in filthy garments and standing before the angel. ⁴But [the angel] responded and spoke to those standing before him, saying, "Take those filthy garments away from him." And [the angel] said to him, "See, I have removed your guilt from you and clothe you with special attire."

NRSV

3 Then he showed me the high priest Joshua standing before the angel of the LORD, and Satan standing at his right hand to accuse him. ²And the LORD said to Satan, "The LORD rebuke you, O Satan! The LORD who has chosen Jerusalem rebuke you! Is not this man a brand plucked from the fire?" ³Now Joshua was dressed with filthy clothes as he stood before the angel. ⁴The angel said to those who were standing before him, "Take off his filthy clothes." And to him he said, "See, I have taken your guilt away from you, and I will clothe you with festal apparel."

3:1. וַיַּרְאֵנִי (then he showed me) has God as its subject (see the Exposition of 2:3 [1:20]). עֹמֵד לִפְנֵי (standing before): It is not clear that this expression is elsewhere a technical term for a judicial standing, but this context gives it such a sense. מַלְאַךְ יְהוָה (the angel of the LORD): See the Exposition of 1:11. וְהַשָּׂטָן (and the adversary): Basic to the root שׂטן is the idea of opposition (Num. 22:22, 32; 1 Sam. 29:4; 1 Kings 11:14, 25; Pss. 71:13; 109:6, 20, 29). The denominative does not, however, always indicate Satan, the archenemy of the people of God, for in most of its occurrences it indicates a human adversary, either in litigatory (Ps. 109:6) or nonlitigatory (1 Sam. 29:4; 2 Sam. 19:23 [22]; 1 Kings 5:18 [4]; 11:14, 23, 25) situations. In the passages traditionally understood to refer to Satan (e.g., Job 1–2) the article is generally affixed to שׂטן, but it is not necessary (1 Chron. 21:1). The context here does not develop the identity of the accuser further than that of an accuser in a legal confrontation (see the Exposition). עַל־יְמִינוֹ (to his right): Psalm 109:6 shows that the adversary stood to the right of the accused in matters of litigation, exercising a prosecutorial role in the controversy. לְשִׂטְנוֹ (to accuse him) underscores this role. The function of the adversary was to accuse Joshua of wrongdoing and, beyond him, the people.

2. וַיֹּאמֶר (and said): ו (and) continues the series of *waw*-clauses that began in verse 1 and continues through verse 7. This sequence marks verses 1–7 as a logical unit. יְהוָה (the LORD) himself utters the imprecation "the LORD rebuke you," which is curious, but we need not think that the Lord and the angel of the Lord were identical in the prophet's mind, for 1:12–16 observes a distinction between them (see the Exposition there). יִגְעַר (rebuke) does not denote only verbal rebuke or the expression of strong disapproval, for the word often involves appropriate action. In Psalm 9:6 [5], for example, it is parallel with "you have destroyed the wicked"; in Malachi 3:11, God's rebuke of the locusts prevents them from destroying the produce of the land. Here in Zechariah, however, the text gives no indication of punish-

---

3:1. The Lord reveals another vision to Zechariah that extends throughout all of chapter 3; I have broken it at verse 7 to reflect the absence of narrative *waw* (and) at the beginning of verse 8. This vision involves Joshua the high priest. While the high priest had great authority throughout much of Israel's history (2 Kings 12:11–13 [10–12]; 22:4; 2 Chron. 26:16–20), the absence of a reigning monarch in the postexilic period appears to have lifted the high priest to even greater prominence, especially in matters relating to the temple, which were at the forefront early in this period of restoration (Ezra 3:9). The prophet Haggai reflects the high priest's authority at this time, speaking of him in the same breath with Zerubbabel, the governor of Judah (1:1, 12, 14; 2:2, 4).

This vision depicts a scene of legal controversy. Since Joshua the high priest is "standing before the angel of the LORD," we may assume that the angel sustains an important role in this dispute. To Joshua's right stands an accuser. The text does not require us to assume that this figure (*haśśāṭān*) is Satan; he may function only as a symbol of an accuser, a role endemic to any legal disputation (see the Exegesis). The description of this figure in the text is too vague for us to draw any other conclusions, and thus the use of this datum in any theological description of Satanology is tenuous (see Unger, *Zechariah*, pp. 57–58). It is enough to know that there was an accuser present when Joshua stood before the angel.

The description of this dramatic court scene is not yet complete, for we learn from verse 4 that there were figures standing before the angel of the Lord ready to do his bidding (see also v. 5). Verse 8 contributes another element, informing us that Joshua's colleagues were seated before him. The dramatic event this vision describes occurred in the presence of a large assemblage. In all probability, the angel of the Lord represents Yahweh as the judge in this court scene (Baldwin, *Zechariah*, p. 113), for it is the angel who carries out the implications of Yahweh's rebuke in verse 2 by removing the nation's guilt (v. 4) and speaking on Yahweh's behalf (v. 7).

2. We learn that Joshua symbolizes the postexilic community because the "stick snatched from the fire" can refer only to the nation recently returned from exile. The choice of the high priest as the representative of the nation calls to mind the character of holiness that Yahweh wished for his people and that the levitical priesthood watched over and emulated (Lev. 21:1–24). Because the people had violated Yahweh's demands for holiness, they had become vile in his sight (v. 4), losing their priestly privilege and falling far short of the original ideal for the nation that they should be "a priestly kingdom" (Exod. 19:6).

We do not hear the accuser's words in this court scene: perhaps he had no opportunity to speak. His standing in the position of the complainant is enough for us to know that he wishes

ment for the accuser. בְּךָ . . . יִגְעַר (rebuke . . . you): יִגְעַר has a jussive sense, expressing a wish (GKC §48g–h) with the intention of imprecating its object. בְּךָ (you): The preposition בְּ is not an essential object indicator with the verb גָּעַר, nor is it always an element in a crystallized collocation like גָּעַר בְּ. It functions here only to indicate the object and provide a seat for the object suffix ־ךְ (you). הַבֹּחֵר (who chooses): For the function of בָּחַר (to choose) in this participial relative clause, see the Exegesis of 1:17. הֲלוֹא (is [this] not) expects an affirmative answer in most occurrences (e.g., Deut. 3:11; Josh. 1:9; 2 Sam. 15:35; BDB, p. 520). Brongers ("H^alō^'") suggests that it also has a polite usage, "as you know," an appropriate sense here, but lacking the force we expect in this litigatory context. אוּד (stick) occurs elsewhere only in Isaiah 7:4 and Amos 4:11. In the former verse, אוּד has a smoking stump or end (lit., tail: זָנָב), probably indicating a stick used to stir a fire. The latter verse gives us little information, stating only that God saved the people from destruction as one would snatch a piece of wood from the fire before it is consumed. Perhaps אוּד designates a small branch used to stir a fire. Here in Zechariah it may represent such a stick rescued from the flames before it

becomes ashes (see the Exposition). מֻצָּל (snatched) in the hiphil and hophal (as here) expresses the idea of taking away. The context determines the degree of urgency in the verbal action. Here, the metaphor of fire pictures urgent removal. Israel was saved from extinction in the exile by divine intervention.

3. צוֹאִים (filthy): This adjectival form occurs only here and in verse 4. The root צוא connotes more than merely soiled, for its related nouns refer to human excrement (Deut. 23:14 [13]; Isa. 36:12 [Qere]; Ezek. 4:12) and vomit (Isa. 28:8). The noun may occur in metaphors depicting sin (Prov. 30:2; Isa. 4:4), as it does here. וְעֹמֵד לִפְנֵי הַמַּלְאָךְ (and [he was] standing before the angel): For the coordinate function of וֹ, see the Exposition.

4. וַיַּעַן (but responded): My translation gives an adversative sense to the particle וֹ because the clause it introduces resolves a tension in the discourse: the soiled garments made Joshua unfit to stand in God's presence, but (וֹ) the speaker commanded their removal. I understand the subject of this verb to be the angel of the Lord, even though Yahweh is the only previous speaker (v. 2). The angel is the nearest logical referent, appearing at the end of verse 3, and the form לְפָנָיו (before him)

---

to accuse the people of wrongdoing and thus establish the legal ground for Yahweh's punitive judgment of them. We do hear a voice—the Lord's—and he silences the accuser.

Expecting an affirmative response (see the Exegesis), the Lord's question, "Is this not [hǎlô'] a stick snatched from the fire?" makes the reality of the captivity the heart of his judicial decision in this disputation. The accuser has no right to expect God to destroy the nation on account of its sin (see v. 4). His accusation is futile because God has already revealed his will for the people by delivering them from the captivity. If he had wished to let them perish for their sin, the Lord would have left them in Babylon; but by snatching them from the flames of exile, he revealed that his grace was greater than their guilt.

3. Our attention now turns to the high priest. We expect to see him clothed in white vestments with the ephod on his chest, but we are shocked at what we see. His garments are soiled with filth, and the description of his condition repulses us (see the Exegesis). The verse repeats the observation of verse 1 that Joshua was standing before the angel, but it intensifies the action of the statement by coordinating it with the previous clause: "Now [waw] Joshua was clothed in filthy gar-

ments, and [waw] standing before the angel." These coordinate clauses intensify the atmosphere of the text by underscoring Joshua's being Yahweh's representative while at the same time being in a disgusting state. Feelings of revulsion turn to wonder: Must not God turn his back on this repulsive sight and vent his anger at this affront to his holiness? It seems that the accuser is justified in calling for God's judgment on the sin this filth represents.

4. The angel responds ('ānâ) to the pitiful condition of the high priest, not in anger or disgust, but in grace, commanding his companions to discard the vile clothes. Perhaps the figures who stand before the angel to do his bidding are the angels who accompanied the angel of the Lord in the vision of 1:7–17 (see the Exposition of 1:8–11). At any rate, we know that they symbolize the agencies by which God removed the people's guilt, clothing them with honor.

The reality behind the symbol of the soiled garments is the guilt of the nation. No doubt the people wondered if their frustrating failures were the result of God's rejecting them because of the disobedience of past generations (1:4). Perhaps the divine anger that had lashed out against them and drove them into exile had not been assuaged. The

places this figure, who is the subject of this verb, directly in the assemblage, a position these visions never give to Yahweh. יַּעַן (responded): The verb עָנָה (to answer, respond) cannot here indicate a verbal response because there is no previous question (see the Exegesis of 1:12); rather, the angel responds to the high priest's pitiful condition. אֵלָיו (to him) refers to Joshua, as the subsequent words of this clause indicate. הֶעֱבַרְתִּי (I have removed): Hiphil עָבַר (to pass away) can be translated "to remove" (2 Chron. 35:24; Zech. 13:2), "to avert" (Ps. 119:37), or "to banish" (1 Kings 15:12). Here, it indicates divine forgiveness or the removal of guilt. מֵעָלֶיךָ (from you; lit., from upon you) is not a necessary adjunct to hiphil עָבַר (remove) where the removal of guilt is concerned (see 2 Sam. 24:10). It intensifies the action of the verb by expressing the locus of the guilt. The translation "remove guilt *from upon* one" provides a deeper sense of the burden of guilt and the relief of forgiveness. עֲוֹנֶךָ (your guilt): עָוֹן (guilt) has a broad range of meaning, including not only the act of sin but its consequence (guilt) as well. This is true of several Hebrew words for sin (McComiskey, "Prophetic Irony," pp. 98–99). וְהַלְבֵּשׁ (and clothe): This infinitive absolute bound with the conjunction ו qualifies the leading verb הֶעֱבַרְתִּי (I have removed) and represents an action distinct from that verb (*IBHS* §35.5; Rubenstein, "Finite Verb"). This infinitive absolute anticipates the action of reclothing Joshua, which the text goes on to describe in the subsequent verse. מַחֲלָצוֹת (with special attire) is a nominal form of the root חָלַץ (to draw off). BDB (p. 323) suggests that this noun relates to its verbal affinity in the sense that something designated מַחֲלָצָה was "taken off in ordinary life"; hence, it is a robe suited only for special occasions. This noun occurs elsewhere only in Isaiah 3:22, where its association with other types of finery indicates a special garment perhaps worn only on festive occasions.

---

removal of the soiled garments speaks to this concern and signifies the expunging of their guilt. Assured of Yahweh's favor, the community could continue their building efforts untrammeled by doubt and uncertainty. The removal of the filthy garments silenced the accuser, making his charge baseless, because the supreme Judge has done the unthinkable: he has removed the guilt of the people by a sovereign act of grace.

Not only do the angels remove the soiled garments; they replace them with rich finery. The high priest now stands in splendor, not abject shame. The forgiveness of sin precedes the bestowal of tokens of glory. So it is with those who are governed by the new covenant: "And all of us . . . seeing the glory of the Lord . . . are being transformed into the same image from one degree of glory to another" (2 Cor. 3:18). Particularly appropriate to the scene here in Zechariah are the words of Romans 8:30: "Those whom he justified he also glorified." The matchless grace of God that expunged Israel's guilt is the same grace that motivates God to expunge in us what he must view as disgusting sin, cleansing and glorifying all who come to him (Rom. 8:28–30).

V. Fourth Vision: The High Priest Symbolizes the Branch (3:1–10)
B. The High Priest's Clean Garments (3:5–7)

McCOMISKEY

⁵And I said, "Let them put a clean turban on his head." So they put the clean turban on his head and dressed him in [the] garments, and the angel of the LORD was standing [there]. ⁶And the angel of the LORD assured Joshua, saying, ⁷"This is what the LORD of hosts says, If you walk in my ways and if you observe my charge, then you shall both judge my house and have charge of my courts, and I will give you free access among these who are standing [here].

NRSV

⁵And I said, "Let them put a clean turban on his head." So they put a clean turban on his head and clothed him with the apparel; and the angel of the LORD was standing by.

⁶Then the angel of the LORD assured Joshua, saying ⁷"Thus says the LORD of hosts: If you will walk in my ways and keep my requirements, then you shall rule my house and have charge of my courts, and I will give you the right of access among those who are standing here.

5. יָשִׂימוּ (let them put): This jussive form expresses the prophet's wish. The plural formation refers to the angels who carry out the symbolic activities in this vision (v. 4). צָנִיף (turban) is related to the verb צָנַף (to wrap) and thus probably represents a turban. It is included in the litany of finery in Isaiah 3:23; in Isaiah 62:3, it is qualified by מְלוּכָה (royal); and in Job 29:14, it is a headdress, probably implying honor. Since it never refers to the headdress of a priest, its function here is to carry out the motif of glory established by the robe. טָהוֹר connotes cleanness, at times ceremonial (Lev. 15:13), moral (Lev. 16:30), or physical (Isa. 66:20). Since this context contrasts Joshua's new garments with the filthy ones he wore previously, this word merely indicates being free from soil. יְהוָה וּמַלְאַךְ (and the angel of the LORD): See the Exposition of 1:11.

6. וַיָּעַד (and assured): Hiphil עוּד indicates a sense of assurance or warning and occurs frequently with בְּ (as here). The preposition, however, does not appear to measurably affect the sense of the verb (for עוּד without בְּ, see Jer. 6:10; 11:7b; Lam. 2:13). The gracious promise of the angel is assuring.

7. כֹּה־אָמַר יְהוָה (this is what the LORD says) underscores the function of the angel as the representative of Yahweh (see the Exposition of 3:2 and 1:14 [10]). צְבָאוֹת (of hosts): See the Exegesis of 1:3 and the comments on Hosea 12:6 [5]. אִם (if) accompanied by the imperfective (תֵּלֵךְ) indicates a condition that may occur in the future (GKC §159l). בִּדְרָכַי תֵּלֵךְ (lit., in my ways you walk): The ways of the Lord are aspects of God's character that he desires humans to emulate (Deut. 10:12; 11:22; see the Exegesis of Hos. 14:10 [9]). וְאִם (and if): The writer had the option of omitting אִם (if) and beginning the second half of the protasis with וְאֵת כִּי can influence both clauses of a conditional sentence: כִּי תִשְׁמֹר אֶת־מִצְוֹת יְהוָה אֱלֹהֶיךָ וְהָלַכְתָּ בִּדְרָכָיו, if you keep the commandments of the LORD your God and walk in his ways; Deut. 28:9). The use of a second conditional particle (אִם) creates two separate conditional clauses and emphasizes the conditional atmosphere of the second אִם (if) clause. מִשְׁמַרְתִּי (my charge), related to the verb שָׁמַר (to keep, guard), denotes something to be kept or observed. In Genesis 26:5, it is more precisely defined by "my commandments," "my statutes," and "my laws." In its secular usages, it connotes responsibility (Num. 3:25; 2 Kings 11:5), a charge

---

5. Zechariah, who up until this point has been only an observer of the vision, now participates in it, speaking to the angel. The prophet has been a participant in previous visions (1:9; 2:2, 4 [1:19, 21]), and now, perhaps emboldened by the optimistic tenor of the revelations, finds himself crying: "Let them put a clean turban on his head." It is an attractive option to view the turban (ṣānîp) as one of the priestly vestments (Keil, *Minor Prophet*, pp. 254–55), but the priest's headdress was called a miṣnepet (Exod. 28:37; 29:6; Lev. 16:4; Ezek. 21:26), not a ṣānîp. While both terms are related to the same root, we have no evidence that the word ṣānîp developed into a designation for the priestly headdress (this word is associated with fine apparel in Job 29:14; Isa. 3:23; 62:3; see the Exegesis). At the time of the vision, the nation had little of the glory that Zechariah's urgent plea called for. The people must have felt shame at the pitiful state of the city and temple. The turban Zechariah requested crowns the high priest's glory, representing the full measure of honor the prophet desired for his people.

The New Testament speaks of the "crown of glory" that completes the believer's process of glorification: "And when the chief shepherd appears, you will win the crown of glory that never fades

away (1 Peter 5:4; see also 2 Tim. 4:8; James 1:12; Rev. 2:10). As Joshua stands before the heavenly assemblage in this vision, he symbolizes his nation, but he foreshadows as well the experience of the believer under the new covenant:

> Clothed in splendor now I stand,
> condemned no more by sin's vile stain;
> here before the heavenly band,
> a crown of glory is my gain.

This vision assured Zechariah that his people would achieve the status of a nation chosen and honored by God. The last words of this verse remind us of the angel's solemn presence. As the representative of God, his presence casts God's approval on the transaction.

6–7. The angel of the Lord speaks again (see the Exegesis of v. 4), uttering words of assurance to Joshua. Because Joshua represents the people, the assurances are in reality directed to them. And since the angel of the Lord is Yahweh's representative, it is God who makes the following promise to his people.

That the Lord speaks in verse 7 is underscored by the messenger formula: "This is what the LORD of hosts says." Since this title depicts Yah-

(Num. 1:53), protection (1 Sam. 22:23; 2 Sam. 20:3), or the keeping of objects for a period of time (Exod. 12:6; Num. 17:25 [10]). When it relates to the Lord, it refers to his requirements, that is, the commands and restrictions he wants observed (Lev. 8:35; 18:30; 22:9; Deut. 11:1; Mal. 3:14). תִּשְׁמֹר (you observe), like the preceding תֵּלֵךְ (you walk), is an imperfective expressing the possibility of fulfillment in the future. וְגַם (then both): וּ (then) frequently introduces the apodosis of conditional clauses and denotes the consequence of the condition (וְהָלַכְתִּי in Judg. 4:8; וְסָר in Judg. 16:17; וְהָיָה in 2 Sam. 15:33). When the particle גַּם occurs in the construction [וְ]גַם . . . וְגַם (both . . . and), as it does here, it differentiates entities that share a broadly conceptual relationship (Gen. 24:44; 1 Sam. 12:14). אַתָּה (you) does not necessarily receive emphasis in this construction (IBHS, p. 301). תָּדִין (you shall judge): The broad semantic range of this verb generally indicates adjudication. Since, however, one cannot adjudicate a temple (בֵּיתִי), the companion clause תִּשְׁמֹר אֶת־חֲצֵרָי (have charge of my courts) gives דִּין the sense of governing (Ps. 72:2) and royal administrative responsibility (Jer. 21:12). בֵּיתִי (my house): The word בַּיִת has several meanings in Zechariah: the temple (1:16; 4:9; 7:2, 3; 8:9), a domicile (5:4; 6:10), a place of lodging (5:11), and the people of God (8:13, 15, 19; 9:8; 10:3, 6). The form בֵּיתִי (my house) in this book can refer to both the temple (1:16) and the people (9:8). Since the high priest is at the forefront in this vision and the courts (חֲצֵרָי) are probably those of the temple, the promise certainly envisions the temple. תִּשְׁמֹר (have charge): When occurring with

components of the temple structure (as it does here), שָׁמַר connotes the act of watching over or guarding the temple precincts (2 Kings 22:4; 25:18; 1 Chron. 9:19; 2 Chron. 34:9; Neh. 13:22; Jer. 35:4). חֲצֵרָי (courts) most frequently refers to the courts of the tabernacle (Exod. 27:9; 38:9; 39:40; Lev. 6:9 [16]; Num. 3:26) and temple (1 Kings 6:36; 7:12; Jer. 36:10; Ezek. 8:16; 10:4; see also 40:14, 19, 32); on occasion it designates the courts of a palace (1 Kings 7:8, 9, 12; 2 Kings 20:4; Esth. 4:11). The combination בַּיִת and חָצֵר always designates components of the temple structure (2 Kings 21:5; 2 Chron. 33:5; see esp. 1 Chron. 28:6). The priestly atmosphere of this text indicates temple courts. The Septuagint translates מַהְלְכִים (free access) as ἀναστρεφομένους (men to walk), understanding it either as a hiphil participle after the analogy of the Aramaic מַהְלְכִין (walking) in Daniel 3:25 or as a piel participle (Eccles. 4:15). The Masoretic tradition points it as a noun form (מַהֲלָךְ) of הָלַךְ (to go). Appeal to another language is speculative, especially since the Masoretic form is attested sufficiently elsewhere (Neh. 2:6; Ezek. 42:4; Jon. 3:3). The second option (piel participle) also presents difficulties, for the only substantival usage of the piel participle (Prov. 6:11) requires an intensive sense akin to tramping because it balances אִישׁ מָגֵן (armed man) in the parallel structure, a sense too strong for the context here. It is best to posit the noun מַהֲלָךְ (going), which can refer to a journey (Neh. 2:6; Jon. 3:3) or a measured distance (Ezek. 42:4). Since מַהֲלָךְ appears only here in the plural, we must look to the context, which colors it with the sense of freedom of movement among "those

weh as commander of legions of the heavenly armies (see the Exegesis of 1:3), he speaks with authority and possesses the power to make the spoken assurance a reality. The assuring words, however, are couched in two conditional clauses: "*If* you walk in my ways, and *if* you observe my charge." The reality that the rich apparel symbolizes—the restoration of the nation's glory—is conditioned on national obedience. This condition, following the act of sovereign grace that resulted in the removal of Joshua's filthy garments, should not surprise us, for after all it was the people's disobedience that flung them headlong from their lofty status as Yahweh's possession to the shameful exile in a foreign land. It is this rebellion that the vision represents as the disgusting stains on the garments of a nation that was originally destined for priestly status (Exod. 19:5–6). The words of Moses that envisioned this

high privilege were themselves cloaked in a condition: "If you obey my voice and keep my covenant . . ." (Exod. 19:5). The postexilic community learned that even though God had removed their sin by an act of grace, they could not expect to achieve his highest goals for them if they neglected his precepts.

The text amplifies the ideal of priestly status by describing the free access the nation will enjoy "among those who are standing [here]." The only group the text pictures as standing are those who carry out the angel's command to remove Joshua's stained garments (v. 4). These figures symbolize the agencies by which God expunges guilt. In Zechariah's day, these agencies were the levitical sacrifices and rituals. The promised freedom of access to these priestly functions is an affirmation of the restoration to priestly privilege that this vision sets forth, assuring the free enjoyment of

standing here." בֵּין (among) connotes some freedom of movement among or access to the assemblage described in the following participial clause

as הָעֹמְדִים (standing). This participle designates the figures who carried out the directives of the angel of the Lord (v. 4). הָאֵלֶּה (these): See the Exposition.

---

the means of grace by which God expunges human guilt.

The promise that Joshua would minister in the temple, having charge of its courts, assumes the successful completion of the building project. Thus, the discourse of 3:1–7 has two major themes: the affirmation that God will not forsake his people, but remain faithful to his covenant

promise by removing their guilt (v. 4); and the assurance that they will complete the building of the temple (v. 7). These themes would have meant much to the struggling community. They knew they would succeed in the work of rebuilding because their past sin had not severed their relationship to their God, and they had his assurance that they would not fail.

V. Fourth Vision: The High Priest Symbolizes the Branch (3:1–10)
C. Significance of the Change of Garments (3:8–10)

McCOMISKEY

⁸"Hear now, Joshua the high priest—you and your companions who sit before you, for they are men of a sign; for look, I am bringing forth my servant, [the] Branch; ⁹for look, the stone that I have set before Joshua—on a single stone are seven eyes. Look, I am engraving its inscription, utterance of the LORD of hosts, and I shall remove the guilt of this land in one day. ¹⁰On that day, utterance of the LORD of hosts, you will invite one another under vine and under fig tree."

NRSV

⁸Now listen, Joshua, high priest, you and your colleagues who sit before you! For they are an omen of things to come: I am going to bring my servant the Branch. ⁹For on the stone that I have set before Joshua, on a single stone with seven facets, I will engrave its inscription, says the LORD of hosts, and I will remove the guilt of this land in a single day. ¹⁰On that day, says the LORD of hosts, you shall invite each other to come under your vine and fig tree."

8. שְׁמַע־נָא (hear now): Lambdin (*Biblical Hebrew*, p. 170) notes that the particle נָא (now) seems "to denote that the command . . . in question is a logical consequence either of an immediately preceding statement or of the general situation in which it is uttered." This is its function here, for the command to hear (שְׁמַע) introduces the reality underlying the symbolic activity this vision describes: what follows is the logical consequence of the preceding. The word *now* in my translation reflects that function of נָא. Even though שְׁמַע is construed as a singular, it addresses Joshua's companions as well as Joshua himself, as the subsequent אַתָּה וְרֵעֶיךָ (you and your companions) shows. Jeremiah 22:2 has a similar construction, and the subsequent plural forms show that the singular שְׁמַע addresses a wide audience. וְרֵעֶיךָ (your companions): The sense of רֵעַ ranges broadly, and can indicate a companion, friend, compatriot, or even the innocuous "another" (v. 10). The following participial clause exerts an influence on this word, giving it greater clarity. הַיֹּשְׁבִים לְפָנֶיךָ (who sit before you): All secular occurrences of the collocation יָשַׁב לִפְנֵי (sit before) denote being in the presence of a superior for the purpose of receiving counsel or instruction (2 Kings 4:38; 6:1; Ps. 61:7 [8]; Ezek. 8:1; 14:1; 20:1; 33:31). כִּי (for) following שְׁמַע (hear) often introduces clauses that state in narrow or broadly causal terms the reason for hearing (Gen. 21:12; Neh. 3:36 [4:4]; Job 34:2, 3; Isa. 1:2; 28:14, 15; Ezek. 40:4; Hos. 4:1; 5:1). Here, the reason is that Joshua and his colleagues symbolize a portentous event that demands their attention. אַנְשֵׁי מוֹפֵת (men of a sign): The word מוֹפֵת (sign) is many times parallel to or associated with אֹת (sign) (Deut. 4:34; 6:22; 7:19; Ps. 78:43), but it does not always refer to a portent. It can describe someone out of the ordinary (Ps. 7:17), and in Ezekiel 12:6 (see also v. 11) and 24:24 (see also v. 27) it occurs in connection with a person, as here. In both passages the prophet Ezekiel is a מוֹפֵת in that he symbolizes future divine activity. The following כִּי clause gives the word that sense here (see below). The construct (men of a sign) connotes relationship; in some way, Joshua and his fellow priests relate to a sign of a future event. הֵמָּה (they): The mode of address to Joshua and his colleagues now curiously changes to the third person. Stylistic changes of person are not characteristic of Zechariah, and it is difficult to understand why the third person appears in a mode of direct address. Perhaps the writer wished to distinguish Joshua from his fellow priests, an idea he could not express if he used the second-person plural אַתֶּם (you) in place of הֵמָּה (they), for that would group Joshua with his colleagues (see the Exposition). כִּי introduces a clause that explains the previous one: they are men of a sign because they represent "the Branch." This כִּי cannot relate directly to שְׁמַע, introducing the reason to hear; thus, the previous כִּי clause is a parenthetical statement: "Hear now, Joshua the high priest—you and your companions who sit before you (for they are men of a sign)—*for* look. . . ." מֵבִיא (am bringing forth): The timeless nature of the participle creates the sense that the

---

8. The summons to hear imparts a sense of expectation to this section: we feel we are going to learn more about the significance and importance of the events we are witnessing. The text intensifies this sense of anticipation by repeating the attention-getting particle *hinneh* (look) three times in verses 8–9 and *nĕʾum yhwh* (utterance of the Lord) twice in verses 9–10, literary devices that do not appear in the first section of the vision. Verses 8–10 resolve this sense of anticipation in the announcement that the Lord will bring forth his servant the Branch, who is somehow involved in the agencies of redemption by which God removes the people's guilt.

The summons to hear is not only directed to Joshua but also to his companions. While the text does not tell us who these are, we may assume that they are associates of the high priest, for the suffix ("your") on *rēʿêkă* (companions) connects them to him. That they sit before (*yāšab lipnê*) him further underscores the connection, for this expression conveys the sense of receiving counsel and instruction, not administrative subordination (see the Exegesis). The conclusion that answers best to the textual data is that Joshua's companions were fellow priests over whom the high priest exercised spiritual authority.

The reason for including Joshua's colleagues in the summons is that "they are men of a sign." We need not wonder why the text refers only to them, apparently omitting Joshua from the explanation of their symbolic function, for we have already learned from verse 3 that he is a sign standing for the nation that was "snatched from the fire." Now we learn that Joshua's companions also serve as a sign. Since the word *hēmmâ* (they) appears at the end of the clause, it may be emphatic: they, too, are men of a sign.

The priestly figures in this vision are "men of a sign" because God will bring forth his servant the

action is moving toward its goal. צֶמַח ([the] Branch) indicates something that sprouts or grows (Gen. 19:25; Ps. 65:11 [10]; Isa. 4:2; Hos. 8:7). Its apposition with עַבְדִּי (my servant) shows that we must understand it metaphorically to refer to a person (see the Exposition; see also the Exegesis and Exposition of 6:12).

9. כִּי (for) introduces a broader causality than the previous כִּי clause. We know only that in some way the reference to the stone continues the explanation of the function of the Branch. הִנֵּה (look), like הִנֵּה in verse 8, does not have the sense of visual observation as the translation "look" may seem to imply. The use of this translational equivalent is an effort to express the emphatic sense of the term. הָאֶבֶן (the stone) may refer to any type of stone, including gems (Exod. 25:7) and building stones (Zech. 5:4). Several commentators suggest a precious jewel (see the Exposition). נָתַתִּי (I have set) continues the first-person references to God that began in verse 6. עַל־אֶבֶן אַחַת (on a single stone): Lipinski ("Recherches," p. 25) favors the translation "at one time—at the same time," a conclusion based on the occurrence of this expression in Judges 9:5, 18, where it seems to indicate that the murders of the seventy sons of Jerubbaal

all took place at one time. There is no convincing reason, however, for denying the literal sense of this expression in Judges, for one particular stone may have served as an execution block. In Judges, עַל אֶבֶן אַחַת may have the secondary meaning "at one time," but that is no guarantee that this is the sole semantic function of this expression (see the Exposition). The reference to a stone in the immediately preceding clause makes it likely that it is the one in this clause. עַל . . . עֵינָיִם (on . . . eyes): עֵינָיִם (eyes) is dual in form, but this does not imply seven pairs of eyes, for the dual often serves as the plural of naturally paired objects (e.g., שֵׁשׁ כְּנָפַיִם, six wings, in Isa. 6:2; see *IBHS*, p. 117). This use of עַיִן (eye) with עַל (on) may indicate either that the eyes are carved on the face of the stone or that they are fixed on (i.e., watching) the stone. The latter view fits the context best and comports with the use of the expression elsewhere in Scripture (2 Sam. 22:28; 2 Chron. 20:12; Job 34:21; Jer. 16:17). The following reference to carving (מְפַתֵּחַ) may appear to support the idea that these eyes were cut into the stone, but this view requires that there are seven eyes on the stone and then awkwardly states that God is in the process of carving them (הִנְנִי מְפַתֵּחַ). If the writer wished to

---

Branch. Both servant and Branch have messianic significance. The servant concept appears for the first time in Isaiah and envisions someone who brings redemption to his people (52:13; 53:8, 10–11) through suffering (53:4–11), accomplishing the will of God in spite of shame (49:7) and humiliation (50:6). Jeremiah envisions the Branch as a king associated with David (23:5; 33:15). The Branch reappears in Zechariah 6:11–12 as a king. The sign function of Joshua and his fellow priests symbolizes the work of this servant-king whom God will bring forth into the arena of world history. We cannot identify the Branch with Joshua the high priest or with any of those who sit before him, for they are symbolic figures; to do so would be to identify the symbol with the symbol, not with the reality to which it points. The Branch stands outside this vision and is foreseen by it. God will yet bring him forth, and in some way he will build the temple and expunge the guilt of his people.

9. Our attention turns now to a stone that God has set before the high priest. *Kî* (for) indicates that in some way the stone is broadly explicative of Yahweh's intention to bring forth the Branch. The following verses develop that explanation.

How are we to imagine this stone? Is it a precious gem with seven facets (Ackroyd, "Zecha-

riah," p. 648), the plate on the high priest's turban (Mitchell, *Zechariah*, pp. 25–29; Petersen, *Zechariah 1–8*, pp. 211–12), or a stone symbolizing the temple reconstruction? The view that it represents an engraved plate on the high priest's turban is attractive because the context refers to engraving ("I am engraving its inscription"), and Exodus 28:36–38, speaking of this plate, associates it with the removal of guilt, an important concept in this verse ("I will remove the guilt of this land"). This plate, however, is not designated *ʾeben* (a stone) but *ṣîṣ*, and it is doubtful that the word *ʿayin* (eye, facet) can refer to the consonants in this plate's inscription (Petersen, *Zechariah 1–8*, pp. 211–12). It is not likely that this is a precious stone, for in each instance where *ʾeben* refers to such a stone the context qualifies it by an immediate modifier such as *yāqār* (precious; 2 Sam. 12:30) or *sappîr* (sapphire; Ezek. 1:26), which is not the case here. On the other hand, there is little in the context that identifies this stone as a building stone. We may observe, however, that the stone is "set before" Joshua, a notation that favors a large object rather than a gem that one would put into the hand or place on the turban. While the word *ʾeben* is a virtual semantic zero in this text, the

say that the eyes were already carved into the stone he could have expressed that idea unequivocally by the use of פִּתַּחְתִּי (I have engraved). Lipinski ("Recherches," p. 29) translates עֵינָיִם as "springs" of water, yielding, "At the same time, seven springs! Behold, I will open their openings" (my translation; see the Exposition). The New Revised Standard Version translates עֵינָיִם as "facets," apparently understanding אֶבֶן as a precious stone. While the word עַיִן can refer to the face of the ground (Exod. 10:5; Num. 22:5), there is no evidence that "facet" is an acceptable translational equivalent for this word. מְפַתֵּחַ (engraving):

Contexts dealing with artistic work give piel פִּתַּח the meaning "to engrave, carve, inscribe" (Exod. 28:36; 1 Kings 7:36; 2 Chron. 3:7). פִּתֻּחָה (its engraving) refers mainly to inscriptions (Exod. 28:11, 21, 36; 39:6, 14, 30), but may also connote representational engravings (1 Kings 6:29). נְאֻם יְהוָה (utterance of the LORD): See the Exegesis of 1:3. יְהוָה צְבָאוֹת (the LORD of hosts): See the Exegesis and Exposition of 1:3. וּמַשְׁתִּי (and I will remove) is the only transitive occurrence of this verb in the qal (see also 14:4); it never elsewhere occurs with עָוֹן (guilt), but one cannot mistake its sense here. הָאָרֶץ־הַהִיא (this land) is postexilic Judah.

---

remote context that deals with the construction of the temple also favors the latter view.

Understanding the stone as symbolic of the building project rather than as part of the priestly apparel complements the two main themes of the first section of the discourse: removal of the nation's guilt (v. 4) and assurance of the successful completion of the temple (v. 7)—resolving them nicely in the mission of the Branch. The function of this second section thus establishes the relationship of the messianic figure, the Branch, to those two prospects (see the Exegesis of the second *kî* clause). The association of the Branch with the construction of the temple is not anomalous to Zechariah, for 6:12 says of him that "he . . . shall build the temple of the LORD." The reference in 4:10 to the seven eyes of the Lord, which represent Yahweh's watchfulness, also occurs in a context dealing with the success of the building efforts and echoes the reference to the seven facets in 3:9 (see the Exposition of 4:10).

Lipinski's suggestion ("Recherches"; see the Exegesis) that *ʿênāyim* represents "springs" rather than "eyes" and that the expression *ʿal ʾeben ʾāḥat* connotes "at one time" gives the sense that from this rock Yahweh will cause seven springs to flow at one time. If, however, *ʿal ʾeben ʾāḥat* modifies *měpattēăḥ pittuḥâ* (I will open its openings), we should expect it to be in the same clause with those words ("look, at the same time I am opening its openings"), not in the previous clause. On the basis of this suggestion we must read the previous clause as "at the same time are seven springs," an awkward translation, especially since *pittuḥâ* (its opening) and its suffix ought to be plural in this case. Lipinski refers this suffix to the collective substantive *sibʿâ* (seven) rather than to *ʾeben* (stone), which is questionable. He also relates *ʿayin* (spring) to the concept of divine forgiveness (I will remove the guilt of this land in a single

day), but *ʿayin* never occurs as a metaphor for cleansing (only *maqôr* [fountain] has that sense; see 13:1). The reference to this stone in 4:7, 10 further complicates this view (see the Exposition). Lipinski's suggestion that there is an analogy with Moses striking the rock in Exodus 17:5–6 is apparent but by no means convincing. The text in no way signals that event, and to refer to it here is speculative. This suggestion also fails to observe that national cleansing is not the only theme of this discourse: the successful completion of the temple is here as well.

The view that best answers to the demands of the discourse is that Yahweh's eyes are watching over the building efforts (the stone). The numeral *seven* would then have its symbolic sense of totality (McComiskey, "Seventy Weeks," pp. 35–40), indicating that God is watching the building efforts intently and will see them through to completion. In all probability, this stone is a finishing stone (a capstone or cornerstone) whose inscription Yahweh is already carving and the placement of which would mark the completion of the structure.

The builders would have gained encouragement from the prophet's assuring word, but the significance of the stone does not end with the completed temple because *kî* (for), beginning this verse, relates the stone to the mission of the messianic figure, the Branch. The stone symbolizes a greater temple whose ministrations effect the removal of guilt—the temple of the Branch (6:12) over which God intently watched. Numerous New Testament concepts intersect with this affirmation, only one of which is the representation of Christ's redemptive work against the background of Old Testament temple ministrations (Heb. 10).

The assurance that God will remove the guilt of the land calls us sharply back to the earlier section of this vision, where the angels removed

10. בַּיּוֹם הַהוּא (on that day): The previous referent of this expression is the time when God will bring forth his servant, the Branch. נְאֻם יְהוָה צְבָאוֹת (utterance of the LORD of hosts): See the Exegesis of 1:3. תִּקְרְאוּ (you will invite): Unless the writer is now addressing his reading audience, this plural construction is directed to Joshua and his colleagues. אִישׁ (one) most frequently indicates a man, but it possesses an individualizing function as well: each (Gen. 10:5) or one (Exod. 34:3). לְרֵעֵהוּ (another): See the Exegesis of verse 8. גֶּפֶן most commonly designates grape-bearing vines (but see 2 Kings 4:39). תְּאֵנָה (fig tree) is frequently compounded with גֶּפֶן in expressions describing abundance of agricultural produce (Deut. 8:8; Joel 2:22), lack of such abundance (Jer. 5:17; 8:13; Hos. 2:14 [12]; Joel 1:7, 12; Hab. 3:17), or undisturbed enjoyment of the land's abundance (1 Kings 4:25; 2 Kings 18:31; Isa. 36:16; Mic. 4:4). The unsuffixed form of these words seems to be nothing more than a poetic mode of speech (Joel 2:22; see also 1:7). Here, the expression is a metaphorical description of the prosperity that will obtain when the prospects of this vision materialize (see the Exposition).

Joshua's soiled garments (v. 4). There, we had only the oblique reference to the "stick snatched from the fire" (v. 2) to indicate that Joshua stood for the nation; now we are certain of that fact, for it is the land that experiences forgiveness. We have learned that Joshua's companions also function as a symbol (v. 8), and we must include them along with Joshua as representatives of the nation that will experience the removal of guilt "in one day." This text does not identify the "one day" that witnesses the expunging of the people's sin; therefore, we must leave the question open at this point. There is, however, a day to which this book refers (13:1; see also 12:10), on which "a fountain shall be opened for the house of David and the inhabitants of Jerusalem, to cleanse them from sin and impurity."

10. The expression *on that day* refers to the period of time that verses 8–9 describe: the time when symbol will give way to reality and the Branch will come. We learn from verse 9 that he will expunge the guilt of his people; now we learn that they will invite one another under vine and fig tree. This metaphor frequently describes great abundance (see the Exegesis), but its collocation with *taḥat* (under) expands its sense to include security (1 Kings 5:5 [4:25]; Mic. 4:4). Jeremiah 23:5–6 and 33:15–16 also speak of the security the Branch will provide for his people. This assurance of security for God's people intersects with the regnal implications of the title "Branch," foreshadowing the kingdom he will establish. We perceive in these assurances an important element in this book: as surely as the temple builders will complete their task, so surely will God bring into time and history the kingdom of his servant the Branch.

It is possible that the word *rēaʿ* in the expression *ʾîš lĕrēʿēhû* (one another) reflects the use of this word in verse 8, where it refers to Joshua's fellow priests. If this is so, those figures are "men of a sign" in that they prefigure the citizens of the kingdom of the Branch who will "invite one another under vine and fig tree." Once again the community learned that they would succeed in their efforts, for God is watching over his work (the stone). We, too, may derive encouragement from this vision, for in a larger way God is watching over the kingdom of Christ and will continue to do so until that day when "he will dwell with them as their God . . . and . . . wipe every tear from their eyes . . . for the first things have passed away" (Rev. 21:4).

VI. Fifth Vision: Gold Lampstand (4:1–14)
A. Description of the Lampstand (4:1–3)

McCOMISKEY

4 And the angel who spoke with me roused me again as one who is awakened from his sleep, ²and he said to me, "What are you seeing?" And I said, "I look, and there is a lampstand all of gold and a receptacle on the top of it and its seven lamps on it and seven lips each to the lamps that are on top of it. ³And [there are] two olive trees beside it, one to the right of the receptacle and one on its left."

NRSV

4 The angel who talked with me came again, and wakened me, as one is wakened from sleep. ²He said to me, "What do you see?" And I said, "I see a lampstand all of gold, with a bowl on the top of it; there are seven lamps on it, with seven lips on each of the lamps that are on the top of it. ³And by it there are two olive trees, one on the right of the bowl and the other on its left."

4:1. וַיָּשָׁב (and again): See the Exposition. וַיְעִירֵנִי (and he aroused me): The contexts in which עוּר occurs give it various nuances: to motivate to action (2 Chron. 36:22; Ezra 1:5; Jer. 51:11; Joel 4:9 [3:9]), to raise up on the scene of world history (Isa. 41:2; 45:13), to rise to action (Job 8:6), to awaken (Pss. 57:9 [8]; 108:3 [2]; Song 2:7), or to rouse up (Deut. 32:11; Ps. 78:38). The comparative כְּ (as [one who is awakened]) shows that the prophet was not actually asleep, but roused by the angel, perhaps to a higher state of prophetic receptivity.

2. וַיֹּאמֶר: This second occurrence of אָמַר in this verse is problematic. The *Kethiv* is translated "and he said," making the subsequent words the angel's, not Zechariah's. The *Qere*, וָאֹמַר (and I said), is preferable because the formula רָאָה + הִנֵּה (see + there is) always appears as the prophet's words in these visions. That the prophet "responded" (עָנָה) in verse 4 does not indicate that the angel had been speaking to that point, because עָנָה can indicate a response to not only a question but also to a statement or situation (1:11, 12; 4:11, 12; 6:4). מְנוֹרַת (lampstand): In all probability we

are to picture this lamp not as a seven-branched menorah, but as a pedestal of some kind suitable to support a receptacle and seven lamps. וְגֻלָּה (and a receptacle): The mappiq in ה in the Masoretic tradition makes the word appear to represent a form גֹּל with a possessive suffix. There is, however, no form גֹּל suitable to this context (unless it designates a curved ornamental decoration). The recurrence of this form without the mappiq in verse 3 makes it all but certain that we must read וְגֻלָּה here. This obscure word refers to springs of water in Joshua 15:19 and Judges 1:15, probably describing the pool into which the springs flowed. In 1 Kings 7:41 and 2 Chronicles 4:12, it describes a globelike decoration at the top of a pillar, under its capitals. In Ecclesiastes 12:6, it is almost certainly a bowl, for it could be broken. These occurrences favor a bowl-shaped container or reservoir for this word, a conclusion that gains support from the pedestal-bowl lamps that North ("Lampstand") describes. שִׁבְעָה וְשִׁבְעָה (seven each; lit., seven and seven) is the typical Hebrew way to express the distributive (e.g., in 2 Sam. 21:20 and

---

4:1. The prophet is conscious of a hiatus in the course of his reception of the visions. We cannot fully understand what occurred; we only know that he again became aware of the mysterious presence of the mediating angel arousing him to prepare for another vision (see Jer. 31:26).

The word *šûb* that begins this verse may mean "return," but it is not likely that it has that sense here, for the text does not previously inform us that the angel left the prophet to return at this point. Since *šûb* has an auxiliary function answering to "again" in 5:1 and 6:1 (Rudolph, *Sacharja*, pp. 103–4; Meyers and Meyers, *Zechariah 1–8*, p. 228; Hamilton, *TWOT*, p. 209), this translation resonates with earlier elements in the account of the night visions—namely, the instances in which the mediating angel lifted the prophet to even greater heights of prophetic awareness by explaining to him the significance of the visions. That the angel again roused Zechariah's prophetic consciousness creates a juncture in the narrative, and it is significant in this regard that the two sections this juncture marks (1:7–3:10; 4:1–6:15) develop the same theological concepts in a roughly similar pattern, both beginning with encouragement to the builders (1:7–17; 4:1–14) and ending with the anticipation of the Branch (3:8–10; 6:9–15). Both sections also have in common the major themes of cleansing from sin (3:1–10; 5:1–10) and Gentile

inclusion in the divine purpose (2:15 [11]; 6:15). It is likely, then, that the words *roused me again* tell us that the angel lifted Zechariah to a renewed state of prophetic awareness.

2. Zechariah saw a golden lampstand supporting seven lamps. We are probably not to picture this lampstand as the seven-branched menorah that stood in the tabernacle (Exod. 25:31–40), but as the pedestal lamps known to us from antiquity (North, "Lampstand"). Zechariah's lampstand also supported a bowl that apparently was a receptacle for the oil. The seven lamps were "on" (ʿal) the lampstand, at its "top" (rōʾšāh), probably arranged around the brim of the receptacle. Since ancient saucer lamps were themselves receptacles for oil, with fluted lips to support the wicks, the lamps in Zechariah's lampstand would have been refilled from the oil in the receptacle. Since this lampstand differs from the one in the tabernacle, we should not press associations with Israelite cultic worship in the interpretation of the vision.

The word *mûṣāqôt* (lips) represents one of the most difficult problems in this passage. The word probably represents the spoutlike lips of ancient saucer lamps (see the Exegesis). The lamps in this vision would thus be the seven-lipped lamps known to us from antiquity. See North's reconstruction ("Lampstand") of Zechariah's lampstand based on archaeological models.

1 Chron. 20:6, שֵׁשׁ וָשֵׁשׁ [six each; lit., six and six] expresses six each of fingers and toes [hence twenty-four]). מֻצָקוֹת (lips) appears elsewhere only in 2 Chronicles 4:3 in a clause (יְצוּקִים בְּמֻצַקְתּוֹ) describing the oxen that ornamented the molten sea. While obscure, this clause answers comfortably to "cast in its [the molten sea's] casting" or "cast in its mold," indicating that the oxen and the molten sea were cast in the same pouring (מֻצַקְתּוֹ). יְצֻקְתּוֹ, the word that corresponds to מֻצַקְתּוֹ (its casting) in the parallel account in 1 Kings 7:24, has the same general sense. Since מֻצַקְתּוֹ is related to יָצַק (to pour), it probably represents a spout and, in the case of lamps, the fluted lips that supported the wicks of ancient saucer lamps (see the Exposition and the photograph of such a lamp in Wiseman, *Biblical Archaeology*, p. 102). רֹאשָׁהּ (on top

of it): The feminine singular suffix *it* (הָ-) refers to מְנוֹרָה (lampstand), not to גֻּלָּה (receptacle), because גֻּלָּה is itself suffixed to מְנוֹרָה, as are all the immediately preceding suffixes, a pattern the writer could have modified by the addition of עַהַגֻּלָּה (on the bowl) if he wished to place the lamps on the bowl at this point in the narrative.

3. עָלֶיהָ (beside it): The subsequent reference to "right and left" makes it clear that עַל means "beside" here. The suffix (ה) has the same referent as the preceding feminine suffix on רֹאשָׁהּ in verse 2, namely, the lampstand. מִימִין . . . עַל־שְׂמֹאלָהּ (to the right . . . on its left): That the prepositions מִן and עַל both appear in this structure does not require the translation "off to [the side]" for מִן, as Nehemiah 8:4 shows.

---

3. The forty-nine flames that crowned Zechariah's lampstand would have produced light of unusual brilliance, emblazoning the gold pedestal and gilding the deep green foliage of the gnarled olive trees. This is not the whole of the vision, however, for we learn from verse 12 that each tree had a conspicuous branch, and two gold spouts conveyed the oil from these branches to the receptacle below. We must await the explanation of these branches.

VI. Fifth Vision: Gold Lampstand (4:1–14)
B. Explanation of the Lampstand's Significance (4:4–6)

McCOMISKEY

⁴And I responded and asked the angel who spoke with me, saying, "What are these my lord?" ⁵And the angel who spoke with me answered and said to me, "Do you not know what these are?" And I replied, "No, my lord." ⁶And he answered and said to me, "This is the word of the LORD to Zerubbabel, Not by strength, nor by power, but by my Spirit, says the LORD of hosts."

NRSV

⁴I said to the angel who talked with me, "What are these, my lord?" ⁵Then the angel who talked with me answered me, "Do you not know what these are?" I said, "No, my lord." ⁶He said to me, "This is the word of the LORD to Zerubbabel: Not by might, nor by power, but by my spirit, says the LORD of hosts.

4. וָאַעַן (and I responded) does not indicate that the prophet is responding to the previous words of the angel (see the Exegesis of v. 2), but to the vision he has just perceived. The plural מָה־אֵלֶּה (what are these) shows that Zechariah viewed this vision as consisting of its several components, not as a complex entity, to which he would have responded, מַה זֹּאת (what is this?): See the discussion of the similar expression in the Exposition of 1:9. אֲדֹנִי (my lord?): See the Exegesis of 1:9.

5. הֲלוֹא (do not) frequently expects an affirmative response (Isa. 40:21, 28) and may even func-

tion as an overt affirmation. For example, in Joshua 10:13, הֲלֹא־הִיא כְתוּבָה (lit., is this not written?) means "surely it is written" (see the Exposition and the Exegesis of 3:2). מָה־הֵמָּה אֵלֶּה (what are these?): See the Exegesis of 1:9.

6. וַיַּעַן (and he answered) does not always connote response to a question (see the Exegesis of 1:10). זֶה (this): Since this demonstrative pronoun "almost always points out a (new) person or thing present" (GKC, p. 442), I understand it to introduce the following words, not to refer to the preceding vision. בְחַיִל (by strength): חַיִל refers

---

4–5. Certainly the prophet's simple question, "What are these?" inquired after the meaning of what he was seeing, but the angel's use of *mâ-hēmmâ ʾēlleh* (what these are) focuses more sharply on the symbolic significance of the objects in the vision than their identity. "Do you not know what these *mean?*" was the angel's question. The perplexed prophet could only answer, "No."

The discourse does not take up the answer to the prophet's question until the end of the chapter (v. 14), leading some scholars to suggest that 4:6–10 contains two oracles that interrupt the original account of the vision (e.g., Smith, *Micah–Malachi*, pp. 203–4; and see the NAB and NEB). While it is possible that 4:6–10 found later placement here in the editorial process, this suggestion raises several literary problems. Not only would the prophet's "No, my Lord" in verse 5 go unanswered in the original oracle (vv. 1–5, 11–14), but the following question about the olive trees in verse 11 would as well, creating an awkwardness in the flow of the discourse that is, at best, suspicious. This suggested arrangement places the three uses of ʿānâ (to respond) in verses 4, 11, and 12 in close proximity, and since the first two occurrences of ʿānâ do not receive a positive response according to the suggested arrangement, we wonder why the word *šēnît* (a second time) does not occur at verse 11 in company with the second response in the original discourse. That it appears where it does (v. 12) makes it likely that verses 11–12 do not follow logically from verse 5. This view regards the words of verse 8, "Then the word of the LORD came to me," as a messenger formula introducing a separate oracle; the text, however, gives it the function of marking a juncture where the direction of the discourse moves from Zerubbabel (vv. 6–8) to the prophet himself (see the Exegesis of v. 8). It is true that the angel's words in verse 6 are not a detailed explanation of

the symbolic elements in the vision, but the angel's explanations to this point (1:10; 2:2 [1:19]; 2:4 [1:21]; 3:2, 9) are not overly specific either. The original oracle would have lacked the spiritual force of verse 6, which is certainly the key verse in this passage. While one can understand how in the editorial process verse 6 could have given added force to the original oracle, this suggested oracle stands before us rather limply, raising more questions than it answers and leaving unanswered the significance of the main segment of the vision, namely, the lampstand and the oil flowing from the trees. There seems to be no reason why the powerful words of verses 6–11 could not have accompanied the account of the vision from its inception in the prophecy of Zechariah.

6. The angel responds (ʿānâ) to Zechariah's perplexity by giving the overall symbolism of the vision, not an explanation of each of its symbolic representations. The word *this* in the angel's reply does not refer back to the vision, but to the words it introduces: "Not by strength, nor by power, but my Spirit"—this is God's word to the people. While these words explain the vision, they do so only in the broadest way, and it is left up to the reader to relate their significance to the objects Zechariah beheld.

This is not difficult to do, for what other sense could the vision have than that the continual supply of oil to the reservoir symbolizes God's supply of what the people needed to complete the building of the temple? This divine aid is "by my Spirit." The word *rûaḥ* has a variety of senses; besides its primary usages relating to the divine and human psyches, it connotes the life force (Ezek. 37:10; Hab. 2:19; Zech. 12:1) and the wind (Hos. 13:15; Amos 4:13; Zech. 6:5). When applied to humankind, it designates that aspect of the human psyche that motivates thought and action (Isa. 66:2; Ezek. 36:26; Hos. 5:4; Zech. 12:10). When it refers to God, it describes the manifesta-

most frequently to physical strength and by extension to wealth (Zech. 14:14) or an army (Ezek. 17:17). The full range of meaning is appropriate to this universal affirmation, for without God's Spirit, all human effort on his behalf is futile. בְּכֹחַ (by power): כֹּחַ is virtually indistinguishable in meaning from חַיִל, both serving here as a hendiadys for human might. בְּרוּחִי (by my Spirit): See the Exposition.

---

tion of the divine personality, actively communicating the divine will and controlling human events (Isa. 61:1; Ezek. 36:27; 37:14; Mic. 2:7). Here, the word *rûaḥ* assures the presence of God in the building project. The postexilic prophet Haggai echoes this in 2:5: "My spirit abides among you; do not fear." Because his Spirit was actively present among the people (v. 6), the success of their work did not depend on their feeble strength. Without God's active presence in history, they could not have overcome the powerful forces that opposed them (Ezra 5:3) nor moved the hearts of kings to help them (Ezra 6:1–12).

While there is disagreement among commentators as to the significance of the lamps, if the oil represents the divine energy that moved the work to completion, the lamps must then represent in some way the work on the temple building and, beyond that, God's glorious kingdom. His work will not fail, nor his promises prove empty. By his active presence among his people, he sustains them, in spite of forces that oppose his kingdom.

The words "not by strength, nor by power, but by my spirit" comprise a verbless clause in which each word stands out, unencumbered by verbal elements. Each is like the pinnacle of a mountain standing high above the surrounding territory. There is more to the angel's reply, however, and we must now wander through the foothills below these mountain peaks to learn more about it.

VI. Fifth Vision: Gold Lampstand (4:1–14)
C. Promise of the Lampstand's Symbolism (4:7–10)

McCOMISKEY

[7]What are you, O great mountain? Before Zerubbabel [you shall become] a plain, and he will bring out the capstone amid shouts of "Grace! Grace!" to it. [8]Then the word of the LORD came to me, saying, [9]"The hands of Zerubbabel have laid the foundation of this house, and his hands will complete [it]. Then you will know that the LORD of hosts has sent me to you. [10]For whoever has contempt for the day of small things will behold with joy the plumb line in the hand of Zerubbabel. These seven are the eyes of the LORD—they move back and forth throughout the earth."

NRSV

[7]What are you, O great mountain? Before Zerubbabel you shall become a plain; and he shall bring out the top stone amid shouts of 'Grace, grace to it!' "

[8]Moreover the word of the LORD came to me, saying, [9]"The hands of Zerubbabel have laid the foundation of this house; his hands shall also complete it. Then you will know that the LORD of hosts has sent me to you. [10]For whoever has despised the day of small things shall rejoice, and shall see the plummet in the hand of Zerubbabel.

7. מִי־אַתָּה (what are you?): מִי (what?) generally inquires after the identity of a person (who?). On occasion, however, it has other translational equivalents: "how?" (Amos 7:5) or "what?" (Deut. 4:7; Judg. 13:17). Perhaps the latter usage applies here, or perhaps מִי betrays personification (who are you, O great mountain?). Whatever the case, the question belittles the great obstacle before the people. הַר (mountain) sometimes metaphorically indicates an obstacle, as it does here (Isa. 41:15; Jer. 13:16). There is no need to apply it to the temple mount (Meyers and Meyers, *Zechariah 1–8*, p. 244). גָּדוֹל (great) appears only here with הַר גָּרוֹז, high, most frequently accompanies הַר. The use of גָּדוֹל here emphasizes the mountain's mass, which is appropriate to its metaphorical function as an obstacle. The text omits the article before הַר (O mountain). Perhaps we are to read אַתָּ הָהָר (GKC §32g), but more likely the article we expect in this vocative has slipped out in transmission because of the unusual number of הs in the sequence לְמִישֹׁר אַתָּה הָהָר. (become a plain): מִישׁר, related to יָשַׁר (to be straight), denotes a level place, sometimes occurring as the antithesis of הַר (as here and in 1 Kings 20:23). Especially important in this regard is Isaiah 40:4 ("every mountain and hill be made low"), where the construction הָיָה ... לְמִישׁוֹר (become a plain) occurs in connection with הַר to depict the removal of all impediments from Yahweh's path. It is not necessary to complicate Zechariah's text by rejecting this straightforward sense of לְמִישׁר and reading לְ as an emphatic particle (Meyers and Meyers, *Zechariah 1–8*, p. 245),

yielding "[you are] surely a platform" (i.e., Mount Zion). The omission of הָיָה before לְ to express "become" is not uncommon (GKC §114h). הָאֶבֶן הָרֹאשָׁה (the capstone) occurs only here, but in this context certainly represents the finishing stone of the temple, thus marking the temple's completion. תְּשֻׁאוֹת (with shouts) denotes a loud noise (Job 36:29) or shouting (Job 39:7; Isa. 22:2). Here, the occurrence of חֵן (grace) gives the word a sense of intelligible shouting, not simply a tumult. Since תְּשֻׁאוֹת is unaccompanied by a preposition, it is difficult to know whether we should translate this pregnant expression as *with* shouts, attributing the implied action to Zerubbabel (compare הוֹצִיא, he will bring out), or *to* (i.e., amid) shouts, attributing the action to the people. Since this verse describes a celebratory event, the latter is preferable. The meaning of the noun חֵן is consonant with its related nuances (Gen. 33:5; Exod. 3:21; Judg. 21:22; Job 19:21; Ps. 67:2 [1]; Prov. 31:30). In its secular (Gen. 33:8; Deut. 24:1; 1 Sam. 1:18) and theological (Gen. 6:8; Exod. 33:13; Ps. 84:12 [11]) usages, it connotes a positive attitude that may result in favorable action or the expectation of such action on the part of the person who is the object of favor. Here, this word affirms God's favor toward the people, which the completion of the temple evinces.

8. וַיְהִי (then came) marks an important juncture in this discourse. To this point, the angel's explanation of the vision related to Zerubbabel (vv. 6–7); now (vv. 8–9) the syntax directs the explanation directly to Zechariah (note the singular con-

---

7. The question is filled with irony: "What are you, O great mountain?" With God's Spirit in the community, no obstacle was too great. The people's lethargy and weakness would soon give way to the Holy Spirit, and the mountain would become level ground: they will complete the temple (see Ezra 6:13–15).

The assurance continues as the words of God anticipate the temple's completion. Zerubbabel will lead the laborers in a festal celebration. Some of them will position the wooden rollers beneath the capstone, while others strain at its ropes. The laborers only have to lift it into place and square it with the other stones to complete the work. It is significant that the people attribute the work to God, crying, "Grace! Grace!" to the stone. They do not celebrate their own abilities or national might, for they had little of that. The people learned of the mighty power of the Holy Spirit at their disposal.

8–9. The angel continues the address to Zechariah. Having learned that God would accomplish the work through the agency of the Holy Spirit, Zechariah also learned that God works through individuals. The task of rebuilding will come to fruition, but not apart from human agency. Zerubbabel's hands laid the foundation; his hands will complete the work. The angel's words to the prophet may be paraphrased this way: "When the temple stands complete, you [Zechariah] will know that God has sent me [the angel] to you [the community]." The finished structure will attest to the validity of the angel as an emissary of God and confirm the word of God that he conveyed to Zechariah, Zerubbabel, and the people who worked alongside them.

The more glorious temple—that is, the kingdom of God—that Zion's temple symbolizes also witnesses to the validity of the angel and the message he brought, for the Branch has come. The

structions אֵלַי [to me; v. 8] and יָדַעְתָּ [you will know; v. 9]) and through him to the people (אֲלֵיכֶם, to you [pl.]; v. 9).

9. יָדָי (hands of): יָד (hand) has the sense of agency as it does in 8:9, 13, and Haggai 2:14, 17. תְּבַצַּעְנָה (will complete [it]) has a variety of senses—cut off, break off, gain by violence (BDB)—which both the qal and piel (the form here) broadly share. It expresses "bringing [God's word] to fruition" (Lam. 2:17) and the completion of God's works (Isa. 10:12). "Cut off" is the apparent sense in Job 6:9 and Isaiah 38:12. It thus connotes bringing to an absolute end. וְיָדַעְתָּ (then you will know) continues the address to Zechariah. ו ties the action of knowing to the act of completing the temple, thus calling for a temporal translational equivalent (then). אֲלֵיכֶם (to you): The plural suffix moves from Zechariah to the people.

10. כִּי (for) has a subtle sense of causality here, justifying the previous statement by exemplifying it (BDB, p. 473). מִי (who?) with the perfect tense בַּז (to have contempt, despise) can function as a desiderative sentence, expecting the answer "no one" to the question "who has contempt for?" (GKC §151 and מִי הֶאֱמִין לִשְׁמֻעָתֵנוּ [lit., Who has believed our report?] in Isa. 53:1, which anticipates the response that few have believed). The New American Standard Bible follows this approach ("who has despised the day of small things") and makes שִׁבְעָה אֵלֶּה (these seven) the subject of וְשָׂמְחוּ (with joy) and וְרָאוּ (behold), but this translation removes the subject from its predicate by a formidable distance and requires the insertion of "these are" before עֵינֵי יְהוָה (the eyes of the LORD), straining the syntax. The interrogative pronoun can answer to "whoever" (Exod. 24:14; 32:24, 26, 33; Ezra 1:3), a sense that

presents no syntactical difficulties. While most of the usages of מִי answering to "whoever" refer to an individual, Exodus 32:24 shows that מִי could be plural in the speaker's mind, as it is here: לְמִי זָהָב הִתְפָּרָקוּ (lit., whoever has gold, let *them* take it off). While the singular verb (בַּז) in the protasis seems to militate against this, Psalm 107:43 betrays a similar plurality, where the first clause is singular (מִי־חָכָם וְיִשְׁמָר־אֵלֶּה, whoever is wise then let *him* give heed to these things), but the second clause is governed by a plural verb (וְיִתְבּוֹנְנוּ, and let them consider), indicating that the writer intended the admonition of the protasis to have a broad application. This verse says literally "Whoever is wise then let him give heed to these things, and let them consider the mercies of the LORD." בַּז לְיוֹם (has despised the day of): בּוּז means basically the same thing with (Prov. 1:7) or without (Prov. 23:22) לְ : "to look down on" (Prov. 1:7; 23:22) or "to despise" (Prov. 6:30; Song 8:7). Since לְ (to, for) transfers the action of the verb to its indirect object, my translation reads "have contempt for." וְשָׂמְחוּ (with joy): ו (untranslated) is a *waw*-consecutive, which appears on several occasions after מִי when that pronoun means "whoever"—but usually only with the imperfective (Exod. 32:24; 2 Chron. 36:23; Hos. 14:10), unlike here, where וְשָׂמְחוּ (will rejoice) is perfective. There is no reason, however, why the writer could not have chosen the perfective with *waw* after מִי, particularly if he wished to communicate strong assurance (perfect of confidence), which this tense often conveys (*IBHS*, p. 490)—thus the use of "shall" in my translation. The plural form of this verb indicates that the speaker had a group in mind: those who despise the day of small things will rejoice.

---

struggle of the people to build a temple against powerful opposition is but a small part of the cosmic struggle in which God's kingdom has come to reality and is sustained against forces beyond our comprehension (Eph. 6:12).

10. The people will know that God has sent his angel to them when they see Zerubbabel holding the plumbline for the laborers as they set the final stone in place, squaring it with the adjacent stones. Those who found the mean, narrow temple foundation to be an offense will rejoice when at last the final stone crowns the second temple. This event will also affirm the presence of God's Spirit with them, imparting his strength to their feeble efforts (v. 6). The greatest of efforts and institutions all have had small beginnings. The

church began with a handful of timorous disciples, and now its domain is the world. Large numbers of adherents or vast amounts of wealth are not necessarily a mark of blessing on a work of God.

As the prophet imagines the installation of the inscribed stone, he thinks again of the earlier reference to this stone in 3:9 and of the "seven eyes" fixed on it. Now he tells us that these eyes represent the eyes of the Lord that range to-and-fro throughout the earth. When we encountered this stone earlier, it held only the prospect of the temple's completion; now as the stone reappears, the text envisions the actual completion of the temple and reminds us that God was watching over

וְרָאוּ (when they see) is coordinate with the preceding וְשָׂמְחוּ (and they shall rejoice). In this construction "the principal idea is introduced only by the second verb, while the first . . . contains the definition of the manner of the action" (GKC, p. 386)—thus my translation: "They shall behold *with joy*." הָאֶבֶן הַבְּדִיל (the plumb line): בְּדִיל, probably tin, clearly refers to some sort of metal: it is the dross removed during the smelting of silver (Isa. 1:25); it can withstand heat (Num. 31:22–23); and it is grouped with other metals (Ezek. 22:18; 27:12). The appositional structure of the phrase הָאֶבֶן הַבְּדִיל is significant, for it identifies אֶבֶן not as a rock but as a metal (GKC §131c–e). The word אֶבֶן probably means "weight" in this difficult construction, as it does in 5:8 (see also 2 Sam. 14:26; Prov. 11:1; 16:11; 20:10, 23). It seems not to indicate a tool such as

a chisel, for neither lead nor tin would be suitable for an instrument that must inscribe stone. In all probability, it is a metal weight used in the building process, hence a plumb line. שִׁבְעָה־אֵלֶּה (these seven) has no stated referent in the preceding context. The writer must, however, have had in mind at this point the stone with the seven eyes in 3:9 (see the Exposition). The resumptive pronoun הֵמָּה (they) refers to the eyes. מְשׁוֹטְטִים (move back and forth): In the intensive stems שׁוּט connotes to and fro motion and describes people searching here and there (Amos 8:12) and running to and fro through a city (Jer. 5:1). It occurs with עֵינֵי יְהוָה (the eyes of the LORD) here and in 2 Chronicles 16:9. בְּכָל (throughout the whole) links with שׁוּט (to move back and forth) whenever the context defines this verb's sphere of action (2 Sam. 24:2, 8; Job 1:7; 2:2; Jer. 5:1; 49:3).

---

the building efforts and, in a larger sense, the advancement of his kingdom.

The verb accompanying ʿênê (eyes), mĕšôṭṭîm, creates difficulty for the view that ʿênê in 3:9 denotes fountains rather than eyes (see the Exegesis and Exposition of 3:9), for it never expresses the concept of flowing. It does, however, occur

with ʿayin in 2 Chronicles 16:9, where it states that "the eyes of the LORD range throughout the entire earth." There is no compelling reason to understand ʿênāyim in 3:9 to refer to anything other than the watchful eyes of God. The prophet continues his quest for the meaning of the vision by asking about the significance of the olive trees.

VI. Fifth Vision: Gold Lampstand (4:1–14)
D. The Olive Trees and Their Branches (4:11–14)

McCOMISKEY

[11] Then I responded and said to him, "What are these two olive trees on the right of the lampstand and on its left?" [12] Then I responded a second time, and asked him, "What are the two branches of the olive trees that are by the two golden spouts, which are emptying out the gold from above them?" [13] And he replied to me, "Do you not know what these are?" And I said, "No, my lord." [14] And he replied, "These are the two sons of oil who are standing by the Lord of all the earth."

NRSV

"These seven are the eyes of the LORD, which range through the whole earth." [11] Then I said to him, "What are these two olive trees on the right and the left of the lampstand?" [12] And a second time I said to him, "What are these two branches of the olive trees, which pour out the oil through the two golden pipes?" [13] He said to me, "Do you not know what these are?" I said, "No, my lord." [14] Then he said, "These are the two anointed ones who stand by the Lord of the whole earth."

11. וָאַעַן (then I responded): See the Exegesis of 1:10, 11; and 4:4. Here, the response is to the symbolic representations whose significance the prophet is seeking to learn. עַל־יְמִין (on the right of): The use of עַל (on) here, instead of מִן (from) as in 4:3, shows that מִן has no special significance there (see the Exegesis of v. 3).

12. וָאַעַן (then I responded): See the Exegesis of verse 11. שִׁבֲּלֵי (branches of) connotes flowing waters (Ps. 69:3 [2], 16 [15]; Isa. 27:12) and ears of grain (Gen. 41:5; Ruth 2:2; Job 24:24; Isa. 17:5). It is doubtful that the former sense obtains here, for streams flowing from the trees would hardly be *by* (בְּיַד) the spouts, but flowing *into* them. Since שִׁבֹּל can refer to ears of grain, it is best to picture not the large branches of an olive tree but the smaller ones that produce the olive clusters. בְּיַד may connote proximity (Job 15:23; Ps. 141:6), but it cannot have its more frequent translation "by the agency of," for then the relative participle הַמְרִיקִים (which are emptying out) would create a sentence lacking a primary verb ("which by the agency of the two golden pipes, the ones emptying out the gold from above them"). צַנְתְּרוֹת (spouts) appears to be a quadriliteral noun, formed with a *t*-infix, related to an unattested root צנר. If so, this word is related

to צִנּוֹר, a water tunnel or conduit (2 Sam. 5:8) or water spouts (Ps. 42:8 [7]). While etymology is not greatly helpful, the context gives צַנְתְּרוֹת the sense of spout or conduit: it is made of gold (זָהָב) and pours out liquid (הַמְרִיקִים). הַמְרִיקִים (which are emptying out): The verb רִיק denotes to empty (Gen. 42:35; Eccles. 11:3; Isa. 32:6; Jer. 48:12; Mal. 3:10). This participle construes צַנְתְּרוֹת as masculine even though it is morphologically feminine. Cases where masculine nouns take feminine inflections are not infrequent (GKC §87p). הַזָּהָב (gold): Since זָהָב empties from the olive branches, it can hardly refer to anything else but the golden oil that fuels the lamps.

13. See the Exegesis of verse 5.

14. בְּנֵי־הַיִּצְהָר (lit., sons of oil): Besides the common "son," בֶּן also functions with substantives and words describing characteristics to express a relationship appropriate to the sense of the adjunctive word (e.g., בֶּן־חַיִל is a mighty man and בְּנֵי־עַוְלָה are sons of violence). Since the branches are symbols, they find their reality in figures who sustain a relationship to oil. יִצְהָר (oil): See the Exposition. אָדוֹן (lord): See the Exegesis of 1:9 and the comments at Hosea 12:15 [14].

11–12. Thus far, the angel's explanation might have satisfied Zechariah that he and his fellow citizens would complete the work. Zechariah must have felt, however, that his knowledge of the vision was incomplete, for the olive trees remained a mystery. Surely they must hold some significance! So he boldly asks their meaning. Does the prophet's rephrasing of the question mean that the angel did not wish to explain the significance of the olive trees? We cannot know. In all likelihood, the second question was for greater specificity (Baldwin, *Zechariah*, p. 123).

The two branches about which he inquired may have borne clusters of olives from which oil flowed through two gold spouts or channels into the receptacle of the lampstand. Having told us that the branches were "by" the gold spouts, verse 12 goes on to define the proximity of these spouts as under the branches, for the golden oil pours out "from above them." That the spouts "empty out" the oil indicates that we are to picture the oil flowing in profusion, not simply dripping from the spouts. This element of the vision underscores the abundant supply of God's Spirit for the task at hand.

13–14. We may wonder about the spirit of the angel's questioning of the prophet, for we ob-

served it also in verse 5, and its insistence is troubling: How could the prophet have understood these symbols? The angel's question is not a sincere inquiry whether the prophet knew the vision's intent, for his previous question, "What are the two branches?" showed that he did not. Nor can the angel's question be purely rhetorical, for the prophet felt obliged to respond to it. In all probability, the sense of the question is, "Surely you know what these are?" (Gen. 44:15; Judg. 15:11; 1 Sam. 20:30; 2 Sam. 2:26; 3:38; 11:20; 19:23 [22]; 2 Chron. 32:13; Isa. 40:21, 28; Mic. 3:1), implying that the prophet should have known the significance of what he was seeing. Perhaps he should have understood that the profuse supply of oil somehow gave promise of divine enablement (v. 6), and that the two branches (v. 12) stood for two personages through whom God would work (v. 14). As condescending as the angel's questions sound, he responded fully to the prophet's queries.

The angel replies that the branches represent the "two sons of oil" (v. 14). Are we to think of the oil that flowed to the lamps or of anointing oil that would point to two anointed leaders in the community? A difficulty in the latter view is that this verse does not use *šemen*, the usual word for anointing oil, but *yiṣhār*, which always connotes oil as a staple or as a symbol of abundance (Deut. 7:13; 14:23; Neh. 5:11). If we follow this latter view, the "sons of oil" are likely Joshua the high priest and Zerubbabel the civil leader. Anointing certainly marked Joshua's induction into his priestly office, but we are not sure that Zerubbabel was an anointed leader (but see May, "Zechariah's Visions"). Since Ezra 3:2 and Haggai 1:1 (see also Matt. 1:12) list him in David's line and since anointing was part of the ceremony for inducting kings into office (1 Sam. 10:1), the designation "sons of oil" may refer to the two leaders, who were to one degree or another associated with anointing. The avoidance of the term šemen in this verse may be a literary device to force our attention on the oil flowing from the olive trees, not to the ritual of anointing. While verse 12 does not refer to that oil as yiṣhār, using the word zāhāb (gold), there is no mistaking the gold as oil. Viewing the oil of verse 12 as a symbol of the abundant supply of divine enablement (v. 6), the "sons of oil" stood in a special relationship to that enablement. The consonance of Joshua and Zerubbabel with the two branches is striking: they stood out from the community as these branches did from the trees, and as "sons of oil" they sustained a relationship to the enabling power of God (see the Exegesis). The discourse does not call for the significance of anointing or for Davidic associations. Its single thrust is that the people will complete the building of the temple.

VII. Sixth Vision: Flying Scroll (5:1–4)
A. Explanation of the Flying Scroll (5:1–3)

McCOMISKEY

5 And I lifted up my eyes again and looked, and there was a flying scroll. ²And he said to me, "What do you see?" And I said, "I see a flying scroll. Its length is twenty cubits and its width ten cubits." ³And he said to me, "This is the curse that goes forth over the face of the whole land, for in accordance with it, everyone who steals will be purged out [in keeping with] the one side, and in accordance with it, everyone who swears [falsely] will be purged out [in keeping with] the other."

NRSV

5 Again I looked up and saw a flying scroll. ²And he said to me, "What do you see?" I answered, "I see a flying scroll; its length is twenty cubits, and its width ten cubits." ³Then he said to me, "This is the curse that goes out over the face of the whole land; for everyone who steals shall be cut off according to the writing on one side, and everyone who swears falsely shall be cut off according to the writing on the other side.

5:1. וָאָשׁוּב (and again): For the meaning "again" for שׁוּב, see the Exposition of 4:1 and the similar function of שׁוּב in Genesis 26:18 ("Isaac dug again the wells of water"). מְגִלָּה denotes a scroll for writing (Jer. 36:2 spells out its basic function). עָפָה (flying): This participle of the common verb עוּף (to fly) depicts the scroll soaring through the air.

2. וַיֹּאמֶר (and he said) sustains the third-person references to the angel (see the Exegesis of 4:14). בָאַמָּה (cubits): The preposition בְּ affixed to אַמָּה has an instrumental sense: *by the cubit* (GKC §134, 3).

3. זֹאת (this) corresponds to the feminine singular מְגִלָּה (scroll) in verses 2–3. אָלָה (curse) has a broad semantic range; it may (Num. 5:21, 23; Deut. 29:20 [21]; 30:7; 2 Chron. 34:24) or may not (Gen. 24:41; 26:28 [par. בְּרִית, covenant]; Lev. 5:1; Neh. 10:30 [29]) include specific penalties or

curses. Here in Zechariah, the curse connected with this oath is clearly present (see the Exposition). עַל־פְּנֵי כָל־הָאָרֶץ (over the face of the whole land), an expression of extent, never elsewhere indicates land but always earth (Gen. 7:3; 11:9; 41:56), thus expressing universal extent. Here we must look to the broad context of the book for help in understanding the extent of אֶרֶץ (see the Exposition). כִּי (for): Like the כִּי beginning 4:10, כִּי here expresses causality only in the broadest sense, exemplifying the previous statement by expanding on the nature of the curse. מִזֶּה . . . מִזֶּה (the one side . . . the other) indicates alternate sides (Exod. 17:12; 25:19; 26:13; Num. 22:24; 1 Sam. 14:4). Although in Exodus 32:15, מִזֶּה וּמִזֶּה indicates the front and back sides of the tablets containing the law, it is not necessary to attribute "from" to the preposition מִן, as does Keil (*Minor*

5:1. The sequence of visions continues as the prophet perceives a scroll rushing through the air to some unknown destination. He does not tell us that he could detect writing on it—perhaps it was moving too rapidly for that—but we know from verse 3 that each side contained intelligible concepts, because the angel conveyed the meaning of each to him.

2. The angel asks the prophet what he sees. Perhaps Zechariah was growing weary at this point. While he had responded alertly to the early visions (1:9, 19; 2:2; 3:5), at 4:1–2 the angel must arouse him and ask him what he sees, and at 5:5 the angel commands him to look. The final vision (6:1–8) involves no such prodding, however.

The dimensions of this scroll, twenty cubits (thirty feet) by ten cubits (fifteen feet), are imposing. The great expanse of this parchment would have awed the prophet, and perhaps it created an overwhelming sense of its importance and possible implications. The prophet must have wondered whether it would bode well for his people.

3. The angel reveals the reality behind the symbolic scroll, saying that it represents a curse (see Brichto, *"Curse" in the Hebrew Bible*). The word *ʾālâ* may refer to an oath in the sense of a sworn agreement as well as to the penalties or curses inherent in the oath, which take effect should one of the parties violate its terms or its spirit (see the Exegesis). It is likely that these oath-curses were always implicit in the *ʾālâ*-oath. For example, 1 Kings 8:31–32 says: "If someone sins against a neighbor and is given an oath [*ʾālâ*] to swear, and comes and swears before your altar in this house,

then hear in heaven, and act, and judge your servants, condemning the guilty by bringing their conduct on their own head, and vindicating the righteous by rewarding them according to their righteousness."

The account of the covenant renewal ceremony in Deuteronomy 29:11 [12] uses the word *ʾālâ* of the Mosaic law, differentiating this word from *bĕrît* (covenant). It is clear that *ʾālâ* refers to the curses of the Mosaic covenant, for verse 19 [20] says that "all the curses [*kōl hāʾālâ*] written in this book will descend on them." It is also clear that the *ʾālâ* in Zechariah refers to the Mosaic law because verse 4 cites two of its legal proscriptions: stealing (Exod. 20:15; Deut. 5:19) and false swearing (Exod. 20:7; Deut. 5:11). The curse of Zechariah's vision is the curse of the law.

What comfort is there in this vision for the laborers on Mount Zion? Does the law threaten their national existence once again, as it did in the past? If it does, would not the reference to the law's curse weaken their efforts rather than encourage them? The text makes it clear that the law's function here is a benign one, purging evil from the people. This affirmation recalls the function of the law in the covenant renewal ceremony of Deuteronomy 29:18–19 [19–20], where the law's curses receive both a national and an individual perspective. Those who hear the words of the *ʾālâ* and refuse to comply with its terms will go unpardoned; the curses of the law will come upon them, and "the LORD will blot out their names from under heaven." The following verse states that the Lord will "single them out from all

Prophets, p. 279): "cleansed away from this side." כָּמוֹהָ (in accordance with it) is composed of כְּ (lit., like, as), מוֹ (BDB, p. 555), and the feminine suffix הָ. The basic sense of this construction is comparison (see the usages in 9:15; 10:2, 7, 8), and thus it frequently occurs in similes (Exod. 15:5; Isa. 30:22; Jer. 13:21). The nearest appropriate syntactical referent for the feminine suffix on this construction is אָלָה (oath, curse). We may thus understand כָּמוֹהָ as "in accordance with [the stipulations of the oath]." The exact nuance of נִקָּה is always determined by context. Verse 4 shows that in this pericope it indicates purging, which is con-

sonant with its usage in Isaiah 3:26, where Jerusalem is purged of its male population and its affluence. הַנִּשְׁבָּע (who swears [falsely]): Taking an oath is not wrong in itself (Gen. 21:31; 26:3; Deut. 1:8; Josh. 6:22), but when נִשְׁבָּע occurs with לַשֶּׁקֶר (Jer. 5:2; 7:9; Mal. 3:5) it means "to swear to a lie" (i.e., false swearing). Even though הַנִּשְׁבָּע is not accompanied in verse 3 by an adjunctive word, it recurs in verse 4 with לַשֶּׁקֶר (to a lie). Since verse 4 reiterates the destructive action of the flying scroll, it creates a conceptual force that shapes the sense of הַנִּשְׁבָּע here in verse 3 as "the one who swears falsely."

---

the tribes of Israel, in accordance with all the curses [*kĕkōl ʾālôt*] of the covenant written in this book of the law." The law thus has a purging effect, expunging from the community those who turn their backs on its demands. This is the function of the law here in Zechariah's vision as well.

The curse of this vision extends over "the face of the whole land." While *ʾereṣ* can connote earth or land (see the Exegesis), I have chosen the latter because of the theology of national cleansing that this book develops. In chapter 13, we read of the time of cleansing that the vision of 5:1–4 anticipates. It is limited to the "house of David and the inhabitants of Jerusalem" (13:1) and to "the land" (vv. 2, 8); and even within the universal scope of

chapter 14, we do not find the promise of cleansing for all the people of the earth. The land here has its counterpart under the new covenant in all who find redemption in the one whom Zechariah describes as "pierced" (12:10; see Isa. 53:5; John 19:37; Rev. 1:7; and see the promise of land as the experience of the believer in Heb. 3–4).

The two proscriptions of the law that this text specifies (stealing and false swearing) are the third and eighth commandments according to the traditional arrangement of the Decalogue, comprising the middle laws of each of the original tablets. They are a symbol: their reality is the entire law, stylistically represented by the scroll.

VII. Sixth Vision: Flying Scroll (5:1–4)
B. Effect of the Flying Scroll (5:4)

[4]I have sent it forth, utterance of the LORD of hosts, and it will enter the house of the thief and the house of the one who swears falsely by my name, and it will lodge in his house and destroy it, both its timbers and its stones.

[4]I have sent it out, says the LORD of hosts, and it shall enter the house of the thief, and the house of anyone who swears falsely by my name; and it shall abide in that house and consume it, both timber and stones."

4. הוֹצֵאתִיהָ (I have sent it forth): The only stated referent for the first-person construction of this verb is the angel of verses 2–3. While the angel possesses great power, we must remember that he acts as the representative of Yahweh (see the Exposition of 1:11). The feminine suffix (הָ־) on this verb finds its closest referent in אָלָה (curse), not in מְגִלָּה (scroll). The repetition of the verb יָצָא (to go out) here (הוֹצֵאתִיהָ) after its occurrence in verse 3 (הַיּוֹצֵאת), where it refers to the curse, supports the conclusion that the curse is the destructive force, not the scroll that contains it. נְאֻם יְהוָה צְבָאוֹת (utterance of the LORD of hosts): See the Exegesis of 1:3. וּבָאָה אֶל־בֵּית (and enter the house of): This phrase may indicate going or coming *to* a house (Josh. 20:6; Judg. 18:15), as well as going *into* a house (Gen. 19:3; Exod. 7:23; Deut. 24:10). Since the verbal action of this collocation culminates in the curse lodging (וְלָנֶה) in the house, it connotes entering in this context. הַנִּשְׁבָּע בִּשְׁמִי

(who swears by my name): When בְּ (by) occurs with נִשְׁבַּע (to swear), the word following it designates the surety of a sworn oath. In most cases the surety is a deity, either the Lord (Gen. 22:16; Lev. 19:12; Josh. 2:12; 1 Kings 2:23) or a pagan god (Amos 8:14; Zeph. 1:5). בִּשְׁמִי (my name) is the surety of the false oath here. To swear "by the name" of Yahweh is the same as swearing by Yahweh himself (see the Exposition). לַשָּׁקֶר (falsely): See the Exegesis of verse 3 and 8:17. The feminine וְלָנֶה (and it will lodge), which finds its referent in the oath-curse (אָלָה), as do the feminine constructions in verse 3, has the sense of temporary lodging (Gen. 32:22 [21]; Num. 22:8; Judg. 19:6). וְכִלַּתּוֹ (and consume it): The sense of absolute termination is always inherent in piel כָּלָה (Deut. 7:22; 2 Sam. 2:29; Lam. 2:22). וְאֶת־עֵצָיו וְאֶת־אֲבָנָיו (both its timbers and its stones) underscores the sense of the previous word.

4. The angel represents Yahweh dispatching this curse to the houses of all the covenant-breakers. The destruction the curse causes is ultimate, consuming all that belongs to these lawbreakers. This vision anticipates the cleansing from sin that 13:1–6 envisions for God's people.

The expression *swear falsely by my name* recalls Leviticus 19:12, which in turn reflects the law's proscription against false swearing in the two accounts of the law (Exod. 20:7; Deut. 5:11). These proscriptions oppose the wrong use of the divine name, that is, using that name for worthless reasons (*laššaw*ᵓ). Zechariah describes the use of the divine name as *laššeqer* (as does Lev. 19:12) and thus specifies the use of the divine name as surety for oaths that are patently insincere. Such oath-taking not only reflected a disregard for the welfare of others but also a lack of concern for the sanctity of God's name as well.

Swearing by the name of a deity is tantamount to swearing by the deity himself (Jer. 12:16), because "the name" is the set of intelligible characteristics that reflects the deity's character and by which he is known and for which he is worshiped (see the Exposition of Hos. 2:19 [17]). Thus, to swear to a lie using Yahweh's name is to violate the third commandment.

The assurance that God will cleanse his people in this fashion would have encouraged the builders, for it meant that God had not abandoned his people to their sin, forgetting his promise to make them a kingdom of priests (Exod. 19:6). We must not forget, however, that the promise of priestly privilege was conditional (Zech. 3:7). Centuries later, the nation was to experience another diaspora (11:4–6). The day of ultimate cleansing dawns when "they look upon the one whom they have pierced" (12:10). The vision here anticipates that day.

VIII. Seventh Vision: Basket That Goes Forth (5:5–11)
A. Explanation of the Basket (5:5–8)

McCOMISKEY

⁵And the angel who spoke with me came forward and said to me, "Lift up your eyes and see what this is that is coming forth." ⁶And I said, "What is it?" And he said, "This is the basket that goes forth." Then he said, "This is their likeness in all the land." ⁷And there was a lead cover lifting up, and this [likeness] was a certain woman crouching within the basket. ⁸And he said, "This is Wickedness." And he pushed her back into the basket and thrust the lead cover back onto its opening.

NRSV

⁵Then the angel who talked with me came forward and said to me, "Look up and see what this is that is coming out," ⁶I said, "What is it?" He said, "This is a basket coming out." And he said, "This is their iniquity in all the land." ⁷Then a leaden cover was lifted, and there was a woman sitting in the basket! ⁸And he said, "This is Wickedness." So he thrust her back into the basket, and pressed the leaden weight down on its mouth.

5. וַיֵּצֵא (and came forward) does not necessarily indicate a pause in the sequence of visions, for when the angel came forward in 2:7 [3] it added a dramatic note to that vision. הַמַּלְאָךְ הַדֹּבֵר בִּי (the angel who spoke with me): See the Exposition of 1:9. מָה (what) does not introduce a question (the translation "what is this?" for מַה־הִיא in v. 6 is inappropriate since we expect to read that the prophet does not know). Rather, מָה here introduces an object clause (see what this is; see Gen. 2:19; 37:20; Num. 13:18; 2 Sam. 24:13; Hab. 2:1). הַיּוֹצֵאת (that is coming forth) shares the sense of its previous occurrence in this verse where the angel "came forward." In 6:1, it describes the approach of the chariots. It is appropriate to translate it as "coming forth," "approaching," or even "coming into view" (Petersen, *Zechariah 1–8*, p. 254: "which is approaching"). הַזֹּאת (this) may be an abstract feminine (GKC §122q) because we are as yet uncertain of what is coming forth; more probably it is feminine because the narrating angel is already aware that it is an אֵיפָה (ephah, basket), which is feminine in gender.

6. מַה־הִיא (what is it?): If הִיא (it) refers to a previous entity, as it usually does, it must be to the basket, indicating that the prophet has already

seen and recognized the basket. אֵיפָה is frequently a unit of dry measure roughly equivalent to two-thirds of a bushel (but see Marenoff, "Ephah"). It can refer to the container as well as to the unit of measure (1 Sam. 1:24 [a skin of wine]; 17:17) in a manner similar to the English word *bushel*. זֹאת הָאֵיפָה הַיּוֹצֵאת (this is the basket that goes forth): הָאֵיפָה is determined by the article, affecting the sense of the entire clause. If the angel wished only to identify the approaching object, the indeterminate אֵיפָה (a basket [going forth]) would have sufficed, but such an answer would not be consonant with the angel's other replies, in which he gives the significance or purpose of the symbolic objects (1:10; 2:2 [1:19]; 4:6, 14; 5:3; 6:5). The significance of the basket is that it goes forth (see the Exposition). וַיֹּאמֶר (then he said): This second occurrence of וַיֹּאמֶר, following so closely after the previous one, probably indicates a juncture in the discourse, signaling a new topic (*Then* he said). זֹאת (this): If the writer wished to retain the same thought here, the construction וְזֹאת (and this) would have established that connection. The directional force of זֹאת depends on one's understanding of the difficult construction of the subsequent word, עֵינָם (their appearance). As it stands in

---

5. The angel draws closer to the prophet, an action that perhaps underscores the importance of what is to follow. Or perhaps the angel wished to point out more clearly the mysterious object that was becoming more distinct in the vision. "See what is coming forth," the angel says.

6. The angel answers the prophet's question, "What is this?" by stating that a basket goes forth. An *ʾêpâ* measured typically about two-thirds of a bushel (see the Exegesis), but in the postexilic period it indicated a basket of any size, in this case, a basket large enough to hold a person.

The significance of this basket is that it goes forth (see the Exegesis), anticipating its removal to a distant location (see vv. 9–11). That this basket is about to go forth is good news for the community, for it signals the removal of wickedness from them. We have seen references to the removal of sin in 3:1–5 and 5:1–4, and in each instance it meant that God would remove the sin that had hindered the people in the achievement of their spiritual and national goals. Once again, the builders learn that God would remove the greatest of all obstacles: their sinful human hearts. The new covenant also sets forth this promise for all who are under its jurisdiction (Jer. 31:33–34).

I understand the second occurrence of *zōʾt* (this) to refer to a topic that the text is yet to introduce (see the Exegesis)—the figure in the basket who represents wickedness. The words *this is their appearance* thus refer to the covenant-breakers, whom the crouching figure represents. The word *ʿayin* (eye, appearance) has the sense of external aspect (Num. 11:7; 1 Sam. 16:7). The words *this is their appearance* thus anticipate the representation of wickedness that the basket contains. The immediate references to the lifting of the lid and to the symbolic figure this action reveals (v. 7) support this perspective.

It is also possible that emendation is in order here (see the Exegesis) and that we are to read *ʿēnām* with the Septuagint and Syriac as *ʿăwônām* (their guilt). But if the directional force of *zōʾt* is forward in the discourse and refers to the figure in the basket, the reading *ʿăwônām* creates an awkward situation, for the woman is then identified twice as the personification of evil—"this is their guilt" (v. 6) and "this is Wickedness" (v. 8)—even though verse 8 appears to initiate her identity in this discourse. If *zōʾt*, however, refers back to the *ʾêpâ*, we wonder why the writer included *wayyōʾmer* (and he said) when *wĕzōʾt* (and this) would have sufficed. The reading *ʿēnām* (their

the Masoretic Text, עֵינָם cannot represent the word עָוֹן (guilt), which always appears with ו as the second radical (Ps. 69:28 [27]; Isa. 13:11; Jer. 31:34; 33:8; Hos. 4:8). The Septuagint reads עֵינָם as עָוֹן: αὕτη ἡ ἀδικία αὐτῶν ἐν πάσῃ τῇ γῇ (this is their iniquity in all the earth). To emend עֵינָם to עָוֹן involves only the substitution of ו for י, and the translation "guilt" fits the context. While the word may have suffered in transmission, the absence of a *Qere* reading is suspicious and warrants a closer examination of the form in the Masoretic tradition. עֵינָם represents the word עַיִן (eye) and may refer to the "appearance" of wickedness as a woman (Num. 11:7; 1 Sam. 16:7). This possibility gains support from the fact that זֹאת and זֶה frequently introduce a new topic into a discussion (see the Exegesis of 4:5), whereas הוּא (he, it) or הִיא (she, it) generally refers to the previous topic (see הִיא [it] in v. 6a). The nearest plural referent for the plural suffix on עֵינָם (ם-) is the covenant-breakers in the previous section (vv. 3–4) of this pericope. While this is a difficult construction, the text as it stands may be understood as, "This [a topic yet to appear in the text] is their [the covenant-breakers'] likeness," referring to the symbolic woman. בְּכָל־הָאָרֶץ (in all the land): For אֶרֶץ as "land," see the Exposition of verse 3.

7. וְהִנֵּה (and there was) draws our attention to the following word, establishing a degree of importance for it in the development of this vision. כִּכָּר indicates a plain, a loaf of bread, or a weight. The commonality in these terms seems to be the idea of roundness (BDB, pp. 502–3), and the context here in Zechariah supports this idea, for the כִּכָּר fits the opening of the basket. While it seems inappropriate for a basket to have a lead cover, the heaviness of this weight symbolizes a sense of finality with regard to the disposition of the wickedness it confines within the basket. נִשֵּׂאת ([that was] lifted up): The niphal of this verb indicates the act of rising or lifting up, with no mention of external agency (Isa. 40:4; Ezek. 1:19, 21). וְזֹאת (and there was) recalls and may resume the referent of the previous זֹאת. If this is so, its sense here is, "This (appearance) was (that of) a woman crouching within the basket." אִשָּׁה אַחַת (a woman): אַחַת may have no other function in this construction than to indicate *a certain* woman (Judg. 9:53). Since this numeral also indicates "alone" (Josh. 22:20; 1 Chron. 29:1), it could be translated "a lone woman." This translation, however, creates an unnecessary redundancy since the singular אִשָּׁה already carries that sense. The translation "certain," indicating an as-yet-unspecified person is more appropriate at this point in the context, because the text has not yet identified the woman. Whatever function we assign אַחַת, it isolates this figure, focusing our attention on her.

8. זֹאת (this) echoes the previous זֹאת, which refers to the figure in the basket. הָרִשְׁעָה (wickedness) has no specific connotations of wrongdoing (Deut. 25:2; Prov. 11:5; 13:6; Isa. 9:17 [18]; Mal. 1:4; 3:15), its generality making it an appropriate title for the evil the figure in the basket represents.

---

appearance) avoids these difficulties and fits comfortably into the fabric of the discourse. The question is a difficult one, but the main thrust of the discourse becomes clear as it develops.

The expression *in all the land* recalls the flight of the scroll "over the face of the whole land," searching out the covenant-breakers (v. 3). If we read *ʿēnām* as "their appearance," the figure crouching in the basket is the symbolic manifestation of their wickedness. Since this wickedness is confined beneath the heavy cover, we are assured that God has already dealt with the sin of his people.

7. The text draws our attention to the sudden upward movement of the heavy lid on the mouth of the basket. We do not know who or what lifts it. It seems to rise mysteriously from its position, and in the basket is the figure of a woman. On the basis of the view taken here, this figure is in some way the symbolic manifestation of the covenant-breakers. The symbol is probably a woman because the word for wickedness (*hārišʿâ*) in verse 8 is feminine.

8. The angel identifies the figure in the basket as "the Wickedness," probably recalling the wickedness of the covenant-breakers to which the first section (5:1–4) of this syntactically unbroken account refers. At this point, the woman must have emerged from the basket or stood up in it, for we read that the angel pushed her back into it. He thrusts the heavy lid back on the basket's opening, thus confining wickedness within it.

VIII. Seventh Vision: Basket That Goes Forth (5:5–11)
B. Disposition of the Basket (5:9–11)

McCOMISKEY

⁹And I lifted up my eyes and looked, and there were two women coming forth, and the wind was in their wings. And they had wings like the wings of the stork. And they lifted up the basket between earth and heaven. ¹⁰And I said to the angel who spoke with me, "Where are they taking the basket?" ¹¹And he said to me, "To build for it a house in the land of Shinar, and there it will be set firmly on its base."

NRSV

⁹Then I looked up and saw two women coming forward. The wind was in their wings; they had wings like the wings of a stork, and they lifted up the basket between earth and sky. ¹⁰Then I said to the angel who talked with me, "Where are they taking the basket?" ¹¹He said to me, "To the land of Shinar, to build a house for it; and when this is prepared, they will set the basket down there on its base."

9. יוֹצְאוֹת (coming forth): The frequent references to going and coming impart an unusual energy to this lengthy section. וְרוּחַ בְּכַנְפֵיהֶם (and the wind was in their wings): The use of רוּחַ (wind) with כְּנָפַיִם (wings) indicates wind, not spirit. הַחֲסִידָה (the stork): The name of this bird is related to a Hebrew word for loving, kind, faithful—qualities appropriate to the stork, which is known for its attentiveness to its young. Perhaps the writer chose the stork because of its large wingspan ("the wind was in their wings").

10. הַמַּלְאָךְ הַדֹּבֵר בִּי (the angel who spoke with me): See the Exegesis of 1:9. הֵמָּה (they) is not emphatic since it is necessary to the further specification of the participle.

11. בַּיִת may refer to a lodging place or a temple. If the former, it is a place of confinement for wickedness; if the latter, it carries connotations of idolatry (see the Exposition). בְּאֶרֶץ שִׁנְעָר (in the land of Shinar): Shinar was an area in Mesopotamia that Daniel 1:1 associates with Babylon, recalling the captivity of Judah after the fall of Jehoiakim. Isaiah 11:11 cites Shinar as one of the nations from which Yahweh will recall the remnant. While these are the only other prophetic references to Shinar, they nevertheless establish the tradition of Shinar as a surrogate for captor nations (see the Exposition). וְהוּכַן (and firmly): Hophal כוּן (to be firm) refers to the establishing of David's throne (Isa. 16:5), to the fastening of pegs in a wall (Ezek. 40:43), to the cinching of a horse's harness (Prov. 21:31), and to the coalescing of a defensive military maneuver (Nah. 2:6). For the sense of "firmly" in my translation, see the discussion of the following word. וְהִנִּיחָה (set), from נוּחַ (to rest), denotes to be rested upon (note the impersonal use of the Hophal perfect in Lam. 5:5: lit., there is not rested upon to us, i.e., we have no rest). Hiphil נוּחַ also means "to set down" (Gen. 39:16; Josh. 4:3; 1 Sam. 6:18). Since this word is coordinate with the previous one, it creates a syntactical configuration in which the second verb conveys the

---

9. Something else draws the prophet's attention, for he lifts up his eyes to look and sees two winged figures approaching. It may have been the sound of their beating wings that caught his attention, for he tells us that "the wind was in their wings." With great wings, like those of a stork, these figures soar with the basket high above the earth toward the heavens. While a woman is the symbol of wickedness in verse 8, women now symbolize deliverance.

10–11. Once again, the prophet relies on the angel's understanding of the vision, asking where these surreal creatures are taking the basket. He learns that they are going to the land of Shinar. The text does not communicate any sense of returning to Shinar as though it were the source of wickedness. If that were the case, we would expect to read that the winged figures carried off Wickedness to *its* house, but instead they must prepare a house for it. Since in the prophetic books Shinar represents oppressing nations (see the Exegesis), it is more suitable to this context to view the winged figures as removing Wickedness to an appropriate place, that is, to where idolatry, oppression, and cruelty already abide. That the basket is ensconced in a house and set firmly on its base conveys a sense of finality. We do not expect Wickedness to reappear.

This passage resonates with contextual elements in 13:1–6, which describe the absolute removal of sin from God's people. There, idolatry is a principal evil. While the words *house* and *base* have no apparent connotations of idolatry in 5:11, 13:1–6 may give them that sense, making *house* a temple and *base* a pedestal for an idol. If we limit our attention to the confines of this text alone, the images of the basket and the flying creatures establish the absolute removal of guilt from the people. The first section of this vision (5:1–4) also affirms the purging of evil from the community. There the evil was disobedience to the law, while here the sense of evil is more general.

The ideal this passage presents did not materialize in the experience of the postexilic community, for we soon find Zechariah inveighing against their lack of spiritual sensitivity (7:1–8:23) and predicting the community's demise (11:1–7; 15–17). Evidently the vision of the basket anticipates a later event, when rebellion against the spirit of the old covenant will be no more because a new covenant will reign (Jer. 31:31–34). The removal of sin will then be absolute, because God will write his law on the hearts of his people and "remember their sin no more."

While they may not have realized the full extent of the vision, the people of Zechariah's day knew that somehow God had removed the iniquity that had driven the nation into exile. The vision would have been meaningless to the builders if its perspective were only future. They could work, encouraged by the assurance of divine aid. Their past sins would not hinder their present efforts.

principal action and the first describes it (see the Exegesis of 4:10 and GKC §120d), yielding "set firmly [וְהֻנִּיחָה]." [וְהוּכַן] מְכֹנָתָה (its base) always denotes the base of a standing object (1 Kings 7:27; 2 Kings 25:13; Jer. 52:17).

IX. Eighth Vision: Four Chariots (6:1–8)
A. Introduction of the Four Chariots (6:1–5)

McCOMISKEY

6 And I lifted up my eyes again and looked, and there were four chariots coming out from between the two mountains, and the mountains were mountains of bronze. ²The first chariot had sorrel horses, and the second chariot had dark horses, ³and the third chariot had white horses, and the fourth chariot had dappled horses. [The horses were] powerful. ⁴And I responded and said to the angel who spoke with me, "What are these, my lord?" ⁵And the angel answered and said to me, "These are the four winds of the heavens going forth after stationing themselves by the LORD of all the earth."

NRSV

6 And again I looked up and saw four chariots coming out from between two mountains—mountains of bronze. ²The first chariot had red horses, the second chariot black horses, ³the third chariot white horses, and the fourth chariot dappled gray horses. ⁴Then I said to the angel who talked with me, "What are these, my lord?" ⁵The angel answered me, "These are the four winds of heaven going out, after presenting themselves before the LORD of all the earth.

6:1. וָאָשֻׁב (and again): See the Exegesis of 5:1. אַרְבַּע (four): For the significance of this numeral in apocalyptic literature, see the Exposition of 2:1 [1:18]. מֶרְכָּבוֹת almost always denotes military chariots. When this term relates to God's activity, it describes his vast might, as in Habakkuk 3:8 and Isaiah 66:15, where chariots represent the forces of God by which he accomplishes his purposes among the nations. הֶהָרִים (the two mountains): It is difficult to understand why הָרִים is determined by the article since we have not encountered these mountains before. Since the text does not develop this definiteness, it is probably best to regard them as mountains that the prophet had already perceived in the vision. הָרֵי נְחֹשֶׁת (mountains of bronze): Once again, the text fails to give the symbol bronze any specific meaning (see the Exposition). We are left to allow our own emotions to resonate with these gleaming peaks.

2. The preposition בְּ on בַּמֶּרְכָּבָה indicates accompaniment: horses *with* chariots. אֲדֻמִּים (sorrel): See the Exegesis of 1:8. שְׁחֹרִים connotes a range of dark shades; the various items identified with the root שׁחר are all dark or black: a raven

(Song 5:11), visages of starving people (Lam. 4:8), and the Shulamite's complexion (Song 1:5–6).

3. The adjective בְּרֻדִּים likely describes dappled or mottled horses (see the Exegesis of 1:8); compare the root ברד (hail) in Exodus 9:23–25; Joshua 10:11; and Psalm 105:32. אֲמֻצִּים ([the horses were] powerful): It is difficult to determine whether this adjective modifies only סוּסִים בְּרֻדִּים (the dappled horses) or all four teams of horses. On the one hand, the writer could have made clear that it modifies only the dappled horses by writing סוּסִים בְּרֻדִּים וַאֲמֻצִּים (lit., horses, dappled and powerful). On the other hand, the addition of כֻּלָּם (all of them) after אֲמֻצִּים would have clearly expressed the other possibility. The construction הָאֲמֻצִּים (the powerful [horses]) in verse 7 is determinative in this regard, for it modifies all the horses in this vision (see the Exegesis of v. 7). The view that אֲמֻצִּים here in verse 3 modifies all the horses, not only the dappled ones, necessitates the removal of a substantive from its modifier by some distance, but the same type of separation of modifying words and phrases occurs elsewhere in Zechariah (note הַנָּבִיא [the prophet] in 1:1 and אֲשֶׁר־בָּאוּ מִבָּבֶל [who have returned from Babylon] in 6:10).

6:1. We come now to the final vision that Zechariah perceived in his prophetic consciousness. These four chariots picture military might rushing forward against the enemy. These chariots were coming out (*yōṣᵉʾôt*). The frequent use of *yāṣāʾ* (to go out) in the visions is striking. Going beyond the cognitive level to the emotional, this verb creates a compelling sense of divine activity (2:7 [3]; 5:4, 5, 6, 9; 6:5, 6, 7).

We look in vain for an explanation of the metallic composition of the two peaks. We should not be quick to impart a symbolic meaning to the bronze, no matter what it may signify in other apocalyptic passages (for various suggestions, see Baldwin, *Zechariah*, pp. 130–31). These imposing bronze mountains add vivid color to the vision, imparting feelings of invulnerability and impenetrability, an image also found in other apocalyptic literature. Apart from their composition, these mountains represent the gateway to and from the presence of God (note v. 5: "after stationing themselves by the Lord of all the earth"). Clifford assigns these mountains a cosmic influence (*Cosmic Mountain*, p. 3).

2–3. Several horses draw each chariot, and we find their colors familiar, for they recall the colors of the horses in 1:8. Unlike the vision of 1:7–17,

which cites three colors, this text mentions four: sorrel, dark gray or black, white, and dappled. Several commentators suggest reasons for this difference. McHardy ("Horses in Zechariah"), for example, posits that abbreviations underlying the text were misconstrued by later copyists. This reconstruction is impressive but complex, and one wonders if efforts to harmonize these sections are true to the spirit of apocalyptic. Perhaps the symbolic significance of the numeral *four* was important to this vision, but not to the one in 1:7–17 (see the Exposition of 2:1 [1:18]). This appears to be the case because verse 5 identifies these varicolored horses as "the *four* winds." The horses represent forces that are active in the world; thus the idea of comprehensiveness, which is appropriate to both the numeral *four* and the figure of the four winds, is consonant with the comprehensiveness of the divine activity that this text establishes. Since the text assigns no cognitive value to the colors, we need regard them as nothing more than motifs that convey a sense of vibrancy and emotion to the drama unfolding before us. The addition of another color need not greatly concern us if it was symbolically necessary to include a fourth horse in the vision.

4. וָאַ֫עַן (and I responded): See the Exegesis of 1:12. הַמַּלְאָ֥ךְ הַדֹּבֵ֖ר בִּ֑י (the angel who spoke with me): See the Exegesis and the Exposition of 1:9.

5. אַרְבַּ֖ע רֻח֣וֹת הַשָּׁמָ֑יִם (the four winds of the heavens): In 2:10 [6], this expression denotes geographical expanse, but that context influences it in that direction (through the use of פָּרַשׂ [to spread out] and כְּ [like]), yielding "spread out like the four winds of the heavens" (see the Exegesis of 2:10 [6]). Here, however, no such forces influence the expression (see the Exposition of vv. 5, 8). מֵהִתְיַצֵּב

(after stationing themselves): Hithpael יָצַב has many nuances: to take a determined stand (Pss. 2:2; 36:5 [4]; Hab. 2:1), to firmly position oneself (1 Sam. 17:16; 2 Sam. 23:12; 1 Chron. 11:14; Job 41:2 [10]), or to present oneself (Exod. 8:16; Deut. 31:14; Josh. 24:1; 1 Sam. 10:19). The collocation יָצַב עַל connotes proximity (Job 1:6; 2:1). מִן (lit., from) places the act of standing before the Lord in the past and focuses only on the activity of the horses after they go forth (see the Exposition).

4–5. Using a symbol to explain a symbol (as in 4:14), the angel answers the prophet's query about the chariots and their varicolored horses: they are "the four winds." If we regard the winds as a virtual semantic zero, we find that they are in some way under the aegis of God and, like their symbolic counterparts, are forces active in the world (v. 8). It is not difficult to understand how the destructive force of nature's wind could become a symbol of divine activity (Isa. 17:13; 41:16; 57:13; 59:19). Jeremiah 22:22 uses wind as an active force, apart from any reference to God, but in 51:1 it represents a divine agency (compare *zārîm*, winnowers, in v. 2), as it does in Isaiah 11:15 and Ezekiel 1:4. Jeremiah 49:36, like Zechariah, uses the four winds as a symbol of God's destructive power. This prophetic concept of the winds is consonant with Zechariah's chariot-winds, for these also represent destructive forces. The chariot-winds are under the supervision of God, for according to Zechariah, they present themselves to God before going into the world. They comprise a complex symbol representing forces active in the world that God uses to his own ends.

IX. Eighth Vision: Four Chariots (6:1–8)
B. Explanation of the Four Chariots (6:6–8)

McCOMISKEY

6"[As for] the one with the black horses, [they] are going to the land of the north, and the white [horses] will go forth after them, and the dappled [horses] will go to the land of the south." 7And the powerful [horses] came forward and they strove to leave to range throughout the earth. Then he said, "Go! Range throughout the earth." And they ranged throughout the earth. 8Then he shouted to me, and spoke to me, saying, "Look! Those that are going to the land of the north have quieted my spirit in the land of the north."

NRSV

6The chariot with the black horses goes toward the north country, the white ones go toward the west country, and the dappled ones go toward the south country." 7When the steeds came out, they were impatient to get off the earth. And he said, "Go, patrol the earth." So they patrolled the earth. 8Then he cried out to me, "Lo, those who go toward the north country have set my spirit at rest in the north country."

6. אֲשֶׁר־בָּהּ ([as for] the one with): That this verse begins with אֲשֶׁר (the one) is suspicious to many commentators and warrants emendation (Petersen, *Zechariah 1–8*; Baldwin, *Zechariah*; Smith, *Micah–Malachi*; see NRSV, NEB, JB). There are, however, several similar usages of this particle in Jeremiah (14:1; 46:1; 47:1; 49:34). בָּהּ (with): The suffix הּ־ (untranslated) has its nearest grammatical referent in מֶרְכָּבָה (chariot) in verse 3. The preposition בְּ expresses the connection of each team of horses to its chariot (vv. 2–3); I have translated it "had." אֲשֶׁר־בָּהּ (lit., which had on it) may be rendered more smoothly, "The one with the [black horses]." יֹצְאִים [they] are going) is plural and must thus refer to the horses, which we must supply (see my translation and the Introduction). This construction is not anomalous, for the Old Testament frequently uses a participle with an unexpressed pronoun when the pronoun's referent has just been cited. Joshua 8:6 says, for example, כִּי יֹאמְרוּ נָסִים לְפָנֵינוּ (for they will say, [They are] fleeing before us). The subject of the participle (fleeing) is the "we" in line 1 of this verse. Here in Zechariah, the reference to the chariot-winds in verse 5 is close enough to the participle יֹצְאִים (are going) to relate to it syntactically. אֶרֶץ צָפוֹן (the land of the north) is not necessarily a surrogate for Babylon, for according to Jeremiah 46:10 and 50:9, it may include other nations to the north of Israel (see also Isa. 41:25; Jer. 1:15). Elsewhere in Jeremiah, this expression connotes the land of exile (3:18; 6:22; 16:15; 23:8) or the direction from which Israel's enemies approached (10:22). Here in Zechariah, the cosmic scope of this passage allows us to think in terms broader than the country of Babylon alone. יָצְאוּ (will go) is not a preterite since the horses do not leave until verse 7. Its perspective is future, and the perfect tense may reflect a sense of certainty (*IBHS*, p. 490). אֶל־אַחֲרֵיהֶם (after them): The collocation אֶל־אַחַר means "to" or "at" the rear (2 Sam. 5:23; 2 Kings 9:18, 19). The form אַחֲרֵיהֶם (after them) is popularly emended (NRSV, JB, NEB; Petersen, *Zechariah 1–8*; and others) to אַחֲרֵי הַיָּם (to the west), requiring the insertion of only one consonant (י), but this conjectural emendation has no manuscript evidence. That two chariots go to the north underscores the emphasis this text lays on that part of the world (v. 8), possibly reflecting the demise of the Assyrian and Babylonian empires. אֶרֶץ הַתֵּימָן (the land of the south): תֵּימָן is a common designation for the south (Deut. 3:27).

7. וְהָאֲמֻצִּים (and the powerful [horses]) cannot refer only to הַבְּרֻדִּים (the dappled [horses]), because that would mean that only they went forth, but verse 6 tells us that the dark and white

---

6. The particle *ʾăšer* that begins this verse seems awkward (see the Exegesis), suggesting to some commentators a corruption in the text. Jeremiah 14:1 begins in a similar fashion, *ʾăšer hāyâ dĕbar-yhwh ʾel yirmyāhû* (that came as the word of the LORD to Jeremiah; NASB), and fits comfortably with the syntactical requirements of this clause. We may understand Zechariah 6:6 similarly; the black horse refers to the first chariot.

The black horses prepare to draw their chariot to the lands to the north, and the white horses follow at the rear. The north had painful associations for the postexilic community, for it was the direction from which their former enemies had entered the land to take the earlier generations into captivity. The dappled horses speed off in the opposite direction. When these horses went forth in 1:11, it was to observe the world from their cosmic perspective; we shall soon learn that their forays also involved active involvement in the world (6:8).

It is not significant that the text fails to inform us that the sorrel horses went forth. The following verse strongly implies that they did. Perhaps the text focuses on the north because of its relevance to the concerns of the postexilic community. The reference to the south may have directed the community's attention to their sometime ally and enemy Egypt. As with the cruel captor nations to the north, Egypt was also no longer a threat to the community.

There are numerous suggestions in the literature as to how we should emend this verse so as to include the four points of the compass (see Baldwin, *Zechariah*, pp. 139–40). The text does not, however, appear to be syntactically or textually assailable (see the Exegesis). The text may cite only the north and south because its scope encompasses the postexilic community and is not primarily universal. Certainly the horses "ranged throughout the earth" (v. 7), but the direction that would have had the most meaning for the community would be that from which their enemies entered the land. We must not impose our concepts of order on a text that meant to encourage a people long beleaguered by intrusions from the north and south.

7. The powerful horses move to the foreground of the vision. Once again the verb *yāṣāʾ* (to go, come out) creates a sense of restless activity (see

horses went out, which strongly implies that they all did (see אֲמֻצִּים [powerful] in v. 3). יָצְאוּ (came forward) does not have a future perspective, as do the two previous occurrences of this form (v. 6), because it is in a new clause and we must posit a verbal action for this verb that is appropriate to the time of the next construction (were eager to go forth). The sense is that they came forward because they were impatient to start out. וַיְבַקְשׁוּ לָלֶכֶת (and were eager to leave; lit., sought to go): The collocation בָּקַשׁ לְ־ expresses a range of meanings, from strongly desiring to effect an action (1 Sam. 23:10; 1 Kings 11:22) to striving after something (2 Sam. 20:19; Esth. 2:21; Zech. 12:9). The latter sense complements the picture of these horses straining at their harnesses, "impatient to get off" (NRSV). לְהִתְהַלֵּךְ (to range): See the Exegesis of 1:10. וַיֹּאמֶר (and he said) carries forward the speech of the angel (see v. 5).

8. וַיַּזְעֵק אֹתִי (then he shouted to me): זָעַק אֶת (to lift the voice) may mean "to summon" (Judg. 4:10; 12:2; 2 Sam. 20:5), but that cannot be its sense here, because the text does not tell us that the prophet was off at a distance. "Shouting" is sufficient in this context, with אֶת indicating the object of the verb's action. In Ezekiel 5:13 and 16:42, הֵנִיחוּ (have quieted) has the sense of causing to rest. In Ezekiel 5:13, God causes his wrath (חֵמָה) to rest (i.e., spends it); in Ezekiel 16:42, this word connotes the calming of God's anger (see also Ezek. 21:22; 24:13). I translate it as a preterite rather than a future verb because of the historical circumstances the text describes (see the Exposition). רוּחִי (my spirit) is construed in the first person in a speech attributed to the angel, not to Yahweh (see the Exposition). רוּחַ (spirit) has a broad semantic range in Zechariah (see the Exposition of 4:6 and 6:8; see also 7:12).

---

the Exposition of 6:1). They thrust forward, straining against their harnesses because they are eager to gallop off to range throughout the earth. The sudden command of the angel frees them to go, and they begin their mysterious journey.

This verse, like the previous one, appears to have suffered in transmission, lacking the word *horses* after *powerful*. A glance at verse 6, however, shows that the lack of the word *horses* is a consistent pattern (see my translation). If we supply the appropriate word in the ellipsis (horses), the text makes good sense.

8. The angel must shout to the prophet, perhaps to be heard over the thundering hooves of the powerful steeds. He tells the prophet that the horses that go to the north (the black and white horses) have quieted God's spirit in that area of the world.

It is tempting to conclude that the quieting of God's spirit refers to the cessation of his anger as in Ezekiel 5:13, but there the text specifically mentions God's anger. Since that is not the case here, we must look in another direction. The Exposition of 4:6 concludes that *rûaḥ* (spirit), when syntactically construed with references to God, refers to the active presence of the divine personality in the world. We may observe God's active presence in the north country when he

drove the people into exile, using the captor nations as instruments of his wrath (Isa. 10:5; 39:6; Jer. 20:4–6; 21:10; 22:25). We see it also when he brought about Babylon's downfall (Isa. 14:22; 47:1–15) and delivered his people from captivity (Isa. 48:14). It was God who raised up King Cyrus of Persia (Isa. 41:25; 44:28; 45:1–7). Now the turmoil in the north has ceased, and the world is at rest.

The first-person suffix (*my* spirit) must refer primarily to the angel of the Lord, not Yahweh, because the text does not mark a change in person. In view of the close association of this angel with Yahweh (see the Exposition of 1:11), however, we do not go astray if we regard the angel's spirit as one with Yahweh's.

This vision would have encouraged the builders on Mount Zion by reminding them that the world was at rest (1:11); they could carry on their building efforts without outside interference. In a larger way, it reminds us today that the destructive forces that human pride and greed unleash into the world are not unseen by God or out of his control. The horses of Zechariah's vision ride forth today, but the God who dwells between the mountains of bronze is still sovereign over human events.

X. A Symbolic Ceremony Prefiguring the Branch (6:9–15)
A. The High Priest as the Branch (6:9–12)

McCOMISKEY

⁹Now, the word of the LORD came to me, saying, ¹⁰Take [silver and gold] from the exiles—from Heldai, Tobijah, and Jedaiah, who have come from Babylon—and go the same day. And you shall go to the house of Josiah son of Zephaniah. ¹¹And take silver and gold and make a crown and place it on the head of Joshua son of Jehozadak the high priest. ¹²And you shall say to him, Thus says the LORD of hosts, Look! A man whose name is Branch. And from his place he will sprout forth, and he will build the temple of the LORD.

NRSV

⁹The word of the LORD came to me: ¹⁰Collect silver and gold from the exiles— from Heldai, Tobijah, and Jedaiah—who have arrived from Babylon; and go the same day to the house of Josiah son of Zephaniah. ¹¹Take the silver and gold and make a crown, and set it on the head of the high priest Joshua son of Jehozadak; ¹²say to him: Thus says the LORD of hosts: Here is a man whose name is Branch: for he shall build the temple of the LORD.

9. וַיְהִי ... אֵלַי (now came to me): For this expression, see the Exegesis of 1:1 and Hosea 1:1. וַיְהִי includes a light *waw* that often begins narrative sections (see 7:1); it does not necessarily establish a conceptual link between this and the previous pericope.

10. לָקוֹחַ (take): This infinitive absolute, occurring in the clause-initial position, functions as a command form (*IBHS*, p. 593). The clause it introduces does not state the object of the "taking" because לָקוֹחַ forms a hendiadys with וּבָאתָ (lit., take and go), thus emphasizing the verbal action (see the discussion below). (A hendiadys is the grammatical interrelating of two distinct verbal actions to create a complex verbal action that may or may not express an object; the verb לָקַח is a frequent member of this construction; Gen. 12:19; 24:51; 27:3; 42:33.) We know from verse 11 that the object is כֶּסֶף־וְזָהָב (silver and gold). The absence of an object in this hendiadys shows that the writer's concern is with the action of the two verbal ideas. The prophet was to take [something] and go. The singular הַגּוֹלָה (the exiles) functions as a collective for all the exiles (Jer. 28:6; 29:4, 20, 31; Ezek. 1:1; 3:11, 15; 11:24; Nah. 3:10). The Septuagint has αἰχμαλωσίας (captivity) here and probably translates וּמֵאֵת broadly as "the things of," which yields a difficult reading ("take the things of the captivity"). The Septuagint offers little help, and if we posit a hendiadys, there is no reason to follow it. The second half of the verse leads off with וּבָאתָ (and go), the second element in the hendiadys headed by the volitional לָקוֹחַ. בַּיּוֹם הַהוּא (the same day) does not mean "this day," that is, the day the prophet received the vision, for that would require זֶה (this), as in Jeremiah 44:10, 22; Daniel 9:15. When הוּא (lit., he, it) accompanies יוֹם, it expresses "that day" (Ezek. 29:21; Hos. 1:5; Zech. 3:10) or "the same day/time" (Jer. 39:10; Ezek. 40:1; Zeph. 1:9). Here, the day is the time of the verbal action determined by לָקוֹחַ ... וּבָאתָ. The prophet was not necessarily to go on the day he received the vision, but at the time that he collected the silver and gold (see v. 11). The presence of וּבָאתָ a second time in the text proves the existence of the hendiadys in the previous clause, for if the writer had omitted it he would have created a separate clause, wresting the previous וּבָאתָ from its relationship with לָקוֹחַ. אֲשֶׁר־בָּאוּ מִבָּבֶל (who have returned from Babylon): The plural form בָּאוּ refers to all the returned exiles cited in this verse; coming at the end of the clause, it recalls the similar function of אַמִּצִים (powerful) in verse 3.

11. וְלָקַחְתָּ (and take) resumes לָקוֹחַ (take) in the previous verse, informing us that its implicit object is כֶּסֶף־וְזָהָב (silver and gold). עֲטָרוֹת (a crown) has several senses, occurring most frequently as a metaphor for glory (Job 19:9; Prov. 4:9; 12:4; Isa. 28:1, 3, 5; Jer. 13:18; Lam. 5:16). In its literal sense it refers to a precious object (Job 31:36), finery (Ezek. 16:12; 23:42), or a royal crown (2 Sam. 12:30; 1 Chron. 20:2; Esth. 8:15; Song 3:11). "Crown" is most appropriate to this text because of its association with the royal terms *Branch, throne,* and *rule* in verses 12–13. The plural form is difficult, but עֲטָרוֹת likely refers to only one crown (in v. 14, it is construed with a singular verb: תִּהְיֶה, shall become; GKC §145h). The inten-

---

9–10. We now move from the visions to a brief section in which the prophet's message comes to us in vivid symbolic activity. He felt the divine impulse to request something from several of his fellow citizens: Heldai, Tobijah, and Jediah. The text calls these men "exiles" and states that they have "come from Babylon." Apparently they were recent returnees, because the reference to their return from Babylon would otherwise be superfluous. They may have taken up temporary lodging at Josiah's house. The names of these men do not appear in the Septuagint (but see the Exposition of v. 14). That Zechariah did not use these men as witnesses is clear from the use of *min* (from) preceding each name.

Zechariah was to go to the house of Josiah, who is also unknown to us. Once again we detect an urgency in the activity the prophet describes, for he was to go at once ("the same day") to Josiah's house. Since they would find Joshua the high priest there, it is possible that Josiah was a priest, who along with Joshua lived in the temple environs (Ezra 2:70).

11. Filling out the command of verse 10, verse 11 now informs us that Zechariah requested silver and gold from the three returned exiles. These men may have prospered in Babylon, bringing valuables to help the struggling community. Zechariah took some of the gold and silver to fashion a crown.

The function of the plural term *ʿăṭārôt* (crown) is unclear. Since it is likely not an abstract plural (see the Exegesis), I regard it as a concrete plural referring to several crowns. Zechariah would not have melded the silver and gold, creating an unstable mass, but probably fashioned a band of gold as well as one of silver, either one of which would singly have served as an insignia of royalty.

sive plural is unlikely here because that function applies mainly to abstract ideas: traits (אוֹנִים [might] in Isa. 40:26; אֱמוּנוֹת [faithfulness] in Prov. 28:20), emotions (חֵמוֹת [wrath] in Ps. 76:11 [10]), and human conditions and experiences (בְּרָכוֹת [blessed] in Prov. 28:20; בְּחֻרִין [youth] in Num. 11:28). It is rare to find an intensive plural relating to a concrete object that is divorced from human experience. There seems to be no reason to regard עֲטָרוֹת as anything other than a simple plural (see the Exposition).

12. כֹּה אָמַר יְהוָה צְבָאוֹת (thus says the LORD of hosts): See the Exegesis of 1:3. הִנֵּה (look!) is an attention-getting particle. It does not denote seeing. אִישׁ (a man) is indeterminate. In relative clauses comprised of suffixed שֵׁם (name) and a related substantive unmarked by the article ("a man whose name is"), the substantive refers to a person or object in the writer's mind not yet—but soon to be—introduced into the events of the narration (e.g., 1 Sam. 9:1: "There was a man of Benjamin whose name was Kish"; see also Josh.

2:1; Ruth 2:1; 1 Sam. 9:1, 2; 17:4, 12; 25:2, 11; 2 Sam. 9:2, 12; 13:1; 16:5; 1 Kings 13:2). Zechariah's reference here to "a man" leads us to expect him to be one who stands apart from the activity narrated in this text. This makes it unlikely that it refers to Joshua, who by virtue of his symbolic role is already a part of the events this text describes. צֶמַח (Branch): See the Exegesis and Exposition of 3:8. וּמִתַּחְתָּיו (and from his place) is related to תַּחַת (the under part; BDB, p. 1065). Here, the word indicates simply the place from which a branch would sprout (in Exod. 10:23, the same construction is a general term for place). This is Zechariah's first use of הֵיכָל to designate the temple (he previously used בַּיִת, house). הֵיכָל has several nuances in postexilic literature: a royal palace (Ezra 4:14), the temple of Yahweh (2 Chron. 3:17; 4:7, 8; 26:16), a pagan temple (2 Chron. 36:7), and the holy place (Neh. 6:10). Elsewhere in Zechariah (8:9), the word refers to the temple structure (see the Exposition).

He may have woven the bands together or joined them in some other way, thus making the simple bands into a more regal crown. In this view, the plural form would indicate the whole, comprised of its several parts (see Baldwin, *Zechariah*, p. 133).

When we observed the high priest earlier, we were struck by the disparity between his filthy condition and the purity we expect of the high priest. Here another disparity confronts us: the high priest wears a crown. This intrusion of a priest into the sphere of royal prerogative clashes with the historic role of the priesthood in ancient Hebrew socioreligious practice. Such an intrusion occurred in the other direction, when King Uzziah usurped the priestly role and experienced the divine displeasure at his encroachment into the prerogative of the priests (2 Chron. 26:16–20).

As the high priest stands crowned before us, we are aware that this event has a significance that transcends the traditional order of things in ancient Israel. The witnesses to this ceremony might have wondered if they were party to a prophetic movement to restore the monarchy or to a well-meaning, but ill-advised, effort to force the conviction on the people that the messianic era had dawned. The prophet's words in the next verse may have seemed to support the latter possibility.

12. A momentous pronouncement accompanies this symbolic ceremony of crowning: "Look!

A man whose name is 'Branch.' " If the prophet had said "the man" instead of "a man," he might have led his hearers to think that Joshua was the Branch, but the indefinite *ʾîš* warrants our looking beyond Joshua to one who yet stands outside these events (see the Exegesis). If Zechariah's theology of the Branch is consonant with the eighth-century tradition (and it is difficult to think otherwise), the Branch is of Davidic lineage (Jer. 23:5; 33:15; see also Isa. 11:1) and therefore could not belong to a priestly (levitical) family as did Joshua the high priest, whose father was Jehozadak, a descendant of Levi (1 Chron. 6:1, 14). This inauguration was thus not a prophetic ploy or intrigue, but a sincere effort to express in vivid symbolism the prophetic messianic hope. As a plant sprouts from the field, so the Branch will emerge on the scene of world history.

Some scholars suggest that Zechariah recognized Zerubbabel as the Messiah (Mitchell, *Zechariah*, p. 104; Lamarche, *Zacharie*). It is possible that Zechariah had such a hope, especially as he observed the progress of the work under Zerubbabel's leadership; perhaps the Davidic kingdom would soon become a reality. Mason ("Proto-Zechariah," p. 136) maintains that such hopes soon faded. The use of the high priest in the prophetic symbolism of this passage, however, makes Zerubbabel an unlikely Messiah, since the point of the symbolism is that the offices of priest and king will peacefully coalesce in the Branch (6:13).

While Zerubbabel was indeed of Davidic lineage, he was not a descendant of a priestly family. It is more likely that the prophet's symbolic act expresses a hope that extends beyond the moment to a figure who more closely fits the symbol.

If the Branch is yet to appear, the temple he builds cannot be the second temple. It is possible that Zechariah believed the Branch would emerge from the community to complete the temple and establish the long-sought-rule rule of Yahweh, but this is not likely. The time of the appearance of the Branch is indefinite and does not seem to be part of the community's immediate expectation. This fact, coupled with the urgency to complete the temple that permeates this book, places the *hêkal* (temple) that the Branch builds outside the purview of the community. The temple is the future domain of the Messiah. In Christian theology, it is the kingdom of God that Christ established (Gal. 4:4).

X. A Symbolic Ceremony Prefiguring the Branch (6:9–15)
B. The Branch as a King-Priest (6:13)

McCOMISKEY

[13]Yes, it is he who will build the temple of the LORD, and it is he who will bear royal honor and will sit and rule on his throne and will be a priest on his throne, and the counsel of peace will exist between the two of them.

NRSV

[13]It is he that shall build the temple of the LORD; he shall bear royal honor, and shall sit and rule on his throne. There shall be a priest by his throne. There shall be a priest by his throne, with peaceful understanding between the two of them.

13. וְהוּא ... יְהוָה (and he ... the LORD): This reiteration of the final clause of verse 12 does not appear to be dittography because of the imperfective form יִבְנֶה (he will build) in place of a *waw*-perfective in the preceding clause and the addition of וְהוּא (and he). The independent personal pronoun וְהוּא (it is he) forcibly recalls the subject of this lengthy sentence, namely, the Branch. That it occurs in a clause that repeats the assertion of the previous clause imparts an affirmatory sense to וְהוּא that I reflect in the translation, "Yes, it is he." The second occurrence of וְהוּא (and it is he) is also emphatic because the writer could have omitted it, continuing the sentence with וְנָשָׂא (and he will bear) as with וְיָשַׁב (and will sit). הוֹד (honor) denotes those aspects of a person or object that elicit emotions of awe or respect. Job 39:20 refers to the snorting of a horse as הוֹד, because it elicits a response of awe. Joshua received הוֹד (authority) from Moses, thus eliciting respect (Num. 27:20). The response this word calls for is shaped by conditions relating to the person or object receiving it. When it is a human trait, הוֹד connotes one's reputation (Prov. 5:9) or, in the case of kings, splendor and majesty (1 Chron. 29:25; Pss. 21:6 [5]; 45:4 [3]). The regnal terminology in this verse exerts a force that makes "royal honor" an appropriate translational equivalent for this word. וְיָשַׁב וּמָשַׁל (and he will sit and rule) is another pair of coordinate verbs similar to those in 4:10 and 5:11 (see the Exegesis there). In this construction, the second verb indicates the principal action. The sense is that the Branch will rule, with the coordinate verb (וְיָשַׁב) describing this action as emanating from his throne: he will rule sitting on his throne. וְהָיָה (and will be): The New Revised Standard Version translates this construction, "There shall be," postulating another figure in the prophetic drama, namely, "a priest by this throne." The Hebrew construction also allows for the translation, "And [he] will be a priest on his throne." Supporting the former option is שְׁנֵיהֶם (the two of them), which seems to refer to two persons (the NASB boldly translates this form "the two offices"). On the other hand, וְהָיָה (and he will be) is a perfective with וְ, as are the preceding verbs וְיָשַׁב (and will sit) and וּמָשַׁל (rule), both of which refer to the Branch. Since the context does not clearly require the introduction of this figure, but signals a continuation of the subject of the previous two verbs (the Branch) by its use of these similar grammatical structures, the introduction of this figure strains the demands of the context. The writer could have clearly expressed that idea with וְכֹהֵן יִהְיֶה (and a priest will be) or וְיָשַׁב כֹהֵן (a priest will sit). כִּסְאוֹ (his throne): The suffix on this form refers to the צֶמַח (Branch). וַעֲצַת שָׁלוֹם (and the counsel of peace): עֵצָה connotes a reasoned conclusion eliciting or urging some action (Judg. 20:7; 2 Sam. 15:31; 16:20; 1 Kings 12:8; Jer. 50:45; Ezek. 7:26). As the writer envisions the uniting of king and priest in the person of Joshua, he symbolizes the two roles as hypothetical figures who counsel peace between themselves. The Branch will combine within his functions the offices of king and priest. שְׁנֵיהֶם (the two of them): The masculine suffixal pronoun הֶם (them) on this form probably does not represent the abstract (or neutrum) functions of some suffixes, referring here to the *offices* of priest and king, for the feminine would be more appropriate in that case. In all probability, this suffix is concrete, referring to the two symbolic personages—king and priest—whom the symbolic figure of the crowned priest combines.

---

13. The emphatic clause that begins this verse draws our attention away from Joshua to the Branch: "It is not Joshua, it is *he*—the Branch—who will build Yahweh's temple." Another emphatic statement follows: "It is *he*—that is, the Branch, not Joshua—who will bear royal honor." We do not expect Joshua the high priest to have such royal privilege; that would have represented a break with tradition. One is coming, however, who will combine these offices in himself. The era of the Branch will be unique, for he will reign in his kingdom as both king and priest. Baldwin ("*Semaḥ*," p. 9) says of the Old Testament writers that "the evidence would seem to prove conclusively that they use the term 'Shoot' when they wish to bring together the offices of both king and priest." The dichotomy between these two Hebrew institutions will be no more. The New Testament affirms the union of these two offices in Christ (1 Tim. 6:15; Heb. 8:1; Rev. 19:16).

X. A Symbolic Ceremony Prefiguring the Branch (6:9–15)
C. The Crown Residing in the Temple (6:14)

McCOMISKEY

¹⁴And the crown shall be in the temple of the LORD a commemoration of Helem and of Tobijah and of Jedaiah and of the favor of the son of Zephaniah.

NRSV

¹⁴And the crown shall be in the care of Heldai, Tobijah, Jedaiah, and Josiah son of Zephaniah, as a memorial in the temple of the LORD.

14. וְהָעֲטָרֹת (and the crown): See the Exegesis and Exposition of verse 11. תִּהְיֶה (shall be) is singular, supporting the conclusion (see the Exposition of v. 11) that the plural עֲטָרֹת (crown) represents a whole, comprised of its separate parts. לְחֵלֶם (of Helem) is another obscurity in this difficult passage. In the similar list of names in verse 10, we find חֶלְדַּי (Heldai) in the first position. The two are almost certainly the same person, for the history of this name witnesses to alternate spellings (see the Exposition). וּלְחֵן (and of the favor of): חֵן is so vastly different from יֹאשִׁיָּה (Josiah), the name we expect here, that it is difficult to explain it as a textual error. The Septuagint witnesses to וּלְחֵן, translating the construction "and for the favor of." Since there is no reason to suspect the intrusion of yet unnamed persons into this verse, the son of Zephaniah is almost certainly Josiah, as in verse 10 (see the Exposition). לְזִכָּרוֹן (for a commemoration): זִכָּרוֹן denotes an object that serves as a reminder of persons (Exod. 28:12; Num. 10:10), events (Exod. 12:14; 13:9), or things (Exod. 17:14; 30:16; Num. 5:15; 31:54). Affixed לְ clearly connotes function: it is to be *for* a commemoration. The לְ affixed to the preceding names is not so clear: it may connote a commemoration *for* (as in Exod. 12:14) or *of* (as in Exod. 28:12). The former option does not fit the context well, for if the crown were a reminder only for the three returnees, why would such an awesome event as the coming of the Branch be only theirs to know—and since they are not designated priests, they probably would not have had access to the temple, where they could see the crown. It is best to view this crown as a commemoration of these three men, in the sense that it memorialized the ceremony of crowning that involved them. Thomas (*Zechariah*, p. 1081) suggests placing חֵן after לְזִכָּרוֹן to read "a sign of favor."

---

14. The crown did not remain on the head of the high priest nor did it become his possession. He, after all, was not the Branch. Rather, the symbolic diadem resided in the temple, where it commemorated the participation of Heldai, Tobijah, and Jedaiah in the momentous event that envisioned the coming of a priest-king (see the Exegesis). We may think that they should have placed the crown in a more conspicuous place as a constant reminder to the community, but that would not have expressed all the significance of this crown. It was appropriate that the temple should house this emblem because the Branch will build the temple of the Lord (see the Exposition of verse 12).

The names of the individuals in this verse are perplexing. I have identified Heldai (v. 10) and Helem (v. 14) as the same person (see the Exegesis). The name appears as Heldai in 1 Chronicles 27:15, but in 1 Chronicles 11:30 it appears as Heled, lacking the hypocoristic (or gentilic) ending *ai*. Evidently the two are forms of the name of one of David's soldiers who was a Netophathite. In 2 Samuel 23:29, however, a Netophathite who, like Heled (1 Chron. 11:30), is a son of Baanah, has the name Heleb. It is thus all but certain that the name Heldai underwent alteration, either as a result of faulty text transmission or dialectical peculiarities. The fact that this name appears with a labial (*b*) in 2 Samuel 23:29 (Heleb) parallels the situation here in Zechariah, where the labial *mem* (*m*) is the final radical. It is possible that a copyist mistook final *d* or *du* for *mem* here, an error that could have occurred during the first to fourth centuries A.D., when inscriptions show yodh as a vertical stroke which with daleth could have been mistaken for mem.

Even though the Septuagint does not translate these entities as names, it witnesses to their presence. The words *tois hupomenousi* (to them that wait patiently) may indicate that the translator regarded *him* (Helem) as a plural noun form of *ḥûl*, which has as one of its connotations to wait patiently. Such a defectively written noun form, however, is unattested. It is much easier to understand how the Septuagint translator could derive *tois chrēsimois autēs* (to the useful men of it [that is, the captivity]) from *lĕṭôbîyâ*, for *ṭôb* (lit., good) may have the sense of *valuable*, and the *y* (yodh) can indicate a plural, while *-â* can function as a feminine suffix (it). The name Jedaiah (*lîdaʿyāh*) appears in the Septuagint as *tois epegnōkosin autēn* (to them that have known it). The translator evidently understood this word as *know* (*yādaʾ*), with *-â* again functioning as a suffix (it).

Far more difficult is the presence of *ḥēn* (favor) in this verse. The uncertainties surrounding this word allow us only to make suggestions regarding its function. Its connection with "the son of Zephaniah" makes it likely that it denotes Josiah (v. 10), Zephaniah's son; it is perhaps an alternate name for Josiah. Dual personal names—perhaps copyists' slips or popular variations—are found frequently in the Old Testament for the same individual: Jorah (Ezra 2:18) and Hariph (Neh. 7:24), Shema (1 Chron. 8:13) and Shimei (1 Chron.

8:21), Jehoaddah (1 Chron. 8:36) and Jarah (1 Chron. 9:42), and Shallum (1 Chron. 9:17) and Meshullam (Neh. 12:25). Another possibility is that *ḥēn* means "grace" or "favor," with the construction *ûlḥēn* meaning "and the favor of." Since *waw* is in sequence with this particle on the preceding names, the crown would have memorialized not only the three participants in the prophetic object lesson, but also the favor that Josiah son of Zephaniah showed in receiving these three returnees, perhaps giving them lodging and graciously opening his home to the prophet for the symbolic ceremony. We must look to the next verse for the reality behind these symbols.

X. A Symbolic Ceremony Prefiguring the Branch (6:9–15)
D. Those Far Off Working on the Temple (6:15)

McCOMISKEY

[15]And those who are far off shall come and work on the temple of the LORD, and you will know that the LORD of hosts has sent me to you. And this will be so if you sincerely obey the voice of the LORD your God.

NRSV

[15]Those who are far off shall come and help to build the temple of the LORD; and you shall know that the LORD of hosts has sent me to you. This will happen if you diligently obey the voice of the LORD your God.

15. וּרְחוֹקִים is an adjective meaning "distant ones" (Isa. 33:13; Jer. 25:26) or exiled Israelites (Dan. 9:7). Here it refers to people at a distance. וּבָנוּ בְּהֵיכַל (and work on the temple): בָּנָה (to work) occurs with the preposition בְּ in this fashion only in Nehemiah 4:4 [10], 11 [17] and means "to work on," not "work within." וִידַעְתֶּם (and you will know) is plural. In the other occurrences of the angel's formula of confirmation (2:13 [9], 15 [11]; 4:9), the significance of the number of the verb יָדַע (to know) is clear because the context names the person addressed. That is not the case here, but the future perspective of the passage and the general call to obedience support an address to all the people. יְהוָה צְבָאוֹת (the LORD of hosts): See the Exposition of 2:12 [8], 15 [11]; 4:9. וְהָיָה (and this will be so) establishes the potential reality contingent on the conditional clause that follows. It has greater force than its more common narrative function of "and it was [that]," conveying instead "and it will take place" (as in Jer. 39:16). אִם (if) followed by an imperfective has the force of possible fulfillment in the future (GKC §159*l*). שָׁמוֹעַ תִּשְׁמְעוּן (you sincerely obey): This use of the infinitive absolute with the imperfective strengthens the verbal action. The verb שָׁמַע (lit., hear) often means "to obey," as "hear" does in English. בְּקוֹל (the voice of): בְּ is frequently collocated with שָׁמַע with no discernible difference in sense between it and collocations with לְ (לְ) in Gen. 3:17 and Judg. 2:20; בְּ in Deut. 4:30 and Jer. 3:13). אֱלֹהֵיכֶם (your God): See the Exegesis of 8:8 for the significance of this divine name.

---

15. The text does not define "those who are far off." We cannot limit this reference to Jewish exiles remaining in the far reaches of the Persian Empire, for that would ignore the important post-exilic theological tradition of a future union of Jews and Gentiles under the aegis of Yahweh. The call of 2:10 [6] to flee from the north may appear to summon Jewish exiles, but our exploration of this and the subsequent verses shows that this call envisions a great influx of Gentiles into the community of God: "Many nations shall join themselves to the LORD on that day, and shall be my people" (2:15 [11]). We reflect the full-orbed theology of Zechariah when we view "those who are far off" as Gentiles who join in the building of the kingdom of God.

These people unite to "work on the temple of the LORD," which is not the Second Temple, but the kingdom of God over which the Branch rules (see the Exposition of 2:13). Haggai also refers to the temple, envisioning a "shaking of the nations" (2:6), in which these foreign peoples will bring their treasures to the Lord's house. This house, he says, will be greater in splendor than Solomon's (2:9)

This union of Jews and Gentiles in God's kingdom confirms the angel's role as an emissary of God: "Then you will know," he says, "that the LORD of hosts has sent me." Two events confirm the angel's mission: the destruction of the nations that held Israel captive (2:13 [9]) and the allegiance of Gentile nations to Yahweh (2:15 [11]). That Gentiles have come in large numbers to the Lord, working in his kingdom, confirms God's presence in the world, fulfilling what Zechariah perceived by prophetic foresight.

These observations shed light on the assertion of verse 14 that the crown memorialized not only the three returnees, but also the favor that Joshua showed in his hospitality both to them and to Zechariah. These three men must have had some significance in the symbolism of Joshua's coronation, but what is the reality behind these individuals who came from afar to join the rebuilding efforts of the community? This verse points to that reality, envisioning people who will come from "far off" to "work on the temple of the LORD." Haggai enriches this symbolism by envisioning the nations bringing silver and gold to the Lord's house (2:7–9), just as Heldai, Tobijah, and Jediah brought silver and gold to the Second Temple. The favor of Josiah, to which verse 14 refers, is then a continuing reminder of God's favor that admitted Gentiles to equal privilege with his ancient people (Eph. 2:11–16).

It seems strange to read that these momentous events will become reality only if the people are obedient, for Gentile inclusion in the promise is a certainty in the Old Testament (Gen. 12:3; 22:17–18; Isa. 49:6). On the other hand, it is true that God's blessings come only to the godly remnant. The union of believing Gentiles with unrepentant Jews is unthinkable. The prophet here establishes that the Lord can work only through a godly remnant. The kingdom of God, which the Branch's temple envisions, is a kingdom in which God dwells and rules over redeemed Jews and Gentiles through the agency of the Branch.

The symbolic visions and events we have witnessed in 1:7–6:15 are a panoramic expression of one theme—a theme that Zechariah's compatriot, Haggai, stated succinctly in 1:13: "I am with you, says the Lord" (see also 2:4). The builders understood that they were part of a vast continuum spanning the ages and culminating in a kingdom whose glory they could not imagine. This realization must have given great urgency to their task, for they knew that if they failed to establish their homeland and that if they should depart Zion's hill to lose themselves among the nations, history would never witness the appearance of the Branch nor the kingdom that Zechariah's crown memorializes.

XI. A Delegation from Bethel Visits the Prophet (7:1–8:23)
A. The Delegation's Question (7:1–3)

McCOMISKEY

7 Now, in the fourth year of King Darius, the word of the LORD came to Zechariah on the fourth day of the ninth month, that is Chislev. ²Now Bethel—[that is in particular] Sharezer and Regem-melech and his followers—had sent to entreat the LORD's favor, ³speaking to the priests who were of the house of the LORD of hosts and to the prophets, asking, "Shall I lament in the fifth month, practicing abstinence as I have done for these—how many years?"

NRSV

7 In the fourth year of King Darius, the word of the fourth day of the ninth month, which is Chislev. ²Now the people of Bethel had sent Sharezer and Regem-melech and their men, to entreat the favor of the LORD, ³and to ask the priests of the house of the LORD of hosts and the prophets, "Should I mourn and practice abstinence in the fifth month, as I have done for so many years?"

7:1. וַיְהִי (now came): See the Exegesis of 1:1.

2. וַיִּשְׁלַח (now had sent): It would be unusual for שַׂר־אֶצֶר (Sharezer) and רֶגֶם־מֶלֶךְ (Regem-melech) to be objects of וַיִּשְׁלַח because of the high degree of consistency with which שָׁלַח (to send) notes its object by the object marker אֶת, which is lacking here. In the absence of this marker, these names stand in apposition to בֵּית־אֵל (Bethel): "Bethel, that is Sharezer and Regem-melech." The verb שָׁלַח frequently describes someone at a distance sending to inquire of another. בֵּית־אֵל in this view is the subject of וַיִּשְׁלַח because the verb is singular. Bethel—that is, its citizens, including Sharezer, Regem-melech, and his followers—sent to Jerusalem. וַאֲנָשָׁיו (and his men): The suffix ו (his) must refer to רֶגֶם מֶלֶךְ, not בֵּית־אֵל, because the latter

option would establish an awkward redundancy since Sharezer and Regem-melech were themselves citizens of Bethel. וַאֲנָשָׁיו thus indicates followers of Regem-melech (see 1 Sam. 18:27). לְחַלּוֹת אֶת־פְּנֵי (to entreat the favor of; lit., to entreat the face of): *Lamed* indicates purpose (see similar constructions in 1 Sam. 22:11; 1 Chron. 19:5). חָלָה פְּנֵי (to entreat the face of): In most contexts, the purpose of the pleading is to entreat one's favor or persuade (Exod. 32:11–12; 1 Sam. 13:12; 1 Kings 13:6; 2 Chron. 33:12; Dan. 9:13; Mal. 1:9). The sense here does not appear to be simply to learn God's will, but to gain his favorable response.

3. לֵאמֹר (speaking) frequently follows שָׁלַח (to send), expressing the content of the message (Amos 7:10). Since no such content follows the

---

7:1. More than two years had passed since Zechariah received his first vision (1:1). The construction of the temple would have been well under way at this time, and the initial frustrations and fears of the people were giving way to the more immediate demands of a maturing community. The population was spreading to cities and towns outside Jerusalem. The people of Bethel were probably not caught up in the immediate concerns of completing the temple structure, and the respite they had from the building activities in Jerusalem allowed time for religious disputation.

The order of the words in this historical notice differs from 1:1, 7 in that the clause *the word of the Lord came to Zechariah* interrupts the references to the year and month. This does not necessarily indicate faulty transmission of the text, because if the writer had united the references to the year and month, placing the words *the word of the Lord came to Zechariah* at the end of the sentence, "Zechariah" would have immediately preceded *wayyišlaḥ* (now had sent), momentarily directing the reader's eye to it as the possible subject of this verb. This would be particularly so in unversified manuscripts. Chislev, the Akkadian name for the ninth month of the Hebrew calendar, appears also in Nehemiah 1:1.

2. The subject of the verb *wayyišlaḥ* (now had sent) is far from clear. I have chosen to regard the personal names as appositional to Bethel (see the Exegesis). It is attractive to understand Bethel as a constituent of the personal name Bethel-sharezer, since this name appears in Neo-Babylonian materials around the time of Zechariah (Hyatt, "Neo-Babylonian Parallel"). Baldwin (*Zechariah*, pp. 141–43) argues effectively for this view, understanding the delegation to have come from Babylon, not Bethel. This view regards Regem-melech

as a royal title, thus requiring the dropping of *waw* (and) before this name, which is only a slight alteration of the text.

The view that the delegation came from Bethel, however, answers nicely not only to the syntactical structure of the Masoretic Text, but to verse 5 as well, where the words *say to all the people of the land and to the priests* indicate that the prophet's concern was not with disseminating his prophetic judgment in Babylon, but in Palestine. He appears to have wished that the spirit that prompted Bethel's dispute would not permeate the land. Since the delegation's visit took place in the ninth month, the fast of the fifth month was now several months behind them. Evidently the question had arisen on or around that fast day and had continued for three months. In this view, we do not know who conveyed the inquiry to Zechariah and the priests; we know only that the disputation involved Sharezer, Regem-melech, and his followers, who sent to the religious authorities at Jerusalem for a ruling on the matter. The citing of Bethel in apposition with the names Sharezer and Regem-melech indicates that the dispute was the concern of the larger community of Bethel as well.

If the expression *to entreat the Lord's favor* means that Sharezer and Regem-melech were expecting a favorable response to their request, it may explain the prophet's impassioned reply to their question. Sharezer is a Babylonian name, *šar-uṣur* (protect the king; 2 Kings 19:37; Isa. 37:38). One wonders if the retention of his Babylonian name indicates that he had not entirely left Babylonian influences behind.

3. The message that the people of Bethel sent to Jerusalem inquired of the priests and prophets about the need to continue the religious practices

first occurrence of לֵאמֹר, it is best to translate it as "speaking" (see my translation). לְבֵית־יְהוָה צְבָאוֹת (of the house of the LORD of hosts): *Lamed* appears to indicate "belonging to." Its exact function is obscure, but it probably refers to the priests who were accredited to the temple, thus having the authority to pronounce judgment in cases such as this. יְהוָה צְבָאוֹת (the LORD of hosts): See the Exegesis of 1:3. לֵאמֹר (asking) introduces the content of the message (see לֵאמֹר above). הַאֶבְכֶּה (shall I lament): בָכָה (to weep) does not occur elsewhere with the sense of mourning on a fast day, but it can have no other sense in this context. The construction is singular because, as I have construed it, Bethel as a corporate entity is the subject. בַּחֹדֶשׁ הַחֲמִשִׁי (in the fifth month): See the Exposition for the significance of this month. הִנָּזֵר (practicing abstinence) is a niphal infinitive absolute functioning as a *casus adverbialis*, defining more

precisely the action of the main verb בָּכָה. The basic verbal action lurking in the several forms of the root נזר appears to be "separation" (Lev. 22:2 is definitive in this regard). This verb occurs in the niphal on only three other occasions (Lev. 22:2; Ezek. 14:7; Hos. 9:10), none with the sense of religious abstinence. The association of this verb with בָכָה, however, indicates that lamenting and abstinence were aspects of self-denial in the fifth month. עָשִׂיתִי (I have done) is singular because its subject is the community of Bethel (see above). כַּמֶּה (so many): This combination of כְּ (as) and מָה (what) frequently introduces questions ("how many?"; Gen. 47:8; 2 Sam. 19:35 [34]; Ps. 119:84), but it may also introduce rhetorical statements (Job 13:23; 21:17; see also Zech. 2:6). The structure here may be a question (These—how many years?) indicating an indefinite number.

---

of the fast of the fifth month. This fast marked the destruction of the temple on the seventh day of that month (2 Kings 25:8–9), and that day became a fast day for the Jewish exiles in Babylon. Now that the temple was on the way to completion, the observation of this fast seemed unnecessary.

Perhaps the question was sincere, suggesting that the people should turn the fast into a cele-

bration of the temple's completion once it was finished. The delegation's vague recollection of the period during which they had observed these fasts ("these—how many years?") indicates otherwise, for these words reflect a weariness with the required abstinences. Zechariah apparently saw the question in this light and answered accordingly.

XI. A Delegation from Bethel Visits the Prophet (7:1–8:23)
B. The Motive for the Question (7:4–6)

McCOMISKEY

⁴And the word of the LORD of hosts came to me, saying, ⁵Speak to all the people of the land, as well as to the priests, saying, When you fasted and mourned in the fifth and in the seventh [months], and this for seventy years, was it really for me that you fasted? ⁶And when you eat and when you drink, are you not the ones eating and you the ones who drink?

NRSV

⁴Then the word of the LORD of hosts came to me: ⁵Say to all the people of the land and the priests: When you fasted and lamented in the fifth month and in the seventh, for these seventy years, was it for me that you fasted? ⁶And when you eat and when you drink, do you not eat and drink only for yourselves?

4. וַיְהִי דְבַר ... אֵלַי (the word came to me): See the Exegesis of 1:1. יְהוָה צְבָאוֹת (the LORD of hosts): See the Exegesis of 1:3. לֵאמֹר (saying) introduces the content of Yahweh's word to the prophet.

5. אֱמֹר (say): Impelled by the force of Yahweh's word, the prophet delivered the following discourse. כִּי (when) has its frequent temporal sense here (Gen. 6:1; 1 Sam. 1:12). צַמְתֶּם (you fasted) always denotes abstaining from food, showing that the word הִנָּזֵר in verse 3 involves abstinence (separating) from food. The plural form of the verb probably indicates that the prophet addressed his words to all the people of the land, not just Bethel. וְסָפוֹד (and mourned) always expresses sorrow. Its most frequent connotation is sorrow over a death (Gen. 23:2; 50:10; 1 Sam. 25:1), but it can also refer to the loss of the land (Jer. 4:8). The loss of someone or something underlies most of the occurrences of this word. For the use of this infinitive construct as an adverbial complement, continuing the action of the preceding verb but distinct from it, see GKC §113z; IBHS, pp. 588–89. וְזֶה (and this for): See the Exposition. הֲצוֹם צַמְתֻּנִי (was it really for me that you fasted?): This use of the finite verb with the infinitive absolute intensifies the verbal action: Was it *really* ... ? The form צַמְתֻּנִי (fasted) contains the rare masculine plural ending ־תּוּ in the suffixed (perfect) conjugation (see also Num.

20:5; 21:5). The suffix ־נִי (for me) does not have an accusative function (fasted me) as we may expect from this construction, but a dative function. It is similar to the English "give me," which is acceptable for "give to me" (see Neh. 9:28; Isa. 27:4). The sense is, "Did you fast for me?" אָנִי (untranslated): This independent personal pronoun stands in apposition to the verbal suffix, serving an emphatic role (IBHS, pp. 299–300; GKC §135e): My translation, "Was it really for me that you fasted?" is an effort to reflect this appositional structure. This emphatic sense is valid because the verbal suffix alone would have sufficed to designate the one to whom it refers.

6. וְכִי (and when): ו connects this clause sequentially to the preceding sentence, thus balancing the two contrasting clauses (me ... you). כִּי (when) sustains the temporal quality of כִּי in the preceding sentence and, in company with the two imperfectives that follow it ("eat and drink"), expresses a nonperfective state in indefinite time that כִּי defines in this sentence. The translation "whenever you eat" is appropriate to the construction. הֲלוֹא (are not?), composed of the question marker (ה) and the negative indicator (לֹא), expresses assurance (is it not so?). It also contributes a measure of emphasis to אַתֶּם (you) by drawing attention to it: "Is it not *you*?"

4–5. Again the prophet felt the divine impulse to speak on behalf of God. He looks beyond the Bethel delegation, speaking to both the priests and the people. He could speak with authority to the priests because, as a prophet of God, he communicated God's will to all.

The word of Yahweh comes as a question referring to the fifth month. Several fast days imposed during the exile and early restoration commemorated recent tragic events that had happened to the Jewish people: the conquest of Jerusalem by Nebuchadnezzar (the fast during the fourth month), the destruction of the temple (fifth month), the murder of Gedaliah, a Judean governor (seventh month), and the beginning of the siege of Jerusalem by Nebuchadnezzar (tenth month). Since the delegation's question related only to the fast day that observed the temple's destruction, it is likely that the progress on the temple prompted their question.

The seventy-year period refers to the same general time span found in 1:12, which was actually sixty-seven years (see the Exposition of 1:12 and Ackroyd, "Historical Problems," pp. 25–27). Here the time extends from 587 B.C. to 518 B.C., the

fourth year of Darius. The words *and this for seventy years* underscores the lengthy duration of these fasts; apparently the exiled community began to observe these fasts shortly after the events occurred. They had become an integral aspect of postexilic worship, and the prophet did not wish to let them go.

The heart of the question Zechariah represents God asking is, "Did you really observe these fasts as unto me?" We shall see (v. 7) that the prophet appeals to the eighth-century prophets who decried the religious formalism of their day. Zechariah championed the traditional prophetic faith and possibly viewed the Bethel delegation's question as betraying a lack of sincere commitment to their Yahwistic heritage.

6. The prophet's questioning continues as he asks the Bethel delegation (and, beyond them, all the people of the land) if it is not true that they eat and drink only to themselves. The prophet's insistent probing moves from the people's failure to take God into account in their fasting (v. 5) to a failure to take him into account when they eat their meals; that is, they do not consider God as the provider of their daily bread. "Eating and drinking" may elsewhere in the Bible have broader application to the affairs of everyday life (see Eccles. 3:13; Jer. 22:15; Luke 17:27–28), but the balancing of these words with fasting in this context limits it to the partaking of food.

XI. A Delegation from Bethel Visits the Prophet (7:1–8:23)
C. Call to Sincere Religion (7:7–12)

McCOMISKEY

⁷Are [these] not the words that the LORD proclaimed through the former prophets when Jerusalem was inhabited and secure, with its towns surrounding it, and the Negeb and the Shephelah were occupied? ⁸And the word of the LORD came to Zechariah, saying, ⁹This is what the LORD of hosts says, Render true judgment, and show kindness and compassion to one another, ¹⁰and do not oppress the widow or the orphan, the alien or the poor, and do not plot in your minds each the harm of others. ¹¹But they refused to listen, presenting an unwilling shoulder, and they stopped up their ears so they could not hear. ¹²And they made their hearts hard so that they could not obey the law and the words that the LORD of hosts sent by his Spirit through the former prophets. Thus, great wrath came from the LORD of hosts.

NRSV

⁷Were not these the words that the LORD proclaimed by the former prophets, when Jerusalem was inhabited and in prosperity, along with the towns around it, and when the Negeb and the Shephelah were inhabited?

⁸The word of the LORD came to Zechariah, saying: ⁹Thus says the LORD of hosts: Render true judgments, show kindness and mercy to one another; ¹⁰do not oppress the widow, the orphan, the alien, or the poor; and do not devise evil in your hearts against one another. ¹¹But they refused to listen, and turned a stubborn shoulder, and stopped their ears in order not to hear. ¹²They made their hearts adamant in order not to hear the law and the words that the LORD of hosts had sent by his spirit through the former prophets. Therefore great wrath came from the LORD of hosts.

7. הֲלוֹא (are not?): See the Exegesis of the preceding verse. אֶת־הַדְּבָרִים ([these] the words): אֵת (these) cannot be the sign of the direct object since the text does not indicate an explicit or implicit verbal idea in association with this particle (Hoftijzer sees it as a connector between this and the previous passage; "Particle ʾt," pp. 76–77). אֵת is occasionally used to emphasize the nominative (2 Chron. 31:17; Neh. 9:19; Dan. 9:13; Zech. 12:10; esp. Ezek. 47:17–19, where אֵת in the recurring phrase וְאֵת פְּאַת [this is the side] functions as the demonstrative pronoun [this]). בְּיַד (through; lit., by the hand of) expresses agency. In Haggai 2:1, it refers to prophetic agency ("the word of the LORD came by the agency of Haggai"), as it does here. בִּהְיוֹת (when was): The infinitive construct of הָיָה with בְ conveys its frequent temporal sense. הָיָה relates to the participle יֹשֵׁב (inhabited), giving it a past progressive sense. יֹשֵׁב (be inhabited): See the Exegesis of 2:8 [4]. וּשְׁלֵוָה (and secure): Basic to this root is the sense of quiet. The adjective שָׁלֵו elsewhere describes security within Jerusalem's battlements (Ps. 122:7; in parallel with שָׁלוֹם, peace), the antithesis of strife (Prov. 17:1), and Judah's security, which prevented her from turning to God (Jer. 22:21). Zechariah's following reference to the cities around Jerusalem favors the translation "secure" for this word rather than "prosperous." יֹשֵׁב (inhabited): See the Exegesis of 2:8 [4] and 9:5.

8. וַיְהִי דְּבַר־יְהוָה אֶל־ (and the word of the LORD came unto): See the Exegesis of 1:11.

9. יְהוָה צְבָאוֹת (the LORD of hosts): See the Exegesis and Exposition of 1:3. The cognate accusative structure מִשְׁפָּט . . . שְׁפֹטוּ (lit., judge a judgment) has to do with the administration of justice: to judge a cause (Lam. 3:59), to dispense justice (Zech. 8:16), to judge on the basis of legal standards (Ezek. 16:38; 23:24; 44:24), or to render legal decisions (1 Kings 3:28). Zechariah 8:16 places the verbal action of this structure in "the gate," applying this expression to Israel's judges (see the Exposition). אֱמֶת (true): Like its verbal affinity אָמַן (to be firm), אֱמֶת conveys a sense of firmness, faithfulness, steadfastness, dependability, consistency, certainty, and, by extension, truth and honesty. The contexts in which this word appears determine its nuancing. For example, in Genesis 24:27, the word applies to God's consistency with his promise (v. 7), and in verse 48, it refers to the way that Abraham's servant took when seeking a wife for Isaac, describing it as דֶּרֶךְ אֱמֶת (the right way),

---

7. It is difficult to know whether "are [these] not the words?" refers to the prophet's questions in verses 5–6 or to the words of the preexilic prophets in verses 9–10. Supporting the former option is the prophetic formula in verse 8, "and the word of the LORD came to Zechariah saying . . . ," which appears to introduce a new section, thus placing verse 7 with the preceding material. The latter view finds support in the questions of verses 5–6, which are specific to matters at issue in the postexilic community. If the prophet's rhetorical question in verse 7 does not relate to verses 9–10, the words of the former prophets appear with no introduction, and we do not know we are reading their words until verses 11–12. The words *they refused to listen* in verse 11 refer to the people of the eighth century; and without the allusion to the eighth-century prophets in verse 7 these words have no previously stated referent, an awkwardness quite uncharacteristic of this book.

It is possible that an editor placed the prophetic formula in verse 8, failing to grasp the flow of the discourse, but it is also possible that this formula indicates that the word of God entered Zechariah's consciousness as he found it in the writings of his prophetic predecessors, particularly the prophecy of Jeremiah. The subsequent discussion shows that the words of verse 9 are a crystallization of Jeremiah's prophetic message. For this and the reasons cited above, the discussion will follow the second line of thought, regarding the words of verses 5–6 primarily as Zechariah's.

Verse 7 envisions the former prophets preaching to their fellow citizens when Jerusalem was still secure and Judah still intact. The surrounding towns and geographical areas functioned as a protective buffer for Jerusalem against invaders. Micah 1:8–16 pictures the gradual dissolution of these buffer towns. The security that Jerusalem enjoyed before the exile will have a bearing on Zechariah's developing response to Bethel's question.

8–9. Perhaps Zechariah perceived in Bethel's inquiry the seeds of the same empty religious formalism—which had produced the bitter fruit of the exile—that the preexilic prophets of verse 7 so vehemently denounced. The words following the formula of verse 8 comprise a collage of prophetic voices that does not appear to contain revelational material original to Zechariah. Although the former prophets never use the words *raḥămîm ʿăśû* (show compassion), Hosea 10:12; 12:7 [6]; and Micah 6:8 call for "kindness" (*ḥesed*), with Hosea 4:1 and 6:4 in particular bemoaning its lack.

that is, the way consistent with God's stated purposes. When it connotes consistency with facts as they are known, "truth" is the appropriate translation (Gen. 42:16; Deut. 13:15 [14]; 17:4; 22:20; Judg. 9:15; Zech. 8:16). The construct relationship is adjectival (characteristic genitive). For a further discussion of this function, see the Exegesis and Exposition of 8:16. וְחֶסֶד (and kindness): Since kindness is an attitude that manifests itself in relation to another individual, חֶסֶד frequently occurs in contexts describing interpersonal relationships (Gen. 19:19; 40:14; Ruth 3:10). It functions here as one of two objects of the imperative עֲשׂוּ (show; lit., do), thus imparting to חֶסֶד the sense of "acts of kindness." וְרַחֲמִים (and mercy) is the second object of עֲשׂוּ and, like חֶסֶד, connotes acts of compassion (see the Exegesis of 1:16). אִישׁ אֶת־אָחִיו (one another): אָח does not here indi-

cate a filial relationship, which the English word *brother* possesses. When it occurs with אִישׁ (lit., man), it simply designates "another," occurring even in hostile contexts (see Hag. 2:22).

10. וְאַלְמָנָה וְיָתוֹם (and the widow or the orphan): ו (and) continues the litany of prophetic utterances. The two nouns are joined by ו (or), as is the following pair, גֵּר וְעָנִי (the alien or the poor). This is the only instance where these four words are joined in pairs (see the Exposition). אַל־תַּעֲשֹׁקוּ (do not oppress), broadly defined, connotes taking wrongful advantage of another. "Defraud" is an appropriate translation in some contexts (Lev. 5:21 [6:2]; 1 Sam. 12:3, 4), but in most instances "oppress" is better because the wrongdoing this expression describes is against a person or nation inferior in strength or station (Deut. 24:14; Ps. 119:122; Prov. 14:31; Isa. 52:4; Mic. 5:2). וְרָעַת אִישׁ אָחִיו (and each

---

It is the voice of Jeremiah, however, that rings most clearly in this collage. Perhaps Zechariah was reading the prophecy of Jeremiah; we noted a similar dependence on Jeremiah at 1:4 (see the Exposition there). The cadences of Jeremiah's prophecy sounded in the prophetic consciousness of Zechariah and the word given by God decades before now received new force as Zechariah shaped that word for the people of postexilic Judah.

The words *judge [true] judgment* (my translation, *render [true] judgment*) appear in Jeremiah 5:28 with reference to the cause of the needy (see also 21:12; 22:3, 15). Jeremiah 7:5 calls for just treatment "one to another" (as does Zechariah) and urges concern for the alien, orphan, and widow (see also 5:28). In 7:25, 26:5, 29:19, 35:15, and 44:4, Jeremiah speaks of the prophets whom the people rejected, a theme that Zechariah takes up in 7:12. Most important in this regard is Jeremiah 7:5–6, which is part of the extensive first temple sermon that began at 7:1. In that sermon Jeremiah decried the people's superstitious dependence on the presence of the temple in their midst, and he called for obedience in a plea reminiscent of Zechariah's words here. If Jeremiah's prophecy influenced Zechariah, Zechariah may have envisioned the temple looming behind Jeremiah as he preached his impassioned sermon to the throngs of worshipers. The temple may have struck a resonant chord in Zechariah's mind, and he may have perceived a similar false security appearing in his community. The rising walls of the nearly completed temple mutely testified to the freedom from external interference that the

Persian Empire had secured. This stability may have reminded Zechariah of the false security the people of the eighth century derived from their "temple theology." And this may be the reason for his reference to the security of preexilic Jerusalem in verse 7. Now that the temple was nearing completion, the people seemed to reflect a growing lack of dependence on Yahweh in their wish to suspend one of the fasts. Zechariah may have viewed the cessation of one fast as breaking a link between the nation and its Yahwistic heritage.

The call to "render true judgment" refers not to the general run of society but to those who had the fate of the less fortunate in their hands. This would include Israel's political leaders and judges. Zechariah 8:16 underscores this conclusion by placing the action of the collocation *mišpaṭ . . . šipṭû* (render . . . judgment) "in your gates," the site of Israel's legal proceedings. True judgments are legal decisions that accord with facts, not judgments perverted by dishonest motives.

10. Zechariah recalls the former prophets' concern for the oppressed classes in their society, but we do not find Zechariah's grouping of these classes (widow and orphan, alien and poor) elsewhere. Deuteronomy regularly speaks of the "orphan, widow, and stranger" (14:29; 16:11, 14; 24:19, 20–21; 26:12–13; 27:19), but Malachi, another postexilic prophet, adds "the hired workers" (3:5) to this grouping. While the former prophets frequently called for compassion toward the poor, Zechariah may have included them in the levels of oppressed in his society because of the severe economic conditions that existed in his day (see Hag. 1:6, 9–11).

the harm of others): רָעַת (harm; lit., harm of) is in the construct state. The sense of this statement leads us to expect the associative noun in this relationship to be אָחִיו (others; lit., his brother), not אִישׁ (each; lit., a man), as this literal translation illustrates: "Do not plot in your minds each [אִישׁ] the harm of another [אָחִיו]." This sense, however, requires a broken construct chain interrupted by אִישׁ. While such broken construct chains do occur in Hebrew (see the commentary on Hos. 6:9; 8:2; 14:3 [2], 8 [7]), it would be highly unusual for such an inversion to occur in a crystallized expression like this one (lit., a man his brother). The structure here in Zechariah 7:10 conveys the same sense as is found in Genesis 9:5: מִיַּד אִישׁ אָחִיו (at the hand of each one's brother), with אָחִיו standing in apposition to אִישׁ. תַּחְשְׁבוּ (do not plot): חָשַׁב (to plot) describes various mental processes. With רָעָה (to harm), it connotes plotting (Jer. 48:2; Mic. 2:3; Nah. 1:11) or intending (Jer. 18:8; 26:3; 36:3) harm against another. בִּלְבַבְכֶם (in your minds): לֵבָב is the center of human cogitation. Paired with חָשַׁב, it places the action of that verb in the mind. This construction forbids any thought processes that entail the harm of others.

11. לְהַקְשִׁיב (to listen): See the Exegesis of 1:4. וַיִּתְּנוּ (presenting; lit., and they gave): נָתַן (to give) sometimes occurs in conjunction with body parts to create various senses, such as turning the neck (back) to flee (Exod. 23:27; 2 Sam. 22:41), turning

away in rejection (2 Chron. 29:6), and presenting a resistant shoulder as a beast of burden might in refusing the yoke (Neh. 9:29). The context here calls for the latter sense. סֹרָרֶת (unwilling) typically connotes a refusal to submit to authority (e.g., a stubborn heifer; Hos. 4:16): הִכְבִּידוּ (they stopped up; lit., they made heavy): While the precise sense of the idiom *make the ears heavy* escapes us, the context makes it clear enough that it connotes unresponsiveness (Isa. 6:10). מִשְּׁמוֹעַ (could not hear; lit., from hearing): מִן (from) directs the action of הִכְבִּיד "away from hearing."

12. וְלִבָּם (and their hearts): ו (and) continues the litany of condemnatory clauses that began in verse 11. לֵב (heart) is the center of cogitation (see v. 7 and Gen. 20:5; Job 11:13; Jer. 17:9). שָׁמִיר (hard) on several occasions refers to thorns or thorn bushes. Isaiah uses it in this sense as a metaphor for desolation (5:6; 7:23, 24, 25) or to describe fuel for fire (9:17 [18]). Only in Jeremiah and Ezekiel does it appear with the sense it has here. The occurrence of this word with צִפֹּרֶן (the point of a stylus) in Jeremiah 17:1 points to a hard substance (probably diamond) suitable for engraving. Ezekiel 3:9 uses it to describe hard stone (probably flint). מִשְּׁמוֹעַ (could not obey; lit., from hearing): See the Exegesis of v. 11 and Isaiah 63:17. שָׁמַע (lit., to hear) frequently means "to obey," as does the English word *hear* (see the Exegesis of 1:4). הַתּוֹרָה, frequently translated "the law," does not here

---

Zechariah goes on to recall the eighth-century prophets' opposition to plotting harm against others. The prophet Hosea speaks of the wrongdoing that transected all levels of society in his day. In 4:1–3 he speaks of the lack of truth, the use of false oaths, and the violence that was common among his fellow citizens. These wrongs are consonant with the "plotting of harm" to which Zechariah refers. Jeremiah 5:26 also condemned the wrong his fellow citizens did to one another:

For scoundrels are found among my people;
　　they take over the goods of others.
Like fowlers they set a trap;
　　they catch human beings.

And in 6:13 he says:

For from the least to the greatest of them,
　　everyone is greedy for unjust gain.

11. The people to whom the former prophets preached did not heed them. Like a recalcitrant

beast turning from the yoke, they stubbornly resisted the prophets' pleas for repentance. This sequence of clauses is a vivid picture of willful refusal to obey God. It allows for no plea of ignorance or misunderstanding on the part of the earlier generations.

12. Once again, the cadences of Jeremiah's first temple sermon resound in Zechariah's prophecy. Jeremiah refers to the prophets (7:25), depicts the people's stubborn refusal to listen to them (7:13, 26), and describes the desolation the land will suffer (7:33)—all elements found in Zechariah 7:12.

Zechariah observes two agents in the communication of God's words in the preexilic period: the Spirit of God and the prophets. The Spirit of God is the manifestation in time of the divine personality (see the Exposition of 4:6), and the prophets, by virtue of their relationship to God's Spirit (Mic. 3:8), were agents of his Spirit, communicating God's will. The wrath of the Lord that resulted from the people's hardness of heart was, of course, the exile.

mean "instruction," for its connection with the words of the prophets indicates that the Torah, the Mosaic law, is in view. שָׁלַח (sent) occurs with two prepositional constructions—בְּרוּחוֹ (by his Spirit) and בְּיַד (through; lit., by the hand of)—pos-

iting both God's Spirit and the prophets as agencies of revelation (see the Exposition). יְהוָה צְבָאוֹת (the LORD of hosts): See the Exegesis and Exposition of 1:2, 15.

XI. A Delegation from Bethel Visits the Prophet (7:1–8:23)
D. Result of the Disobedience of the Forefathers
(7:13–14)

McCOMISKEY

¹³And so it was that as I called, and they did not respond; so they would call and I would not respond, says the LORD of hosts, ¹⁴and I blew them away over all the nations that were not familiar with them. So the land [they left] behind them was bereft of [travelers] going back and forth. So they made a pleasant land into a desolation.

NRSV

¹³Just as, when I called, they would not hear, so, when they called, I would not hear, says the LORD of hosts, ¹⁴and I scattered them with a whirlwind among all the nations that they had not known. Thus the land they left was desolate, so that no one went to and fro, and a pleasant land was made desolate.

13. קָרָא (he called) has as its nearest logical subject יְהוָה צְבָאוֹת (the LORD of hosts) in the previous verse. The action of this perfective verb is constative, viewing Yahweh's calling as a complete situation (*IBHS*, p. 480). שָׁמֵעוּ (they respond) sustains the plural reference to the people that began in verse 11 and continues throughout the pericope. Like קָרָא (he called), this perfective views the people's failure to respond as a complete situation. For the meaning of this word, "to respond, obey," see the Exegesis of verse 12. יִקְרָאוּ (they would call) and its companion verb אֶשְׁמָע (I would [not] respond) are imperfectives. Keil (*Minor Prophets*, p. 310) translates them as futures ("so will they cry and I shall not hear"), but this is hardly likely in view of the following clause's reference to the past ("and I blew them away"). Comrie (*Aspect*, p. 28) views the nonperfective "not as an incidental property of the moment but, precisely, as a characteristic feature of the whole period." If that sense of the nonperfective holds true here, and there is little reason (other than pure stylistic variation) to think otherwise, the imperfectives indicate a "past customary non-perfective" (*IBHS*, p. 503), yielding "so they would call, and I would not answer." יְהוָה צְבָאוֹת (the LORD of hosts): See the Exegesis of 1:3.

14. וְאֵסָעֲרֵם (and I blew them away): The qal stem occurs only three times, denoting a literal (Jon. 1:11) or figurative (Isa. 54:1; Hab. 3:14) storm. This is the only occurrence of the word in the piel. Since the context posits a destination for the action of this verb (to all the nations), the piel must be more directive than the qal and (at least in this context) indicate "storming the people," that is, blowing the nations by a violent wind. עַל (over) may mean "to" on occasion, especially with verbs of motion (Gen. 24:49; 1 Sam. 2:11; Jer. 14:3), but "over" seems more appropriate in this context, which pictures a violent windstorm scattering debris over the ground. לֹא־יְדָעוּם (not familiar with them; lit., did not know them) may also indicate that the Israelites did not know these nations. This is not entirely consonant with the structures of this context, however, since the third-person plural suffixes in this sentence consistently refer to the people of Israel. נָשַׁמָּה (was desolated) connotes severe deprivation. When מִן follows this verb, it indicates what the land has been deprived of, in this case מֵעֹבֵר וּמִשָּׁב (from passing through and returning). That is, the land has been deprived of traversal of its territory (compare the similar construction in Ezek. 33:28). The elliptical expression אַחֲרֵיהֶם (behind them) requires that we supply an appropriate verbal idea ("they left behind them"). וַיָּשִׂימוּ . . . לִשְׁמָּה: The collocation שִׂים לְ frequently means "to make into" (Mic. 4:7). חֶמְדָּה (pleasant): The related verb חָמַד means "to desire," which gives rise to the sense of "desirable" or "pleasant" for the noun. This word is here the antithesis of שַׁמָּה and thus conveys the idea of a land of pleasant prospect. שַׁמָּה (desolation), like its counterpart above, connotes deprivation.

---

13. The comparison clause in this verse ("as . . . so") marks the widening breach between Yahweh and his people. As he called to them through the voices of the prophets, he observed little response; and as conditions grew worse for the nation and the exile became a growing certainty, the people would cry out to their God, but he would turn a deaf ear. Their hearts, now adamant, had separated them from their God.

14. So great was the stormy breath of God that scattered the people over foreign lands that it also laid waste their homeland. Merchants and travelers no longer traversed the now desolate and forbidding land. Neither nature nor invading armies had laid the land waste—it was the people themselves who were responsible. They lost their inheritance because they proved untrue to the covenant that assured on condition of obedience (Exod. 19:5–6) their continuation in the land.

The construction *nāšammâ . . . mēʿōbēr ûmiššāb* is difficult to translate. It does not say that the land was so desolate that travel was impossible, but that the land was "desolated from traversing it." That is, it was deprived of travel over its territory. This expression does not tell us why the land was not traveled, only that it was not.

XI. A Delegation from Bethel Visits the Prophet (7:1–8:23)
E. God's Repopulating Zion (8:1–6)

McCOMISKEY

8 Now the word of the LORD of hosts came, saying, ²This is what the LORD of hosts says, I am jealous for Zion—extremely jealous—and with great anger I am jealous for it. ³This is what the LORD says, I shall return to Zion and dwell in Jerusalem, and Jerusalem shall be called the City of Truth, and the mountain of the LORD of hosts, the Mount of Holiness. ⁴This is what the LORD of hosts says, Old men and women will again sit in the streets of Jerusalem, each with cane in hand because of [their] length of days. ⁵And the streets of the city will be full of boys and girls playing in its streets. ⁶This is what the LORD of hosts says, If it should seem incredible to the remnant of this people in those days, should it also seem incredible to me? utterance of the LORD of hosts.

NRSV

8 The word of the LORD of hosts came to me, saying: ²Thus says the LORD of hosts: I am jealous for Zion with great jealousy, and I am jealous for her with great wrath. ³Thus says the LORD: I will return to Zion, and will dwell in the midst of Jerusalem; Jerusalem shall be called the faithful city, and the mountain of the LORD of hosts shall be called the holy mountain. ⁴Thus says the LORD of hosts: Old men and old women shall again sit in the streets of Jerusalem, each with staff in hand because of their great age. ⁵And the streets of the city shall be full of boys and girls playing in its streets. ⁶Thus says the LORD of hosts: Even though it seems impossible to the remnant of this people in these days, should it also seem impossible to me, says the LORD of hosts?

8:1. וַיְהִי (now came) marks a juncture in the reception of the prophetic word. Contrary to 7:9–10, which betrays dependence on the former prophets (see the previous discussion), the text now shows no direct dependence and is thus the prophet's own response to the situation at hand. יְהוָה צְבָאוֹת (the LORD of hosts): See the Exegesis of 1:3.

2. קִנֵּאתִי לְ־ (I am jealous for Zion): See the Exegesis of 1:14. קִנְאָה (jealous) is a cognate accusative that, by virtue of its reexpressing the action of the verb, carries an emphatic sense. גְדוֹלָה (lit., great) enlarges the sense of emphasis in the cognate accusative (extremely jealous): Yahweh is overwhelmed with feelings of undivided loyalty to his people. וְחֵמָה (and with anger): Related to the verb יָחַם (to be hot), this noun expresses a range of meaning, from "heat" to "intense anger" (Gen. 27:44; Jer. 21:12; 30:23; Lam. 2:4; Ezek. 3:14). It functions here as an internal accusative expressing the action of its verb (the following קִנֵּאתִי, I am jealous). לָהּ (for her) indicates Zion.

3. שַׁבְתִּי (I shall return to): The context gives this construction the meaning "return to" (not "turn to" as in 1:16). These are the references to Yahweh's jealousy, indicating his continued allegiance to his people (see the Exegesis and Exposition of 1:14) and the promise that he will dwell in Jerusalem, which would recall his previous residence there. The perfective שַׁבְתִּי (I shall return) indicates a situation complete in future time, conveying the writer's confidence that the verb's action will become a reality. וְשָׁכַנְתִּי (and dwell) and its companion verb וְנִקְרָאָה (and shall be called)

8:1–2. As Yahweh's word comes to him again, the prophet moves from the history of his people to the present. Zechariah's statement rings with assurance, reaffirming Yahweh's loyalty to his people. This affirmation recalls the assurances of the angel of the Lord in 1:14–15, where, speaking for the community, he echoes their deep concerns. The affirmation there that Yahweh is jealous for his people and angry with the nations reflects the community's concern that Yahweh had transferred his loyalty to the nations that were now at rest (see the Exposition of 1:14–15).

Why should the prophet re-echo that assurance here? It implies that the people of Bethel, as well as all the people of the land, continued to doubt Yahweh's allegiance as they did at the beginning of Zechariah's ministry. Did the progress on the temple not allay their fears? It appears it did not. The reason is because the frustrating inaction of the people regarding the reconstruction of the temple was not the only discouraging situation that seemed to belie Yahweh's interest in the welfare of the community. They were in severe economic depression, and it is this situation to which this discourse moves (v. 10). The postexilic prophet Haggai (1:6) says of this desperate economic situation: "You have sown much, and harvested little; you eat, but you never have enough; you drink, but you never have your fill; you clothe yourselves, but no one is warm; and you that earn wages earn wages to put them into a bag with holes."

In this discourse the prophet Zechariah looks beyond the wretched poverty in the community to a future bright with prosperity (vv. 12–13)—an outlook based on the faithfulness of his God. As he did earlier (1:14), Zechariah expresses this idea in terms of divine jealousy. Yahweh has not become tolerant of the nations, rejecting his people to favor their erstwhile enemies. Indeed, his loyalty to his people is so fierce that it burns with fury against those who would harm them. "Zion," a reference to God's ancient people, may be extended to represent the church (see the Exposition of 2:10–17 [6–13]). God's promise of absolute loyalty to his people is the church's promise, as are other assurances in this passage (Porteous, "Jerusalem-Zion").

3. The emotions that spark Yahweh's response to his people are his intense loyalty to them and the anger he feels toward the nations. We found these same emotions in 2:12–13 [8–9], where they also precede the affirmation that Yahweh will dwell with his people (2:14 [10]). His returning to them is the physical display of these emotions.

This text refers to Jerusalem as the City of Truth. The sense of 'ĕmet is not immediately apparent. The subsequent verses of this discourse, however, establish a situation to which this word answers nicely. The previous chapter (7:14) left us with a mental picture of the land lying in eerie desolation during the captivity. In the discourse here, however, we have a different picture: Jerusalem's streets ring with the voices of playing children as elderly people look on. As long as Jerusalem was desolate it was a stark witness to God's unfulfilled promises. Where was the prospect of a multitude of descendants to Abraham (Gen. 15:5–6)? And was Isaiah's assurance (54:1) of great repopulation for Jerusalem only an empty promise? The once desolate city and its present mean condition seemed to be inconsistent with Yah-

describe actions consequent to the collocation שׁוּב אֶל (to return to). Yahweh's returning to his people initiates these verbal actions. וְנִקְרְאָה (and will be called): Typical of the niphal, no agent accompanies this verb. We have only the general statement that Jerusalem will be known by the following characterizations. עִיר־הָאֱמֶת (city of truth): This construct relationship broadly associates Jerusalem with truth. אֱמֶת (truth): See the Exegesis of 7:9. וְהַר יְהוָה צְבָאוֹת (and the mountain of the LORD of hosts): While the mountain of the Lord is sometimes indistinguishable from the city of Jerusalem itself (Isa. 2:3; 66:20; Dan. 9:16; Joel 2:1), the Old Testament's emphasis on Yahweh's residence in the temple (Deut. 12:11; see also Ezek. 43:6–7) and the theology of the divine presence, the word שָׁכֵן (to dwell; Exod. 25:8; 1 Kings 8:12; Ps. 68:17 [16]; Joel 4:17, 21 [3:17, 21]) makes it likely that the mountain of the Lord of hosts represents the temple mount. הַר הַקֹּדֶשׁ (the mount of holiness): The root קדשׁ indicates "the essential nature of that which belongs to the sphere of the sacred and which is thus distinct from the common or profane" (McComiskey, TWOT, p. 1990).

4. עַד יֵשְׁבוּ (will again sit): עַד (again) signals continuance in the past, present, and into the future. With the imperfective יֵשְׁבוּ (will sit), it signals imperfective continuance (i.e., the situation that עַד יֵשְׁבוּ describes is not complete; thus the "sitting" will yet take place). זְקֵנִים וּזְקֵנוֹת (old men and women): The text belabors the advanced age of these people by the statement מֵרֹב יָמִים (because of [their] length of days) and by references to their "sitting" (יֵשְׁבוּ) and depending on canes. בִּרְחֹבוֹת (in the streets): The root רחב has the basic sense of width. The singular רְחוֹב designates an expanse, such as a public square (Gen. 19:2; Deut. 13:17 [16]; Judg. 19:15; 2 Sam. 21:12), which may be in front of a city gate (2 Chron. 32:6; Neh. 8:1; Esth. 4:6; Job 29:7) or the temple (Ezra 10:9). The plural רְחֹבוֹת means "streets" in most if not all its occurrences (Prov. 1:20; 5:16; Isa. 15:3; Jer. 50:30; Lam. 2:11; Amos 5:16).

5. וּרְחֹבוֹת (and the streets of): See the Exegesis of verse 4. מְשַׂחֲקִים (playing) frequently means "to laugh," with concomitant nuances of derision and rejoicing. In the piel (the form here), it means "to play," with the related nuances to make sport (Judg. 16:25), to deride (Jer. 15:17), and to frolic (1 Sam. 18:7). Here the sense must be that of children playing games in the streets.

6. יְהוָה צְבָאוֹת (the LORD of hosts): See the Exegesis of 1:3. כִּי (if): When this particle introduces a conditional clause with an imperfective verb in the protasis as here (יִפָּלֵא), the imperfective gives the condition the sense of possible fulfillment (GKC §159b); it does not impart to it a sense of reality. The word *should* in my translation reflects this modal function of the imperfective. יִפָּלֵא (it is incredible): In the niphal, this verb's

---

weh's words. But the city will once again enjoy conditions consistent with his promises, and this consistency with known facts is truth (see the Exegesis). When the bright picture the prophet paints in verses 4–5 becomes a reality, Jerusalem will be a "city of truth," affirming the veracity of Yahweh's word.

The temple mountain will be a "Mount of Holiness." Holiness is separation from the common and profane (see the Exegesis). During the exile the temple mount was no longer holy because the destroying armies had profaned it, and the rude piles of stones on its summit were no longer Yahweh's abode. Even at the present time, the temple was still unfinished and Yahweh still did not live in his holy dwelling on Mount Zion. This will all change, however, when the Lord fulfills his purposes for Jerusalem. These assurances have their ultimate fulfillment in the church, which is spiritual Jerusalem. In this sense, "Jerusalem" has been vastly repopulated, and God dwells again in an earthly temple (2 Cor. 6:16; see also Lev. 26:11–12; 1 Peter 2:5).

4–5. Once more the "LORD of hosts" speaks, the title reminding us of the great power he possesses. The prophet represents Yahweh assuring the people that he will repopulate Jerusalem. The picture Zechariah paints of children playing, while old people sit in front of their houses and look on, creates a sense of one generation succeeding another in a placid environment. God's promise of great repopulation of Jerusalem is before us once more (see the Exposition of 2:8 [4]).

6. A conditional clause underscores the ability of Yahweh of hosts to bring to reality the happy prospect of the previous verse. If when the great repopulation occurs the people who witness it regard it as incredible, God will not deem it so. The implication is that it will not be too difficult for God to accomplish. Since we may find here the prospect of Gentile inclusion in the redemptive promises of God—that is, the church (see the Exposition of v. 4 and 2:8 [4])—we may regard the inception of the church in the world, with its myriad of adherents, as an incredible phenomenon.

range of meanings includes that which is beyond normal ability or comprehension, thus impossible from the human standpoint. Nothing is beyond God's ability (Gen. 18:14; Jer. 32:17), but there are things that may be beyond the abilities of some humans to perform (Deut. 17:8; 2 Sam. 13:2). When God performs acts that are beyond human ability or comprehension, they may elicit responses of wonder in those who witness them (Ps. 118:23). The vast majority of niphal participles of פלא denote God's wonders. בְּעֵינֵי (lit., in the eyes of) is most frequently translated "in the estimation of" (Gen. 6:8; 16:4, 5, 6; 18:3; 38:7; Zech.

11:12), but some contexts allow for "seem" (Hag. 2:3; Zech. 11:12). The hypothetical atmosphere of this text, established by the conditional clause, encourages this translation. שְׁאֵרִית (the remnant): Basic to this word is the sense of a remainder. Here (as in Hag. 1:12; 2:2) the word refers to the small number of returning exiles compared to the larger numbers that went into exile. הָהֵם (those) refers to future days, not the present, which would require בַּיָּמִים הָאֵלֶּה (in these days). גַּם (also) reflects its basic sense of addition here: will the condition of the apodosis also be true of God?

The root pl has a wide range of nuances. The word incredible, however, captures the basic sense of this root, which describes activity "beyond normal ability or comprehension" as well as the awe that such activity may inspire (see the Exegesis). Yahweh of hosts will not regard the promise of Jerusalem's great repopulation as "incredible" because it is not beyond his power to fulfill it.

XI. A Delegation from Bethel Visits the Prophet (7:1–8:23)
F. God's Bringing His People to Zion from Faraway Lands (8:7–8)

McCOMISKEY

[7]This is what the LORD of hosts says, Look! I shall deliver my people from the land of the rising [of the sun] and from the land of the setting sun. [8]And I will bring them [here], and they will dwell in Jerusalem, and they will be my people, and I will be God to them, in truth and in righteousness.

NRSV

[7]Thus says the LORD of hosts: I will save my people from the east country and from the west country; [8]and I will bring them to live in Jerusalem. They shall be my people and I will be their God, in faithfulness and in righteousness.

7. יְהוָה צְבָאוֹת (the Lord of hosts): See the Exposition of 1:3. הִנְנִי (look!): This attention-getting particle underscores the importance of the affirmation it introduces. מוֹשִׁיעַ ... מֵאֶרֶץ (save from the land): The collocation יָשַׁע מִן (to save from) never means "to bring from" (which hiphil בּוֹא would satisfy; see v. 8); it always connotes deliverance from a threatening situation: captivity (Jer. 30:10), the lion's mouth (Ps. 22:22 [21]), distress (Ps. 107:13), or one's detractors (Ps. 109:31). Here the sense is that of delivering from nations that hold the people captive. מִזְרָח indicates the direction of the sun's rising (the east), and מְבוֹא הַשָּׁמֶשׁ its setting (the west). This construction, coupled with the previous one, connotes the farthest reaches of the earth.

8. וְהֵבֵאתִי (and I will bring): The context requires only a consecutive sense for this perfective with ו, stating another divine act in the sequence of events initiated by Yahweh's coming to the aid of his people (v. 7). The same is true of the subsequent perfectives וְשָׁכְנוּ (and they will dwell) and וְהָיוּ (and they will be). For the signification of the imperfective אֶהְיֶה (I will be), see the following discussion. לְעָם (people): While it is difficult to determine the precise function of לְ, it probably means "in respect to"—that is, as to their relationship to me, it is as a people. This sense is adequate for the occurrences of this construction in other contexts. For example, in Deuteronomy 7:6, the construction seems to carry no other connotation than "to be to him a people—a treasured possession" (see also Deut. 14:2; 26:18). In Genesis 28:21, when Jacob says (literally), "and Yahweh will be to me in respect to God," the context requires nothing more than that Yahweh will be his God, that is, that Jacob would acknowledge and worship Yahweh as God. In Exodus 4:16, the hypothetical construction (lit., he will be to you in respect to a mouth, and you will be to him in respect to God) carries the sense "he will be (function as) your mouth and you will be (function as) his God." The expression here in Zechariah 8:8 occurs throughout the Old Testament. It occurs

---

7. Verse 7 reminds us of the call in 2:10 [6] summoning the people to leave the nations. Indeed, the response of Zechariah to Bethel's theological question echoes several themes that appear in chapters 1–2: the importance of heeding the prophets (1:4; 7:7), the captivity occurring as a result of sin (1:6; 7:13–14), Yahweh's jealousy for Jerusalem (1:14; 8:2), his turning to Zion in compassion (1:16; 8:3), his dwelling in Jerusalem (2:14 [10]; 8:3), and many nations coming to Jerusalem (2:15 [11]; 8:22). These concepts comprise the bank of theological ideas from which much of the message of this book derives.

8. The gathering of the remnant (v. 6) is an important prophetic theme (Isa. 11:11–12; Mic. 2:12–13; 4:6–7). Here, it is the first act following the statement of Yahweh's resolve to deliver his people. We learn in verse 3 that Yahweh will dwell in Jerusalem; now we learn that his people will dwell there as well. The divine acts that the series of waw-clauses in verses 7–8 establish culminate in the actualization of the promise that Yahweh will be God to his people.

This promise, stated first (albeit partially) in Genesis 17:7–8, establishes the presence of God among his people in an intimate relationship with them. His presence provides the protection and spiritual benefits that the name Elohim conveys:

This great statement is the heart and soul of the promise because all the gracious benefits of the promise derive from the loving power and volition of God expressed in the intimate and mysterious relationship with him that the people of faith enjoy. (McComiskey, *Covenants of Promise*, p. 57)

The New Testament affirms the ultimate fulfillment of this promise in the church (2 Cor. 6:16; Heb. 8:10; Rev. 21:3). The preacher may span the eras of time proclaiming the message of this discourse with the same urgency and relevance with which Zechariah proclaimed it to the band of laborers on Mount Zion.

God will be God to his people "in truth and in righteousness." Because he will restore Jerusalem, his words will be "truth"; no longer will they appear to be empty promises. And he will act in "rightness" (*ṣĕdāqâ*) toward his people, dealing with them in accordance with his nature. Yahweh's promises will come to fruition, and the Jerusalem he establishes will never perish. The church is always a witness to the truth of God's words and the rightness of his dealings with his people:

Within Jerusalem's walls,
  God with his people dwells;
secure whate're befalls,
  his truth their doubt dispels.

for the first time in Genesis 17:8, requiring the sense of "I will be their God" (see also Exod. 6:7; 29:45; Jer. 11:4; and the Exposition here as well as of Hos. 1:9). לִי (my) has the common possessive function (BDB, pp. 512–13): you shall be in relation to me (לִי) a people (i.e., my people). וַאֲנִי (and I) possesses a degree of emphasis that indicates a change of subject from "they" to "I." If the writer intended no emphasis, he could have used the form וְהָיִיתִי (and I will be) (as in Gen. 17:8). אֶהְיֶה (I will be): The change from the perfective with ו (וְהָיוּ) to the imperfective (אֶהְיֶה) appears to have no exegetical significance, both serving only to indicate the future. When the expression "I will be their God and they will be my people" occurs in a clausal sequence requiring הָיָה plus ו in the clause-initial position, הָיָה is perfective (e.g., Gen. 17:8). Since the apodosis usually begins with an independent pronoun construed with ו in this expression (e.g., וַאֲנִי here and וְאַתֶּם in Lev. 26:12), the verb הָיָה in the apodosis is not construed with ו and thus is not perfective because the perspective of the clause is future. When, however, the verb in the protasis does not occur in the clause-initial position (as in Ezek. 34:24), it does not carry ו and

appears as a nonperfective (imperfect). לֵאלֹהִים (God): For לְ, see the previous discussion of לְעָם (people). In the Pentateuch, the divine name אֱלֹהִים describes God in terms more transcendent than those of the more personal יְהוָה (Yahweh, the LORD). For Yahweh to be God to his people means that he will be all that God is, exercising his sovereign power on their behalf and receiving their worship. בֶּאֱמֶת (in truth): See the Exegesis of 7:9. The preposition בְּ indicates that truth will be the sphere of Yahweh's relationship to his people as God (see the Exposition). וּבִצְדָקָה (and in righteousness): Once again the preposition בְּ indicates the sphere in which Yahweh will relate to his people as God. The root צדק generally connotes rightness, whether in the court, government, ethical response to God, or the marketplace. It can refer to divine (Judg. 5:11; Ps. 145:6–7; Jer. 9:23 [24]; Dan. 9:16; Mic. 6:5) or human (2 Sam. 8:15) activities. God's צְדָקָה here is nuanced by אֱמֶת (truth), creating the idea that God's restoration of his people will be consistent with his promises and the righteous standards by which he acts on behalf of his people.

XI. A Delegation from Bethel Visits the Prophet (7:1–8:23)
G. Encouragement in View of the Current Hard Times
(8:9–10)

McCOMISKEY

⁹This is what the LORD of hosts says, Let your hands be strong, you who have been hearing in these days these words from the mouth[s] of the prophets who [were there] when the foundation of the house of the LORD of hosts was laid—the temple to be rebuilt. ¹⁰For before those days no wage was realized for a person, and there was no wage for a beast, and for the one going out and the one coming in, there was no peace from the enemy, and I set all the people one against another.

NRSV

⁹Thus says the LORD of hosts: Let your hands be strong—you that have recently been hearing these words from the mouths of the prophets who were present when the foundation was laid for the rebuilding of the temple, the house of the LORD of hosts. ¹⁰For before those days there were no wages for people or for animals, nor was there any safety from the foe for those who went out or came in, and I set them all against one other.

9. יְהוָה צְבָאוֹת (the Lord of hosts): See the Exegesis of 1:3. תֶּחֱזַקְנָה יְדֵיכֶם (let your hands be strong) connotes either courage (2 Sam. 2:7; 16:21; Zech. 8:13) or physical strength (Jer. 32:21; Ezek. 3:14; 22:14). Because the work on the temple is not in view, the context here does not require the sense of increasing physical strength for this expression; it requires, rather, the sense of taking courage because dismal economic conditions (v. 10) will eventually give way to happier times (vv. 12–13). הַשֹּׁמְעִים (you who have been hearing): This participle, construed with the article and standing in apposition to the pronominal suffix (כֶ-), comprises a relative clause: "the ones hearing" or "you who are hearing" (Davidson, *Hebrew Syntax*, p. 133). מִפִּי הַנְּבִיאִים (from the mouth[s] of the prophets): The apparently singular פִּי (mouth of) frequently occurs with plural substantives in construct relationship (2 Chron. 18:21–22). אֲשֶׁר (who [were there]): The relative clause this particle introduces is elliptical, requiring the reader to insert a verb appropriate to the action the sentence describes. Most frequently, this construction suppresses the copula (to be) before a preposition (Gen. 7:23; 46:31; Isa. 27:1; Jer. 52:32; Ezek. 9:6), but in Obadiah 20, אֲשֶׁר־כְּנַעֲנִים (who [are among] the Canaanites) shows that the ellipsis may be bolder. Here in Zechariah, we must supply a verbal idea that places these prophets at the time of the founding of the temple. The somewhat innocuous "were there" fills the simple requirements of this construction (NRSV: "who were present"; NASB: "those who spoke"). (For further discussion of ellipsis, see the commentary on Hos. 5:8; 8:1, 10; 9:3, 4, 6.) בְּיוֹם יֻסַּד (in the day when the foundation was laid): It is unusual to find בְּיוֹם (in the day) creating a temporal clause with a finite verb (it usually takes the infinitive), but this construction is not completely unattested (Pss. 102:3 [2]; 138:3). The temporality is not strange, however, for we may read the clause "in the day the foundation was laid"; since there is no other linguistic signal of temporality, that may be how the Hebrew ear heard this construction. When יוֹם (day) occurs in the singular, it envisions a period of time that the writer conceived of as encompassing a single event (Zech. 2:15 [11]; 3:9, 10; 9:16; 11:11; 12:3, 4, 6, 8, 9, 11; 13:1, 2, 4; 14:1) or as possessing a single characteristic (4:10; 14:3), whereas the plural envisions a period of time consisting of indefinite extension. הַהֵיכָל (the temple): See the Exegesis and Exposition of 6:12. לְהִבָּנוֹת (to be rebuilt) is an infinitive of purpose, which envisions the time from the temple's founding through the period of its reconstruction (see the Exposition).

10. כִּי (for) does not directly introduce the reason why the people should take courage, but rather introduces proximate causation. That is, the reason why they should "strengthen their hands" is set in both the negative terms of this verse and the positive terms of verse 11. לִפְנֵי הַיָּמִים הָהֵם (before those days): The plural יוֹם (day) expresses the time beginning with the laying of the foundation and continuing through the period of building (the same period designated by the

---

9. Yahweh speaks again. This time the prophet represents him as encouraging the people to be strong. It is as though Zechariah turns from Bethel's representatives to the whole nation, for he addresses those who have been hearing the words of the prophets from the inception of the work on the temple. This verse takes us back to the completed foundation, which is always the connotation of the plural *yāsad* (found) (1 Kings 6:37; Ezra 3:6; Hag. 2:18). The infinitival construction, the temple *to be rebuilt*, betrays the writer's looking beyond the laying of the foundation, through the years of its neglect, to the continuation of the work on the temple building. The prophets to whom the text refers are Haggai and Zechariah, who were present before the construction of the foundation and whose words Zechariah's contemporaries were still hearing.

Zechariah encourages the present generation to be strong. He does not place them back before the foundation of the temple as he does himself, because many of his hearers had been born since that time and were now entering adulthood. Zechariah and Haggai, however, well remembered those days, having a perspective on the course of the temple's construction that would place in stark contrast both the dismal conditions of the period when the temple foundation lay unfinished and the bright prospects described in verses 12–13. Because of these prospects he can urge his contemporaries to take courage.

10. In this verse the prophet states the reason for the encouraging admonition of the previous verse. His explanation, which extends through verse 13, comprises a negative (v. 10) and a positive (vv. 11, 13) perspective. Here, in verse 10, he looks back to the time "before those days," that is, before the days of rebuilding that commenced after the long period of inactivity, and he recalls the bleak economic conditions that existed then.

construction in v. 9). שָׂכָר (wage) not only denotes compensation for labor rendered (Gen. 30:28) but also a reward (Gen. 15:1; Isa. 40:10). That the word also applies to animals in this verse indicates that it can refer to tangible results from the labor of humans and beasts. נִהְיָה (lit., was made to be) is the niphal passive of הָיָה (to be). The sense is that wages were not actualized or realized by them; they received no remuneration for their work. וּשְׂכַר (and wage): See the previous discussion of this word. אֵינֶנָּה (no): The feminine suffix on this negative particle refers to the feminine הַבְּהֵמָה (cattle), not to the masculine שָׂכָר (wage). וְלַיּוֹצֵא (and

for the one going out): The Masoretic Text points this participle as a substantive; the *lamed* relates conceptually to שָׁלוֹם (peace; i.e., "no peace for" as in Jer. 12:12). וְלַבָּא (for the one coming in) is the same construction as the previous participle. שָׁלוֹם (peace): The occurrence of this word with הַצָּר (the enemy) gives the nuance of safety or security (from the enemy). וָאֲשַׁלַּח (and I set) is collocated with בְּ (בְרֵעֵהוּ), which sometimes requires the translation "send against" (e.g., Yahweh sent hornets [Deut. 7:20] and serpents [Num. 21:6] against the people).

Zechariah's contemporary, Haggai, also recalls the time of economic depression before the people began to work on the temple (1:4–11). Evidently Zechariah understood the period before the commencement of the reconstruction work to initiate the period of hard times, because relief from these conditions is still a promise of this text. In this way Zechariah is again like his contemporary, in that Haggai also viewed the period of economic depression as extending from the early period of inaction to his present (2:15–19).

The prophet describes the early days of hardship as yielding no "wage" for man or beast. So difficult were those times that the unyielding earth provided little for humans to subsist on and produced only meager forage for the cattle. He reminds the people also that those were unsettled times, for in their going out and coming in they had no peace from their enemy. "Going out and coming in" is an expression that can designate everyday activities (2 Kings 19:27; Ps. 121:8), military activities (Num. 27:17; 2 Sam. 3:25), all one's undertakings (Deut. 28:6, 19), and widespread distress (2 Chron. 15:5). The sense of the expression here is that the people met with trouble "coming and going." The reference to the "enemy" warrants our understanding this expression more nar-

rowly than a general expression for trouble, for it refers specifically to hostile forces. It is difficult to know precisely how the enemy caused insecurity both externally and internally. Perhaps the external hostility came from the local tribespeople, who harassed the farmers and herders who "went out" to labor in the fields. Ezra 4:4 speaks of the people of the land who made them afraid to build. Ezra 4–6 contains an account of hostility that the people had to face within their community as their leaders in Jerusalem struggled with governmental opposition to their building project. Whether one went out or returned home, there was no respite from the hostile forces that sought the destruction of the Jewish community.

Zechariah continues his dismal recital of the early conditions of the nation by pointing out that there was also internal strife, for Yahweh set one against another. By representing Yahweh as the immediate cause of this strife, the writer reveals an important prophetic concept that underscores the immanence of God in history. The prophet Haggai also saw God's hand in all this: "I [Yahweh] struck you and all the products of your toil. . . . I will bless you" (2:17–19; see also Amos 4:6–11).

XI. A Delegation from Bethel Visits the Prophet (7:1–8:23)
H. A Promise in View of the Hard Times (8:11–15)

McCOMISKEY

[11]But now, I will not [be] to the remnant of this people as I [was] in the former days, utterance of the LORD of hosts, [12]for the seed of peace, [namely] the vine, will yield its fruit, and the earth will yield its produce, and the heavens will give their dew; and I will cause the remnant of this people to inherit all these things. [13]And it will be that as you were a curse among the nations, O house of Judah and house of Israel, so I will deliver you, that you may become a blessing. Do not fear. Let your hands be strong. [14]For this is what the LORD of hosts says, As I resolved to do harm to you when your fathers provoked me to anger, says the LORD of hosts, and I did not relent, [15]so I have resolved again in these days to do good to Jerusalem and the house of Judah. Do not fear.

NRSV

[11]But now I will not deal with the remnant of this people as in the former days, says the LORD of hosts. [12]For there shall be a sowing of peace; the vine shall yield its fruit, the ground shall give its produce, and the skies shall give their dew; and I will cause the remnant of this people to possess all these things. [13]Just as you have been a cursing among the nations, O house of Judah and house of Israel, so I will save you and you shall be a blessing. Do not be afraid, but let your hands be strong.

[14]For thus says the LORD of hosts: Just as I purposed to bring disaster upon you, when your ancestors provoked me to wrath, and I did not relent, says the LORD of hosts, [15]so again I have purposed in these days to do good to Jerusalem and to the house of Judah; do not be afraid.

11. וְעַתָּה (but now): ו requires an adversative sense here because of the contrasting picture it introduces. עַתָּה frequently introduces judgment sayings (see the Exposition of Hos. 6:2), but here it introduces the point at which a reversal of Yahweh's negative attitude toward his people occurs. The phrase כַּיָּמִים הָרִאשֹׁנִים אֲנִי requires the unexpressed copula in translation: "As I was in the former days." לִשְׁאֵרִית (to the remnant): See the Exegesis of 8:6. יְהוָה צְבָאוֹת (the LORD of hosts): See the Exegesis of 1:3.

12. כִּי (for) continues the causal sense established by כִּי in verse 10, explaining why the people should take courage. זֶרַע (the seed): Besides referring to seed for planting (Gen. 1:11; Amos 9:13) and human reproduction (Gen. 3:15; 7:3), זֶרַע may even indicate a mature plant (Job 39:12) or the act of sowing (Gen. 8:22; Lev. 26:5). It is attractive to view this expression as connoting a peaceful sowing in contrast to the hostility the workers faced on the farms outside Jerusalem (v. 10), but the grammatical construction does not greatly favor

this view. In view of כִּי־זֶרַע הַשָּׁלוֹם (lit., for the seed of peace), it is difficult to maintain the definiteness of הַשָּׁלוֹם by reading זֶרַע as sowing. If this clause refers to sowing, we would expect the subsequent clause to begin with ו, introducing a new subject. The absence of ו indicates the likelihood that the two clauses are appositional: "For the seed of peace, [namely,] the vine." This type of apposition (permutation) defines the previous substantive (as in Isa. 42:25: וַיִּשְׁפֹּךְ עָלָיו חֵמָה אַפּוֹ, and he poured out on him wrath, [namely,] his fury; see GKC §131k). הַגֶּפֶן (the vine): See the Exegesis of 3:10. יְבוּלָהּ (its produce), related to יָבַל (to bear along), probably denotes what the land or plant bears or produces. שְׁאֵרִית (the remnant): See the Exegesis of 8:6. אֶת־כָּל־אֵלֶּה (all these things): The causal nature of the hiphil sometimes calls for the double accusative, here introduced by the particle אֵת.

13. וְהָיָה (and it will be) continues the sequence of bright prospects God's people have; this time, however, these prospects appear to be more applicable to the postexilic community than the

---

11. The dismal days of fruitless toil and economic woes will give way to a brighter time. The use of the word ʿattâ (now) signals Yahweh's determination to bring this bright prospect to reality. The theological theme of Yahweh's immanence in time appears again. Yahweh set the people one against the other (v. 10), "but," says Yahweh, "I will not [be] to . . . this people as I [was] in the former days." It is Yahweh's relationship with his people that determines their welfare. Even though the copula is suppressed in this construction, the personal pronoun ʾănî (I), standing starkly alone, is all we need. It encompasses all the wealth of Yahweh's love and covenant loyalty to his people.

This "I," with all its connotations of power, stands over against the word remnant, which reminds us of the community's limited population. The recurring term LORD of hosts underscores Yahweh's might. Truly it was "the day of small things" (4:10), but Yahweh is about to reverse that situation.

12. The second kî (for) in this discourse (see v. 10) introduces in more positive terms the reason for taking heart (v. 9). We may represent this reason broadly, as times have been bad (v. 10), but they will greatly improve (vv. 11–13). Verse 12 represents the improvement metaphorically in terms of agricultural abundance. The vine sometimes has such a sense, standing for peace and prosperity (1 Kings 4:25; Isa. 36:16; Mic. 4:4; Zech.

3:10), and this is the sense the appositional construction the seed of peace [namely] the vine creates. On the basis of this view, then, the prospects of the community are not simply plentiful harvests, but an abundance of peace and security from the hand of God.

If we limit the sense of abundant fructification only to favorable weather conditions and fruitful harvests, we lose the flow of the discourse because this section (vv. 11–12) must answer to the previous one (v. 10), which described the bad times the community experienced. Besides the lack of economic prosperity, verse 10 says that in these days the people had no "peace from the enemy." Thus, if we understand the references to the vine, the earth, and dew as metaphorical depictions of God's provision, the vine, which symbolizes peace as well as prosperity, complements more fully the foregoing section of this discourse. The observation that the people "will inherit all these things" seems rather flat if the agricultural motifs refer only to a succession of bountiful harvests. God's provision for the people reverses the way the nations view them, making them a blessing to the nations (v. 13). Yahweh's blessing on the people must include the spiritual benefits his people enjoy from his hand. These benefits belong to the believer today, multiplied a thousandfold by the guarantees of the new covenant (Jer. 31:31–34).

13. The abundant bestowal of spiritual blessings on God's people will reverse their fortunes.

broader family of God. הֱיִיתֶם (you have been) is a perfective verb describing a complete situation. This is appropriate to the changes the next clause introduces. קְלָלָה (a curse): The root קלל (slight or trifling) probably connotes something that is unworthy of attention or despised. This word may designate a malediction (1 Kings 2:8), the misfortune that may come in response to such a curse (Deut. 28:15), or the object of a curse (Jer. 24:9; 25:18; 26:6). The latter meaning is always present when it occurs with a form of הָיָה (to be), as it does here (2 Kings 22:19; Jer. 42:18; 44:8, 12, 22; 49:13). בַּגּוֹיִם (among the nations) underscores the foregoing conclusion about the sense of קְלָלָה, for the people were not a curse upon the nations, but among them, as an object of God's evident displeasure. בֵּית יְהוּדָה וּבֵית יִשְׂרָאֵל (O house of Judah and house of Israel): Coordinate ו (and) creates the possibility that the writer conceived of Judah and Israel as separate entities here, not different names for the same entity (as in 2:2 [1:19]; see the Exposition). כֵּן (so) introduces the apodosis of the comparison clause that כַּאֲשֶׁר (as) establishes, the correspondence being God's activity with regard to his people. אוֹשִׁיעַ (I will deliver): See the Exegesis of 8:7. בְּרָכָה (a blessing): Unlike its companion word קְלָלָה, this word does not connote the object of its action receiving a blessing. Rather, when it occurs with הָיָה (to be), as it does here, it conveys the idea of being a blessing (Gen. 12:2). תֶּחֱזַקְנָה יְדֵיכֶם (let your hands be strong): See the Exegesis of verse 9.

14. כִּי (for) continues the reasons that the previous two particles establish for strengthening the hands. יְהוָה צְבָאוֹת (the LORD of hosts): See the Exegesis of 1:3. כַּאֲשֶׁר (as): See the Exegesis of verse 13. זָמַמְתִּי (I resolved): See the Exegesis of 1:6. לְהָרַע (to do evil): Besides indicating "doing evil" (1 Kings 14:9), secular hiphil connotes treating wrongfully or harmfully (Gen. 43:6; 44:5). The sense of doing harm as punishment (Jer. 25:29; Zeph. 1:12) is not endemic to the word, for it is sometimes used of God (Exod. 5:22; Num. 11:11; Ruth 1:21). The sense of harm as punishment for disobedience is an important part of this text. בְּהַקְצִיף (provoked to anger): In 1:2, qal קצף denotes Yahweh's anger with the fathers (see the Exposition). The infinitive construct with the preposition בְּ creates a temporal clause ("when your fathers"). יְהוָה צְבָאוֹת (LORD of hosts): See the Exegesis of 1:3. נִחָמְתִּי (and I relent): Piel נחם means "to comfort" (see the Exegesis of 1:7). The niphal form (as here), however,

---

The prophet recalls the times when the nations considered Israel and Judah a curse (a reference to the captivities of the two kingdoms, when it appeared that Yahweh had cursed his own people). "Israel" and "Judah" are not designations of only postexilic Judah (see the Exposition of 2:2 [1:19]), because the construction here is different, and verse 14 betrays the fact that the prophet's perspective extends back beyond the laying of the foundation of the Second Temple to the time when the forefathers provoked God to wrath and brought about the demise of their nations. From his prophetic perspective far above the span of history, Zechariah views the long course of his nation, addressing the ancient kingdoms of Judah and Israel as though they stood before him represented corporately in the postexilic community.

The prophet does not repeat the words *among the nations* when he says that the people will become a blessing, but this is certainly implied. To whom else could they be a blessing? We have only to read a few verses farther (vv. 20–23) to learn how the reversal of the fortunes of God's people will affect the nations (see also 2:15 [11]). In his postresurrection appearance, Christ pictured the benign effect the gospel will have on the nations as it goes forth, beginning at the very city in which Zechariah penned his prophecy (Luke 24:47).

The prophet again urges his hearers to let their hands be strong (v. 9). They learned that Yahweh had not abandoned his people or his promise. They would take heart and expend every effort to complete the temple, little realizing that the nations (Gentiles) would find eminent spiritual blessing in a temple far greater than the builders could imagine: the temple that Messiah himself will build (see the Exposition of 6:12).

14–15. The Lord of hosts speaks again, establishing a comparison between past and present. His resolve to do harm to the kingdoms of Israel and Judah resulted in their captivity. That awful event became a reality because Yahweh did not relent. The "fathers" (i.e., the preexilic generations) stubbornly continued to believe that Yahweh would not do harm to the nation, especially to the city that housed his temple (Jer. 7:4; Mic. 3:11). The Lord, however, did not stay the tide of events that engulfed the people; he continued to be angry with "the fathers" because they did not do what was necessary to assuage his anger, namely, respond to him in heartfelt obedience (Jer. 7:5–7; Hos. 14:1–3; Mic. 6:8). The word *qāṣap* (anger) appears in connection with the fathers in

can also answer to that sense, as well as to "relent" or "change the mind." Since the historical event to which this text alludes is the punishment of the captivity and since Yahweh did not become less severe in his dealings with his people, but allowed the captivity to become a reality, I have chosen the word *relent*.

15. כֵּן (so) introduces the apodosis of the comparison clause verse 14 introduces. שַׁבְתִּי (again;

lit., turn): See the Exposition of 4:1. זָמַמְתִּי (I have resolved): See the Exegesis of verse 14. לְהֵיטִיב (to do good): Influenced by the contrast with לְהָרַע (to do evil) in verse 14, this verb creates the prospect of positive action on behalf of God's people. אֶת־יְרוּשָׁלַם וְאֶת־בֵּית יְהוּדָה (Jerusalem and the house of Judah): Perhaps influenced by the growing population outside Jerusalem, the writer refers to the people of God by this expanded designation.

Zechariah 1:2, where its qal form depicts Yahweh's anger against them. Here, the hiphil form presents the other side of the coin: the fathers provoked Yahweh to anger.

The second part of this comparison clause sets Yahweh's earlier resolve (*zāmamtî*) in verse 14 against his present resolve to do good to the peo-

ple. The prophet's perspective changes from the earlier days to "these days," the time in which he lived; the "good" Yahweh intends to do reflects the affirmations of verse 12. Because of the strong determination the prophet attributes to the sovereign God, he can end this verse with the admonition "Do not fear."

XI. A Delegation from Bethel Visits the Prophet (7:1–8:23)
I. Another Call to Sincere Religion (8:16–17)

McCOMISKEY

16These are the things that you must do: speak truth one with another; in your gates render truth and judgment[s] of peace; 17and do not devise harm against others in your hearts; and do not love a false oath, for all these are what I hate, utterance of the LORD.

NRSV

16These are the things that you shall do: Speak the truth to one another, render in your gates judgments that are true and make for peace, 17do not devise evil in your hearts against one another, and love no false oath; for all these are things that I hate, says the LORD.

16. הַדְּבָרִים (the things): Accompanied by the verb תַּעֲשׂוּ (you must do), דָּבָר has its rather frequent meaning of "thing, matter." אֱמֶת (truth): See the Exegesis of 7:9. אִישׁ אֶת־רֵעֵהוּ (one with another): See the Exegesis of 3:10. אֶת is a preposition meaning "with as" (Gen. 17:3, 22; 34:8). The second occurrence of אֱמֶת appears textually questionable, especially since it is not construed with וְ (and) and the writer rarely fails to structure clauses with this coordinate particle (BHS suggests deleting אֱמֶת). The Septuagint, however, witnesses to the presence of אֱמֶת without וְ: ἀλήθειαν . . . καὶ κρίμα εἰρηνικὸν κρίνατε (judge truth and peaceful judgment). Hebrew usage is not so mechanical as to require וְ here, for literary style may call for infrequent rhythmic patterns to provide an esthetic quality (see the Exposition). וּמִשְׁפַּט שָׁלוֹם (and judgments of peace) is a construct relationship that functions adjectivally (note "bronze mountains" in 6:1, "peaceful seed" in 8:12, and "false oath" in 8:17). Peaceful judgments are legal decisions that

lead to peace. שִׁפְטוּ (render): In 7:9, this verb occurs with מִשְׁפָּט (judgment) as here. בְּשַׁעֲרֵיכֶם (in your gates): See the Exposition.

17. וְאִישׁ . . . בִּלְבַבְכֶם (and in your hearts): See the Exegesis and Exposition of 7:10. וּשְׁבֻעַת (oath, something sworn): This binding obligation played an important role in Israel's religious and civil life (Lev. 5:4; Num. 5:19; 30:3 [2]). שֶׁקֶר (false) indicates concepts like empty or vain (1 Sam. 25:21; Pss. 33:17; 119:118; Prov. 31:30; Jer. 10:14), profitless (Jer. 3:23), and falsehood or deceit (Isa. 28:15; Jer. 5:2, 31; Hos. 7:1). It is difficult to detect the commonality in these connotations. Perhaps a false oath was an empty one, devoid of honest intention, or vain in the sense that it would never come to fruition. אַל־תֶּאֱהָבוּ (do not love) is a jussive that, coming from the lips of a superior, has the force of a command, not necessarily counsel or exhortation (*IBHS*, p. 568). כִּי (for) introduces the reason why they are not to love these things. To see אֶת as the sign of the direct object of the verb שָׂנֵאתִי (hate)

---

16. God's resolve to do good to his people is not divorced from their obedience: "These are the things you must do." If they continue to do the things he hates (v. 17), they may not expect his benefits—that is what their forefathers learned (1:6). Yet God's sovereign will encompasses an obedient people. Sovereignly he will establish a believing remnant, providing for them a way of forgiveness (12:10–13:9) and a means of obedience. The new covenant reflects God's sovereign provision for his people's obedience: "I will put my law within them, and I will write it on their hearts" (Jer. 31:33). Only the most hardened hearts could reject God's will and fail to be touched by the compassion he longed to see in his people.

God calls his people to "speak the truth [ʾĕmet] one with another," that is, to say what is consistent with facts as one knows them (see the Exposition of 7:9). Lying may be endemic to some societies and governments, but when God's people lie, they do something that God hates (v. 17) and that threatens their spiritual welfare.

The second injunction seems textually suspect (see the Exegesis), but the Masoretic Text makes sense as it stands. While the words ʾĕmet ûmišpaṭ šālôm šipṭû (render truth and judgment[s] of peace) do not begin with waw (and), neither does the phrase ḥesed ûmišpaṭ šĕmōr (observe lovingkindness and justice) in Hosea 12:7 [6]. The construction is not greatly different from mišpaṭ ʾĕmet šĕpōṭû (render true judgment) in Zechariah 7:9, which calls for legal decisions in accordance

with facts and uncorrupted by devious motives. Judging "truth and judgment[s] of peace" conveys the sense of legal decisions that are honest and fair, taking into account the facts and thus resulting in peaceful resolutions, not one-sided decisions that engender strife and dissatisfaction.

Job 31:21 illustrates the results of such a biased decision: "If I have raised my hand against the orphan, because I saw I had supporters at the gate." Ancient people often brought their legal disputes to the city gates, where the elders sat in judgment (Ruth 4:1–2; 2 Sam. 19:8; Job 29:7; Ps. 127:5; Prov. 22:22; 24:7; Isa. 29:21; Jer. 38:7; Amos 5:10).

17. We now hear the negative side of Yahweh's requirements. God's people are not to engage in dishonest practices or devise ways of harming others. Taken with the admonitions of the previous verse, Yahweh's will is that his people treat one another with genuine concern for their welfare. The prophet thus crystallizes an important aspect of the Mosaic covenant (Exod. 20:12–17; Deut. 10:12–22; see also Matt. 22:39).

This covenant strongly prohibits falsity in interpersonal relations (Exod. 20:16; 23:7; Lev. 5:22 [6:3]; 19:12; Deut. 19:18). Failure to fulfill the spoken intent of an oath can cause great harm, and such empty oaths must have been common in Zechariah's day. The people of postexilic Judah learned that they, like their forebears, were imperceptibly moving away from their obligations to their God. Zechariah does not hesitate to hold before them the dismal example of their fathers (1:4; 8:14).

would create an untranslatable sentence, since אֲשֶׁר (what) has this function (GKC, p. 365). We must see אֶת with its emphasizing function here, drawing attention to the things that the Lord hates (see the Exegesis of 7:7). כָּל־אֵלֶּה (these; lit., all these): It is unusual for כָּל to refer to only two entities, namely, the two objects of divine hatred in the previous clauses; we expect it to refer to three or more (but see the Exposition). אֲשֶׁר (what) requires the insertion of the unstated copula (are), which is not uncommon with אֲשֶׁר clauses (Exod. 16:23; 20:4; Hag. 1:9; Zech. 1:8; 4:2, 12; 6:6). The sentence states: "All these [are] what (אֲשֶׁר) I hate." נְאֻם יְהוָה (utterance of the Lord): See the Exegesis of 1:3.

Evidently there were those who loved (te'ĕhābû) to devise evil against others. They remind us of the people of the eighth century of whom the prophet Micah says:

Alas for those who devise wickedness
    and evil deeds on their beds!
When the morning dawns, they perform it,
    because it is in their power.   (2:1)

The people of the postexilic community must learn the lessons of an earlier time if they are going to survive. God hated what he was seeing among them. We must not restrict these words only to Zechariah's day. Has God changed? Does he not still hate "all these things"? God's people today need to give heed to the chastising words of this ancient prophet. These words are the "utterance of the Lord," and they continue to thunder over the centuries that divide us from the community that first heard them.

It is rare for kōl (all) to govern only two entities (plotting evil and loving false oaths), but it does occur in the Old Testament. In Jeremiah 14:33, for example, this word governs two elements of the text, namely, the rhetorical questions referring to two hypothetical sources of rain:

Are there among the idols of the nations giv-
    ers of grain?
Or do the heavens (apart from God) give
    rain? . . .
But you made all these things. (my translation)

The mind of the writer appears to envision more than the heavens and the showers that fall from them—in fact, all things that exist in the realm of nature. The words all these things here appear to extend the prohibitions beyond the two Zechariah cites to include all that falls within the category of dishonest dealing with and ill-treatment of one's fellow citizens.

XI. A Delegation from Bethel Visits the Prophet (7:1–8:23)
J. Fasts Becoming Feasts (8:18–19)

McCOMISKEY

18And the word of the LORD of hosts came to me, saying, 19This is what the LORD of hosts says, The fast of the fourth [month] and the fast of the fifth [month] and the fast of the seventh [month] and the fast of the tenth [month] shall be for the house of Judah for joy and for gladness and for pleasurable feasts. So love truth and peace.

NRSV

18The word of the LORD of hosts came to me, saying: 19Thus says the LORD of hosts: The fast of the fourth month, and the fast of the fifth, and the fast of the seventh, and the fast of the tenth, shall be seasons of joy and gladness, and cheerful festivals for the house of Judah: therefore love truth and peace.

18. וַיְהִי דְּבַר (and the word came): See the Exegesis and Exposition of 1:1; Hosea 1:1; and Joel 1:1. יְהוָה צְבָאוֹת (the LORD of hosts): See the Exegesis of 1:3.

19. לְשָׂשׂוֹן (for joy) is a general word for joy, often connoting rejoicing over Yahweh's benefits (Pss. 51:14 [12]; 105:43; 119:111; Isa. 12:3). וּלְשִׂמְחָה (and for gladness) is also a general word for joy. The repetition of these near-synonyms appears to be for effect. וּלְמֹעֲדִים (and for feasts): A מֹעֵד is an appointed time: an appointment (1 Sam. 20:35), an assembly (Num. 16:2; Isa. 14:13), and the sacred seasons and festivals in Israel's worship (Lev. 23:2). They were occasions of holy convocation (see the Exposition). וְהָאֱמֶת (so truth): Since ו introduces a clause that reiterates the injunctions of verses 16–17, I translate it "so." Attached to the noun rather than the verb, it emphasizes the noun. It is not that the people are to *love* truth and peace rather than hate them; rather it is *truth and peace* (as opposed to the false oaths and ill-treatment of others) that they are to love. אֱמֶת: See the Exegesis of 7:9. It is difficult to know why the writer makes this word and its companion definite (lit., the truth). Perhaps he wishes to emphasize the truth and peace of which he has spoken (v. 16), or perhaps he wishes to establish them as a class of virtues: *the* truth and *the* peace.

18–19. Once again, Yahweh of hosts speaks to his prophet, referring to the fasts that prompted Bethel's question (7:3) and Zechariah's response. It is here that we find the heart of the prophet's resolution of the dispute at Bethel. He says, in effect, that if the people of the land observe Yahweh's precepts, loving what he loves and hating what he hates (vv. 16–17, 19), God will so abundantly bless them that the gloom of past events will fade in the light of present blessing. The prophet does not say that the events these fasts commemorated will be forgotten, but they will become times of celebration and rejoicing. If they should learn the lessons their forefathers failed to learn (1:6; 7:7–14), enjoying the fruits of obedience to their God, they will rejoice in the captivity, for its painful example will be the motivation of their heartfelt response to God. In their humble obedience, they will see the captivities of the two kingdoms not as cruel strokes from an uncaring God, but as the discipline of a loving God, angered that his people should forfeit the treasures of his love for the worthlessness of pagan idols and unjust gain. Instead of regarding the fasts as burdensome religious obligations that had lost their purpose and relevance (as some at Bethel thought), Zechariah viewed them as perpetually relevant because they were a continuing witness to Yahweh's activity in history. When their hearts were at last transported by joy, they would thank God for his intervention, painful as it was, and rejoice in all the ways of God, even if they could not comprehend them.

Time has not erased the captivity of Israel and Judah from human memory, and it conveys to us the same message it did then. The highest station in life is humble submission to God. When we walk in obedience to him we shall perceive, even within the gloom, that he "is preparing for us an eternal weight of glory beyond all measure" (2 Cor. 4:17).

XI. A Delegation from Bethel Visits the Prophet (7:1–8:23)
K. Nations Flocking to Jerusalem (8:20–23)

McCOMISKEY

²⁰This is what the LORD of hosts says, Nations will yet come, and the inhabitants of many cities, ²¹and the inhabitants of one [city] will go to another, saying, "Come! Let us go to entreat the LORD and to seek the LORD of hosts—I also am going." ²²And many peoples and mighty nations will come to seek the LORD of hosts in Jerusalem and to entreat the LORD. ²³Thus says the LORD of hosts: In those days, ten men from all the languages of the nations will grasp—they will grasp the garment of a Jewish man, saying, "We will go with you, for we have heard that God is with you."

NRSV

²⁰Thus says the LORD of hosts: Peoples shall yet come, the inhabitants of many cities; ²¹the inhabitants of one city shall go to another, saying, "Come, let us go to entreat the favor of the LORD, and to seek the LORD of hosts; I myself am going." ²²Many peoples and strong nations shall come to seek the LORD of hosts in Jerusalem, and to entreat the favor of the LORD. ²³Thus says the LORD of hosts: In those days ten men from nations of every language shall take hold of a Jew, grasping his garment and saying, "Let us go with you, for we have heard that God is with you."

20. צְבָאוֹת יְהוָה (the LORD of hosts): See the Exegesis of 1:3. עֹד (yet): See the Exegesis of 8:4 (where an imperfective verb also accompanies this particle). אֲשֶׁר (untranslated) frequently follows prepositions (אַחַר and יַעַן) or adverbial particles (עֵקֶב) and is translated "that." The clause literally reads: "[It will be] still that nations will come."

21. נֵלְכָה הָלוֹך (Come! Let us go): The infinitive absolute הָלוֹך with the volitional נֵלְכָה renders the volition more forceful. לְחַלּוֹת אֶת־פְּנֵי יְהוָה (to entreat the LORD): See the Exegesis of 7:2. וּלְבַקֵּשׁ (and to seek): To seek God is to make him the object of one's allegiance and desire (see the commentary on Hos. 3:5). יְהוָה צְבָאוֹת (the LORD of hosts): See the Exegesis of 1:3. גַּם־אָנִי (I also): גַּם, indicating "addition," occurs frequently before independent personal pronouns. When it appears before a personal pronoun at the beginning of a clause, accompanied by a verb, it may function as a deictic element in the discourse, connoting an addition to what has been said ("moreover"). When it precedes a personal pronoun creating a nonverbal subordinate clause (as here), it almost invariably means "also" (Gen. 4:4; 20:5; 27:31, 34; 30:3; Deut. 3:20; Judg. 3:31).

22. וּבָאוּ (and will come): Whereas the previous verse pictures the nations going (וְהָלְכוּ) from one city to another, this verb pictures them from the prophet's perspective in Jerusalem. עֲצוּמִים (mighty) indicates strength more in terms of number than military might (Exod. 1:9; Num. 22:6; Deut. 26:5; Ps. 35:18; Isa. 60:22). לְבַקֵּשׁ אֶת־יְהוָה צְבָאוֹת (to seek the LORD of hosts): See the Exegesis of verse 21. וּלְחַלּוֹת אֶת־פְּנֵי יְהוָה (and to entreat the LORD): See the Exegesis of verse 21.

23. יְהוָה צְבָאוֹת (the LORD of hosts): See the Exegesis of 1:3. בַּיָּמִים הָהֵמָּה (in those days) indicates the time when Gentiles come to God in large number (vv. 20–22). Although אֲשֶׁר does not here follow an adjective or adverbial particle, it functions somewhat similarly to אֲשֶׁר in verse 20 (see the Exegesis there). It requires the insertion of the copula: "In those days [it will be] that [אֲשֶׁר] ten men. . . ." The first occurrence of יַחֲזִיקוּ חָזַק, will grasp) is not collocated with the preposition בְּ (as is the second occurrence of this verb: וְהֶחֱזִיקוּ, and they will grasp), and so the action of this verb stands starkly isolated from the object it anticipates, creating a pleasing literary pattern. לְשֹׁנוֹת (the languages of): See the use of לָשׁוֹן (language; lit., tongue) in Isaiah 66:18.

---

20. A new paragraph begins here, but it continues the same thought as the preceding section of the discourse, describing the blessings of obedience. The renewal of God's people will have a benign effect on the nations (v. 13), affecting the way the people of the world view God. This is a Deuteronomic ideal, for Deuteronomy 4:1–8 states that if the people obey the law's precepts, the nations round about will say, "For what other great nation has a god so near to it as the LORD our God is?"

So it is with God's people today. The world judges our God by our actions. When the people and their leaders falter in their obedience, the world judges not only them but also their God. We must, however, remember that these words are part of God's sovereign will for his people, for he has resolved (v. 15) to do these things. Today, Gentiles have come in great numbers to the Lord in fulfillment of the ancient promise (Gen. 12:3) the prophet reflects here.

21–22. Verse 21 expands the promise that Judah and Israel will be a blessing to the nations (v. 13) in language that is less prosaic than that of verse 20, containing a strong emotional undercurrent. We see Gentiles in great numbers streaming from one city to another, encouraging others to join them in seeking the Lord. The words *I also am going* strengthen the mutual encouragement the clause already indicates with the volitional *nēlkâ* (let us go), creating an atmosphere of excitement and keen anticipation. The Books of Isaiah (2:2–4) and Micah (4:1–4) contain a common prophetic oracle reflecting the same mutual encouragement of the nations to seek the Lord.

Verse 22 reiterates the prospect of Gentile nations coming to Yahweh, adding two elements: these are mighty nations, and they come to Jerusalem. The word *mighty* underscores the vast numbers of people who will come to Jerusalem. (For the significance of Jerusalem, see the Exposition of 2:8 [4].)

23. The prophet concludes the bright picture of Gentiles coming to the Lord in great numbers with a hypothetical picture that conveys the sense of excitement that verse 21 created with the words *I also am going*. So great will be the desire of Gentiles to know God that ten will grasp the garment of one Jew in the keen desire to know his God. The metaphor of many taking hold of one appears also in Isaiah 4:1. Once again we find a motif that underscores the theme of great multitudes of people coming to God that runs throughout this section. In Zechariah this metaphor pictures the

Judaic roots of the church, reminding us that Gentiles have come in great numbers today to worship the God of ancient Israel, finding in him the abundant spiritual blessings the prophet portrays in metaphor in verse 12. It is Israel's God who brings forth the Branch (6:12), who raises up a good shepherd (11:15), and who identifies himself closely with one who is pierced (12:10). The apostle Paul affirmed the union of Jews and Gentiles in an eternal promise: "But if some of the branches were broken off, and you [Gentiles], a wild olive shoot, were grafted in their place . . . do not boast over the branches" (Rom. 11:17–18).

XII. First Oracle: Announcement of Zion's King (9:1–17)

A. Divine Activity among the City-States of Syria–
Palestine (9:1–8)

McCOMISKEY

9 The word of the LORD is against the land of Hadrach, and Damascus is its resting place (for the LORD's eye is on humankind, as well as [on] all the tribes of Israel); ²and Hamath also, [which] borders on it; Tyre and Sidon, though it is very wise. ³For Tyre has built for itself a siegework and has heaped up silver like dust and gold like dirt from outdoors. ⁴Listen! The LORD will dispossess it, and cast its wealth into the sea; it will be consumed by fire. ⁵Ashkelon will see and fear, and Gaza will writhe in great [anguish], and Ekron because its hope has withered. And the king will perish from Gaza, and Ashkelon will not be inhabited, ⁶and the illegitimate one will dwell in Ashdod, and I will cut off the pride of the Philistines. ⁷And I will remove his blood from his mouth and his abominations from between his teeth, and moreover he will be left for our God and will be as a clan chieftain in Judah, and Ekron [will be] like the Jebusite. ⁸But I will encamp at my house as a posted guard [to protect them] from [those] who march back and forth, and an oppressor will not march over them again, because now I have seen with my eyes.

NRSV

9 An Oracle.

The word of the LORD is against the land
  of Hadrach
  and will rest upon Damascus.
For to the LORD belongs the capital of
  Aram,
  as do all the tribes of Israel;
² Hamath also, which borders on it,
  Tyre and Sidon, though they are very
  wise.
³ Tyre has built itself a rampart,
  and heaped up silver like dust,
  and gold like the dirt of the streets.
⁴ But now, the Lord will strip it of its possessions
  and hurl its wealth into the sea,
  and it shall be devoured by fire.

⁵ Ashkelon shall see it and be afraid;
  Gaza too, and shall writhe in anguish;
  Ekron also, because its hopes are withered.
The king shall perish from Gaza;
  Ashkelon shall be uninhabited;
⁶ a mongrel people shall settle in Ashdod,
  and I will make an end of the pride of
  Philistia.
⁷ I will take away its blood from its mouth,
  and its abominations from between its
  teeth;
it too shall be a remnant for our God;
  it shall be like a clan in Judah,
  and Ekron shall be like the Jebusites.
⁸ Then I will encamp at my house as a
  guard,
  so that no one shall march to and fro;
no oppressor shall again overrun them,
  for now I have seen with my own eyes.

9:1. מַשָּׂא (an oracle): For the sense of this word, see the Exposition. It is likely, though far from certain, that we should understand מַשָּׂא as a formal title—"an oracle"—rather than (with the NASB) simply another element in the construct chain מַשָּׂא דְּבַר־יהוה (the burden of the word of the LORD) (see the Exposition). מַשָּׂא has a titular function in Proverbs 30:1 and 31:1, and in 2 Kings 9:25 and Jeremiah 23:33–34 it occurs as a formal designation of God's word apart from any immediate association with דְּבַר־יהוה. Indeed, Jeremiah 23:33 shows that the construction מַשָּׂא יהוה (the oracle of the LORD) functions similarly to דְּבַר־יהוה, both designating the content of the divine revelation.

When someone asks, "What is the oracle of the Lord?" Jeremiah is to reply, "As to what the oracle is—'I will abandon you,' utterance of the Lord" (my translation). Thus, associating מַשָּׂא directly with דְּבַר־יהוה may create a redundant expression. חַדְרָךְ (Hadrach): For the significance of this and the other place-names in this section, see the Exposition. כִּי (for) introduces proximate causation, giving the broad reason for the divine activity, not the immediate reason for the word of God resting upon Hadrach. God's word has become active because he observes humankind. Since this clause interrupts the otherwise tightly sequenced arrangement of place-names, I have rendered it as

---

9:1. I regard *maśśāʾ* (oracle) as a title introducing the subsequent section (see the Exegesis). It is impossible to determine the extent of this oracle. It may end with the judgment on Ekron in 9:7 or continue to the following oracle at 12:1.

Maśśāʾ may refer to a wise (Prov. 30:1; 31:1) or authoritative saying (2 Kings 9:25; Jer. 23:33). According to 2 Kings 9:25–26, a *maśśāʾ* is a declaration of God expressing judgment on an individual, spoken by a prophet (see also 1 Kings 21:19). Jeremiah 23:33 is definitive in this regard (see the Introduction and the Exegesis). *Maśśāʾ* in Jeremiah 23:33 is also a declaration of divine judgment, reflecting the earlier affirmation of Judah's abandonment in 12:7. The subsequent verses (23:34–37) assert that only one to whom the Lord has entrusted his word can utter a *maśśāʾ*; all others must inquire only as to what the Lord said—they cannot utter an oracle. In this context, the oracle is also a declaration of God through a prophet expressing divine judgment. The various oracles in Isaiah 13–30 have the same function, pronouncing divine judgment on non-Israelite nations. In Zechariah 12:1, the word *maśśāʾ* introduces an extensive prophetic statement that affirms hope for Israel in a context of judgment on the nations; depending on its extent, the oracle that begins in 9:1 is similar. There are two commonalities in the occurrences of the *maśśāʾ* in connection with the prophets: it is an authoritative divine utterance, and it contains pronouncements of judgment.

The word of the Lord also rests on Damascus, the capital of Syria. Known chiefly as a mercantile center, Damascus continued to be the major city of Syria during the Persian period. That the word of Yahweh "rests" on Damascus reflects the theology of "word" we encountered first in 1:6 (see the Exegesis). In the Old Testament, the word of

Yahweh is a cognitive force active in the affairs of nations, effecting Yahweh's purposes in history.

Kî (for) introduces a clause stating the reason for this divine activity. This clause confronts us with several difficulties, foremost of them being the relationship of the phrase ʿên ʾādām (lit., eye of man) to the rest of the sentence. It seems wise in this instance to preserve the difficult reading, understanding ʿên in a construct relationship with ʾādām. Smith agrees (*Micah–Malachi*, p. 251), but understands the construct relationship to be subjective: "the eyes of Gentiles and all the tribes of Israel should be on Yahweh." This seems a more natural sense of ʿên ʾādām, but it is not clear that the possessive *lamed* with a construct ever has a modal sense ("should"). The reading otherwise—"the eye of man and all the tribes of Israel belong to Yahweh"—is obtuse. The textual emendation to ʿry ʾrm (the cities of Aram), which the New Revised Standard Version and many scholars adopt, is attractive, fitting the reference to the other Syrian cities in this text, but it lacks significant witness. The Septuagint supports the Masoretic Text: *dioti kyrios ephora anthrōpous* (for the Lord looks upon men). Dahood ("Zechariah 9:1") offers an attractive solution, suggesting that ʿên means "aspect" or "surface" (see the Exegesis of 5:6; see also Exod. 10:5, 15; Num. 22:5, 11). In construct with ʾādām, which he regards as a masculine form of "ground" (usually the feminine ʾădāmâ), the phrase thus connotes the surface of the earth. It is not clear, however, that this word for earth ever occurs in the masculine. In the passages he cites (Gen. 16:12; Job 11:12; 36:28; Prov. 30:14; Jer. 32:20), ʾdm could as easily mean "man."

The flow of the discourse establishes a conceptual pattern with which an objective genitive fits comfortably. If we represent the statement baldly

a parenthetical statement. לַיהוָה עֵין אָדָם does not say "the eye of humankind is toward [לְ] the LORD" because אֶל (toward) is the preposition that would create this sense (Pss. 25:15; 34:16 [15]; Isa. 17:7). לְ frequently expresses possession (Isa. 22:5; 28:2; 34:2, 8; Jer. 6:25; Hos. 4:1; Mic. 6:2), a nuance that may be present here. The construct state may indicate an objective genitive (eyes on), which fits the flow of the discourse (see the Exposition) and yields the translation, "For the LORD's eye is on humankind." On this view, what God possesses is "an eye on humankind" (i.e., an objective genitive; see Obad. 10). וְכֹל שִׁבְטֵי יִשְׂרָאֵל (as well as [on] all the tribes of Israel): וְ means "as well as" in the phrase בַּקַּיִץ וּבָחֹרֶף (in summer as well as winter) in 14:8.

2. וְגַם (and also): גַּם calls us back to the text's flow after the brief parenthetical observation in the previous verse. תִּגְבָּל־בָּהּ (borders on it) also transits the parenthetical clause, finding its referent in דַּמֶּשֶׂק (Damascus) in the previous verse. כִּי (for): If this particle introduces the reason for Tyre's visitation by the word of Yahweh, that reason is Tyre's vaunted wisdom. חָכְמָה (it is wise) is singular, indicating that the writer thought only of the more important Tyre.

3. וַתִּבֶן (for has built): Having no intrinsic meaning, וְ functions only as a clause coordinate, and because it introduces a clause that appears to

illustrate Tyre's wisdom, the translation "for" is appropriate. מָצוֹר (a fortress) may indicate a siege (Deut. 20:19; 2 Kings 24:10) or siegeworks (Deut 20:20), both senses reflecting confinement. The מָצוֹר is built (וַתִּבֶן), thus connoting a place of confinement against attack. וַתִּצְבָּר (and has heaped up) describes piling up the dead frogs of the Egyptian plague (Exod. 8:10 [14]), heaping up rubble (Hab. 1:10), storing up grain (Gen. 41:35, 49), and amassing wealth (Job 27:16; Ps. 39:7 [6]). The following construction, כֶּעָפָר (like dust), indicates that we are to retain the imagery of "heaping up." חָרוּץ (gold) always occurs in poetic contexts and always in parallel with כֶּסֶף (silver) (Ps. 68:14 [13]; Prov. 3:14; 8:10, 19; 16:16; note Ugaritic ḥrṣ ([Gordon, *Ugaritic Textbook*, p. 405]). כְּטִיט (like dirt): טִיט may designate several forms of dirt: that under the runners of a sledge (Job 41:22 [30]), mire (Pss. 40:3 [2]; 69:15 [14]; Isa. 57:20; Jer. 38:6), and miry clay (Isa. 41:25; Mic. 7:10; Nah. 3:14). חוּצוֹת (from outdoors): This plural designation of the outside (Deut. 23:13 [12]) frequently connotes a city's streets (Isa. 15:3; 51:20; Jer. 5:1; 7:17; Lam. 2:19; Amos 5:16), but Proverbs 8:26 shows that the plural form may simply connote "out-of-doors" (see the Exposition).

4. הִנֵּה (Listen!) conveys the urgency the writer felt as he reflects on Tyre's fate. אֲדֹנָי (Lord): See the Exegesis of 1:9 and 4:14. The plural suffix (יִ-)

---

as "the LORD has an eye in relation to man and all the tribes of Israel," we may understand it to say that Yahweh's eye is focused on all humankind as well as on Israel. It leads us to expect Yahweh to act in some way with regard to these entities, and that is the point of this discourse, for Yahweh creates upheaval among the localities in verses 2–7, but in verse 8 we read that he protects Israel. This reference to Israel ends with the observation that "now I have seen with my own eyes." If this does not create a purposeful inclusion with "the LORD's eye" here in verse 1, at least it resonates with the sense of the objective genitive: "The LORD's eye is on humankind." It also corresponds to the first vision (1:7–17), which represents Yahweh's cognizance of the course of events in the arena of the nations, and affirms as well his loyalty to his people. On the basis of this view, the reason for the intrusion of Yahweh's active word into history is that he is cognizant of his people and intervenes in history on their behalf. The name *Israel* recalls the ancient heritage of postexilic Judah (see the Exposition of 2:2 [1:19]).

2–3. Hamath was an important Syrian city as well as a province in the Persian Empire. It appears from this verse that the territories of Damascus and the province of Hamath shared a border. Tyre and Sidon were the two most important cities of Phoenicia. The singular *hokmâ* (wisdom) indicates that the writer thinks mainly of Tyre, possibly reflecting his view of Tyre as overshadowing Sidon in the history of these two cities. It is clear that Tyre alone is before us in verses 3–4. Ezekiel 27:8 speaks of Tyre's wise men, while Isaiah 23:7–9 and Ezekiel 26:12 and 27:3–25 reflect its greatness.

Verse 3 depicts Tyre's wealth in vivid simile. She has amassed great riches as easily as one would sweep dust from a house and gather dirt from the streets and in abundance equal to that metaphorical language. The word *ṭîṭ* (dirt) probably does not refer to mud, but to the dusty soil that abounds in the holy land.

4. The word *hinnēh* (Listen!) calls our attention to a startling fact: the wealth of Tyre will sink into the sea, and fire will destroy this fortressed city. Zechariah's words intersected with

probably is the plural of majesty (see the Exegesis of Hos. 12:15 [14]). יוֹרִשֶׁנָּה (will dispossess her) generally connotes taking possession of or inheriting. The causative hiphil probably conveys the idea of causing others to inherit, that is, to dispossess (BDB, p. 440). It is difficult to determine whether חֵילָה refers to Tyre's wealth (Zech. 14:14), which verse 3 says was heaped up like dust, or to the might of its siegeworks (v. 3). An apparent chiasmus in verses 3–4 supports the former sense, for verse 3 refers first to Tyre's siegework and then its wealth, while verse 4 refers to the loss of Tyre's חֵיל and then to the destruction of the city's siegeworks by fire, indicating that חֵילָה perhaps answers in this structure to Tyre's wealth in verse 3. At any rate, Tyre will suffer the loss of all that represents its vaunted position among the world's proud city-states.

5. וְתָחִיל (and will writhe in anguish) denotes bodily movement, which may find expression in dancing or writhing in pain (Isa. 26:17) or anguish (Deut. 2:25). The companion word in this context, וְתִירָא (and fear), gives וְתָחִיל the sense of writhing in anguish over the threatened calamity. וְעֶקְרוֹן (and Ekron) does not govern a verb and thus shares the verbal action of the previous localities. Like Ashkelon and Gaza, Ekron will writhe in fear. כִּי (because) introduces the reason for Ekron's reaction, as the singular suffix on מֶבָּטָה (its hope) shows. הֹבִישׁ (has withered) may derive from the

hiphil of any of three verbs: בּוֹשׁ (to be ashamed, put to shame; Jer. 10:14), יָשַׁב (to sit, marry; Ezra 10:14—a meaning that makes little sense in this context), or יָבֵשׁ (to be dry, withered). While most instances of the latter verb are transitive ("make dry" [Isa. 42:15] or "cause to wither" [Ezek. 19:12]), in Zechariah 10:11 it is intransitive ("will dry up") and in Joel 1:10, 12, 17 it certainly requires an intransitive sense in an interplay between this verb and בּוֹשׁ, which extends through verse 12 (see the Exegesis of Joel 1:10). מֶבָּטָה (its hope): This noun, related to the root נבט (to look), connotes the object of looking, that is, expectation or hope. לֹא תֵשֵׁב (will not be inhabited): For the sense of יָשַׁב as "be inhabited," see the Exegesis of 2:8 [4].

6. מַמְזֵר (the illegitimate one) occurs elsewhere only in Deuteronomy 23:3 [2] in a context describing inappropriate conditions for admission to the assembly of the Lord. The Aramaic words מַמְזְרָא (a person of illegitimate birth) and מַמְזֵרוּת (incest) support the sense of illegitimacy for מַמְזֵר. Since, according to verse 5, the population of Philistia will be decimated, it is likely that מַמְזֵר refers to an illegitimate people, that is, non-Philistines who will inhabit Philistia after its demise. וְהִכְרַתִּי (and I will cut off): With this construction, the third-person expressions of the divine will that began in verse 1 now become first-person constructions, and continue so through verse 13 (for a discussion

---

reality when Alexander the Great placed Tyre under siege, constructing a causeway through the sea to Tyre, which at that time was situated on an island off the coast of the Mediterranean Sea. The prophet Ezekiel envisioned the same event (26:5–6).

5. The litany of impending destruction continues with Ashkelon, a Philistine city located on the Mediterranean coast. It will observe Tyre's demise and fear for its own safety. This section cites four of the cities that comprised the Philistine pentapolis, omitting Gath (as do Amos 1:6–8; Jer. 25:20; Zeph. 2:4–6). Perhaps Gath dropped out of these late lists of Philistine cities because it fell to Uzziah during his military expeditions in Philistia's northern plain (2 Chron. 26:6) or had suffered the loss of hegemony because of Ashdod's increasing importance. Whatever the case, this section portends the end of Philistia's national might and glory. Gaza, also located on the Mediterranean coast southwest of Jerusalem, will writhe in fearful anguish because of the yet undefined fate it faces. Ekron, too, will writhe in fear

because any hope of avoiding the onslaught will perish.

Zechariah says that Gaza's king will be no more and that Ashkelon will be uninhabited. The inscriptions of Nebuchadnezzar (605–562 B.C.) refer to the king of Gaza, who continued to serve the Babylonian court. Zechariah's prophecy concerning Gaza shows that its hegemony continued in the postexilic period, in spite of its checkered history.

6–7. As for the Philistine city of Ashdod, people not native to the land will occupy it as it becomes bereft of its original inhabitants. Viewing all of Philistia, the writer concludes that its vaunted pride will be no more, for Yahweh will cut it off. Archaeological excavations have yielded little evidence of Philistine national glory, and the biblical data rarely place the Philistines in a positive light, but Philistia could boast of a history of military prowess and seafaring, and the light, airy Philistine pottery reflects artistic appreciation. When pride applies to nations, it represents "the magnificence of a nation—its history, wealth, ter-

of shifts in person in the Old Testament, see the Introduction to Amos and the Exposition of Amos 7:10). When applied to nations, גְּאוֹן (the pride of) denotes something in which a people may glory or boast (Ps. 47:5 [4]; Isa. 13:19; 16:6; Jer. 13:9; Hos. 5:5; 7:10). Hosea uses this word to describe the magnificence of Israel's wealth, institutions, and heritage (see the Exposition of Hos. 5:5; 7:7). Here, all the glory and power of Philistia will come to naught before the vague but certain onslaught.

7. דָּמָיו (his blood): The third-person suffix (his) must refer to the Philistines viewed corporately, not to מַמְזֵר (illegitimate one) in the previous verse. The plural דָּמָיו connotes blood that has been shed (GKC §124n). וְשִׁקֻּצָיו (and his abominations) denotes something detestable, most frequently the abominations of idols and their worship (Deut. 29:16 [17]; 1 Kings 11:5; Isa. 66:3; Jer. 4:1; Ezek. 5:11) or other types of false worship (2 Kings 23:24). In Hosea 9:10, it refers to what Israel became as a result of idol worship; in Nahum 3:6, it refers to filth that one casts at another. Since the שִׁקּוּצִים are said to be between his teeth, the word connotes sacrifices offered to idols. Associating this element of the text with דָּמִים gives דָּמִים the force of sacrificial blood, not blood shed by violence. וְנִשְׁאַר (and he will be left): In the niphal, שָׁאַר (qal: to remain) means "to be left or left over." When collocated with לְ, it yields "left in relation to God" (e.g., 2 Chron. 21:17: no son was left to him). Here, what remains of the Philistines after the devastation will belong to Israel's God. גַּם (also) frequently occurs before pronouns (e.g., Gen. 4:4; 20:5) to connote addition

ritory, and institutions" (see the Exposition of Hos. 5:5). All this Yahweh will destroy.

Verse 7 pictures the Philistines as an individual, devouring the meat of a sacrificial animal offered to his god (see Judg. 16:23). The picture is a disgusting one, representing the Philistine with the blood of the animal dripping from his mouth. It intensifies the revulsion we feel by using the word *šiqqûṣîm* (abominations), which reflects the writer's disgust for pagan sacrifices. The text forces our attention on the teeth of the Philistine, where we can see the shreds of the meat he is devouring.

We turn from this disgusting picture, sharing the writer's revulsion for the bloody pagan orgy he depicts. But as we turn we hear that God will remove the blood and shreds of flesh from the Philistine's mouth. The text does not tell us how God will do this—it is a sovereign act. It relieves our revulsion, however, and as we look back at the figure cleansed of the disgusting remnants of the sacrifice, we understand that God will expunge evil not only from his own people (5:1–4, 5–11), but that he will also impose his will on the pagan world. That the Philistines will be as a clan chieftain in Judah emphasizes this fact, for they will become a part of the political structure of God's people, occupying the role of a minor official.

The recital of doom on Philistia ends with the assertion that Ekron will become like the Jebusites, a nation about which we know little. The biblical accounts place them in the hill country of Palestine (Josh. 11:3), and they occupied the city of Jerusalem until David drove them out. The remaining Jebusites were absorbed by the Judahites and became forced laborers (2 Chron. 8:7–8).

A commonality in the fates of the Philistines and Jebusites begins to become apparent in the parallelism, for both national entities will become part of the societal structure of God's people. This appears to be the reason behind the text's use of the Jebusites, and it is certainly what "clan chieftain" means with regard to Philistia's fate. The text envisions that time when "the LORD will become king over all the earth; on that day the LORD will be one and his name one" (Zech. 14:9), and when "there shall be inscribed on the bells of the horses, 'Holy to the LORD'" (14:20).

Numerous commentators note the consonance between the order of the cities listed in verses 1–7 and the conquests of Alexander the Great in Syria–Palestine (see Delcor, "Les Allusions"). When we view the text against that event, we can understand how these city-states would be so fearful of the threat of Alexander's military might. There is little doubt that Zechariah's prophecy of the fates of these cities intersects with the course of Alexander's bold military expeditions against Syria–Palestine in 333 B.C. Taking Tyre after a seven-month siege, he captured Gaza before proceeding on to Egypt. Certain aspects of Zechariah's prophecy do not, however, resonate in complete harmony with Alexander's conquests, for we do not observe such an absorption of the Philistines into Judah as this text describes, and the subsequent section (vv. 8–10) affirms that these events will come to fruition in the kingdom of Messiah.

The conquests of Alexander, momentous as they are in the annals of history, are but an earnest of the conquests of Christ's kingdom, which burst into time when a star streaked across the

("also" or "moreover"). The latter sense is preferred because it does not tell us that another nation in addition to the Philistines will be left for Israel's God. לֵאלֹהֵינוּ (to our God): See the Exegesis of 8:8. כְּאַלֻּף (as a clan chieftain): Outside Zechariah, אַלֻּף is a clan chieftain (BDB, p. 49). Apart from 12:5–6, there is no clear evidence that it has this sense in Zechariah. וְעֶקְרוֹן (and Ekron) is governed by the previous וְהָיָה (shall be). כִּיבוּסִי (like the Jebusite): See the Exposition.

8. וְחָנִיתִי (but I will encamp): Since the text now moves from Yahweh's judgment on these city-states to his benign activity on behalf of his people, "but" is an appropriate translation of ו. חָנִיתִי receives the force of a military encampment from the use of מַצָּבָה (as a posted guard). לְבֵיתִי (at my house) cannot refer to the temple because the plural suffix on עֲלֵיהֶם (over them) betrays the writer's having people in mind. The use of בַּיִת (house) here is thus similar to its occurrences in 8:13, 15, 19, where it designates the covenant people. The first-person suffix is important because it gives בַּיִת a sense of familial relationship (Hos. 8:1). Affixed ל with חָנָה (to encamp) yields the sense of proximity (Num. 2:34). מַצָּבָה (as a posted guard): According to the Masora, this form represents מִצָּבָא (i.e., מִן צָבָא), the preposition מִן yielding "[encamp] *because* of an army" or

"[protect] *from* an army." In 1 Samuel 14:12, consonantal מצבה appears to indicate a posted guard. Throughout 1 Samuel 13:23–14:15, מַצָּב refers to the Philistine garrison as a whole, whereas אַנְשֵׁי הַמַּצָּבָה in 14:12 designates the posted guard of the garrison who called to Jonathan to come up to their position, perhaps the very soldiers whom Jonathan and his armor bearer later killed (v. 13). They appear to have comprised an outpost and not the garrison itself, because verse 15 tells us that the מַצָּב "trembled" when it witnessed the slaughter of these men, thus placing the אַנְשֵׁי הַמַּצָּבָה at some distance from the garrison (see the Exposition). In Zechariah's construction, מצבה functions as an internal accusative expressing comparison (GKC §118m, q, r). The Septuagint reflects the consonantal text in its reading: καὶ ὑποστήσομαι τῷ οἴκῳ μου ἀνάστημα (and I will set up a structure [a defense] for my house). מֵעֹבֵר וּמִשָּׁב (from [those] who march back and forth): See the Exegesis of 7:14. If I am correct in my understanding of the initial words of this verse, מִן affixed to עֹבֵר now creates the assertion, "I will encamp at my house as a guard against [מִן] those who march back and forth." Since this participle is singular in number, we must supply a plural subject for it (as in the identical expression in 7:14). The collocation עָבַר עַל may mean to pass by (Exod. 33:22),

---

heavens heralding his birth. When at last the dominion of Christ spans the new heavens and the new earth, righteousness will prevail. The disgusting picture of the Philistine devouring the sacrifice becomes a heartening one when we view it in this light, because it pictures the ultimate destruction of all that is false and dishonoring to God, and the destruction of Philistia's pride (v. 6) represents the end of the glory of all the nations.

8. It is Yahweh, the God of covenant love and loyalty, who posts himself as a guard by his people. What have they to fear? The city-states that appear in this section will fall before the might of conquerors, but God's people will be safe because Yahweh stands guard over them. As observed in the previous verse, this section looks far beyond the conquests of Alexander to envision the people of God in all ages. Thus, God protects his people today (2 Thess. 3:3; 1 Peter 1:5).

The promise that "an oppressor will not march over them again" is hollow if we limit it to the time of Alexander the Great, for Palestine remained under the oppressor's boot for centuries after Alexander's conquests. The promise of God's watchful care over his people continued in the

preservation of his ancient people until Jerusalem witnessed a king entering its gates on the foal of a donkey (v. 9). When Christ fulfilled the hope this text creates (Matt. 21:1–11; Mark 11:1–11; Luke 19:28–40; John 12:12–19), he initiated the conquest of our greatest oppressor—the sinful human heart—and by his submission to death on the cross he enabled God to "forgive their iniquity, and remember their sin no more" (Jer. 31:34). No type of oppression can overcome the protection God gives his "house" (Heb. 3:6) today. The apostle said: "For I am convinced that neither death, nor life, nor angels, nor rulers, nor things present, nor things to come, nor powers, nor height, nor depth, nor anything else in all creation, will be able to separate us from the love of God in Christ Jesus our Lord" (Rom. 8:38–39).

The prophet represents the Lord saying, "Now I have seen with my eyes." This statement is an anthropomorphic representation of God's immanence in history, recalling the affirmation of verse 1 that Yahweh's eyes are on the nations as well as on Israel. Whether it is an intended inclusion, it rounds out this passage nicely, reassuring us that God is aware of the course of human events. The

to overlook (Hos. 10:11), to pass on (2 Sam. 15:18), to come upon (Num. 5:14, 30; Deut. 24:5), or to pass over (Ps. 124:4; Jon. 2:4). It is difficult to know whether the oppressor (נֹגֵשׂ) comes upon the people or passes over them. In all probability the rhythm of the previous clause (march back and forth) carries over to this one and we are to think of an oppressor rolling over the nation to go on to other conquests. עַתָּה (now) functions, as does the same particle in 8:11, to signal a reversal of Yahweh's attitude toward his people.

---

entire passage illustrates the assertion of verse 1 that Yahweh's eyes are on all humankind as well as on Israel, for verses 1–7 give evidence of Yahweh's cognizance of the nations, while verse 8 assures us that his eyes are on his people. Even though Tyre had amassed such riches and erected such great fortifications, the Lord is watching, and she will not withstand the onslaught he directs against her.

XII. First Oracle: Announcement of Zion's King (9:1–17)
B. Zion's Coming King (9:9–10)

McCOMISKEY

⁹Rejoice greatly, O daughter Zion! Shout, O daughter Jerusalem! Listen, your king comes to you. Just is he and victorious; humble and riding on a donkey and on a colt, the foal of a donkey. ¹⁰And I shall cut off the chariot from Ephraim and the horse from Jerusalem, and the war-bow will be cut off, and he will speak peace to the nations, and his dominion [will be] from sea to sea and from the river to the ends of the earth.

NRSV

9 Rejoice greatly, O daughter Zion!
      Shout aloud, O daughter Jerusalem!
   Lo, your king comes to you;
      triumphant and victorious is he,
   humble and riding on a donkey,
      on a colt, the foal of a donkey.
10 He will cut off the chariot from Ephraim
      and the war horse from Jerusalem;
   and the battle bow shall be cut off,
      and he shall command peace to the nations;
   his dominion shall be from sea to sea,
      and from the River to the ends of the earth.

9. בַּת־צִיּוֹן (O daughter of Zion): See the Exegesis of 2:14–15 [10–11]. גִּילִי (rejoice) colors the companion word הָרִיעִי with the sense of shouting for joy (see the Exegesis of Hos. 5:8). בַּת יְרוּשָׁלַ͏ִם (O daughter of Jerusalem) stands in parallel to בַּת־צִיּוֹן and shares its meaning. הִנֵּה (listen) underscores the importance of the statement it introduces. It is difficult to find a satisfactory translational equivalent for this particle. "Listen" does not connote audition, but functions only in the sense of demanding one's attention. יָבוֹא (comes): The aspect of this imperfective is wide-ranging, encompassing the indefinite future. צַדִּיק (just): See the Exegesis of 8:8. וְנוֹשָׁע (and victorious): This niphal form of יָשַׁע always indicates the passive sense of "be delivered" (Num. 10:9; 2 Sam. 22:4; Ps. 33:16; Isa. 45:17). We need not attempt to find a conceptual commonality between צַדִּיק (just) and נוֹשָׁע (victorious), even though both appear to be balanced in this quaternity of attributes, and the third and fourth are clearly correlative. Hebrew poetry is not so exact that we can force the semantic functions of words into unyielding molds. The first two words may have only the broadest of symmetrical relationships, denoting regal characteristics of Israel's king. Most frequently in the Old Testament עָנִי (humble) means "afflicted" or "poor," but nothing in this text

---

9. The encouragement to God's people to rejoice flows out of the previous affirmation of his concern for them. Because God's eye is on his people he will direct the events of history so that from those events there will emerge a king who will fulfill the promise of verse 8. Isaiah also envisions an end to oppression under the aegis of a messianic king (9:3 [4]). The words of this verse resound in the triumphal entry of Christ into Jerusalem as the early Christians' faith led them to see Christ in this ancient prophecy (Matt. 21:5; John 12:15).

The messianic king is both "just" and "victorious." We should not attempt to force a rigid conceptual commonality on these words (see the Exegesis). The king will be just, reigning over his people in a manner that befits his righteous character, and he will be victorious in that he will be delivered from his foes. The passive verb *nôšaʿ* (victorious) does not state the agency that will give him victory; it is enough to know that he will conquer all his enemies.

The context does not clearly require the word ʿānî to mean "afflicted," although it is an attractive option in view of the afflictions of the figure in Zechariah 11–13 and the Servant of Isaiah. Only the companion clause referring to Zion's king riding on a donkey appears to influence this word toward the meaning "humble," but this is not certain. Lipinski ("Recherches," p. 51) claims that the donkey was a royal mount, and in the period of the judges it is clear that persons of rank rode donkeys (Judg. 5:10; 10:4; 12:14). Lipinski's evidence, however, comes from the second millennium B.C. (Baldwin, *Zechariah*, p. 166), which, like the references in Judges, is removed from the postexilic period by a formidable span of time.

The donkey appears to express humility in this context, because verse 10 states that the Lord will cut off the horse from his people, ending their misplaced trust in implements of war. Since Zion's king establishes peace among the nations (v. 10), it would be anomalous for him to ride an animal that symbolizes war. The donkey, on the other hand, stands out in this text as a deliberate rejection of this symbol of arrogant trust in human might, expressing subservience to the sovereignty of God. We must view Jerusalem's king in contrast to Alexander the Great and the other proud conquerors of history. The reference to his riding a beast of burden, not a white charger, underscores this sense of the word ʿānî. Jerusalem's king is of humble mien, yet victorious, and so it has always been that the church does not effectively spread the gospel by sword or by arrogance, but by mirroring the humble spirit of its king and savior.

Matthew adapts this verse to his recital of the triumphal entry of Jesus into Jerusalem (21:5), representing it in a way that appears to be more a loose rendition of the Hebrew text than the Greek. He alone of the Gospel writers posits two animals in his account—a donkey (*onos*) and the foal of a donkey (*pōlos*). The structural arrangement of the relevant clauses in the Hebrew text is

> [and] riding on a donkey
> and on a colt the foal of a donkey

Although governed by one verb (riding), the parallel clauses need not require close synonymity for "donkey" and "colt." There are numerous instances of this structure in Zechariah, in which verbally governed sustantives are different entities: silver and gold (9:3), blood and abominations (9:7), chariot and war horse (9:10), grain and new wine (9:17), showers and vegetation (10:1), fire pot and flaming torch (12:6). On the other hand, the

gives it this sense. The reference to the donkey, however, is significant in this regard (see the Exposition). עַיִר (a colt) denotes a young male donkey (Gen. 49:11; Job 11:12) used for bearing burdens (Isa. 30:6) and laboring in the field (Isa. 30:24). בֶּן־אֲתֹנוֹת (the foal of a donkey): בֶּן (lit., son) designates the young of animals as well as humans (Lev. 22:28; 1 Sam. 6:7). אֲתֹנוֹת denotes a female donkey (Gen. 12:16), the plural apparently functioning as an "indefinite singular" (GKC §124o; IBHS, p. 122 n. 15; compare שְׁעָרֶיךָ, your gates; Deut. 16:5).

10. וְהִכְרַתִּי (and I shall cut off) connotes absolute separation (Exod. 8:5 [9]; Ps. 109:13; Isa. 48:9; Zech. 13:2; Mal. 2:12). The Septuagint reads this verb as הִכְרִית (he will destroy), attributing the work of "cutting off" to Zion's king, not Yahweh. It is difficult to be certain of the correct reading, but the Masoretic Text seems superior, for it is consistently Yahweh, not Zion's king, who intervenes directly on behalf of his people in this section (vv. 6–13), while the dominion of the messianic king is pictured only in terms of universal peace. In this way the passage is similar to Micah 5:9 [10], where Yahweh cuts off the horses and destroys the chariots through the agency of his earthly king. It is thus likely that Zechariah represents Yahweh as the speaker, who announces the coming of Israel's king in verse 9. רֶכֶב: It is difficult to know why the writer uses this term for chariot rather than מֶרְכָּבָה—perhaps because רֶכֶב also includes the more abstract sense of chariotry (BDB, p. 939), while מֶרְכָּבָה, more often than not, designates "individual chariots" (W. White, TWOT, p. 2163). מֵאֶפְרַיִם (from Ephraim): See the Exposition. וְדִבֶּר (and he will speak): This shift to the third person represents the messianic king as speaking. וּמָשְׁלוֹ (and his dominion): This noun form occurs elsewhere only in Daniel 11:4, where it refers to the dominion of Alexander the Great. Since מֹשֶׁל is the object of the verb מָשַׁל (to rule) in Daniel 11:4 the translation "exercise dominion" is suitable to that context and also in Zechariah 9:10. מִיָּם עַד־יָם (from sea to sea): See the Exposition. וּמִנָּהָר עַד־אַפְסֵי־אָרֶץ (and from the river to the ends of the earth): See the Exposition.

---

parallel clauses of Zechariah 13:7 require close synonymity between their substantives: "O sword, awake against my *shepherd* / against the *man*, my associate." Zechariah 9:9 must fall into the latter class because "riding upon" would not likely refer to two animals. The occurrence of this verb (rākab, to ride) in Habakkuk 3:8 may seem to militate against this conclusion, but it refers there to riding in chariots and its scope may be iterative of God's past and present activity. There is little doubt that we are to envision only one animal in Zechariah's proclamation of the coming king and that the foal of a donkey. (For a discussion of Matthew's interpretation of this verse, see Carson, "Matthew," p. 438.)

10. One of the beneficial results of the rule of this king will be that Yahweh will cut off the chariot from Ephraim. The tribe of Ephraim grew to become the most influential of all the tribes of the northern kingdom. Indeed "Ephraim" became a surrogate for the name Israel itself (see the Exposition of Hos. 5:3, 5, 11). By balancing Ephraim with Jerusalem, the capital of the southern kingdom, the writer envisions the eventual union of these erstwhile kingdoms, reflecting an ideal that other prophets share. In a prophetic act representing the end of the historic rift between the two nations, Ezekiel joined two sticks together (37:16–20), one representing the northern kingdom and designated Ephraim, and the other representing the southern kingdom. Jeremiah envisioned the union of Israel and Judah under the jurisdiction of the new covenant (31:31), a prospect the writer of Hebrews affirms for all believers (10:15–17). And Isaiah saw an end to the jealousy between the two states (11:13) under the aegis of the "root of Jesse" (11:10). Zechariah 11:14 develops this concept further (see the Exposition there).

When this king establishes his kingdom, Yahweh will cut off all instruments of war from his people, freeing them from dependence on their own might (4:6). This is in keeping with the humble character of this one who conquers not by force of arms but by gentleness of spirit. Micah 5:10–15 envisions a similar prospect, showing that the success of God's kingdom does not depend upon physical strength (Zech. 4:6) or military power.

The lowly scene verse 9 creates encapsulates the nature of the kingdom that Christ established. The suffering, humiliation, and death that unfolded on the palm-strewn road he traveled would eventuate in the conquest of countless human hearts and in his ultimate rule over new heavens and a new earth. Little did the onlookers at the "triumphal entry" of Christ into Jerusalem that first Palm Sunday understand the full import of what they were witnessing. While many shouted "hosanna!" some must have looked—and wondered.

> It is a jest—A king come riding on a donkey's
>   foal?
> He only mocks at thrones of pomp and great
>   renown.
> No more! As written first in ancient scroll,
>   through lowliness of heart he gains a crown.

The expression *from sea to sea* may have had its origin in the territorial boundaries of the Mediterranean Sea and the Dead Sea. Amos 8:11–12 so restricts it, balancing it with "north" and "east" and limiting it to the land. But this expression can connote universal extent (Ps. 72:8; Mic. 7:11–12). This universal sense may reflect the ancient belief that primordial seas bounded the extremities of a flat earth. "The river" is the Euphrates (Exod. 23:31; 1 Kings 4:21). The sense here in Zechariah 9:10, then, is not that the messianic king's dominion will extend to the limits of the land, thus representing the believer's landedness in Christ (Heb. 3–4), but that it will be of vast extent, encompassing people "from every tribe and language and people and nation" (Rev. 5:9).

XII. First Oracle: Announcement of Zion's King (9:1–17)
C. God's Defending His People (9:11–17)

McCOMISKEY

¹¹Moreover, as for you, because of the blood of your covenant, I will set your prisoners free from the pit that has no water. ¹²Return to the stronghold, O prisoners of hope. This very day I declare that I shall restore twofold. ¹³For I will bend Judah for myself, as a bow I will stretch Ephraim, and I will incite your sons, O Zion, against your sons, O Greece, and I will make you like a hero's sword. ¹⁴And the LORD will appear above them, and his arrow shoot forth like lightning, and the Lord GOD will sound the trumpet and march in the windstorms of the south. ¹⁵The LORD of hosts will defend above them, and they will eat, and they will repulse the slingstones and will drink, they will roar as if with wine, and they will be full like the temple bowls, like the corners of the altar. ¹⁶And the LORD their God will deliver them in that day as the flock of his people: for they are stones of a crown displayed on his land. ¹⁷For how [great] its goodliness and how [great] its beauty! Grain will make the young men flourish, and new wine the maidens.

NRSV

¹¹ As for you also, because of the blood of my covenant with you,
    I will set your prisoners free from the waterless pit.
¹² Return to your stronghold, O prisoners of hope;
    today I declare that I will restore to you double.
¹³ For I have bent Judah as my bow;
    I have made Ephraim its arrow.
I will arouse your sons, O Zion,
    against your sons, O Greece,
    and wield you like a warrior's sword.

¹⁴ Then the LORD will appear over them,
    and his arrow go forth like lightning;
the Lord GOD will sound the trumpet
    and march forth in the whirlwinds of the south.
¹⁵ The LORD of hosts will protect them,
    and they shall devour and tread down the slingers;
they shall drink their blood like wine,
    and be full like a bowl,
    drenched like the corners of the altar.

¹⁶ On that day the LORD their God will save them
    for they are the flock of his people;
for like the jewels of a crown
    they shall shine on his land.
¹⁷ For what goodness and beauty are his!
    Grain shall make the young men flourish,
    and new wine the young women.

11. גַּם־אַתְּ (moreover, as for you): גַּם (moreover) does not introduce a different referent into the discourse as it does in verse 2, because the feminine אַתְּ (as for you) sustains the previous reference to בַּת־צִיּוֹן (daughter of Zion) in verse 9. Rather, it signals an activity of Yahweh in addition to those that verse 10 cites. אַתְּ in this construction gives strong emphasis to the feminine suffix on אֲסִירַיִךְ (your prisoners) (see the Exegesis of 7:6; GKC §135e; Eccles. 2:15). בְּדַם־בְּרִיתֵךְ (because of the blood of your covenant) cannot have the sense of instrumentality, for it would be awkward to state that the blood of the covenant is the instrument by which Yahweh will free the prisoners. Rather, it is the basis of Yahweh's action; thus translational equivalents such as "on account of" or "because of" (Gen. 18:28; Deut. 9:4; 2 Sam. 3:27) seem accurately to portray the function of cove-

nant in God's dealings with his people. בְּרִיתֵךְ (your covenant): The feminine suffix reminds us that the writer continues to address בַּת־צִיּוֹן (daughter of Zion) in verse 9. בְּרִית: See the Exposition. מִבּוֹר (from the pit): בּוֹר connotes a deep depression that could be a cistern (Gen. 37:24; Lev. 11:36; Deut. 6:11), general excavation (Exod. 21:33, 34), natural hollow (1 Sam. 13:6; 2 Sam. 23:20), or dungeon (Jer. 38:6). It may also be a metaphor for a condition of restraint (Pss. 7:16 [15]; 40:3 [2]; Lam. 3:53, 55) or death (Ps. 28:1; Isa. 14:15). The reference to the absence of water in this pit indicates a dry cistern, but this text also gives it a metaphorical sense (see the Exposition).

12. שׁוּבוּ לְבִצָּרוֹן (return to the stronghold): The writer reverts to the masculine plural as the address now turns from בַּת־צִיּוֹן (daughter of Zion) to אֲסִירֵי (prisoners). בִּצָּרוֹן (the stronghold), occur-

---

11. Not only will the Lord free Zion from a faithless dependence on her own strength (v. 10), but he will also loose her from a waterless pit. This metaphor expressing confinement recalls Zion's subservience to national powers. This theme appears also in 8:13–14. When the once proud kingdoms of Israel and Judah collapsed before the onslaught of cruel conquerors, there began a period of Gentile domination that existed even in Zechariah's time. That the metaphorical pit contains no water complements the hope this text holds for Zion. If it did contain water, we would not expect Zion to survive. Joseph's brothers cast him into a pit (bôr) that contained no water (compare Zechariah's ʾên mayim bô with ʾên bô māyim with Gen. 37:24). Evidently, Joseph's brother, Reuben, chose to hold Joseph in a dry cistern, so that his brother would not drown and he could later rescue him. Zion's treatment at the hands of her enemies would not terminate her existence in the world. The basis of that assurance is the blood of the covenant.

But which of Israel's covenants does the writer have in mind? According to this context, it must be a covenant ratified by blood that unconditionally guarantees the continued existence of God's people. Although the shedding of blood was an expiatory function of the Mosaic covenant, that covenant could not guarantee the continuation of the nation because it was conditioned on human obedience (Exod. 19:5, 8). The captivities of Israel and Judah that resulted from their failure to obey the Mosaic covenant attest to that fact. We must look rather to unconditional covenants, particularly the Abrahamic, which guarantees that God

will never terminate the promise that Abraham's offspring will be as numerous as "the stars of the heaven and as the sand that is on the seashore" (Gen. 22:17; see also Hos. 2:1 [1:10]). The shedding of blood was an element in the ratification of the Abrahamic promise as a formal covenant (Gen. 15:7–10). The Davidic covenant, also unconditional, forms a continuum with the Abrahamic covenant and, like it, is eternal (2 Sam. 7:13, 16, 24–25, 29; see also Gen. 17:7 and McComiskey, *Covenants of Promise*, pp. 21–25). As we trace the development of covenant into the New Testament, we find the writer of Hebrews speaking of "the blood of the eternal covenant" (13:20; see also 10:29). God could not let the nation of Israel perish at the hands of her enemies, for that would violate his promise, and the "Zion" over which the lowly monarch reigns today (9:9) may rejoice that God remembered his promise, preserving the line through which Zion's king would come.

12. The elements of hope this discourse establishes with its reference to the waterless pit (v. 11) continue here in the term *prisoners of hope*. Because the pit contained no water, there was no hope of survival. Now these prisoners learn the substance of their hope. Once the nations oppressed them, but now they will find a place of security and strength. God will restore twofold (Isa. 54:1; Hos. 2:1–2 [1:10–11]) the great losses the nation sustained during the exile when they were bereft of wealth and population (Hos. 2:11 [9]; 9:11–14).

The words *this very day* represent Yahweh's resolve as immediate (see the Exegesis). His resolve did not depend on human volition or the

ring only here, must refer to a secure place, as indicated by the verb בָּצַר (to cut off, make inaccessible; BDB). אֲסִירֵי הַתִּקְוָה (O prisoners of hope): אָסִיר is a general word for prisoner. Its relationship to הַתִּקְוָה (hope) must be that of a characteristic genitive (hopeful prisoners) rather than possessive, because of the anomaly of being imprisoned by hope. גַּם־הַיּוֹם (this very day; lit., moreover today): The emphasis on הַיּוֹם places Yahweh's resolve to restore his people in the immediate present. מַגִּיד ([I] declare): The omission of אֲנִי (I) before the participial clause is not unusual (GKC §116s).

13. כִּי (for) introduces a broad causality: The reason Zion will enjoy a restoration of divine favor is that Yahweh will impart great strength to it (see the Exegesis of 9:1). דָּרַכְתִּי לִי (I will bend for myself) is an "accidental perfective" (IBHS, p. 490) or perfect of confidence that views a future condition as complete. It imparts a sense of conviction to its assertion. On the view taken here regarding the position of קֶשֶׁת in this sentence, לִי (lit., to me) is not possessive (my bow), but reflexive (for myself). קֶשֶׁת (as a bow): Lacking a preposition, this noun functions as an accusative, speci-

fying the manner of the verb's action. The accent (yĕthib) is disjunctive, placing קֶשֶׁת with clause b in this line. My discussion follows the Masoretic arrangement of the clauses, not that of the Septuagint (also the Targum and Vulgate), which reads, "I have bent you, O Judah, for myself as a bow; I have filled Ephraim." Perhaps the reason for the latter clausal arrangement is the temptation to understand מִלֵּאתִי (I will fill) to refer to a quiver, thus causing קֶשֶׁת to fit more naturally with דָּרַכְתִּי. Since Zechariah's expression occurs nowhere else in the Old Testament, it is likely an elliptical form of the fuller expression in 2 Kings 9:24 (where מִלֵּאתִי does appear in connection with a bow). This sense complements the companion word דָּרַכְתִּי and may be elliptical for reasons of poetic symmetry. וְעוֹרַרְתִּי (and I will incite): Poel עוֹר may mean "to incite to activity" (BDB, p. 735). עַל (against) imparts a hostile sense to this verb. יָוָן (O Greece): Originally the name of one of the sons of Japheth (Gen. 10:2), this word functioned later as a designation of Greece (Dan. 8:21). גִּבּוֹר (a hero) designates a person of strength and courage (Zech. 10:5).

fortuitous course of human events, but existed at the time the writer spoke. It is this same resolve that guaranteed that the blood of the new covenant would be the instrument that effected the resurrection of Christ (Heb. 13:20). The apostle Peter observes that the resurrection gives believers "a living hope," restoring to them what they lost through their former sinful state, namely, "an inheritance that is imperishable, undefiled, and unfading" (1 Peter 1:3–4). Like the "prisoners of hope" who "return to the stronghold" (Zech. 9:12), Peter says that believers are "protected by the power of God through faith for a salvation ready to be revealed in the last time" (1 Peter 1:5).

13. We learn now how Zion will come to prominence and power among the nations: Yahweh will use her as a war bow. He will do this "for himself"; that is, Zion cannot depend on weapons of war (9:10) or conquer on her own; it is only as God uses her as an instrument of war for himself that he will advance Zion's cause in the arena of the nations. This affirmation recalls 8:11, which signals a change of attitude toward his people.

I have chosen to follow the accents in line 1 (see the Exegesis). If we override the accents, placing qešet (bow) with the preceding clause, the resulting b clause is flat:

For I will bend Judah as my bow,
I will fill Ephraim.

Whereas observing the accents creates a pleasing symmetry:

For I will bend Judah for myself,
as a bow, I will fill [the hand with] Ephraim.

To fill the hand with a bow connotes drawing the bow, but we need not regard Ephraim as a quiver "filled" with arrows, for both Ephraim and Judah appear to function as weapons in this vivid metaphor (see the Exegesis). Ephraim's role is thus not passive, as it would be if the text represented it as a quiver.

Once again the nation of Greece appears hauntingly in this lengthy oracle. We have already observed a consonance with Alexander's conquests (vv. 1–5); now we learn that Zion will engage Greece in battle and be successful (vv. 14–15). History intersects with the prophet's vision in the struggle of the Jews against the Hellenists in 165 B.C., but that cannot be the event that brings this prophecy to total fruition. "Zion" represents the people over whom the king rules (9:9), and these events must find their final resolution in the triumph of the kingdom he established. The vic-

14. יֵרָאֶה (will appear): This passive of רָאָה (to see) occurs frequently with reference to God. His appearance always signals a momentous event in the life of an individual or nation (e.g., Gen. 12:7; 2 Sam. 22:11; 1 Kings 3:5). חִצּוֹ (his arrow) is singular and may be collective, but more likely the arrow signals the beginning of battle since it goes forth when Yahweh sounds the trumpet. וַאדֹנָי יְהוִה (the Lord God): The word אָדֹן (Lord) connotes a superior (see the Exegesis of 1:9 and 4:14). Its combination with יְהוִה (here pointed with the vowels of אֱלֹהִים) strengthens the concept of deity in this statement. בַּשּׁוֹפָר יִתְקָע (sound the trumpet): שׁוֹפָר, a ram's horn, has various functions, one of them being to summon to battle (Job 39:25; Amos 2:2, see the Exegesis of Hos. 5:8). בְּ (untranslated) is collocated with יִתְקָע (lit., to thrust or strike). In this context, the collocation represents the act of thrusting air through a horn. בְּסַעֲרוֹת (in the wind-storms) functions metaphorically as a representation of the destructive power accompanying Yahweh's intervention in history (Isa. 29:6; Jer. 23:19; 30:23).

15. יְהוָה צְבָאוֹת (the LORD of hosts): The military connotations of this divine name (see the Exegesis of 1:3) are appropriate to the martial atmosphere of this context. יָגֵן עֲלֵיהֶם (will defend above them): Qal יָגֵן occurs elsewhere with עַל (over, against) with the meaning "to defend," not "to defend over." Since, however, verse 14 tells us that Yahweh will "appear above them," we may understand him to defend over (עַל) them. וְאָכְלוּ (and they will eat) appears not to have the sense of consuming the people's enemies because it is balanced in the text by וְשָׁתוּ (and will drink); it contributes to the atmosphere of unbridled celebration of newfound military might and prowess. It begins a series of perfective verbs with ו related to the imperfect יָגֵן that describe the divine actions accompanying Yahweh's defense of his people. וְכָבְשׁוּ (and they will trample) in the qal means "to subdue" (Gen. 1:28; 2 Chron. 28:10; Neh. 5:5; Esth. 7:8; Jer. 34:11; Mic. 7:19). The verb does not here mean "to tread down" (i.e., "to tread on fallen slingstones"), but rather "to subdue" the slingstones by overcoming their onslaught (hence my translation, "repel"). וְשָׁתוּ (and will drink) is coordinate with הָמוּ ([and] roar) without the copula. In this construction, in which the second verb "represents the principal idea" (GKC, p. 386), the sense is that they roar as from drinking intoxicants (see the Exegesis of 8:15). כְּמִזְרָק (like the

---

tory of the Jews over the Hellenists is an earnest of God's being at work in history and moving events toward the final manifestation of his rule (see the Exposition of 9:7).

14. Zion is assured of divine aid in her conflict with the nations, for the Lord appears over his people. As the Jews in 165 B.C. defeated the Hellenists by a power greater than human might, so the kingdom of God, ruled by its lowly king, will advance because God will fight for it against its enemies. Like a cosmic warrior, God stands above his people—their victory is assured.

Zion's warrior-God signals the start of the battle by sounding a trumpet blast and shooting an arrow that pierces the sky with the speed of lightning. The text adds to this vivid display of divine might the depiction of Yahweh marching triumphantly in the middle of the roaring winds of a southern storm.

15. The Lord of hosts defends his people, standing over them as a mighty protector. The sequence of verbs related to this action begins with the assertion "they will eat." It is difficult to understand how Yahweh's defense of his people relates to their eating, but we must not lose sight of the twofold description of God's people in verses 11–12: first weak and emaciated from their incarceration in the waterless pit, deprived of food and drink, but then restored to a place of security. Now the writer deftly unites these facets of Yahweh's provision for his people. Freed from their long imprisonment, these starving people will eat, drink, and be full. The once emaciated people will eat, and thus strengthened by Yahweh's provision they can repulse the enemy's sling stones. Once weakened by thirst, the people now roar defiantly as though emboldened by wine. Once hungry, they will be full as the bowls of the temple and the corners of the altar.

This last depiction of God's people is unlike the previous two in that its construction is a comparison, not a sequence of verbal actions (eat, repulse; drink, roar). The words *be full* in this bilateral structure answer not only to the words *eat* and *drink*, but to the conquests of God's people over their enemies in that the qualifying phrase ("like the temple bowls, like the corners of the altar") expands its sense to being full of blood. Both the temple bowls and the corners of the altar recall profusion of sacrificial blood (see the Exegesis). Thus satisfied by Yahweh's provision, the people of God wage war victoriously, covered by the blood of their conquered foes. In this case, the verb *māləʾû* connotes "filled" in relation to their

temple bowls): מִזְרָק usually refers to the bowls used in sacrificial rites; only in Nehemiah 7:70 and Amos 6:6 does it not have that sense. Its association here with the four corners of the altar (as in Exod. 27:2–3; 38:2–3; Num. 4:13–14) and its identification with the altar in Zechariah 14:20 make it all but certain that the sense is sacrificial bowls (see the Exposition). כְּזָוִיֹּת מִזְבֵּחַ (like the corners [of the altar]): זָוִית (corner) occurs elsewhere only in Psalm 144:12, where it likely refers to corner figures of a palace, thus describing a side or supporting corner rather than the corner of a flat surface. Taken in conjunction with Leviticus 1:5, which describes the act of dashing (זָרַק) blood all around (סָבִיב) the altar, this word apparently describes the side corners of the altar on which the priests splashed the blood of the sacrifices from bowls (Lev. 9:12, 18). The apposition of כַּמִּזְרָק and כְּזָוִיֹּת מִזְבֵּחַ creates a conceptual overlap that recalls this priestly duty.

16. וְהוֹשִׁיעָם (and will deliver them) continues the series of waw-perfectives describing the complex of events related to Yahweh's defense of his people that began in verse 15. It rounds out the sequence nicely, informing us that Yahweh's defense of his people will result in total victory.

בַּיּוֹם הַהוּא (in that day) indicates when Yahweh comes to the defense of his people. כְּצֹאן עַמּוֹ (like the flock of his people): See the Exposition. כִּי (for) is probably broadly causal, introducing the reason why Yahweh will deliver his people (see the Exposition). אַבְנֵי־נֵזֶר (stones of): אֶבֶן can refer to any type of stone; when linked to the word נֵזֶר, it indicates a precious stone (Exod. 35:27). נֵזֶר indicates a consecration (Lev. 21:12; Num. 6:7), a royal crown (2 Sam. 1:10; 2 Kings 11:12; 2 Chron. 23:11; Pss. 89:40 [39]; 132:18; Prov. 27:24), an inscribed plate attached to the priest's turban (Exod. 28:36–38; 29:6; 39:30; Lev. 8:9), or human hair (Jer. 7:29). Consecration seems to lie at the heart of the root נזר (separate, Nazirite, consecrated person). It is difficult to understand how a royal crown relates to consecration, but perhaps the crown is an insignia of consecration to royal office. Not every occurrence of the word in this sense, however, carries the connotation of consecration (2 Sam. 1:10; 2 Chron. 23:11; Ps. 89:40 [39]; Prov. 27:24). Since contexts describing the priests' נֵזֶר (Exod. 29:6; 39:30; Lev. 8:9; see also Exod. 28:36–38) make no mention of inset jewels, the נֵזֶר here is likely a royal insignia, especially since the land is *his* land (אַדְמָתוֹ), that is, Yahweh's sovereign terri-

---

eating and "covered" in relation to the bloodiness of their victorious conflicts. This verb has the latter sense in Isaiah 1:15 ("your hands are filled/covered with blood") and 34:6 ("the sword of the LORD is also filled/covered with blood"). Pairing these concepts as it does, this literary structure spans the restoration of Zion from subservience to the hostile nations to triumphant victory under the protective leadership of their God.

16. The series of events that surround Yahweh's resolve to defend his people (v. 15) includes the assurance that he will deliver them: he will rescue them as "the flock of his people." The writer does not extend the pastoral imagery of this metaphor beyond sōʾn (flock), for such an unbroken metaphor could convey the notion that Yahweh's people are defenseless sheep, an idea incompatible with the bold metaphors in verses 15–16. Rather, he mixes the reality (people) with the imagery (sheep); by breaking the metaphor in this way, the writer reminds us that a mighty people are before us, and while invincible, they nevertheless remain under his watchful care.

The affirmation that Yahweh will deliver his people may seem superfluous in view of the preceding description of their bloody conquests, but the text has thus far stopped short of affirming

total victory for them. And lest we think they vanquished their foes in their own strength, we learn that Yahweh gains the victory for them. This text bids us look up to the colossal figure who battles above his people (v. 15). It reminds us that when the dust has settled and the foe is vanquished that "the battle is the LORD's" (1 Sam. 17:47).

Causal kî (for) begins the second line of this verse, introducing the reason why Yahweh will deliver his people: because they are "stones of a crown." This is a royal crown (see the Exegesis), thus giving ʾabnê (stones) in this construct relationship the sense of precious stones. The verb mitnôṣṣôt (displayed) is perplexing; quite possibly it is a biform of mitnôṣṣôt (sparkling), a sense that fits the context well. If one wishes, however, to preserve more closely the orthography of the Masoretic Text, one reaches a conclusion equally as uncertain but also compatible with the context: Yahweh's people are crown jewels "displayed" on his land. In all likelihood this broken metaphor conveys the sense that the land is Yahweh's crown—the royal insignia of his sovereignty—and the people are the jewels of his crown. The two broken metaphors in this pericope depict the Lord as the shepherd-king and warrior.

tory. The masculine suffix continues the third-person singular reference to Yahweh in this verse, which עַמּוֹ (his people) in turn takes up. מִתְנוֹסְסוֹת (displayed): The verb נָסַס appears elsewhere only in Psalm 60:6 [4], a verse almost as uncertain as the one here, where it describes an action related to נֵס (standard, banner). Since the context of Psalm 60:6 [4] seems to favor "display" for נָסַס and since the cognate noun נֵס may represent a standard that marks a rallying point for troops pressed in battle (Exod. 17:15; Isa. 30:17), Zechariah's use of the term may require this expansive sense of hithpoel נָסַס (see the Exposition).

17. כִּי (for) probably relates to the immediately preceding clause rather than answering to וְהוֹשִׁיעָם (and will deliver them), as does the previous כִּי. It thus introduces a broadly causal statement explaining why Yahweh's people are likened to crown jewels—because they are goodly in his sight. מַה (how [great]) is exclamatory. The sense is "how great its goodliness"; the suffix must refer to the nearest masculine referent, namely, the crown, which by extension represents the people of the Lord (see the preceding discussion). טוּבוֹ (its goodliness) describes physical beauty (Hos. 10:11). יָפְיוֹ (its beauty): Always conveying the sense of physical beauty, in apposition to טוּבוֹ this word underscores the sense of beauty. The crown is both goodly and beautiful. דָּגָן is a general word for edible grains and probably has no specificity in this passage. וְתִירוֹשׁ (and new wine) refers most frequently to new wine, but its semantic range may be broad enough to include fermented wine (Judg. 9:13). Its association here with דָּגָן may indicate new wine or grape juice. יְנוֹבֵב (flourish) means "to bear fruit" in the qal (Pss. 62:11 [10]; 92:15 [14]; Prov. 10:31). Zechariah's context gives this poel form a similar metaphorical sense. Since the subject is formed by the coordination of דָּגָן and תִּירוֹשׁ, the verb can be singular (Gen. 3:8).

The reason for Yahweh's deliverance of his people, then, is that they are the precious tokens of his sovereignty arrayed on the land he promised them (Isa. 62:3 presents a similar concept). Difficult as this verse is, it is not too obtuse, for it unveils the commitment of Yahweh, the Warrior-King, to the defense of his kingdom as a shepherd. The powerful forces opposing Christ's kingdom may have periodic successes, but they will never vanquish that kingdom because it is the royal insignia of God's sovereign rule in the world. The church is a witness to God's being at work in history, fulfilling his promise of offspring to Abraham (Gen. 22:17; see also Rom. 9:6–18). The Warrior-King does not come to deliver his people because of their beauty or intrinsic worth, but because they are symbols of his sovereign domain.

17. Once again, the writer breaks a metaphor, moving from the crown as a symbol of the land to the land as the reality behind the metaphor. How great the goodness and beauty of Yahweh's land! Its rich abundance will cause the youths to flourish. This affirmation stands in contrast to the picture of the emaciated people in verse 11. The figure of grain and wine always stands for the staples the land produces (Gen. 27:28, 37; Num. 18:12; Deut. 33:28; 2 Kings 18:32; Isa. 36:17; Hos. 7:14), underscoring the conclusion that *tîrôš* is new wine—the first pressings of the grape—not wine as an intoxicant (see the Exegesis).

Yahweh, the Warrior-King, does not act alone in winning the victory for his people and providing them with great abundance. It is only when the lowly king of verse 9 comes to establish his dominion that the import of these predictions is felt. The historical events we observed intersecting with the predictions in this passage (see the Exposition of verses 6–7, 13) are adumbrations of the kingdom of Christ, in which the power and blessings of God come to his people through one who was despised and rejected by others (Isa. 53:3)—a man of suffering and acquainted with infirmity.

The citizens of Christ's kingdom as well as God's ancient people are a landed people. Hebrews 3 and 5 make this clear, affirming the believer's landedness in the gospel—"at-homeness in Christ." Today, the fruit of the land that causes its citizens to flourish is the fruit of salvation.

XIII. God Will Act on Behalf of His People (10:1–12)
A. The People Wandering for Lack of a Shepherd (10:1–2)

McCOMISKEY

10 Ask from the LORD rain in the time of spring rain—the LORD who makes the storm clouds—and he will send them showers of rain, to each one vegetation in the field. ²For the teraphim speak vanity, and the diviners see a lie and relate false dreams; they give vain comfort. Therefore [the people] wander like sheep; they suffer affliction because there is no shepherd.

NRSV

10 Ask rain from the LORD
  in the season of the spring rain,
from the LORD who makes the storm
    clouds,
  who gives showers of rain to you,
  the vegetation in the field to everyone.
² For the teraphim utter nonsense,
  and the diviners see lies;
the dreamers tell false dreams,
  and give empty consolation.
Therefore the people wander like sheep;
  they suffer for lack of a shepherd.

10:1. שֲׁאֲלוּ (ask), having no immediate referent in the preceding discourse, is a general command to the people. מַלְקוֹשׁ denotes the latter rain, the rain that falls in the spring months (מָטָר is the general word for rain). חֲזִיזִים (the storm clouds) occurs elsewhere only in Job 28:26 and 38:25, each time in association with קֹלוֹת (thunders) and in parallel with a reference to rain. In Zechariah's context, however, חָזִיז is not accompanied by קֹלוֹת and occurs in a context having to do entirely with the natural fructification of rain. While this word is problematic, "storm clouds" fits the context comfortably. עֵשֶׂב בַּשָּׂדֶה (vegetation in the field): עֵשֶׂב may indicate vegetation in general (Exod. 10:12, 15; Deut. 32:2; Ps. 105:35; Jer. 12:4 [with שָׂדֶה]; Amos 7:2) or edible plants (Gen. 1:29–30; 9:3; Deut. 11:15 [with שָׂדֶה]; Ps. 104:14). Here, the accompanying לְאִישׁ (to each one) gives עֵשֶׂב the sense of edible vegetation.

2. כִּי (for) introduces the reason why the people are to seek rain from the Lord—because diviners and false gods are incapable of predicting the onset of rain. הַתְּרָפִים (the teraphim) are household gods (see the Exposition). אָוֶן (evil) spans a wide range of meaning that includes misfortune (Num. 23:21), mourning (Hos. 9:4), wickedness (Job 4:8; Jer. 4:14; Hos. 12:12 [11]), and associations with falseness (Job 11:11; Isa. 41:29) and idols (1 Sam. 15:23; Isa. 66:3). Influenced by the words שֶׁקֶר (lie) and שָׁוְא (false) and the emphasis of verse 1 on the worthlessness of seeking rain from any source other than Yahweh (v. 1), this word indicates falseness or vanity. חָזוּ (see): While this verb sometimes includes the physical act of seeing (Exod. 24:11; Ps. 58:9 [8]; Prov. 24:32; Isa. 33:20; 57:8), it also encompasses mental apprehension: to see hypothetically (Prov. 22:29; 29:20; Isa. 48:6), experience (Job 24:1; Ps. 58:11 [10]; Isa. 26:11), choose (Exod.

10:1. It seems strange to hear a postexilic prophet call the people to seek rain from the Lord and warn them against teraphim and diviners. His words are reminiscent of the early prophets (Isa. 30:22–23; Jer. 5:24; 14:22; 51:15–19; Joel 2:23), and we wonder if he is simply reechoing their words to support the theological principle of Yahweh's supremacy over nature. Could the postexilic community so soon have reverted to practices that had deceived their preexilic ancestors into believing a lie?

2. Verse 2 informs us that such was the case, for the use of diviners is a present reality in these verses, not a literary device. The discourse does not flow in the direction of Yahweh's rule over nature, but the failure of Israel's leaders. It is sad to read of this spiritual defection, but out of this account will emerge a message of hope.

We are not to think that the shepherd-leaders that this discourse condemns were only diviners, for its concept of leadership is broader than that. The lack of leadership must be political leadership, because that is what 10:4 says God will provide. The young lions of 11:3 must also be political leaders, and the leaders of verse 4 have far greater control over the people than would soothsayers. Evidently Israel's leaders forsook Yahweh to gain guidance in the occult.

The exhortation to ask the Lord for rain indicates that some time has elapsed since the writing of the pre-oracle section of the book (chaps. 1–8). While Haggai also refers to a drought (1:5–6, 10–11), it cannot be the one here, because Haggai 1:14 makes a point of the effectual leadership the peo-

ple had in the dismal days before they resumed work on the temple, making it apparent that the verse before us in Zechariah refers to a late period of declension. Gone are the pleas to work on the Lord's house; the people's rejection of Yahweh seems ultimate (11:7–17; see also 1:4), and their hope is thrust into the distant future. The plea to seek Yahweh's help is sincere, but the prophet knows that it will go largely unheeded until the Lord sovereignly intervenes to come to the aid of his people.

The reason for the prophet's urgent plea to seek the Lord for the fulfillment of their needs is that the leaders had turned to teraphim and diviners. References to teraphim occur throughout the Old Testament (Gen. 31:19, 34–35; 35:2; Wright, *Biblical Archaeology*, p. 25). Here in Zechariah, however, the divinatory function of the teraphim is at the fore, a function of the teraphim that is especially clear in 2 Kings 23:24 and Ezekiel 21:26 [21] (see also Judg. 17:5, 13; 1 Sam. 15:23). As for the diviners, other prophets affirm, as did Zechariah, that these self-styled foretellers of the future spoke lies (Jer. 27:9–10; 29:8–9; Mic. 3:7).

Because the pronouncements of these diviners and the teraphim they consult are devoid of truth, the comfort the people derive from these pronouncements is hollow. Thus the people do not have proper guidance, but wander like a flock of sheep. It is not a harmless wandering, for as the text views the course of their leaderless condition it tells us that they "suffer affliction." On previous occasions diviners had brought suffering on the nation, for in the preexilic period these sooth-

18:21), or, most frequently, see with the inner vision (Num. 24:4, 16; Job 15:17; 34:32; Ps. 46:9 [8]; Isa. 1:1; 30:10; Lam. 2:14; Ezek. 13:7, 8; Amos 1:1; Mic. 1:1). It is thus suitable to the mental perception of prophets and diviners. שֶׁקֶר (a lie): See the Exegesis of 8:17. הַשָּׁוְא (false) carries connotations of emptiness (see the Exegesis of Hos. 12:12 [11]). Here, the diviners relate dreams devoid of truth. הֶבֶל (vain) is closely synonymous with שָׁוְא (Prov. 21:6; Isa. 57:13). The numerous occurrences of this word in Ecclesiastes are generally translated "worthless," "vanity," or "meaningless." Linked, as it is here in Zechariah 10:2, to words that share the general force of emptiness, the word must describe comfort that is worthless. עַל־כֵּן (therefore) introduces the result of the worthlessness of the teraphim and diviners. נָסְעוּ (wander) basically means "to journey" (Gen. 33:17), "to depart" (Gen. 37:17), "to proceed" (Num. 10:5), and "to leave" (Num. 12:15). The words כְּמוֹ־צֹאן (like a flock of sheep) are thus necessary to a more precise definition of the action it describes. The perfective aspect of נָסְעוּ views the situation as a whole: the people wander aimlessly. יַעֲנוּ (they suffer affliction), on the other hand, is nonperfective and represents its action as ongoing.

---

sayers predicted a benign future for the people, while in reality the nation was headed for ruin (Jer. 27:9–10; 29:9–10; Mic. 3:5–7).

Today, the church must seek its blessings and power from the Lord, just as Zechariah urged his people to do. Blinded by middle-class values, the people of God may seek their direction in methods that successfully build corporations, but that may neglect biblical principles and fail to reflect the spirit of Christ. We are surprised by Zechariah's plea to return to the Lord. How could these people so quickly turn again to forces that earlier had led to their national demise? Perhaps the church should view itself with the same surprise as it observes its failure to show the self-effacing, forgiving love for which its Savior called.

Since verse 3 says that God is angry at the "shepherds," the lack of a shepherd that verse 2 decries must refer to true shepherds. The people had leaders in this time, but their counsel was false. As in the eighth century, the nation of Zechariah's day was following its false prophets headlong into ruin.

XIII. God Will Act on Behalf of His People (10:1–12)
B. God's Empowering His People (10:3–7)

McCOMISKEY

³My wrath is kindled against the shepherds, and I will attend to the male goats; for the LORD of hosts will attend his flock, the house of Judah, and make them like his majestic steed in battle. ⁴From him the cornerstone, from him the peg, from him the battle bow, from him will go forth every ruler together. ⁵And they will be like warriors trampling in the dust of the streets in battle, and they will fight because the LORD is with them, and they will put to shame the riders of horses. ⁶And I will strengthen the house of Judah and deliver the house of Joseph, and I shall restore them because I shall have had mercy on them, and they will be as though I had not rejected them, for I am the LORD their God, and I will respond to them. ⁷Then Ephraim will be like a warrior, and their heart[s] will rejoice as with wine, and their children will see [it] and rejoice—their heart[s] rejoice in the LORD.

NRSV

3 My anger is hot against the shepherds,
   and I will punish the leaders;
for the LORD of hosts cares for his flock,
   the house of Judah,
   and will make them like his proud war
   horse.
4 Out of them shall come the cornerstone,
   out of them the tent peg,
out of them the battle bow,
   out of them every commander.
5 Together they shall be like warriors in
   battle,
   trampling the foe in the mud of the
   streets;
they shall fight, for the LORD is with
   them,
   and they shall put to shame the riders
   on horses.

6 I will strengthen the house of Judah,
   and I will save the house of Joseph.
I will bring them back because I have
   compassion on them,
   and they shall be as though I had not rejected them,
   for I am the LORD their God and I will
   answer them.
7 Then the people of Ephraim shall become
   like warriors,
   and their hearts shall be glad as with
   wine.
Their children shall see it and rejoice,
   their hearts shall be glad as with wine.
Their children shall see it and rejoice,
   their hearts shall exult in the LORD.

3. הָרֹעִים (the shepherds) is another designation of the deceitful leaders about whom we read in verses 1–2. חָרָה אַפִּי (my wrath is kindled): חָרָה always relates to intense emotion, especially anger. Aramaic and Arabic witness, though not strongly, to a sense of burning (*TWOT*, p. 736); regardless, it clearly indicates the rise or intensification of anger. אַפִּי (my anger; lit., my nose; Assyrian *appu*, face) is the most frequent way to indicate anger in the Old Testament. Perhaps חָרָה אַפִּי refers to the reddening of the face in anger. וְעַל . . . אֶפְקוֹד (and I will attend to): When פָּקַד is collocated with עַל and has one object, as here, the attention of the initiator of the action enters the experience of the object, which is always indirect (e.g., Isa. 10:12). While "punish" is a translational equivalent compatible with the judgment atmosphere of Zechariah 10:3, "attend to" better reflects the concepts of cognition and implicit response this collocation possesses in both blessing and judgment sayings (see the Exegesis and Exposition of Hos. 1:4 and McComiskey, "Prophetic Irony"). הָעַתּוּדִים (the male goats): Jeremiah 50:8 depicts עַתּוּדִים as leaders of the flock ("like male goats leading the flock"), probably reflecting the basis of the metaphorical use of this term for political leaders. The parallel structure here (shepherds/male goats) gives the word the sense of leader. כִּי (for) does not introduce direct causality, informing the reader as to why Yahweh will attend to the leaders; rather, we learn that he will come to the aid of his people. The function of כִּי

appears to include the destruction of the political leaders as a necessary concomitant of his blessing the people: Yahweh will attend to the leaders because (כִּי) he intends to bless his flock. פָּקַד (will attend): The context removes any sense of punishment from פָּקַד. It has rather the function of preceding the bestowal of divine blessing (Gen. 21:1; Exod. 4:31), signaling both God's cognizance of a situation and an appropriate response on his part. Thus, the word *attend* adequately reflects the sense of this verb. יְהוָה צְבָאוֹת (the LORD of hosts): See the Exegesis of 1:3. אֶת (untranslated) marks the two objects of פָּקַד, determining their apposition. Yahweh's flock is the house of Judah. וְשָׂם (and make): ו (and) is coordinate, the verb שָׂם (make) sharing the same future time as כְּסוּס הוֹדוֹ פָּקַד. (like his majestic steed; lit., like the steed of his majesty): The suffix (his) affixed to the final member of this construct pair exerts its influence on the whole construction and yields "of his majestic steed" (*IBHS*, p. 304).

4. פִּנָּה indicates a corner, a cornerstone (Job 38:6; Ps. 118:22; Isa. 28:16), a tower (Zeph. 1:16; 3:6), battlements (2 Chron. 26:15), or (metaphorically) a leader (Judg. 20:2; 1 Sam. 14:38; Isa. 19:13). When פִּנָּה refers to a leader, it is always qualified by a reference to persons, a metaphorical use based on the corner as a supporting point in a structure. The immediate association of this noun with another supporting object, namely, יָתֵר (peg), creates a symmetrical pair indicating support. יָתֵר is a pin or nail (Num. 3:37; Judg. 4:21) or (meta-

---

3. The false leaders of the postexilic community will feel the burning heat of Yahweh's anger, and he will attend to (*pāqad ʿal*) them. This collocation does not primarily meaning "to punish," but carries a sense of divine cognition and implicit response (see the Exegesis and also the Exegesis and the Exposition of Hos. 1:4). The cognitive aspect of the verb *pāqad* is particularly clear in structures where it balances *zākar* (to remember; see Jer. 14:10). The reason Yahweh will vent his anger against the leaders is that his turning his attention to them is the prelude to great blessing that will eventuate in the appearance of a good shepherd (11:7–14). The complex of events involved in coming to the aid of his people will include the termination of false leaders, a theme found again in this book (11:8; 13:4–6). Oppressed as they were through the years, the Lord will make his people like a majestic steed, awesome and powerful, straining to charge into battle.

4. When the Lord visits his flock, he will send forth the cornerstone, the peg, and the bow of war. The clausal structure of this verse suggests that these figures are metaphors for leaders rather than general expressions of national stability. Line 1 of this structure lacks stated verbs and thereby anticipates the verb *yēṣēʾ* (will go forth) in line 2, creating the possibility that this verb embraces line 1 conceptually. The verse could be paraphrased this way: "From him the cornerstone, from him the peg, from him the bow of war; indeed from him will go forth [*yēṣēʾ*] every type of ruler, all of these together." The adverb *yaḥdāw* (together) must embrace all the elements of this verse, not only *nôgēś* (ruler), and thus views its constituents collectively, not as separate entities that come "together." This adverb would otherwise be superfluous if it represents only *nôgēś* (ruler), since *kōl* (every) already does that.

While *waw* (and) is lacking between the first two clauses of this verse (from him the corner-

phorically) a place of security (Ezra 9:8; Isa. 22:23). נֹגֵשׂ always means "oppressor" (e.g., Exod. 3:7; Job 3:18; Isa. 9:3 [4]). Here the oppression that goes forth from Yahweh is against his foes, thus from Israel's perspective, the נֹגֵשׂ is a ruler.

5. וְהָיוּ (and they shall be) is plural and conso-nant with the previous grammatical plurals that began in the third line of verse 3 and that have their referent in בֵּית יְהוּדָה (the house of Judah) in the second line of that verse. כְגִבֹּרִים (like war-riors): See the Exegesis of 9:13. וְהֹבִישׁוּ (and they will put to shame) grammatically sustains the ref-erence to God's people. Hiphil בּוֹשׁ (to be ashamed) occurs elsewhere in parallel with words connoting the defeat of enemies (Pss. 44:8 [7]; 53:6 [5]). We should not, however, understand it to lose its sense of shame.

6. וְגִבַּרְתִּי (and I shall strengthen): This perfec-tive with ו continues the series of waw-perfectives that began with וְהָיוּ (and they shall be) in verse 5 and that describes the various aspects of the affir-mation "they shall be like warriors." That its root is the same as גִּבֹּרִים (warriors) in verse 5 does not necessarily indicate strength in a military sense (e.g., Eccles. 10:10). The conceptual overlap be-tween גִּבַּרְתִּי (I shall strengthen) and אוֹשִׁיעַ (I shall deliver) broadens the semantic force of גִּבַּרְתִּי, cre-ating the sense of increased strength that has as its end the deliverance of God's people. הוֹשְׁבוֹתִים (I shall restore them) is an anomalous form and likely reflects an error in transmission. If the first waw is original, the verb it indicates is יָשַׁב (to sit, dwell) and the meaning of the hiphil is "to be set-tled or give a dwelling place." If, however, the

stone/from him the peg), they are nevertheless united by their common expression of stability, and are thus conceptually one. The war bow does not share this commonality and thus creates a con-ceptually separate clause. The clausal scheme is:

From him the cornerstone, from him the peg;
From him the bow of war;
From him will go forth every ruler. . . .

5. The colorful depiction of the transformation that will occur in God's people when he comes to their aid continues as we observe them in the heat of battle, the dust of the streets swirling around them. The dust in this depiction does not repre-sent the enemy on whom they tread, but height-ens the intensity of the fighting the text pictures. This text uses several devices besides the swirling dust to heighten its emotional pitch: it designates the people as "warriors," pictures them "in bat-tle," and views their enemies as suffering shame-ful defeat. We must not forget that these are the citizens of the kingdom the humble king of 9:9 establishes. Its leaders will be a "bow of war," and its citizens warriors.

The reason for the people's confidence in battle is that the Lord is with them. The cornerstone, peg, and war bow come forth from Yahweh, not the people, because he cuts off the war bow from them (9:10) and it is he who sovereignly supplies their needs (9:8, 11–16; 10:3, 6, 8–12). We see again in this verse the colossal figure who defends above them (9:15), and we recall that God acts on behalf of his people as they put their hands to the task (4:6). The Book of Zechariah is a tapestry on

which unfolds the dramatic depiction of the mar-riage of divine sovereignty and human agency.

6. God will overcome the weakness and afflic-tion of his people that resulted from their lack of moral leadership by strengthening and delivering them. The parallel structure of the clauses in which the verbs *strengthening* and *delivering* appear gives them a semantic range that extends the connotation of each beyond its essential meaning, for the strengthening of the people is conceptually one with God's deliverance, which does not occur apart from his impartation of strength to them. Once again divine sovereignty and human agency meet in this prophecy of hope.

The titles *house of Judah* and *house of Joseph* are designations of the southern and northern kingdoms, respectively. The tribe of Ephraim was the most influential one in Israel and frequently lends its name to the whole northern kingdom; here "Joseph," the father of Ephraim, serves the same purpose. We encounter again the prophetic ideal of the eventual reuniting of the divided king-doms (see the Exposition of 9:10). Zechariah 11:14 envisions the dissolution of this union (see the Exposition there). That the historic kingdoms of Israel and Judah are not in view here is clear from the perspective of this text, which is the restora-tion of the people of God resulting from the benign rule of the messianic king (9:9). These kingdoms play a role in a dramatic motif in this book, in which there rises above these historical entities a spiritual kingdom, sharing characteris-tics with them but different from them in that it witnesses the fulfillment of God's promises to his people. We read about the historic kingdoms in 1:12; 2:2 [1:19]; 2:4 [1:21], but it is not long before

waw in the second syllable is original, the verb is שׁוּב (to return) and the meaning of the hiphil is "to restore or return." It is impossible to be certain, but since the discourse calls for a restoration of the people to their original status ("they will be as though I had not rejected them"), neither of these options greatly affects the direction of the discourse. In all probability, we are to read the hiphil of שׁוּב here (see the Exposition). כִּי (because) introduces the reason why the people of God will enjoy these benefits: because of God's mercy. רִחַמְתִּים (I shall have had mercy on them): Since this perfective verb refers to the future deliverance of the people, it is best understood as a future perfect (*IBHS*, p. 491; see the Exegesis of 1:12). כַּאֲשֶׁר לֹא זְנַחְתִּים (as though I had not rejected them): In this hypothetical clause, the perfective זְנַחְתִּים (I had rejected them), with its emphasis on the completion of the verbal action in its time frame, depicts the past rejection of the nation as a settled reality (see the Exposition). כִּי (for) prepares us for the reason for

God's bestowal of the gracious benefits this passage describes. אֲנִי יְהוָה אֱלֹהֵיהֶם (I am the LORD their God): There is no need to place this verbless clause in the future, because the prospect of God's deliverance is based on the fact that he *is* their God now. If he were not, there could be no such offer of help. וְאֶעֱנֵם (and I will answer them): The context contains no petition to which the Lord might reply; therefore this verb has the sense of responding to a situation or condition that is explicit or implicit in the context (see the Exegesis of 1:10–12 and Hos. 2:23 [21]).

7. וְהָיוּ (then will be) establishes another step in the sequence of actions in this discourse. כְגִבּוֹר (like a warrior): See the Exegesis of 9:13. אֶפְרַיִם (Ephraim): See the Exposition. וְשָׂמַח (and will rejoice) is construed as a singular in agreement with אֶפְרַיִם, but the following לִבָּם (their heart[s]) betrays the writer's thinking of them as individuals. כְּמוֹ־יָיִן (as with wine): See the Exegesis of 9:15.

---

we find intimations in the text of a greater significance for these entities (see the Exposition of 2:16 [12]). The houses of Judah and Joseph find a significant counterpart in the kingdom of Christ, which realizes the ideals of the ancient prophets.

God will restore his people on the basis of his mercy. The anomalous verbal form *hôšbôtîm* (I shall restore them) does not refer only to restoration to a homeland, but to the renewal of divine favor (see the Exegesis). Returning his people to the land seems too narrow a concept to balance *zānâ* (reject) in the antithetical clause ("they will be as though I had not rejected them"), for Yahweh's rejection of his people involved more than their expulsion from the land. He rejected them as his people, cut them off from his promise, and resolved not to be their God (Hos. 1:4–9). The words *I am the* LORD *their God* assure more than resettlement in the land; they envision the restoration of a relationship to God in which he empowers his people (v. 4), accompanies them in battle (v. 5), delivers them (v. 6), and gives them a place to dwell (10:9–10). Ultimately, however, the words *I am the* LORD *their God* encompass the restoration of the people to the benefits of the promise to Abraham (Gen. 17:7–8; Exod. 6:7; Jer. 31:33). Zechariah 9:12 uses hiphil *šûb* (to return, restore) to refer to far more than restoration to the land (see the Exposition there), and Psalm 60:3 [1] places *šûb* in antithesis to *zānâ* (to reject), as does the verse here in Zechariah. God will restore his people to fellowship with him

because he has compassion on them. The hypothetical statement "they will be as though I had not rejected them" is a powerfully emotive concept, expunging the negative effects the exile had on the people. The restored people of God will become such a powerful force among the nations that past humiliations and defeats will fade in the light of their conquests.

Motivated by his compassion, Yahweh will respond to his oppressed people. The word *ʿānâ* implies response to a need or situation (see the Exegesis). The condition to which the Lord responds in this context is the state the people are in as a result of their ineffectual leaders. The subsequent chapters expand on the Lord's response to the people's leaderless state.

7. It is difficult to know with certainty why only the northern kingdom (Ephraim) appears here. Perhaps it is because Israel went into captivity before Judah and the writer wishes to cover the entire span of the exile with divine compassion and concern, extending God's response to his people to the beginning of his rejection of them. The first kingdom to go into exile will also experience a restoration to divine favor. The joy that God's people experience will not be momentary, for future generations will experience it as well: "Their children will see it." The appearance of the lowly king in history and the unparalleled might of his kingdom should bring joy to his people today because the fulfillments of the predictions of this oracle attest to God's activity in history.

XIII. God Will Act on Behalf of His People (10:1–12)
C. God's Restoring His People (10:8–12)

McCOMISKEY

⁸I will whistle for them and gather them, for I shall have redeemed them, and they will multiply as they have multiplied, ⁹and I shall sow them among the nations and in distant lands they will remember me, and along with their children they will live, and they will return. ¹⁰And I will bring them out of the land of Egypt, and from Assyria I will gather them, and to the land of Gilead and Lebanon I will bring them, and no [room] will be found for them. ¹¹And he will pass through the sea of affliction and smite the waves of the sea, and all the depths of the Nile will dry up. And the pride of Assyria will be brought low, and the scepter of Egypt will depart. ¹²And I will strengthen them in the LORD, and in his name they will walk—utterance of the LORD.

NRSV

8 I will signal for them and gather them in,
      for I have redeemed them,
   and they shall be as numerous as they
      were before.
9 Though I scattered them among the na-
      tions,
   yet in far countries they shall remem-
      ber me,
   and they shall rear their children and
      return.
10 I will bring them home from the land of
      Egypt,
   and gather them from Assyria;
   I will bring them to the land of Gilead and
      to Lebanon,
   until there is no room for them.
11 They shall pass through the sea of dis-
      tress,
   and the waves of the sea shall be struck
      down,
   and all the depths of the Nile dried up.
   The pride of Assyria shall be laid low,
   and the scepter of Egypt shall depart.
12 I will make them strong in the LORD,
   and they shall walk in his name, says
      the LORD.

8. אֶשְׁרְקָה (I will whistle): שָׁרַק denotes making a sound with the mouth and may mean "to astonish" (1 Kings 9:8; Jer. 19:8; 49:17; 50:13), summon (Isa. 5:26; 7:18), express scorn (Lam. 2:15), or frighten away (Job 27:23). Only "to summon" fits this context (see the Exposition). The lengthened form ה֑ "lays stress on the determination underlying the action" (GKC, p. 319). כִּי (for) establishes the basis for the gathering of the people: because God has redeemed them. פְּדִיתִים (I have redeemed them): The settled action of this perfective form establishes the sphere in which the preceding imperfectives אֶשְׁרְקָה and אֲקַבְּצֵם come to reality and operate. Not only does this verbal form reflect Yahweh's resolve to reclaim ownership of his people, but it encompasses the actions by which he carries out that resolve. Since Yahweh's activity on behalf of his people is yet future, the translation "shall have redeemed them" reflects the temporal aspect of this verb in the context as well as its completed aspect. The range of meaning of פָּדָה (to redeem) is broad. In the levitical legislation (Lev. 27:27), it includes purchasing back by an exchange of some kind (usually monetary). The exchange of ownership may also take place by force (Deut. 9:26). Frequently, however, the sense is to deliver with no implication of an exchange of any kind. It is likely that the sense of ownership is never far from any occurrence of this word. Here פָּדָה appears to connote more than simple deliverance, which שָׁרַק and קָבַץ imply; rather, פָּדָה supplies the basis for that deliverance. The word then must reflect the sense that God redeems the people because they are his own. וְרָבוּ כְּמוֹ רָבוּ (and they will multiply as they have multiplied): The second perfective רָבוּ (they have multiplied) points to a period in the past when the nation increased greatly in number (see the Exposition).

9. יִזְכְּרוּנִי (they will remember me) frequently includes in its range of meaning taking appropriate action (Gen. 9:15; Num. 15:40; Isa. 44:21–22; Ezek. 6:9; 16:60, 61; Hos. 9:9; Hab. 3:2). וְחָיוּ אֶת (and along with . . . they will live): חָיָה (live) cannot have its infrequent meaning "to reside" (Gen. 47:28), for the idea of generations residing in foreign lands is out of place between זָכַר (remember) and שׁוּב (return), which refers to a return to the land (see the Exposition).

---

8. Verses 3–7 relate how the Lord will transform his feeble flock into triumphant warriors, erasing from their experience the effects of their subjugation to the nations. The discussion here in verses 8–12 spans the same events, for it begins with the Lord's whistling for his wandering flock and ends with their triumphant deliverance. It is unlikely that šāraq (to whistle) is a summons to the victorious army of verse 7 because this discourse does not sustain the reference to their military triumphs, but pictures Yahweh as acting on behalf of his feeble flock, whom he himself rescues (v. 10) and strengthens (v. 12).

That the people have yet to experience great population growth indicates that the writer views them as a remnant (8:6, 11–12). Having assured the remnant of the prospect of victory (vv. 5, 7), the Divine Warrior now promises them that they will increase greatly in number, for he says that they will multiply as they have multiplied in the past. There are two periods in Israel's early history in which the historian makes a point of telling us that the people increased greatly in number: the period of bondage in Egypt (Gen. 47:27; Exod. 1:7, 12, 20) and the time when the people were on the threshold of Canaan (Deut. 1:10). There can be no question as to what the text intends here, for its perspective is clearly the Egyptian bondage (v. 10).

When we read promises of great repopulation we must not fail to see the church, for the promise to Abraham of great posterity includes redeemed Gentiles. This is consonant with Pauline theology (see the Exposition of 2:8 [4] and 8:4–8). Thus, the promises of victory for God's people and the subsequent promise of landedness not only belong to the ancient people, but to God's people today, who also inherit the promise that the Lord will be God to his people.

There is a marked parallel between this passage and 8:2–8. In both sections we learn that God affirms his ownership of his people (8:2; 10:8), that he will repopulate them (8:5; 10:8), that they will escape from the nations (8:7; 10:9), and that they will become a landed people (8:8; 10:10)—all because of the Lord's promise to be their God (8:8; 10:6).

9. This verse continues the promise of population growth with a vivid metaphor: the Lord will sow his people as one sows seed. It is doubtful that zāraʿ means "to scatter" here (NASB: "when I scatter them") because elsewhere it always indicates sowing seed. The metaphor of sowing elsewhere expresses population growth (Jer. 31:27; Ezek. 36:9–10; Hos. 2:25 [23]), and it amplifies the similar assurance in verse 8 by designating "the nations" as the sphere of that growth.

10. אֲקַבְּצֵם (I will gather them): There appears to be no difference in sense between this imperfective verb and the earlier perfective with וֹ: וַהֲשִׁבוֹתִים (and I will bring them out). If the writer had not placed *waw* in the clause-initial position (וּמֵאַשּׁוּר) it would otherwise attach to a perfective form of קָבַץ (gather) and refer to the future. גִּלְעָד

וּלְבָנוֹן (Gilead and Lebanon): See the Exposition. מָצָא (will be found) has no subject, but the context makes it clear enough that we must supply this ellipsis with the idea of "enough room." See the similar use of this verb in Joshua 17:16 (for the function of ellipsis in Hebrew, see the commentary on Hos. 5:8 and 9:11).

Not only will the remnant increase in number among the nations, but they will "remember" the Lord. The action of remembering in the Old Testament may include far more than simply recalling (see the Exegesis). We may understand it here to convey the sense of responding positively to God and his conditions for the spiritual welfare of his people. Without this response they could not experience the "life" of which the next clause speaks.

In the Mosaic legislation, life is "continued participation of the nation or the individual in the blessings of the inheritance" (McComiskey, *Covenants of Promise*, p. 121). The nation lost this vital relationship to the promised inheritance (Gen. 12:7) when it went into exile, rejected by God; but when it returns to him it will again know the security of landedness. Once again we observe the theme of divine sovereignty and human agency. The God who battles with and for his people will not return them to the land until they remember him. This concept of life as the vitality of the relationship of the nation to the promised inheritance may be found throughout the Old Testament. It is especially prominent in Deuteronomy (4:1; 5:33; 8:1, 3; 16:20; see also Rom. 10:5–13).

The prospect of a renewed relationship to the promise of land extends to the children as well. The picture is one of generations enjoying the security and rest that landedness entails (8:4–5). Throughout this oracle, we have observed another people who stand as the spiritual inheritors of the promises of this oracle—the church—for Hebrews 3–4 reflects a clear land consciousness, setting forth the "rest" of which they speak as the gospel (4:2)—at-homeness in Christ.

Once again, the words of this book intersect future events, paralleling the history of the kingdom that the lowly Messiah established (9:9). By his death, he triumphed over the forces of evil (John 12:31) to establish a spiritual kingdom (John 8:36; 1 Peter 2:5, 9–10) whose subjects reside among the nations. Throughout the ages, God calls those he has redeemed (Zech. 10:8; Rom. 8:29–30) to the landedness of which Hebrews 3–4

speaks. The period of dispersal in the world parallels the history of the church from its inception to its culmination.

10. The words *I will bring them out of the land of Egypt* reflect a philosophy of history in which persons, places, and events stand for similar entities in the future (see the Exposition of 2:10 [6]). The bondage in Egypt was an event in the distant past, and Assyria, the first land of exile, no longer existed. Yet, freed from their historical associations, these nations continued to live in the prophet's mind as symbols of oppression.

Not only do these nations recall cruel oppression, but Assyria in particular recalls how empty God's promises of land and offspring must have seemed to the exiles as they forsook their homeland. It is these associations with exile—oppression and seemingly failed divine promises—that the passage universalizes and overcomes. Verses 8–10 affirm the restoration of God's promises of landedness and offspring, while verses 11–12 affirm that God will bring to an end the bondage and oppression that Egypt and Assyria represent. No longer can an oppressing power sever God's people from their spiritual inheritance. So today, surrounded by hostile powers that may suppress its proclamation for a time, the church will continue its course, empowered by God, until its final triumph.

> From age to age Christ's kingdom stands,
>   While evil foes assail;
> Though scattered throughout farflung lands
>   His people will prevail.

God does not bring the people back to Israel, but to Gilead and Lebanon, which stand in antithesis to Egypt and Assyria. These localities are not likely a metonomy for Israel, because it is doubtful that Israelite hegemony ever extended far into Lebanon or the Lebanon range and Gilead was located to the east of the Jordan: neither name is an unmistakable surrogate for the northern kingdom. The terms must be understood metaphorically. Both Lebanon and Gilead were noted for their fertility (Song 4:15; Isa. 29:17; Jer. 22:6;

11. וְעָבַר (and he will pass): The New Revised Standard Version follows the Septuagint's plural καὶ διελεύσονται ἐν θαλάσσῃ στενῇ (and they will pass through a narrow sea), but it is not necessary to change the number even though the transition seems abrupt. Verse 12 demonstrates that Yahweh is the subject of the action of this pericope ("I will strengthen them"; see also v. 6), and the destruction of the nations is the exclusive province of Yahweh in this book. בַיָּם (through the sea): בְּ (through) channels the action of עָבַר (to pass) to

its object. צָרָה always connotes trouble or affliction. Its use with יָם (sea) probably reflects the awesome power of the sea and the dangers that lurk in its depths. The Masoretic tradition does not represent יָם and צָרָה as a construct chain (sea of distress) but as an appositional relationship, which defines "more exactly . . . the one by the other" (GKC §131a). This construction defines the sea more properly as affliction and excludes several senses that the construct relationship may convey. We should not, for example, regard the

---

Ezek. 31:16; Nah. 1:4), and Gilead provided abundant pastureland for flocks (1 Chron. 6:80; Song 4:1; 6:5; Mic. 7:14). Even though the imagery of sheep is present in this discourse (see the Exposition of 10:8), these two localities do not represent the rich provision that God has prepared for his flock, for while Gilead is associated with flocks (Num. 32:1) and is a metaphor for God's provision for his sheep (Mic. 7:14), Lebanon has no such associations. It is associated with the promised land (Deut. 1:7; 11:24; Josh. 1:4), but Gilead is not, making it difficult to assume that the writer intends an idealized extension of the land God promised his people. Only one commonality exists between Gilead and Lebanon—both are metaphors for the Restoration, the time when the blessings of the new covenant became a reality. Lebanon is a metaphor of restored Zion (Isa. 60:13), and Isaiah 35:10 speaks of the time when the ransomed (including Lebanon in 35:2) of the Lord will return to Zion. Gilead is a metaphor for the Shepherd-King's provision for his flock (Jer. 50:19–20; Mic. 7:14).

The promise of great repopulation, "they will multiply as they have multiplied" (10:8), appears again: the people will be so numerous that there will not be enough room for them in the land to which God will bring them. The highly metaphorical language of this section is the vehicle for two aspects of the Abrahamic promise: the offspring, which asserts that Abraham would become the father of a multitude (Gen. 15:5), and the promise of land (Gen. 15:18). The theological perspective of the New Testament affirms the Christian's participation in the promise (see the Exposition of v. 8). Restored Zion includes those who are under the jurisdiction of the new covenant and have found the forgiveness it assures (Jer. 31:34) and the landedness it promises (Jer. 32:37, 41). For further discussion of the church as restored Zion, see the Exposition of 2:15 [11].

11. I understand the Lord to be the subject of the singular verb ʿābar (to pass through), in spite of the plural form in the Septuagint, whose translators stumbled over the idea of God experiencing affliction. The point of this metaphor is not that Yahweh suffers affliction, but that he breasts its billows to bring affliction to an end. It is scarcely possible to attribute that action, coupled with the destruction of the nations, to the people. It is his people's affliction that the Lord conquers.

It is possible that the writer intended "the sea of affliction" to recall the Red Sea and its association with the Egyptian bondage, but we cannot be certain. The Masoretic tradition makes a studied effort to identify this sea as a metaphor of affliction (see the Exegesis). The Red Sea may have been lurking in the writer's mind, but it is not at the forefront. The drying up of the Nile cannot be a direct reference to the exodus because nothing like that occurred when the plagues came on Egypt. That both Assyria and Egypt reappear in this text immediately after their function as symbols of oppression (v. 10) favors the same usage for them here. The sea of affliction does not represent suffering in general, but rather the affliction the people suffered at the hands of their oppressors, for when Yahweh smites the sea, Egypt and Assyria, symbols of Israel's bondage and captivity, come to an end.

The promise that oppression will cease recalls the words of 9:8: "No oppressor shall again overrun them, for now I have seen with my own eyes." To bring an end to oppression, the Lord sends his king (9:9), reminding us that this lowly monarch is not absent from the text here. In a way that we cannot yet fully comprehend, the Lord experiences affliction, but he emerges from it, having brought it to an end.

That oppression will cease assures us that no earthly tyrant, no matter how strong, can force the citizens of Christ's kingdom from their landed status as Assyria and Babylon had done to Israel

affliction as vast as the sea. Rather, he will pass through a sea—that is, affliction—or pass through affliction as through a sea (see the Exposition). בַּיָּם: בְּ in this second occurrence of יָם can function as the object marker of הִכָּה (to smite; Exod. 17:6), yielding "and he will smite the sea [as to its] billows," but this is unlikely because the same element in the preceding parallel clause places the action of the verb עָבַר in the sea. If we give it the same function here, this clause reads, "he will smite in the sea billows" (i.e., "he smites the billows that are in the sea" or "from his position in the sea he smites the billows"). The connection of this clause with the parallel clause favors the latter view. Related to מְצֻלָה (hollow) in 1:8, מְצוּלוֹת (the depths of) may refer to watery depths (Job 41:23 [31]; Pss. 68:23 [22]; 69:16 [15]) or to deep mire (Ps. 69:3 [2]). Its association with כֹּל (all) underscores the intensity of the action of the verb הֹבִישׁוּ (dry up). גָּאוֹן (pride): See the Exegesis of 9:6. A שֵׁבֶט is a staff (Exod. 21:20), the shaft of a spear (2 Sam. 18:14), or a shepherd's staff (Mic. 7:14). In parallel with גָּאוֹן, however, which stands here for all that characterized Egypt at the height of its power—its might, authority, magnificence, and wealth—שֵׁבֶט must stand for the symbol of Egypt's hegemony, namely, a scepter.

12. וְגִבַּרְתִּים (and I will strengthen them) can refer only to Yahweh and recalls the same word in verse 6, where Yahweh is clearly the subject. בַּיהוָה (in the LORD): It may seem strange to encounter this third-person reference to Yahweh after the first-person וְגִבַּרְתִּים, but this phenomenon is not uncommon in the prophets and is well represented in Zechariah (1:17; 2:15 [11]; 8:9; 9:6–8 [see also vv. 1–4], 11–13 [see also vv. 14–16]; 10:3–5, 6–7, 8–11). וּבִשְׁמוֹ יִתְהַלָּכוּ (and in his name they will walk): שֵׁם (name), when used of the true God or a pagan deity, can signal the embodiment of the deity's character, encompassing the attributes by which he is known and by which he receives cognitive existence in the physical world (Isa. 9:5 [6]; Ezek. 36:21; 39:7, 25, 27; 43:8; Joel 2:26; Amos 2:7; Mic. 5:3 [4]; Zeph. 3:12; Mal. 1:11; 2:5; 3:16). This word occurs with הָלַךְ (to walk) elsewhere only in Micah 4:5, where the context gives the collocation הָלַךְ בְּשֵׁם (to walk in the name) the broad sense of identification with and participation in the sphere of attributes that characterize the mental comprehension of a deity. Here in Zechariah, however, the parallel structure relates שֵׁם to the divine attribute of strength. יִתְהַלָּכוּ is nonperfective, stating the consequence of the people's walking in the divine name, but the nonperfective nature of this motion verb goes further, for it is not merely that they will so walk (perfective), but an incomplete action, therefore a continuing activity. נְאֻם יְהוָה (utterance of the LORD): See the Exegesis of 1:3.

---

and Judah. Under the aegis of Messiah, the oppression of sin comes to an end (Rom. 6:9), death loses its sting (1 Cor. 15:55), and his people find peace greater than any human monarch can secure (John 14:27). The hope that Zechariah 10:11 proclaims recalls Isaiah's words in 9:3, 5 [4, 6]:

For the yoke of their burden,
  and the bar across their shoulders,
the rod of their oppressor,
  you have broken as on the day of Midian. . . .
For a child has been born for us,
  a son given to us;
authority rests upon his shoulder.

12. Yahweh now speaks, as the expression *utterance of the LORD* indicates. The text does not say that he will strengthen his people "in himself," but "in the LORD," allowing this revered name to ring in the people's ears, reminding them of all the attributes his name entails (Exod. 3:14–15). He does not strengthen them in themselves—because he takes from them everything in which they might find strength or of which they may boast (Zech. 9:10). Rather, as the people continue in the world, participating in the kingdom of Messiah, they enjoy the strength of their God, empowered by a power greater than their own (4:6).

XIV. The Good Shepherd (11:1–14)
A. Poetic Prelude (11:1–3)

McCOMISKEY

11 Open your gates, O Lebanon, that fire may consume your cedars. ²Wail, O cypress, because the cedar has fallen, for the glorious [trees] are despoiled. Wail, O oaks of Bashan, for the dense forest has come down. ³The sound of the shepherds' wail—for their glory is despoiled. The sound of the roaring of young lions—for the pride of the Jordan is despoiled.

NRSV

11 Open your doors, O Lebanon,
   so that fire may devour your cedars!
² Wail, O cypress, for the cedar has fallen,
   for the glorious trees are ruined!
Wail, oaks of Bashan,
   for the thick forest has been felled!
³ Listen, the wail of the shepherds,
   for their glory is despoiled!
Listen, the roar of the lions,
   for the thickets of the Jordan are destroyed!

11:1. דְּלָחֶיךָ can indicate either a door (1 Sam. 3:15) or a gate (Deut. 3:5). Since Lebanon was a region, not a city, the word is metaphorical. וְתֹאכַל (that . . . may consume): ו with this imperfective verb represents the logical consequence of opening the gates, thus the translation "that."

2. הֵילֵל (wail) is usually translated "wailing" because of realized or impending destruction (Isa. 13:6; Jer. 47:2; Amos 8:3); only in Isaiah 52:5; Hosea 7:14; and Micah 1:8 is it otherwise. The content of this pericope makes it clear that we are to understand it in this more common sense. כִּי (for) begins a clause that explains why the cypress is to wail: because the other mighty trees of the forest have fallen. The particle אֲשֶׁר should not be translated as "whose" (whose glorious ones are despoiled), referring to the cedar, but as "for" or "forasmuch," stating that the cedar has fallen forasmuch as all the mighty trees of the forest are destroyed. The latter sense maintains a precise balance with the b clause of line 2 (also beginning with יְלָל, to wail), which refers to the forest as a whole, not to specific trees. אַדִּרִים (the glorious trees): אַדִּיר in the plural always refers to glorious or mighty persons or objects. Among other things, it describes the waters of the sea (Exod. 15:10; Ps. 93:4) and leaders (Neh. 3:5; Jer. 30:21; Nah. 3:18). See the Exposition. כִּי (for) introduces the reason for the oaks to wail. יָרַד (has come down), like the preceding נָפָל (has fallen), is perfective, viewing its action as an established event. יַעַר הַבָּצוּר (the dense forest): The Kethiv (the consonantal text) represents בצור as a qātûl form while the Qere points it as a qātîl, namely, the substantive בָּצִיר

(vintage; the AV has "the forest of the vintage"). I understand the qātûl form to represent a qal passive participle that functions adjectivally in the attributive position. While this verse is obscure, there appears to be no convincing reason to depart from the consonantal text. The sense of impenetrability or inaccessibility that lurks in the frequent uses of the qātûl form of this word and expresses "fortified" applies comfortably to a dense forest (BDB, p. 131: "made inaccessible"), and the association of vintage with a forest is in itself difficult.

3. יְלָלָת (wail), like its verbal counterpart (יְלָל) in verse 2, expresses wailing because of destruction. כִּי (for) introduces the destruction that יְלָלָת anticipates. שֻׁדְּדָה אַדַּרְתָּם (their glory is despoiled): Echoing the somewhat similar words in the previous verse, these words attribute to the shepherds (leaders) a fate similar to the trees in that verse. אַדַּרְתָּם (their glory), while this word is related to the same root as אַדִּרִים (glorious [trees]) in verse 2, it has a different emphasis, referring most frequently to a mantle (Zech. 13:4) with few observable connotations of glory. In Ezekiel 17:8, however, it describes a majestic vine and thus is appropriate to the context here. כְּפִירִים denotes young lions (Judg. 14:5; Amos 3:4), but never cubs. As a metaphor, it has a broad range, including the righteous (Prov. 28:1), warriors (Nah. 2:14 [13]), and enemies (Jer. 2:15). Nahum 2:12 [11] uses the word of foreign princes, and in Ezekiel 19:5–6 it refers to an Israelite prince (see the Exposition). גְּאוֹן (the pride of): See the Exegesis of 9:6.

11:1–2. A somber poetic piece forms a prelude to chapter 11. The destruction this section depicts is not against the regions of Lebanon and Bashan, but against the trees for which these regions were celebrated (2 Chron. 2:8; Pss. 29:5; 92:13 [12]; Isa. 2:13; Ezek. 27:6). In this surreal depiction, these symbols of glory crash, charred and smoking, to the forest floor, their personified wails piercing the sound of the rushing flames. This vivid picture creates the feeling that the vaunted objects of human pride are collapsing, and this hypothetical destruction stirs emotions within us that we carry into the actual destruction of verse 3. The word ʾaddirîm (glorious) refers to the trees of the forest, but it foreshadows Israel's leaders in verse 3.

3. The metaphorical commands to the dense forest to wail (v. 2) give way to the actual wailing of shepherds. These shepherds are Israel's leaders whom we encounter first in 10:2–3. They bemoan

the loss of their glory, not the loss of their sheep. The root ʾdr (glory) reappears: referring to the stately trees of the forest in verse 2, here it relates to Israel's leaders and carries the same connotations of ruined glory. The word šuddĕdâ (is despoiled), likewise appearing in verse 2, links the despoliation of the trees with that of the shepherds here in verse 3.

A sound distracts us from the shepherds' lament—the roar of lions. The clausal structure balances kĕpîrîm (young lions) with hārōʿîm (the shepherds). Since kĕpîrîm can mean "prince" (see the Exegesis) and since it is balanced by hārōʿîm, we may understand it as another reference to leaders. The lions roar because the pride of the Jordan is despoiled. The root šdd (to despoil) appears for the third time in verses 1–3, creating a verbal link with the destruction of the forests in verse 2.

The reference to the "pride of the Jordan" introduces yet another river into this lengthy discourse. The reference to the Nile in 10:11 extends to the whole of Egypt (which stands in that context for oppression) because the drying up of the Nile would have devastated the entire region (this is confirmed by the reference to the scepter of Egypt in the same verse). This is also true of the reference to the Jordan. The pride of the Jordan is not the river itself; this expression personifies it, referring to that in which the Jordan may take pride: the topography through which it flows—its beautiful valleys and hills—hence the land itself. This concept balances ʾaddartām (their glory) in the companion clause, relating to it only broadly but nevertheless influencing its sense in the direction of the land. The land—the jurisdiction over which the leaders (shepherds) ruled—was their glory. All this is to come to ruin.

XIV. The Good Shepherd (11:1–14)

B. God's Rejecting the Inhabitants of the Land (11:4–6)

McCOMISKEY

⁴This is what the LORD my God says, Shepherd the flock of slaughtering ⁵whom their buyers slaughter and are not held guilty, and those who sell them say, "Blessed be the LORD, for I am rich"—and their shepherds do not spare them—⁶for I shall no longer spare the inhabitants of the land. Utterance of the LORD. Now listen! I am going to cause each man to fall into the hand of another and into the hand of his king, and they will strike the land, and I will not deliver them from their hand.

NRSV

⁴Thus said the LORD my God: Be a shepherd of the flock doomed to slaughter. ⁵Those who buy them kill them and go unpunished; and those who sell them say, "Blessed be the LORD, for I have become rich"; and their own shepherds have no pity on them. ⁶For I will no longer have pity on the inhabitants of the earth, says the LORD, I will cause them, everyone, to fall each into the hand of a neighbor, and each into the hand of the king; and they shall devastate the earth, and I will deliver no one from their hand.

4. רָעָה (to shepherd): While this verb generally means "to feed or pasture," there are enough occurrences of it to show that it also has a more general meaning of "to tend or shepherd" (1 Sam. 16:11; 17:15; 25:16; Jer. 23:2). Since Israel's leaders are in view, the general sense is appropriate to this context. הַהֲרֵגָה (slaughtering): See the Exposition.

5. אֲשֶׁר קֹנֵיהֶן יַהֲרְגֻן (whose buyers slaughter [them]; lit., whom their buyers slaughter): If אֲשֶׁר

(whose, whom) introduces an independent relative clause, the resulting translation ("those who buy them slaughter [them]") is appropriate. The writer could, however, have said that by omitting אֲשֶׁר altogether, which would have achieved a more precise symmetrical balance with מֹכְרֵיהֶן (those who buy them/those who sell them). It is possible that אֲשֶׁר should be translated "for" (as in v. 2), but the absence of an object suffix on יַהֲרְגֻן

---

4. The prophet feels the divine impulse to "shepherd the flock." Since the motif of shepherd in this discourse represents Israel's leaders, we wonder whether he actually took a position of civil or religious leadership in the community or simply portrayed the part of a shepherd in symbolic activity. When we read that he "banished three shepherds in one month" (v. 8), we feel a sense of reality, as though he used the influence of public office to rid the community of several pernicious officials. That Israel's leaders soon tired of him and that he became frustrated with them (v. 8) also favors this possibility. On the other hand, the activity in the subsequent section (vv. 15–16) is entirely symbolic, for the shepherd he portrays there foreshadows a foolish leader whom God has yet to raise up, and the prophet would not have actually become one of the unwise officials who so plagued Israelite society. Evidently the words *take again the implements of a foolish shepherd* in verse 15 mean to play the part of this future ruler.

If the prophet had actually become an official of the community and the relationship eventually soured, we wonder how the events of this chapter, which would thus be largely fortuitous, could so precisely prefigure future events. The prophet did not shape his concept of the future as he reviewed his past experiences, because he took on the role of shepherd knowing that it was because God no longer had pity on the inhabitants of the land (v. 6). The shepherds' staffs fit more comfortably with symbolic activity than with an official role in the community.

We may bring these constituents of the discourse together if we understand them as aspects of a prophetic protest against the community's corrupt leaders that the prophet acted out in public, probably over a period of time. Verse 13 points to the temple environs as the likely location of this protest (see also Jer. 7:1–4; 26:1–6). This activity would be similar to Ezekiel's public role-playing (Ezek. 4:1–17; 5:1–4; 12:1–7). This crusade may have succeeded in expelling several leaders from

office. That the expulsion of these leaders does not figure in the prophet's development of analogous future events may limit its significance only to his time.

The prophet may have worn shepherd's garb, flailing his staffs as he cried out to the throngs entering the temple, warning them of the treacherous path on which their officials were leading them. One can understand how these leaders would find his tirades tiresome after a while (v. 8) and begin to view the prophet's strange behavior as more a threat than an annoyance. In one dramatic event, in which he hewed his staffs in two, he symbolized the destiny of his community. The people had returned from exile with high hopes: their former enemies no longer existed, and it seemed that ancient prophetic visions of Yahweh's reign would become reality. How bitter must this prophet's words and actions have seemed to the onlookers when they heard him say that another enemy would enter their land!

The command that commences this verse relates the flock to slaughter. Unpitied by their leaders (v. 5), this "slaughter flock" represents the entire nation, for we learn from verses 5–6 that as the leaders do not spare the people, but let them out to slaughter, so God will not spare "the inhabitants of the land." That the entire nation is destined for slaughter is also clear from verses 9 and 16.

5. The picture is that of a sheepmarket, with buyers and sellers haggling over the sheep. Those who buy them do not put them out to pasture, but slaughter them wholesale, threatening the flock with extermination—and no one holds them accountable for this waste. The merchants count their profits, blessing God for their newfound wealth, while the shepherds who tended this flock spare none of them. These shepherds have no compassion for the sheep, but let them go to the slaughter, enriching the coffers of those who buy and sell them. The merchants and buyers stand apart from the shepherds—the leaders in Israelite

(slaughter) is suspicious. If we understand אֲשֶׁר to resume the reference to צֹאן (flock) in verse 4, the translation "whom their buyers slaughter" is smooth and fits comfortably in the textual environment. The object suffix would thus be unnecessary on יַהֲרְגֻן, the function of the object being taken up by אֲשֶׁר, as in 12:10. The semantic range of יַהֲרְגֻן is broad; it does not always connote intense killing (Eccles. 3:3), for it may be used matter-of-factly of slaying animals (Lev. 20:15). This paragogic form (וּ-) expresses "contrastivity" (J. Hoftijzer as quoted in *IBHS*, p. 517), that is, "exceptions to normal practice." It is not usual for one to buy sheep only to slaughter them. יֶאְשָׁמוּ (held guilty) connotes both the commission of wrong and being held liable for wrong (i.e., being guilty), as in Hosea 4:15. The context here, with its negative (לֹא), creates the sense of going guilt-free or not being held guilty. יֹאמַר (say) is singular, though construed with the plural מֹכְרֵיהֶן (those who sell them). BHS suggests reading the plural, and it is possible that this is a textual corruption influenced by the following singular וְאַעְשִׁר (I am rich). Plural participles, however, sometimes appear with a singular predicate to represent each individual in the assertion, rather than a class of individuals (GKC §145*l*). That this distributive function occurs with יַחְמוֹל (do not pity) argues against textual corruption. יֹאמַר and the preceding imperfectives express what is going on in the author's present. Only rarely (e.g., 1 Sam. 15:15) is the sense of compassion indiscernible in the collo-

cation חָמַל עַל. Here, the context—with its emphasis on the Lord's letting his people go and "not delivering them"—enforces the translation "to spare," but the idea of compassion is not absent either. For the singular construction of this verb, see the discussion of יֹאמַר above.

6. כִּי (for): For the function of this particle, see the Exposition. אֶחְמוֹל (I shall spare): See the Exegesis of verse 5. עוֹד (longer): Denoting continuance, this particle with לֹא (no) and the nonperfective אֶחְמוֹל extends the sense of continuance over the indefinite expanse of the nonperfective, hence "no longer." This construction creates a sense of ultimacy. נְאֻם־יְהוָה (utterance of the LORD): See the Exegesis of 1:3. וְהִנֵּה אָנֹכִי מַמְצִיא (Now listen! I am going to cause to fall): Since the event this lengthy participial clause describes is yet future, the translation "I am going to" is appropriate. הִנֵּה (listen) adds vividness to the construction. רֵעֵהוּ (another): Sometimes referring to a friend or companion (see the Exegesis of 3:10), this word takes the weaker translation "another" when it occurs in conjunction with אִישׁ (each). וְכִתְּתוּ (and they will strike) possesses a strong verbal action: shattering a jar (Isa. 30:14), crushing the golden calf (Deut. 9:21), or beating metal (Isa. 2:4). Here it describes the devastation of the attack to which this context refers. The plural construction of this verb can refer only to רֵעֵהוּ (another) and מַלְכּוֹ (his king), who are the only agents of destruction in the immediate context.

---

society—and must represent the influential or wealthy members of the community in this time.

6. We find dark statements of divine resolve similar to this one elsewhere in the prophets (Hos. 1:6; Amos 8:2), and they raise questions about God's grace. Does the ultimacy of the words *I shall no longer spare the inhabitants of the land* mean the cessation of the ancient promises to Abraham? The answer is, of course, no, for hope lies ahead. The withdrawal of compassion this verse affirms relates to the "inhabitants of the land." God may allow a generation to go into captivity, but he will not forsake his promise. Leviticus 26:44 assures us of that: "Yet for all that, when they are in the land of their enemies, I will not spurn them, or abhor them so as to destroy them utterly, and break my covenant with them."

This verse begins with the causative particle *kî* (for). It is best to refer this particle back beyond the explanatory material in verse 5 to the command to become shepherd of the flock in verse 4, thus giving the reason for that command. If we relate it only to the immediately preceding words, "their shepherds do not spare them," it creates the illogical assertion that their leaders do not spare them because (*kî*) God will not. Connected with the command to shepherd the flock, however, the sense is: "Take the role of a shepherd, *because (kî)* just as Israel's leaders do not spare them, I shall not spare them." Viewed in this way, the prophet's role-play served to signify the severance of God's relationship to the nation.

XIV. The Good Shepherd (11:1–14)

C. The Shepherd's Rejecting the Nation (11:7–9)

McCOMISKEY

⁷So I became shepherd of the flock of slaughtering, thereby the afflicted of the flock, and I took two staffs; one I named Favor, the other I named Bonds, and I proceeded to shepherd the flock. ⁸And I got rid of three of the shepherds in one month. Now I became impatient with them, and moreover they loathed me. ⁹And I said, "I will not continue to shepherd you; what is dying will die, and the perishing perish, and as for those who remain, they will devour one another's flesh."

NRSV

⁷So, on behalf of the sheep merchants, I became the shepherd of the flock doomed to slaughter. I took two staffs; one I named Favor, the other I named Unity, and I tended the sheep. ⁸In one month I disposed of the three shepherds, for I had become impatient with them, and they also detested me. ⁹So I said, "I will not be your shepherd. What is to die, let it die; what is to be destroyed, let it be destroyed; and let those that are left devour the flesh of one another!"

7. וָאֶרְעֶה (so I became shepherd): ו with this imperfective denotes consequence. The word *became* is an effort to reflect the aspect of this nonperfective form. הַהֲרֵגָה (slaughtering): See the Exegesis of verse 4. לָכֵן (thereby), which answers most frequently to "therefore," seems awkward since there is no clear logical conclusion that it introduces. The Septuagint combines לָכֵן with the following עֲנִיֵּי (the afflicted of) to form the word לכנעניי, which it translates εἰς τὴν Χαναανῖτιν (in the [land of] Canaan). This reading leaves unexplained the presence of הַצֹּאן (the flock) in the Masoretic Text, and "Canaan" serves no apparent purpose in the text. More attractive is BDB's suggestion (p. 489) that כנעני is a merchant (see Hos. 12:8 [7]). The New Revised Standard Version follows this reconstruction, translating לכנעניי הַצֹּאן "on behalf of the sheep merchants," an idea appropriate to the context. While this translation is compatible with the consonants of the Masoretic Text, it raises several questions regarding the sense of the discourse (see the Exposition). If we accept the reading לָכֵן, the contextual environment calls for it to have a sense that logically connects "the flock of slaughtering" with "the afflicted of the flock," while preserving the integrity of the latter, which appears again as an entity in this discourse in verse 11 (see the Exposition). מַקְלוֹת (staffs) has a broad range of meaning: the branch of a tree (Gen. 30:37), a walking staff (Exod. 12:11), a weapon (1 Sam. 17:43), or a scepter (Jer. 48:17). It does not refer elsewhere to shepherds' implements, but the context here gives it that sense. נֹעַם (favor): The verbal form of this word connotes something pleasant or delightful (Gen. 49:15). While most occurrences of the noun share these senses, in Psalm 90:17, because it occurs in a prayer for divine blessing on the nation, it means "favor"—a connotation that still falls within the semantic range of "delight" but translates that concept into the tangible display of the emotion. Here in Zechariah, the word also means "favor," for when the prophet breaks the staff "Favor" he signals the end of Yahweh's protection of the nation. חֹבְלִים must mean bonds or cords because the breaking of the second staff severs a relationship (v. 14). וָאֶרְעֶה (so I proceeded to shepherd) does not view the prophet's experience from beginning to end, as might the perfective. The activities that follow fall within the comprehension of וָאֶרְעֶה, thus the use of "proceeded" in the translation of this verb.

8. וָאַכְחִד (and I got rid of): Hiphil כָּחַד (to hide; Job 20:12) can indicate the complete destruction of an enemy (Exod. 23:23; 1 Kings 13:34; 2 Chron. 32:21; Ps. 83:5 [4]). Evidently the prophet succeeded in expelling several officials from office. אֶת־שְׁלֹשֶׁת הָרֹעִים (three of the shepherds): The

---

7. In obedience to the divine impulsion, the prophet became shepherd of the "flock of slaughtering" (v. 4), a descriptive term that the text relates logically (*lākēn*) to the "afflicted of the flock." The New Revised Standard Version translation, "on behalf of the sheep merchants," fulfills the requirements of the consonantal text but raises a question as to how the prophet acted on behalf of these heartless merchants: What did he do in their interest or as their representative? The preposition *lamed* on this proposed reconstruction does not possess a function that answers satisfactorily to what he actually did regarding them, that is, to intervene on behalf of the flock and take the place of the shepherd-leaders who were neglecting the people. If we read *lākēn*, in accordance with the Masoretic tradition, we must ask if this adverb meets the context's requirements. It appears that it does, for another possible translation of this adverb is "that being so" (BDB, p. 486) as in 1 Samuel 27:6. This function of *lākēn* creates the sense that when the prophet became shepherd of the flock of slaughtering (i.e., of the nation that was destined for destruction), he also became shepherd of the oppressed of the nation. Verse 11 identifies the afflicted as a class within the postexilic society, not the nation as a whole. A paraphrase of this is: "I became shepherd of the flock of slaughter [i.e., the nation], thereby [*lākēn*] becoming shepherd of the afflicted of the flock [i.e., the oppressed of the nation]." Because he shepherds the entire nation, he thereby tends its afflicted. The expulsion of the three shepherds (v. 8) may have been a display of his concern for the oppressed. The New American Standard Version expresses an idea similar to this by using the word *hence* for *lākēn*. (Finley, "Sheep Merchants," argues for the reading "Canaanites" to mean "merchants.")

As he begins his symbolic activity the prophet fashions two staffs to which he gives names. Perhaps he inscribed these names on the staffs or referred to them in his preaching. His hearers would wonder at the significance of these names: Does the staff "Favor" herald divine blessing? The people would soon learn its significance.

8–9. The reconstruction of the events we are following leads us to a point of confrontation. The

translation "the three shepherds" is also permissible grammatically, but unlikely since there is no previous reference to three shepherds, which this construction would resume (a similar construction occurs in Exod. 26:9). וַתִּקְצַר נַפְשִׁי בָּהֶם (now I become impatient with them): The verb קָצֵר sometimes means "to be short" (Isa. 28:20; Ezek. 42:5). When it occurs with נֶפֶשׁ, as it does here, it has the sense of being impatient (Num. 21:4; Judg. 10:16; 16:16) and expresses a limit to the emotion נֶפֶשׁ communicates. נַפְשִׁי has a broad range of meaning; most frequently it refers to nonphysical aspects of the human being. It is possible but not certain that its basic notion is to breathe (compare Gen. 1:30 and Akkadian *napasu*, to breathe out). It may often refer to oneself (Gen. 49:6), probably reflecting the consciousness of one's own existence, and in these instances it is a surrogate for "I." בָּהֶם (with them): It is uncertain as to whom this refers. Is it the three expelled leaders, the leaders who remained in power, or the nation as a whole? The immediate grammatical reference is to the leaders he expelled from office, but it would be strange for him to become impatient with them after their expulsion: it was his frustration

with them that led him to rid the nation of their influence. In all likelihood the writer has Israel's current leaders in mind, of whom the expelled leaders were a part, but the nation is never far from his thoughts either. בָּחֲלָה (wearied) occurs only here. While its inherent sense is uncertain, the context clearly calls for a negative response to the prophet (see the Exposition).

9. אֶתְכֶם (you): This plural construction must encompass the entire nation (v. 7). הַמֵּתָה (what is dying) is a feminine singular participle agreeing in gender with צֹאן (flock) in verse 7. While it is possible that the feminine form is abstract, denoting whatever dies, the deliberate use of the feminine אִשָּׁה instead of the more general masculine אִישׁ in the expression *one another's* (see the masculine in v. 5) betrays the writer's thinking about the nation as feminine. תָּמוּת (will die) is not jussive in form and thus has the general sense of the nonperfective: the dying will die. וְהַנִּכְחֶרֶת (and the perishing), like הַמֵּתָה, is a feminine participle with the same force as that participle in this sentence. אִשָּׁה . . . רְעוּתָה (one another's): See the Exegesis of 3:10.

---

prophet succeeded in expelling three of the community's leaders (shepherds) from office (for a summary of various interpretations of these shepherds, see Baldwin, *Zechariah*, pp. 181–83). That this happened within one month may have encouraged him to believe that the nation was on the verge of a new beginning, but he had reached the limit of his successes. As the prophetic protest wore on, the leaders still in power must have grown tired of the upstart prophet, and he, seeing that he could accomplish no more, reached the point of frustration. The text conveys his impatience by saying that his *nepeš* had reached its limits. *Nepeš* describes humans as conscious beings, for numerous times the term refers to functions of the human consciousness (or psyche), especially the emotions or, more broadly, feelings (see the Exegesis; Deut. 23:25 [24]; Hos. 9:4). That *nepeš* refers to the human consciousness is clear

from its frequent association with emotions: desire (Hos. 4:8), hatred (Jer. 14:19), or sorrow (Jer. 13:17). Whatever emotions of benevolence or patience the prophet felt became "shortened" (*qāṣar*), that is, they reached their limit (Judg. 16:16). The word *nepeš* occurs also with reference to the leaders' reaction to the prophet. Deep within their emotional consciousness they reacted against his castigation of them. This depth of feeling finds a suitable translation in the word *loathing*.

Verse 9 brings us to a crucial point in the prophet's symbolic activity, for he resolves no longer to tend the flock. Their rejection of him runs deep in their hearts, and in words that echo over centuries to come, he abandons the dying nation to its fate and pictures an impending situation so dire that the people will resort to cannibalism in order to subsist.

XIV. The Good Shepherd (11:1–14)
D. Significance of the Staff, Favor (11:10–11)

McCOMISKEY

10So I took my staff Favor and cut it [in two] in order to break the covenant that I had made with all the nations. 11And it was broken that very day. And thus the afflicted of the flock, those who heeded me, understood that this was the word of the LORD.

NRSV

10I took my staff Favor and broke it, annulling the covenant that I had made with all the people. 11So it was annulled on that day, and the sheep merchants, who were watching me, knew that it was the word of the LORD.

10. מַקְלִי (my staff): See the Exegesis of verse 7. נֹעַם (favor): See the Exegesis of verse 7. וָאֶגְדַּע (and cut up) never clearly means "to break" but always "to cut." In the qal it refers to the severing of an arm (1 Sam. 2:31) or the cutting off of a beard (Isa. 15:2). It refers figuratively to the cutting down of a tree (Isa. 10:33) and to the cutting off of God's anger (Lam. 2:3). The sense, then, is of severing the rod into two or more pieces. Since the word does not clearly connote hewing in pieces, "cut in two" is adequate. לְהָפֵיר (to break): While this construction really signifies the breaking of the covenant, the action is so immediate in the prophet's mind that he can picture the cutting of the staff as the breaking of the covenant. The first words of the next verse underscore the immediacy of the action. בְּרִיתִי (my covenant): See the Exposition. The first-person suffix on בְּרִית cannot refer to the prophet, although he is the immediate grammatical referent, but must refer to Yahweh, who alone controls the nations (1:11–12, 15; 2:12–13 [8–9]; see the Exposition). כָּרַתִּי (I had made; lit., to cut) is the common word for making a covenant. הָעַמִּים (the nations): Zechariah consistently uses the plural of this word to refer to the nations surrounding Israel (8:20, 22; 10:9; 12:3, 6; 14:12).

11. וַתֻּפַר (and it was broken): This feminine form can refer only to the feminine בְּרִית (covenant), not the מַקֵּל (staff), which is masculine. כֵן (so): The context calls for this particle to function

10. Taking his staff "Favor," Zechariah severed it, symbolizing the breaking of a covenant between God and the surrounding nations. In the Old Testament, a covenant is "a relationship involving obligation" (McComiskey, *Covenants of Promise*, p. 63). Since it is impossible to find in Scripture a covenantal agreement that Yahweh entered into with the nations, the covenant here must consist of unilateral strictures placed on them by God. There is no explicit reference to such a covenant in the postexilic literature, but the Book of Zechariah refers to unilateral strictures that God placed on the nations. These divine strictures prohibited the nations from invading the postexilic community, thus providing the people with a context in which to work unimpeded on the temple. Even though not called such, these strictures fall into the category of *bĕrît* (covenant). For a discussion of these strictures, see the Exposition of 2:4 [1:21] and 6:8.

In this dramatic moment, the broken staff symbolized the end of divine impositions, allowing hostile nations again to invade the land. We have already read of a real, but vaguely defined catastrophe awaiting the nation (vv. 6, 9), and verses 15–16 are disquieting, envisioning a wicked leader "in the land." The staff has been severed and the land lies open to the invader.

The reference to "my covenant" within a series of first-person suffixes referring to the prophet is unusual. We cannot refer this suffix to him, for only Yahweh could exercise control over the nations. Evidently the prophet looks beyond the symbol of the staff to its reality.

11. There is a sense of frustration throughout this section, portrayed by both the resolve to leave off shepherding the flock and the broken staff. There is, however, more than simple impatience

here, for the prophet was portraying Yahweh's attitude toward the nation. The reality behind the broken staff was that the nation's God had given them up. The wicked leaders would not have accepted this idea, but the oppressed members of the postexilic community who had found in this prophet a champion perceived that his rustic symbols conveyed an awful truth—Yahweh's obligation to protect the nation had ceased. It must have been with heavy hearts that these oppressed people watched as the prophet left the shattered staffs lying scattered on the ground, ending his prophetic crusade.

The dismal events the prophet depicted in his symbolic activity did not come to reality in his lifetime, nor for some time to come. As we scan the years following the prophet's protest, we do not observe a significant invasion of the holy land until the Seleucid period, when forces under Antiochus IV Epiphanes entered Palestine intending to impose Hellenistic religion and ideals on the Jews. This effort, which struck at the heart of the Jewish religion, soon fomented rebellion. After the ultimate blow to the Jewish faith—the desecration of the temple—Jewish resistance to efforts at Hellenization mounted. Led by the Maccabees, the Jews successfully defeated forces sent by Antiochus to Palestine. Taking advantage of these victories, Judas Maccabeus moved quickly to Jerusalem, cleansing the temple and expunging the nation of symbols of the Hellenistic religion.

While this interference by an outside power in Jewish affairs reminds us of the significance of the breaking of the prophet's staff, attesting to the termination of Yahweh's obligation to shut out hostile powers, it does not answer to all the elements of the text, and thus cannot be the central event that the prophet's activity anticipated. The main

as a hinge between the symbolic breaking of the staff and the reaction of the oppressed classes. Since their reaction results from their observation of the prophet's symbolic act, the translational equivalent "so" answers the text's demands. עֲנִיֵּי (the afflicted): See the Exposition of verse 7. הַשֹּׁמְרִים (those who heeded me): When the object

marker אֵת accompanies שָׁמַר (to keep, guard), it connotes meaningful and responsive attention to the object, often with appropriate action. Since the afflicted whom this verb (שָׁמַר) describes comprehended (יָדַע) that the symbolic act represented God's word, the translation "heed" answers nicely to the context.

---

reason for this is the victory the Jews achieved. We do not find them falling into the hands of a foreign king (v. 6), nor did they perish as a nation (v. 9), and the words *I will not deliver them from their hand* (v. 6) were not true in view of the Jews' stunning victory.

The next significant invasion of Palestine meshes with the constituents of this text: the invasion led by the Roman emperor Titus, who in A.D. 70 succeeded in taking Jerusalem after a lengthy siege. Jewish historian Josephus recounts events from that dark page in Jewish history that resonate with the statements here in Zechariah 11. The conditions described in verse 6 match Josephus's record of the seditions and civil wars that raged in Palestine, especially Jerusalem, at

this time. In this ideological strife, Jews robbed and killed one another: "For barbarity and iniquity those of the same nation did no way differ from the Romans" (*Works*, p. 527). Josephus describes the famine in a way that invokes horror: "When those that were most dear were perishing under their hands, they were not ashamed to take from them the very last drops that might preserve their lives" (*Works*, p. 564). The description of an act of cannibalism underscores the pitiable condition of the people (*Works*, p. 579), recalling Zechariah's words that "they will devour one another's flesh" in verse 9. The assertion that "I will not deliver them from their hand" (v. 6) found awful reality in this dark period of Jewish history.

XIV. The Good Shepherd (11:1–14)
E. Rejection of the Shepherd (11:12–13)

McCOMISKEY

[12]And I said to them, "If it seems good in your eyes, give me my wages, but if not, don't bother." And they weighed out as my wages thirty silver pieces. [13]And the LORD said to me, "Throw it to the potter"—the magnificent amount at which I was valued by them. So I took the thirty silver pieces and threw it toward the house of the LORD to the potter.

NRSV

[12]I then said to them, "If it seems right to you, give me my wages; but if not, keep them." So they weighed out as my wages thirty shekels of silver. [13]Then the LORD said to me, "Throw it into the treasury"—this lordly price at which I was valued by them. So I took the thirty shekels of silver and threw them into the treasury in the house of the LORD.

12. אֲלֵיהֶם (to them): The discussion in verse 8 leads to the conclusion that this and the subsequent plural constructions in this verse refer to the leaders of the community. חֲדָלוּ (to cease or leave off): Since the context calls for the meaning "to forebear" (Jer. 40:4), that is, to hold back from initiating an action, the translation "don't bother" is faithful to the context and reflects the prophet's frustration. שְׁלֹשִׁים כָּסֶף (thirty silver pieces) was the amount of compensation the law required for a slave who had been killed (Exod. 21:32): See the Exposition.

13. הַשְׁלִיכֵהוּ (throw it): When this verb is construed in the hiphil, it always describes forcible motion: throwing (Num. 35:22), expelling (2 Kings 13:23), forcing into a pit or dungeon (Gen. 37:22; Jer. 38:9), or removing forcefully (Ps. 2:3). With אֶל (to), the motion is directed in a manner appropriate to the indirect object: into (Gen. 37:22), upon (Deut. 29:27 [28]), to (Lev. 14:40; 2 Sam. 20:22; Isa. 2:20). הַיּוֹצֵר (the potter) presents a textual problem. BHS suggests reading הָאוֹצָר (the treasury) with the Syriac. The Septuagint is far afield from the Masoretic Text, reading Κάθες αὐτοὺς εἰς τὸ χωνευτήριον, καὶ σκέψαι εἰ δοκιμόν ἐστιν (put them into the furnace that I may see if it is good). While the reading הָאוֹצָר fits comfortably with this text, the witness of only the Syriac is not persuasive. The Masoretic Text remains our best control, and we should work within its parameters before emending the text (see the Exposition). אֶדֶר (the magnificent): See the Exegesis of verse 3. The root אדר undoubtedly reflects irony here. הַיְקָר (amount) has several senses, including honor and preciousness. The word does not indicate strictly price, but since it is the object of the verb יָקַר (to be valued) its sense here is akin to the value of the prophet's employment. יָקַרְתִּי (I was valued): See the comment above. This verb is in the first person and occurs in a sentence in which Yahweh is the speaker. There is no syntactical break between this clause and the preceding one, and since we observed a close interaction between God and

---

12. Still acting out the part of a shepherd, the prophet asks the sheepmasters for his wages. While thirty shekels of silver was the value of a slave, we cannot be sure that the prophet regarded this sum as "slave wages." Much depends on how long he envisioned himself to have worked as a shepherd. The irony in the description of the sum as "magnificent" (v. 13) is sufficient to show that he considered it paltry compensation for his work.

13. The prophet felt a divine impulsion to relinquish the thirty silver pieces. But did he throw the coins into the temple *treasury* or cast them to a *potter?* The reading *treasury* certainly complies with the context's basic requirements, but its support is tenuous (see the Exegesis and Torrey, "Second Temple").

There is no reason, however, to conclude that *potter* is inappropriate, because we cannot be certain that artisans had no immediate association with the temple. There is no need to think of the potter working within the temple (which could have indicated by affixing the preposition bĕ [in] to bêt [house]). The use of the adverbial accusative (see the Exegesis), lacking as it does a stated preposition, instead appears to be a convention enabling the writer to avoid two indirect objects governed by ᵓel (to), which might have created confusion as to which of the two was the principal object to which he threw the coins. Since the adverbial accusative is adjunctive in a sentence (IBHS, p. 163), it can share the same directional force as the prepositional clause, but not rob that clause of its principal function. The choice of this convention favors a similar directional sense for both the ᵓel-clause and the adverbial accusative: to (ᵓel) the potter, toward the temple. This view allows us to imagine the potter's shop somewhere in the environs of the temple, perhaps on the way to it or in its immediate vicinity. He could have been a temple artisan, fashioning vessels for use in the temple worship or for the use of worshipers.

It is unlikely that the prophet would have deposited the money in the temple's collection box (the treasury), for that would have contributed to the support of the religious leaders he so vehemently opposed. By casting the money to a lowly potter, he underscored how mean was the compensation he received. Whether he used actual coins or simply pretended to throw them we cannot know, but some in his audience captured something of the significance of what he was doing (see v. 11).

The complex symbolic activity thus far contains several levels that we must explore if we are to grasp its full impact. One of the levels within this rustic symbolism is the immediacy of the presence of God. The reference to the covenant "that *I* had made" (v. 10) shows the immediacy of the divine presence in the prophet's consciousness, for he can move easily from his words to

the prophet in verse 10, there is no reason to apply this construction exclusively to the Lord. מֵעֲלֵיהֶם (by them; lit., from upon them): This compound preposition never means the simple instrumental "by," but connotes removal from. It is difficult to reflect this sense in English, and so the word *by* in my translation. We are warranted, however, in seeing a sense of release in this form (e.g., 1 Sam. 6:20). Taking the verb and

its compound preposition together, the expression *they paid off* approximates the construction here. אֹתוֹ (it) is singular, probably viewing the coins as the wage he received. בֵּית יְהוָה (toward the house of the Lord): Lacking a preposition, this construction comprises an adverbial accusative. The accompanying verb and object determine the sense that a preposition would normally provide (see the Exposition).

---

those of Yahweh. The afflicted of the land perceived God's word in the prophet's symbolic activity. The words *the Lord said to me* (vv. 13, 15) reflect an intimacy that the formulas *thus says the Lord God* or *the word of the Lord came to me* do not. The words *I am valued* may refer to God as well as the prophet (see the Exegesis).

There is another level, however: the reality the symbols portray. This symbolism intersects with several historical occurrences. The land was despoiled (v. 3) in the invasions of Antiochus and of Titus, and the slaughter that occurred during the Roman siege gives profound significance to the slaughtering in verses 4–5. The people fell into each other's hands (vv. 6, 9) and became subject to a foreign king (v. 6). God's protection of the nation from invaders then ceased, recalling the words of verse 10.

We have not yet inquired about the significance of the principal symbol in this activity, namely, the prophet himself, who took the role of a shepherd. The interplay between the two shepherds in this discourse—the one who figures in verses 4–13 and the wicked shepherd of verses 15–16—influences us to think of the former as a good shepherd. When we look for a shepherd-leader whom the nation's rulers rejected for thirty pieces of silver at a time when the nation fell into foreign hands, the New Testament stands insistently before us, urging us to look at Christ, the Good Shepherd (John 10:11), who was betrayed for thirty pieces of silver (Matt. 26:15; 27:3, 9). Only forty years after his rejection by the civil and religious leaders of his time, the cruel events of A.D. 70 occurred. The land became despoiled, and the metaphorical timbers fell (v. 2).

XIV. The Good Shepherd (11:1–14)

F. Significance of the Staff, the Bonds (11:14)

McCOMISKEY

[14]Then I cut up my second staff, the Bonds, to break the brotherhood between Judah and Israel.

NRSV

[14]Then I broke my second staff Unity, annulling the family ties between Judah and Israel.

14. וָאֶגְדַּע (then I cut up): See the Exegesis of verse 10. הַחֹבְלִים (the Bonds) has the article here, perhaps reflecting more of a direct reference to its significance than merely being a name: the brotherhood existing between Judah and Israel (see the Exegesis of verse 7). לְהָפֵר (to break): See the Exegesis of verse 10. הָאַחֲוָה (the brotherhood): Occurring only here, this word (related to אָח, brother) conveys a brotherly relationship, which the text observes was broken.

---

14. The prophet cut his other staff, "Bonds." This act symbolized the end of a brotherly relationship between Israel and Judah. There is little evidence of brotherhood between these kingdoms. Deep-seated antipathies and even hostilities continued until the demise of the northern kingdom. Nevertheless, since the eventual union of the two kingdoms was a prophetic ideal (Ezek. 37:16–23; Zech. 10:6), we must inquire into the significance of the breaking of the second staff in this context.

The breaking of the first staff portended invasion by hostile powers. It does not, however, adequately explain everything that was in store for the nation, for the context foresees not only the hostility of foreign powers, but also the horrible prospect of the people turning one against another (v. 6), which the context cites just before the taking of the two staffs (v. 7). The severing of the staff "Bonds" would permit this other aspect of the context to become an awful reality.

XV. The Foolish Shepherd (11:15–17)
A. The Foolish Shepherd's Neglecting the People (11:15–16)

McCOMISKEY

[15]Then the LORD said to me, Take yet the implements of a foolish shepherd, [16]for look, I am raising up a shepherd in the land. He will not attend the perishing nor search for the lost nor heal what is broken. What is standing he will not provide for, and the flesh of the fat he will eat and tear off their hooves.

NRSV

[15]Then the LORD said to me: Take once more the implements of a worthless shepherd. [16]For I am now raising up in the land a shepherd who does not care for the perishing, or seek the wandering, or heal the maimed, or nourish the healthy, but devours the flesh of the fat ones, tearing off even their hoofs.

15. עוֹד (yet) signals continuance. It may occupy several positions in a clause (see the Exegesis of Hos. 3:1): at the end of a *wayyqtl* clause (as in Gen. 46:29) or in the clause-initial position (1 Kings 22:44 [43] and esp. Zech. 1:17). If the former here, it yields "the LORD said to me again"; if the latter, then "take yet the implements" is the translation. The former option is unlikely because the writer could have stated that concept unequivocally by placing עוֹד after וַיֹּאמֶר (then said), as in Exodus 3:15. The avoidance of that option favors the placement of עוֹד at the beginning of the second clause. "Again" is too narrow for עוֹד in the second clause, for it implies that the prophet had taken the implements of a foolish shepherd on a previous occasion. This particle is, however, frequently translated "yet" (see the Exegesis of 8:4, 20; and Hos. 1:4; Jon. 3:4; Mic. 6:10; Hab. 2:3). He was yet to take the implements of another shepherd, in this case, a foolish one. כְּלִי (implements) is a broad term, answering sometimes to "things"; it may refer to weapons (Jer. 21:4), vessels (Ezek. 4:9), or musical instruments (Amos 6:5). We do not know what the prophet's implements were. Perhaps they were cudgels for killing wild animals. אֱוִלִי (wicked): The Wisdom Literature frequently gives the root אול (to be foolish) a moral connotation, describing someone who is outside the sphere of godly wisdom. Zechariah's context emphasizes the sense of "foolish," for the shepherd it describes is so senseless as to neglect his flock and even forsake the sheep that have wandered off. The meaning "wicked" may, however, be lurking in the word as well because the neglect of the nation by this unwise leader can only bring evil on the land. In this way, the foolish shepherd is like Israel's leaders, whom verse 5 describes as neglectful shepherds.

16. כִּי (for) gives the reason for the command to take up other implements: because another shepherd comes into the picture. הַנִּכְחָדוֹת (the perishing): This verb appears in verse 8 in the piel as "to make to hide," that is, "to get rid of." Here, the niphal form means "to be hidden, efface, annihilate" (BDB, p. 470). לֹא־יִפְקֹד (he will not attend): The primary sense of פָּקַד is not "to tend" but "to give attention to" (McComiskey, "Prophetic Irony," p. 95; see also the Exegesis of 10:3). הַנַּעַר (the lost) cannot mean "youth," for the word never refers to the young of animals, but always to humans. Another root, נער (to shake), means "to scatter or shake off" (Neh. 5:13; Isa. 33:9, 15). The noun may thus have the sense of scattering, referring to sheep that wild animals may have scattered. While we cannot be sure of either the integrity of this form or its connotation, it must be appropriate to the verbal action of בָּקַשׁ (to seek), as is the word "lost" in my translation. וְהַנִּשְׁבֶּרֶת (what is broken), from שָׁבַר (to shatter), refers to injured sheep with broken limbs. הַנִּצָּבָה (what is standing) is in opposition to וְהַנִּשְׁבֶּרֶת and refers to the sheep that are standing, that is, the uninjured sheep. Even these he neglects. Neither sense of יְכַלְכֵּל, "to contain" (1 Kings 8:27) or "to provide for" (Gen. 45:11; 2 Sam. 19:33), occurs with reference to sheep. If it has the former sense here, the foolish shepherd does not guard his flock, but allows them to wander. If it has the latter sense, then this shepherd does not provide the sheep with food. The context favors the sense of providing for the sheep because the clauses that describe this foolish shepherd's neglect of the flock otherwise include no reference to feeding them, an unusual omission. If the word connotes containing the flock, preventing them from wandering off, it would more appropriately follow the clause stating that he will not seek the lost, and would be connected to it by ו (and).

15–16. The prophet felt impelled to take the part of another shepherd who stands over against the good shepherd in this discourse. This is an unwise shepherd who does not care for his flock. That Yahweh raises up this shepherd "in the land" is significant in view of the earlier description of the successful invasion of the land in verse 6. It is impossible to place this section historically, but viewed against the events of A.D. 70 we find a figure consonant with the description here—the emperor Titus, who violated the principles of benign authority in allowing his forces to treat the inhabitants of the land with intense cruelty, and beyond him all the emperors and officials of Rome who imposed their will on the people of the land.

XV. The Foolish Shepherd (11:15–17)
B. Imprecation against the Foolish Shepherd (11:17)

McCOMISKEY

17Woe to the worthless shepherd who forsakes the flock. A sword on his arm and on his right eye! His arm shall become useless, and his right eye shall become sightless.

NRSV

17 Oh, my worthless shepherd,
   who deserts the flock!
May the sword strike his arm
   and his right eye!
Let his arm be completely withered,
   his right eye utterly blinded!

17. הוֹי (woe): See the Exegesis of 1:10 [6]. This interjection does not convey a single conceptual idea, but receives its force from the context. Originally it was probably a shout or expression of lament. Because punishment awaits the foolish shepherd, "woe" is an appropriate equivalent. הָאֱלִיל (worthless): The derivation of this word is uncertain. On several occasions, it clearly conveys the idea of worthless (Job 13:4; Jer. 14:14). On all other occasions it refers to idols, probably as worthless objects of worship. Here, then, is a shepherd who is incapable of leading the flock. חֶרֶב עַל־זְרוֹעוֹ (a sword on his arm): This verbless clause may be either an assertion, "A sword [will be] on his arm," or a precative expressing a wish (as my translation construes it) (GKC §141f). Since הוֹי-clauses do not merely wish misfortune but pronounce it, we may regard the impending judgment on this shepherd as real in any case. זְרֹעוֹ יָבוֹשׁ תִּיבָשׁ (his arm shall become useless): Since this clause does not begin with ו (and) affixed either to זְרֹעוֹ (his arm) or to the verb יָבוֹשׁ (become useless), we cannot understand its assertion as a direct consequence of the preceding verbless clause (as in Jer. 50:36a). Rather, this clause comprises an independent thought reasserting the reality of the threat against this shepherd (see my translation).

---

17. The prophet pronounces woe on this worthless shepherd who harms the flock. The imprecation is directed against both arm and eye: the arm, because this foolish shepherd does not "attend" the sheep, reaching out to heal "what is broken" or "providing for" the well sheep (v. 16), and the eye, because he does not "search for the lost" (v. 16). The parts of the body symbolizing this shepherd's neglect are themselves struck. If the prophecy of verses 15–17 envisions the Roman Empire embodied in its emperors, this imprecation portends the fall of the empire. It is as though its arm became useless and its eye sightless, as Roman emperors attempted vainly to hold the far-flung empire together and tame its conquered tribes. Blind to the needs of its masses, the empire at last succumbed to internal decay. The early church— the kingdom of the lowly Messiah—replaced Roman ideals in many minds, and with the decline of Rome established a foothold in a hostile world.

XVI. Second Oracle: The Destiny of the People of God (12:1–14:21)

A. God's Making Judah and Jerusalem Impregnable (12:1–9)

McCOMISKEY

12 The word of the LORD concerning Israel. The utterance of the LORD who stretches out the heavens and lays the foundation of the earth and fashions the spirit of a person within him or her. ²Look! I am making Jerusalem a bowl of staggering for all the nations round about. And this will also be [so] concerning Judah in the siege against Jerusalem. ³And it will be in that day that I will make Jerusalem a heavy rock for all the nations; all who lift it will be severely lacerated, though all the peoples of the earth should gather against it. ⁴In that day, utterance of the LORD, I will strike every horse with confusion and their riders with madness. But on the house of Judah I shall open my eyes, and every horse of the nations I will strike with blindness. ⁵And the leaders of Judah will say in their hearts, "The inhabitants of Jerusalem are my strength in the LORD of hosts their God." ⁶In that day I shall make the leaders of Judah like a firepot on a pile of wood and like a flaming torch on sheaves, and they will consume all the surrounding nations to the right and to the left, and Jerusalem will continue to dwell on its site at Jerusalem. ⁷And the LORD will deliver the tents of Judah first, so that the glory of the house of David and the glory of the inhabitants of Jerusalem may not supersede [that of] Judah. ⁸In that day, the LORD will protect the inhabitants of Jerusalem, and the one among them who stumbles in that day will be as David, and the house of David as God—as the angel of the LORD before them. ⁹And it will be in that day that I shall seek to destroy all the nations that come against Jerusalem.

NRSV

12 An Oracle.

The word of the LORD concerning Israel: Thus says the LORD, who stretched out the heavens and founded the earth and formed the human spirit within: ²See, I am about to make Jerusalem a cup of reeling for all the surrounding peoples; it will be against Judah also in the siege against Jerusalem. ³On that day I will make Jerusalem a heavy stone for all the peoples; all who lift it shall grievously hurt themselves. And all the nations of the earth shall come together against it. ⁴On that day, says the LORD, I will strike every horse with panic, and its rider with madness. But on the house of Judah I will keep a watchful eye, when I strike every horse of the peoples with blindness. ⁵Then the clans of Judah shall say to themselves, "The inhabitants of Jerusalem have strength through the LORD of hosts, their God."

⁶On that day I will make the clans of Judah like a blazing pot on a pile of wood, like a flaming torch among sheaves; and they shall devour to the right and to the left all the surrounding peoples, while Jerusalem shall again be inhabited in its place, in Jerusalem.

⁷And the LORD will give victory to the tents of Judah first, that the glory of the house of David and the glory of the inhabitants of Jerusalem may not be exalted over that of Judah. ⁸On that day the LORD will shield the inhabitants of Jerusalem so that the feeblest among them on that day shall be like David, and the house of David shall be like God, like the angel of the LORD, at their head. ⁹And on that day I will seek to destroy all the nations that come against Jerusalem.

12:1. מַשָּׂא (an oracle): See the Exegesis of 9:1. דְּבַר־יְהוָה עַל־יִשְׂרָאֵל (the word of the LORD concerning Israel): Since the content of the oracle introduced by this clause is positive regarding Israel, we must translate עַל "concerning," not "against" as in 9:1. נְאֻם־יְהוָה (utterance of the LORD): See the Exegesis of 1:3. Occurring elsewhere in Zechariah unpredicated, it must have נֹטֶה (who stretches out) as its predicate, for no other reconstruction is possible. רוּחַ־אָדָם (the spirit of man): The association of רוּחַ (spirit) with the creation formula, "who stretches out the heavens" (as in Isa. 42:5), gives it the sense of the life principle (the animus). The context does not warrant our understanding the word to have the directive force it has elsewhere (see the Exposition of 4:6 and 6:8).

2. הִנֵּה (Look!) draws our attention to the assertion it introduces, as in its other occurrences in this book. סַף־רַעַל (a bowl of staggering): The only context that clearly defines סַף is Exodus 12:22, where it is a bowl into which one could dip hyssop (see Honeyman, "Hebrew סַף"). וְגַם (and also): See the Exegesis of 8:6. עַל (concerning) cannot mean "against" here, because verse 4 tells us that God will protect Judah (see the subsequent discussion). יִהְיֶה (will be): We must posit a subject for this verb that will reflect the sense of addition (also, moreover) in the construction וְגַם that begins this clause, as well as the function of עַל. The simplest solution is to regard וְגַם as imparting a sense of reiteration to עַל in verse 1: as the word concerns Israel there, here in verse 2 it also (וְגַם) concerns Judah. This view requires דְּבַר־יְהוָה (the word of LORD) in verse 1 to be the subject of יִהְיֶה (will be). בְּמָצוֹר (in the siege): See the Exegesis of 9:3.

3. בַּיּוֹם־הַהוּא (in that day) always refers back to a previously mentioned or implied period of time (see the Exegesis of 3:10). The reference is to the time of siege mentioned in verse 2. מַעֲמָסָה describes a stone (אֶבֶן) that is difficult to lift. שָׂרוֹט יִשָּׂרְטוּ (will

---

12:1. The previous chapter left us with questions concerning Israel's future. The breaking of the staff "Favor" opened the way for hostile powers to invade the land (v. 10) and for the nation to fall into the hands of an uncaring shepherd (v. 16). The oppressive regime of this shepherd will come to an end, but we do not know of Israel's destiny. Have the prophet's people suffered final rejection by their God? Does historic Jerusalem give way to the heavenly Jerusalem? If Zechariah's book ended at 11:17 there would be a void of uncertainty as to the nation's future and the fealty of God to his promises. The subsequent chapters round out the message of the book, bringing it to a triumphant conclusion.

Chapter 11 recounts events that relate specifically to historical Israel, and we expect the material now before us to resolve our uncertainties as to the nation's future. We have found, however, that sections of this book adumbrate the church, and that is true here as well (see the Exposition of 13:9).

Verse 1 introduces another *maśśā'* (oracle), which we expect to announce hope for Israel while proclaiming judgment on the nations (see the Exposition of 9:1). The "word" (*dābār*) this oracle announces is from Yahweh, who stretches out the heavens and founds the earth. This description of the creation of the physical universe imparts a sense of great power to the name *Yahweh* and assures us that he can perform what this oracle envisions.

The text reminds us that God created humankind. This is important to the flow of the discourse because the events it describes take place in the human arena, and the observation that God imparts life to human beings signifies that because they came from his hand he controls their activities. The oracle thus begins with a sense of Yahweh's invincible power over his created realm.

2. That Jerusalem becomes a "bowl of staggering" to the surrounding nations has its explanation in the words *in the siege*. When besieged by her adversaries, Jerusalem will become like a vessel containing an intoxicant: the hostile nations that drink from Jerusalem will reel back like drunken people and be unable to take the city. This oracle begins by affirming the future impregnability of Jerusalem. The clause *and this will also be concerning Judah* appears almost as an afterthought, as though the writer must explain that because God will make Jerusalem impregnable he must do the same for the region of which it is the capital. This construction thus applies the hypothetical siege to both Jerusalem and the province of Judah.

3. Another metaphor describes Jerusalem's impregnability: God will make the city like a heavy rock. The function of the last clause in this verse ("though all the peoples of the earth gather against her") is difficult to determine. The clause-initial perfective with *waw (wĕne'espû)* may be an affirmation that all the peoples of the earth will

be severely lacerated): The verbal form of the root occurs elsewhere only in Leviticus 21:5 in a context referring to shaving or cutting parts of the body. וּבִבְשָׂרָם (and in their flesh) gives the verb the sense of scratching or lacerating the skin. The infinitive absolute with the finite verb strengthens the verbal idea ("*severely* lacerated"). וְנֶאֶסְפוּ (though gather): The perfective with ו fills the role of the concessive ("though") in enough places in the Old Testament to establish its validity here (e.g., Lev. 5:2, 17 [neg.]; Hos. 7:10). גּוֹיֵי (the peoples of): It is sometimes difficult to differentiate this word from עַמִּים (nations), but its association with אֶרֶץ (earth) makes it clear that it connotes distant nations (see the Exposition).

4. בַּיּוֹם הַהוּא (in that day) continues the references to the time of Jerusalem's impregnability. נְאֻם־יְהוָה (utterance of the LORD): See the Exegesis of 1:3. בַּתִּמָּהוֹן (with confusion) occurs elsewhere only in Deuteronomy 28:28 (also with נָכָה, to strike) to express a condition of the mind that the following verse expands further as bewilderment. בַּשִּׁגָּעוֹן (with madness) occurs also in Deuteronomy 28:28. The connection of this word with the root שָׁגַע (to be mad) leaves no doubt as to its nuance here. וְעַל־בֵּית יְהוּדָה (but on the house of Judah): ו

calls for an adversative sense because the clause it introduces expresses a benign attitude on the part of God as opposed to the negative attitude in the previous clause. The expression אֶפְקַח אֶת־עֵינַי (I shall open my eyes) conveys the sense of being aware of (Jer. 32:19) or giving attention to (2 Kings 19:16; Isa. 37:17; Dan. 9:18). בַּעִוָּרוֹן (with blindness): Occurring also in Deuteronomy 28:28, the word connotes blindness.

5. וְאָמְרוּ . . . בְּלִבָּם (and will say in their hearts): To "say in the heart" goes beyond mere proclamation or affirmation (for which אָמַר [to say] alone would suffice) to the forces of reason and emotion that control the processes of thought. This expression connotes reasoning to a conclusion (Deut. 7:17; 8:17; 9:4; 18:21; Isa. 47:8, 10; Hos. 7:2; Zeph. 1:12; 2:15). אַמְצָה (strength) is not attested elsewhere. The Masoretic tradition represents it as a feminine noun of אָמֵץ (to be strong), while the Septuagint appears to relate it to מָצָא (to find), resulting in an awkward reading: "We shall find for ourselves the inhabitants of Jerusalem in the Lord Almighty their God." The form here is consonant with the feminine noun pattern, and we may not reject a reading on the basis of its infrequent occurrence. בַּיהוָה צְבָאוֹת (in the LORD of

come against Jerusalem. This assertion, however, is contrary to verses 2 and 6, which establish a line of thought that limits the hypothetical attack to the surrounding nations (*ʿammîm*). The transition from *ʿammîm* to *gôyim* (peoples) at the end of this verse does not favor the identification of these peoples of the earth with the attacking nations, as the continued use of *ʿammîm* would have done. This departure from the line of thought that establishes the "surrounding nations" as the attackers to the use of the more expansive "peoples of earth" favors a hypothetical idea compatible with a concessive ("though all the peoples of earth should gather"). Hebrew grammar allows the perfective with *waw* to indicate the concessive (e.g., Lev. 5:2; see the Exegesis). On this basis the sense of the clause is that even if all the peoples of the earth should attempt to conquer Jerusalem, they will turn away, bloodied by their futile efforts.

4–5. The metaphors of Jerusalem's impregnability continue with a reference to the attacking horses and riders. It is a picture of mass confusion, with the horses shying in terror, their riders unable to carry the battle to success because they are confused like madmen. As Yahweh fights on behalf of his people, he does not strike about

indiscriminately, for he "opens his eyes" on the house of Judah, protecting them in this onslaught.

The perspective changes in verse 5 from the battle raging outside Jerusalem to the situation within it. Observing the conquest of their foes at the hand of their Divine Warrior, the leaders of Judah give praise to the inhabitants of Jerusalem for the support they have imparted to them. We nowhere read that these inhabitants of the city engage in the battle; only the leaders do so (v. 6). The support is evidently united moral support, a situation different from the attitude of many of the people of Zechariah's time toward their leaders (11:11). The strength they give is not apart from God, but in the sphere of Yahweh of hosts. It is not without Yahweh's sovereign intervention in the siege that the people unite in support of their leaders.

The leaders of Judah do not merely acknowledge this support, but affirm it "in their hearts." It is a reasoned conclusion based on evident circumstances. There may be an element of emotion in the expression as well, such as gratitude to the inhabitants of Jerusalem and praise to God. The absence of *bayyôm hahû* (in that day) at the head of this verse indicates that its thought is an extension of that of verse 4.

hosts): See the Exegesis of 1:3. The preposition בְּ (in) channels the concept of strength to the sphere of the divine name and all that this name entails.

6. בַּיּוֹם הַהוּא (in that day) introduces a new aspect of the depiction here (see the Exposition of v. 5). אַלֻּפֵי יְהוּדָה (the leaders of Judah): See the Exegesis of verse 5. כְּכִיּוֹר (like a fire pot): Unaccompanied by אֵשׁ (fire), a כִּיּוֹר is a pot or basin, even a laver (e.g., Exod. 30:18; 1 Kings 7:30). When associated with אֵשׁ, it is probably a container for carrying burning material, perhaps to ignite a fire. וּכְלַפִּיד (and like a torch): Denoting a torch, the addition of אֵשׁ intensifies its force in the context (Gen. 15:17). וְיָשְׁבָה . . . עוֹד (and will continue to dwell): This perfective with ו, along with the previous perfective with ו (וְאָכְלוּ), expresses consequence, each introducing a result of the imperfective אָשִׂים (I shall make) at the head of this verse. וְיָשְׁבָה (and will dwell) does not have the sense of being inhabited, as it does in 2:8 [4], for the accompanying form תַּחְתֶּיהָ (on its site) views Jerusalem corporately as a population center, rather than as a group of inhabitants. יָשַׁב means "to be

situated" (as in Nah. 3:8). תַּחַת indicates the locale of a community (Deut. 2:22; Isa. 25:10) and functions as an adverbial accusative ("on its site"). עוֹד cannot mean "again," because nothing in the context signals a hiatus in Jerusalem's existence.

7. וְהוֹשִׁיעַ (and will deliver) does not have a soteriological sense in Zechariah, but always connotes deliverance from foes (8:7, 13; 9:9, 16; 10:6). The flow of the discourse, with its emphasis on military action (vv. 1–6), is compatible with this sense of the word here. לְמַעַן (so that) frequently signals the purpose inherent in a preceding action. תִּפְאֶרֶת (the glory of): Both beauty and glory mingle in this word. Since the intent of the verb וְהוֹשִׁיעַ has nothing to do with beauty, the sense of תִּפְאֶרֶת is glory. בֵּית־דָּוִיד (the house of David): See the Exposition.

8. בַּיּוֹם הַהוּא (in that day): See the Exegesis of verse 3. יָגֵן . . . בְּעַד (will protect): See the Exegesis of 9:15. יָגֵן appears there in collocation with עַל, not בְּעַד (as here), but with no discernible difference in meaning. הַנִּכְשָׁל (who stumbles): When the niphal occurs in contexts referring to physi-

---

6. The words *in that day* resume the references to the time of Jerusalem's impregnability. In that time, Israel's leaders will contribute to her defense. They will be like flames that touch off a fire in a woodpile or in dry sheaves, and the conflagration will consume their foes. This metaphor describes the ease with which they will exercise their military power. Because of this commingling of divine sovereignty and human effort, Jerusalem will continue to exist as a political entity. The two references to Jerusalem at the end of this verse state that the city known as Jerusalem will continue to exist on the site it occupies, an existence that is also affirmed in Daniel 9:26 (see the Exposition of 14:1).

7. The phrase *house of David* has several connotations in the Old Testament: the reigning Davidic king (Isa. 7:2, 13), the Davidic dynasty (1 Kings 12:19–20, 26; 13:2; 14:8; 2 Kings 17:21; 1 Chron. 17:24, 27; Ps. 122:5), and David's household (Isa. 22:22) and family (2 Sam. 3:1, 6). Little in this discourse resonates with any of these connotations, but we may observe a pattern in the discourse centering around the term *inhabitants of Jerusalem*. In verse 5, this term occurs in connection with "leaders of Judah," but here and in verse 10 "house of David" accompanies this term. It appears that at this point in the discourse "house of David" has replaced "leaders of Judah" as a descriptive term for Judah's leaders, becoming

another designation for them. The expression would thus be a metonomy for Israel's leaders, idealizing them in Davidic trappings. Several prophets idealize future persons and events in a similar fashion (Isa. 9:6 [7]; Jer. 17:25; Ezek. 34:23–24; Amos 9:11–12). Jeremiah's reference is particularly relevant here, for he couches the prospect of benign leadership for God's people in Davidic terminology. The reference to the house of David envisions Israel's future leadership in terms of a restoration of the Davidic monarchy.

In this metaphorical warfare, Yahweh acts first on behalf of Judah so that the family of David and the citizens of Jerusalem will not have the greater glory. This discourse already reflects a studied effort to establish Judah's equality with its capital city (vv. 2, 5). It is impossible to determine with certainty the sociological conditions that lie behind this affirmation. Perhaps the people living in the country at this time felt inferior to the citizens of Jerusalem, and the affirmation that Judah, not Jerusalem, will receive Yahweh's attention first establishes the equality of all whom Yahweh comes to deliver.

8–9. The discourse now turns to the inhabitants of Jerusalem and affirms their protection. In highly metaphorical language, the text depicts the strength the people will possess when Yahweh comes to their aid. Once again Zechariah intertwines divine sovereignty and human agency. The

cal strength, it connotes the antithesis of strength (1 Sam. 2:4; Isa. 40:30): feebleness. Since David appears in this verse as a metaphor of strength, we may understand this participle to indicate physical weakness. כֵּאלֹהִים (as God): See the Exegesis of 8:8. כְּמַלְאַךְ יְהוָה (as the angel of the LORD): See the Exposition of 1:11.

9. בַּיּוֹם הַהוּא (in that day): See the Exegesis of verse 3. אֲבַקֵּשׁ לְהַשְׁמִיד (I shall seek to destroy): See the Exegesis of 6:7.

---

reference to David recalls his numerous military successes and the stability he brought to the kingdom he governed. Viewed from the perspective of the returned exiles, Jerusalem was impregnable in David's time, and Zechariah affirms the renewal of that condition. Even the weakest of Jerusalem's inhabitants will be as mighty as David. Then, referring to the leaders of the people ("the house of David"), the text states that they will be like God; they will govern with supernatural strength and discernment. The appositional statement *the angel of the LORD before them* recalls references to the angel who went before the people and prepared the way to the land of promise (Exod. 23:20, 23; 32:34; 33:2). By elevating the strength of Judah's leaders to the level of divine activity, the writer underscores by bold metaphor how great will be Jerusalem's impregnability. Verse 9 concludes the long affirmation of this impregnability in an expansive summary statement.

XVI. Second Oracle: The Destiny of the People of God (12:1–14:21)

B. The People's Intense Mourning for One They Have Pierced (12:10–14)

McCOMISKEY

¹⁰And I will pour out on the house of David and on the inhabitants of Jerusalem a spirit of grace and supplications, and they will look upon me, the one they pierced, and mourn for him like the mourning for an only child, and be in bitterness for him as bitterness for a firstborn.

¹¹In that day the mourning in Jerusalem will be great, as the mourning of Hadad-rimmon in the valley of Megiddo, ¹²and the land will mourn, family by family alone: the family of the house of David alone and their wives alone, the family of the house of Nathan alone and their wives alone, ¹³the family of the house of Levi alone and their wives alone, the family of the Shimeite alone and their wives alone. ¹⁴All the other families, family by family alone, and their wives alone.

NRSV

¹⁰And I will pour out a spirit of compassion and supplication on the house of David and the inhabitants of Jerusalem, so that, when they look on the one whom they have pierced, they shall mourn for him, as one mourns for an only child, and weep bitterly over him, as one weeps over a firstborn. ¹¹On that day the mourning in Jerusalem will be as great as the mourning for Hadad-rimmon in the plain of Megiddo. ¹²The land shall mourn, each family by itself; the family of house of David by itself, and their wives by themselves; the family of the house of Nathan by itself, and their wives by themselves; ¹³the family of the house of Levi by itself, and their wives by themselves; the family of the Shimeites by itself, and their wives by themselves; ¹⁴and all the families that are left, each by itself, and their wives by themselves.

10. עַל שָׁפַכְתִּי (and I will pour out on): שָׁפַךְ may have a metaphorical sense of pouring out fury (Hos. 5:10) and hatred (Job 12:21) or refer to the diffusion of God's Spirit (Ezek. 39:29; Joel 3:1–2 [2:28–29]). דָּוִיד בֵּית (the house of David): See the Exposition of verse 7. רוּחַ (a spirit of): See the Exposition. חֵן (grace): See the Exegesis of 4:7 and Ap-Thomas, "Root *hnn*". וְתַחֲנוּנִים (and supplications) always connotes earnest entreaty for some favor (e.g., Ps. 28:2). The collocation אֵלַי וְהִבִּיטוּ ("to look at") has several nuances: to look for support (Isa. 22:11), to give attention (Isa. 66:2), or to look at approvingly (Hab. 1:13). אֵלַי (unto me): The suffix on this preposition finds its logical referent in the first-person constructions that began at verse 9, which can refer only to Yahweh. It is inconceivable that anyone other than he can destroy all of Jerusalem's enemies. The Septuagint reflects the reading of the Masoretic Text: καὶ ἐπιβλέψονται πρός με (and they will look upon me). There is no significant textual witness to another reading of the consonantal text (see the Exposition). אֲשֶׁר אֵת (the one): אֲשֶׁר alone can function as an object, but the addition of אֵת particularizes it, yielding "him whom" or "the one whom" (see the Exegesis of 7:7). דָּקָרוּ (they pierced): The qal stem always con-

notes killing or wounding by piercing with some kind of instrument: a sword (Judg. 9:54; 1 Sam. 31:4; 1 Chron. 10:4) or a spear (Num. 25:8). The Septuagint translates the phrase ἀνθ᾽ ὧν κατωρχήσαντο ("because they treated him despitefully," "or because they mocked him"). It is difficult to reconstruct the Septuagint's *Vorlage*, but the translator(s) likely read דקר (to pierce) as רקד (to skip or dance). Since the word κατορχέομαι can mean "to dance in triumph over one, treat despitefully," it is likely that the Septuagint translation conveys the sense of treating with despite or mocking. While it is permissible to understand אֲשֶׁר as a causative particle, the Septuagint's translation is suspect because it construes κατωρχήσαντο without an object, a grammatical condition appropriate to the reading of the Masoretic Text (whom they pierced), but creating a somewhat awkward Greek rendering. The Septuagint thus witnesses to the unsuffixed verb in the Masoretic Text. Since the Masoretic Text represents a valid Hebrew construction and the Septuagint does not appear to be a comfortable rendering of the Hebrew text, the Masoretic Text is superior in this verse. וְסָפְדוּ (and mourn for him) refers always to mourning for the dead (Gen. 23:2).

---

10. The Lord's activity on behalf of Judah and Jerusalem will not occur apart from their spiritual renewal. In a sovereign act of grace, the Lord will infuse the inhabitants of Jerusalem and their leaders with "a spirit of grace and supplications." The word *rûaḥ* is not marked by references to God as it is in 4:6, 6:8, and 7:12, so we must be cautious about identifying it in this context with God's Spirit. The effusion of spirit described here effects an awakening in the human psyche, prompting the people to look to God in supplication and heartfelt sorrow.

Rûaḥ can designate the psyche, particularly that aspect of the mind that is directive (see the Exposition of 4:6). By infusing the inhabitants of Jerusalem and their leaders with a spirit of grace, the *rûaḥ* creates within them a comprehension of God's grace, as in 4:6–7, where the people realize that they will complete the temple by divine grace, not by their efforts alone. Awakened to the fact that it is God who aids them in their struggle, the inhabitants of Jerusalem respond with supplications to him. They have a new spirit, prompting them to a heart response to God (see Ezek. 36:26). We do not know for what favor they so earnestly entreat God, but the immediate reference to their

sorrow points to their seeking his forgiveness for the piercing the text describes.

The juxtaposition of the pronouns in the phrases *look upon me* and *mourn for him* have firm textual attestation. The text represents Yahweh as the speaker, for no linguistic signal or discourse indicator intervenes to alter the subject. It thus confronts us with a startling affirmation: it is not the hostile nations that have pierced Yahweh, but "the house of David and the inhabitants of Jerusalem." It is unlikely that this piercing is metaphorical, referring to God's anguish over the sin of his people, because in all its occurrences the verb *dāqar* (to pierce) has a concrete sense, referring to actual piercing, usually by a sword. This implicit reference to a sword strongly implies the death of this individual, as does the sword motif in 13:7 (see the Exposition there). That the figure of 13:7 is a shepherd makes it a virtual certainty that the figure there and here in 12:7 is the shepherd of 11:4–14, for if he were not, the figure the prophet portrays in chapter 11 would remain vague, with no apparent connection to the flow of the discourse.

The close association between Yahweh and the angel of the Lord (see the Exposition of 2:15 [11]) raises the possibility that the figure of this

or to misfortune that is anticipated (Jer. 4:8) or experienced (Jer. 49:3). כְּמִסְפֵּד (like the mourning): The noun מִסְפֵּד carries the same general connotations as its verbal counterpart. עָלָיו (for him): The third-person masculine suffix on this preposition is curious in view of the previous first-person suffix on אֵלַי (upon me), but no significant manuscript evidence contests its integrity. וְהָמֵר עָלָיו (and be in bitterness for him): In its other occurrences in the hiphil, this verb has the sense of embitter (Ruth 1:20; Job 27:2), but that sense is inappropriate to this context. The preposition עַל must carry the meaning "for." This infinitive with ו represents a situation subordinate to the leading verb (*IBHS*, p. 596), though coordinate with it. Thus being in bitterness is a component of וְסָפְדוּ (and mourn).

11. בַּיּוֹם הַהוּא (in that day): See the Exegesis of verse 3. הַמִּסְפֵּד (the mourning): See the Exegesis of verse 10. הֲדַד־רִמּוֹן (Hadad-rimmon): See the Exposition.

---

verse is that angel. This is unlikely, however, because of the striking consonance between the figure here and the redemptive figure of 3:8–10 called the Branch. The angel of the Lord stands apart from the Branch in 3:8–10, envisioning his future appearance with no hint that the angel and the Branch are identical. It is difficult to understand how the nation could have pierced this angel, for there is no hint of his rejection by them and the shepherd of chapter 11, who suffers rejection, stands before us as a person, not an angelic figure. Zechariah 12:10 thus affirms that God is not a stranger to suffering, but knows it from experience. The mystery this verse creates is almost incomprehensible, for it tells us that God brings redemption to his people by entering into the experience of human suffering. The New Testament also affirms that God is not a stranger to suffering, because in the mystery of the incarnation he lived a human life, knowing even death on a cross. That the suffering described in this verse strikes one who is close to God (note the juxtaposition of pronouns) reminds us of the Servant of the Lord's being pierced (Isa. 53:5) and suffering death on behalf of his people (Isa. 53:8).

The New Testament refers to Zechariah 12:10 twice. John 19:37 applies the piercing of this verse to the piercing of Jesus' side by Roman soldiers, and Revelation 1:7 also alludes to this event: "Every eye will see him, even those who pierced him." The New Testament thus penetrates the obscure corners of this verse with light from the cross.

The sovereign activity of God within their hearts will impel Jerusalem's inhabitants to look to this pierced figure in sorrow. That the mourning of this verse is not hopeless anguish over their rejection of him, but heartfelt repentance, is clear from the resultant cleansing from sin that the discourse goes on to describe (13:1–6).

11. The litany of references to "that day," the time of Jerusalem's impregnability, continues with a description of the mourning to which verse 10 refers. The identity of Hadad-rimmon is not known. We can be certain only that it is a linguistic function in the text that underscores the intensity of the mourning for the pierced figure of verse 10. The name *Hadad-rimmon* may be a compound of West Semitic *Hadad* (an alternate name in the Ras Shamra texts for Baal, the fertility god) and Akkadian *Ramman* (the storm god). Greenfield ("Aramean God") sees this verse as a ritual mourning for this god. If we understand Hadad-rimmon to be a pagan god, it is difficult to grasp why a prophet from postexilic Judah would liken a divinely initiated sorrow to the intensity of pagan ritual, unless it had become a popular metaphor for mourning.

On the other hand, it is possible that Hadad-rimmon is a place-name. The syntax of the clause *kĕmispad hădad-rimmôn* (lit., like the mourning of Hadad-rimmon) may seem to preclude this possibility, requiring the sense of mourning for that deity, but Hosea 1:4 uses a similar construct relationship before a place-name to refer to an event that occurred there: "And I will visit the bloodshed of Jezreel [*dĕmê yizrĕ'e'l*] on the house of Jehu." Jerome identified Hadad-rimmon as Rummane near Jezreel, and a Rimmon once existed in the region of Megiddo. Perhaps the words *in the valley of Megiddo* have the purpose of differentiating this Rimmon from others of the same name (Josh. 15:32; Zech. 14:10). Mourning is associated with Megiddo in 2 Chronicles 35:21–25, where lamentation over the death of the good king Josiah continued up until the editing of the Chronicles. That Josiah died from piercing by arrows may be significant, for the writer may have viewed Josiah as an adumbration of the pierced figure of Zechariah 12:10. Other explanations may be found in the literature (see Baldwin, *Zechariah*, p. 193; and Delcor, "Deux Passage Difficile"), but the view that Hadad-rimmon is a place-name seems most appropriate to the text.

12–14. הָאָרֶץ (the land) can refer to the inhabitants of the land (see Lev. 19:29; 1 Sam. 14:25; Ezek. 14:13; and the Exegesis of Hos. 1:2). מִשְׁפָּחוֹת מִשְׁפָּחוֹת (family by family): This repetition of nouns is distributive, as in Deuteronomy 14:22, where שָׁנָה שָׁנָה connotes "year by year." לְבָד (alone): Joined with בַּד, which connotes separation, the preposition לְ yields "by itself" (compare Exod. 26:9: "curtains by themselves").

12–14. All the people of the land join in this time of mourning, not only the inhabitants of Jerusalem. The family of David and the family of Levi encompass both the royal and the priestly houses. Nathan is not likely the prophet (2 Sam. 7:2), but a son of David (2 Sam. 5:14), because, as Keil notes (*Minor Prophets*, p. 391), the words *mišpaḥat haššimʿî* (the family of the Shimeite) appear in Numbers 3:21 with reference to the grandson of Levi, thus balancing a family progenitor with a descendant. Keil suggests that the reference to the family branches as well as to the main family shows that everyone mourns. The summary reference to all the other families indicates that the writer's purpose is to establish the absolute universality of the mourning he describes.

The discourse thus far describes the formation of a godly remnant energized by the pierced figure of 12:10. We must be cautious about identifying this event or basing unwarranted conclusions on it. We cannot comprehend the full significance of these events, which must forever remain in God's hands (see the Exposition of 13:9). We can be certain that this book establishes a philosophy of history that has its goal in a suffering figure who represents the intrusion of divine redemption into history. The Christian response to this philosophy of history is that Christ is this suffering figure and that his presence in human history enlightens the words of this ancient prophet, giving them meaning and life for subsequent generations. Coming as it does before the events of chapter 14, which I understand to refer primarily to the eternal state, the repentance of the Jewish remnant described in 12:10–14 may occur in the climactic events that precede the new heavens and the new earth (see the Exposition of 14:10).

XVI. Second Oracle: The Destiny of the People of God (12:1–14:21)
C. God's Cleansing His People from Sin (13:1–6)
1. Cleansing Fountain (13:1)

McCOMISKEY

13 In that day a fountain will be opened for the house of David and the inhabitants of Jerusalem for sin and uncleanness.

NRSV

13 On that day a fountain shall be opened for the house of David and the inhabitants of Jerusalem, to cleanse them from sin and impurity.

13:1. בַּיּוֹם הַהוּא (in that day): See the Exegesis of 12:3. מָקוֹר (fountain) is a naturally flowing source of water (Hos. 13:15; see also Lev. 12:7; 20:18; Jer. 8:23 [9:1]). Since this מָקוֹר is opened (נִפְתָּח), we are to think of a spring of water. לְבֵית דָּוִיד (for the house of David): See the Exposition of 12:7. לְחַטָּאת (for sin): The word חַטָּאת is a general word for transgressing God's standards. Since it frequently occurs in the prophets in association with other words for sin, we should not press nuances this context may not allow. וּלְנִדָּה (and for uncleanness): This word occurs in the legal literature primarily with the sense of the ritual uncleanness incurred during menstruation or childbirth (e.g., Lev. 12:2, 5). It is a metaphor for impurity (2 Chron. 29:5; Ezra 9:11).

13:1. Continuing references to "in that day" remind us that we are still in the time when the land will be impregnable and when the people will mourn because of the piercing of the figure of 12:10. The metaphorical fountain of cleansing is thus an element in the complex of events connected by the discourse link "in that day." We cannot divorce this cleansing from the previous events, and we do not stray from the flow of the discourse if we connect the cleansing of this verse with the sorrow over the death of Yahweh's representative in 12:10. Against the background of this metaphor of cleansing, the sorrow of 12:11–14 becomes repentance. Likened to a gushing spring, this divine forgiveness cleanses from sin and uncleanness. Not only are the people and their leaders cleansed of their overt disobedience to God (*ḥaṭṭᵊʾt*), but also of the uncleanness that their disobedience created. When this rushing fountain opens it will cleanse the land of all uncleanness.

XVI. Second Oracle: The Destiny of the People of God (12:1–14:21)
C. God's Cleansing His People from Sin (13:1–6)
  2. God's Purging the Land of Idols and False Prophets (13:2–6)

McCOMISKEY

²And it will be in that day, utterance of the LORD of hosts, that I will cut off the names of the idols from the land, and they will be remembered no longer, and also the prophets and the spirit of uncleanness will I expel from the land. ³And it will be if a man still prophesies, his father and his mother—the ones who begot him—will say, "You shall not live, because you have spoken falsely in the name of the LORD." And his father and mother who begot him will pierce him when he prophesies. ⁴And it will be in that day that the prophets will be ashamed, each of his vision when he prophesies, and they will not put on a hairy cloak in order to lie. ⁵And he will say, "I am not a prophet; I am one who tills the soil, for a man has hired me out from a youth." ⁶And if one says to him, "What are those wounds between your hands?" he will say, "Those I received in the house of my friends."

NRSV

²On that day, says the LORD of hosts, I will cut off the names of the idols from the land, so that they shall be remembered no more; and also I will remove from the land the prophets and the unclean spirit. ³And if any prophets appear again, their fathers and mothers who bore them will say to them, "You shall not live, for you speak lies in the name of the LORD"; and their fathers and their mothers who bore them shall pierce them through when they prophesy. ⁴On that day the prophets will be ashamed, every one, of their visions when they prophesy; they will not put on a hairy mantle in order to deceive, ⁵but each of them will say, "I am no prophet, I am a tiller of the soil; for the land has been my possession since my youth." ⁶And if anyone asks them, "What are these wounds on your chest?" the answer will be "The wounds I received in the house of my friends."

2. בַּיּוֹם הַהוּא (in that day): See the Exegesis of 12:3. נְאֻם יְהוָה (utterance of the LORD): See the Exegesis of 1:3. צְבָאוֹת (of hosts): See the Exegesis of 1:3. אֶת־שְׁמוֹת הָעֲצַבִּים (the names of the idols): See the Exposition. וְלֹא יִזָּכְרוּ עוֹד (and they will be remembered no longer): For the function of the nonperfective (יִזָּכְרוּ) with עוֹד, see the Exegesis of 11:6. רוּחַ הַטֻּמְאָה (the spirit of uncleanness): Whether רוּחַ denotes an actual spirit that drove the false prophets to lie (1 Kings 22:22–23) or the mental disposition of these prophets (see the Exposition of 4:5 and 12:10), we can be sure that its function in this text is to designate the motivating force behind the false prophets' deceptive words. God will drive these prophets from the land, along with the deceptive spirit that inspired them to lie.

3. וְהָיָה כִּי־יִנָּבֵא (and it will be if . . . prophesies): כִּי with the nonperfective can introduce true contingency (*IBHS*, p. 510), presenting here a hypothetical situation (if, when). עוֹד (still): See the Exegesis of verse 2. שֶׁקֶר (falsely; lit., a lie): See the Exegesis of 8:17. בְּשֵׁם (in the name of) indicates the representative of Yahweh (Jer. 14:14; 29:23). וּדְקָרֻהוּ (and will pierce him): See the Exegesis of 12:10.

4. בַּיּוֹם הַהוּא (in that day): See the Exegesis of 12:3. אִישׁ (each): See the Exegesis of 3:10. מֵחֶזְיֹנוֹ (of his vision): חִזָּיוֹן overlaps somewhat with חָזוֹן, the latter designating a visionary mode of prophetic

---

2. The text focuses this cleansing particularly on idols and false prophets. Their "spirit of uncleanness" shows these prophets to be false, even though the text does not specify them as such. It is Yahweh who cuts off the names of the idols and expels the lying prophets; thus, the fountain is a metaphor of his activity on the people's behalf.

The "name" of an idol is what gives cognitive reality and identity to it, transforming even a rude pillar into an object that the mind invests with spiritual reality and energy. An image is not a representative of deity until the mind designates it as such. Thus, the reference to the erasing of the idols' names from the memories of the people shows that it is this cognitive value that the text envisions. Once an object bore the name of a god, it took on a spiritual energy that could affect human consciousness and society in general. In this way, early Israel's toleration of idols led to societal decay (see the Exposition of Hos. 2:19 [17]).

The discourse progresses from the reference to idols to the influence of the false prophets, indicating that their lying prophecies will no longer trouble the people (vv. 3–6). Not only will Yahweh expel these prophets, but he will also eliminate the motivating energies that led the people astray. Since neither idolatry nor false prophesying appears to have been a major problem in this time, these references to manifestations of Israel's earlier disobedience to God are likely metaphors for the absolute cleansing Yahweh will eventually effect for the nation.

That this cleansing occurs "in that day," referring to the piercing of the figure of 12:10 and the subsequent mourning over his death, recalls the reference to a future "day" in 3:1–10, where the Lord of hosts will remove the guilt of the land in one day. In the prophetic symbolism that prompted this statement, there appears a figure called "the Branch." Like the pierced one of 12:10, the Branch bears a close relationship to Yahweh, who calls him "my Servant," and in striking consonance with the cleansing fountain in this passage, the Lord removes the guilt of the land in a single day. Other references to the expunging of evil from the land also receive energy from this prospect of a cleansing fountain (13:1), for the flying scroll of 5:1–4 and the ephah of 5:5–11 both depict the end of the evil that plagued the people.

3. The prophet has established the certainty of the end of false prophetism among his people, but wishing to underscore that certainty he pens a hypothetical account that assures the reader that a false prophet will never reappear in restored Israel (for a similar literary device, see the Exposition of Hos. 9:12). Should a lying prophet arise (but none will), his parents will pierce him through. Nothing will stand in the way of the complete elimination of false prophecy—not even an emotion as strong as parental love.

4–6. Not only will false prophets die in this time, but they will be ashamed of the content of their visions; so much so that they will eschew their profession. No longer will they put on a hairy mantle to deceive people into thinking they are true prophets. As a result, the people of the restoration will not follow prophets who lie in the name of Yahweh. Fearful for his life, this hypothetical prophet will claim another profession, owning to being a hired hand who has worked the fields all his life. By going back to his earlier years he allows no time in his life when

reception (Joel 3:1 [2:28]). חִזָּיוֹן refers to night visions (2 Sam. 7:4, 17; Job 4:13) and is parallel with חֲלוֹם (dream) in Job 7:14 and 20:8 and apposite to it in Job 33:15. The context here does not call for any nuance more specific than a prophetic revelation. The collocation יֵבֹשׁוּ ... מֶחֶזְיֹנוֹ uses מִן (lit., from) to yield "to put to shame by" (Isa. 1:29; Jer. 2:36). אַדֶּרֶת שֵׂעָר (a hairy cloak): Elijah the prophet wore an אַדֶּרֶת (outer garment or mantle; 2 Kings 2:8; see also Gen. 25:25). לְמַעַן (in order) depicts the reason for the donning of the prophetic mantle—to deceive the people into thinking he is a true prophet.

5. לֹא נָבִיא אָנֹכִי (I am not a prophet): As with all noun clauses, we must infer the time of this clause from the context. It is clear that this denial is present to the circumstances of this context. כִּי (for) introduces a broadly causal clause giving the reason why this hypothetical prophet is a tiller of the soil: because he was hired from his youth (הִקְנַנִי מִנְּעוּרָי). This is the only occurrence of hiphil קָנָה (to acquire, buy). The hiphil seems suspect because a literal translation, "caused to acquire me," seems awkward. The Septuagint's ὅτι ἄνθρωπος ἐγέννησέν με (a man brought me up) apparently understood קָנָה as broadly parallel to יָלַד (to beget). There are several suggestions as to how we should understand this form. The New Revised Standard Version's "land has been my possession" appears to follow the conjecture of BHS, reading קִנְיָנִי (something acquired). It is possible, however, to retain the Masoretic Text's הִקְנַנִי without vio-

lating the text or the structures of grammar by understanding this hiphil form to indicate selling (lit., cause to acquire), after the analogy of qal שָׁבַר (to buy grain; BDB), but hiphil הִשְׁבִּיר (to sell grain), that is, "to cause someone to acquire grain" (Gen. 42:6; Amos 8:5). If we understand הִקְנַנִי in this way, the idea is that the tiller was indentured (sold) to a farmer or hired out to farmers over the course of his lifetime. The perfective verb does not militate against a habitual use of the perfect (hired out over his lifetime), for there are enough occurrences of the perfect with נְעוּרִים (youth) to establish its validity (1 Kings 18:12; Job 31:18; Pss. 71:17; 129:1, 2; Jer. 3:25). The perfective would view the situation as a reality. מִנְּעוּרַי always means "from a youth," never "in one's youth" (compare NASB). These observations lend support to the view that the tiller of this text was hired out to others over a lifetime.

6. וְאָמַר (and if one says) is a conditional clause in English (GKC §159g), but the Hebrew ear may have heard something akin to "and one says," understanding it as a hypothesis. הַמַּכּוֹת is a general word for wound. בֵּין יָדֶיךָ (between your hands) envisions the hands as stretched out; hence "between the hands" refers to the back or chest. In the Ugaritic material (Gordon, *Ugaritic Text* §68.14, 16), the words *bn ydm* (between the hands) occur in parallel with *ktp* (shoulder). מְאַהֲבָי (my friends): Related to אָהַב (to love), this word refers largely to friends, with few nuances beyond that sense.

---

he served as a prophet. Should someone wonder about the lacerations on the back of this false prophet (1 Kings 18:28; see the Exposition of Hos. 7:14), the response will be so lame as to bring a smile to the face: "Wounds? Oh these! These are wounds I received in the house of my friends." One wonders what sort of friends this prophet had. The lameness of this excuse is so

obvious that it creates a sense of the weakness of false prophetism in restored Israel. Certainly his guise will not stand up under close scrutiny, especially with such a defense as this. He will surely suffer death. While this is not an account of an actual occurrence, it does underscore the absolute cleansing of the remnant who turn to God in repentant sorrow.

XVI. Second Oracle: The Destiny of the People of God (12:1–14:21)

D. God's Restoring His Scattered Flock (13:7–9)

McCOMISKEY

⁷O sword, awake against my shepherd, against the man, my associate, utterance of the LORD of hosts. Strike the shepherd that the sheep may be scattered, but I shall turn my hand to the little ones. ⁸And it will be that in all the land, utterance of the LORD, two parts of it will be cut off, will perish, and the third part of it will remain. ⁹And I shall bring the third part into the fire and refine them as silver is refined, and I shall purify them as gold is purified. It will call on my name, and I shall answer it. I will say, "It is my people," and it will respond, "The LORD my God."

NRSV

7 "Awake, O sword, against my shepherd,
   against the man who is my associate,"
      says the LORD of hosts.
Strike the shepherd, that the sheep may
      be scattered;
   I will turn my hand against the little
      ones.
8 In the whole land, says the LORD,
   two-thirds shall be cut off and perish,
   and one-third shall be left alive.
9 And I will put this third into the fire,
   refine them as one refines silver,
   and test them as gold is tested.
They will call on my name,
   and I will answer them.
I will say, "They are my people";
   and they will say, "The LORD is our
      God."

7. חֶרֶב (O sword): Occurring in the clause-initial position, this word receives a degree of emphasis (see the Exposition). וְעַל־גֶּבֶר עֲמִיתִי (against the man, my associate): Few occurrences of גֶּבֶר reflect the meaning of its root ("to be strong") (1 Chron. 24:4; 26:12; Job 38:3; 40:7; Jer. 41:16). More often than not it is a general term for a man, with no specific nuances apparent. עֲמִיתִי (my associate) occurs elsewhere only in Leviticus, where it indicates various levels of personal association: the other party in a transaction (5:21 [6:2]; 19:15; 25:14–15), an acquaintance (18:20), a fellow citizen (19:17), and "another" (19:11; 24:19; 25:17). The first-person suffix creates a sense of personal association with Yahweh, who speaks throughout this section. נְאֻם יְהֹוָה (utterance of the LORD): See the Exegesis of 1:3. צְבָאוֹת (hosts): See the Exegesis of 1:3. הַךְ (strike) is masculine but addresses the feminine חֶרֶב, probably because the unexpressed reference to the sword followed the

verb in the writer's mind, a grammatical situation in which gender agreement may lapse (*IBHS*, p. 109; GKC §144a; Mic. 1:13). וּתְפוּצֶיןָ (that may be scattered): For the ending ־ן instead of ־נָה in the third-person feminine plural of the imperfect, see GKC §47*l*. Prefix-conjugation verbs with ־ן following an imperative (הַךְ) may have a jussive force: "that" (*IBHS*, p. 577). וַהֲשִׁבֹתִי (but I shall turn my hand): The translation of ו depends on whether one translates this construction in a positive or negative sense. The collocation שׁוּב יָד עַל may indicate hostile intent (Ezek. 38:12; Amos 1:8) or God's gracious activity on behalf of his people (Isa. 1:25). הַצֹּעֲרִים (the little ones): The verb צער occurs elsewhere only in Job 14:21 and Jeremiah 30:19, where it is the antithesis of כָּבֵד (to honor), and thus indicates smallness or insignificance. Since the context here deals with sheep, it designates lambs (as does the related noun צָעִיר [little] in Jer. 49:20 and 50:45).

---

7. A voice suddenly sounds, driving the account of the false prophet from our minds. It is the voice of the Lord, summoning a sword to strike the shepherd. The first word the voice cries in the Hebrew text is "Sword!" The effect is chilling, bursting into the almost humorous section we have left, to introduce a tragic picture of a shepherd pierced by a sword, his flock scattering in confusion. The sword is a metaphor for physical harm (Zech. 11:17) as well as death (Amos 9:4). The discourse does not clearly state that this figure dies, but it is difficult to conclude otherwise because of the intensity of the people's mourning in 12:11–14 and because their mourning is like that "for an only child" (12:10), an analogy that implies a child's death. In this way, the pierced figure of this verse is similar to the figure of Isaiah 53, whose piercing and death lead to the redemption of "the many." The pierced one of 12:10 is to be identified with the shepherd in 13:7 (see the Exposition of 12:10).

This shepherd is in some way an associate of the Lord. We do not learn how this is so; the text only makes that assertion and does not further explain it. By this juxtaposition of pronouns, however, Zechariah 12:10 establishes a strikingly intimate association between the Lord and the pierced one (see also John 6:46; 10:30). This discourse contains strong implications that the relationship between the Lord and the shepherd is one of cooperative redemption, for the restoration of God's people does not occur apart from the intervention of one who suffers the shedding of blood.

The purpose of the shepherd's smiting is that the sheep may scatter. Viewed against the account that begins to unfold at 11:1, the sheep are the people and the shepherd is a leader. Recalling the account of the betrayal of the shepherd in 11:4–12, which portends the loss of national integrity for the people, we now learn that a dispersion of the people will take place as well. Several prophetic statements in this book intersect with events that occurred beyond the writer's time (see the Exposition of 9:7, 13); now we find a striking consonance with the dispersion of the population of Judea in A.D. 70 when the Roman emperor Titus sacked Jerusalem. This event, occurring roughly forty years following the crucifixion of Christ, is strikingly consonant with the words *strike the shepherd that the sheep may be scattered*. If one believes that the disciples of Jesus manipulated events to make it appear that he fulfilled Old Testament predictions, it is difficult to fit this anticipation of a future diaspora into such a framework of belief.

In Matthew 26:31 and Mark 14:27, Jesus applied this prophecy more specifically to the disciples' desertion of him on the eve of the crucifixion. This adaptation of an Old Testament prediction is typical of the New Testament, which allows prophetic statements to have validity beyond their stated intent if certain factors verify such an application. For example, Isaiah addressed the words of 29:13 directly to the empty religious formalism of his times, but in Matthew 15:7–9 Jesus applied Isaiah's words to the Pharisaical reli-

8. נְאֻם־יְהוָה (utterance of the LORD): See the Exegesis of 1:3. פִּי (mouth): The associated numeral calls for the sense of portions or parts (Deut. 21:17; 2 Kings 2:9). יִגְוָעוּ (will die): It is difficult to distinguish this verb from מוּת (to die). In all likelihood, they are virtually synonymous. גוע stands here as an independent verbal clause together with יִכָּרֵתוּ (will be cut off), uncoordinated by ו. In these constructions, neither verbal clause is conceptually subordinate to the other, each having the same force in the sentence (see Exod. 15:9; Job 29:8). It does, however, define with greater precision what will be cut off.

9. וּצְרַפְתִּים (and refine them). Both this verb and the following בָּחַן (purify) have to do with the processes by which one eliminates dross from silver or gold, thus purifying them. These verbs clearly connote more than melting or working metal because the process leads to spiritual renewal. הוּא (it) is singular, departing from the plural third-person references in the previous lines. This interchange appears awkward, but the writer likely reverts to the dominant motif of the flock and views the people corporately. יִקְרָא בִשְׁמִי (will call on my name) indicates communicating with God (Joel 3:5 [2:32]; Zeph. 3:9), a privilege stemming from a valid relationship to him (Pss. 79:6; 116:17). אֶעֱנֶה (I will answer): See the Exegesis of 1:11. אָמַרְתִּי (I will say): When אָמַר (to say) follows עָנָה (to respond), it introduces the verbal content of the action that עָנָה initiates (see 1:10, 12; 3:4; 4:4, 5, 6, 11, 12; 6:4, 5). Unlike these instances, however, אָמַרְתִּי and אֶעֱנֶה are not coordinated by ו, which would create "I will answer him and say" (see the Exposition).

---

gion of his day, evidently because of the striking similarity of Pharisaical formalism to the spiritual conditions confronting Isaiah.

The expression *turn my hand to* may connote a negative reaction from God, referring to punishment, or it may indicate that he will aid the lambs of the flock (see the Exegesis). It is this latter sense that obtains here, for if Yahweh were to destroy even the little ones of the flock (NASB: "turn my hand against"), there would be none left of the nation. Yet, verse 9 establishes that God will preserve a remnant to whom he gives the privilege of being his people.

8. Nothing in this context signals an expansion of the word *ʾeres* to encompass the world; it continues to refer to the land. This text depicts a decimation of the population in which two parts will perish. We need not take this division literally; it tells us only that God will not terminate all the population, but will establish a remnant through whom he will continue to accomplish his redemptive purposes. The existence of a remnant guarantees the continuation of God's ancient promise to Abraham.

9. We cannot be sure that the fire represents a period of suffering for the remnant of the flock. We can be sure only that the Lord will refine them, making them like pure silver and gold. Viewing the flock as a corporate entity (my translation, "it"), the text affirms that they will enjoy a viable relationship with the Lord in which they call and he answers. That the following clause ("I will say") is not coordinated to this clause by *waw* (and) creates the possibility that it does not state the content of God's response to their calling

upon him, but describes a separate action. Viewed in this way, this following clause does not comprise an answer to their prayer, but expresses a separate divine affirmation ("it [the flock] is my people") that includes them in the blessings of the Abrahamic promise (for a discussion of this statement of the promise, see the Exposition of 2:15 [11] and 8:8).

Thus far, I have understood Jerusalem in this lengthy discourse to include in its symbolism the literal city that will continue to exist in spite of the hostilities it will experience. There is validity to this because the oracle begins by announcing that it concerns "Israel" (12:10), which designates the historical nation (2:2 [1:19]; 8:13; 9:1; 11:14), and because the prophet's own people would certainly predominate in his frame of reference. We must always ask first how the prophet's hearers would have understood his words. We have found, however, instances in this book in which Jerusalem and Judah function as concrete realities that envision a prospective level of reality that, from a New Testament perspective, admits the church to its sphere of meaning (see the Exposition of 2:8 [4]; 15–16 [11–12]; 8:3–8; 9:9–17; 10:6). Galatians 4:26–27 and Hebrews 12:22–23 show that New Testament writers could perceive the church in Jerusalem's symbolic range. In Pauline theology, the key that unlocks the presence of the church in an Old Testament text is its allusion to elements of the Abrahamic promise (see the Exposition of 2:8 [4]). We do not immediately find promise elements in this discourse, but when we reach this verse we hear its familiar cadences: "I will say, 'They are my people'; / and they will say, 'The LORD is our God.' "

It is these words that unite the church and the restored Jewish remnant in a common hope and a shared inheritance, their experiences in the world being remarkably parallel. Like the remnant (12:2–4), the church faces hostility, but it enjoys security from hostile forces that may hinder its progress but never bring it to an end (Mic. 5:7–8; Matt. 16:18). The leaders of the church have struck fire in the world in spite of their frailties and shortcomings. Christians look to a suffering figure for their spiritual cleansing, confessing that, like the remnant, they too have pierced him, and in sorrowful repentance they find in him their redemption.

XVI. Second Oracle: The Destiny of the People of God (12:1–14:21)

E. Final Siege of Jerusalem (14:1–3)

McCOMISKEY

14 Listen! A day is coming for the LORD when your plunder will be divided in your presence, ²for I will muster all the nations against Jerusalem for battle, and the city will be taken, and the houses looted, and the women raped, and half the city will go into captivity, but the rest of the people will not be cut off from the city. ³And the LORD will go out and fight against those nations as the day of his fighting on a day of battle.

NRSV

14 See, a day is coming for the LORD, when the plunder taken from you will be divided in your midst. ²For I will gather all the nations against Jerusalem to battle, and the city shall be taken and the houses looted and the women raped; half the city shall go into exile, but the rest of the people shall not be cut off from the city. ³Then the LORD will go forth and fight against those nations as when he fights on a day of battle.

14:1. הִנֵּה (Listen!) marks this statement off from others, thus warranting our careful attention. לַיהוָה (for the LORD): The preposition לְ directs the action of the verb בָּא (is coming) to Yahweh, but not in the sense that it comes upon him, but *to* him in that it is his day. This is a surrogate expression for בַּיּוֹם הַהוּא (the day of the LORD) that we find frequently in the prophets. שְׁלָלֵךְ is the plunder taken from you, not plunder previously belonging to you (see Ezek. 29:19). The suffix is singular, continuing the references to the nation as a corporate entity (see 13:9). בְּקִרְבֵּךְ (among you) adds an emotional value to this assertion by placing the unidentified enemy in the land.

2. וְאָסַפְתִּי (and I will muster) is the only first-person construction in this section (14:1–21) that refers to the Lord, all the others being third person. It is difficult to know why this is so, but it does serve to create a sense of Yahweh's immediacy in the events the prophet describes. *Waw* connects this construction to a clause that explains how the spoiling of Jerusalem will come about, thus the translation "for." כָּל־הַגּוֹיִם (all the nations) refers to the nations within the writer's purview, because verse 14 describes Israel's enemies as "the surrounding nations." It is not necessary to posit a worldwide conflagration here.

3. כְּיוֹם הִלָּחֲמוֹ (as the day of his fighting): The context does not specify a particular day of fighting for this infinitive following the noun יוֹם (day) in the construct state. The indefiniteness of בְּיוֹם קְרָב (on a day of battle) also does not warrant our searching for a specific battle of Yahweh against his enemies.

14:1. It seems strange to move from the previous affirmations of Jerusalem's impregnability to this section, which describes enemy soldiers distributing the spoil they have taken from Jerusalem. Is it possible that this section was misplaced or from the hand of another? Verse 2 is particularly intense in its description of pillage, rape, and exile, making even more obtuse the connection this section has with the impregnability of Jerusalem celebrated in chapter 12.

Daniel 9:24–27 sets forth a similar destiny for Jerusalem, affirming the continued existence of the city after the return from the exile, but in a time of trouble (see McComiskey, *Seventy "Weeks" of Daniel*, pp. 25–41). At the end of Jerusalem's historical existence, an eschatological figure (probably the Antichrist) will effect unparalleled destruction on the city, but at the same time he will meet his end. This event will bring the peace to Jerusalem for which Daniel prayed and herald the long-expected kingdom. Zechariah 12:1–14:21 has a similar pattern, affirming Jerusalem's continued existence (impregnability) and envisioning a final onslaught against the city that will herald the new heavens and the new earth.

The day of the Lord in prophetic literature designates any time when Yahweh steps into the arena of human events to effect his purposes. Here it encompasses his stirring up the nations to conquer Jerusalem (v. 2) and do battle against them. The devastating events the city will experience are not outside his control.

This chapter presents the interpreter with difficult challenges. How far may we take its symbolism, and what is its perspective? In some ways, chapter 14 reflects the history of the church, the people of the new covenant who endure hostility (vv. 1–2) yet enjoy God's protection (v. 3). They have a refuge in him (vv. 4–5) and possess spiritual life (v. 8). As spiritual Jerusalem, they drink living waters (v. 8) and dwell securely (v. 10). There are, however, elements in this chapter that urge on us another perspective. The dimensions of the cataclysm of 14:1–3 transcend any of the historical military invasions at which the book has hinted thus far (9:7, 13). The intervention of God into human history, represented by the words *the LORD my God will come, all the holy ones with [him]*, coupled with the cosmic upheavals that will occur, bespeak a time when the natural order will undergo great changes. That this time is known only to God (v. 7) implies that it is beyond previous human experience. That the Lord becomes king over the whole earth and is without rival (v. 9) does not answer adequately to his present reign over his church. The New Testament perspective found in the Book of Revelation depicts the new Jerusalem and the new heavens and the new earth in the eternal state.

2–3. The plundering of Jerusalem will occur because "all the nations" will come against the city to do battle. We should not understand *kōl* (all) too clinically, taking it to refer to every nation on the face of the earth. It is enough to know that Jerusalem's enemies in this final onslaught will be numerous. The slaughter and rapacity this verse describes are shocking, and the prospect of Jerusalem's citizens going once more into exile must have been particularly galling to the readers of this oracle.

There is, however, a strong note of hope in the assurance that "the rest of the people will not be cut off from the city." In the Old Testament tradition of the remnant, we learn that it is not God's intention to terminate his people. In spite of the intensity of this invasion, he will continue his promises in those who remain in the city. There is hope also in the affirmation that Yahweh will fight for his people as on a day of battle. We need not look to Israel's previous history to find such a day (see the Exegesis). It is enough to know that he will fight with the fervor and intensity a warrior would display in battle.

XVI. Second Oracle: The Destiny of the People of God (12:1–14:21)
F. God's Rescuing His People (14:4–5)

McCOMISKEY

⁴And his feet will stand that day on the Mount of Olives, which is before Jerusalem on the east. And the Mount of Olives will be cleft in the middle from east to west [forming] a very great valley. And half the mountain will remove northward, and half southward. ⁵And you will flee to the valley of my mountains, for the valley of the mountains will stretch to Azel, and you will flee as you fled from the earthquake in the days of King Uzziah of Judah. And the LORD my God will come, all the holy ones with you.

NRSV

⁴On that day his feet shall stand on the Mount of Olives, which lies before Jerusalem on the east; and the Mount of Olives shall be split in two from east to west by a very wide valley; so that one half of the Mount shall withdraw northward, and the other half southward. ⁵And you shall flee by the valley of the LORD's mountain, for the valley between the mountains shall reach to Azal; and you shall flee as you fled from the earthquake in the days of King Uzziah of Judah. Then the LORD my God will come, and all the holy ones with him.

4. הַר הַזֵּתִים (the Mount of Olives): See the Exposition. מֵחֶצְיוֹ מִזְרָחָה וָיָמָּה (in the middle from east to west): חֶצְיוֹ (middle; Exod. 27:5; Ruth 3:8) indicates the chasm formed as the mountain splits east and west.

5. וְנַסְתֶּם (and you will flee): The Masoretic tradition recognizes this construction as a second-person masculine plural of נוּס (to flee), but it is possible to read these consonants with the Greek as a third-person masculine singular niphal perfective of סָתַם: "will be stopped up" (see the Exposition). גֵּיא (to the valley of): If one understands וְנַסְתֶּם as "you will flee," גֵּיא is an adverbial accusative (to). It is not clear that we should understand such an accusative to convey any idea other than the goal of the action of the verb נוּס (to flee): "to the valley" (NRSV and NASB, "by"). The verb נוּס occurs with Jerusalem as an adverbial accusative meaning "to" (1 Kings 12:18; 2 Chron. 10:18). The context does not specify that the egress from the city is by the way of this valley to a particular location (see the Exposition). הָרַי (my mountains): If we understand וְנַסְתֶּם as "flee," the first-person suffix refers to the mountains formed in the cataclysmic activity of God this text describes. כִּי (for): The sense one gives this particle depends on one's understanding of וְנַסְתֶּם. If we understand it as "stopped up," כִּי introduces a broadly defined reason for this stopping up: because the newly formed valley extends to the side of "the valley of my mountains," thus blocking it up (see the Exposition). אָצַל (Azel) adds to the complexities of an already difficult passage. Many emend to אָצְלוֹ (its side). The view taken here is that it is a place-name (see the Exposition and Abel, "Asal dans Zacharie"). The Revised Standard Version reads "the side of it," but this form never refers to the side of an object; it always expresses proximity. If it were an absolute (side), we would expect a suffix on אָצַל (its side), rather than the vague "a side" that would thus exist in the text. וְנַסְתֶּם (and you will flee): For the significance of the second-person plural to the interpretation of this verse, see the Exposition. קְדֹשִׁים (holy ones): See the Exegesis of 2:16 [12] and 8:3 and the Exposition of 14:5. עִמָּךְ (with you): The absence of a separate verb (will be) with this preposition favors its collocation with וּבָא (and will come), creating "the holy ones will come with you." Construed in this way, the singular suffix addresses God, not the people. Interchanges of person are not uncommon in this book.

---

4. Like a mighty colossus the Warrior-God stands on the summit of the Mount of Olives. The violent changes that occur in this mountain create a great valley that provides the inhabitants of Jerusalem with a refuge from the violence within the city. Anthropomorphic representations of Yahweh's entry into the arena of human history may be found in the prophets (Joel 4:16 [3:16]; Amos 1:2; Mic. 1:3–4), and we need not understand them literally. So here in Zechariah we may look beyond the apocalyptic symbolism to the reality it portrays. This symbolism affirms that God will not allow his people to perish but will enter into time to preserve a remnant. The context gives no significance to the Mount of Olives other than its location "before Jerusalem." The choice of a more distant mountain would provide no egress for Jerusalem's inhabitants. The geological shift of the mountain northward and southward creates an awareness of awesome power, a vivid pictorial representation of the activity of the invisible God in history.

5. Verse 5 presents some of the greatest difficulties in this chapter. The crux of the difficulty is the first occurrence of wěnastem, which I translate "And you will flee," not "and will be stopped up," which creates the sense that the earth's convulsions result in a great rift in the Mount of Olives and also fill in an unnamed valley between "my mountains," probably making easier the escape of the people from the city of Jerusalem. It would be strange if the writer used the form nastem once to say "will be stopped up" when two forms identical to it in this verse unmistakably mean "you will flee." To make this meaning clear, changing the number of the second and third occurrences of nastem would have alerted the earliest readers to a juncture in the narration.

In addition, the appearance of two unnamed mountains in the text, designated "my mountains," is suspicious. That a textually unspecified valley should be filled in, touching the side of an unidentified mountain adds little to the logical coherence of the discourse. The failure of the writer to specify the "valley of my mountains" as the Kidron or some other valley makes it likely that it is the one just mentioned, namely, the rift in the Mount of Olives. The view that nastem means "stopped up" also leaves us uncertain as to where Jerusalem's inhabitants flee; is their flight in confused terror with no haven to protect them, or does the Warrior-God provide a place of security for them?

These perplexities disappear when we read *wěnastem* in keeping with its companion forms in this verse to say "and you will flee." Understanding the word *valley* as an adverbial accusative (see the Exegesis), Jerusalem's beleaguered inhabitants flee *to* the valley that the convulsion in the Mount of Olives creates. The valley is their refuge and defense (as in Jer. 21:13; 48:8). "My mountains" are thus the two that the Lord creates as he forms the great rift. They are his by virtue of his creating them (Ps. 24:1).

The word *ʾāṣal* is a problem for either view. I construe it as a place-name, though its existence is not well attested. Keil (*Minor Prophets*, p. 404) points to Bethezel in Micah 1:11, noting that *bêt* (house of) "is frequently omitted from names of places constructed with it." If this word functions as a place-name, it indicates that the valley will be extensive enough to provide refuge for all who escape to it.

The superscription to the prophecy of Amos (1:1) refers to an earthquake that occurred during the reign of Uzziah. In all likelihood this is the earthquake about which Zechariah 14:5 speaks. Its dreadful results were not forgotten in the postexilic period. Fleeing in terror from the rapacity in Jerusalem, the refugees will find security in the valley that Yahweh's intervention creates for them.

The symbolism of the valley represents the activity by which God will protect this remnant from extermination in the turmoil of the day of the Lord. In a sense, it represents the climax of that activity, for God has been at work throughout the ages forming a people for his own, preserving them against hostile forces. Little do we know how God's people have been sheltered in valleys of refuge within the upheavals of history.

We wonder why the writer observes that "the LORD my God will come" when he has already entered into time by setting foot on the Mount of Olives. Evidently he comes to his people who have found refuge, for verse 3 places him earlier outside the city engaging the enemy. He has provided security for his people; now they enjoy his presence. The text does not define the "holy ones." We can be sure only that they are figures associated with God, as the form *ʿimmāk* (with you), referring to God, and the parallel structure of Psalm 89:8 [7] show:

a god feared in the council of the holy ones (*qědōšîm*)
great and awesome above all that are around him

XVI. Second Oracle: The Destiny of the People of God (12:1–14:21)

G. New Heavens and New Earth (14:6–9)

McCOMISKEY

⁶And it will be in that day that there will be no light; the glorious things will congeal. ⁷And it will be a singular day; it will be known to the LORD—no day and no night—and it will be that at evening time there will be light. ⁸And it will be on that day that living waters will go out of Jerusalem, half of them to the eastern sea, and half of them to the western sea. It will be so in summer as well as winter. ⁹And the LORD will become king over all the earth in that day. The LORD will be one, and his name one.

NRSV

⁶On that day there shall not be either cold or frost. ⁷And there shall be continuous day (it is known to the LORD), not day and not night, for at evening time there shall be light.

⁸On that day living waters shall flow out from Jerusalem, half of them to the eastern sea and half of them to the western sea; it shall continue in summer as in winter.

⁹And the LORD will become king over all the earth; on that day the LORD will be one and his name one.

6. בַּיּוֹם הַהוּא (in that day) is the day of the Lord (v. 1). יְקָרוֹת (the glorious things): See the Exegesis of 11:13. The function of this word in this context is not clear, but since they congeal and are associated with the absence of light, we are probably not in error to identify these יְקָרוֹת with the heavenly bodies. The word thus intersects with the root's indication of glory (Job 31:26; Ps. 37:20). "Glorious things" is an apt description of heavenly bodies. Qere וּקְרוֹת, from קרר (to be cold), perhaps reflects the plural of קָרָה (coldness). The Qere has וּקְפָּאוֹן (congelation) for יִקְפָּאוּן (will congeal), probably referring to frost (NRSV: "there shall not be either cold nor frost"). The Septuagint reflects the same readings, placing the resulting substantives (cold and frost) in the next clause (v. 7). If the word אוֹר (light) originally stood between these hypothetical substantives as אוֹ (or), this translation would be valid, but the Septuagint witnesses to the integrity of אוֹר, thus making the reading conjectural. As Keil (*Minor Prophets*, p. 405) shows, simply pointing יקפאון as a verb, יִקְפּוֹן (will congeal), resolves the problem posed by two substantives standing together. While the disparity in gender is problematic to this view, one finds such examples elsewhere (e.g., Prov. 2:10).

7. יוֹם־אֶחָד (a singular day): It makes little sense to translate אֶחָד by the numeral one, for the context does not develop the numerical concept. It does, however, develop the uniqueness of that day, stating that God knows it (see below). אֶחָד has the sense of unique or singular (Job 23:13; Song 6:9), the sense being that a person or object is "one" in that no other exists.

8. מַיִם־חַיִּים (living waters): See the Exposition. חֶצְיָם (lit., their half) indicates half of them. הַיָּם הַקַּדְמוֹנִי (the eastern sea) is the Dead Sea (Ezek. 47:18; Joel 2:20), and הַיָּם הָאַחֲרוֹן (the western sea)

---

6. Great changes in the heavens will result in the diminution of light. Such cosmic changes characterize other prophetic descriptions of divine intervention, even when that intervention portends immediate judgment on Israel and Judah (Isa. 30:26; Jer. 4:23–27; Joel 2:1–2; Amos 5:20; Zeph. 1:4, 7–15) or on other nations (Isa. 13:9–10; Ezek. 30:3–4; 32:7–8). Particularly instructive in this regard is Jeremiah 4:23–26, where darkened heavens are symbolic precursors of Jerusalem's exile. This symbolism creates an emotive response in the reader that conveys the writer's sense of the profound significance of the events he describes. To take them always as literal depictions of actual physical phenomena is to miss the nature of prophetic language in general and of apocalyptic symbolism in particular. Zechariah 14:6 is charged with emotion; it is as though mere words fail the writer, and he depicts his vision of the future in bold, surreal imagery.

The surreal nature of this prophetic depiction is apparent in the existence of light (v. 7), even though the luminaries have grown cold and their light has been extinguished. It is as though the prophet says that the new Jerusalem will not need sun or moon. Darkness will not prevail, however, for there will be light, but not astral light. John takes up a similar thought in Revelation 21:23: "And the city has no need of sun or moon to shine on it, for the glory of God is its light."

The translation option "there shall not be either cold nor frost" (NRSV) is attractive (see the Exegesis), but the flow of the discourse renders it tenuous because the context does not go on to develop this concept. It does, however, develop the concept of light. That verse 7 says there will be continuous light in this day supports the idea that something has caused the celestial luminaries to no longer have their normal function. Thus the translation "the glorious things will congeal," referring to these luminaries, is compatible with the flow of the discourse.

7. Since this day is unique (ʾeḥād), never having occurred before, it is beyond human experience or comprehension. Struggling in symbol to convey the nature of this day, the prophet can only leave its effects in the hands of God. It is known to the Lord and that is sufficient. Without the transition from day to night, it will always be light, even at evening. This statement foresees an end to the cosmic order as we know it (Jer. 31:35–36). All that the prophetic symbol of darkness conveys— divine wrath (Ezek. 32:8; Zeph. 1:15), gloom (Amos 5:18), portents (Joel 2:2), oppression (Isa. 9:1 [2]; 42:7), distress (Isa. 5:30)—all this will be no more.

There is a finality about this day that signals the beginning of the eternal state when "there will be no more night" (Rev. 22:5). This congealing of the astral bodies resonates with Revelation's affirmation that there will be no need of "the light of the sun" (22:5). Known only to God are the glories of that day when the light of God will dispel the darkness of pain, oppression, tears, and evil.

8. The vivid symbolism continues as the prophet envisions living waters flowing from Jerusalem. Jeremiah refers to living waters in 2:13

is the Mediterranean (Deut. 11:24). The ancient Hebrews oriented themselves eastward in determining the points of the compass.

9. וְהָיָה . . . לְמֶלֶךְ (and will become king): See the Exegesis of 2:9 [6]. אֶחָד (one): See the Exposition.

Gordon ("His Name Is One") suggests that אֶחָד represents the name of God. וּשְׁמוֹ (and his name): See the Exposition of 5:4 and 13:2 and the Exegesis of 10:12.

(see also 17:13), applying the expression to God, the source of these waters. The people of Jeremiah's day had forsaken the life God offered the nation, going their own way, hewing out cisterns that could not provide them with the essence of their life as a nation. In the Old Testament law, the symbol of life "connotes the viability of the relationship of the nation or the individual to the promised inheritance" (McComiskey, *Covenants of Promise*, pp. 152, 121–28). Living waters symbolize the spiritual nourishment that vitalizes God's people, sustaining them in their relationship to the inheritance and symbolizing God's provision for this people (Ps. 46:5 [4]; Ezek. 47:1–12; Rev. 22:1–2).

Zechariah 14:8 depicts the life-giving water flowing eastward and westward, never ceasing to provide for the people because it flows continually, both "summer and winter." Once again a sense of finality pervades the text. The viability of the relationship of God's people to their promised inheritance will not come to an end as it did when Israelites and Judahites went at sword point into exile. As we envision these waters, we may imagine John who, in his vision of the eternal state, described "the river of the water of life . . . flowing from the throne of God and of the Lamb" (Rev. 22:1). At last the people of God have realized their inheritance in heaven, and force and oppression no longer threaten them. Zechariah sets this hope in symbols relating to the land, for the waters flow to the Mediterranean as well as to the Dead Sea. These seas functioned as boundaries of the promised land (Num. 34:12; Deut. 11:24; 34:2). This, as well as the use of Jerusalem as a motif, brings the promised land before us. As we view the land in prospect here, we learn that the inheritance of land has its ultimate function, representing the climax of the inheritance, namely, landedness in the eschatological kingdom of God.

9. We have reached the pinnacle of the discourse. That the Lord will be one and his name one guarantee the bright prospects this chapter holds out to God's people. He alone will reign over the new heavens and the new earth, with no rivals vying with him for power. The earth over which he rules will undergo great changes, introducing a new era when there is no need of the sun and when the people of God drink from ever-flowing waters of life. There is no curse, and they will enjoy absolute security (v. 11). The old order of the universe is no more, for there is a new earth. The words of Revelation 21:1 again resound: "Then I saw a new heaven and a new earth; for the first heaven and the first earth had passed away" (see the Exposition of v. 7). Just as John beheld the new Jerusalem in his vision (21:2), so we see it in Zechariah 14:11. We hear also the words of the ancient promise (Rev. 21:3) coming to final reality as we do in Zechariah 14:8, and the affirmations that "the first things have passed away" (Rev. 21:4) and that there will no longer be a curse (Rev. 22:3) resound in Zechariah 14:11 as well.

The prophet gives us a glimpse of heaven in symbols that fall far short of reality, but whose emotional force reach a deep level of our comprehension. It is as though we are observing a stained glass window depicting a person or event. The images of colored glass represent objective reality, and while they pulsate with brilliant light, they forever remain symbols. So with apocalyptic, for now we must wait to behold its realities. Beautiful as they are, these figures, like pieces of stained glass diffusing the light of the sun, can only suggest "what no eye has seen nor ear heard" (1 Cor. 2:9).

XVI. Second Oracle: The Destiny of the People of God (12:1–14:21)

H. New Jerusalem (14:10–11)

McCOMISKEY

[10]And all the land from Geba to Rimmon south of Jerusalem will change, [becoming] like a plain, and it will rise and remain in its place from the Gate of Benjamin to the site of the first gate—to the Corner Gate—and from the Tower of Hananel to the King's Winepresses. [11]And they will live in it, and there will no longer be a curse, for Jerusalem will dwell secure.

NRSV

[10]The whole land shall be turned into a plain from Geba to Rimmon south of Jerusalem. But Jerusalem shall remain aloft on its site from the Gate of Benjamin to the place of the former gate, to the Corner Gate, and from the Tower of Hananel to the king's wine presses. [11]And it shall be inhabited, for never again shall it be doomed to destruction; Jerusalem shall abide in security.

10. יָסוֹב (will change): The basic meaning of this word is "to go around." While the idea of change is unusual for this word, the accompanying preposition on כָּעֲרָבָה gives this collocation the meaning "to change into." כָּעֲרָבָה (like a plain): The definiteness of this form in the Masoretic tradition may indicate "the Arabah," perhaps referring to the Jordan Rift Valley; on the other hand, it may indicate "an ʿărābâ" or plain, in which case the definiteness of the form denotes

---

10. Geba, located in the tribe of Benjamin (Josh. 21:17), is identified with modern Jebaʿ, five miles north of Jerusalem. Rimmon, which the text locates south of Jerusalem to distinguish it from other towns of the same name, is likely En-Rimmon (Neh. 11:29), identified with Umm er-Ramāmīn, nine miles north of Beersheba (J. F. Prewitt, *ISBE*, vol. 2, p. 104). A line drawn between Geba and En-Rimmon includes the hills north of Jerusalem, the ridge on which Jerusalem is situated, and the hilly country extending into southern Judah.

An ʿărābâ is usually an arid steppe, but this word may also be a proper name designating the rift valley of the Jordan River that extends from Mount Hebron to the Gulf of Aqabah. Several translations are possible for the first clause of this verse:

"And all the land will change, becoming like the plain (ʿărābâ) from Geba to Rimmon south of Jerusalem."

"And all the land from Geba to Rimmon south of Jerusalem will change, becoming like the Arabah (ʿărābâ)."

"And all the land from Geba to Rimmon south of Jerusalem will change, becoming like a plain (ʿărābâ)."

The first option is doubtful because the topography from Geba to Rimmon is mainly hilly country. The second and third options, while somewhat awkward in their representation of the Hebrew word order, are nevertheless more compatible with the context. The second option reflects the definiteness of ʿărābâ and may convey the sense that the hill country between Geba and Rimmon will become "like the Arabah," that is, the Jordan Rift Valley, which, except for a stretch of some five miles near Samaria, is comparatively fertile. The sense of this translation would be that the waters flowing from Jerusalem and the tributaries of the Jordan will make the land fertile. The allusion in verse 8 to the waters is, however, separated from verse 10 by the climactic affirmation in verse 9 of the Lord's universal reign, which does not facilitate the continuation of the theme of living waters into this verse.

The third option complements the concept of Jerusalem's security by understanding the definiteness of kāʿărābâ (like the ʿărābâ) to designate a class (GKC §126*l*–p), thus yielding "like a plain" as in Isaiah 33:9. The sense is that the hilly country extending northward and southward from Jerusalem will undergo great convulsions, becoming a plateau that will establish the city on a secure geological base uninterrupted by hills and valleys. This idea is consonant with the next statement that Jerusalem "will rise and remain in its place" and with verse 11, which says that Jerusalem's inhabitants will "dwell secure," thus creating a sense of stability and security. The new Jerusalem will be eminently secure, a concept reflected in Revelation's allusions to the "great high wall" of the new Jerusalem" (21:12) and to the security its inhabitants will enjoy "forever and ever" (22:5).

The next section of this verse presents the exegete with numerous difficulties, not the least of which is the identity of the "first gate." This gate may have been one that existed in the old wall, whose site the people remembered but whose identity is lost to us (see Meyers and Meyers, *Zechariah 9–14*, p. 445, and Baldwin, *Haggai, Zechariah, Malachi*, p. 204). This view would explain why the writer refers to the "site" (mā-qôm) of this gate, not to the gate itself as with the Corner Gate. However, if this gate was important enough to list as a landmark in the prophet's description of Jerusalem, we wonder why we do not find it in other accounts of the environs of Jerusalem. It is possible that the first gate is one with the Old Gate of Nehemiah 3:6 and 12:39, which O. Bahat places to the south of the Tower of Hananel (*Atlas* p. 36), but which LaSor (*ISBE*, p. 1020) and Paton and Simons (Bahat p. 30) locate farther to the west in the northwest district of the city. The evidence for this identification of the first gate with the "Old Gate," however, is not compelling. The syntax of ûmigdal (and the tower) is equally troubling: waw may coordinate šaʿar happinnîm and migdal ḥănanʾēl to yield "the Gate of the Corners and the Tower of Hananel" (Meyers and Meyers, *Zechariah 9–14*, p. 408) or it may introduce another clause meaning "and from the Tower of Hananel." It is diffi-

a class (GKC §126*l–p*; Isa. 33:9; see the Exposition). וְרָאֲמָה (and it will rise): An א sometimes appears in ע"ו verbs (e.g., קָאם/קוּם); here the verbal root is רוּם (to be high). See the Exegesis of Hosea 10:14. This form and וְיָשְׁבָה (and remain) have no stated subject, but it is certain that it is Jerusalem, because it "remains in its place" with boundaries that define only Jerusalem, and according to verse 11, "they will live in it . . . for Jerusalem will dwell secure." In all likelihood וְיָשְׁבָה views the city as a corporate entity, as it does in 12:6 (see the Exegesis there), not primarily as individuals who inhabit the city. עַד מְקוֹם . . . עַד שַׁעַר (to the city of . . . to the gate of . . .): See the Exposition.

---

cult to pinpoint the various landmarks this verse cites, but even so, the former reading of the line makes it difficult to perceive a clearly defined progression when proceeding westward from the Benjamin Gate to the Gate of the Corners and then eastward to the Tower of Hananel before again going west around the southern extremity of the city past the king's winepresses and the First Gate, coming full circle to terminate the circuit at the king's winepresses. On the other hand, understanding *ûmigdal* to initiate a new clause allows for a complete circuit of the city with no reduplication of its perimeter.

Before suggesting a solution we must discuss the locations of these landmarks:

1. The Gate of Benjamin was in the north wall because Benjamin lay to the north of Jerusalem (see Jer. 37:13).
2. The location of the first gate was likely known to Zechariah's audience, but its identity is now lost to us (Meyers and Meyers, *Zechariah 9–14*, p. 445; Baldwin, *Zechariah*, p. 204). One wonders, however, why the writer refers to the "site" (*māqôm*) of this gate, not to the gate itself. And why was this gate important enough to list in this description of Jerusalem, but not in other accounts of the environs of Jerusalem? It is possible that this gate is the Old Gate of Nehemiah 3:6 and 12:39, which was south of the Tower of Hananel (Bahat, *Atlas*, p. 36) or farther to the west in the northwest district of the city (W. S. LaSor, *ISBE*, vol. 2, p. 1020; L. B. Paton and J. Simons in Bahat, p. 30). The evidence for this identification of the first gate with the Old Gate is not compelling.
3. The Gate of the Corners is no doubt the same as the Corner Gate. It was likely at the confluence of the north and west walls of the city (W. S. LaSor, *ISBE*, vol. 2, p. 1020).
4. The Tower of Hananel was located in a northerly wall of Jerusalem.
5. The king's winepresses were most certainly in the south in the vicinity of the king's garden (Neh. 2:14; 3:15).

If these last two landmarks describe part of Jerusalem's circumference, the text reduplicates part of Jerusalem's perimeter. It is more likely that these landmarks do not describe a circuit but an imaginary line extending from north to south through the city. If the Tower of Hananel stood on the north wall, a line drawn from it southward to the king's winepresses would roughly trace the course of another line of walls, namely, the west walls of the temple compound and the city of David.

Like the territory of Benjamin, Ephraim also lay to the north of the city, creating the likelihood that the Benjamin Gate and the Ephraim Gate were identical at the time this verse was written (Keil, *Minor Prophets*, p. 409). According to 2 Kings 14:13, the Gate of Ephraim was four hundred cubits from the Corner Gate. If these gates were identical, it seems strange that the writer would define the limits of Jerusalem only from this gate to the nearby Corner Gate. It is possible, however, that the writer imagined a circuit starting at the Corner Gate, passing through the Benjamin/Ephraim Gate, circuiting the east and south sides of the city and continuing back to the Corner Gate, which the words the *first gate* now designate as the starting point of the circuit. If *ûmigdal* marks a new clause, the previous clause would thus read, "From the Gate of Benjamin to the site of the first gate, that is, to the Corner Gate." This reconstruction relies on the collocation *ʿad mĕqôm . . . ʿad* (to the site of . . . to), which appears elsewhere only in Genesis 12:6: "Abram passed through the land to the place at Shechem (*ʿad mĕqôm šĕkem*), to (*ʿad*) the oak of Moreh." In other words, Abram went to Shechem, but more precisely to the oak of Moreh. If this construction has the same sense in Zechariah, the writer delineates the restored border of Jerusalem as stretching through the Benjamin/Ephraim Gate, circuiting the city back to the first gate in his imaginary circuit, more precisely to (*ʿad*) the

11. וְיָשְׁבוּ (and they will live in it): Since יָשַׁב (to live) can mean "to be inhabited" in this book (7:7; 9:5) and no stated plural subject precedes it, we must understand the subject to be the people ("they"). וְחֵרֶם (a curse) denotes something devoted either to God (Lev. 27:21; Num. 18:14) or to total destruction (Deut. 7:26; Josh. 6:17; 7:12; 1 Kings 20:42; Isa. 43:28). That there will no longer be a ban (curse) guarantees the perpetual security of the new Jerusalem. וְיָשְׁבָה (will dwell): See the Exegesis of 12:6 and 14:10.

Corner Gate. This demarcation encompasses the entire city and supports the sense that Jerusalem's walls will be secure and the new Jerusalem will be unmovable on its newly formed foundation.

11. This verse continues to underscore the security the new Jerusalem will enjoy. The city will be populated, and its citizens will not be under the threat of a curse. The *ḥerem* (curse, ban) that led to Israel's demise (Isa. 43:28) cannot ever hang over the heavenly community because the curse will be no more, thus guaranteeing the city's security. Revelation 22:3 echoes this assurance, probably reflecting the Septuagint's translation of *ḥerem* by *anathema* (curse). The context of Revelation's assurance that there will be no more curse does not define the curse. We can be sure, however, that the *ḥerem* in Zechariah is total destruction. It is comforting to know that the inhabitants of heaven will be forever safe from the fears and threats of mortal existence.

XVI. Second Oracle: The Destiny of the People of God (12:1–14:21)
I. Punishment on the Attacking Nations (14:12–15)

McCOMISKEY

¹²Now this will be the plague with which the LORD will strike all the peoples who waged war against Jerusalem: his flesh rots while he stands on his feet, and his eyes will rot in their sockets, and his tongue will rot in his mouth. ¹³And it will be in that day that there will be great confusion from the LORD among them. One man will seize the hand of his comrade, and his hand will rise against the hand of his comrade. ¹⁴And Judah will also fight at Jerusalem, and the riches of all the surrounding nations will be gathered—gold and silver, and garments in great abundance. ¹⁵And the plague on the horse, the mule, the camel, and all the cattle, which will be in these camps, will be the same as this plague.

NRSV

¹²This shall be the plague with which the LORD will strike all the peoples that wage war against Jerusalem: their flesh shall rot while they are still on their feet; their eyes shall rot in their sockets, and their tongues shall rot in their mouths. ¹³On that day a great panic from the LORD shall fall on them, so that each will seize the hand of a neighbor, and the hand of the one will be raised against the hand of the other; ¹⁴even Judah will fight at Jerusalem. And the wealth of all the surrounding nations shall be collected—gold, silver, and garments in great abundance. ¹⁵And a plague like this plague shall fall on the horses, the mules, the camels, the donkeys, and whatever animals may be in those camps.

12. הַמַּגֵּפָה (the plague): From the verb נָגַף (to strike), this noun can connote a blow or a plague. The physical effects described in this verse give this word the sense of plague. צָבְאוּ (who waged war) may be either a gnomic (who attack) or a past perfective (who attacked). The context is determinative (see the Exposition). הָמֵק (rots): From מָקַק (to rot, fester) this hiphil infinitive absolute names an action, literally, "a causing to rot." We know only that some unnamed force causes the flesh of the enemy to decay. בְּשָׂרוֹ (his flesh): The person indicators revert from the plural to the singular. It is as though the writer focuses on one member of the attacking forces in order to intensify our perception of what is transpiring. Denoting a hole, only here does בְּחֹרֵיהֶן indicate the eye socket. בְּפִיהֶם (in their mouths) with its plural suffix rounds out the verse by reminding us that the writer has the entire invading army in mind.

13. בַּיּוֹם הַהוּא (in that day) indicates when the Lord destroys all hostile forces (v. 12). מְהוּמָת has a broad range of meaning: tumult, panic, confusion, and discomfiture; this context, with its description of soldiers fighting their companions, calls for the translation "confusion." וְהֶחֱזִיקוּ (and raise [his hands] against): See the Exegesis of 8:23. אִישׁ (one man): See the Exegesis of 3:10 and 7:9. וְעָלְתָה (and will rise) has as its feminine subject יָד (hand).

14. תִּלָּחֵם בִּירוּשָׁלָ͏ִם (will fight at Jerusalem): The collocation נִלְחַם בְּ may have a hostile sense ("fight against"—14:3) or a local one ("fight at"—2 Chron. 20:17). The former cannot be valid here, for it would violate the relationship between Judah and Jerusalem that 12:2, 7 and 14:21 establish. חֵיל (the riches): See the Exegesis of 9:4 (see also Hag. 2:7).

15. וְכֵן (lit., and so) with כְּ (כַּמַּגֵּפָה) establishes a comparison: "And so the plague on the animals will be as this plague." That is, the plague of verse 12 will also strike the animals in the camps of the attacking armies. מַגֵּפַת (the plague on): See the Exegesis of verse 12.

12–13. The picture of the new heavens and the new earth fades as the discourse brings us back to an earlier event—the defeat of the hostile nations that waged war against Jerusalem (only hinted at in v. 3). It is possible that the verb ṣāb'û is a gnomic perfective ("wage war") referring to any nation that might attack the new Jerusalem, thus further establishing the security its citizens will enjoy. This is unlikely, however, for if we view it in this way, the discourse leaves the fate of the nations of verses 1–3 undetermined.

The disgusting description of bodies rotting even before they fall to the ground creates a scene of absolute destruction. Yahweh's might is so great that his enemies cannot stand before him. In this way, those who oppose the people of God will come to an end. No force—no matter how great—will stay them from their inheritance in glory. When God destroys these powers hostile to his church and his ancient people (see the Exposition of 13:9), great panic will ensue. Foes will turn one against the other, thus defeating themselves. This vivid symbolic language depicts the absolute power God displays in his triumph over his foes.

14. Once again we learn that Judah is on an equal footing with Jerusalem. The people of God will be unified in their resistance against the enemy, and the riches of the nations "will be gathered." While the text does not tell us who receives the wealth of the nations, the implication is that the nations yield up their riches to the kingdom (vv. 9–11). We see in prospect in this verse the final conquest of the Gentile world powers as God reigns supreme.

The gathering of the world's wealth is an important concept in postexilic theology, especially Haggai 2:7, which refers to the upheaval among the nations that accompanied the inception of the church in the world. The Gentile mission of the church caused great upheaval among the nations, altering forever the course of history. This shaking of the nations that preceded the reign of God in his church foreshadows the ultimate shaking of the nations that will herald the eternal reign of God over the new heavens and the new earth.

15. In order to convey a sense of the total annihilation of all opposition to God, the writer extends the plague of verse 12 to the animals these nations possess. The obscure symbols serve only to show how complete the destruction of evil will be when the eschatological kingdom dawns. We need not think of a literal plague that will leave animal carcasses decaying in the fields, but of the blessed freedom from oppression that God's people will experience. A similar motif is found in 13:4–6, where the prophet expresses the absolute cleansing of his people in a hypothetical allusion to false prophets.

XVI. Second Oracle: The Destiny of the People of God (12:1–14:21)

J. Gentile Nations Worshiping the Lord (14:16–19)

McCOMISKEY

¹⁶And it will be that all who are left of the nations that have come against Jerusalem will go up yearly to worship the King, the LORD of hosts, and observe the Feast of Booths. ¹⁷And it will be that whoever of the families of the earth does not go up to Jerusalem to worship the King, the LORD of hosts, there will be no rain upon them. ¹⁸And if the family of Egypt does not go up and does not come, then [there will be] no [rain] upon them—the plague with which the LORD strikes the peoples who do not go up to observe the Feast of Booths. ¹⁹This will be the punishment for Egypt, as well as the punishment for all the nations that do not go up to observe the Feast of Booths.

NRSV

¹⁶Then all who survive of the nations that have come against Jerusalem shall go up year after year to worship the King, the LORD of hosts, and to keep the festival of booths. ¹⁷If any of the families of the earth do not go up to Jerusalem to worship the King, the LORD of hosts, there will be no rain upon them. ¹⁸And if the family of Egypt do not go up and present themselves, then on them shall come the plague that the LORD inflicts on the nations that do not go up to keep the festival of booths. ¹⁹Such shall be the punishment of Egypt and the punishment of all the nations that do not go up to keep the festival of booths.

16. הַבָּאִים (that have come): Since the nations no longer attack Jerusalem (v. 14), we must give this participle the translation "have come" (as in Jer. 28:4), not "coming." מִדֵּי (untranslated): Without this particle שָׁנָה בְשָׁנָה alone would have sufficed to express "yearly." The addition of מִדֵּי seems to add nothing to the expression. יְהוָה צְבָאוֹת (the LORD of hosts): See the Exegesis of 1:3. חַג הַסֻּכּוֹת (the Feast of Booths): See the Exposition.

17. יְהוָה צְבָאוֹת (the LORD of hosts): See the Exegesis of 1:3. הַגֶּשֶׁם is a general word for rain (not necessarily seasonal rains).

18. וְאִם . . . תַעֲלֶה (and if . . . go up): The protasis of this conditional clause is complex, containing both an imperfective (תַעֲלֶה) and a perfective (בָאָה). The perfective follows logically from the condition the imperfective תַעֲלֶה (go up) establishes: if they do not go up (imperfective), it follows (perfective) that they will not come. וְלֹא עֲלֵיהֶם (then [there will be] no [rain] upon them; lit., and not upon them): The apodosis of this conditional clause is difficult to construe. If we read the text as it stands it says, "If the family of Egypt does not go up, . . . then the plague with which Yahweh strikes the nations will not come upon them," a concept that contradicts the earlier part of the discourse. It is possible, however, that וְלֹא עֲלֵיהֶם is elliptical, requiring the reader to insert הַגֶּשֶׁם (the rain) from verse 17. Such ellipsis is not foreign to the book (omission of הָיָה [to be] occurs in 4:7; 8:9; and 9:7; see also 3:4; 7:7). It is also possible that the text has suffered in transmission (for the possibility that the problem results from the influence of the neighboring passage, see Naor, "Paired Passages"). הַמַּגֵּפָה (the plague): See the Exegesis of verse 12. חַג הַסֻּכּוֹת (the Feast of Booths): See the Exposition of verse 16.

19. חַטַּאת (the punishment for; lit., sin) illustrates the way in which Hebrew words for sin indicate punishment.

---

16. In terms reminiscent of the religious observances of ancient Israel, the text affirms that redeemed Gentiles will share in God's kingdom, worshiping him in obedience. We cannot fully understand why the writer cites the Feast of Booths, but it is likely that this feast, which recalls the wilderness experience, functions as a motif for the childlike obedience that sometimes marked the Israelites' response to God in their earliest history. The returned exiles observed the Feast of Booths even before beginning construction on the foundation of the temple (Ezra 3:4, 8) to ensure their security from the surrounding tribespeople. In the new heavens and the new earth, all the people of God will live in obedience to him. Nothing external (the nations) or internal will threaten the integrity of the kingdom of God.

17–19. In this time when God's reign is universal, nations that refuse to worship him will experience drought. Again, a hypothetical allusion underscores the prophet's efforts to convey a sense of absoluteness. Like the allusion to the termination of false prophetism in 13:3–6, the hypothetical allusion here envisions the end of all rebellion against God. No such nations will exist in this time, of course, but, by way of example, should such rebellion arise it will not continue to exist in God's eternal kingdom. The hypothetical allusion continues with Egypt as an example of one of the nations from which God will withhold rain. Egypt stands for all the hypothetical nations that disobey God's rule. Again, the prophet's allusion affirms the absolute rule of God.

XVI. Second Oracle: The Destiny of the People of God (12:1– 14:21)

K. Holiness Pervading God's Eternal Kingdom (14:20–21)

McCOMISKEY

²⁰In that day there will be [inscribed] on the bells of the horses, "Holy to the LORD," and the bowls in the house of the LORD will be like the vessels before the altar. ²¹And it will be that every bowl in Jerusalem and in Judah will be holy to the LORD of hosts. And all those who sacrifice will come and take from them and cook in them, and there will not be a Canaanite anymore in the house of the LORD in that day.

NRSV

²⁰On that day there shall be inscribed on the bells of the horses, "Holy to the LORD." And the cooking pots in the house of the LORD shall be as holy as the bowls in front of the altar; ²¹and every cooking pot in Jerusalem and Judah shall be sacred to the LORD of hosts, so that all who sacrifice may come and use them to boil the flesh of the sacrifice. And there shall no longer be traders in the house of the LORD of hosts on that day.

20. מְצִלּוֹת (the bells of): With several related words connoting cymbals, this word designates bells or other metallic ornaments capable of being inscribed. קֹדֶשׁ (holy): See the Exegesis of 2:16 [12]. הַסִּירוֹת (the bowls): The reference to the temple indicates that these are vessels used in the Israelite cultus (Exod. 27:3; 38:3; 1 Kings 7:45); see the Exegesis and Exposition of 9:15.

21. סִיר (bowl): See the Exegesis of verse 20. קֹדֶשׁ (holy): See the Exegesis of 2:16. יְהוָה צְבָאוֹת (the LORD of hosts): See the Exegesis of 1:3. כְּנַעֲנִי (a Canaanite): See the Exposition.

---

20. The expression *holy to the* LORD was inscribed on the gold plate on the high priest's turban. This inscription expressed the special state of holiness that marked the priestly office. When God establishes his eternal kingdom, no semblance of evil will exist. So pervasive will be the rule of righteousness in the new order that even the most common objects will be holy to God. Nothing will belong to the sphere of the common or profane (see the Exegesis of 8:3). Even the trappings on the horses will be holy to God.

The prophet turns from the objects of everyday life to the most prominent of the levitical institutions—the temple. Even the cooking vessels in the temple will be as holy as those used to sprinkle blood before the altar (see the Exposition of 9:15). Just as we do not expect literal horses in the eternal state, we need not think in terms of a literal temple. These allusions express in comprehensible terms something that was not yet incomprehensible. There will no longer be a difference between the holy and the secular, for holiness will pervade all aspects of life.

21. Continuing the affirmation that holiness will be the ruling element in eternity, the prophet turns again to objects of everyday life: even the cooking pots in the new Jerusalem will be holy to the Lord. The absence of a separation between the holy and the profane appears again as we imagine those who use sacrificial bowls before the altar cooking food in the same vessels.

Kěnaʿănî has two possible meanings in this text: Canaanite or merchant (see the Exegesis of 11:7 and Hos. 12:8 [7]). The latter choice has no correspondence with the flow of the discourse, which has nothing to do with trading and is particularly anomalous to the "house of the LORD of hosts." On the other hand, this discourse is particularly concerned with the pervasiveness of holiness in the eternal state, and uses temple motifs to express that concept (vv. 16–19). The abominations of the Canaanites were not forgotten in the postexilic period and found their way into the restored community, tarnishing the purity of the "holy seed" that had mixed with the "peoples of the lands" (Ezra 9:1–2). The assurance that no Canaanite will exist in God's temple guarantees the end of every threat of impurity in the kingdom of God and further underscores the absolute rule of God over the new Jerusalem.

Malachi

Introduction

Author

Nothing is known about the personal life of the author of the Book of Malachi. Indeed, it is not even absolutely certain that Malachi is the author's name. The superscription (Mal. 1:1) is somewhat ambiguous, for the Hebrew text can be translated either as "A message: the word of Yahweh to Israel through Malachi" or "A message: the word of Yahweh to Israel through my messenger." In other words, מַלְאָכִי (mal'ākî) can be regarded as either a proper noun (Malachi) or a common noun with a pronominal suffix (my messenger). Most early Greek versions took it as a common noun, ἀγγέλου αὐτοῦ (angellou autou, of his messenger), whereas two important later Greek revisions (Symmachus and Theodotion) regarded the word as a proper noun: μαλαχιου (malachiou, of Malachi). The testimony of Symmachus and Theodotion cannot be accepted without question, however, since both saw their task as updating the Septuagint to conform more closely to the Masoretic Text and its ongoing tradition of interpretation. Through the centuries, this tradition gradually developed into the consistent practice of treating מַלְאָכִי as a proper noun.

There was, however, good reason for this congealing of opinion, since as a name מַלְאָכִי conforms to the typical "-i hypocoristicon" pattern and is the shortest form in a series of successively shortened names: מַלְאָכִיַהוֶה (Malachiyahweh: "messenger of Yahweh"), מַלְאָכִיָהוּ (Malachiyahu: "messenger of Yahu"), and מַלְאָכִיָה (Malachiah: "messenger of Yah"). Proper names that link a common noun with the name of the Israelite God (Yahweh) in this manner (via the Hebrew construct form) occur by the hundreds

To Gayle, who manifests God's love.

Contributor:
Douglas Stuart
B.A., Ph.D.
Professor of
Old Testament,
Gordon-Conwell
Theological Seminary

throughout the Old Testament, indicating that מַלְאָכִי falls within a common category of Hebrew names.

There is little to support the frequently advanced theory that the name in 1:1 is borrowed from 3:1 ("I am sending *my messenger* [מַלְאָכִי] to prepare the way before me"), since the latter verse speaks of the divine covenant messenger who introduces the cataclysmic Day of the Lord, not someone associated with prophesying in Malachi's day. Least useful for resolving the question is the evidence of Targum Jonathan, an expansionistic and periphrastic fifth-century A.D. Aramaic translation of the Hebrew, which reads in 1:1, "By my messenger whose name is Ezra the scribe." This identification of מַלְאָכִי with Ezra comes from medieval Jewish speculative historicizing rather than from factual data. It is far more likely that מַלְאָכִי in 3:1 is independent of 1:1, in the same way that the name Isaiah contains the Hebrew verbal root *yšᶜ* (to save), but *yšᶜ* appears dozens of times in the Book of Isaiah with no reference to the prophet's own name. It is remotely possible that מַלְאָכִי in 3:1 is a play on words, but the context gives no hint of that. Moreover, the word מַלְאָךְ (*malʾāk*, messenger, angel) is such a common word in the Old Testament that one can hardly conclude that its appearance in a book composed of prophetic oracles must refer to the author of the book rather than to the subject matter of the oracle in which it occurs.

It is often argued that several of the prophetic books in the Old Testament have anonymous appendages (e.g., so-called Second Isaiah, Deutero-Zechariah, and Trito-Zechariah). By this reasoning, Malachi is treated as an anonymous appendage to Zechariah or to the Minor Prophets as a whole. It is alleged that the similarity of the titles in Zechariah 9:1, 12:1, and Malachi 1:1 indicates that these prophecies were all originally anonymous, with two of them attributed to Zechariah and one to "Malachi," a word borrowed from Malachi 3:1 and made into a proper name by a late, anonymous editor/redactor. Scholars who hold this view sometimes contend that מַלְאָכִי would not have been a normal Hebrew name, an assertion that does not stand up to careful scrutiny (see Stuart, "Names, Proper"). The theory that Malachi is an anonymous addition to the Minor Prophets has several weaknesses:

1. The assertion that any of the prophetic books contain secondary appendages is unprovable. Such supposedly nongenuine parts of books are typically identified by the appearance of contrasting theological outlooks—a sufficiently subjective enterprise that it is debatable in every case. Since many competent scholars defend the unity and integrity of Zechariah and maintain that Zechariah 9–14 is not a secondary addition to Zechariah 1–8 (e.g.,

Baldwin, *Malachi*, pp. 211–15; see also Verhoef, *Maleachi*, pp. 9–16), the argument that Malachi is a tertiary addition to Zechariah 9–14 is much less tenable.

2. Malachi has such a distinct structure and perspective that one can hardly doubt its unity, as opposed to the purportedly anonymous additions to other prophetic books that tend to reflect closely the style or perspective of the book to which they have been, in theory, added.

3. Malachi's superscription, which has the simple form found in several other prophetic books, especially Haggai (1:1), sets it off as a distinct prophetic work, in spite of the similarity of three of its words with Zechariah 9:1 and 12:1. Naturally, one cannot prove that the superscription is not a secondary addition, but none of the other supposed secondary additions occurring at the end of prophetic books has such a superscription. As Childs notes, "Its separate status is deeply rooted in the book's own tradition" (*Introduction to the Old Testament*, p. 492).

4. The tradition that Malachi is a proper name is based on ancient understanding: Symmachus, Theodotion, the Vulgate, and the Syriac Peshitta all interpreted מַלְאָכִי as a proper name. In addition, 2 Esdras, a second-century A.D. noncanonical work, lists the last three books of the Old Testament as "Haggai, Zechariah, and Malachi" (1:40).

5. The tradition that Malachi is a proper name is also based on the grammar of the superscription: מַלְאָכִי follows בְּיַד (*bĕyad*, through, by), a typical expression for indicating the human instrument of divine revelation.

In the final analysis, the absence of a compelling reason to overturn or doubt the validity of the traditional reading of 1:1 requires the acceptance of the likelihood that a prophet named Malachi, otherwise unknown from the Old Testament, authored the book that now occupies the final position among the Minor Prophets.

Form and Structure

Malachi is comprised of a superscription and six prophetic disputation speeches, the last of which may also contain a summary challenge related to the message of the book as a whole. This structure is one of the simplest and most repetitive in the Old Testament prophetic corpus, matched in simplicity only by the shorter Book of Haggai, which contains four chronologically dated oracles, and Obadiah, which is a single, self-contained foreign-nation oracle. That an entire prophetic book should be characterized by the exclusive use—six times over, indeed—of a single prophetic speech form is without parallel. That the speech form in question is one of the rarer prophetic speech forms, namely, disputation, is one of the unique features of Malachi. Here, then, is a book of oracles delivered by the last of the Old Testament writing prophets, consisting of six oracles, all with the same basic literary form that is seldom employed by the prophets.

The disputation (more fully, rhetorical disputation) speech form has four elements: assertion, questioning, response, and implication. These four elements are well illustrated by the first disputation (1:2–5):

assertion (by God)	"I have loved you" (1:2a)
questioning (by Israel)	"How have you loved us?" (1:2b)
response	"Is not Esau . . . the people with whom the LORD is angry forever?" (1:2c–4)
implication	"Your own eyes shall see it . . . beyond the borders of Israel!" (1:5)

It is important to note that this disputation structure is remarkably unobtrusive in each of the six main passages of the book. In other words, the structure, while easily visible, does not govern the content but serves it. Such a structure is so simple and allows for so much variation that a great deal of unique material is found in each of the six passages. They are hardly mirror images of one another even though they share the same overall format. The rhetorical disputation is essentially a question-and-answer structure, allowing for the coverage of almost any sort of content. (For further discussion of the disputation form, see the Exposition.)

There are no grounds for estimating how many of a prophet's oracles found their way into the Scriptures. Malachi may have preached on hundreds of occasions, while he, his disciples, or some other collector selected only six of his many prophecies for inclusion in the book that bears his name. Alternatively, the six disputation speeches may represent the entirety of his public ministry. Moreover, we do not know the extent to which the canonical prophets were faithful in their preaching. Perhaps Malachi delivered some "prophecies" on certain occasions that were not actual messages from God, either because he was not entirely adept at discerning the Spirit's inspiration, or because he improperly modified what he heard the Spirit say, or because his sinful mind led him now and again to preach some things for personal reasons rather than under true inspiration. These would not be appropriate for inclusion in Scripture. In the end, it doesn't matter. Whether the Book of Malachi contains only prophetic disputations as the result of some elaborate process of selection or whether it represents the sum total of a prophet's inspired oral ministry, it is what God, the ultimate Author of all Scripture, wanted included.

The component parts of the book may be summarized as follows:

Superscription (1:1)	Malachi is the vehicle for the divine message: Yahweh is the source, Israel the audience, and Malachi the intermediary.
First Disputation (1:2–5)	An oracle against Edom, showing God's covenant love and power and his distinction between the good (seen in his faithfulness to his covenant love for Israel) and the wicked (seen in his international power via his judgment on one of Israel's key enemies, Edom).
Second Disputation (1:6–2:9)	An oracle against the Jerusalem priests concerning their unfaithfulness to the covenant: they ignore various provisions of the Sinai covenant, cooperating with the people in a system of profaning the sacrificial system and thus violating the covenant with Levi.
Third Disputation (2:10–16)	An oracle against the people of Judah concerning their unfaithfulness to the covenant: they intermarry with pagan women or divorce their first wives.
Fourth Disputation (2:17–3:5)	An oracle against the people of Judah concerning their unfaithfulness to the covenant: they are unrighteous and unjust; the Day of the Lord will bring judgment against all evildoers, including them.
Fifth Disputation (3:6–12)	An oracle against the people of Judah concerning their unfaithfulness to the covenant: they fail to provide tithes and adequate offerings to God; the oracle also contains promises of great blessing for the faithful (implicitly following the arrival of the Day of the Lord).
Sixth Disputation (3:13–21 [3:13–4:3])	An oracle against the people of Judah concerning their unfaithfulness to the covenant: they fail to fear and honor God and they doubt that God distinguishes between the good and the wicked; the oracle also includes a warning of the coming of the Day of the Lord.
Summary Challenge (3:22–24 [4:4–6])	A summary of the two main themes of the book: the need to keep the law of Moses (the primary theme of disputations 1–3) and the need to be prepared for the coming Day of the Lord (the primary theme of disputations 4–6).

The chapter divisions in English translations are notoriously inept. The book is obviously structured by the disputations, and the chapter divisions so abuse this that the reader of the book must learn to pay little attention to them. This is especially the case at the end of the book, for what is designated 4:1–3 in English versions (following the Septuagint tradition) is in fact the continuation of the final disputation (3:19–21 in the Hebrew text).

More debated is the question whether the final three verses of the book (3:22–24 [4:4–6]) are distinct from the other disputations, constituting an epilogue of some sort. Most scholars believe that these verses, with their command to obey the Mosaic law and the prediction of the coming of Elijah, are best understood as an independent conclusion to the entire book rather than the conclusion of the sixth disputation, to which they seem only modestly connected.

It becomes evident when one studies the structure of Malachi that its disputations are arranged chiastically: the first disputation is comparable to the sixth disputation, the second to the fifth, and the third to the fourth. The chiastic arrangement of the book represents a careful, intentional pairing of the various disputations. The following chiastic scheme is adapted from Hugenberger's *Marriage as a Covenant* (p. 25):

Matching Chiastic Units		Common Themes
Superscription (1:1)	Summary Challenge (3:22–24 [4:4–6])	Yahweh has a message for Israel.
First Disputation (1:2–5)	Sixth Disputation (3:13–21 [3:13–4:3])	God distinguishes between the good and the wicked; the proof of his covenant love is his sparing the righteous and condemning the wicked.
Second Disputation (1:6–2:9)	Fifth Disputation (3:6–12)	The double assertion-questioning pattern at the beginning of each disputation; improper, begrudging offerings condemned; promise of reversal of blessing; the Lord's name to be great among the nations.
Third Disputation (2:10–16)	Fourth Disputation (2:17–3:5)	The Lord is a witness relative to marriage fidelity; Judah is unfaithful.

It is not possible to be sure who created this arrangement. Malachi could have done it, being keenly aware of how the messages God had given him corresponded in certain ways to one another. But any disciple or later scribe with a reasonable amount of insight and judicious investment of time could have done the same.

Is the arrangement chronological? Again, it is not possible to be certain. Perhaps God gave the six disputations to Malachi in the order in which they now stand in this book, but there is also nothing to suggest otherwise. We know that they are organized thematically; we simply cannot tell if the order is the result of chance or intent, or even whether it is chronological.

At any rate, we must not give the concentric organization of the material in the book too much weight, in spite of its surface visibility. The concentric structures in Scripture are not more important, complicated, or elementary than other portions. They are simply organized to facilitate memorization. We must not conclude that chiastic patterning is the sole or even dominant factor in the presentation of the content itself. The pattern serves the content, not vice versa.

The same is true of the rhetorical-disputation format that houses each of the six passages that comprise the book. That Malachi's oracles are in the form of disputations does not imply anything about the book's topics, significance, relationships with other doctrines of Scripture, or any other matters that fall within the category of "content" as distinct from "form." The inspired prophet's message is not controlled by the format adhered to. The rhetorical-disputation format gives each oracle its general structure, but the content whose purpose is to communicate truth effectively and not to fit an idealized norm, is far more important than the form. The oracles do not simply mirror their chiastic pairs, as is evident especially in the implication section of each of the six disputations, which are topically and stylistically free, with no impingement of the structure on them.

Style and Unity

The oracles in Malachi appear to contain a relatively high proportion of repeated vocabulary, which is unparalleled in other prophetic books (for full lists of these repetitions, consult the introduction to each major section in the Exposition). There is no consensus about the distribution of prose and poetry in Malachi. Modern English translations such as the New International Version and the New Revised Standard Version recognize no poetry in the book. Glazier-McDonald treats the entire book as essentially parallelistic, whether typical poetry or parallel prose, while Verhoef sees in it a good deal of poetic parallelism. BHS treats the majority of the book as poetry. My analysis finds clear evidence of poetic parallelism only in the following parts:

1:2–5 (the entire first disputation)
1:6–9 (the opening of the second disputation)
2:6–9 (the close of the second disputation)
2:10 (the opening verse of the third disputation)

If this analysis is correct, then the distribution of poetry is limited to the early disputations and perhaps only to the first two (2:10 is not as clearly poetic as the other sections). The presence of poetry in some sections of Malachi's oracles might have been one of the bases for the present ordering of the book (poetry at the beginning, prose toward the end). For the organizer of the book, the pattern of poetic distribution may have reinforced (or even suggested) the chiastic structure noted above. There is, however, insufficient evidence for a definitive conclusion.

One thing is sure: the style of the book is remarkably consistent. Each oracle follows a four-part disputational outline, and each is characterized by extensive repetition of vocabulary. Each is more or less chiastic, and each reflects classic pentateuchal doctrines and themes. The oracles are linked by chiastically paired catchwords and characterized by the same sorts of messenger formulas, especially "Yahweh of the Armies said" (אָמַר יְהוָה צְבָאוֹת, ʾāmar yhwh ṣĕbāʾôt). In these ways, the consistency of the book obviates any speculation about lack of integrity or multiple authorship.

Date and Situation

As with Joel, Obadiah, Jonah, Nahum, Habakkuk, and Zephaniah, one must date the Book of Malachi by inference. No statement in the book ties it indisputably to a distinct period. Prior to the second century A.D. (i.e., 2 Esdr. 1:40), we find no reference to Malachi as a person or a book. Because he faced so many of the issues that Ezra and Nehemiah had to contend with, it is widely held that Malachi lived close to the time of these leaders. On the assumption that Malachi preceded the reforms of Ezra (who arrived in Palestine in 458 B.C.) and Nehemiah (who arrived in 444 B.C.; on these two dates, see Cross, "Judean Restoration"), I conclude that a date of approximately 460 B.C. for this book is probable. Several particulars suggest a date around this time:

1. Malachi 1:10 and 3:1–8 assume the existence of the Second Temple and thus reflect a date after its completion in 516 B.C.
2. Malachi 1:2–6 reflects the era after the Edomites lost the territorial claims they had made at the expense of Judah in the sixth century B.C., suggesting a fifth-century date.
3. Malachi 1:6–2:9 reflects the same concern for the corruption of the priesthood that occupied Nehemiah (Neh. 13:4–9, 29–30).
4. Malachi specifically mentions the covenant with Levi (2:4) to which Nehemiah 13:29 alludes.

5. Malachi excoriates marriages of Israelites to pagans (2:11–12), a problem addressed and at least temporarily resolved by both Ezra (9–10) and Nehemiah (10:30; 13:1–3, 23–27).
6. Malachi speaks of the need for godly offspring (2:15) in a manner that comports with Nehemiah's concern over Israelite–pagan marriages that produced children who could not even speak Judean Hebrew properly (13:23–24).
7. Malachi preaches against the social injustices of his day, including abuse of the poor and the dependent (3:5)—abuse that Nehemiah tried to end (5:1–13).
8. Malachi's criticism of the failure of his contemporaries to pay their full tithes reflects the concern of Nehemiah (10:32–39; 13:10–13).

These parallels suggest that Malachi was a contemporary of Ezra and Nehemiah, preaching either at the same time that they were implementing their reforms or, more likely, slightly in advance of them. He would thus have been inspired to prepare the hearts of the people for the needed corrections to the faith and practice that Ezra and Nehemiah would eventually undertake.

In the mid-fifth century B.C., Judah was not necessarily a satisfactory place to live (Neh. 9:32–37). The first waves of captives had returned from Babylon in 538 B.C. (2 Chron. 36; Ezra 1–2) to a small territory (Judah was only about twenty miles by twenty-five miles) with a population numbering around 150,000 (Yamauchi, "Ezra, Nehemiah," p. 568). Almost immediately the returned exiles encountered well-organized opposition to their plans to rebuild the temple and the city of Jerusalem (Ezra 4–5) from the people of the surrounding territory. By 516 B.C., the Jews had succeeded in rebuilding the temple, though it did not compare with Solomon's temple (Ezra 3, 6). Their success was due in part to the preaching of Haggai and Zechariah (Ezra 6:14; Zech. 2:10–13; 6:9–15; 8:9–23). Jerusalem itself, however, lay in ruins, its walls broken, inhabited only here and there by squatters (Neh. 1:3; 2:13–17; 3; 4; 11). The great hopes of the late sixth century were only memories.

Judging from the Book of Haggai, Nehemiah 5, and Malachi 3:8–12, agriculture had not adequately rebounded after the exile; drought, pests, and blight had long hampered economic recovery. Poverty was widespread (Neh. 1:3; 2:3, 17; 4:2; 5:1–5; 9:36–37; Mal. 3:5). Politically, Judah was just a minor province among the 120 provinces of the vast Persian Empire, forced to endure a discouraging subjugation to a foreign power that did not appear likely to end (Neh. 1:3; 9:36). Indeed, Judah never became independent again, except for the brief period of the Maccabean revolt in the second century B.C. The Edomite incursions of the prior century, though finally at an end (Mal. 1:2–5), had left Judah impoverished and vulnerable to the neighboring states. Persian taxes, tolls, and annual tributes wrung from the local economy the resources that might have allowed an earlier return to economic prosperity (Neh. 9:37).

Far more ominous than the economic and political hardships the people faced was their spiritual distress. The prophecies of Haggai and Zechariah place great emphasis on the early stages of the restoration era (520 and beyond), as well as on the coming of the Messiah and the renewed presence of God among his people. These promises, rightly understood, were absolutely true; but wrongly understood (as they undoubtedly were in Malachi's day), they seemed a cruel mockery. Things had not improved since the final decades of the sixth century. The Messiah had not yet come, and the people had by and large given up trusting God to do anything (Mal. 3:14–15).

Moreover, the priesthood had become corrupt, failing to enforce the sacrificial laws and the other aspects of their solemn covenant duty (Mal. 1:6–2:9). The people no longer regarded the priests with respect, but with scorn (2:9), a situation that led the priests to accept imperfect animals from the people as a matter of course simply in order to put food on their tables (1:12–14; 2:13; 3:4). Thus, both clergy and laity were cooperating in a violation of the law of Moses (3:22 [4:4]). In addition, the Lord had not yet "come to his temple" (3:1), so it was as devoid of the divine presence as it was earlier when God's glory departed from Jerusalem (Ezek. 10; see also Mal. 3:17). Though the priests knew the law of Moses, they were not observing it themselves or helping the people observe it (Mal. 2:7–8).

It is evident that the temple had high priests during the fifth century B.C. (Neh. 12:10–11), yet Malachi does not mention them apart from general references to priests and Levites. The high priests evidently supported the corruption that pervaded the rank and file, and so Malachi included them within the sweeping condemnations of his prophecy. He did not single them out for special notice or exception. Malachi thus reflects the style of Deuteronomy and several other prophetic books, most notably Jeremiah and Ezekiel (but see Neh. 12:23), in not emphasizing the distinction between priests and Levites.

One area of life that demonstrated the religious decline of the era was tithing. Stinting on tithing went along with tough times, and—though most Israelites of Malachi's day were not conscious of it—actually contributed to them (3:8–12). The tithe was also a concern of Nehemiah (Neh. 10:37–39; 12:44; 13:5, 10–13) and is one of the factors linking Malachi to Nehemiah's era (see no. 8 in the list above). Israel's worship required finances to support the tribe of Levi and defray the costs of the temple. The Levites likely constituted one-twelfth of the population of fifth-century Judah and thus would have required around 8 percent of the nation's income if they were to be proportionately supported. The additional cost of maintaining the temple system meant that approximately 10 percent of the nation's wealth would be needed for the worship system to function as the Mosaic law required. When contributions fell short of the tithe, the nation's cultus and its ministers were deprived. Accordingly, Malachi, like his contemporaries Ezra and Nehemiah, paid a great deal of attention to the correct functioning of the priests. Giving less than the tithe was intolerable because it undermined the people and their praise of God.

There was one bright spot in the Judean religion in Malachi's time: the people had apparently abandoned formal idolatry once and for all. They may well have continued some of the mentality and practices associated with idolatry (see the Exegesis and Exposition of 2:13) but, judging from the complete lack of reference to it in the Books of Ezra, Nehemiah, and Malachi, the practice of idol worship, which had so often corrupted the nation in its past, was now gone. The religious tolerance of the Persians meant that the lesson of the folly of idolatry, learned the hard way in exile, could continue to be taught in successive generations in Judah. To date, Palestinian archaeological investigation confirms this. No indication of Israelite idolatry or other cultic practices has been found from periods after the exile.

The worship of Malachi's time was not heartfelt, however, and the people's offerings were inadequate. Lack of tithing meant lack of true obedience to God. Freedom from idolatry was not accompanied by vibrant orthodoxy. The earlier era of hope had yielded to a widespread attitude of disaffection with faith in Yahweh. The people to whom Malachi preached were saying, in effect, "God doesn't seem to care anymore. And if he doesn't care, why should we?"

Text

The state of preservation of the text of Malachi is somewhat below the quality found in the average prophetic book, mainly because of the great difficulty posed by the wording of several phrases in 2:11–15. Since the Septuagint also reflects the majority of these difficulties, it would appear that most of the textual difficulties in the book arose before the second century B.C., when the Septuagint was produced. The Septuagint is helpful, however, in restoring the text at 1:6, 2:2–3, and 3:5, among other places. On the other hand, many Septuagint manuscripts omit 3:21 [4:3]. This is probably due to haplography, since the balance of the evidence for the originality of the verse supports the

Hebrew Masoretic Text. Perhaps the most famous problem in the text of Malachi is the Targum Jonathan's addition of "whose name is Ezra the scribe" after מַלְאָכִי in 1:1. As noted above, this speculative addition preserves nothing original.

Malachi's Contribution to Biblical Revelation

Though Malachi is a relatively short book, it contributes to biblical revelation in a number of ways. In particular, eleven of the book's themes are noteworthy for their uniqueness or for their interconnectedness with major doctrines of the Bible. These themes are developed in greater detail throughout the commentary, but for purposes of overview are listed here in summary form:

1. The divine election of nations (1:2–5) vis-à-vis Israel and Edom is foundational for Paul's development in Romans 9–11 (esp. 9:13) of the concept of the sovereign election of Israel—and the true Israel, the church—from among the peoples of the earth.
2. The judgment on the priesthood (1:6–2:9) anticipates Christ's assumption of the priestly role, a concept developed especially in Hebrews 7–8.
3. The necessity of implementing the sacrificial system with perfect offerings (1:6–2:9) is sounded often in the New Testament, notably in Hebrews 9–10.
4. Malachi's inspired condemnation of divorce based on aversion (2:10–16) anticipates and undergirds Jesus' condemnation of the practice in Matthew 19.
5. The emphasis on the unacceptability of religious intermarriage (2:10–16) both reinforces the teaching of the Pentateuch and presages the similar emphasis in the New Testament (e.g., 1 Cor. 7; 2 Cor. 6).
6. The role of the coming Messiah as purifier of a people (2:17–3:5) is widely reflected in the New Testament (e.g., 2 Cor. 6:14–18; Phil. 4:8; 1 John 3:3).
7. The dual concept of the Day of the Lord as providing cleansing and burning and also as a time of great joy and reward for the faithful (2:17–3:5; 3:13–24 [3:13–4:6]) complements the more common prophetic descriptions of the day using language related to darkness, gloom, warfare, and the like.
8. Malachi's emphasis on the failure to tithe as a form of defrauding God (3:6–12) forcefully undergirds the biblical doctrine that support of the Lord's work is a sacred obligation (see Acts 5:1–11; 2 Cor. 8–9).
9. The emphasis on keeping the Mosaic covenant (3:22 [4:4]) both reinforces the message of the prophets and antici-

pates the work of Christ in fulfilling the law so that a new covenant could be introduced on behalf of a new people.

10. The strong contrast of the respective fates of the righteous and the wicked (3:13–24 [3:13–4:6]) gives depth to the biblical doctrine of judgment as developed throughout the Bible, especially in the New Testament.

11. The prediction of the ministry of the second Elijah (3:23–24 [4:5–6]), fulfilled by John the Baptist (Matt. 11:14), is a unique prophetic word that held both hope and warning before the faithful for the five centuries that elapsed between the end of the era of classical prophecy and the inauguration of the new covenant.

Malachi's Knowledge and Use of the Pentateuch

Hugenberger (*Marriage as a Covenant*, pp. 48–50) identifies nine connections between Malachi and the Book of Deuteronomy:

1. Only Malachi and Deuteronomy among the Old Testament books begin with an address to all Israel.

2. The Book of Malachi concludes with a deuteronomic injunction mentioning Horeb (3:22 [4:4]), the deuteronomic word for Sinai (Deut. 4:10–14).

3. Malachi and Deuteronomy emphasize in a similar way Yahweh's special love for Israel (Mal. 1:2–5; Deut. 4:37; 7:6–10).

4. Malachi's reference to the name of Yahweh (1:6–2:9) reflects the well-known deuteronomic "name theology."

5. Malachi and Deuteronomy uniquely emphasize the fatherhood of God (Mal. 2:10; Deut. 8:5; 14:1; 32:6).

6. Malachi's treatment of priests and Levites without rigorous distinction between the terms reflects the practice in Deuteronomy, and his appeal to the covenant with Levi (2:8) finds part of its background in Deuteronomy 33:8–11.

7. Malachi's concern for tithing (3:6–12) is comparable to Deuteronomy 26:19, especially in regard to the promise of blessing that accompanies proper tithing.

8. Malachi's reference to Israel as God's property or special possession (3:17) reflects what some scholars call the "grant" concept in Deuteronomy 7:6, 14:1–2, and 26:18. Deuteronomy 14:1–2, like Malachi 3:17, also speaks of Israel's sonship.

9. The prominence of various aspects of the covenant in Malachi ties it closely with Deuteronomy, including a significant corpus of shared vocabulary (e.g., "love," "hate," "father," "son," "cursed," "great king").

Beyond these connections to Deuteronomy, three other kinds of connections to the Pentateuch are prominent in Malachi. First, Malachi relies heavily on the pentateuchal curse and blessing types (discussed below). Second, Malachi frequently alludes implicitly and explicitly to the Mosaic covenant—and not merely to the portion of it that is called Deuteronomy. The assumption of a covenantal relationship between God and his people affects each of the six disputations and is especially overt in the summary statement of Malachi 3:22 [4:4]: "Remember the teaching of my servant Moses, the statutes and ordinances that I commanded him at Horeb for all Israel." Third, in his second disputation (1:6–2:9) excoriating the priests of his day for their failure to faithfully perform the duties assigned them by the law of Moses, Malachi alludes carefully and at length to three passages from the Pentateuch (Num. 6:24–26; 25:12–13; Deut. 33:8–11). It is evident that Malachi knew the Pentateuch well.

Malachi and Pentateuchal Curses and Blessings

Like the other Old Testament prophets, Malachi was a "covenant enforcement mediator," a term that defines "prophet." He was God's spokesperson (mediator) relative to the enforcement (via curses and blessings, also known as "sanctions") of the Mosaic covenant. The sanctions portion of an ancient Near Eastern covenant contained groups of curses (i.e., predictions of distress and disaster that would ensue if the covenant was not kept) and blessings (i.e., predictions of good fortune and happy circumstances that would ensue if it was kept). The Old Testament, however, makes a distinction between blessings that would accompany Israel during its sojourn in the promised land (initial blessings) and those that would come only after the unleashing of whatever punishments were needed (restoration blessings). Virtually all the blessings in the prophetic books have to do with restoration following conquest and exile and its attendant miseries; they are not blessings to be expected instead of judgment in the short run. None of the Old Testament prophets created curses or blessings; rather, God had already revealed them to the Israelites through Moses. It was necessary only to allude to one of the Pentateuch's twenty-seven types of curses to indicate that doom awaited those who broke the covenant. It was equally necessary only to allude to one of the Pentateuch's ten types of restoration blessings to indicate that abundance awaited those who remained faithful to the covenant. The following list provides a numbering system that I will follow in this commentary (for a more substantial discussion of the topic of covenantal curses and blessings, see Stuart, *Hosea–Jonah*, pp. xxxi–xlii):

Curses	Leviticus	Deuteronomy
1. anger and rejection from Yahweh	26:17, 24, 28, 41	4:24–25; 29:19, 23, 26–27 [20, 24, 27–28]; 31:17–18, 29; 32:16, 19–22, 30
2. rejection and destruction of the cult	26:31	
3. war and its ravages		
a. general	26:17, 25, 33, 37	28:25, 49, 52; 32:23–24, 30, 41–42
b. siege	26:25–26, 29	28:52–53, 55, 57
4. fear, terror, and horror	26:16–17, 36–37	28:66–67; 32:25
5. occupation and oppression by enemies and aliens	26:16–17, 32	28:31, 33, 43–44, 48, 68; 32:21
6. agricultural disaster and nonproductivity		
a. drought	26:19	28:22–24
b. crop pests		28:38–42
c. general	26:20	28:17–18, 22, 40; 29:22 [23]
7. starvation and famine	26:26, 29, 45	28:53–56; 32:24
8. illness, pestilence, and contamination	26:16	28:21–22, 27–28, 35, 59–61; 29:21 [22]; 32:24, 39
9. desolation		
a. of holy places	26:31	
b. of cities and towns	26:31, 33	
c. of the land	26:32–35, 43	28:51; 29:22 [23]
10. destruction by fire		28:24; 32:22
11. harm from wild animals	26:22	32:24
12. decimation and infertility		
a. of family	26:22	28:18, 59
b. of cattle	26:22	28:18, 51
c. of population generally	26:22, 36	4:27; 28:62; 32:36
13. exile and captivity		
a. of the people	26:33–34, 36, 38–39, 41, 44	4:27; 28:36–37, 41, 63–64, 68; 29:27 [28]; 30:4; 32:26
b. of the king		28:36
14. forced idolatry in exile		4:28; 28:36, 64
15. futility	26:16, 20	28:20, 29–31, 33, 38–41
16. dishonor and degradation	26:19	28:20, 25, 37, 43–44, 68

Curses	Leviticus	Deuteronomy
17. loss of possessions and impoverishment		28:31
18. loss of family		28:30, 32; 41; 32:25
19. helplessness and stumbling	26:36–37	28:29, 32; 32:35–36, 38–39
20. psychological afflictions		28:20, 28, 34, 65–67
21. lack of peace and rest		28:65
22. denial of burial		28:26
23. becoming like the cities of the plain		29:22 [23]
24. death and destruction	26:36, 39	4:26; 28:20–22, 44, 48, 51, 61; 29:19 [20]; 30:15, 18–19; 31:17; 32:25–26, 35, 39, 42
25. general and unspecified		4:30; 28:20, 24, 45, 59, 61, 63; 29:18, 20–21 [19, 21–22]; 31:17, 21, 29; 32:23, 35
26. general punishment, curse, and vengeance	26:41, 43	28:16, 20–21, 27; 30:19; 32:35, 41, 43
27. multiple punishment	26:18, 21, 24, 28	
Restoration Blessings	**Leviticus**	**Deuteronomy**
1. renewal of Yahweh's favor, loyalty, and presence	26:42, 45	4:29, 31; 30:3, 9
2. renewal of the covenant	26:42, 44–45	4:31
3. restoration of true worship and ability to be faithful		4:30; 30:6, 8
4. population increase		30:5, 9
5. agricultural bounty	26:42	30:9
6. restoration of general prosperity, well-being, and wealth		30:3, 5, 9; 32:39
7. return from exile and repossession of the land		30:3–5
8. reunification		30:3–4
9. power over enemies and aliens		30:7
10. freedom and restoration from death and destruction	26:44	30:6; 32:39

No single prophetic book contains all twenty-seven types of curses or all ten types of restoration blessings. The shorter books normally contain few of either. Malachi, on the other hand, contains a fairly high proportion of both types relative to its length, confirming what readers of the book have long noticed: the Book of Malachi is closely concerned with fidelity to the covenant and the consequences (thus curses and blessings) of keeping or breaking the law of Moses. In Malachi, the curses and restoration blessings are distributed as follows:

1:3	"I have hated Esau."	curse type 1	anger and rejection from Yahweh
1:3	"I have made his hill country a desolation and his heritage a desert for jackals."	curse type 9c	desolation of the land
1:4	"They may build, but I will tear down."	curse type 15	futility
1:4	"They are called the wicked country, the people with whom the LORD is angry forever."	curse type 16	dishonor and degradation
1:5	"Your own eyes shall see this."	restoration blessing type 9	power over enemies and aliens
1:9	"Will he show favor to any of you?"	curse type 1	anger and rejection from Yahweh
1:10	"I will not accept an offering from your hands."	curse type 2	rejection and destruction of the cult
1:11	"Incense is offered to my name, and a pure offering."	restoration blessing type 3	restoration of true worship and ability to be faithful
1:14	"Cursed be the cheat who has a male in the flock and vows to give it, and yet sacrifices to the Lord what is blemished."	curse type 25	general and unspecified
2:2	"I will send the curse on you and I will curse your blessings."	curse type 2	rejection and destruction of the cult
2:2	"I will curse your blessings."	curse type 15	futility
2:3	"I will rebuke your offspring."	curse type 12a	decimation and infertility of family
2:3	"I will . . . spread dung on your faces."	curse type 16	dishonor and degradation
2:9	"I make you despised and abased before all the people."	curse type 16	dishonor and degradation
2:12	"May the LORD cut off from the tents of Jacob anyone who does this."	curse type 24	death and destruction
2:12	"May the LORD cut off from the tents of Jacob anyone who . . . bring[s] an offering to the LORD of hosts."	curse type 2	rejection and destruction of the cult

3:1	"The Lord whom you seek will suddenly come to his temple."	restoration blessing type 1	renewal of Yahweh's favor, loyalty, and presence
3:2	"Who can endure the day of his coming, and who can stand when he appears?"	curse type 24	death and destruction
3:2	"He is like a refiner's fire and like fullers' soap."	curse type 10	destruction by fire
3:3	"He will purify the descendants of Levi and refine them like gold and silver, until they present offerings to the LORD in righteousness."	restoration blessing type 3	restoration of true worship and ability to be faithful
3:5	"I will draw near to you for judgment."	curse type 26	general punishment, curse, and vengeance
3:7	"I will return to you."	restoration blessing type 1	renewal of Yahweh's favor, loyalty, and presence
3:9	"You are cursed with a curse."	curse type 26	general punishment, curse, and vengeance
3:10–11	"I will . . . pour down for you an overflowing blessing. . . . Your vine in the field shall not be barren."	restoration blessing type 5	agricultural bounty
3:12	"All nations will count you happy, for you will be a land of delight."	restoration blessing type 6	restoration of general prosperity, well-being, and wealth
3:17	"They shall be . . . my special possession."	restoration blessing type 1	renewal of Yahweh's favor, loyalty, and presence
3:17	"I will spare them as parents spare their children."	restoration blessing type 10	freedom and restoration from death and destruction
3:19 [4:1]	"The day is coming, burning like an oven."	curse type 10	destruction by fire
3:20 [4:2]	"The sun of righteousness shall rise, with healing in its wings. You shall go out leaping like calves from the stall."	restoration blessing type 6	restoration of general prosperity, well-being, and wealth
3:21 [4:3]	"You shall tread down the wicked."	restoration blessing type 9	power over enemies and aliens
3:24 [4:6]	"So that I will not come and strike the land with a curse."	curse types 9c and 24	desolation of the land; death and destruction

Analysis

    Superscription (1:1)

  I. First Disputation (1:2–5)

    A. The People Question the Lord's Love, and He Responds with a Question (1:2–3a)

    B. The Lord Will Make Edom Desolate (1:3b–4)

    C. Israel Will Learn That the Lord Is Not a Territorial Deity (1:5)

  II. Second Disputation (1:6–2:9)

    A. Three Questions Deserve an Answer (1:6)

    B. The Lord Responds to Israel's Question (1:7–8a)

    C. The Priests Should Know It Is Wrong to Offer Defective Sacrifices (1:8b–9)

    D. The Priests Are Warned by God (1:10–2:5)

    E. The Priests Will Become Despised Because They Have Corrupted Their Office (2:6–9)

  III. Third Disputation (2:10–16)

    A. Because of the People's Unfaithfulness, the Lord Will Not Accept Their Sacrifices (2:10–13)

    B. The Lord Will Not Accept Their Offerings Because He Must Enforce the Covenant (2:14)

    C. The People Must Preserve Their Spirit and Not Be Unfaithful (2:15–16)

  IV. Fourth Disputation (2:17–3:5)

    A. The People Doubt the Lord's Justice (2:17)

    B. When the Messenger Comes, the Lord Will Display His Justice (3:1–5)

  V. Fifth Disputation (3:6–12)

    A. In Spite of the People's Disobedience, the Lord Does Not Change (3:6–7a)

    B. The People Can Return to God by Restoring to Him Their Tithes and Offerings (3:7b–12)

  VI. Sixth Disputation (3:13–21 [3:13–4:3])

    A. The People Have Overruled God (3:13)

    B. The People Believe It Is Useless to Serve God (3:14–15)

    C. The Faithful People of Malachi's Day Have a Covenant Renewal Ceremony (3:16–21 [3:16–4:3])

  VII. Concluding Summary (3:22–24 [4:4–6])

    A. The People Are Exhorted to Remember the Law of Moses (3:22 [4:4])

    B. The People Receive a Promise of Elijah and a Warning of Destruction (3:23–24 [4:5–6])

Select Bibliography

Ackroyd, P. R. "The History of Israel in the Exilic and Post-Exilic Periods." Pp. 320–50 in *Tradition and Interpretation*. Edited by G. W. Anderson. Oxford: Clarendon, 1979.

_____. "Two Old Testament Problems of the Early Persian Period." *Journal of Near Eastern Studies* 17 (1958): 13–37.

Adamson, J. T. H. "Malachi." Pp. 804–9 in New Bible Commentary. Revised and edited by D. Guthrie. London: InterVarsity, 1970.

Adinolfi, M. "Il ripudio secondo Mal 2:14–16." *Bibbia e oriente* 12 (1970): 246–56.

Allen, C. J. *Hosea–Malachi*. BBC 7. Nashville: Broadman, 1972.

Allison, D. C., Jr. "Elijah Must Come First." *Journal of Biblical Literature* 103 (1984): 256–58.

Alonso Díaz, J. "El bautismo de fuego anunciado por el Bautista y su relación con la profecía de Malaquías." *Estudios bíblicos* 23 (1965): 319–31.

Alt, A. "Die Rolle Samaria bei der Entstehung des Judentums." In Vol. 2, pp. 316–37, *Kleine Schriften zur Geschichte des Volkes Israel*. Munich: Beck, 1953.

Althann, R. "Mal 2:13–14 and UT 125,12–13." *Biblica* 58 (1977): 418–21.

Andersen, F. I. *The Verbless Clause in the Pentateuch*. JBL Monograph Series 14. Nashville: Abingdon, 1970.

Andrew, M. E. "Post-Exilic Prophets and the Ministry of Creating Community." *Expository Times* 93 (1982): 42–46.

Archer, G. L., Jr. "Old Testament History and Recent Archaeology from the Exile to Malachi." *Bibliotheca Sacra* 127 (1970): 291–98.

Baldwin, J. G. *Haggai, Zechariah, Malachi: An Introduction and Commentary*. Tyndale Old Testament Commentary. London/Downers Grove, Ill.: Tyndale/InterVarsity, 1972.

_____. "Malachi 1:11 and the Worship of the Nations in the Old Testament." *Theologische Beiträge* 23 (1972): 117–24.

Bamberger, B. J. "Fear and Love of God in the Old Testament." *Hebrew Union College Annual* 6 (1929): 39–53.

Bartlett, J. R. "From Edomites to Nabataeans: A Study in Continuity." *The Palestine Exploration Quarterly* 3 (1979): 53–66.

_____. "The Brotherhood of Edom." *Journal for the Study of the Old Testament* 2 (1977): 2–27.

Begg, C. T. "The Classical Prophets in the Chronistic History." *Biblische Zeitschrift* 32 (1988): 100–107.

Bennett, T. M. "Malachi." Pp. 366–94 in BBC 7. Edited by C. J. Allen. Nashville: Broadman, 1969.

Bergen, R. V. *The Prophets and the Law.* Monographs of the Hebrew Union College 4. Cincinnati, Ohio: Hebrew Union College, 1974.

Berquist, J. L. "The Social Setting of Malachi." *Biblical Theological Bulletin* 19 (1989): 121–26.

Bewer, J. A. "The Book of the Twelve Prophets." Vol. 2. Harper Bible. New York: Harper & Row, 1949.

Blake, R. D. *The Rhetoric of Malachi.* Diss. Union Theological Seminary, 1988. No. 11, 3395–96.

Blenkinsopp, J. *A History of Prophecy in Israel.* London: SPCK; Philadelphia: Westminster, 1984.

Boeker, H. J. "Bemerkungen zu formgeschichtlichen Terminologie des Buches Maleachi." *Zeitschrift für die alttestamentlich Wissenschaft* 78 (1966): 78–80.

Bossard, E., and R. G. Kratz. "Maleachi im Zwolfprophetenbuch."*Biblische Notizen* 52 (1990): 27–46.

Botterweck, G. J. "Die Sonne der Gerechtigkeit am Tage Jahwes, Auslegung von Mal 3:13–21." *Bibel und Leben* 1 (1960): 253–60.

_____. "Ideal und Wirklichkeit der Jerusalemer Priester, Auslegung von Mal. 1:6–10; 2:1–9." *Bibel und Leben* 1 (1960): 100–109.

_____. "Jakob habe ich lieb—Esau hasse ich. Auslegung von Malachias 1,2–5." *Bibel und Leben* 1 (1960): 28–38.

_____. "Schelt- und Mahnrede gegen Mischehen und Ehescheidung, Auslegung von Mal. 2:2, 10–16." *Bibel und Leben* 1 (1960): 179–85.

Brichto, H. C. *The Problem of "Curse" in the Hebrew Bible.* JBL Monograph Series 13. Philadelphia: SBL, 1963.

Broecker, H. J. "Bermerkungen zur formgeschichtlichen Terminologie des Buches Maleachi." *Zeitschrift für die alttestamentliche Wissenschaft* 78 (1966): 78–80.

Brooks, A. "The Influence of Malachi upon the New Testament." *Southwestern Journal of Theology* 30 (1987): 28–31.

Broome, E. C. "Nabaiati, Nebaioth and the Nabataens: The Linguistic Problem." *Journal of Semitic Studies* 18 (1973): 1–16.

Browning, I. *Petra.* London: Chatto & Windus, 1974.

Bruno, A. *Das Buch der Zwölf Eine rhythmische und textkritische untersuchung.* Stockholm: Almquist, 1957.

_____. "Zum Text der drier letzten kleinen Propheten." *Zeitschrift für die alttestamentliche Wissenschaft* 26 (1906): 1–28.

Buhl, F. "Einige textkritische Bemerkungen zu den kleinen Propheten." *Zeitschrift für die alttestamentliche Wissenschaft* 5 (1885): 179–84.

Bulmerincq, A. "Die Mischehen in B. Maleachi." Pp. 31–42 in *Oriental Studies Published in Commemoration of the Forti-*

eth Anniversary (1883–1923) of Paul Haupt as Director of the Oriental Seminary of the Johns Hopkins University, Baltimore, MD. Edited by Cyrus Adler and Aaron Ember. Baltimore: Johns Hopkins, 1926.

_____. *Einleitung in das Buch des Propheten Maleachi: Die Theologie des Buches.* Dorpat: Acta et Commentationes, Univ. Dorpat. 1926, pp. 225–355.

_____. *Kommentar zum Buch des Propheten Maleachi.* Tartu: Kommissionsverlag von J. G. Krueger, 1932.

Burrows, M. *The Basis of Israelite Marriage.* American Oriental Society Series 15. New Haven, Conn.: American Oriental Society, 1938.

Cameron, D. "A Message from Malachi." *Expository Times* 32 (1920–21): 408–10.

Carmignac, J. "Vestiges d'un pésher de Malachie?" *Revue de Qumran* 4 (1963): 97–100.

Chary, T. *Les prophetes et le culte a partir de l'exil.* Paris: Desclée, 1955.

Childs, B. S. *Memory and Tradition in Israel.* SBT 37. London: SCM, 1962.

_____. *Introduction to the Old Testament as Scripture.* Philadelphia: Fortress, 1979.

Clark, D. G. *Elijah as Eschatological High Priest: An Examination of the Elijah Tradition in Mal 3:23–24.* Diss. University of Notre Dame, 1975.

Collins, J. J. "The Message of Malachi." *The Bible Today* 22 (1984): 209–15.

Coppens, J. "Malachi's Messenger Not Jesus." *Theology Digest* 22 (1974): 145–50.

Cresson, B. C. "The Condemnation of Edom." Pp. 125–48 in *The Use of the Old Testament in the New.* W. F. Stinespring's Festschrift. Edited by J. M. Efird. Durham, N.C.: Duke University Press, 1972.

Cross, F. M., Jr. "A Reconstruction of the Judean Restoration." *Journal of Biblical Literature* 94 (1975): 4–18.

DeLang, N. R. M. "Some New Fragments of Aquila on Malachi and Job [plates]?" *Vetus Testamentum* 30 (1980): 291–94.

Dell'Oca, E. C. "El sacrificio de la Misa según Mal 1,10s." *Revista Bíblica con Sección Litúrgica* 18 (1956): 127–33, 187–92.

Derrett, J. M. D. "Herod's Oath and the Baptist's Head: With an Appendix on Mk 9:12–13; Mal 3:24; Micah 7:6." *Biblische Zeitschrift* 9 (1965): 49–59, 233–46.

Devescovi, U. "L'alleanza di Jahvé con Levi." *Biblica et orientalia* 4 (1962): 205–18.

Drinkard, J. F., Jr. "The Socio-Historical Setting of Malachi." *Review and Expositor* 84 (1987): 383–90.

Dumbrell, W. J. "Malachi and the Ezra–Nehemiah Reforms." *Reformed Theological Review* 35 (1976): 42–52.

Eybers, I. H. "Malachi—The Messenger of the Lord." *Theologia Evangelica* 3 (1970): 12–20.

_____. "The Use of Proper Names as a Stylistic Device." *Semitias* 2 (1971): 82–92.

Faierstein, M. M. "Why do the Scribes Say that Elijah Must Come First?" *Journal of Biblical Literature* 100 (1981): 75–86.

Fensham, F. C. "Widow, Orphan and the Poor in Ancient Near Eastern Legal and Wisdom Literature." *Journal of Near Eastern Studies* 21 (1962): 129–39.

_____. "Peḥâ in the Old Testament and the Ancient Near East." *Studies in the Chronicler*. OTWSA 19. Pochefstroom: Pro Rege, 1976, pp. 44–52.

Fischer, J. A. "Notes on the Literary Form and Message of Malachi." *Catholic Biblical Quarterly* 34 (1972): 315–20.

_____. "Understanding Malachi." *The Bible Today* 66 (1973): 1173–77.

Fishbane, M. "Form and Reformulation of the Priestly Blessing." *Journal of the American Oriental Society* 103 (1983): 115–21.

Fransen, I. "Le messager de l'Alliance, Mal 2,17–3,14." *Bible et vie chrétienne* 16 (1956): 53–65.

Freedman, B. "An Unnoted Support for a Variant to the MT of Mal 3:5." *Journal of Biblical Literature* 98 (1979): 405–6.

Fuller, R. "Text-Critical Problems in Malachi 2:10–16." *Journal of Biblical Literature* 110 (1991): 47–57.

Gehman, H. S. "The 'Burden' of the Prophets." *Jewish Quarterly Review* 31 (1940–41): 107–21.

Geller, S. A. *Parallelism in Early Biblical Poetry*. Harvard Semitic Monograph 20. Missoula, Mont.: Scholars, 1979.

Gemser, B. "The *Rîb* or Controversy Pattern in Hebrew Mentality." *Vetus Testamentum Supplement* 3 (1955): 124–37.

Glazier-McDonald, B. "Intermarriage, Divorce, and the *bat-'el nekar*: Insights into Mal 2:10–16." *Journal of Biblical Literature* 106 (1987): 603–11.

_____. "Malachi 2:12: *er we oneh*—Another Look." *Journal of Biblical Literature* 105 (1986): 295–98.

_____. *Malachi: The Divine Messenger*. Atlanta: Scholars, 1987.

Gray, J. "The Day of Yahweh in Cultic Experience and Eschatological Prospect." *Svensk exegetisk årsbok* 39 (1974): 5.

Gray, W. "Useless Fires: Worship in the Time of Malachi." *Southwestern Journal of Theology* 30 (1987): 35–41.

Greenfield, J. C. "Two Biblical Passages in Light of Their Near Eastern Background—Ezekiel 16:30 and Malachi 3:17." *Eretz-Israel* 16 (1982): 56–61 [Hebrew].

Gruber, M. I. "The Many Faces of Hebrew *nasa' panayim,* 'lift up the face.'" *Zeitschrift für die alttestamentliche Wissenschaft* 95 (1983): 252–60.

Habel, N. C. *The Book of Job: A Commentary.* Old Testament Library. Philadelphia: Westminster, 1985.

Habets, G. "Vorbild und Zerrbild. Eine Exegese von Maleachi 1,6–2,9." *Teresianum* 41 (1990): 5–58.

Halevy, J. "Le prophete Malachie." *Revue sémitique* 17 (1909): 1–44.

Hammond, P. C. *The Nabataeans—Their History, Culture and Archaeology.* Studies in Mediterranean Archaeology. Vol. 37. Gothenberg, Sweden: Paul Åstroms Förlag, 1973.

Harrison, R. K. *Introduction to the Old Testament.* Grand Rapids: Eerdmans, 1969.

Hausmann, M. "Der grosse und schreckliche Tag des Herrn." Pp. 85–91 in *FS S. Ben-Chorin: Israel hat dennoch Gott zum Trost.* Edited by Gotthold Müller. Trier: Paulinus, 1978.

Heflin, J. N. "The Prophet Malachi, His World and His Book." *Southwestern Journal of Theology* 30 (1987): 5–11.

Hendrix, J. D. "'You Say': Confrontation Dialogue in Malachi." *Review and Expositor* 84 (1987): 465–67.

Hengstenberg, E. W. *Christology of the Old Testament.* 4 vols. Translated by T. Meyer and James Martin. Edinburgh: T. & T. Clark, 1872–78. Reprinted Grand Rapids: Kregel, 1956.

Hernando, E. "Profecía y Apocalíptica. Un estudio sobre el libro de Malaquías en su relación con la Sabiduría y la Apocalíptica." *Lumen* 20 (1971): 210–30.

Herranz, A. "Dilexi Jacob, Esau autem odio habui." *Estudios bíblicos* 1 (1941): 559–83.

_____. "El Profeta Malaquías y el sacrificio de nuestros altares." *Estudios bíblicos* 2 (1930): 283–300.

_____. *Treaty Curses and the Old Testament Prophets.* BibOr 16. Rome: Pontifical Biblical Institute, 1964.

Holladay, W. L. *The Root ŠUBH in the Old Testament: With Particular Reference to Its Usages in Covenantal Contexts.* Leiden: Brill, 1958.

Holtzmann, O. "Der Prophet Maleachi und der Ursprung des Pharisäerbundes." *Archiv für Religionswissenschaft* 29 (1931): 1–21.

Huffmon, H. "The Covenant Lawsuit in the Prophets." *Journal of Biblical Literature* 78 (1959): 285–95.

Hugenberger, G. B. *Marriage as Covenant: A Study of Biblical Law and Ethics Governing Marriage Developed from the Perspective of Malachi.* VTSup 52. Leiden: Brill, 1994.

_____. "Malachi." Pp. 883–89 in *New Bible Commentary Twenty-first Century Edition* [4th ed.]. Edited by D. A. Carson

et al. Leicester, England: InterVarsity; Downers Grove: Inter-
Varsity, 1994.

Hunt, B., Jr. "Attitudes toward Divorce in Post-Exilic Judaism."
Biblical Illustrator 12 (Summer 1986): 62–65.

Hvidberg, F. F. *Weeping and Laughter in the Old Testament.*
Leiden: Brill, 1962.

Isbell, C. D. *Malachi.* Grand Rapids: Zondervan, 1980.

Jagersma, H. "The Tithes in the Old Testament." Pp. 116–28 in
Remembering All the Way . . . OTS 21. Leiden: Brill, 1981.

Janzen, W. "asre in the Old Testament." *Harvard Theological
Review* 58 (1965): 215–26.

Kaiser, W. C., Jr. *Micah–Malachi.* Vol. 21. The Communicator's
Commentary. Dallas: Word, 1992.

_____. *Malachi: God's Unchanging Love.* Grand Rapids: Bak-
er, 1984.

_____. "The Promise of the Arrival of Elijah in Malachi and
the Gospels." *Grace Theological Journal* 3 (1982): 221–33.

Keller, C. A. "Religionswissenschaftliche Betrachtungen zu
Maleachis Kritik an der Opferpraxis seiner Zeit." Pp. 79–91 in
Studien zum Opfer und Kult im Alten Testament. Edited by
A Schenker. 1992.

Kline, M. G. *Treaty of the Great King: The Covenant Structure
of Deuteronomy.* Grand Rapids: Eerdmans, 1963.

König, E. *Stilistik, Rhetorik, Poetik in Bezug auf die biblische
Litteratur.* Leipzig: T. Weicher, 1900.

Kooy, V. H. "The Fear and Love of God in Deuteronomy." Pp.
106–16 in *Grace upon Grace.* L. J. Kuyper's Festschrift. Edited
by J. I. Cook. Grand Rapids: Eerdmans, 1975.

Krieg, M. *Mutmassungen Uber Maleachi. Ein Monographie.* Ab-
handlungen zur Theologie des Alten und Neuen Testaments,
80. Zurich: Theologischer Verlag, 1993.

Kruse-Blinkenberg, L. "The Book of Malachi according to Codex
Syro-Hexaplaris Ambrosianus." *Studia theologica* 21 (1967):
62–82.

_____. "The Peshitta of the Book of Malachi." *Studia theolog-
ica* 20 (1966): 95–119.

Lescow, T. *Das Buch Maleachi. Texttheorie, Auslegung, Kanon-
theorie. Mit einem Exkurs Uber Jeremia 8, 8–9.* Stuttgart: Cal-
wer, 1993.

_____. "Dialogische Strukturen in den Streitreden des Buches
Maleachi." *Zeitschrift für die alttestamentliche Wissenschaft*
102 (1990): 194–212.

Limburg, J. "The Prophets in Recent Study: 1967–77." *Interpretation* 32 (1982): 56–68.

Lindblom, J. *Prophecy in Ancient Israel.* Oxford: Oxford University Press, 1962.

Long, B. "Two Question and Answer Schemata in the Prophets." *Journal of Biblical Literature* 90 (1971): 129–39.

Mackenzie, S. L., and H. H. Wallace. "Covenant Themes in Malachi." *Catholic Biblical Quarterly* 45 (1983): 549–63.

Malchow, B. V. "The Messenger of the Covenant in Mal 3:1." *Journal of Biblical Literature* 103 (1984): 252–55.

_____. "The Prophetic Contribution to Dialogue." *Biblical Theology Bulletin* 16 (1986): 127–31.

Margalioth, E. "Eschatology in the Book of Malachi." In *Sepher M. H. Segal.* Jerusalem (1964): 139–43. [Hebrew].

Matthews, J. G. "Tammuz-Worship in the Book of Malachi." *Journal of the Palestine Oriental Society* 2 (1931): 42–50.

Meinhold, A. "Die theologichen Vorspruche in den Diskussionsworten des Maleachibuches." Pp. 197–209 in *FS J. J. Boecker,* 1993.

_____. "Zustand und Zukunft des Gottesvolkes im Maleachibuch." Pp. 175–92 in *FS S. Wagner,* 1991.

Michel, J. "I Will Send You Elijah." *The Bible Today* 22 (1984): 217–22.

Miklik, J. "Textkritische und exegetische Bemerkungen zu Mal. 3,6." *Biblische Zeitschrift* 17 (1926): 224–37.

Moran, W. L. "The Ancient Near Eastern Background of the Love of God in Deuteronomy." *Catholic Biblical Quarterly* 25 (1963): 77–87.

_____. "The Scandal of the 'Great Sin' at Ugarit." *Journal of Near Eastern Studies* 18 (1959): 280–81.

_____. "The Use of the Canaanite Infinitive Absolute as a Finite Verb in the Amarna Letters from Byblos." *Journal of Cuneiform Studies* 4 (1950): 169–72.

Morgenstern, J. "Jerusalem—485 B. C." *Hebrew Union College Annual* 28 (1975): 15–47.

O'Brien, J. M. *Priest and Levite in Malachi.* Diss. Duke University, 1988, No. 8, 2270.

Ogden, G. S. "The Use of Figurative Language in Mal 2.10–16." *The Bible Translator* 39 (1988): 223–30.

Or, D. "Malachi—Last of the Prophets, and His Link to Moses." *Beth Mikra* 31 (1985–86): 316–19 [Hebrew].

Petersen, D. L. *Late Israelite Prophecy: Studies in Deutero-Prophetic Literature and in Chronicles.* SBLMS 23. Missoula, Mont.: Scholars, 1977.

Pfeiffer, E. "Die Disputationsworte im Buche Maleachi." *Evangelische Theologie* 19 (1959): 546–58.

Pierce, W. "A Thematic Development of the Haggai/Zechariah/Malachi Corpus." *Journal of the Evangelical Theology Society* 27 (1984): 401–11.

_____. "Literary Connectors and a Haggai/Zechariah/Malachi Corpus." *Journal of the Evangelical Theology Society* 27 (1984): 277–89.

Rábanos, R. "El sacrificio eucarístico profetizado por Malaquías." *Cultura biblica* 5 (1948): 151–54.

Rabinowitz J. J. "The 'Great Sin' in Ancient Egyptian Marriage Contracts." *Journal of Near Eastern Studies* 18 (1959): 73.

Radday, Y. T., and Moshe A. Pollatschek. "Vocabulary Richness in Post-Exilic Prophetic Books." *Zeitschrift für die alttestamentliche Wissenschaft* 92 (1980): 333–46.

_____. *An Analytical Linguistic Key-Word-in-Context Concordance to the Books of Haggai, Zechariah, and Malachi.* The Computer Bible 4. Wooster, Ohio: Biblical Research Associates, 1973.

Redditt, P. L. "The Book of Malachi in Its Social Setting." *Catholic Biblical Quarterly* 56 (1994): 240–55.

Rehm, M. "Das Opfer der Völker nach Mal 1:11." Pp. 193–208 in *Lex Tua Veritas.* Festschrift für H. Junker. Edited by H. Gross and F. Mussner. Trier: Paulinus-Verlag, 1961.

Rembold, A. "Die eucharistische Weissagung des Propheten Malachias." *Theologie und Glaube* 16 (1924): 58–70.

Renaud, B. "Le jour du Seigneur, Mal 3, 19–20." Pp. 64–70 in 33 Dimanche ordinaire = Assemblées du Seigneur 64. Paris: Éd. du Cerf, 1969.

_____. "Reproches aux prêtres, Mal 1,14b–2,2b8.–11." Pp. 6–12 in Assemblées du Seigneur 62. Paris: Éd. du Cerf, 1970.

Renker, A. *Dic Tora bei Maleachi. Ein Beitrag zur Bedeutungsgeschichte von Tora im AT.* Freiburger Th. St. 112. Freiburg: Herder, 1979.

Reventlow, H. v. "Mal 3,13–21." *Wissenschaft und Praxis in Kirche und Gesellschaft* 59, 11 (1970): 113–19.

Reynolds, C. B. *Malachi and the Priesthood.* Diss. Yale University, 1993.

Rinaldi, G. "La profezia di Mal 1,11 e la S. Mesa." Pp. 23–30 in *Il Misterio dell'Altare nel peniero e nella vita della Chiesa.* Edited by A. Piolanti. Rome: Desclée, 1957.

Robinson, A. "God the Refiner of Silver." *Catholic Biblical Quarterly* 11 (1949): 188–90.

Ross, J. F. "The Prophet as Yahweh's Messenger." Pp. 98–107 in *Israel's Prophetic Heritage: Essays in Honor of James Muilenburg.* Edited by B. W. Anderson and W. Harrelson. New York: Harper & Brothers, 1962.

Rudolph W. *Haggai—Zacharja 1–8—Sacharja 9–14—Malachi.* Kommentar zum Alten Testament. Neukirchen: Neukirchener Verlag, 1976.

_____. "Zu Malachi 2:10–16." *Zeitschrift für die alttestamentliche Wissenschaft* 93 (1981): 85–90.

Saydon, P. P. "Assonance in Hebrew as a Means of Expressing Emphasis." *Biblica* 36 (1955): 36–50, 287–304.

Scalise, P. J. "To Fear or Not to Fear: Question of Reward and Punishment in Malachi 2:17–4:3." *Review and Expositor* 84 (1987): 409–18.

Schreiner, S. "Mischehen—Ehebruch—Ehescheidung: Betrachtungen zu Malachi 2:10–16." *Zeitschrift für die alttestamentliche Wissenschaft* 91 (1979): 207–28.

Sellin, Ernst. *Das Zwölfprophetenbuch.* Kommentar zum Alten Testament 12. Leipzig: Deichert, 1929–30.

Selms, A. van. "The Inner Cohesion of the Book of Malachi." *Die Ou Testamentiese Werkgemeenskap in Suid-Afrika* 13 (1975): 27–40.

Seraphimus ab Ausejo. "De matrimoniis mixtix apud Mal. 2,10–16." *Verbum domini* 11 (1931): 367–73.

Sessolo, P. "Particolarismo ed universalismo di salvezza nel libro di Malachia." *Euntes Docete* 31 (1978): 80–107.

Skrinjar, A. "Angelus Testamenti." *Verbum domini* 14 (1934): 40–48.

Smalley, W. A. "Translating 'Thus Says the Lord.'" *The Bible Translator* 29 (1978): 222–24.

Smith, J. M. P. *A Critical and Exegetical Commentary on the Book of Malachi.* ICC. Edinburgh: T. & T. Clark, 1912, repr. 1961.

Smith, R. L. *Micah–Malachi.* Word Biblical Commentary 32. Waco: Word, 1984.

_____. "The Shape of Theology in the Book of Malachi." *Southwestern Journal of Theology* 30 (1987): 22–27.

Snyman, S. D. "Antitheses in Malachi 1:2–5." *Zeitschrift für die alttestamentliche Wissenschaft* 98 (1986): 436–38.

_____. *Antithesis in the Book of Malachi.* Diss. University of Pretoria, 1985, No. 10, 3066–67.

_____. "Chiasmes in Mal. 1:2–5." *Skrif en Kerk* (1984): 17–22.

_____. "Haat Jahwe vir Esau? ('n Verkenning van Mal. 1:3a." *N* 25 (1984): 358–62.

Spoer, H. H. "Some New Considerations towards the Dating of the Book of Malachi." *Jewish Quarterly Review* 20 (1908): 167–86.

Stamm, J. J. "Ein ugaritisch-hebräisches Verbum und seine Ableitungen." *Theologische Zeitschrift* 35 (1979): 5–9.

Starcky, J. "The Nabataeans: A Historical Sketch." *The Biblical Archaeologist* 18 (1955): 84–106.

Steinmann, J. *Le Livre de la Consolation d'Israel et les Prophetes du Retour de l'Exile.* LectDiv 28. Paris: Editiones du Cerf, 1960.

Stiassny, M. J. "Le prophete Élie dans le Judaïsme." Pp. 199–255 in *Élie, le Prophete*. Edited by G. Bardy et al. Bruges: Desclée de Brouwer, 1956.

Stuart, D. *Studies in Early Hebrew Meter*. HSM 13. Missoula, Mont.: Scholars, 1976.

_____. "The Old Testament Prophets' Self-Understanding of Their Prophecy." *Themelios* (1980–81): 9–14.

_____. *Hosea–Jonah*. Word Biblical Commentary 31. Waco: Word, 1987.

_____. "Names, Proper." Vol. 3, pp. 483–88 in the *International Standard Bible Encyclopedia*. Edited by Geoffrey W. Bromiley et al. Grand Rapids: Eerdmans, 1986.

_____. "The Sovereign's Day of Conquest." *Bulletin of the American Schools of Oriental Research* 221 (1976): 159–64.

Stuhlmueller, C. "Sacrifice among the Nations." *The Bible Today* 22 (1984): 223–25.

Sutcliffe, E. F. "Malachi's Prophecy of the Eucharistic Sacrifice." *IER* 5 (1922): 502–13.

Swetnam, J. "Malachi 1:11: An Interpretation." *Catholic Biblical Quarterly* 31 (1969): 200–209.

Tate, M. E. "Questions for Priests and People in Malachi 1:2–2:16." *Review and Expositor* 84 (1987): 391–407.

Teeple, H. M. *The Mosaic Eschatological Prophet*. SBLMS, Vol. 10. Philadelphia: Society of Biblical Literature, 1957.

Thompson, J. A. "Israel's Haters." *Vetus Testamentum* 29 (1979): 200–205.

Tillman, W. M., Jr. "Key Ethical Issues in Malachi." *Southwestern Journal of Theology* 30 (1987): 42–47.

Torrey, C. C. "The Edomites in Southern Judah." *Journal of Biblical Literature* 17 (1898): 16–20.

Tosato, A. "Il Ripudio: Delitto e Pena (Mal 2:10–16)." *Biblica* 59 (1978): 548–53.

Utzschneider, H. "Die Schriftprophetie und die Frage nach dem Ende der Prophetie. Uberlegungen anhand von Mal 1,6–2,16." *Zeitschrift für die alttestamentliche Wissenschaft* 104 (1992): 377–94.

Utzschneider, H. *Kunder oder Schreiber? Eine These zum Problem der "Schriftprophetie" auf Grund von Maleachi 1,6–2,9*. Beitrage zur Erforschung des Alten Testaments und des Antiken Judentums, 19. Frankfurt am Main: P. Lang, 1989.

Vaccari, A. "Matrimonio e divorzio in un contrastato versetto del profeta Malachia (2:15f)." *Civilta Cattolica* 114 (1963): 357–58.

Van Der Woude, A. S. "Malachi's Struggle for a Pure Community: Reflections on Malachi 2:10–16." Pp. 65–71 in *Tradition and Reinterpretation in Jewish and Early Christian Litera-*

ture: Essays in Honour of Jurgen C. H. Lebram. Edited by J. W. Van Henten et al. Studia Post-Biblica 36. Leiden: Brill, 1986.

Van Selms, A. "The Inner Cohesion of the Book of Malachi." Pp. 27–40 in *Studies in Old Testament Prophecy*. OTWSA. Edited by W. C. van Wyk. Potchefstroom: Pro Rege, 1975.

Van Seters, J. *Abraham in History and Tradition*. New Haven, Conn.: Yale University Press, 1975.

Vattioni, F. "Mal 3,20c e un mese del calendario fenicio." *Biblica* 40 (1959): 1012–15.

Vattioni, F. "Malachia 3,20 e l'origine della giustizia in Oriente." *Revista bíblica* 6 (1958): 353–60.

Vaux, R. de. *Ancient Israel: Its Life and Institutions*. Translated by John McHugh. New York: McGraw-Hill, 1961.

Verhoef, P. A. "Some Notes on Malachi 1:11." *OTWSA* (1966): 163–72.

_____ . *The Books of Haggai and Malachi*. NICOT. Grand Rapids: Eerdmans, 1987.

_____ . *Maleachi Verklaard* . Commentar op het Oude Testament. Kampen: Kok, 1972

Viberg, A. "Waking a Sleeping Metaphor: A New Interpretation of Malachi 1:11." *Tyndale Bulletin* 45 (1994): 297–319.

Villalón, J. A. "Sources Vétéro-documentaires de la doctrine qumranienne des deux Messies." *Römische Quartalschrift* 8, no. 29 (1972): 53–63.

Vriezen, T. C. "How to Understand Malachi 1:11." Pp. 128–36 in *Grace Upon Grace*, L. J. Kuyper's Festschrift. Edited by J. Cook. Grand Rapids: Eerdmans, 1975.

Waldman, N. M. "Some Notes on Malachi 3:6; 3:13; and Psalm 42:11." *Journal of Biblical Literature* 93 (1974): 543–49.

Wallis, G. "Wesen und Struktur der Botschaft Maleachis." In *Das Ferne und Nahe Wort*. Fest. L. Rost. Ed. Fritz Maass. BZAW 105. Berlin: Töpelmann (1967): 229–37.

Waltke, B. K., and Michael O'Connor. *An Introduction to Biblical Hebrew Syntax*. Winona Lake, Ind.: Eisenbrauns, 1990.

Watts, J. D. W. "Introduction to the Book of Malachi." *Review and Expositor* 84 (1987): 373–81.

Weiner, A. *The Prophet Elijah in the Development of Judaism*. London: Kegan Paul, 1978.

Weinfeld, M. *Deuteronomy and the Deuteronomic School*. Oxford: Clarendon, 1972.

Wendland, E. "Linear and Concentric Patterns in Malachi." *The Bible Translator* 36 (1985): 108–21.

Whedbee, J. W. "A Question-Answer-Schema in Haggai 1: The Form and Function of Haggai 1:9–11." Pp. 184–94 in *Biblical and Near Eastern Studies*. Fest. W. S. LaSor. Edited by G. A. Tuttle. Grand Rapids: Eerdmans, 1978.

Williams, D. T. "The Windows of Heaven. [Mal 3,10]." *Old Testament Essays* 5 (1992): 402–13.

Yamauchi, E. M. "Ezra, Nehemiah." Vol. 4, pp. 565–771 in *The Expositor's Bible Commentary*. Edited by Frank I. Gaebelein. Grand Rapids: Zondervan, 1988.

Ziegler, J. *Beiträge zum griechischen Dodekaprophetom*. Göttingen, 1942.

Zimmerli, W. *The Law and the Prophets*. Oxford: Oxford University Press, 1965.

Superscription (1:1)

STUART

1 A message: Yahweh's word to Israel through Malachi.

NRSV

1 An oracle. The word of the LORD to Israel by Malachi.

1:1. מַשָּׂא (message): The form is the maqtal nominal from the root נשא and means, literally, "burden," with the derived meanings of duty, pronouncement, oracle, message, and revelation (BDB, p. 672; KB, p. 604: utterance, oracle; RSV, NRSV, NAB, NEB: oracle). The term מַשָּׂא is used thirty-four times in the Old Testament prophetic books to refer to a divinely revealed message. In all probability this stems from the prophetic concept that a prophet is, by definition, a messenger sent from God, thus transporting as his or her "burden" the word of Yahweh from sender to recipient. The term is used sixteen times at the outset of the superscriptions of prophetic oracles, as it is at the beginning of Malachi. In such a position it functions as an overall description of the contents of what follows, whether a particular section in a book (e.g., Isa. 13:1, "The Message of Babylon") or, as in Malachi, an entire small book of prophecy (e.g., Nah. 1:1, "The Message of Nineveh"; Hab. 1:1, "The Message That Habakkuk the Prophet Saw"). This definition is not universally accepted, however. Some scholars have argued that מַשָּׂא means "threatening prophetic speech" or the like (so Gehman, "'Burden' of the Prophets," p. 110; Kaiser, *TWOT*, 2:602; Hengstenberg, *Christology of the Old Testament*, 4:139–228). This assumption of a negative conno-

---

1:1. The superscriptions (titles, incipits) of prophetic books often provide useful biographical and chronological information. The superscription of the Book of Malachi, on the other hand, raises questions and is sufficiently laconic in its wording as to leave us uncertain as to whether we even know the name of the author. The book's superscription can be translated in several ways, but I judge the best rendering to be "A Message: Yahweh's Word to Israel through Malachi." In any case, there are three components to the superscription: content, sender, recipient. The content is a divinely revealed message, the sender-author of the message is Yahweh, and the intended recipient is his people Israel.

Three special questions are raised by the title of the book (1:1): (1) Is there a significance to the use of *maśśaʾ* (message/burden) at the outset of the book that sets Malachi apart from any other prophetic book or links it to any others in some way? (2) Is *malʾākî* (Malachi) a proper name or merely a descriptive noun for an anonymous prophet? (3) Does the precise wording at the beginning of the superscription (*maśśāʾ dĕbar-yhwh*, a message: Yahweh's word) link Malachi with the final chapters of Zechariah, where we find the same wording introducing that book's final two sections, so that it should not be seen as an independent book but as an appendage to the Book of Zechariah?

The answer to the first question must surely be no. Beginning a book of prophecy or a section of a prophetic book with *maśśaʾ* is much too common an option. A key to how it is used in prophetic contexts is Jeremiah 23, where the term appears repeatedly with overtones of the messenger speech concept, the common Old Testament prophetic claim that a true prophet is a messenger from Yahweh delivering exactly his word, as memorized, in the manner of an ancient messenger who "ran" from one person to another with a memorized message or "burden." The word *maśśaʾ* in Jeremiah 23 seems to refer specifically to a revelation from Yahweh given to his prophet—with emphasis on the strict unoriginality of the message. Indeed, *maśśaʾ* might in many or most prophetic contexts best be translated "revelation" (Isbell, *Malachi*, p. 25).

The third question, namely, whether the use of the first three words of the superscription indicates that Malachi is in fact an appendage to the Book of Zechariah, must in the final analysis be answered in the negative. The precise three-word title phrase (*maśśāʾ dĕbar-yhwh*, a message: Yahweh's word) occurs only in Zechariah 9:1 and 12:1 and here, and in each instance in a title line or superscription for a major section of prophecy. But what follows these three words is different in each case:

Zechariah 9:1	*maśśāʾ dĕbar-yhwh bĕʾereṣ ḥadrāk wĕdam-meśeq*	a message: Yahweh's word against Hadrach and Damascus
Zechariah 12:1	*maśśāʾ dĕbar-yhwh ʿal-yiś-rāʾēl*	a message: Yahweh's word concerning Israel
Malachi 1:1	*maśśāʾ dĕbar-yhwh ʾel-yiś-rāʾēl bĕyad malʾākî*	a message: Yahweh's word to Israel through Malachi

It is difficult to ignore the fact that the Book of Zechariah closes with two superscriptions starting with the same three words and that Malachi begins likewise. However, the similarity hardly points to a unity of composition. What could, alternatively, account for such a proximity? In all likelihood, the placement of Malachi directly after

tation for מַשָּׂא fails to appreciate the actual nature of the semantic contexts in which the word occurs. De Boer's idea that מַשָּׂא indicates a burden imposed by a (despotic!) master is surely extreme ("Meaning of the Term מַשָּׂא"). The context of Jeremiah 23:33–38 is decisive: what the people Jeremiah describes are looking for is not a harsh word of command or some sort of information that is difficult to accept; rather, they are seeking revelation—a "message" from Yahweh. In a wordplay on מַשָּׂא, Jeremiah replies that the people have become a "burden" to Yahweh that he will cast off, but otherwise clearly indicates that his opponents, including false prophets and priests, are purporting to utter "messages" from Yahweh when in fact their words are merely their own creations.

A second question raised by the superscription is more difficult to answer. Is מַלְאָכִי a proper noun (Malachi) or a common noun (messenger) with a first-person singular possessive pronominal suffix (my messenger)? The earliest versions of the Septuagint took it as a common noun (angellou autou, "[of] his messenger," reflecting, conceivably, מלאכו [maľako, his messenger, rather than maľaki, my messenger] in the Vorlage of the Septuagint—but see below), whereas two major Septuagint revisions (Symmachus, Theodotion) rendered the word as a proper noun: malachiou (of Malachi). The latter evidence is hardly decisive, however, since all three revisions were undertaken precisely to conform the Septuagint more closely with the Masoretic Text and its ongoing interpretation tradition, which, as time passed, became fixed on taking מלאכי as a proper noun. They are not, in other words, independent witnesses to the interpretation of the original text.

Zechariah is the result of editorial ordering of the two books, as part of the ordering of the Twelve, on the basis of the so-called catchword principle. By this favored principle of organization, evidenced widely in such books as Proverbs, some vocabulary or thematic feature of one unit of literature that is also shared by another is seen as a good and sufficient basis for placing the two units of literature side by side in a final setting. But was the catchword principle used to link whole books in the Minor Prophets? The answer, again, must surely be yes. Catchword ordering, in loose combination with chronological ordering, was in fact the dominant criterion for establishing the current order of the twelve Minor Prophets (see Stuart, Hosea–Jonah, pp. xlii–xlv). In other words, there is nothing in Malachi's content, style, or placement to suggest that it was once part of Zechariah, or that it, along with the material in Zechariah 9–14, once circulated independently and anonymously, eventually to be viewed as a self-contained book of prophecy for the convenient purpose of getting the number of Minor Prophets up to an even dozen.

Finally, we note that the superscription of the Book of Malachi is in all likelihood editorial. The compiler of the Minor Prophets, the book of the Twelve in Jewish tradition, surely felt the freedom to shape the wordings of the superscriptions in modest ways. The longer prophetic book superscriptions are often quite similar in style, typically identifying the prophet, his family lineage and/or hometown, and the kings during whose reign he prophesied. The shorter books, likewise, are similar in the relative brevity of their superscriptions, being normally just a few words in length, and identifying the prophet and providing some sort of summation of his subject matter. The tendency was toward consistency: the prophetic incipits were to be relative to the lengths of the books. Within this restriction, the employment of the common prophecy term maśśāʾ on the basis of the catchword principle in light of the proximity to the end of Zechariah, along with a typically brief description of the author and the content, is in fact just what we might expect to find in the first verse of the Book of Malachi.

The fact that Israel, not Judah, is named as the recipient of the prophetically carried message, even though Malachi was surely an inhabitant of postexilic Judah, reflects the common prophetic view that God's people, north and south, were a unity in spite of the long history of political separation after the death of Solomon and in spite of the north's preemption of the title Israel until its demise at the hands of the Assyrians in 722 B.C. This may be demonstrated in part statistically. The prophets use the word Israel 511 times and the word Judah 300 times even though most of them are Judeans and most of them prophesied after the eighth-century conquest of the north. This is in no small measure surely a reflection of the prophetic dependence on the Pentateuch ("Israel" occurs seventy-one times in Deuteronomy as compared to four occurrences of Judah, for

The weightiest argument in the discussion of whether מלאכי is a name (Malachi) or a common noun with suffix (my messenger) is not linguistic but literary. The fact that the term occurs in a prophetic book's superscription strongly tilts the argument in favor of the interpretation that the term is a name. What do we find in the superscriptions of all other prophetic books that actually have superscriptions (i.e., all prophetic books other than Ezekiel, Daniel, Jonah, Haggai, and Zechariah)? We find the name of the prophet. Moreover, without exception, descriptions of Yahweh's speaking his word "through" (בְּיַד) a prophet or prophets (e.g., Isa. 20:2; Hos. 12:10; Zech. 7:7, 12) are consistently third person in form. The mix

of third-person speech ("Yahweh's word to Israel") and first-person speech ("through my messenger"), required if מלאכי were to be translated as the common noun with suffix, would have no parallel elsewhere in prophetic diction. It may in fact be the case that the Septuagint rendering *angellou autou* (his messenger) derives not from a different Hebrew *Vorlage* but from a translator's decision that the first-person suffix he saw before him simply had to be corrected in light of the unacceptable awkwardness that would otherwise result from the mixing of persons in the superscription. Accordingly, I judge that מלאכי means Malachi, a prophet's name.

---

example). The prophets always prophesied on the basis of and consistent with the Pentateuch's paradigmatic teaching. The following table illustrates the overall tendency to assign the name *Israel* to God's people, in spite of variations among the individual prophetical books and the fact that some references to Israel or Judah are not reflections of prophetic outlook but simply geographical notations within narrative parts of the books:

	Israel (*yiśrā'ēl*)	Judah (*yĕhûdâ* or *yĕhûd*)
Isaiah	91	31
Jeremiah	125	183
Ezekiel	186	15
Daniel	4	8
Hosea	44	15
Joel	3	6
Amos	30	4
Obadiah	1	1
Jonah	0	0
Micah	12	4
Nahum	1	1
Habakkuk	0	0
Zephaniah	4	3
Haggai	0	4
Zechariah	5	22
Malachi	5	3
Total	511	305

Even postexilic narratives such as Ezra and Nehemiah, clearly cognizant of the fact that Israel as a political entity existed no longer (being replaced in the political terminology by Samaria and other titles), nevertheless refer often to "Israel" rather than "Judah." Ezra mentions Israel forty times and Judah fifteen; Nehemiah refers to Israel twenty-one times and Judah twenty-nine.

Malachi, not surprisingly, shares this perspective. God's people is the Israel of the patriarchal promises, the Israel of the Pentateuch, the true Israel, as distinguished by the apostle Paul so carefully in Romans and his other letters. In Malachi's day all that was left of political Israel was in fact Judah. But the remnant of God's people was truly "Israel," not merely the Persian administrative district named Judah to which groups of Mesopotamian exiles had been returning since the days of the decree of Cyrus (Ezra 1:2–4) in 539 B.C.

I. First Disputation (1:2–5)

A. The People Question the Lord's Love, and He Responds with a Question (1:2–3a)

STUART

2 I love you, Yahweh said.
You say, "In what way do you love us?"
Isn't Esau Jacob's brother? (states Yahweh).
I loved Jacob, 3but Esau I hated.

NRSV

2I have loved you, says the LORD. But you say, "How have you loved us?" Is not Esau Jacob's brother? says the LORD. Yet I have loved Jacob 3but I have hated Esau.

2–3a. אָהַבְתִּי אֶתְכֶם אָמַר יְהוָה (I love you, Yahweh said): Verbs of perception and attitude often have a present meaning in the perfect tense, as the first verb אהב (love) does here (cf. Driver, *Treatise on the Use of Tenses in Hebrew* §11; GKC §106g; Waltke and O'Connor, *Biblical Hebrew Syntax* §30.5.1). The verse's first messenger formula, אָמַר

יְהוָה, is preferably rendered in the past tense (Yahweh said), however, since it is a standard statement by which the prophet reminds his audience that he is simply repeating to them what he has already been told in the (immediate) past by Yahweh, rather than making up the message himself. וַאֲמַרְתֶּם בַּמָּה אֲהַבְתָּנוּ (you say, "In what way do you

---

2–5. Malachi 1:2–5 forms a unit with a clearly discernible beginning and ending, and there has emerged no argument against regarding it as a self-contained oracle. It appears to be poetic, and Elliger arranged it as poetry in the BHS. Major modern translations, such as the Revised Standard Version, New Revised Standard Version, and New International Version, treat it as prose, ignoring the consistent parallelism. All three major types of semantic parallelism are present (synonymous, vv. 3, 4; antithetical, vv. 2, 2–3, 4; and synthetic, v. 5) and the metrical count shows the sort of overall balance that bespeaks a purposeful poetic structure.

The passage represents a combining of literary forms. From the point of view of the essential topic, the passage is an oracle against a foreign nation, one of dozens found in the prophetic books. Indeed, in one manner or another, every one of the sixteen prophetic books of the Old Testament contains at least one full or partial oracle against foreign nations. In this case the foreign nation in question is Edom, which because of its especially long history of enmity with Israel is the most frequently attacked by the prophets of all of Israel's enemies. It may in fact be noted that the prophets often employed Edom as a synecdoche for Israel's enemies in general, because Edom was the earliest, latest, closest, and most consistently hostile of all Israel's enemies. The following listing demonstrates the remarkable level of attention paid to little Edom in the prophetical oracles against foreign nations.

Prophetic Oracles Against Foreign Nations

Ammon
  Isa. 11:14; Jer. 25:21; 49:1–6; Ezek. 25:1–7; Amos 1:13–15; Zeph. 2:8–11 (with Moab)
Arabia
  Isa. 21:13–17; Jer. 25:24; 49:28–32 (with Hazor)
Aram Damascus
  Isa. 7:7; 8:4; 17:1–14; Jer. 49:23–27; Amos 1:3–5; Zech. 9:1–2

Assyria
  Isa. 10:15–19; 10:25; 14:24–27; 30:31; 37:21–25; Mic. 5:5–6; Nah.; Zeph. 2:13–15; Jon. 3:4; Zech. 10:11
Babylon
  Isa. 13:1–22; 14:3–23; 21:1–10; 47:1–15; Jer. 50:1–46; 51: 1–64; Hab. 2:4–20
Cush (Nubia)
  Isa. 18:1–7; 20:1–5 (with Egypt); Zeph. 2:12
Edom
  Isa. 11:14; 21:11–12; 34:1–17; Jer. 25:21; Lam. 4:21; 49:7–22; Ezek. 25:12–14; 35:1–15; Joel 4:19 [3:19]; Amos 1:11–12; Obad. 1–21; Mal. 1:2–5
Egypt
  Isa. 19:1–25; 20:1–5 (with Cush); Jer. 46:1–26; Ezek. 29:1–21; 30:1–26; 31:1–18; 32:1–32; Joel 4:19 [3:19]; Zech. 10:11; 14:18–19
Elam
  Jer. 49:34–39
Moab
  Isa. 11:14; 15:1–9; 16:1–14; Jer. 25:21; 48:1–47; Ezek. 25:8–11; Amos 2:1–3; Zeph. 2:8–11 (with Ammon)
Philistia
  Isa. 11:14; 14:28–32; Jer. 25:20; 47:1–7; Ezek. 25:15–17; Amos 1:6–8; Obad. 19; Zeph. 2:4–7; Zech. 9:2–8
Sidon
  Isa. 23:1–18 (with Tyre); Jer. 25:22 (with Tyre); Ezek. 28:20–23;
Tyre
  Isa. 23:1–18 (with Sidon); Jer. 25:22 (with Sidon); Ezek. 26:1–21; 27:1–36; 28:1–19; Joel 4:4–8 [2:4–8]; Amos 1:9–10
The Nations in General
  Isa. 10:12–14; 24:1–23; 34:1–17 (via the synecdoche of Edom); 63:1–16; Jer. 25:15–38; Ezek. 38:1–23 (via the figure of Gog); 39: 1–28 (partly via the figure of Gog); Joel 4:9–16 [3:9–16]; Mic. 7:8–17; Hag. 2:20–22; Zeph. 1:2–3; Zech. 12:1–9; 14:12–19

While Edom does not have the most space devoted to prophecies against it in total number of verses (Egypt has that honor, thanks to Ezekiel), it

love us?"): It is not likely that Malachi is actually quoting a conversation that had occurred in which people had said these words to him. Rather, he is characterizing their attitude by speaking for them in a dialogue format, a common prophetic device characteristic of each of the rhetorical disputation oracles that comprise the book. The translation "In what way do you love us?" is to be preferred over such alternatives as "How do you/have you love(d) us?" since the latter in English could imply

doubt about being loved at all, whereas the emphasis here is on the specific manner rather than the fact of Yahweh's love. הֲלוֹא־אָח עֵשָׂו לְיַעֲקֹב נְאֻם־יְהוָה ("Isn't Esau Jacob's brother?" [states Yahweh], or equally translatable, "Esau is, of course, Jacob's brother, states Yahweh"): While הֲלוֹא can be translated "isn't?/doesn't?," and so on, its use in Hebrew is routinely idiomatic as a means of conveying emphasis (of course, surely, certainly) much like the colloquial English "Esau

has the widest distribution among the prophetic books. From Isaiah 34 in particular it is clear that Edom can be used by the prophets to stand as a synecdoche for "all the nations" (Isa. 34:2). Thus, the point of the oracle is that the will of any or all of Israel's enemies—including but not necessarily limited to Edom—cannot alter God's plan to redeem his people Israel.

From the point of view of the structure of the passage, on the other hand, the form is that of a disputation, and more specifically, a rhetorical disputation (see the Introduction). This first of the book's six rhetorical disputations displays the general format that consistently characterizes the passages of the book: (1) assertion; (2) questioning of the assertion; (3) response to the questioning; (4) implication. The passage may be outlined as follows:

1:2a	assertion by Yahweh	"I have loved you."
1:2b	questioning by Israel	"How have you loved us?"
1:2c–4	response	(1) Yahweh's alliance with Israel and enmity with Edom (vv. 2c–3a), (2) the desolation of Edom (v. 3b), (3) futility curse on Edom's desire to rebuild (v. 4).
1:5	implication	Israel will learn that Yahweh is not a limited territorial deity.

With regard to the presence of quotations in this structure, we must not assume that the original audience would have thought that Malachi meant literally to quote his audience in verse 2 or to quote the Edomites in verse 4. Rather, he is characterizing their attitude via a theoretical (rhetorical) dialogue, a common prophetic device (see Isa. 19:11; 36:7; 40:27; Jer. 2:23, 35; 8:8; 13:21–22; 42:13; 48:14; Ezek. 18:19, 25; etc.) and a common feature of the remaining five rhetorical disputations in the book. The translation in verse 2 "In

what way do you love us?" is thus preferable to "How do you love us?" since the latter in English would tend to imply doubt about being loved at all, whereas the emphasis here is surely on the specific manner rather than the fact of Yahweh's love. In verse 4, where Edom is quoted, the style is somewhat in parallel to the manner in which Israel is quoted in verse 2. The rhetorical disputation format emphasizes dialogue, in which one party's statement is contradicted by the statement of another. Such a mode of discourse is well suited to the context, in which Israel is portrayed as needing reassurance that God's blessing has not been withdrawn. And this reassurance involves the promise that no matter what the Edomites may say about it, they will never again be a threat to God's people. The quotation of Edom's words, like that of Israel's words in verse 2, is thus patently rhetorical. That which large numbers of Edomites could be assumed to be thinking is effectively worded as if it were their actual collective speech.

Since the passage is an oracle against a foreign nation, it would be wise to keep in mind the basic purpose of such oracles wherever they are found in the prophetic books. That purpose is reassurance. The basic motive is not vindictiveness toward enemies, or hatred of foreigners, or God's delight in crushing groups who have rejected his will. It is reassurance to the chosen people. Though at the time defeated and weak, hated or even forgotten among the nations, their history was still central to God's great plan of redemption for the world. Any thoughtful, orthodox Israelite during the years 760–460 B.C., when the prophets preached—and Israel's fortunes as a people were almost steadily in decline—would naturally have wondered whether the increasingly marginal, insignificant remainder state of Israel could ever hope to see the grand promises of the Pentateuch fulfilled.

These promises, that God would preserve a covenantal relationship with his people forever,

sure is Jacob's brother, isn't he?" or "Is Esau Jacob's brother, or what?" The second messenger formula of the verse, נְאֻם־יְהוָה ("states Yahweh," lit., "statement of Yahweh"), is common to prophetic oracles, occurs rather randomly in terms of its placement within oracles, and serves, like אָמַר יְהוָה, to remind the audience that the prophet is reporting a revelation rather than declaring anything of his own invention. This particular messenger formula is invariably extrametrical wherever it occurs in poetic contexts. It is hardly unique that two messenger formulas should occur in a single verse of a prophetic oracle. In addition to the present verse, אָמַר יְהוָה and נְאֻם־יְהוָה occur together in a single verse fourteen times in the prophetic books (Jer. 16:5; 23:2; 29:32; 30:3; 31:16, 37; 34:17; 35:13; 49:2; Hag. 2:9; Zech. 1:3, 4, 16; 8:6). The sometimes advanced proposal, reflected in the BHS notes, to delete נְאֻם־יְהוָה on metrical grounds is typical of the worst sort of conjectural textual criticism. The antonyms אהב (love) and שׂנא (hate) here are employed as they are characteristically in ancient Near Eastern language of diplomacy and international relations—not to indicate petty emotion, but to depict alliance and enmity between or among nations. First Kings

5:15 [1] provides a parade example of the use of this vocabulary in that Hiram of Tyre is said to have been a "lover" of David (אֹהֵב הָיָה חִירָם לְדָוִד) all his life. The point is that Hiram was an ally. The references to Jonathan's "love" for David, likewise, are simply employing characteristic language for political alliance (1 Sam. 18:1, 3, etc.). In the allegory of Hosea 2, Israel's "lovers" are the gods she allied herself with and whom she served (Hos. 2:7, 9, 12, 14, 15 [2:5, 7, 10, 12, 13]). Conversely, those who oppose God or his people are frequently called "haters" (Lev. 26:17; Deut. 33:11; 2 Chron. 19:2). Moreover, as Thompson ("Israel's Haters," pp. 200–205) and others have pointed out, love–hate terminology is also used routinely in both the Old Testament and New Testament to indicate what English would express by such semantic pairs as like–dislike, accept–reject, or approve–disapprove. Compare, for example, Genesis 29:30–33, where Rachel is loved more and thus Leah considers herself שְׂנוּאָה "hated," that is, disapproved of; Deuteronomy 21:15–17, where in the case of two wives, one is אֲהוּבָה "loved" and the other שְׂנוּאָה "hated" or disliked; Matthew 6:24 and parallels, where two masters cannot be served because the slave will

---

that they would function as a blessing to the nations, and that they would be great in number, seemed unlikely to be proved true in the days of successive Assyrian, Babylonian, and Persian control of the Fertile Crescent. They probably seemed especially futile in Malachi's time (ca. 460 B.C.), when Judah was all that was left of Israel (the north having been repopulated by foreigners long before; 2 Kings 17) and had been reduced to a defenseless, financially depressed fringe province within the vast Persian Empire.

Its capital city, Jerusalem, had been looted, burned, and largely razed a century and a quarter before, and still lay mostly in ruins. Its decimated population lived a hardscrabble existence on marginal land. Having made the mistake of defying the word of the Lord through Jeremiah (Jer. 27) by trying to hold out against Nebuchadnezzar's armies during the Babylonian conquest of Syria–Palestine (2 Kings 24–25), Judah had been more severely destroyed and depopulated than most of its neighbor states, including Edom. The situation surely seemed hopeless from a human point of view. Yet God encouraged the little remnant via Malachi's preaching of this brief oracle against Edom (and, as noted above, implicitly against any and all of Israel's enemies). God was still their

ally, and Edom—and nations like it—would not prevail against Israel, because Yahweh, Israel's God, was "great beyond the country of Israel." (v. 5).

2–3a. The book's first disputation begins with a chiasm (reverse or inverted parallelism) that may be schematized as follows:

A "I love you,"
B Yahweh said.
B' You say,
A' "In what way do you love us?"

This is one of many chiasms in the book, which itself is generally chiastic in overall structure (see the Introduction). The presence of chiastic structures confirms the precision of the composition, since chiasms are relatively precise structures that do not tend to occur automatically in everyday speech or writing. But in themselves they are merely stylistic variations on the usual correspondences between poetic lines, and do not convey any special emphasis or meaning. To say something in a chiastic format is not to change the meaning in any way as compared to saying it in a more typical, nonchiastic way.

"Isn't Esau Jacob's brother?" (states Yahweh).

invariably "hate" (μισήσει) the one and "love" (ἀγαπήσει) the other. In such contexts, "hate" really means "disapprove of" or "reject" while "love" means "accept" or "favor" whether or not two vocabulary words expressing "hate" and "love" are explicitly employed in direct contrast. For instance, compare Matthew 10:37, "Whoever loves [φιλῶν] father and mother more than me [ὑπὲρ ἐμὲ] is not worthy" with the parallel in Luke 14:26, "Whoever comes to me and does not hate [οὐ μισεῖ] father and mother." Matthew and Luke render Jesus' Aramaic or Hebrew words using different Greek words but conveying the same point, and neither expression indicates literal petty human emotions.

God's love is mentioned dozens of times in the

The reference of the rhetorical question is to a history that all Israelites knew well. Esau and Jacob were the twin sons of Isaac (Gen. 25:19–34) from whom the nations of Edom and Israel were descended. Clearly, however, the interest of the rhetorical question is not primarily genealogical, but international. It is the historical relationship of the two "brother" nations, rather than the original twinship of Isaac's sons, that is the focus of Malachi's oracle. The present situation—the divine rejection of Edom and the election of Israel—got its start in the hostility between the twin brothers (Gen. 27) but came to fruition in the many generations of enmity between the two people groups (Num. 20:14–21), both of whom eventually became settled nations. One might have expected that two nations that both traced their ancestry to a common patriarch would have a natural tendency for alliance with one another. In fact, the exact opposite had happened.

A bitter, consistent, and permanent blood feud between Israelites and Edomites characterized all their relationships. If there was one nation that could always, immediately, be identified as Israel's enemy, it was Edom. There was, in fact, never a time when the two nations were allies (2 Kings 3 describes a time when Edom was a vassal state to Israel), and in spite of the fact that the nations bordered one another, there was never a time when they were not hostile, either via "hot" or "cold" war. Thus we must keep in mind that when Malachi's audience heard these words, they knew very well what kind of "brothers" Esau and Jacob really were.

"I loved Jacob/But Esau I hated." The words of this second line of the couplet, within the line itself ("internally") synonymous and chiastic, are not about personal attraction and affection. They are not words of assurance to a psychologically insecure Israel who needs to know that God still cares. They are not to be personalized or universalized so as to give to a modern audience the feeling that we should never doubt God's love in Christ, or that we should be aware that God loves us personally, or other notions taught elsewhere—but not here. These words are about national election and alliance within the history of redemption.

In the diplomacy of the ancient Near East, the language of "love" and "hate" was employed not to indicate personal emotion or affection, but routinely to convey the concepts of alliance or enmity among nations. Kings spoke about "loving" one another as a way of describing their networks of alliances and coalitions. A king's claim to "hate" another had no reference to personal attraction or lack thereof, but described instead a state of hostility between their respective lands. The Old Testament, in both the Law and the Prophets, also employs the terms ʾāhēb (love) and śānēʾ (hate) in this way, as part of the normal semantic field of the two words (see Moran, "Love of God"; Thompson, "Israel's Haters"). Thus the statement, "Yet I have loved Jacob but Esau I have hated" could just as well be rendered, "Yet I have allied myself with Jacob and Esau I have made my enemy." Esau is thus cursed via curse type 1 (anger, rejection from Yahweh).

The fact that "Jacob" and "Esau" are used here instead of "Israel" and "Edom" emphasizes the original ethnic relationship between the nations of Israel and Edom, both being descendants of the twin children of the patriarch Jacob. Malachi uses the words Esau and Edom as terms indicating the nation, rather than one indicating the nation and one the individual eponymous ancestor of the nation. "Israel" and "Jacob" are employed comparably in Malachi—as the nation and not the person.

In the same way that several personal and place names are used for Israel in the Old Testament (Jacob, Joseph, Ephraim, the children of Israel, Judah and Samaria, the land of promise, etc.), so Edom is also represented by a variety of terms. In the Old Testament as a whole, Edom is used ninety-two times to refer to the nation; Esau is used eight times in this way, the classic statement of equivalency being found in Genesis 36:8, "Esau is Edom." Seir is used thirty-seven times to refer to Edom, and Teman six. In the prophetic books, the distribution runs as follows:

Old Testament, most commonly with the object of that love being proto-Israel in the person of the patriarchs (e.g., Deut. 4:37; 10:15) or Israel as a people (e.g., Deut. 7:6–8, 13; 23:5; Ps. 47:5 [4]; Isa. 43:4; Jer. 31:3; Hos. 11:1; 14:5; Mal. 1:2; 2:11). It should be noted that Paul's use of the present verse in Romans 9:13 is precisely in the context of a lengthy discussion of why Israel *as a nation* was not responding to Christ as the chosen people would be expected to do.

	Edom	Esau	Mount Esau	Seir	Mount Seir	Teman
Isaiah	5			1		
Jeremiah	8	2				2
Lamentations	2					
Ezekiel	8				4	1
Daniel	1					
Joel	1					
Amos	5					1
Obadiah	2	4	2			1
Habakkuk						1
Malachi	1	2				
Total	**33**	**8**	**2**	**1**	**4**	**6**

As might be expected, nearly all these terms occur in those parts of the prophetic books containing oracles against foreign nations. In the Old Testament, Edom, with its very long and remarkably consistent history of enmity to Israel, is treated virtually as the paradigm of all enemy nations. Prophetic books that contain a grouping of foreign nation oracles normally include Edom in the group. To leave out Edom would be to leave out the most obvious member of the group.

I. First Disputation (1:2–5)
B. The Lord Will Make Edom Desolate (1:3b–4)

STUART

I made his mountain lands a desolation,
his territory desert for jackals.
4 For Edom says, "We are shattered
but we will build the desolate places
again."
Yahweh of the Armies says this:
They may build, but I will destroy.
They will be called The Wicked Land and
The People that Yahweh Cursed Forever.

NRSV

I have made his hill country a desolation
and his heritage a desert for jackals. 4If Edom
says, "We are shattered but we will rebuild
the ruins," the LORD of hosts says: They may
build, but I will tear down, until they are
called the wicked country, the people with
whom the LORD is angry forever.

3b. וָאָשִׂים (I made . . .) is pointed by the Masoretes (followed by the ancient versions) as a converted imperfect with past meaning, entirely likely in the context, even though the consonantal text could be imperfect (future) as well. הָרָיו (mountain lands) connotes a region rather than

merely the mountains per se (compare the very common title הַר אֶפְרַיִם, mountain lands of Ephraim). For הָרָיו the Septuagint has τὰ ὅρια αὐτοῦ (his borders), a simple internal Greek copy error for τὰ ὄρεια αὐτοῦ (his mountains). נַחֲלָתוֹ (his territory) may also be rendered "his possession" or

---

3b. Verse 3 depicts Edom as a "desolation," and adds a typical biblical image used to suggest desolate, uninhabited areas—a reference to the presence of characteristic wilderness animals, the jackals (Jer. 49:33, "Hazor will become a haunt of jackals, an everlasting waste; no one will dwell there, no one will sojourn in it"; see also Ps. 44:20 [19]; Isa. 34:13; Jer. 9:10 [11]; 10:22; 51:37). This is an allusion to the fulfillment of the covenant curse type 9, that of desolation (Lev. 26:33, "your land will be laid waste"; Deut. 29:22 [23], "the whole land will be a burning waste"). Edom is further described in verse 4 as shattered and in need of rebuilding. Malachi was composed, as we have suggested, about 460 B.C. But earlier Old Testament prophecies, though consistently predicting the eventual doom of Edom, portray it in their time (i.e., prior to the early fifth century B.C.) as a vigorous enemy of the Israelites, expanding into Judean territory and thriving at the expense of Judah during the Neo-Babylonian era (609–540 B.C.) For example, Joel 4:19 [3:19] looks forward to the day when Edom "will become" (tihyeh, Heb. imperfect) a desolate wilderness "because of the violence done to the people of Judah, in whose land they have shed innocent blood." In Joel's day (probably ca. 595–580 B.C.) Edom was ascendant and Judah mortally weakened as regards their respective national statuses. Jeremiah 49:7–22 (ca. 594 B.C.) also characterizes Edom's destruction as yet to come. Edom must not "go unpunished" (v. 12) and "will become" an object of horror (v. 17) because of its oppression of Judah. Likewise, Ezekiel 25:12 (ca. 587 B.C.) speaks of Edom as having taken "revenge" on Judah, possibly during the time that the Judean army was trapped inside Jerusalem under siege by the Babylonians (2 Kings 25:1–4) and thus unable to protect the bulk of the country. Although Ezekiel voices God's promise that Edom will in the future be "desolated . . . by the sword," its destruction certainly had not yet happened by the beginning of the second decade of the sixth century. Obadiah predicts future destruction for Edom, which at the time of his prophesying (ca. 586 B.C.) is "proud" (v. 3), "aloft like the eagle" (v. 4), boastful about Judah's distress (v. 12), and enriched in territory

and material goods at the expense of the Judeans after the fall of Jerusalem in 586 (vv. 13–14).

What happened between 600–586 and 460? How had Edom, such a threat to Judah and a conqueror of parts of her territory in the decades immediately after 600, fallen to the status of a non-nation by 460? What means did God use to fulfill his promise through the prophets that Edom, once a formidable foe encroaching on Judean territory, would end up desolated a century and a half later? Recent and ongoing archaeological investigation provides some of the answers. Archaeological excavations in the eastern and western Negev and the southern Transjordan have produced some helpful perspectives on late Edomite history.

From the closing decades of the seventh century B.C. to the early decades of the fifth century B.C., Edomite commercial interests in southern Judah were numerous. Indeed, there exists substantial evidence that Edomites controlled some portions of the Negev until 550 B.C., at least in the sense that their pottery and other material remains predominate over those of the Judeans in a number of sites. There may even have been actual politically separate Edomite enclaves of some sort within territory nominally controlled by the Judeans.

The culture of the southern Transjordan and the Negev of Judah from the late eighth to the early sixth centuries B.C. was influenced by Assyria, Judah, and Edom. Material remains reflecting each of these influences are present archaeologically. The three cultures intermingled in various ways. Inscriptions have been unearthed in the region in the respective languages of Edomite and Israelite (Hebrew), and certain local pottery types are clear imitations of Assyrian styles.

The evidence suggests that toward the end of the seventh century B.C., the Edomite influence in the eastern and western Negev began to decline. Apparently, seminomadic groups appeared in the area in such numbers as to overwhelm the Edomites in competition for the land and general economic resources. There is no evidence that these groups drove out the Edomites militarily. At

"his inheritance." Where the Masoretic Text has לִתַנּוֹת מִדְבָּר (for wilderness jackals), the Septuagint translates εἰς δόματα ἐρήμου as "into wilderness roofs/houses/dwellings." The translator is following the Masoretic Text exactly, but is obviously puzzled by the word תַנּוֹת. Some commentators have assumed that the translator may have considered the only proper plural of תַן (jackal) to be תַנִּים (the common form) rather than the word appearing here (תַנּוֹת—an unusual form), and was thus misled to assume that the consonantal Hebrew תנות was a t-prefixed biform of נאות (pastures). But δόμα is never a Septuagint translation for any of the Hebrew words meaning "pasture" or the like and the concept of pasture does not fit the parallelism of the couplet at all. Normally δόμα translates גג (roof). It is more likely that the translator simply guessed at the meaning, lacking any knowledge of what תנות was supposed to mean. The Septuagint translator(s) of the Minor

---

first, they probably merged into Edomite areas of control and then gradually gained dominance. Edomite presence declined first in the southern Transjordan and eastern Negev and later in the western Negev and Shephelah (southern Judah). This movement relates to the situation described in the Book of Obadiah. In Obadiah's time (586) Edomites were moving north and west, into southern Judah proper, not merely because southern Judah contained crop and grazing land that they had always coveted, but also because they had little choice. Their own territories around the southern end of the Dead Sea were being gradually invaded by outsiders, and in order to survive the Edomites found it necessary, in turn, to invade elsewhere. Judah, relatively defenseless and partially depopulated after the Babylonian conquest of 588–586, offered a soft underbelly into which displaced Edomites could penetrate.

Just who were the seminomadic groups that pushed the Edomites into Judah? The answer remains elusive. Some scholars call them "Arab seminomads," others "proto-Nabateans," and others refuse to identify them, so limited is the archaeological evidence that might be used to make an identification. Could the Babylonians have played a part in the course of their extensive wars of conquest throughout the Mediterranean end of the Fertile Crescent during the early decades of the sixth century? There is no sure answer. What we do know is that by the end of the sixth century B.C., for all intents and purposes classical Edomite culture was at an end, and that by the early fourth century B.C., the people known as the Nabateans were in control of the city of Petra and most of the former Edomite regions. Material and linguistic remains easily demonstrate this control. This scenario comports with what little we can glean about late Edomite history from Assyrian sources (mainly the annals of the Assyrian kings from Adad-Nirari III to Ashurbanipal, i.e., to 609 B.C.) and the Old Testament.

The various forces that drove the Edomites out of their original southern Transjordan and Dead Sea homeland and into Judah in the late seventh and early sixth centuries B.C. provided for a time the impetus for a considerable degree of Edomite influence in southern Judah. Recent excavations at Khorbet Qitmit have unearthed the first Edomite religious shrine in the eastern Mediterranean world, ten kilometers south of the biblical city of Arad. This shrine served as an Edomite worship center (right in southern Judah!) from about 595 to 575 B.C., and thereafter was abandoned. The shrine was not merely a "high place" located in part of a city. No evidence of domestic inhabitation is present at the site. Instead, the site is that of a special worship center, a holy place independent of any single town or city, built for the use of several towns or cities. The excavator, Itzak Beit-Arieh, has reasoned that the presence of a separate, self-contained Edomite sanctuary in this location implies clearly that Edomites were living in southern Judah in such large numbers as to require a shrine to which they could go to worship from the surrounding towns and cities, many of which they in all likelihood controlled. Beit-Arieh concludes that Edom, at the beginning of the sixth century, had "dominion" over major parts of Judah's southern Hebron hill country, its Shephelah (western lowlands), and its Negev, judging from Edomite remains found at a dozen sites in southern Judah in addition to Khorbet Qitmit.

This rather profound level of infiltration of Edomites into Judah may account in part for the frequency with which anti-Edomite oracles appear in some of the Judean prophets. Through these prophets God assured his people that his plan of redemption would eventuate in the elimination of Edom, an assurance much needed, apparently, by Judeans who were witnessing in their own day what must have seemed like just the opposite—a waxing rather than a waning of Edomite influence. For people who asked, "If our God is so powerful, how come the Edomites are taking over?"

Prophets often reveals evidence of a limited Hebrew vocabulary.

4. The word כִּי here may be taken as either as a conjunction (for) or as a conditional particle ("If Edom says . . ." or "Edom may say . . ."). Since in the context Israel is imagined as speaking indicatively rather than conditionally ("You say . . .", v. 2), it seems likely that Edom is also imagined as speaking indicatively rather than modally, such as that Edom *might* express determination to rebuild, or the like. However, the imperfect verb form always potentially bears the modal sense (may, might, could, etc.). For רֻשַּׁשְׁנוּ (we are shattered) the Septuagint and the Vulgate rightly took the root as רשש, to be shattered/crushed/destroyed, and the like. The Syriac and Targum, one possibly following the other, wrongly assumed the root ראש, "to be poor," and translated accordingly (Edom says, "We are poor . . ."). The second couplet begins with a standard messenger formula (Yahweh of the Armies says this:). A messenger formula is a standard phrase or clause spoken by a prophet to remind his audience that he is merely repeating what he has been told by God. Although we indicate such formulas in parentheses since they are virtually always parenthetical to the main points of the passage, this one has been fitted by Malachi into the general poetical structure. The Hebrew word גְּבוּל can mean border, territory, region, country, area, and the like. I translate it here "land" because in the context that translation seems most idiomatic (see NIV; RSV: country). The definition of זעם in the final clause of verse 4 is difficult to establish exactly, since זעם has a rather broad range of meaning and can connote "curse," "be angry," "be indignant," "speak against", "condemn," and the like. The Edomites are either those "whom Yahweh has cursed" or those he "is indignant against" in perpetuity. Since Hebrew, like Greek, has no single term to indicate actual infinite duration, the term עַד־עוֹלָם at the end of the verse cannot be translated "forever" unless one understands the English term "forever" loosely. עַד־עוֹלָם means "on and on" or "in perpetuity," indicating a duration of indefinite but not necessarily infi-

---

the prophetic predictions of Edom's full demise would be encouraging—if, that is, the people believed the word of the Lord via his prophets. By Malachi's day, surely, there could be no doubt that God had spoken the truth through his prophets about Edom. Esau had indeed been cursed with desolation of its land (curse type 9c).

4. Verse 4 makes three points: (1) the Edomites would try to rebuild; (2) God would frustrate their attempts to do so; and (3) the permanence of their demise would serve as a reminder of God's judgment against nations who oppose him. The implication of these points taken together is that in Malachi's day there was still an identifiable Edomite population in or near parts of Judah, and that their destruction as a people was recent enough that they were hopeful of resurgence. Both Israel (Judah and the bits of traditionally Ephraimite and Benjaminite territory now appended to it) and Edom had gone through a great deal since the early sixth century. Israel, worse off at first, had come back from the Babylonian exile and had gradually rebuilt as a people under the generally benign Persian administrative system. Edom, on the other hand, while having taken advantage of Judah's misfortunes at the beginning of the sixth century and while never experiencing the massive Babylonian exiles that so decimated Israel, nevertheless was far worse off by the middle of the fifth century.

They had not been officially displaced by a superpower and then allowed to return and rebuild. Rather, their displacement was local and unofficial, at the hands of some sort of Arab seminomadic group or groups. In the providence of God it was thus a situation that official Persian policy could not and would not be bothered with. The Judeans had Persian permission and support in their rebuilding campaign (Ezra 1:1–11; 4:3; 6:1–15; 7:11–28; Neh. 2:7–9; 13:6). That was God's doing. The Edomites had no such help, which was also God's doing and which sealed Edom's fate as a people forever.

Similar language can appear among other oracles against foreign nations in the Old Testament as well. Hosea 9:12 ("even if they bring up children, I will bereave them until no one is left") is an example of a futility curse somewhat similar to Malachi 1:4 ("they may build, but I will demolish"). This is pentateuchal curse type 15, exemplified by Deuteronomy 28:29 ("you will be unsuccessful in everything you do") and Deuteronomy 28:30 ("you will build a house but will not live in it"). The prediction of eternal disgrace for an enemy nation here ("they will be called the Wicked Country, the people Yahweh cursed in perpetuity") is an instance of the pentateuchal curse type 16, dishonor/degradation (Deut. 28:37: "you will become a thing of horror, and an object of scorn and ridicule to all the nations.").

nite length (see 1 Sam. 27:12, where "lifetime" is the meaning; Gen. 49:26, where "long-enduring" is the meaning). It is possible that Malachi employed intentional assonance via word endings in the second of the pejorative titles that he predicts Edom will bear: The People That Yahweh Cursed Forever (הָעָם אֲשֶׁר־זָעַם יְהוָה עַד־עוֹלָם). Even if the assonance were essentially accidental—and there is a great deal of accidental assonance in Hebrew as the result of the many common ending sounds of words—the negative appellation may have been all the more memorable as a result.

I. First Disputation (1:2–5)
C. Israel Will Learn That the Lord Is Not a Territorial Deity (1:5)

STUART

NRSV

5 Your own eyes will see it and you will say, "Yahweh is great beyond the land of Israel!"

[5]Your own eyes shall see this, and you shall say, "Great is the LORD beyond the borders of Israel!"

5. מֵעַל לִגְבוּל (beyond the country of): Some commentators have suggested emending מֵעַל לִגְבוּל (beyond the country of) to מֵעַל גְבוּל (same meaning) on the premise that מֵעַל לְ is less typical Hebrew (so BHS notes). This proposal is obviated by the fact that מֵעַל לְ occurs a dozen times in the Hebrew Bible (e.g., Gen. 1:7; 1 Sam. 17:39; Ezek. 1:25; Jon. 4:6; etc.). The insistence of Smith (*Malachi*, p. 23), followed more recently by Verhoef (p. 206), that מֵעַל should mean "above" or "over" rather than "beyond" is unlikely in the context, especially if Malachi 1:11 and 1:14 are properly understood as describing Yahweh as the supreme God over all the nations. It is certainly true that מֵעַל often means simply "above" and that the Septuagint (ὑπεράνω) apparently so renders it here, although "above and beyond" can also be the sense of the Septuagint. The Vulgate's *super* is ambiguous since Latin *super* can mean "beyond" as well as "above." The Syriac and the Aramaic support the translation "beyond." The question ultimately boils down to what sense is made by speaking of Yahweh's greatness *above* Israel, in contrast to the sense made by the declaration that he has power beyond Israel's borders—the very point, indeed, of the first disputation. Unless one judges that Malachi is asserting something about Yahweh's power in the sky above Israel, or that he is to be understood as hovering over his people in some sort of protective way, "beyond" is the clear choice for rendering מֵעַל לְ here.

---

5. God promises Malachi's audience that they will witness what verses 3 and 4 describe ("your own eyes will see it."). This suggests that the Edomites as of Malachi's time had not yet been entirely destroyed. Some sort of invasion had obviously overrun them, but considerable numbers of Edomites, though displaced and subjugated, must have been left in the vicinity of Judah. Their desire to rebuild as expressed in verse 4 suggests that their defeat or displacement was recent and that they fully hoped to bounce back from it. In Malachi's time, then, or just prior to it, Jews had witnessed the overrunning of former Edomite territories and were wondering how permanent the Edomite setback would be. God's word through Malachi assured them that it would, in fact, be permanent.

As time went by (and it may have required generations for the idea fully to sink in) the realization that Edom was in fact permanently crushed surely became widespread among the people of Judah. Obadiah 10 and many other prophetic oracles predicting the permanent demise of Edom had been fulfilled (see also Amos 9:12). True believers within the nation could then recall Malachi's word that their own eyes would see the permanence of Edom's demise and glorify God by the confession "Yahweh is great beyond the country of Israel." Other ancient Near Eastern nations might hold to the widespread notion that their gods had limited areas of influence, and could project their power only in those geographical areas they were worshiped. Faithful Israelites knew better. Their God was universal in his sovereignty, and had proved it by eliminating for good their most tenacious national enemy, in the manner of restoration blessing type 9 (power over enemies).

II. Second Disputation (1:6–2:9)
A. Three Questions Deserve an Answer (1:6)

STUART

6 A son honors his father
and a servant his master.
If I am a father,
where is my honor?
If I am a master,
where is my respect?
Yahweh of the Armies says this to you
priests who despise my name.
You say, "How have we despised your
   name?"

NRSV

6A son honors his father, and servants
their master. If then I am a father, where is
the honor due me? And if I am a master,
where is the respect due me? says the LORD
of hosts to you, O priests, who despise my
name. You say, "How have we despised your
name?"

6. אָב (his father; lit., a father): While it would be possible to imagine the more explicit wording אָבִיו (his father) here, the Hebrew idiom does not require it and the meter of the first couplet was constructed using the terse noun without the suffix. One might think of neutralizing the non-divine gender language of this first couplet by translating "a child honors its parent and servants their masters." However, even the New Revised Standard Version cannot here follow its usual practice of neutralizing nondivine gender because the term אָב (father) is repeated immediately in the next couplet in reference to God and paralleled thereafter by אֲדֹנִים (master), with emphasis clearly on a combination of the fact of male authority in the ancient world as a paradigm for divine authority over Israel. אדֹנִים is twice presented in the plural in the verse because the masculine plural is the most common way of indicating the abstract in Hebrew (it is not, contrary to many commentators, a so-called plural of majesty), and the singular (אֲנִי אָדוֹן) could tend to mean only "I am Lord" rather than "I am a master," especially in the poetic context, where the presence of the article would be rare if not awkward. Hebrew seems naturally to prefer the plural over the singular for this word throughout the Old Testament, in a thirty to one ratio. Because the second couplet mentions "my honor" in parallel to the use of the root in the third masculine singular verb (honors) in the first couplet, and the third couplet mentions "my respect," it is tempting to conclude that a third masculine singular form of ירא (fear/respect) might have fallen out of the second half of the first couplet. The Sinaiticus Codex of the Septu-

1:6–2:9. The second of the book's six rhetorical disputations concerns the Jerusalem priesthood's neglect of their duties. Priests were responsible for the education of the people in the law, the administration of the provisions of the law (legal rulings and enforcements), and proper worship (see also the Introduction). In each of these areas they had failed and thus deserved the punishment in kind that God would mete out to them.

The only serious challenge to the idea that 1:6–2:9 is a self-contained, integral pericope within the book was offered by Sellin (Das Zwölfprophetenbuch), who opined that 1:6–14 and 2:1–9 should be separated since otherwise the unit is double the average length of the other disputations. There is no doubt that 1:6–14 concentrates somewhat more on the indictment (condemnation) of the priests and 2:1–9 somewhat on their punishment, but this is entirely in accord with what one would expect in a judgment oracle, which this disputation, like the first, surely is. (In 1:2–5 it is v. 5 that delivers the judgment sentence. Here it is 2:2–9, a much longer judgment sentence but otherwise exactly what was to be expected. However, there are elements of both indictment and judgment in both halves of the oracle.) Judgment oracles invariably cite what is wrong (i.e., how the covenant has been broken) before presenting the divine sentence of judgment, so Sellin accomplished nothing by simply breaking the oracle artificially into its two major constituent parts (his approach has gained few adherents). The passage is in fact highly unified with a variety of vocabulary con-

nections, topical consistencies, and a straightforward logical progression. Glazier-McDonald (Malachi, pp. 42–44) outlines an elaborate rhetorical structure that points up the unity of the passage while at the same time overstressing the details of that unity via microanalysis.

The passage may be outlined as follows:

1:6a–b	assertion by Yahweh	"Where is the honor due me? . . . Where is the respect due me?"
1:6c	questioning by Israel	"How have we despised your name?"
1:7a	response by Yahweh	"By offering polluted food on my altar."
1:7b	questioning by Israel	"How have we polluted it?"
1:7c–8a	response by Yahweh	"By thinking that the LORD's table may be despised" and by offering defective animals on the temple altar.
1:8b–2:9	implication	The priests will learn that Yahweh's law is not to be condemned; they will be punished for their disobedience to the priestly covenant.

Although this structure has two questionings and two responses (matching the pattern in the fifth disputation, to which it corresponds chiastically), and although it has a much longer implication section than any of the other disputations, including yet more rhetorical quotations charac-

agint does indeed have "a servant fears [φοβ-ηθήσεται] his master" and the Vulgate likewise supplies "fears" (timebit). One might then be tempted to restore the initial couplet of verse 6 as follows: בֵּן יְכַבֵּד אָב וְעֶבֶד יִירָא אֲדֹנָיו ("a son honors his father and a servant respects his master") This throws off the meter, however. It becomes 5:7 instead of 5:5 (the MT as it stands being vocalized in Malachi's day as follows: אֲדֹנָיו אָב

וְעֶבֶד אֲדֹנָו יְכַבֵּד). Moreover, Codexes Vaticanus and Alexandrinus do not have the third masculine singular word for "fear" in verse 6a, nor do any of the other ancient versions. Thus it seems most likely that the Sinaiticus and the Vulgate readings are secondary and expansionistic and that the Masoretic Text as it stands is to be preferred. One verb governing both halves of a couplet is not an anomaly, but so common a feature

---

terizing the priests' attitudes, its structure is essentially identical to that of the other five disputations. Malachi 1:2–5 is the simplest disputation, and this is the most complex, but they all follow the same basic pattern.

Both the opening section of the disputation (1:6–9) and three verses near the end (2:6–8) are poetry, as evidenced by regularity of meter, clear parallelism, and extensive assonance. However, it is not obvious whether any other parts are poetry. There are some relatively parallelistic phrasings (e.g., 2:2, 5), which could conceivably be poetic, but the bulk of the material seems prosaic, and the presence of an isolated poetic couplet here or there in the midst of a predominantly prose oracle, while not without precedent, would represent a rarity, hard to prove under the best of circumstances. I have thus treated all material other than 1:6–9 and 2:6–8 as prose. Scores of prophetic oracles begin in poetry and change to prose, and back again (or vice versa), so there is nothing unusual in this regard about the present passage (see Isa. 22; 23; 29; 30; Jer. 11; 22; 23; 31; Ezek. 18; 21; 24; 27; etc.).

We have no way of knowing in what order Malachi may have preached the component parts of the book. That the shortest disputation is found first and the longest second determines nothing. The order could be an editorial decision on the part of Malachi or a disciple. It may also reflect chronology. From the point of view of date and provenance, the present passage is one in which certain of the general clues to the dating and place of origin of the book are found (see also the Introduction). The passage portrays an active priesthood, offering sacrifices regularly. To the best of our knowledge, this could only be referring to events in Jerusalem, at the temple, to which sacrifice was confined in the postexilic era. (Had the sacrifice been at some illegal sanctuary—of which no other record exists—it would be amazing that Malachi should not mention that fact along with his condemnation of the actions of the priests involved.) Surely, also, the Persian period (539–

333 B.C.) is in focus, since only during this time do we know of a governmental system in Judah that involved a "governor" (peḥâ), the local Persian district governor. Finally, it would seem that a likely date for the passage would be sometime before the arrival of Ezra (458 B.C.) and Nehemiah (444 B.C.) since both of them did so much to reform the religious practices of the postexilic Judean community. (See also the Introduction.)

There are eleven messenger formulas in the passage (1:6, 8, 9, 10, 11, 13 [twice], 14; 2:1 [2], 4, 8), which is a higher frequency than found elsewhere in Malachi and certainly than found in most prophetic books (see the Introduction). In his prophecies Malachi generally favors the formula "said Yahweh of the Armies" but employs the shorter "said Yahweh" as well. In this passage Malachi uses the longer formula exclusively (see the Exegesis of v. 13). Malachi's messenger speech style included frequent reminders that he was merely a spokesperson for God, repeating verbatim what God had revealed to him, but here Malachi obviously emphasizes his messenger role. Why? Probably because he is addressing the clergy. Since the priests were official religious leaders with absolute authority in many matters (including the handling of sacrifices—the very topic of the passage), Malachi's inspired attack on their behavior was virtually guaranteed to spur resistance. They had permanent, inherited, recognized, professional, legal standing. From a human point of view, Malachi had no credibility at all other than what people might give his words if they believed them. He needed all the support he could get, and his only real credential was that he spoke for God. Frequent verbal reminders of this were his sole weapon of influence.

From all the evidence available to us from ancient Near Eastern letters and from the Old Testament it appears that messengers had some freedom to insert, or not to insert, messenger formulas in their speeches as they saw fit, and reading through the prophetic books, it is easy to see that some messengers (prophets) obviously tended

of Hebrew parallelism as to require no emendation. אַיֵּה מוֹרָאִי . . . אַיֵּה כְבוֹדִי (Where is my honor? . . . Where is my respect?) could also be translated "Where is the honor due me? . . . Where is the respect due me?" (see GKC, §135m). Here the Syriac reads slightly periphrastically ("that you are fearing me") but still seems to support the Masoretic Text. For מוֹרָאִי the Targum mistakenly reads מראי (my vision, image), as if the word

were from the root ראה (to see). אָמַר יְהוָה צְבָאוֹת לָכֶם (Yahweh of the Armies says this to you"): Here the Syro-Hexapla idiosyncratically reads לָכֶם, as if לְ were a vocative particle instead of the preposition ("says the LORD Almighty, You priests who despise my name"). The four-word clause is a messenger formula worked into the poetic structure and meter of the oracle. I therefore do not render it in parentheses as I would if it were

---

to employ the various formulas more than others. It stands to reason that a messenger feeling the need to remind an audience of the identity of the source of the message he or she was repeating might find it advantageous to employ a relatively larger number of messenger formulas than usual. In the circumstance of the present passage, a prophet was delivering a judgment excoriation to the entire priestly community of Judah! If there was any portion of the population likely to have the self-confidence to ignore Malachi or dismiss his words as uninspired, it was the priests. Eleven messenger formulas in an eighteen-verse oracle provided at least a little ammunition against that self-confidence.

Where might Malachi have delivered this oracle? Where else, indeed, but the temple complex. That is where the largest number of priests could be found at any given time, and there we can imagine Malachi gathering as many priests as would stop to listen. Would lay onlookers have been present? Almost certainly, since unless Malachi himself were a priest he would have had no different access to the temple than any other non-priest, and would have preached in one of the outer courtyards where the general crowds were allowed and where priests were present to classify, inspect, and assign offerings for presentation at the altar (see the Exposition of v. 10 for a discussion of the layout of the temple complex).

Some of the vocabulary employed in this oracle has a special function. It is derived, quite intentionally, from the Pentateuch, and notably from three passages. The first is the famous Aaronic blessing of Numbers 6:24–26 ("Yahweh bless you and keep you; Yahweh shine his face on you and be gracious to you; Yahweh raise his face to you and give you peace") and from the two brief verses that surround that blessing (Num. 6:23, 27). The second is the levitical "covenant of peace" (Num. 25:12–13 and the two verses that introduce it, vv. 10–11). The third is Deuteronomy 33:8–11, in which Moses poetically pronounces blessing on

the tribe of Levi and on the teaching and sacerdotal functions of the priests.

Fishbane has reviewed the way in which Malachi 1:6–2:9 is an inner-biblical "divine exegesis" of the first of these passages, the Aaronic blessing (Biblical Interpretation in Ancient Israel, pp. 329–34; cf. also his "Form and Reformulation of the Priestly Blessing"). Fishbane posits some vocabulary connections between the two texts and within the Malachi oracle that no one in the audience could possibly have noticed. For example, he tends to regard any two Hebrew words that share two contiguous consonants, regardless of vowel sounds and other consonants, as purposely linked. A listener would never be able to pick this up from the actual spoken words, since human speech moves too rapidly for people to notice and consciously evaluate successions of consonants in parts of words, unless rhyme or another obvious connection is present, let alone connect the word in which they occur to a different word in a different context that happens to share some, but not all, the same consonants. Accordingly, it would have been useless for the oracle to contain such minute nuances, since they are only discoverable (in a forced way) by painstaking analysis of the consonantal written text—not the spoken sounds. On the other hand, in many other cases the key words and concepts of Numbers 6:24–26 are obviously reused and played upon ironically, sometimes repeatedly, in Malachi 1:6–2:9. These connections are made in a manner that would be easy to detect as Malachi spoke his words—indeed, they would be hard to miss—and therefore Fishbane's argument is convincing to the extent that one major component of Malachi 1:6–2:9 is its ironic reuse of Numbers 6:23–27.

Beyond Fishbane's individual linguistic connections, we would note that the Aaronic blessing of Numbers 6:24–26 was a piece of Scripture that was undoubtedly closely associated with the priests in the minds of all Israelites. It was a pronouncement that most priests probably made

an extrametrical messenger formula, nor do I translate אָמַר by the past-tense translation, "said" as is usual for straightforward messenger formulas. The verse is heavy with alliteration via the letter א, used thirteen times at the outset of words. Alliteration is often accidental or incidental in Hebrew writing, but here it seems purposeful and prominent. The incorporation of the mes-

senger formula beginning with ʾalep (אָמַר) was probably partly determined by the desire for alliteration. The purpose of alliteration is, of course, memorability. It does not alter meaning, but calls attention to the fact that the verse is unified and its words carefully chosen for their concise impact.

---

many times a day—indeed, it was in all likelihood the single set of words they most often publicly said. Worshipers at the temple regularly heard this blessing spoken directly to them, probably at the end of the worship process as they were ready to exit the temple. In other words, everybody knew it by heart. Taking advantage of this familiarity, God inspired Malachi to produce an excoriation of the priests, in the same overall disputation format that governs all the passages of the book, but incorporating terminology and themes from a famous blessing closely associated in everyone's mind with the priests. The connections as we see them (eliminating some elements from and adding some to Fishbane's listing) are as follows:

Num. 6:23–27	Mal. 1:6–2:9
Aaron and his sons (v. 23)	priests (1:6; 2:1, 7)
bless (root brk vv. 23, 24)	your blessing (root brk 2:2)
keep (root šmr v. 24)	keep (root šmr 2:7, 9)
Yahweh (each verse of the blessing)	Yahweh (13 times in the passage)
shine/light (root ʾwr v. 25)	light (start fire, root ʾwr 1:10)
face (pānîm vv. 25, 26)	face (pānîm 1:8, 9; 2:3, 4, 9)
be gracious (root hnn v. 25)	accept/be gracious (root hnn 1:10)
raise face/accept (root nśʾ + pānîm v. 26)	raise face/accept (root nśʾ + pānîm 1:8, 9; 2:9)
raise (root nś [in above phrase])	carry (root nś 2:3)
give (root sym vv. 26, 27)	determine (root sym 2:2 [twice])
peace (šālom v. 26)	peace (šālom 2:5, 6)
my name (šēm v. 27)	my name (šēm 1:6, 11 [twice], 14; 2:2, 5)
I will bless (root brk v. 27)	I will curse (root ʾrr 2:2)
bless [as above]	cursed (root ʾrr 1:14)

It would go far beyond the facts to suggest that Malachi 1:6–2:9 is largely governed by Numbers 5:23–27 or that in its totality it is nothing but a

reworking thereof. The Aaronic blessing is, however, one of the three most important background texts for the passage. Although this curse on the priests is accomplished within Malachi's standard rhetorical disputational style, with many particulars appropriate only to the specific things that the priests were doing in Malachi's day, the point of the passage is made by means of ironically employed terms and concepts from the first and most famous priestly blessing in the Bible. God curses the priests using much of the very language they themselves routinely used in pronouncing their blessings! This is a comeuppance, a satirical dig, a turning of the tables subtly yet artfully accomplished. On the two other important background passages (Num. 15:10–13 and Deut. 33:8–11), see below.

The first three couplets of verse 6 form an a fortiori argument (if x is something, then y is, by definition, more so). If a father deserves honor from his son and a master from his servant, surely God deserves honor and respect (or fear) because he is an even greater father and an even greater master. The language does not state openly that God is a greater father and master than any human, but this is implicitly assumed. God does not warrant merely the respect due a human father and master. It is not that he is *also* a father and master, but that he warrants the respect due a *divine* father and master. On the Old Testament concept of God as father of his people, see Exodus 4:22–23; Deuteronomy 32:5–6, 18–19; Isaiah 1:2; 43:6; 63:16; Jeremiah 2:4; Hosea 11:1; he is called "master" or "lord" almost six hundred times in the Old Testament, most often in the phrase "[my] Lord Yahweh" (ʾădōnay yhwh), translated in most English versions as "Lord God," and otherwise in such contexts as Exodus 3:12; 9:1; Leviticus 25:55; 1 Samuel 3:9; 1 Kings 8:66; Zephaniah 3:9.

The word here translated "servant," Hebrew ʿebed, can also mean "slave." Since in the ancient world a son had no choice but to obey his parents and a slave had no choice but to respect his master, or indeed "fear" him, we are not presented here with an illustration of voluntary behavior or attitude improvement. God is not suggesting to the priests, who are about to be named as those whom this disputation concerns, that they ought to take a clue from sons and servants/slaves and improve their "awareness" or sensitivity to God's feelings. Rather, the priests are being excoriated for disobeying their Father and Master, something that obviously demands a severe penalty. As the last full couplet in 1:6 makes clear, this very group that should have been most keen to give Yahweh the respect he deserves was failing to do so. The charge that they have "despised my name" is not merely a statement of an insult to God's reputation or the like, but is equivalent to saying "they have defied my authority and disobeyed my will."

"Name" (šēm) is a concept so rich and substantial in biblical theology that no brief discussion can do it justice. The words for "name" in Hebrew and Greek can suggest the conceptual semantic range contained in any and all of the following terms: identity, character, significance, power, authority, presence, essence, representation. The Bible contains what has sometimes been referred to as the "name theology," especially strongly represented in Deuteronomy, Kings, the Gospels, Paul, and Revelation, but commonly used in other parts of Scripture as well. The essential idea of name theology is that God's greatness is unmeasurable, so that he cannot be circumscribed or comprehended by human intelligence. Therefore when we encounter the living God we encounter his gracious manifestation of an essence or representation of himself, for which the Bible uses the term *name*. Our minds cannot recognize, comprehend, or remember the fullness of God. But he can represent his fullness to us so that we have *some* appreciation—limited but truly representative—of who he is. Thus Solomon could say of the Jerusalem temple: "But will God indeed dwell on the earth? Behold, heaven and the highest heaven cannot contain you; how much less this house which I have built! . . . Yet . . . you have said, 'My name shall be there'" (1 Kings 8:27–28). God's "name" is his representative, authoritative essential presence, and to despise it is to reject and disobey him

II. Second Disputation (1:6–2:9)
B. The Lord Responds to Israel's Question (1:7–8a)

STUART

7 By offering on my altar polluted food!
   You say, "How have we polluted you?"
   By your saying, "Yahweh's table can be
      despised"!
8 When you offer blind animals for sacri-
      fice, isn't that evil?
   When you offer crippled or sick animals,
      isn't that evil?

NRSV

7By offering polluted food on my altar.
And you say, "How have we polluted it?" By
thinking that the LORD's table may be despised. 8When you offer blind animals in sacrifice, is that not wrong? And when you offer
those that are lame or sick, is that not
wrong?

7. מַגִּישִׁים (by offering): The hiphil of נגשׁ is here employed with the meaning "offering" consistent with its usage in the Pentateuch (e.g., Lev. 2:8) and elsewhere in Malachi (1:8; 11; 2:12; 3:3). At the end of the verse Codex Alexandrinus adds καὶ τὰ ἐπιτιθέμενα ἐξουδενώσατε (and what was set on it you have despised); some other codexes read καὶ τὰ ἐπιτιθέμενα βρώματα ἐξουδενώμενα (and the food set on it may be despised). Is the Hebrew text haplographic, or is the Septuagint expansionistic? Most probably the extra wording in the Greek is a Septuagint conflation from verse 12 and thus the shorter Hebrew is the more original. This conclusion comports with the well-known tendency of the Septuagint to be expansionistic in the Minor Prophets. נִבְזֶה (can be despised): This is a legitimate modal translation of the participle, which can also be translated "despisable" (see also the

Exegesis of v. 12). In the middle couplet of the verse, most commentators have chosen to emend בַּמֶּה גֵאַלְנוּךָ (how have we polluted you ?) to בַּמֶּה גֵאַלְנוּהוּ (how have we polluted it?) on the basis of the Septuagint reading ἐν τίνι ἠλισγήσαμεν αὐτούς (how have we polluted them?), followed also by the Old Latin, assuming that the singular–plural difference (it–them) is merely a matter of idiomatic treatment of the collective concept of sacrifices. However, as has often been noted, αὐτούς (them) could just as well be an inner-Greek corruption for ἄρτους (bread), reflecting a dittography of לֶחֶם (bread). Moreover, the Masoretic Text, with its translation "how have we polluted you" (followed by the Vulgate and Peshitta), makes sense in light of Malachi's emphasis in the context that despising the sacrificial system is a direct way of despising God himself (see the Exposition). It

---

7. What in actual fact had the priests been doing to deserve such a charge? They were disobeying the fundamental Mosaic law that God gets the best as his possession. The Old Testament perspective on all wealth is that the best and first of it *never has* belonged to its temporary human controller ("owner"), but always has belonged to God. The firstfruits of one's labors, the firstborn of one's flocks, and the best quality of one's possessions are God's innate property. Like shop clerks or bank tellers who handle money not their own, the Israelites handled wealth not their own for a time, and were obligated to hand it over to God on demand, both in the form of the yearly tithe as well as the periodic temple offering. Nobody knew this better than the priests, who were the collectors of the tithe and the processors of the offerings, and who were paid and fed by means of a share of each (Lev. 2:3, 10; 6:9, 11, 19, 22 [16, 18, 26, 29]; 7:6–10; 14, 31–34). Indeed, both priests and worshipers shared in eating virtually all the sacrificial meals other than those few that were the token "whole burnt offerings" (Lev. 1).

This raises a question: Why would priests accept defective animals, including as Malachi states specifically, some who were "blind," "crippled," and "sick," and why would worshipers bring such animals, knowing that they themselves would be eating part of them? The answer has to be, quite simply, that aside from some of the sick ones, they all tasted the same, and thus priests were cutting deals with worshipers to receive such animals with some sort of quid pro quo. Farmers have always eaten blind and lame

animals, and Israelite farmers were certainly used to doing so. The point was that God would not accept them *as offerings*. An offering is more than just a meal. It is a symbol of one's dedication to God, a constantly repeated lesson in the nature of his holiness, and a means of atonement for sin.

Why, then, would priests fall into the practice of accepting unworthy sacrifices? The possibilities are some combination of the following: (1) The sick animals were the ones chosen as whole burnt offerings, since no one actually had to eat them. (2) Bribes accompanied the submission of the lower-quality animals, which were just as edible but otherwise useless to the farmers because they would not keep much longer or were below breeding quality. (3) Larger numbers of lower-quality animals were accepted as equal to a smaller number of proper animals, giving both priests and worshipers more to eat as their respective share of the sacrificial meals. (4) By making offering easier, the priests got a much higher income, since the people were, like all people, selfish and stingy when it came to giving to God. (5) The Canaanites, Philistines, and other neighbors of the Judeans allowed loose standards for sacrificial animals, making it doubly hard for the Judeans to hold to the more costly, higher standards of the Mosaic law. (This was certainly the case with the standards on marriage; Ezra 9–10; Neh. 8–13.) Culling the herd and getting worship credit from God for what was not worth keeping anyway was like killing two birds with one stone. The alternative—giving up the very best of what one owned, the finest breeding stock and the healthiest individual animals—was something

should be noted that מִזְבְּחִי (my altar) and שֻׁלְחַן יְהוָה (Yahweh's table) are synonymous pairs and do not indicate different concepts (see Ezek. 41:22).

8a. אֵין רָע (Isn't that evil?): Many modern translations prefer "wrong" for רָע, and indeed the word can be translated "bad," "unpleasant," and the like; it need not have moral overtones. Nevertheless, since the word can describe in its range of meaning moral failure, "evil" surely fits this context especially well. The problem is not accidental mistakes; the problem is willful disobedience. The word could, grammatically, be translated with the New English Bible and Glazier-McDonald,

however, "[declaring it] 'not bad!'" on the assumption that these words are what the priest who received the animal for sacrifice would avow about the animal upon inspecting it. However, since Malachi quotes people extensively in his prophecy with appropriate attributive wording (mainly one of the forms of אָמַר [say]) it seems highly unlikely that he would suddenly omit any indication here that אֵין רָע was what the priest said, rather than being, in the context of a divine speech of excoriation, God's own rhetorical question to the priests.

---

plenty of Israelites probably were simply not willing to do. So the compromise worked. People and priests were both advantaged, and worship attendance increased. Only God was the loser. As Zechariah had said sixty years earlier concerning the eating of sacrifices at the temple: "When you were eating and drinking, were you not just feasting for yourselves?" (Zech. 7:6).

"Priests who despise my name" (v. 6b) sharply contrasts with the instructions accompanying the original Aaronic blessing, that the priests were to "put my name on the Israelites" (Num. 6:27).

8a. There is an obvious ironic slant to the charges and challenges of verse 8. What the priests are doing is so unsatisfactory that there is no way it could be called right, if only they would be honest about it. And the proof is to be found in the fact that they know very well that a human being they desire to please (the Persian appointee governor) would reject what they are offering to God, whom they should much more desire to please! The governor would regard the imperfect offering as an insult and would thus not accept or show favor to those bringing it. How ironic, then, that the priests could think that God should be willing to accept and show favor to them and the worshipers they represent. The Old Testament sacrificial laws clearly prohibit offering animals that are faulty physically (Exod. 12:5; 29:1; Lev. 1:3; 22:18–25; Num. 6:14; 19:2; Deut. 15:21; 17:1). In these

laws one or two types of physical deficiencies, such as blindness or lameness, are typically mentioned in the manner of a synecdoche, but the clear implication is that imperfections of whatever sort cannot be tolerated. This would include sick animals (ḥōleh), even though that specific adjective is not used of prohibited sacrifices in the Pentateuch. Leviticus 22:20 is the most broad in stating that any sort of imperfection (mûm) in an animal was something Yahweh could not accept (ršh, as here in v. 8). The priests knew these sacrificial laws by heart, as was required for their job. Ignorance was not the problem. God was not advising them of considerations that were new to their thinking. Malachi, like all the orthodox prophets, was not calling his audience to new standards, but back to old ones. The problem was not a need to acclimate to new ways of doing things, but to return to the practice of the Mosaic covenant as divinely—and unambiguously—revealed already a full millennium earlier. Accordingly, it would have been hard for any of the priests to deny Malachi's inspired words on the basis of what the Scriptures taught. Thus the later charge that the priests had corrupted the covenant with Levi (2:8) was the underlying problem. Disbelief, not accidental failure to maintain standards, was the priests' real fault. Tradition had replaced the word of God; an evolved system of worship had gradually replaced a revealed one.

II. Second Disputation (1:6–2:9)

C. The Priests Should Know It Is Wrong to Offer Defective Sacrifices (1:8b–9)

STUART	NRSV
Try offering that to your governor! Would he be pleased with you or accept you? (said Yahweh of the Armies). ⁹ Now implore God to be gracious to us. Since this is what you offered, should he show you favor? (said Yahweh of the Armies).	Try presenting that to your governor; will he be pleased with you or show you favor? says the LORD of hosts. ⁹And now implore the favor of God, that he may be gracious to us. The fault is yours. Will he show favor to any of you? says the LORD of hosts.

8b. לְפֶחָתֶךָ (to your governor): The term is frequently used in the Old Testament to denote a regional administrator, appointed by a foreign emperor, during one of the times that Israel was subject to foreign domination. In the Persian system, a "governor" was probably lower in status than a "satrap," although how these ranks and their terminology would have been employed in Judah is another matter (Fensham, "*Peḥâ* in the Old Testament"; and Alt, "Die Rolle Samarias"). הֲיִרְצֶךָ (Would he be pleased with you?): Here some parts of the Septuagint tradition, followed by the Vulgate, read "Would he be pleased with *it?*" (εἰ προσδέξεται αὐτό). It is quite possible that this reflects the more original reading (הֲיִרְצֵהוּ) and since either reading makes perfect sense in the context, there is no good way to decide between them.

9. חַלּוּ־נָא פְנֵי־אֵל (implore God): The piel of חלה here echoes, probably more accidentally than purposefully, the adjectival חֹלֶה (sick) in verse 8 but with the very different meaning that the piel verb form carries (lit., to make soft, weak, thus more abstractly to appeal, implore). The full expression, "implore God," in this same or similar wording occurs widely in the Old Testament (Exod. 32:11; 1 Sam. 13:12; 1 Kings 13:6; 2 Kings 13:4; Jer. 26:19; Dan. 9:13; Zech. 7:2) and thus cannot be considered an expression composed for purposes of vocabulary linkage in this context. The plural imperative undoubtedly refers to the priests as a group—there is no other assumption possible in the context—rather than the nation as a whole or a select group of righteous priests being urged to intercede for the remainder of the nation. וִיחָנֵּנוּ: The initial *waw* is the *waw* of result, indicated in my translation by the infinitival construction, "to be gracious to us." In the second half of the verse the relation between clauses is asyndetic (lit., from your hand was this, will he accept you?). In the context the first clause is dependent and precursory and must be translated accordingly ("since . . ."). The expression הֲיִשָּׂא מִכֶּם פָּנִים (should he accept you?) is not materially different from הֲיִשָּׂא פָנֶיךָ (would he accept you?) in verse 8 above. The difference in wording between them is due to the demands of the poetic meter in their respective verses rather than a change in meaning (מִכֶּם does not mean "because of you" or "to any of you" [RSV] or the like).

8b. As for the governor whom the priests are rhetorically challenged to present with their imperfect animals, his identity is unknown. We know a few of the names of the Judean governors of the Persian era (see Cross, "Judean Reconstruction"), such as Sheshbazzar (538 B.C.; he may well have died en route or shortly after arriving in Judah from Babylon; Ezra 1:8, 11; etc.), Zerubbabel (538–520, at least; Ezra 2:2, etc.; Neh. 7:7, etc.; Hag. 1:1, etc.; Zech. 4:6–10), Nehemiah (444–431, at least), and Bagohi (also known as Bagoas, named in several letters from the late fifth-century Elephantini papyri; see *ANET*, pp. 491–92). But we do not know the identity of any Judean governors in the fifth century prior to Nehemiah's arrival (444 B.C.) and if our dating of Malachi at around 460 B.C. is correct, we remain in the dark as to the governor that Malachi's original audience would have had in mind when they heard these words preached.

The suggestion that the governor would not accept the priests (lit., raise their faces), using the idiom *nāśāʾ pānîm*, is an ironic echo of the language of the Aaronic blessing, "Yahweh raise his face to you" in Numbers 6:26.

9. Twice in verse 9 and once in verse 8 Hebrew expressions for "favoring" or "respecting" are used in establishing a compound a fortiori argu-ment. The argument may be simplified as follows: What a governor would reject, God certainly wouldn't accept, so why don't you priests stop thinking that God is accepting (*nāśāʾ panîm*, again satirically echoing Num. 6:26) your inferior offerings and repent of the practice, appealing for mercy? The national favor with God is jeopardized by your behavior! With verse 9 the poetic section of the oracle comes to an end, but this does not mark a major division in the oracle of 1:6–2:9. The prose part of the oracle will go on to reinforce what the poetic part has introduced, so the use of prose and poetry is more a device of emphasis than of contrast in meaning.

Moreover, it would be wrong to assume that God was prepared to let the priests go free from punishment by merely praying for forgiveness for their despising him ("Now implore God to be gracious to us"). As the immediate context as well as the overall context of the oracle make clear, nothing short of full repentance (change of thinking and practice) will forestall the curse the priests deserve for their disobedience. The rhetorical question posed to the priests at the end of this verse ("Should he show you favor?") implies a curse of anger/rejection from Yahweh (curse type 1), anticipating the more overt curses against the priests yet to come in the passage.

II. Second Disputation (1:6–2:9)
D. The Priests Are Warned by God (1:10–2:5)

STUART

¹⁰One of you ought to shut the doors, so that you would not light worthless fires on my altar! I am not pleased with you (said Yahweh of the Armies), and I will accept no offering from you. ¹¹For from where the sun rises to where it sets, my name will be great among the nations. Everywhere, incense will be offered to my name, and a pure offering, for my name will be great among the nations (said Yahweh of the Armies). ¹²But you are profaning it by saying, "The Lord's table can be defiled and its food is not important." ¹³When you say, "What a bother!" you mistreat me! (said Yahweh of the Armies). You bring injured, crippled, or sick animals when you bring the sacrifice. Should I accept that from you? (said Yahweh of the Armies). ¹⁴Cursed is the cheater who has a male in his flock and vows to give it, but then sacrifices a defective animal to the Lord. For I am a great king (said Yahweh of the Armies), and my name will be feared among the nations.

2 And now: This commandment is for you, priests. ²If you don't listen, and if you are not zealous to honor my name (said Yahweh of the Armies), I will send a curse upon you and I will curse your blessing. Yes, I am cursing it, because you have not been zealous. ³I am going to cut off your descendants. I will spread dung on your faces, the dung from your festivals, and I will carry you to it. ⁴Then you will know that I have sent you this command, so that my covenant with Levi might continue to exist (said Yahweh of the Armies). ⁵My covenant with him was life and peace. And I gave him fear and he feared me and was terrified of my name.

NRSV

¹⁰Oh, that someone among you would shut the temple doors, so that you would not kindle fire on my altar in vain! I have no pleasure in you, says the LORD of hosts, and I will not accept an offering from your hands. ¹¹For from the rising of the sun to its setting my name is great among the nations, and in every place incense is offered to my name, and a pure offering; for my name is great among the nations, says the LORD of hosts. ¹²But you profane it when you say that the Lord's table is polluted, and the food for it may be despised. ¹³"What a weariness this is," you say, and you sniff at me, says the LORD of hosts. You bring what has been taken by violence or is lame or sick, and this you bring as your offering! Shall I accept that from your hand? says the LORD. ¹⁴Cursed be the cheat who has a male in his flock and vows to give it, and yet sacrifices to the Lord what is blemished; for I am a great King, says the LORD of hosts, and my name is reverenced among the nations.

2 And now, O priests, this command is for you. ²If you will not listen, if you will not lay it to heart to give glory to my name, says the LORD of hosts, then I will send the curse on you and I will curse your blessings; indeed I have already cursed them, because you do not lay it to heart. ³I will rebuke your offspring, and spread dung upon your faces, the dung of your offerings, and I will put you out of my presence.

⁴Know, then, that I have sent this command to you, that my covenant with Levi may hold, says the LORD of hosts. ⁵My covenant with him was a covenant of life and well-being, which I gave him; this called for reverence, and he revered me and stood in awe of my name.

10. נַם מִי (one of you [ought] . . .): Here the Septuagint (Διότι [because]) apparently read כִּי נַם, and contextually construed the first verb as a niphal plural (συγκλεισθήσονται, "will be shut"), but can otherwise be viewed as supporting the consonantal Masoretic Text. The Septuagint is slightly periphrastic in the remainder of the verse, as are the Vulgate and the Syriac, again without calling into question the accuracy of the Masoretic Text. Both imperfect verb forms in the first half of the verse (וְיָסְגֹּר ,תָּאִירוּ) are properly translated modally (ought to shut, would not light). What is called for is a condition contrary to fact: מִי plus נַם (intensifying adverb) plus the imperfect expresses a wish, literally, "O that there were at least one among you who. . . ." God does not actually want a cessation of offerings, but the cessation of *improper* offerings, which are worse than nothing. מִנְחָה (offering) is the word used most often in the Old Testament to express the concept of offering in general, without any particular qualification as to which of the wide range of specific offerings was in mind. Here its use is consistent with the broad-scale condemnation of the way that the priests were, in general, violating the offering laws. חִנָּם (worthless): The clause " would not light worth-

less fires" could also be translated "would not fruitlessly light fires," since חִנָּם modifies the verb. Either way, it is clear that the faulty sacrifices are without effect. The Essene community at Qumran self-servingly interpreted this verse as invalidating the practice of sacrificial offerings altogether, a convenient understanding in light of their self-imposed exile from the temple: "None of those brought into the covenant shall enter the temple to put fire to his altar in vain. They shall bar the door, since God said, 'Who among you will bar its door?' and 'you shall not put fire to my altar in vain.'"

11. כִּי (for): The New International Version and some other versions translate this particle as indeed," but this does not demonstrate as clearly the connection between verse 11 and what precedes. The priests are willing to insult Yahweh in part because they are missing the whole direction of history (see the Exposition). מִמִּזְרַח־שֶׁמֶשׁ וְעַד־מְבוֹאוֹ: The Revised Standard Version/New Revised Standard Version translation "from the rising of the sun to its setting" could be misunderstood to refer to the length of a day rather than to the breadth of the earth and therefore the translation "from where the sun rises to where it sets" is

---

10. It would be better to close the temple complex than to continue worship that insults God. The doors (here dual, indicating a pair of doors) of the temple complex presumably refer either to the doors that led to the inner courtyard, where the offerings were actually offered on the altar by the priests on behalf of the worshipers, or the outer courtyard, where the worshipers gathered while the offering was done for them and where they ate their share of the resulting cooked meals. We do not know exactly how these courtyards were laid out, but there were two of them in both the First and Second Temples (1 Kings 6:36; 7:12) and in Ezekiel's idealized symbolic temple (Ezek. 40–44) so that lay worshipers did not occupy the same courtyard as priests. Ezekiel makes much of the importance of the temple doors (40:19, 22, 32, 35; 46:2, 9; 48:34); other parts of the Old Testament also indicate the importance of controlled access to the worship site for which professional guards, under the authority of the priests, were employed (Ezra 2:70; 7:7; Neh. 7:73; 10:29, 40 [28, 39]; Ps. 84:11 [10]). The priests alone had access to the actual sacrificial area. The "doors" cannot refer to those of the roofed temple sanctuary, viewed as the symbolic dwelling place of God, since the concern here is for sacrifices, which were offered out-

doors (worship was essentially an outdoor practice in Bible times), not for incense, occasionally offered inside the roofed structure, by selected priests. According to 2 Chronicles 28:24, Ahaz had actually done what the current passage envisions, shutting the doors of the temple, but for very different reasons. He was trying to suppress true Yahwism, not restore it. Whereas the poetic section posed the dissatisfaction of God mainly in the form of questions (vv. 7–9), verse 10, prose, now bluntly states that God is "not pleased" and "will not accept" the polluted offerings being brought to him. This consititutes a curse of rejection/destruction of the cult (curse type 2). The priests and people may have tried to fool themselves into thinking that what they offered would earn God's favor. But Malachi was inspired to say that there was no chance of that. Malachi's audience would have heard in the use of the Hebrew verb ʾôr (light [worthless fires]) a subtle echo of the same verb in Numbers 6:25.

11. While the verb tenses of this verse may be ambiguous, the concepts are not. God here proclaims to the priests that their inadequate and thus insulting worship is completely inconsistent with what will one day be the case: he will be worshiped reverently—and properly—the world

preferable. The phrase is a merism indicating totality (of place) via polarity (cf. Pss. 50:1; 113:3; Isa. 45:6; 59:19). The Phoenician inscription from Karatepe (tenth century B.C.?) has a parallel wording, *llmsʾ šmš wʾd mbʾy* (where the sun rises to where it sets), for vastness of territory. In Amarna letter 288 (early fourteenth century B.C.) the expression is already known and linked to the concept of name: "my lord has set his name at the rising of the sun and at the setting of the sun." It occurs as well in the Mari letters (seventeenth century B.C.) and in Panammu 2.13 (eighth century B.C.) Its parallels in the verse, which is parallelistic prose, are בְּכָל־מָקוֹם (everywhere) and בַּגּוֹיִם (among the nations). Functioning from narrow and idealistic notions of how the Hebrew language works, some commentators have suggested

that מֻקְטָר מֻגָּשׁ (burnt offering/incense is/will be offered) is awkward grammatically, since it represents two hophal participles in juxtaposition. While this kind of construction is not commonplace, it is hardly awkward. The first participle (מֻקְטָר) is used substantivally, as the noun *burnt offering*. (Not *incense*; Hebrew words from the root קטר refer to offerings that are allowed to burn up in their entirety rather than those eaten after cooking. This can include, but is not limited to, "incense."). See 1:14 for a nearby instance of a hophal participle used as a noun (מָשְׁחָת, "defective animal"). That nouns are sometimes constructed from participial morphologies is so basic to Hebrew as to require no further discussion. Of greater importance is the question of the time reference of the verbs in the verse, including the

over. His name (*šēm*) will be great everywhere, as the priests should have been making it among the Israelites (Num. 6:27).

Some commentators, holding to the notion that the verbless clauses had to indicate a present practice, have thought that the verse suggested a theology that welcomed ancient pagan worship in Malachi's day as somehow honoring the one true God. Some have speculated that these words reflect the syncretistic Persian era concept of a kind of loose monotheism in which a "high God" was shared by all faiths (a concept not easily proved). Others have opined that Malachi was asserting that God beneficently received all sacrifices from all nations given to whatever god or goddess as his own (even less likely in light of the emphasis in the present context against sacrifices that were in any way faulty, and against syncretism in 2:10–16). Still others have assumed that these words were intended to indicate that the widely dispersed Jews of Malachi's day (there were Jews in Africa, Europe, and Asia, after all) were faithfully worshiping "around the world" in contrast to the priests at Jerusalem, and that the "burnt offerings" were limited to incense burned at various synagogues. Another theory holds that Malachi is referring to people of foreign origin who had converted to Judaism, who were honoring Yahweh while the priests were not.

None of the approaches—taking the verse as referring to a situation that prevailed in Malachi's own time—is convincing. In particular, the idea that Malachi (or even an interpolator, as some have argued) would somehow believe that anyone worshiping any god anywhere in the world was merely worshiping Yahweh by another name is

unsupportable. This would make verse 11 out to be the most syncretistic, universalistic material in the entire Bible, in contrast to all the other prophets and in contrast to the rest of Malachi's own prophecies.

Instead, we must appreciate here the presence of eschatological messianic universalism, that is, the common Old Testament doctrine that the true God would one *future* day reign over all peoples, who would have no choice but to acknowledge his sovereignty (restoration blessing type 3). Such a view is the consistent outlook of the prophets (Isa. 2:2–4; 11:10–12; 42:1–9; 45:1–3, 15, 22–23; Jer. 3:17; Mic. 4:1–2; Zeph. 3:8–9; Hag. 2:7; Zech. 8:20–23; 14:16; compare the oracles against foreign nations throughout the prophetic books) and is also widely represented elsewhere in Scripture (e.g., Exod. 9:16; Pss. 22:28 [27]; 95–99). Since it is entirely within the grammatical boundaries of the language of this verse to consider that it points to the future rather than to the present (see the Exegesis), there is every reason to regard the verse as a prediction rather than as a description of current events, as a future contrast to a present reality. Three times in the verse the greatness of God's name is mentioned. This reprises the emphasis of verse 6, that his name (reputation, honor, authority) was being insulted by the self-serving, improper worship conducted by the priests. The eventual greatness of God's name, universal recognition thereof, is a theme often associated with predictions of the future in Scripture (Isa. 29:23; 48:11; 52:6; Jer. 44:26; Amos 9:12; Acts 9:15; 15:17; Rom. 9:17; Phil. 2:10).

The priests were ignorant of the whole direction of history. They could treat Yahweh as a petty god

implicit verb *to be*. Does the wording of the verse mean to say that Yahweh was actually worshiped everywhere in Malachi's day? Such a universalism would surely contrast with the sentiments of 1:2–5. Some commentators have tried to argue, again on supposedly grammatical grounds, that the absence of specifically future verb forms requires taking the verse as stating present realities. This is highly unlikely for several reasons, not the least of which is that verbless clauses are usually not explicit as to tense (Anderson, *Verbless Clause in the Pentateuch*; compare GKC §114f). Context then bears the burden of establishing the tense. What is that context? The universal acknowledgment of Yahweh's sovereignty, which elsewhere in Malachi is clearly a future matter and which generally in the prophets is a future expectation (see the Exposition).

12. מְחַלְּלִים (are profaning): The verb חלל is a synonym for גאל, which is used both here and previously in the passage (v. 7) to indicate the concept of pollution or defilement. Both the participles מְגֹאָל and נִבְזֶה are best construed in a modal sense (can be defiled, can be despised; or, less idiomatically, defilable, despisable). שֻׁלְחַן אֲדֹנָי מְגֹאָל הוּא (the Lord's table can be defiled): These four words carefully parallel—intentionally—the final four words of verse 7, שֻׁלְחַן יְהוָה נִבְזֶה הוּא (Yahweh's table can be despised). Nothing different is being said here about the priests' attitude than was said in verse 7. The two wording substitutions are characteristic of Hebrew style, which generally favors making a point a second time by alternative wording. No theological truth is being added by the different term for God. וְנִיבוֹ נִבְזֶה אָכְלוֹ (lit., its fruit [?]

can be despised, its food): There is reason to doubt the reliability of the Masoretic Text at this point, for three reasons: (1) the grammar is genuinely unusual, the singular verb being surrounded by two singular subjects; (2) the rare term נִיב (fruit?) is known elsewhere in the Old Testament only in Isaiah 57:19, where its meaning is also uncertain; (3) the ancient versions do not seem to support the reading וְנִיבוֹ (and its fruit). The Septuagint reads differently: καὶ τὰ ἐπιτιθέμενα (and what is put on it), part of the same wording it adds at the end of verse 7 by conflation from this spot. Is the Septuagint translator guessing, or did he have before him something like וַאֲשֶׁר עָלָיו (and what is on it) in his Hebrew *Vorlage*? We cannot know for certain, but there is reason to believe that the translator was doing nothing more than fumbling to translate an already garbled text. It must be noted that וְנִיבוֹ is not reflected in either the Targum or the Syriac, and some Hebrew manuscripts do not contain it as well. The common suggestion that וְנִיבוֹ resulted from a dittography of the first two letters of the following word נִבְזֶה (can be despised), which was then "made sense of" by subsequent scribes who made it into the word נִיבוֹ (its fruit) and linked it syntactically by ו (and) to the context remains the only explanation that is even remotely plausible for this admittedly difficult wording. Most of the English translations simply smooth over the problem by ignoring נִיבוֹ (its fruit).

13. וַאֲמַרְתֶּם (When you say . . .): The first clause, paratactically coordinated to the main clause by *waw*, is best understood as dependent and temporal, as is also the next-to-the-last clause in the

---

whose laws were bendable. God rebukes them by the assertion that he will one day control all the world, and thus deserves current sacrifices worthy of his future recognition. They should be ashamed to do so little for so great a Sovereign. He is—and will be—too great to be treated so contemptuously. What could have made the priests so inclined to think so little of God? To many Jews in Malachi's time, including the priests, Judah must have seemed insignificant, and therefore its national God, Yahweh, of little influence once Jerusalem had fallen in 586 B.C. to the Babylonians and Judah had been incorporated thereafter into the Persian Empire as merely one of many administrative districts in the great empire. But they were thinking only in present terms and not in terms of the great sweep of the history of God's redemption. The eschatological future would show them otherwise.

The time would come when everyone would honor God better than they were!

12. Verse 12 is a prose restatement of the essential points of verse 7, reemphasizing that what the priests are doing is illegal and not accidental. "Profaning *it*" refers to the name of God ("my name") mentioned three times in verse 11. To profane Yahweh's name (*ḥālal šēm*) is commonly used elsewhere in the Old Testament to mean "insult God" in any of a variety of ways (Lev. 18:21; 19:12; 20:3; 21:6; 22:2, 32; Prov. 30:9; Isa. 48:11; 56:6; Jer. 34:16; Ezek. 20:9, 14, 22, 39; 36:20–23; 39:7; Amos 2:7). "The Lord's table" is the sacrifice altar, as in verse 7, and "its food" is the sacrificial food prepared on it for eating by priests and worshipers.

13. Verse 13 is a prose restatement of the essential points of verse 8 (as v. 12 was of v. 7) and thus

verse (see below). מַתְּלָאָה (What a bother!): The ת is doubled because the expression is a contraction of מַה תְּלָאָה . וְהִפַּחְתֶּם אוֹתוֹ (you mistreat me; [some: and you cause it to blow/sigh [?]]): The meaning of the hiphil of נפח is debated. It might mean "and you cause [it] to blow" or the like, which could refer to something about the altar, although the context leaves us in doubt as to what it could possibly be. It might also mean "and you cause [me] to puff" or the like, that is, you enrage me/make me mad. Again, this meaning is essentially speculative. Some have concluded that the expression is akin to English "sniff at," an expression of disgust (so RSV/NRSV/NIV), but this is little more than an attempt to find a negative expression related to the movement of air that might fit the context. "Sniff at" is otherwise not a likely meaning for נפח. It means "to cause to breathe hard," that is, "to weary," or "to overwork" or "to mistreat" (not "cause the death of," as RSV/NRSV think) in Job 31:39, the only other place where the hiphil of נפח is found in the Old Testament (see Habel's translation, "cause to despair"; *Job*, p. 425). Who or what, then, is being mistreated? The Hebrew scribes thought it was Yahweh, and corrected אוֹתוֹ to אוֹתִי ("it" to "me"). For the same expression the Septuagint reads καὶ ἐξεφύσησα αὐτά (and I have scorned them), which may be nothing more than an ancient translator's attempt to render a puzzling verb and object pronoun contextually. Could the consonantal Masoretic Text conceal an original וְהִפַּחְתִּים (and I have gotten enraged at them [?]) and the object suffix אוֹתוֹ (it) have been added later when the verb was mistakenly construed as a sec-

ond plural? We simply do not have the facts to make a sure decision. The translation "and you mistreat me" has a low level of certainty (especially about the word *me*) but is nevertheless the most likely. גָּזוּל (injured): Some translations read "stolen" or "taken by violence" since גזל can mean not only "ripped" but "ripped off" in roughly the same idiomatic sense that English slang "ripped off" means "stolen." Since verse 13 so closely parallels verse 8, however, which exclusively describes faulty sacrifices in terms of the imperfections of the animals themselves rather than how they were obtained (how could a priest recognize a stolen animal?), it is most likely that גָּזוּל refers to some kind of defect here as well, and "injured" is the preferred translation. וַהֲבֵאתֶם (when you bring the sacrifice): In the syntax of the sentence, it is most likely that the clause is subordinate and temporal, as clauses of this type introduced by *waw* have the potential to be. אָמַר יְהוָה (said Yahweh [of the Armies]): Because some medieval Hebrew manuscripts as well as the Septuagint and part of the Syriac tradition reflect the word צְבָאוֹת (armies; archaic "hosts") after יְהוָה, it is likely that it was originally present in the passage and was dropped by haplography. The best evidence, then, suggests that Malachi employed a single messenger formula (all eleven times) throughout the passage.

14. אָרוּר (cursed): In the Old Testament context the term means "subject to the punishment of God" or "under God's condemnation." It frequently denotes, as here, a promise that punishment will eventually be rendered, but without

it shares several vocabulary connections with verse 8 (see the Exegesis). The priests have taken the easy road of compromise, and have allowed inferior worship in the form of inferior sacrificial animals. The "evil" (v. 8) that they do is given voice in the rhetorical quotation of their despicable attitude ("What a bother!") as well as in God's own words of condemnation ("you wear me out!"). As verse 8 ends with a question about acceptance ("Would he [the governor] accept you?"), verse 13 concludes similarly ("Should I [God] accept that from you?"). In verse 8 mention is made of "blind" animals. Here the broader term *injured* is substituted. Since injured animals could not even be eaten in everyday, nonreligious settings (Exod. 22:30 [31]; Lev. 7:24; 17:15; 22:8; Ezek. 4:14; 44:31; see also Gen. 31:39; Acts 15:20, 29; 21:25), they certainly could not be brought

legitimately as sacrifices. Yet this is exactly what the priests were doing.

14. To this point, the focus of the oracle has been the priests' sins while the lay worshipers who bring the inferior animals to the priests have been under criticism only by implication. Now, for a moment, the lay worshipers come into focus—yet the priests do not retreat entirely to the background. What the priests do is part of a sordid cooperative system in which the people also participate. The people choose to bring the inferior sacrifices and the priests choose to accept them for offering to God. The priests are supposed to be the inspectors who see that the people's offerings are sound. When the inspectors relax their standards, the people can openly relax theirs But God has not relaxed his! This practice violated the clear instruction of the Mosaic covenant in Leviticus 27:9–12:

any specificity as to the nature and timing of the punishment. זָכָר (male): It has occasionally been proposed that this word be emended to זָכֶה (pure), the opposite of the term מָשְׁחָת (defective) used later in the verse, since that would clarify the contrast under discussion. However, males were the primary sacrificial animals (see the Exposition), and there is no reason to emend the text other than a desire for overt symmetry of antonyms. Without the emendation, the contrast between what is vowed (a given male) and what is offered (an inferior substitute, and incidentally, almost

---

If what [a worshiper] vowed is an animal that is acceptable as an offering to the LORD, such an animal given to the LORD becomes holy [must be offered]. He must not exchange it or substitute a good one for a bad one, or a bad one for a good one; if he should substitute one animal for another, both it and the substitute become holy. If what he vowed is a ceremonially unclean animal— one that is not acceptable as an offering to the LORD—the animal must be presented to the priest, who will judge its quality as good or bad. Whatever value the priest then sets, that is what it will be. If the owner wishes to redeem the animal, he must add a fifth to its value.

It is possible to imagine that Malachi turned away from the priests toward lay people standing nearby and began to address them at this point. But this cannot be demonstrated. The overall oracle is still addressed to the priests, and the statements in this verse are for their benefit. They are the teachers of the law who should be instructing the people about the nature of proper sacrifice.

Note that the verse does not say that all the people are cursed. Only those people who brought inferior animals were to be cursed (in the manner of the general/unspecified curse that I count as curse type 25). The priests were responsible for what the worshipers were allowed to offer, but not the other way around. The priests were surely processing many animals that were perfectly fit for sacrifice from many righteous worshipers. But because they also accepted a percentage of animals that were unfit, from fraudulent worshipers, they were disobedient to God. They would be dim-witted indeed if they failed to see that a curse on *some* worshipers meant a curse on *all* of them. The priests' crime was that they were accepting all sacrifices, fit and unfit. In so doing they condemned themselves uniformly, even though not all worshipers were subject to condemnation.

The illustration of improper sacrifice used in this verse is that of a defective animal substituted for a male that was vowed. The same standards for sacrificial animals are involved: first, healthy, flawless males were to be offered (Exod. 12:5; 29:1; Lev. 1:3, 10; 3:1, 6; 4:3, 12–32; 5:15–18; 6:6; 9:2–3; 14:10; 22:19; Num. 19:2; 28–29, passim; Deut. 15:21; 17:1; etc.); second, vowed animals had to be of no less quality than other sacrificial animals (Lev. 22:18–25). The fact that the animals were vowed is important as a key to the passage's meaning because a vow is a promise to God. Various vow sacrifices were practiced in ancient Israel, from the Nazarite vow to remain ritually pure for a period of one's life in order to dedicate one's living to God, with its attendant sacrifice of a perfect animal (Num 6:14); to the simple vow of gratitude, which was a promise to provide a succession of sacrifices to God in the future for what he had done for the worshiper in the present (e.g., Num. 15:5–8; 2 Sam. 15:7–8; Ps. 50:14; Prov. 7:14; Eccles. 5:4; Jon. 1:16). To vow an animal, a worshiper would make a promise before a priest to bring for sacrifice at some date (possibly indefinite) in the future an unblemished male from his or her flock. The worshiper could not vow what already belonged to God (the firstfruits and tithes); a vowed animal was voluntarily given as "freewill gift" in addition to the annual requirements. Nevertheless, it had to meet every standard of quality otherwise set for sacrifices. Substituting an inferior animal for the unblemished one vowed was, of course, cheating (nkl). Thus Malachi asserts that the priests were actually helping worshipers cheat on God.

The designation of males as the main sacrificial animal was an accommodation of kindness by God to an agrarian society. Flocks and herds need all the females they can get because the females give the milk and bear and nurse the young. Any flock or herd needs a few males for breeding, but most males can be separated out for eating. Males were, in other words, less valuable *on average* to farmers than were females. However, we must not forget that the worshipers were required by the law to offer only *perfect* males—the very best breeders—and could not offer just any males. This does not mean that female animals were never sacrificed. Fellowship offerings could be of any large male or female animals (Lev. 3:1–6), because these were purely voluntary offerings. If someone

certainly a male as well) is clear enough. נוֹרָא (is to be feared): The participle following the implicit verb *to be* is ambiguous as to time (past, present, or future) just as is the case with several verb forms in verse 11. Equally possible from a strictly grammatical point of view are the translations "is feared" or "will be feared." In verse 11, construing the verbs in the present tense leads to a condition contrary to fact. Here the issue is more debatable (see the Exposition).

2:1. וְעַתָּה (and now:): While this compound usually means just "now," "so," or "furthermore," it was sometimes used in Hebrew and Aramaic letters to introduce the main point (or one of the main points) of the letter, and was apparently also sometimes used in legal documents to introduce the ruling (judgment sentence) against the accused. Both וְעַתָּה and לָכֵן (or its synonym עַל־כֵּן) seem to function this way from time to time in

prophetic judgment oracles, the terms probably having been borrowed by the prophets from Israelite legal affairs. For וְעַתָּה in the sense of "here is a/the judgment sentence," see Isaiah 5:5; 16:14; 47:8; Jeremiah 18:11; 26:13; 27:6; 42:15, 22; 44:7; Hosea 2:12 [10]; 5:7; 8:8, 13; Amos 6:7 [with לָכֵן]; 7:16; Nahum 1:13; Zechariah 8:11. But in Malachi וְעַתָּה can also have the simple meaning "now" or "so" (1:9; 3:15); it by no means automatically signals the beginning of a judgment sentence. מִצְוָה (commandment): In the Pentateuch this word always denotes a legal commandment given by God and, while it can certainly refer to commands given by human rulers (e.g., Solomon or David; see 1 Kings 2:43; Neh. 12:24), in the context of an oracle directed to priests it would seem most likely to carry its covenantal connotation of a "legal commandment." While some commentators have suggested that it ought here to carry the

---

wanted to express his or her fellowship with God via the more valuable female animals, why not? Guilt offerings, on the other hand, could only be female, whether goats or lambs (Lev. 4:28, 32; 5:6). The guilt offering demanded an especially worthy offering—one whose loss would always hurt the farmer—a female. Virtually all other offerings were male.

The end of the verse brings to a climax a theme that has appeared once already in this passage (v. 11) and that concluded the prior oracle (v. 5): the greatness of Yahweh. Two points are made of him here: (1) he is a great king; (2) he is (and/or will be) a source of fear among the nations (his name will be feared among them—another echo of Num. 6:27). Both these claims, properly understood, recall those of verse 5 and verse 11. I would not suggest that Malachi's audience had verse 5 from the prior oracle in mind when they heard these words, though surely they had verse 11 and Numbers 6 in mind. Rather, a theme Malachi was inspired to convey surfaces in both oracles—the theme of Yahweh's great power, something the defeated, suppressed, pessimistic Judeans of 460 B.C. tended not to believe but certainly needed to hear.

The claim "for I am great king" has overtones that the words in English do not convey. In the ancient Near East, a great king was a supernational emperor who held sway over lesser kings. The expression "I am a great king" is more than saying "As kings go, I'm great." It is more like, "I am the royal suzerain and all other kings and people are my vassals" (compare Assyrian *šarru rabu*;

Hos. 5:13; 10:6; Kline, *Treaty of the Great King*). The universal kingship of Yahweh is a common theme in the Psalter (e.g., Pss. 10:16; 47:3 [2]; 95:3) as is the concept that he ought to be feared by other nations (e.g., Pss. 9:21 [20]; 102:16 [15]).

Though most of the world did not know it, Yahweh was in fact the world's king. That Israelite priests, who should have known it, failed to act as if they did, is reason for the criticism, and cursing, they are about to receive in 2:1–9.

2:1. These words do not imply that what preceded (1:6–14) was somehow not addressed to the priests. Nor do they function merely as a reminder of the main audience of the oracle, as if 1:14, concerning the judgment against fraudulent lay worshipers, was a parenthetical aside that might have somehow distracted the priests from concern for their own guilt. Rather, these words introduce the oracle's "judgment sentence" ("sentence" in the legal sense of the judge's ruling; see the Exegesis).

Priests worked every day with commandments (*mišpāṭ*). It was part of their job to interpret the commandments of the law for the people. Questions from people about ritual cleanness after exposure to a polluting substance (Lev. 5:2–13), or diagnosis of a skin disease (Lev. 13:1–44), or the proper valuation of a tithe or redemption (Lev. 27:2–23), or the disposition of a defendant accused of a crime addressable by vengeance (Num. 35:6–28), or the acceptability of an offering (Lev. 27:11–12)—these were all matters about commandments. What the priests were used to dealing with, God would now use against them. In effect,

meaning "decision" or "verdict," it would appear to do so only secondarily. The word was surely chosen for its covenant overtones and for its relation to daily priestly practice (see the Exposition).

2. The dominant vocabulary of this verse is repetitive, providing emphasis and having to do with zeal to honor God and the certainty of coming under a divine curse if that zeal is not forthcoming. אִם־לֹא תִשְׁמְעוּ (if you don't listen): In Hebrew as well as in English, the range of meaning for the terminology of listening can include responding/obeying and not merely hearing (compare English "Don't listen to him; he's not telling the truth," in which "listen" means "heed" rather than "hear"). אִם־לֹא תָשִׂימוּ . . . עַל־לֵב (if you are not zealous): The Revised Standard Version translation ("if you will not lay it to heart") is accurate but represents somewhat archaic English. Also possible are translations like "if you do not determine . . ." and "if you don't make sure that. . . ." לָתֵת כָּבוֹד לִשְׁמִי (to honor my name): Many expressions involving שֵׁם (name) have appeared in the passage already, but this one (נתן [give] + כָּבוֹד [glory] + divine element [here, "my

name"]) is slightly different. It has a special idiomatic sense that goes beyond "to use my name respectfully." "Give glory to God/his name" sometimes has the sense "to humble yourself before [God]" or "do what is right" or even "be honest" (e.g., Josh. 7:19; see also John 9:24). הַמְּאֵרָה (a curse): The noun is essentially collective (not to mention definite) and does not mean only "a single given curse" but "cursing." The latter English word cannot easily be employed in translation, however, since it has come to refer to foul language almost exclusively in typical modern English. וְאָרוֹתִי אֶת־בִּרְכוֹתֵיכֶם (lit., I will curse your blessings): The singularity of the referential pronoun in the following statement (Yes, I am cursing *it*) indicates that the Hebrew text originally contained the singular, בִּרְכַתְכֶם (your blessing), rather than the plural, בִּרְכוֹתֵיכֶם (your blessings). The singular form (εὐλογίαν, blessing) in the Septuagint confirms this. וְגַם אָרוֹתִיהָ (Yes, I am cursing it): The Septuagint translates contextually, with a future verb, καταράσομαι (I will curse), since the overall perspective of the verse concerns a coming curse. Most English translations timidly employ

---

God says, "You priests who are so used to applying commandments to other people—now I have a commandment for *you!*"

2. Curse pronouncements were one of the most common kinds of statements prophets were called upon to make (see the Introduction). Now that which Malachi's audience knew had to be coming is unleashed in earnest. The priests are to be cursed. A curse is a pronouncement of divine punishment. All prophetic curses are based on the curses announced in the Mosaic covenant (especially Lev. 26; Deut. 4; 28–32; see the Introduction). The present verse contains two types of curses: rejection/destruction of the cult, or curse type 2 (compare, however, also type 26; e.g., Deut. 28:16; 29:20–21, 27; 30:19) and one that we call a futility curse (type 15; "I will curse your blessing. Yes I am cursing it;" compare, e.g., Deut. 28:20, 29). The function of a general curse is to emphasize that the miscreant will not get away with his or her sin (Lev. 26:41, 43: "they will pay for their sin"). A futility curse focuses on the frustration of one's plans and efforts as a divine punishment (Deut. 28:29: "You will be unsuccessful in everything you do"; "You will build a house but will not live in it").

How would "curse your blessing" be a futility pronouncement on the priests? Precisely because blessing was their business, as we have already

noted in connection with the comments above on Numbers 6:23–27. In the most general sense, people went to priests for blessing. The priests served as the intermediaries between the people and God (Exod. 28–29; cf. 1 Sam. 2:28) and in that sense were authorized to pronounce his blessing on the people. Blessing is the result of proper worship. And, specifically, the priests were pronouncers of blessing statements, declarations of benefit and well-being. It was their job, on request, to say blessings for the people who came to them. The Aaronic blessing was probably the high point, and probably also the conclusion, of a worshiper's experience at the temple. Were it to fail, to be withheld, or to be reversed in effectiveness so that it functioned like a curse (i.e., so that people went home after a blessing only to experience disasters of various sorts), this priestly key role would be rendered futile. A futility curse, like the reversal of blessing, is, of course, well within God's power. Indeed, the opposite—the divine turning of a curse into a blessing—is also demonstrated elsewhere in the Old Testament (the main example being Balaam's curses; compare Deut. 23:6 [23:5]; Neh. 13:2). God is the controller of blessing and curse. The priests' blessing pronouncements were only their verbal acquiescence to the will of God. If they disobeyed his will, he would not honor their blessing pronouncements. This is the point of

the past tense and gratuitously supply a clarifying adverb (e.g., RSV/NRSV: "Indeed, I have already cursed them"; NIV: "Moreover, I have already cursed them"). But this is a typical case of a Hebrew verb with the form of the perfect tense but a meaning that involves, as an intrinsic result of the action, a present or future status for the object of the verb (GKC §§106 g, m–o). Thus a present or future translation is not only possible, but preferable in this context. The Septuagint contains an entire sentence immediately after אָרוֹתִיהָ וְגַם (Yes, I am cursing it) that is not represented in the Hebrew text: καὶ διασκεδάσω τὴν εὐλογίαν ὑμῶν καὶ οὐκ ἔσται ἐν ὑμῖν (and I will scatter your blessing and it will not be among you). This sentence does not seem to be expansionistic, but reads more like the sort of translation-style Greek that the Septuagint normally contains. It might reflect an original Hebrew, lost by haplography via homoioteleuton, which began with one of several first-person singular words for scattering people, such as וְאָפוּץ or וְאֱזָרֶה, and continued with a wording like בְּרַכְתְּכֶם וְלֹא תִהְיֶה בָכֶם . If the original autograph contained such a statement, it would represent yet a further variation on the already repetitive curse vocabulary of the verse.

3. הִנְנִי גֹעֵר לָכֶם אֶת־הַזֶּרַע (I am going to diminish your descendants): For the verb of this clause the Septuagint read ἀφορίζω (mark off, set apart, banish) for what appears in the Masoretic Text as גֹעֵר (rebuke). What Hebrew word was before the Septuagint translators? Most likely it was the participle of גרע (trim, diminish, reduce, take away). It is impossible to decide if this is a metathesis of the consonantal Masoretic Text or if the Masoretic Text is a metathesis of גרע. The Septuagint *Vorlage* might also have been the participle of גדע (cut off, break off) since *dalet* and *reš* are confused hundreds of times in the Old Testament text because of their similarity in appearance at virtually all stages of Hebrew writing. In place of the final word of this clause, the bulk of the Septuagint tradition, followed also by the Vulgate, read τὸν ὦμον (shoulder, arm) for what appears in the Masoretic Text as הַזֶּרַע (the offspring, descendants, seed). Here the matter is simply one of vocalization. The Septuagint read the consonantal Masoretic Text but assumed the vocalization הַזְּרֹעַ (arm). Between the Hebrew and the Greek, then, we have several

---

Numbers 6:27, which says "They will put my name on the Israelites and I will bless you"—presumably including both people and priests.

But what exactly was the nature of the "blessing" referred to here? And what would a "curse" on that blessing actually result in? The so-called Aaronic (priestly) blessing of Numbers 6:24–26 promises God's care, favor, presence, and peace. If these elements at least generally reflect what people expected from God when they received a priestly blessing, then the opposite is what they would get if God were to curse the priests' blessing: in other words, God's neglect, disfavor, absence, and various miseries.

Since "blessing" is a general term, however, we cannot ignore the possibility that it also included material benefits. The corporate blessings of the Old Covenant included prosperity (Deut. 28:3–6) and the curses included economic disaster (Deut. 28:16–19). Since the priests and some worshipers were motivated by greed to relax their standards on the quality of sacrifices, it is fitting that they should receive as part of their punishment an economic blow. God would set to naught both their functions and the expected outcomes therefrom.

3. There are two curse types pronounced against the priests in this verse: decimation/infer-

tility of family (type 12a) and dishonor/degradation (type 16). The first curse is given in the words "I am going to cut off your descendants" (RSV/NRSV: "I will rebuke your offspring"). This punishment envisions loss of lineage, the extinction of one's family line. Israelites, like many ancient peoples, were extremely concerned with family line. The many carefully preserved full and partial genealogies of the Old Testament (Gen. 36; Num. 1–2, 7, 26; Ruth 4:13–22; 1 Chron. 1–12; Ezra 2, 8, 10; Neh. 7, 10, 12) and the New Testament (Matt. 1; Luke 3) make this clear. Genealogical concern could grow to such heights that preoccupation with "endless genealogies" might sabotage thoughtful religious discourse (1 Tim. 1:4; cf. Titus 3:9). Boaz's transaction with Naomi's next of kin hinged on the necessity of marrying Ruth to preserve the all-important lineage of a male Israelite (Ruth 4:5, 10). Levirate (brother-in-law) marriage succession laws also provided for the preservation of lineage (Deut. 25:5–10).

Beyond the general societal concern with loss of family lineage, the priests would be especially sensitive to this type of curse. Their office was hereditary. Only by lineage could a person become a priest. Only those born into the tribe of Levi, and only those Levites born into Aaron's branch

options for what the original might have said. They are:

I am going to rebuke your seed [for planting].
I am going to diminish your seed [for planting]
I am going to cut off your seed [for planting].
I am going to rebuke your descendants.
I am going to diminish your descendants.
I am going to cut off your descendants.
I am going to rebuke your arm.
I am going to diminish your arm.
I am going to cut off your arm.

Obviously, some of these are more plausible than others in the context. With regard to those that are most likely, the following observations may be made. If the original were either "I am going to diminish your seed" or "I am going to cut off your seed," the curse would fall within the category of an agricultural disaster curse (type 6c; see Lev. 26:20; Deut. 29:23). Since such a curse would affect everyone, not just the priests, it is not likely to be the intended meaning here. If the original were either "I am going to diminish your descendants" or "I am going to cut off your descendants," it would represent either a decimation/infertility curse (type 12a; see Deut. 28:18, 59; or type 12c; see Deut. 4:27; 28:62) or a closely related type, the loss of family curse (type 18; see Deut. 28:41; 32:25), depending only on the nuance of the verb. If the original were "I am going to rebuke your descendants," then the curse (a remarkably weak one) would presumably be of the dishonor/degradation sort (type 16; see Lev. 26:19; Deut. 28:37). If it were "I am going to cut off your arm" (where "arm" might stand either for strength,

of the Levites, could be priests (Num. 3:5–10). All other priests were false and subject to condemnation (cf. 1 Kings 12:31–13:4). Thus a prediction of extinction of line to the priests meant to them not only a loss of their personal reputations and standing (name), but a loss of the distinct family office of honor as well.

Was this primarily a rhetorical threat, something said to scare the priests into reform, or was it a literal promise from God of the elimination of the priesthood? The answer must be that it was both. It was a rhetorical threat precisely because it was conditional (v. 2: "*If* you don't listen and *if* you are not zealous to honor my name"). Priests who reformed their ways and once again carried out the worship of Yahweh as the Mosaic law specified might be spared. In the short run, virtually immediately after Malachi's ministry, the priesthood was reformed by Ezra (arrived 458 B.C.) and Nehemiah (arrived 444 B.C.), who set the course of worship properly back where it should have been and greatly benefited the struggling remainder state of Judah accordingly. They removed rebellious priests and purified worship in Jerusalem.

It was also primarily a rhetorical threat because of the nature of curses in general. They are—all twenty-seven types—ways of predicting general and unspecified doom. Any single curse implies the possibility of all the others, and all the curses together are merely ways of saying that the judgment of God will be unleashed on the disobedient. This is not to say that curses have no meaning or only vague meaning. It is to say that the biblical evidence shows us that curses functioned mainly in the manner of synecdoches—suggestive partial descriptions of the fuller picture that could not be stated briefly, but that lay behind any of the particular curses. This is the way that they are presented in Leviticus 26 and Deuteronomy 28–32, as collages of specific types presenting in the sum a general picture of the wrath of God. This is the way that the prophets employ them—one type here, another type there, some seemingly "fitting the crime," while other times only generally applicable to the specific sins cited or apparently employed more for variety's sake than for any correspondence to the situation under condemnation. Accordingly, we cannot with confidence assume that Malachi or his hearers would have thought that these inspired words were meant to predict the total, final extermination of the descendants of all Israelite priests in Jerusalem, whether immediately or slowly as time wore on. Everyone hearing this curse would understand that God was going to punish the priests, but the extent and the exact nature would be more in doubt.

But in a broader sense, the priesthood was, in fact, doomed as an institution. What Malachi was inspired to preach against was not an isolated aberration. The human priesthood could never accomplish what the great divine plan of redemption called for (Heb. 8–10). The priests would indeed lose their lineage in terms of its validity as an office when Christ's sacrifice, the only eternally acceptable one, was accomplished. In the overall plan of God there was not to be an eternal human priesthood. The Aaronic office was by design temporary. Basic though it was to the life

power, authority or relate to the motions associated with giving a priestly blessing), it would represent presumably a helplessness curse (type 19; see Deut. 28:32; 32:36). This option would have the logic that cutting off the arm makes a priest physically imperfect and therefore unfit to serve in the temple as well as unable to raise his arms in blessing. There have been scholarly advocates—at great length—for all these options, and choosing among them is not an easy task. It is our best judgment, however, that the overall context of the oracle as well as the immediate context of the verse make the translation "I am going to diminish your offspring" the most likely (see the Exposition). וְנָשָׂא אֶתְכֶם אֵלָיו (lit., and they [one] will carry you to it): Here the Septuagint (followed by the Syriac) reads καὶ λήμψομαι ὑμᾶς εἰς τὸ αὐτό (and I will carry you to it). Following the Septua-

gint for the verb and a commonly suggested emendation without textual evidence of the final word of the clause, אֵלָיו (to it) to מֵעָלַי (from me), the Revised Standard Version/New Revised Standard Version and New International Version have come up with "and I will remove you from my presence," a translation that is cleverly manipulative but of no credibility. The Septuagint probably reflects the more original wording, which was וְנָשָׂאתִיכֶם אֵלָיו (and I will carry you to it). The splitting and reconstrual of וְנָשָׂאתִיכֶם (and I will carry you) into the nearly identical וְנָשָׂא אֶתְכֶם (and they [lit., one] will carry you) was presumably secondary. The difference is not great. The curse is that the priests will be taken where the dung goes, whether or not Yahweh is the one who does the taking personally.

of the people of ancient Israel, it was not to last. Something better would supplant it, the priesthood of all believers, and in that sense Malachi's curse had a long-range, literal perspective.

The second curse, one of dishonor/degradation, is expressed in the words, "I will spread dung on your faces, the dung from your festivals." The term translated here as dung is *pereš*, which refers to inedible animal innards, especially the contents of the stomachs of ruminants, and intestines and their fecal contents, which were removed from the sacrificial animals prior to roasting on the altar. Some commentators are convinced that the meaning of *pereš* is limited to fecal matter, and it is quite possible that such is the meaning here, perhaps even in the manner of a euphemism (compare English "waste"). In the present context, the *pereš* thus was either the totality of or the worst of the waste innards that were specially taken outside the camp (far from the temple) and burned as entirely unclean.

Therein lies the special humiliation at having it thrown on the priests' faces. In contrast to the positive images of *pānîm* (face) in both Numbers 6:23–27 and generally in Malachi 1:6–2:9, especially in the divine lifting of the face, signifying acceptance and blessing, here is a picture of priests' faces splattered with animal dung—and it is God who has thrown it there! How could the picture of divine rejection and cursing be any clearer? But further, the special requirement of priestly ritual cleanliness lies behind the appropriateness of this image. Priests had to be cleaner than anyone else. Their cleanliness symbolized their holiness before a holy God. Dung was about

as unholy as a substance could be, and thus their humiliation and disgrace were complete.

Why add the explanatory statement "the dung of your festivals"? Is this merely a scribal gloss that should be excised as valueless? Hardly. The reasons for its presence in all probability is that it suggested a higher volume. A festival (*ḥag*) was a time of much greater sacrifice activity than occurred at the lesser daily, Sabbath, or new moon celebrations. The word *ḥag* (festival) is the term most often used in the Old Testament to refer to the three great annual worship feasts of Passover, Pentecost, and Tabernacles, where the crowds were by far the largest, the numbers of animals by far the greatest, and the excrement by far the most voluminous. Huge amounts of dung were what the priests could expect on their collective faces! It is not a pretty image, but it is the point of the added phrase, "the dung of your festivals."

As for the final clause, "and I will carry you to it," this represents a continuation of the dishonor/degradation curse (type 16) since it suggests that God will not allow the priests to become ritually clean again, but will forcibly put them outside the camp/temple in the unclean area where the dung is dumped. "I'll confine you to the dump" would be a periphrastic way of indicating the intended meaning. In verse 9, the statement "I make you despised and humiliated before all the nations," clearly the language of dishonor and degradation, confirms in its overall summation of the passage's curses what the end of verse 3 suggests in more narrow focus.

4. Why has God spoken so critically and threateningly to the priests? Because their disobedience

4. The converted perfect וִידַעְתֶּם can mean any of the following: "then you will know," "you should/must know," "know this," "so that you may know," and the like. The simplest way to take the form is in consecution with what precedes, so that verse 4a reads, "Then you will know that I have sent you this commandment,"

thus nicely completing the thought introduced in 2:1 ("This commandment is for you, priests"). The Septuagint and other versions confirm the Masoretic Text of the entire verse. The only difficulty is the meaning of לִהְיוֹת (usually "to be") at the outset of verse 4b. Many scholars have asked how the single commandment that is referred to

---

threatens the continuation of something very important that he is concerned to preserve: the levitical covenant. This covenant will be described again in verses 5–7 and the failure of the priests to keep it will again be recited in verse 8. Here it is only introduced as a topic. Thus verse 4 is a transitional statement. It concludes discussion of the "commandment" first mentioned in verse 1 (i.e., the curse on the priests) and brings up the issue of the covenant with Levi, heretofore not explicitly under consideration. It is important to note that in verses 4–7 the priests are personified in the singular ("Levi," "he," "him," etc.), a means of emphasizing their corporate identity and responsibility—as well as guilt—under the covenant that they have with God (v. 5).

What would the priests have understood by the term "my covenant with Levi" ("the covenant of Levi" in v. 8)? On the one hand, it is likely that they would have understood it to mean the whole arrangement that made them priests in Israel—the entire body of Mosaic law that defined Israel's religion, its national offices including the priesthood, its worship regulations, and its specifications of priestly duties (including such special tasks as employing the Urim and Thummim and superintending the cities of refuge, for example). This full sense of the term is surely that employed by Nehemiah, who followed Malachi by perhaps two decades, when he refers to "the covenant of the priesthood and of the Levites" (Neh. 13:29). The priests would be aware that certain passages in the law, such as the story of the setting aside of the Levites in Exodus 32:26–29 or Moses' blessing on the Levites in Deuteronomy 33:8–11, were principial in establishing the tribe of Levi as the designated priestly tribe by divine decree. But if they sought a single *locus classicus*, a passage of institution par excellence, they would probably have thought in terms of the famous "covenant of peace" made with Aaron's son Phinehas (Num. 25:11–13):

Phinehas, son of Eleazar, son of Aaron, the priest, has turned my anger away from the Israelites, for he was as zealous as I am for

my honor among them, so that in my zeal I did not put an end to them. Therefore tell him I am making my covenant of peace with him. He and his descendants will have a covenant of a lasting priesthood, because he was zealous for the honor of his God, and made atonement for the Israelites.

This brief passage from Numbers, with a bare preamble and prologue and simple stipulations, does not spell out all the implications of the covenant in full, giving all the stipulations pertaining to priestly duties, but it does summarize the overall essential features. A parallel would be the Davidic covenant in 2 Samuel 7:11–16, which has enormous implications but hardly covers all that needs to be said about the role of the king in Israel. The supportive details are found at various locations in the Mosaic covenant, just as they are in the case of the covenant with the priest in Numbers 25.

Among the prophets, Jeremiah provides the most explicit reference to a "covenant with the Levites" (Jer. 33:20–22) prior to Malachi:

This is what the LORD says: If you can break my covenant with the day and my covenant with the night, so that day and night no longer come at their appointed time, then my covenant with David my servant—and my covenant with the Levites who are priests ministering before me—can be broken and David will no longer have a descendant to reign on his throne. I will make the descendants of David my servant and the Levites who minister before me as countless as the stars of the sky and as measureless as the sand on the seashore.

This language suggests that, like Malachi, Jeremiah is cognizant of the essential provisions of Numbers 25:12–13, namely, peace (care and protection) and life (the ongoing nature of the priesthood). On these two features, see the Exposition of verse 5.

in 2:1 and again in 2:4a could be called "my covenant with Levi." They assume a translation of the Masoretic Text as follows: "Then you will know I sent you this commandment to be my covenant with Levi." The covenant with Levi is clearly much more than a single commandment and is described otherwise in verses 5–7. The threat commandment directed at the priests in verses 1–3 is something different—a commandment, to be sure, but hardly anything that could be identified as the divine covenant with Levi. This translation problem has led to many attempts to emend לִהְיוֹת to such forms as לְחַיּוֹת (to keep alive), or לְחַתֵּת (to shatter [continuing the curse idea]), or even מִהְיוֹת

Note that the present verse (4) explains that the purpose of covenant punishment ("this commandment") is covenant renewal ("so that my covenant with Levi might continue to exist"). The idea is fundamental in the Old Testament. God does not punish because he intrinsically likes to cause misery. He punishes in order to purify. The decimation of the nation and its years of captivity allow a new, purified people to form (Deut. 4:29–31; 30:1–10). The destruction of the wicked leaves those who are righteous and who are motivated to keep the covenant (Deut. 32:36–43; Mal. 3:16–18). More of this will be evident later in Malachi.

5–8. Verse 5 begins with a reference to a historic "covenant" of "life and peace." The actual wording of verses 5–8 in reference to this covenant makes the connection with the Numbers 25 "covenant of peace" hard to miss. Malachi's second disputation carefully reuses some of the themes of Numbers 25:11–13, many with the exact vocabulary, in a manner similar to the way it reuses the Aaronic blessing from Numbers 6.

Here are the correspondences that would have leapt out at Malachi's audience and alerted them to the ironical nature of this disputation.

Num. 25:11–13	Mal. 1:6–2:9
son of Aaron/priest v. 11	priest/priests 1:6; 2:1; 2:7
turn back (hēšîb) v. 11	turn [back] (hēšîb) 2:6
be zealous (qnʾ) v. 11	be zealous (sîm ʾal lēb) 2:2
give (ntn) v. 12	give (ntn) 2:2
covenant vv. 12, 13	covenant 2:4, 5, 8
peace v. 12	peace 2:5, 6
descendants v. 13	descendants 2:3
priesthood v. 13	priest, priests 1:6; 2:1, 7
made atonement v. 13	turned many away from sin 2:6

It must again be noted that Malachi's second disputation is not *merely* a reworking of pentateuchal material related to priests. Just as God's curse of the priests uses *some* of the imagery, themes, and vocabulary of the Aaronic blessing, it also uses *some* of these elements of the priestly covenant of peace. It is not just a mechanistic ironical passage, however. Features of Numbers 6:22–27 and Numbers 25:11–13 are subtly woven into the larger concerns of Malachi 1:6–2:9. But they do not dominate it as if it had no point of its own, nor do they exclude many other influences on the passage from the Pentateuch such as Deuteronomy 33:8–11. There are also important correspondences between the present passage and Deuteronomy 33:8–11, the Levi portion of the famous Blessing of Moses, the third of the three key pentateuchal background texts that help elucidate the meaning of the present text. Malachi's audience would surely have seen in these shared themes and vocabulary a key to the oracle's message: God was reversing the ancient blessing pronounced by Moses on the tribe of Levi, the priestly division of the children of Israel.

Deut. 33:8–11	Mal. 1:6–2:9
Levi v. 8	Levi (vv. 4, 8)
father/child (ʾāb, ben) v. 9	father/son (ʾāb, ben) (1:6)
know (ydʾ) v. 9	know (ydʾ) 2:4; knowledge (ydʾ) 2:7
guard/keep (šmr) v. 9	guard/keep (šmr) 2:9
covenant v. 9	covenant 2:4, 5, 8
guard (nṣr) v. 9	guard (šmr) 2:9
teach (yrh) v. 10	law (tôrâ) 2:6, 7, 8, 9
law (tôrâ) v. 10	law (tôrâ) 2:6, 7, 8, 9
put/place (sîm) v. 10	put/place (sîm) in "be zealous" 2:2
altar (mzbḥ) v. 10	altar (mzbḥ) 1:7, 10
bless (brk) v. 11	your blessings (brk) 2:2
accept v. 11	accept/be pleased 1:9, 13

Even though the number of vocabulary connections is fairly substantial, it is my judgment that the Deuteronomy 33 blessing of Levi is somewhat less directly determinative of the themes and vocabulary of Malachi 1:6–2:9. This is admittedly a subjective judgment, and the reader should be alert to the fact that at any given point in Malachi 1:6–2:9 the proper question is, "Which back-

(from existing [so that my covenant will not exist any longer]). The best solution is simply to recognize that the semantic range of the qal infinitive of היה goes beyond merely "to be" to include such meanings as "to continue/to endure/to remain/to continue to exist" (see Bernhardt, *TDOT*, 3:373; Gen. 17:7; Josh. 7:12; 1 Sam. 19:8; 2 Sam. 7:29; 1 Chron. 17:27; 2 Chron. 6:6; 7:16; Esth. 1:22; Ezek. 17:14; 44:7). Since *lamed* often creates a purpose clause with the infinitive, לִהְיוֹת can then mean in context "in order that [my covenant with Levi] might continue to exist." Revised Standard

Version/New Revised Standard Version "may hold" is intended to reflect this durative sense of the infinitive of היה.

5. הַחַיִּים (life): The masculine plural form used here is the most common way in Hebrew of indicating abstract nouns. Both הַחַיִּים (life) and הַשָּׁלוֹם (peace) from a grammatical standpoint must be predicate nominatives corresponding to בְּרִיתִי (my covenant), indicating that these two concepts constitute key constituents of "the covenant with Levi." A third element, מוֹרָא (fear), also must be a predicate nominative, although it is placed after

---

ground text is relevant here?" rather than, "Which background text is more influential overall?"

5. A full covenant document in the ancient Near Eastern world of the first millennium B.C. had six elements: preamble (identification of parties), prologue (background to the relationship being established), stipulations (terms of the arrangement), list of witnesses (normally divine), sanctions (blessings and curses for obedience or disobedience, respectively), and a document clause (provision for regular reading of the covenant). Large-scale covenant documents like Exodus 20–Leviticus 26 or Deuteronomy (and many parallels outside Israel) have all six elements. Smaller descriptions of covenants usually omit the final three (witnesses, sanctions, document clause), because these play little role in defining the particular covenant, but are somewhat more "all-purpose" elements that do not always vary greatly from covenant to covenant. What defines a particular covenant are the first three elements: the parties (preamble), the reason they have come together (prologue), and the terms (stipulations). Indeed, the essential parts are actually only two, the preamble and the stipulations, and sometimes these two are worked together in the wording, or else the parties are so implicit in the overall context that they are not identified in a consciously separate way. Most covenants preserved from the ancient world are those in which a superior (suzerain) grants a covenant to an inferior (vassal).

Numbers 25:11–13 fits the pattern of such a suzerainty covenant, in which the sovereign (suzerain) agrees to protect the subject (vassal) and the subject agrees to serve the sovereign. It records God's gift of a covenant to those obviously inferior to him, the priests. Both parties have obligations, God's being to grant life and peace and the priests' being to "fear" (obey fully so as to honor). Numbers 25:11–13 is, then, unmistakably a description of a covenant, from which we know

major details: the parties (God and the priests), the reason they are together (the priests—specifically in the person of Eleazar—turned the people from sin), and the terms (life and peace—just as Mal. 2:5 states—given to the priests, and fear, given to God).

Malachi gives the terms of the priestly covenant in shorthand form (2:5), using just two key words, because he is referring to something very well known to his audience. But the meaning of these two words is rich. "Life" (*ḥayyîm*) obviously indicates more than just being alive. The priests were alive when the events described in Numbers 25 took place. It is not as if they were to be willed into existence. What they were granted, of course, is *long* life—the perpetual priesthood of which Numbers 25:13 speaks: "a covenant of a lasting priesthood." They were also granted "peace" (*šālôm*; see Num. 25:12, "Therefore I am making my covenant of peace with him"). This, too, is shorthand for "care and protection," "favor," and the like. No English word does justice to the grand range of meaning that Hebrew *šālôm* conveys. The priesthood was established and protected, provided with perpetual sustenance via the tithes of all the people, given special cities within the various tribal territories, and guaranteed a portion of every sacrifice save for the whole burnt offerings of which no human ate. This is what "peace" means in the present context.

In turn, the priests had a responsibility. The covenant was hardly one-sided (indeed, there is great debate as to whether or not any biblical covenants are actually entirely one-sided). Their task is also summarized in Malachi 2:5 by two key words: "fear" (*yrʾ*) and "terror" (*ḥtt*, niphal). These signify much more than the emotion of being frightened. They are ways of indicating the serious responsibility of the priests to supervise worship, enforce various provisions of the covenant, and keep the nation holy, that is, "make atone-

the verb and its resumptive pronoun ("I gave them to him"). Presumably this placement is intended to indicate by location that it is part of the covenant in a parallel but distinct way—that is, not as the divine sovereign's obligation but as the human vassal's obligation (see the Exposition). מוֹרָא וַיִּירָאֵנִי (fear and he feared me): The lack of an explicit verb is not very disturbing in such carefully styled prose, since "gave" (נתן) in the first half of the verse implicitly governs "fear" as well as "life" and "peace." It might also be possible to translate "reverence and he revered me" or the like since the semantic range of ירא includes "reverence," "be in awe," and so on. But the notion of

severe accountability in this Hebrew word is very strong, and serious fear of the consequences of disobeying God is not well rendered by the weaker "reverence" or "awe" vocabulary used in most of the modern English translations. נְחַת (was terrified of) is the third-person masculine singular niphal perfect of חתת (be shattered, struck down, terrified). "Stood in awe of" (RSV/NRSV/NIV) and similar translations in English are, again, too gentle to convey the sense of real terror at failure to honor God that is implied in the context. Modern English translations are generally too eager to avoid picturing the consequences of angering God as fearsomely as the Bible actually does.

---

ment for the Israelites" (Num. 25:13). To "fear" God is to worship and obey him, to make him primary over other interests so that he is honored above all. Among its most minimal implications was certainly the responsibility of the priests to be utterly careful about how they handled the sacrificial system. The fact, as we have already seen,

that they profaned miserably the sacrificial system (1:6–14) means that they violated the priestly "covenant of peace" and could therefore expect to lose the benefits provided by the sovereign under that covenant—as Malachi 2:3, 9 makes explicit. But what does it mean to be "terrified" of God's "name"?

II. Second Disputation (1:6–2:9)

E. The Priests Will Become Despised because They Have Corrupted Their Office (2:6–9)

STUART

6 True law was in his mouth
and no iniquity was found on his lips.
Perfectly and consistently he served me
and turned many away from sin.
7 For the lips of a priest should preserve
knowledge,
and people should seek the law from his
mouth,
because he is the messenger of the LORD of
the armies.
8 But you have gone the wrong way
and have caused many to stumble in regard to the law.
You have corrupted the covenant with
Levi (said Yahweh of the Armies).
9 So I am making you despised and humiliated before all the nations, as a result
of your not keeping my ways and
showing favoritism in regard to the
law.

NRSV

6True instruction was in his mouth, and
no wrong was found on his lips. He walked
with me in integrity and uprightness, and he
turned many from iniquity. 7For the lips of a
priest should guard knowledge, and people
should seek instruction from his mouth, for
he is the messenger of the LORD of hosts.
8But you have turned aside from the way;
you have caused many to stumble by your
instruction; you have corrupted the covenant of Levi, says the LORD of hosts, 9and so
I make you despised and abased before all
the people, inasmuch as you have not kept
my ways but have shown partiality in your
instruction.

6. This verse is free of grammatical and textual problems. תּוֹרָה (law): The term can refer to the whole Mosaic law (the Sinai covenant plus Numbers and Deuteronomy), any part thereof, or any priestly instruction in conformity with the law. Here it seems to connote what we might render in English as "religious instruction," in line with the priests' duties to keep the nation holy by teaching its people what their full responsibility toward Yahweh was. When the priests failed to do their duty to teach the תּוֹרָה, the prophets had to fill the void (Isa. 9:14 [15]; Zech. 7:12). שָׁלוֹם (peace): Again, we confront a term so rich in semantic value that a single English word does not fully convey its meaning. The idea of completeness and perfection is usually inherent in the term, and this aspect of its semantic range is apparently in view here. Weinfeld (*Deuteronomy and the Deuteronomic School*, p. 76) has drawn attention to the fact that the entire expression בְּשָׁלוֹם וּבְמִישׁוֹר הָלַךְ

אִתִּי (in peace and uprightness he walked with me) has a close parallel in an Akkadian saying about priestly duties in worship: *qirbi ekurrātišu šalmeš littalakma lišallimma parṣīšu* (let him serve perfectly in his sanctuaries and let him perform completely his rights; see *CAD*, vol. 1 [A], p. 325). It is especially noteworthy that *šalmeš littallakma* (lit., let him walk perfectly) is almost a calque of בְּשָׁלוֹם הָלַךְ אִתִּי (lit., he walked with me perfectly). Idiomatically, these expressions for "walk with" are ways of saying "attend" or "serve." As for בְּמִישׁוֹר (consistently), this term literally means "in levelness/in straightness" and can convey, abstractly, the sense of righteousness or fairness. But its most basic sense is that of consistency (evenness) and thus "consistently" seems the best translation for the phrase. On the basis of the Akkadian parallel, Weinfeld translates the verse as follows: "he served me with integrity and equity." His translation is plausible, but fails to

---

6–8. The entire group of three verses is highly parallelistic in the manner of normal Hebrew semantic parallelism, and thus constitutes a three-verse poem (four couplets followed by two triplets, with nine-syllable meter predominating) that combines reference to the past, faithful service of the priests (v. 6), the ideal statement of what a priest ought to do (v. 7), and a description of how far short of this standard the priests of Malachi's day had fallen (v. 8).

6. This verse, the beginning of the three-verse poem of verses 6–8, expands poetically on the historic responsibilities of the priesthood begun in verse 5, mentioning three principal elements that constitute what a priest who truly fears God is supposed to be like: (1) truthful and accurate teaching on the law and rendering of legal decisions ("true law was in his mouth and no iniquity was found on his lips"), (2) full and consistent obedience in various tasks ("perfectly and consistently he served me"), and (3) preservation of the holiness of God's people ("and turned many away from sin").

With regard to the priests' teaching, their pentateuchal job description included the broad, general responsibility to inculcate knowledge of the covenant to the people (compare the use of *daʿat* , knowledge, in v. 7; note the fact that *daʿat*, knowledge, and *tôrâ*, law, are used in parallel in Gen. 2:9, 17 and Hos. 4:6). This is especially evident in the instructions of Deuteronomy 31:9–13, which assigns to the priests (with the support of the Levites and elders) the job of reading the law

periodically before the people and ensuring that knowledge of it is passed down from generation to generation.

With regard to their obedience, some of the material in Exodus 20–23, virtually all of the material from Exodus 24 through the end of Leviticus, and much of Numbers and Deuteronomy, in one way or another, involves the priests, whether as intermediaries in the rituals, as inspectors of animals and people (Lev. 14), or as regulators of tithes, offerings, and redemption payments (Num. 18). They were to practice what was true (ʾĕmet; Exod. 18:21; Ps. 119:142).

With regard to keeping the nation holy, the priests were called upon daily to give many legal decisions (*tôrâ*) to the people about what was holy and what was not (on this sense of the word *tôrâ*, see Lev. 6:2, 7 [9, 14]; 10:10–11; Ezek. 7:26; 44:23). Haggai 2:11–13 gives a parade example of how priests had to rule on the principles of holiness (defilement can be contagious; holiness is not). Because the priests had the Pentateuch to refer to, they should have been able to help shape the behavior of the nation according to divinely revealed standards. Unfortunately, their neglect of the law, which Malachi was inspired to attack, allowed any number of distortions and outright contradictions to what was proper to flourish.

In all these ways, the priests "served" (hālak ʾet) God. The expression recalls the story of Enoch, who "served" (lit., walked with) God, and was honored for it, as well as Noah, who is described also as one who "served" (hālak ʾet)

bring out strongly enough the factor of precision and exactitude that the context demands. Thus I prefer "perfectly and consistently." מֵעָוֹן (from sin): The word עָוֹן is used widely in the Old Testament to refer to any sort of sin, iniquity, unrighteousness, and the like. It refers broadly to that which is wrong and displeases God. The priests were to keep the people holy on all fronts.

7. Both plural imperfect verb forms, יִשְׁמְרוּ (should preserve) and יְבַקְשׁוּ (should seek), are best translated modally rather than by the simple present or future. מַלְאַךְ יְהוָה (messenger of Yahweh): This is a term with major theological overtones. It is routinely translated in many parts of the Old Testament as "the angel of the Lord,"

referring to the supernatural heavenly messenger who speaks the very words of God, so that frequently the narrator of a passage hardly distinguishes between this angel and Yahweh himself (dozens of times, and prominently in postexilic prophecy in Zech. 1:11–12; 3:1, 4–5; 12:8). It also, much less frequently, indicates a prophet (2 Chron. 36:15–16; Isa. 44:26; Hag. 1:13, two of these references being postexilic). Both the angel of the Lord and the true prophet speak only the Lord's words. That is, of course, what the priests should have done.

8. The verse begins with nonconsecutive syntax (ו +nominal אַתֶּם), thus "*But you....*" הִכְשַׁלְתֶּם רַבִּים בַּתּוֹרָה (you have caused many people to

---

God. When Micah summarizes the responsibility of the man or woman of God toward their Lord as "to serve humbly your God," he employs the same Hebrew idiom, halāk 'et. The point is that the priests were servants. They were not authorized to change God's commands or reinterpret them for new times or situations. They were not allowed to be innovators or adapters. What Aaron and his sons had originally done in Moses' day is what the descendants of Aaron were supposed to be doing in Malachi's day.

7. This verse takes the form of a poetic triplet in which the first two lines are related synonymously and the second and third (thus also the first and third) synthetically. This is a common sort of parallelism in triplets, and it effectively emphasizes what a priest ought to do (lines A and B) and why (line C). The theme, and even vocabulary, of verse 7 closely follow on the theme of verse 6a, just as the theme and vocabulary of verse 8 expand on that of verse 6b. "Law" (tôrâ) "mouth" (peh), and "lips" (śĕpātayim) are shared by verse 6a and verse 7. The topic in both is the proper role of the priest as orthodox teacher of proper thinking and behavior.

Glazier-McDonald (*Malachi,* pp. 71–72) has argued that since the term "messenger of Yahweh" (mal'āk yhwh) is used three times in the postexilic era (taking Isa. 44 as postexilic) to refer to a prophet, the fact that Malachi uses it here to describe the role of a priest is evidence that Malachi is advocating a "translation of the role of intermediary *par excellence* from the prophet to the priest," based on "an awareness on his part of the decline of prophetic influence" after the return from exile. This is a rather great leap of logic, since in fact the converse is the case. Malachi's second disputation, in which these words occur, is

a thorough denunciation of the priests, the very opposite of a proposal to transfer to them the prophetic office.

The dominant semantic background for the term *messenger of Yahweh* as it appears here and as Malachi's audience would have understood it, is surely the fifty times in the Old Testament that it indicates the angel of the Lord, God's supernatural spokesman, and, secondarily, the three times that it denotes a prophet, God's human spokesman. By applying the term to priests (here alone in the Old Testament), what this verse is saying about priests is that they, too, were supposed to be spokesmen for God just as angels and prophets were—though they had failed utterly in Malachi's time to honor that role.

Priests should have joined with prophets and angels in faithfulness to the Word of God. This is comparable to the point made in Jeremiah 18:18 (where the triad is priest, wise person, and prophet), Ezekiel 7:26 (where it is priest, prophet, and elder), and Micah 3:11 (where it is leader, priest, and prophet). In all these contexts, priests are listed because of their crucial societal role as religious leaders whose proper influence was essential to a godly course for the nation. They were expected to be honest and true to the law. The fact that they failed to do this most basic, most central obligation was unforgivable.

Many commentators have suggested that this verse represents the highest estimation of the role of the priesthood in the Old Testament. It would be more accurate to say that it affirms the high calling of the priesthood set out in the Pentateuch, from which the priests had fallen far by Malachi's time.

8. Verse 8 represents in part a contrastive expansion on the theme and vocabulary of verse 6,

stumble in regard to the law): כָּשַׁל (stumble) is a common metaphor in the Old Testament for action constituting failure or disobedience—even sin (Isa. 8:14; Ezek. 7:19; see also 1 Cor. 10:32; cf. also "stumbling block" from the same Heb. root,

e.g., Ezek. 44:12). בְּרִית הַלֵּוִי (the covenant with Levi): There is no essential difference between this expression for the levitical covenant, employing the objective genitive via the construct, and the one in verse 4, בְּרִיתִי אֶת־לֵוִי (my covenant

---

somewhat more from verse 6b than verse 6a, just as verse 7 developed some of the concepts mainly of verse 6a. The correspondence may be represented as follows:

2:6b	2:8
"served me" (lit., walked with me)	"gone the wrong way" (lit., left the road)
"turned many from sin"	"caused many to stumble"
"perfectly and consistently served"	"corrupted the covenant"

In addition, we note that verse 8, like verses 6, 7, and 9, also includes reference to the "law," reflecting the overarching theme of lawbreaking in verses 6–9.

The verse makes three main accusations: (1) what the priests are doing constitutes disobedience ("you have gone the wrong way"); (2) they are causing many nonpriests to sin in the process ("you have caused many to stumble in regard to the law"); (3) they have broken the covenant that makes them priests ("you have corrupted the covenant with Levi").

The first of these accusations is the sort of excoriation that characterizes the pericope as a whole. It summarizes the fact that what the priests have done is by God's definition—and it is ipso facto definitive—wrong. They cannot on any grounds justify their behavior. It is not justifiable; it is sin. And, sadly, it is just the opposite of what they could have done. The true priests had set the pattern (v. 6). There was no mystery about what constituted obedience to the divinely revealed law. There is nothing in the sense of "gone the wrong way" (sûr min derek) that would suggest anything accidental about the priests' error. The idiom itself could be used in a neutral context to indicate a mistaken course of action, but in this context it has the clear force of "deviation," "turning away."

The second accusation emphasizes the implications of the priests' disobedience: a large number of people are led to sin as well (as already noted in one sense in 1:14). This is the very opposite of what should have been the priests' function according to Numbers 6:27: "place my name over

the Israelites" (i.e., keep them obedient to God). It is the very opposite, also, of what the true priests had done historically (turned many away from sin, v. 6). Can there be any doubt that such behavior deserves to be punished? Can there be any question that the intermediary role of the priests has been profaned? Their very purpose was to serve in such a relationship to God and his people that they would represent his holiness to them and bring them into his presence for the blessing that it entailed (Num. 6:27, "then I will bless them").

The third accusation states that the covenant has been violated. In the ancient world, a declaration of covenant violation was the precursor to the declaration of punishment (curse). A covenant remained intact until one of the parties corrupted it. The suzerainty covenants, via which vassals agreed to serve great kings (see v. 14), were enforced by the kings, not the vassals. If the vassals failed to live up to the contract, the suzerain declared the covenant violated and unleashed the punishment described in the sanctions. (Verse 9 will deal with that very eventuality.)

Was Malachi conveying God's Word to a few renegade priests? Were some black sheep spoiling it for the others? Was the misbehavior mentioned in these verses an isolated aberration to which a fanatical prophet overreacted? Hardly. It is useful to note the census statistics on priests and Levites that are provided in Ezra concerning those who returned from exile in 538 B.C. (thus perhaps eighty years before Malachi). According to Ezra 2:36–58, there were 4,289 priests, 341 Levites, and 392 temple and palace servants. (The recording of a slightly different number of Levites in Neh. 7:39–60 is a classic instance of the way that numbers, which mean nothing in themselves to a copyist, can get miscopied in the long process of the transmission of the text. The list in Neh. 12:1–26 of those who returned with the first wave back from Babylon gives no numbers, and thus does not indicate the priestly population.) Ezra does not seem to have brought a large number of priests with him (a few dozen?) when he returned shortly after the time of Malachi's prophesying (458 B.C.) judging from Ezra 8:2–3 and his inventory of the priests and Levites he found upon return also does not quantify their population.

with Levi). The difference in wording aside from the pronoun *my* in verse 4 does not change the meaning.

9. וְגַם־אָנִי (so I): The syntax is disjunctive, emphasizing that Yahweh's action is in response and contrast to that of the priests (but you have gone the wrong way [v. 8] . . . so I . . . [v. 9]). נָתַתִּי אֶתְכֶם (I am making you): The verb נתן, usually

translated "give," includes "make" in its range of meaning in English. The Hebrew perfect in a verb like this (one that describes a continuing process) can include past, present, and future in its tense coverage. The action has begun, is continuing, and will have future effect. Thus "am making" (RSV make) is preferable to "have made" (NIV). נִבְזִים (despised): This niphal participle, used adjectivally

---

The point here is that Malachi was criticizing a large and long-established (or reestablished) group, numbering in the thousands, supported by hundreds of Levites and other temple workers, and clearly well-entrenched in terms of their official status. There is no evidence in the descriptions of the priests' involvement in the laying of the foundation of the Second Temple, described in Ezra 6, to suggest that those priests were not properly concerned to obey the law of God, though admittedly this is an argument from silence. On the other hand, it seems clear that by the time of the return to Judah of Ezra (458 B.C.) and Nehemiah (444 B.C.), both zealously orthodox and deeply concerned for the restoration of true worship in Jerusalem, serious problems among the priests were readily discovered. Ezra had to force large numbers of them to conform their behavior to the law with regard to intermarriage outside the people of faith, an egregious crime for a priest (Ezra 10:18–24; see also 9:1; Neh. 13:4–5). It is likely that the severe degeneration in faithfulness to the Mosaic stipulations for priestly service had occurred more between 538 and 460 than between 1440 and 538.

This does not mean that every single priest was in some way apostate by the mid-400s. The picture in Nehemiah of priestly and levitical faithfulness in the rebuilding of the wall (Neh. 3) and the teaching of the law to the people (Neh. 8–9) seems relatively positive (though this, too, is an argument from silence, and the positive statements are in contexts that speak mainly of Levites as opposed to priests). Whatever compliments we can pay the priests on the basis of the evidence in Nehemiah, however, are more than balanced by the fact that Nehemiah had to require a covenant to keep the covenant—involving priests (10:1–8) and Levites (10:9–13) as well as the general population. It was necessary to have a covenant renewal ceremony of the sort Nehemiah describes precisely because those involved had not, on balance, been keeping the covenant as they should have been (Neh. 10:29–40 [28–39]). Indeed, Nehemiah's closing statements in the memoir that bears his name

make it clear that the priesthood was in spiritual decline prior to his reforms:

> Remember them, O my God, because they defiled the priestly office and the covenant of the priesthood and of the Levites. So I purified the priests and the Levites of everything foreign, and assigned the duties, each to his own task. I also made provision for contributions of wood at designated times, and for the firstfruits.

It is fortunate for Israel that the preaching of Malachi was followed by the faithfulness of a priest (Ezra) and governor (Nehemiah) who did everything they could to be sure that faithfulness was generalized among the people. All of the things verse 8 attributes to the priests contrasts to what true priests once did and still should do. The covenant with Levi was instituted in the past, endured by reason of the faithfulness of the priests over time (God's faithfulness, the other ingredient for the endurance of the covenant, is of course assumed without comment), but now in Malachi's day had been corrupted (broken). It was time for divine judgment.

9. The lack of normal poetic parallelism shows that this conclusion to the oracle is prose. There are two close thematic parallels with 2:8:

2:9	2:8
your not keeping my ways (*dĕrākay*)	you have gone the wrong way (*mîn-had-derek*)
your showing favoritism in regard to the law	caused many to stumble in regard to the law

Moreover, the verse contains two obviously intentional ironic contrasts with the Aaronic blessing of Numbers 6:

2:9	Num. 6
I am making you despised and humiliated	I will bless them (v. 27)
showing favoritism (*nś' pānîm*)	raise his face to you (*nś' pānāyw*) (v. 26)

in parallel with שְׁפָלִים (humiliated), can refer to something that is, or even should be, contemptible and to be avoided (Isa. 53: 3). לְכָל־הָעָם (before all the nations): This is a miscopy for the original plural, לְכָל־הָעַמִּים, reflected in the Septuagint and Vulgate as well as many medieval Hebrew manuscripts. בַּתּוֹרָה (in regard to the law): On the grammar, see verse 8. אֵינְכֶם (you're not): This semi-verb form does double duty, governing both of the following participles, just as נָתַתִּי אֶתְכֶם (I am making you) earlier in the verse governs two adjectives. נֹשְׂאִים פָּנִים בַּתּוֹרָה (showing favoritism in regard to the law): Glazier-McDonald argues that since נשׂא + פָּנִים can mean "to regard, consider" as in Prov-

erbs 6:35, the meaning of the last three words in verse 9 is "nor do you have consideration with regard to the instruction" (nor do you consider the law). She concludes that the point of these words is that the priests "resorted not to legal precedent but looked to themselves only" (*Malachi*, p. 73). While it is true that the priests neglected the law (what else is 1:6–2:9 about?), that is not what these three words say. First, although נשׂא + פָּנִים can mean "to regard, consider," it more commonly means "to favor," or in the negative sense "show favoritism." Second, the idiom נשׂא + פָּנִים does not mean "consider" in the sense of "think about" or "take account of" but "consider" in the

---

Note that the latter idiom occurred also in 1:8, in one of its permutations meaning "accept." The presence of certain key wordings woven carefully throughout this prophecy, almost in the manner of paronomasia, is one of its special identifying features in the original.

The topic of the verse, conveyed in part via these artful constructions, is God's punitive judgment against those who have broken his covenant. For God to say that the priests were "not keeping my ways" is to render a blanket condemnation. What broader statement could be made? They were not doing what God wanted done and could no longer be benefited and protected by their levitical covenant.

Judgment brings curse: "I have made you despised and humiliated." The specific Mosaic curse type involved is type 16, dishonor/degradation . The concept of divine judgment/condemnation of priests is hardly unique in prophetic literature (Jer. 20:1–6; Amos 7:10–17). Perhaps especially parallel is Hosea 4:6–9, where God through his prophet condemns the priesthood in the era of Jeroboam II (793–753, three centuries earlier) for their having "rejected knowledge/ignored the law of your God" (compare Mal. 2:5–8) and for the fact that "they feed on the sins of my people and relish their wickedness" (compare Mal. 1:14). Hosea also mentions "prostitution" (his metaphor for covenant infidelity), false divination, and illegal sacrifices (Hos. 4:13; compare Mal. 1:6–2:9 *passim*). The question may then be raised: If Hosea and Amos predicted doom for the priests in the eighth century and Jeremiah in the seventh, how is it that Malachi is doing the same in the fifth? Are these predictions of doom only symbolic or, perhaps, empty threats?

The answer is that they were not empty threats and that each came true fully. The situations and the punishments they produced may be summarized as follows:

Prophet	Date	Location	Result
Amos	ca. 760 B.C.	Israel (north)	fall of north, end of priesthood (2 Kings 17)
Hosea	ca. 760 B.C.	Israel (north)	fall of north, end of priesthood (2 Kings 17)
Jeremiah	ca. 600 B.C.	Judah (south)	fall of Judah, exile of priesthood
Malachi	ca. 460 B.C.	Judah (south)	punitive reform of priesthood by Ezra and Nehemiah

The extent to which Ezra and Nehemiah swept aside the corrupt priesthood that they found upon their arrival in Jerusalem should not be underestimated. Ezra 7–10 and Nehemiah 8–13 describe nothing less than a takeover of the priesthood by the newly arrived priest and governor. They systematically humiliated those priests who had degenerated from orthodoxy, and placed in power those who would handle themselves differently with regard to the law of God. The heterodox indigenous Palestinian priesthood fell to the imposed control of the imported, orthodox version brought back from Babylon. Priests who had never practiced in the temple in their lives gave orders to those who had grown up there. The ones who knew only what Scripture said about worship (a far more valuable knowledge) supplanted the ones who had developed their own convenient ways of worshiping (a truly useless knowledge). This was indeed a humiliating judgment on the priests to whom Malachi preached God's Word, and it occurred in fulfillment of the inspired words of Malachi 1:6–2:9.

sense of "regard highly." Third, that is not the expression at the end of verse 9, as if תּוֹרָה (law) were functioning in the manner of a direct object. The exact expression is נשׂא + פָּנִים + ב (show favor[itism] in regard to), which is not analogous to that of Proverbs 6:35 and cannot be translated as if it were.

III. Third Disputation (2:10–16)
A. Because of the People's Unfaithfulness, the Lord Will Not
Accept Their Sacrifices (2:10–13)

STUART

10 Don't we all have one father?
Didn't one God create us?
Why are we unfaithful to one another,
so as to violate the covenant with our
forefathers?
11Judah has been unfaithful, and abomination has been committed in Israel and in Jerusalem; for Judah has violated Yahweh's sanctuary, which he loves, and has married the daughter of a foreign god. 12May Yahweh cut off the person who does this, every single one, from the tents of Jacob even if he brings an offering to Yahweh of the Armies.

13And this second thing you do: you cover Yahweh's altar with tears, with weeping and groaning, because he no longer regards the offering or takes it with favor from your hand.

NRSV

10Have we not all one father? Has not one God created us? Why then are we faithless to one another, profaning the covenant of our ancestors? 11Judah has been faithless, and abomination has been committed in Israel and in Jerusalem; for Judah has profaned the sanctuary of the LORD, which he loves, and has married the daughter of a foreign god. 12May the LORD cut off from the tents of Jacob anyone who does this—any to witness or answer, or to bring an offering to the LORD of hosts.

13And this you do as well: You cover the LORD's altar with tears, with weeping and groaning because he no longer regards the offering or accepts it with favor at your hand.

10. הֲלוֹא (Don't? Didn't?): As in 1:2, this idiomatic interrogative expression is not a question seeking an answer out of ignorance, but a means of emphasis. Thus the first half of the verse could also be translated "We all surely have one father and one God created us!" Part of the Septuagint tradition has the second-person plural instead of the first-person plural at the end of each line of the first couplet (all of *you* . . . create *you*). This could be simply the result of inner-Greek corruption (ὑμῶν from ἡμῶν and then analogically ὑμᾶς from ἡμᾶς) rather than a reflection of the original Hebrew. However, the Septuagint also reads the second-person plural (ἐγκατελίπετε, have *you* forsaken) for the finite verb in verse 10b, and again ὑμῶν (your [fathers]) at the end of the verse, thus

---

10–16. Malachi's third disputation returns to conveying God's Word to the people of Judah in general (as in 1:2–5). Its topics are three sins: interfaith marriage (vv. 10–12), pagan-style worship (vv. 12–13), and aversion-based divorce (vv. 14–16). The first and last receive the most attention, but each is defined and delimited so as not to be misunderstood. Marriage with people of other nations is attacked not because of ethnic, racial, or national bias, but because (and only to the extent that) it represents the compromising of the true revealed faith by conjoining a pagan and a believer (however nominal) as one flesh. Pagan worship is objectionable to God because it employs manipulative, emotionalistic displays of sorrow instead of being based on a righteous relationship with the true God who is worshiped. Divorce is condemned not because it could never be accomplished under the Old Covenant but because (and only to the extent that) it was based on aversion for a man's legitimate spouse.

Because the second disputation (1:6–2:9) and the third (2:10–16) share both the theme and terminology of covenant as well as several other words and concepts, they were presumably placed one after the other on the basis of the common Old Testament era technique usually referred to as "the catchword principle." By this principle, both small units (e.g., scores of the sayings in Proverbs) and large units (e.g., entire prophetic books) were ordered conveniently and, more important, memorably. A theme or some vocabulary that appears in each of two (or more) literary units was used as the basis for linkage. This does not deny that the six oracles in the Book of Malachi are also organized according to a manifestly chiastic pattern. It merely helps explain why the particular chiastic structure that we observe in Malachi was selected by the prophet or a disciple—at whatever point in time. There are twelve possible permutations of three groups of pairs, and the structure of Malachi represents only one of twelve possible chiastic options for the six pericopes (see the Introduction).

In particular, I note the following "catchwords" that provided more than enough reason for the third disputation to be chosen to follow directly on the second:

Catchword	Second Disputation	Third Disputation
father	1:6	2:10
altar	1:7, 10	2:13
favor, accept	1:8, 10, 13	2:13
covenant	2:4, 5, 8	2:10, 14
offspring	2:3	2:15
guard, preserve	2:7	2:15, 16

The basic structure of this disputation follows the four-part pattern of the others in the book:

2:10–13	assertion by the prophet	Covenant is profaned by being "faithless to one another" (i.e., intermarriage and divorce; v. 10); sanctuary is desecrated by intermarriage (v. 11); pagan manner of worship results in divine rejection (v. 13).
2:14a	questioning by Israel	"Why?"
2:14b	response	Yahweh is the covenant witness (i.e., enforcer).
2:15–16	implication (including the divine decree on aversion divorce; v. 16)	The people must preserve their spirit and not be unfaithful.

Although Malachi again follows his disputational style, he does so with artistry and a considerable degree of freedom of expression. Moreover he does so within a loosely chiastic patterning, which may be represented as follows (modified from Hugenberger, *Marriage as a Covenant*, pp. 99–100):

a he who is one (ʾeḥād) father and one (ʾeḥād) God created (bārāʾ) his people;

systematically rendering the verse in the second-person plural. Since there is no linguistic reason for the Hebrew to become so thoroughly misconstrued, it would appear that the Septuagint translator altered the person of these forms in a pious attempt to exclude Malachi from the indictment of covenant unfaithfulness. In fact, the prophet is simply including himself in the generalization

about the nation's sins rather than addressing his personal guilt, a prophetic style that has a great many parallels (e.g., Isa. 6:5; 42:24; 53:6; 59:12; 64:6 [5]; Jer. 3:25; 8:14; 14:7, 20; Dan. 9:5, 8, 11, 15; etc.). נִבְגַּד (are we unfaithful): The vocalization with *patah* rather than *holem* is idiosyncratic, as if the verb were seen by the Masoretes as a stative, but the meaning is unaffected. The range of mean-

---

general condemnation of unfaithfulness (*bāgad*) (10)

b specific sin condemned: unfaithfulness (*bāgad*) via intermarriage (11)

c curse: being cut off in spite of bringing offerings (*minḥâ*) (12)

c′ curse: rejection of offerings (*minḥâ*) given in emotional worship (13)

b′ specific sin condemned: unfaithfulness (*bāgad*) via divorce (14)

a′ one (*ʾeḥād*) made (*ʿāśâ*) the one (*hāʾeḥād*); general condemnation of unfaithfulness (*bāgad*) (15–16)

It is noteworthy that this passage, unlike the prior two, does not begin with divine speech but with the voice of the prophet. In fact, Yahweh is quoted here only in verse 16, and thus the passage includes only a single messenger formula ("says Yahweh of the Armies"). Too much must not be made of this, however. By this point in the book and by the very nature of his gifts and calling, Malachi is recognizable, to all who understand legitimate prophecy, as a spokesperson for God. The fourth disputation, while containing a greater percentage of direct divine speech, is likewise introduced by the prophet's own speech.

As noted in the Introduction, Malachi's style includes the repetition of key words. In this disputation, the most prominent, *bgd*, "to be unfaithful, betray," appears five times (vv. 10, 11, 14, 15, 16). The word *ʾeḥad*, "one," is found four times (twice each in vv. 10 and 15) and *rûaḥ*, "spirit," appears three times (vv. 15 [twice], 16) as does *ʾēšet*, "wife of" (vv. 14 [twice], 15). Several significant words are employed twice, including *ksh*, "cover" (vv. 13, 16), *bĕrît*, "covenant," (vv. 10, 14), *hillēl*, "defile, pollute" (vv. 10, 11), *minḥâ*, "offering" (vv. 12, 13), and the full expression *nišmartem bĕrûḥăkem weloʾ/ʾal-yîbgod/tigbodû*, "preserve your Spirit and do not be unfaithful" (vv 15, 16). The effect of this sort of repetition is both clarity and emphasis: The hearer/reader gets the point of the disputation easily, and understands

its repetitions as underscoring the severity of what is said.

The disputation begins with two poetic couplets (v. 10) and then changes to prose for the remainder (vv. 11–16). The first and second disputations also began with poetry; the first continuing it throughout, and the second changing to prose for the bulk of the remainder. Since most poetry in the ancient world was musical poetry, it is possible that Malachi sang the beginning of these disputations (perhaps even as a means of attracting an audience, though more probably for the variety that characterizes artistry).

Nothing in the passage helps us fix its date relative to the other disputations. However, much in the passage relates to a key problem encountered by Ezra and Nehemiah upon their respective returns to Judah, namely, intermarriage, and for that reason this section of the book appears to provide further evidence for a date in the mid-fifth century B.C. Because the passage addresses the people in general, we can only speculate that it might have been preached where they most often gathered, in Jerusalem, and perhaps at the temple complex where the largest crowds could be expected at any one time. The mention of the "Lord's altar" in verse 13 does not necessarily locate this oracle at the temple, since it wasn't necessary for people to be at the temple to visualize the altar and understand what Malachi was referring to when he told them that their worship was pagan in its style.

The authenticity of this third disputation has not generally been challenged (it has more often simply been "spiritualized" as if it did not literally concern actual intermarriage and divorce), except with regard to verse 10. Because verse 10 is poetic in style in contrast to the rest of the disputation, and because it refers so strongly to covenantal obligations in a way that scholars of a bygone era or mentality have thought was beyond the purview of Israelite prophets, some commentators have concluded that it is inauthentic, a later addition to Malachi's words (e.g., Elliger, Horst, Nowack, Sellin, Smith). Their skepticism

ing of בגד includes "betray, be disloyal, cheat, renege, double cross, prove untrustworthy," and generally connotes the sense of failure to live up to an agreement or expectation, thus often "act faithlessly." It is used in three broad ways in the Old Testament (all three among its five occurrences in this single passage!): to indicate marital unfaithfulness (Exod. 21:8; Jer. 3:20; Mal. 2:14), covenant unfaithfulness (including covenants explicit or implicit between human beings; e.g., Ps. 73:15; Jer. 12:1), and unfaithfulness to God in any way (including covenantally; e.g., Isa. 24:16; Jer. 3:20–21; 9:1; Hos. 5:7; 6:7). It can function as a synonym for חטא (sin; 1 Sam. 14:33), is used in parallel to the notion of failure to keep God's law (Ps. 78:57), and not uncommonly indicates full-

---

is based on an anti-empirical, idealistic concept of the origins of prophetic literature in Israel, and must be dismissed as unconvincing, to say the least.

This third disputation brings together two sins most prominently: religious intermarriage and aversion divorce. For Ezra, and presumably for Malachi as well, the solution to religious intermarriage was divorce—sending back to their homes those women who had been illegally married in the first place (Ezra 9–10; see the Exposition of v. 11). But this was in no way a typical sort of divorce, and lest anyone think that this very specialized divorce could be used to justify divorce in general, Malachi also attacks the far more common aversion-based divorce as an equally heinous sin. Of course, both sins are related in the sense that they both fall within the general category of violations of the Mosaic covenant's marriage laws.

10. Again Malachi reminds his audience of the special relationship Israel enjoyed with Yahweh. First, he was their father (1:6). If a father commands respect in 1:6, that respect is no less appropriate in 2:10. Moreover, he was their *only* father ("Don't we *all* have one father?"). This rhetorical question anticipates the argument against entanglement with a "foreign god" (v. 11). Malachi's audience needed to be reminded that they were to answer to and be devoted to Yahweh alone. With this principle established, an attack on religious intermarriage would flow logically.

Some commentators have assumed that the "one father" mentioned here is to be identified as Adam, and other have suggested that it is Abraham or even Jacob. Adam is never otherwise called Israel's (or even humanity's) father, and there is simply nothing in the passage to indicate that he is in mind. While Abraham is called Israel's father in a variety of contexts (Josh. 24:3; Isa. 51:2 and widely in the New Testament— Matt. 3:9; Luke 1:73; 3:8; 16:24, 30; John 8:39; Acts 7:2; Rom. 4:12, 16; James 2:21) God is also called Israel's father (Exod. 4:22–23; Deut. 32:6, 18; Isa. 63:16; 64:7 [8]; Jer. 2:27; 3:4, 19; 31:9; and

also widely in the New Testament). It is noteworthy that Isaiah 63:16 contrasts the notion of Abraham's fatherhood of Israel with God's fatherhood (the greater factor) as does John 8:39–42. Decisive for the question in Malachi of who "father" refers to is 1:6—where there is no doubt it is God.

And there is a further value here in the use of the term *father* (ʾāb). In the ancient world, one's marriage was arranged by one's father. Sometimes, both parents could be involved (Judg. 14:2–10) but always the father—only if he were living, of course (Ruth 3:1)—would be the principal negotiator for the marriage of a child in the family. Thus to remind the audience that Yahweh was their father was to remind them, in a marriage context, that *he* was in charge of whom they were to marry. Disobedience to what he had chosen for them would be untenable—and eminently punishable. (See as well the Exposition of vv. 14–15.)

The question "Didn't one God create us?" (bĕrāʾānû) also emphasizes the principle of Yahweh's exclusive ownership of the Israelites. Since bārāʾ (create) is used exclusively in the Old Testament for divine creation of the existing world and its contents (including people), some commentators have suggested that "create us" means "us humans," that is, all people in general, and that this statement is further evidence (along with 1:11) of a supposed universalism in Malachi. However, this conclusion betrays ignorance of the important Old Testament doctrine that God's people (Israel) are a special part of the creation of the world—its final stage or even pinnacle—and thus the verb bārāʾ and other verbs for divine creation are commonly associated with Israel in creation contexts (Deut. 32:6; Pss. 78; 121; 124; 135; 148, Isa. 43:1, 7, 15; 44:2; 63:16; 64:7 [8]; cf. Eph. 2:10). Accordingly, Malachi here addresses the fact that the people of Judah in the mid-fifth century B.C. represent God's special people and on that basis must not do anything that dishonors his special covenantal relationship with them.

In the second half of the verse Malachi makes it abundantly clear that this third disputation concerns a broad-scale covenant violation. The charge

blown violation of the Mosaic covenant (Hos. 6:7). It is important to note from these examples that it does not necessarily refer to a national covenant or law, but can indicate disloyalty to any personal obligation or covenant. חִלֵּל בְּרִית (violate the covenant): The same expression is found in Psalm 89:35 [34] and a similar expression is found in Hosea 6:7, with עבר (transgress) employed instead of חלל. Any damaging, profaning, polluting, desacralizing, or ruining from holiness can be characterized by חלל. בְּרִית אֲבוֹתֵנוּ (the covenant with our forefathers): This wording, parallelling that of Deuteronomy, can only refer to the Sinai covenant, Israel's constitution (Deut. 4:31, בְּרִית אֲבוֹתֶיךָ, "the covenant with your forefathers"; and the long Old Testament tradition of linkage of this vocabulary for "covenant" and "forefathers" to

the Sinai covenant: Deut. 5:3; 7:12; 8:18; 29:24 [25]; 31:16; Judg. 2:20; 1 Kings 8:21; 2 Kings 17:15; Jer. 11:10; 31:32; 34:13). It does not refer to any covenant with a near prior generation, nor the covenant with the patriarchs (as some have tried without success to argue, notably, notably Van Seters, in his *Abraham in History and Tradition*, pp. 265–77). It means *the* covenant with the original wilderness generation (explicit in Jer. 31:32 and 34:12), who accepted, on behalf of all future generations, the Mosaic covenant at Mount Sinai. Malachi knows the Sinai covenant well, and it is that divine contract that he holds before his hearers at this point.

11. The Septuagint translates בָּגְדָה (is unfaithful) somewhat oddly (ἐγκατελείφθη, has been forsaken) but still attests to its reading. יְהוּדָה (Judah)

---

that *"we* are unfaithful to *each other"* and the statement that there had been a desecration of "the covenant with *our* forefathers" leaves no room for doubt that the offense is general (national) and serious (a breaking of the Sinai covenant). The specifics of the crime have not yet been described. They will follow immediately. But the severity of the offense has been announced, and therefore by implication the severity of the breach of relationship with Israel's father and creator. (On the connection of covenant breaking with "faithlessness, betrayal," see Ps. 78:57; Jer. 9:1 [2]; Hos. 6:7.)

But since in the Old Testament the present terminology (*bāgad*) also can, more narrowly, connote unfaithfulness in marriage, that is, faithlessness toward or betrayal of either one's wife (Exod. 21:8) or husband (Jer. 3:20), it is likely that Malachi carefully chose this term as his inspired thinking shaped the wording of verse 10. In other words, while the verse does not explicitly tell us what crime the people have committed against the covenant, it hints via several key terms that it has something to do both with marriage and the way that marriage practices indicated the violation of Israel's general covenant faithfulness to God.

11. This verse communicates the fact that in Malachi's day Judeans were committing a widespread, serious covenant violation that profaned Israel's relationship with her God, namely, religious intermarriage.

That it was general to Judea is indicated by the use of "Judah" in both halves of the verse, once in the masculine and once in the feminine, as well as by the comprehensive phrase "in Israel and in

Jerusalem." Thus the original listener could not have missed the point that this was no isolated or limited practice. That it was a serious covenant violation is indicated by the use of the verb *has been unfaithful (bāgĕdâ)*, by the use of the noun *abomination (tôʿēbâ)*, and by the use of the verb *has violated (ḥillēl)* for a second time in the oracle (see v. 10). Each of these terms comes from the vocabulary associated with the Sinai covenant's emphasis on the necessity of Israel's faithfulness to its sovereign, Yahweh, and its avoidance of the damnable practices of the pagans. That it damaged Israel's favor with Yahweh is conveyed in the reference to harming "Yahweh's sanctuary, which he loves" (*qōdeš yhwh ʾăšer ʾāhēb*). That it was religious intermarriage that was the problem is clearly denoted in the final words, "has married the daughter of a foreign god" (*bāʿal bat-ʾēl nēkār*).

Four questions raised by the verse remain to be answered: (1) Just how widespread was religious intermarriage at this time? (2) How exactly did religious intermarriage break the covenant? (3) What is meant in this context by "Yahweh's sanctuary" (*qōdeš yhwh*)? (4) What motives prompted intermarriage?

The first question is answered mainly from the evidence in the Books of Ezra and Nehemiah, where we note that religious intermarriage was of such concern—because of its blatancy and extent—that it occupied the intention of both leaders upon their return from exile. In fact, once Ezra returned, settled in, and got behind him the immediate task of delivering valuables to the temple (Ezra 7–8) the rest of his account (chaps. 9–10) was entirely devoted to his struggle to rid Judah of intermarriage. The problem was so serious that

is treated as feminine in its first occurrence in the verse (thus the feminine singular verb form בָּגְדָה, is unfaithful) and masculine in its second (thus the masculine singular verb חִלֵּל, violated). Rather than being the result of a copy error, this is in all probability an intentional merism by which the entire population, male and female, is indicted. Indeed, the first half of the verse is essentially "feminine" in gender and the second half predominantly "masculine" with the same effect. The grammar is not at issue, since there are many cases in the Old Testament of nations being construed as either masculine or feminine (e.g., Edom as feminine in 1:4). תּוֹעֵבָה (abomination): This word is used in the Old Testament to indicate something that God will not under any conditions

---

Judean leaders, as a delegation, appealed to him to make dealing with it his first priority:

> The leaders came to me and said, "The people of Israel, including the priests and the Levites, have not kept themselves separate from the neighboring peoples with their abominations [tô⁽ăbōthêhem]. ... They have taken some of their daughters as wives for themselves and their sons, and have mingled the holy race with the people around them. And the leaders and officials have led the way in this unfaithfulness." (Ezra 9:1–2)

The picture is disturbing. All strata of society were involved, the sin had official support via the widespread involvement of the tiny nation's officials (and thus no enforcement of laws against it), and the clergy was just as guilty as the laity (thus not teaching that the practice was wrong). The rest of chapters 9–10 describes Ezra's elaborate task of leading the nation in repentance, formal covenant renewal, and then, finally, enforcement of the covenant via the stringent practice of forcing those who had taken nonbelieving wives to divorce them. The very fact that the Book of Ezra ends with a list of people guilty of intermarriage is a profound reflection of the degree to which the issue was central for the mid-fifth-century B.C. Judean community.

Nehemiah had to address the problem as well. Ezra's reforms, extensive as they were, had not entirely eradicated the practice, which presumably increased again after his retirement and probably especially while Nehemiah was back in Babylon (Neh. 13:6, 432 B.C. until ?). Nehemiah's first return (444 B.C.) followed Ezra's (458 B.C.) by only fourteen years, and the two were thus contemporaries toward the end of Ezra's life, but by the time of Nehemiah's second return (sometime in the 420s?) at least thirty years had gone by and intermarriage was on the increase once again. The extent was not minimal, according to Nehemiah 13:23:

> Moreover in those days I saw men of Judah who had married women from Ashdod, Ammon and Moab. Half of their children spoke the language of Ashdod of the language of one of the other peoples and did not know how to speak the language of Judah.

Nehemiah 13:15–17 describes Nehemiah's strict approach to eradicating the problem, incorporating physical punishment and public shame by forcible balding, indicating that he regarded the problem to be a serious threat to Judean morality. His citation of the great Solomonic sin of idolatry (13:26) and his description of the intermarriage as "this great evil" (hārā⁽âh haggĕdôlâ hazzo⁾t) and unfaithfulness (m⁽l) in 13:27 reinforce this interpretation. If my view that Malachi slightly predates Ezra's return is correct, what Ezra and Nehemiah had to deal with is clear evidence that intermarriage was truly widespread in Malachi's time.

It is important not to confuse religious intermarriage and ethnic intermarriage. Ruth, Rahab, Abigail, Moses' Cushite wife, and undoubtedly many other non-Israelite women were welcomed into the people of God because they accepted the true faith of Israel. It was, however, normally the fact that any woman from another culture brought with her pagan beliefs and practices, which she continued when she married into Israel (1 Kings 11:1–8; 16:31; Neh. 13:26). Since every other ethnic group in the ancient world practiced what the Old Testament calls the "abominations" connected with idolatry, polytheism, pantheism, and the like, it was virtually automatic that an Israelite man who married a foreign woman was compromising his obedience to the Sinai covenant. Indeed, it was the both the first and second commandments that stood to be violated—the first by reason of introduction of foreign gods into Israel and the second by reason of the introduction of idolatry, always and everywhere the mode of religious practice among non-Israelites.

As for the second question, did the covenant clearly—not merely by implication—forbid (reli-

tolerate, an "automatic" covenant violation that earns its practitioners serious guilt. The pagan ways of Israel's neighbors were the prime source of these abominations, against which they were warned firmly prior to their entrance into the promised land (Deut. 18:10–13). Among such were idolatry, child sacrifice, various magical rites with sexual overtones (boiling a kid in its mother's milk; sowing a field with two kinds of seed so as to "mate" them), violations of basic family decency (e.g., temple prostitution, incest), and other degenerations that the Israelites were tempted to borrow from their neighbors against God's will. The Old Testament employs the term in such a way as to indicate that commission of such abominations will virtually automatically defile the people (Exod. 34:15–16; Num. 25:1–5; Deut. 7:1–2) or the temple (Lev. 20:2–3; Ezek. 8:10–16)—or as here, both. חִלֵּל קֹדֶשׁ יְהוָה (violated Yahweh's sanctuary): Though קֹדֶשׁ by itself can

certainly refer to the tabernacle or temple, as dozens of occurrences of the term in the Old Testament confirm (e.g., Exod. 28:43; 29:30; Pss. 20:2 [3]; 150:1; Ezek. 42:14; 44:19) that is not its meaning here. The full expression חִלֵּל קֹדֶשׁ יְהוָה is found in only one other place, Leviticus 19:8, where it surely refers to ruining God's people (see the Exposition). בַּת־אֵל נֵכָר (daughter of a foreign god): The full expression occurs only here in the Old Testament, but the poetic expression אֵל נֵכָר (foreign god—אֵל is an older, even archaic, word for "god," employed usually in poetic contexts) is attested in Deuteronomy 32:12 and Psalm 81:10 [9] and its more common parallel אֱלֹהֵי נֵכָר (foreign god—a form that is neither automatically prose nor poetry) is more widely attested still. The Septuagint seems bothered by this expression בַּת־אֵל נֵכָר (daughter of a foreign god) and apparently resorts to translating contextually (ἐπετήδευσεν εἰς θεοὺς ἀλλοτρίους, has gone after foreign gods), fol-

gious) intermarriage, the answer is yes, and explicitly so. Citing most often the Canaanites as a synecdoche for foreign idolatrous nations, the law forbids intermarriage with foreigners in a variety of contexts (Exod. 34:16; Lev. 21:14; Num. 36:6; Deut. 7:3; 13:6–9; see also Gen. 24:37–40; 27:46; 28: 1, 6). If there had been more willingness to take the law seriously in Malachi's day, the practice of religious intermarriage would have been curtailed. But, as we have already seen in the case of the second disputation, the Mosaic covenant was by Malachi's time understood as a quaint, archaic document too restrictive to be taken seriously and inapplicable to a "modern" age—virtually the same way that most people in modern Western societies view the Bible today.

The third question raised above (What is meant by "Yahweh's sanctuary"?) may be answered as follows. In the present context, it denotes the nation of Israel as a whole (God's holy people is his sanctuary), in contrast to its far more usual meaning of the temple or the holy city of Jerusalem. The doctrine that the land of Israel and its people constitute Yahweh's sanctuary, while only rarely represented, is nonetheless well fixed in the Old Testament, and it is this less common sense that stands behind the wording of the present verse. The exact expression "violate Yahweh's sanctuary" (ḥillēl . . . qōdeš yhwh) means "to profane/violate God's people" in the one other place in the Old Testament where it occurs, Leviticus 19:8 (and thus that verse calls for death or banishment as a punishment for such a violator, since he

is a polluter of the people if he remains among them). On the idea that Israel and its promised land can in their entirety constitute Yahweh's sanctuary, see Exodus 15:17 and Isaiah 63:18. On the parallel language in Malachi 2:10–11 involving breaking the covenant and profaning the sanctuary, see Zephaniah 3:4.

The parenthetical statement "which he loves" (ʾăšer ʾāhēb), echoes the assurance of the Lord's choice of Israel as his chosen people in 1:2, and is further evidence that the sanctuary in question is the nation, not the temple.

As to the final question raised by the verse, there were probably two main motives for intermarriage: money and sex. Regardless of whether any particular Judean's intermarriage involved a first marriage, or the taking of a second, additional wife, or the divorcing of a first wife and remarriage to a foreigner (included in vv. 14–16), money and sex drove the process.

Money was probably the main motive. It came from the establishment of marriage ties with landed non-Israelites, who would favor their in-laws in business dealings in general and the granting of jobs in particular. During the last two-thirds of the sixth century B.C., Judah had suffered far more than her neighbors at the hands of the Babylonians, because Judah had led regional opposition to Babylonian imperialism and because Jerusalem had held out so long against the Babylonian siege of 588–586 B.C. Not only did Judah suffer the ravages of conquest and exile, but the Jews who returned from exile beginning in 538 B.C. (Ezra 1–

lowed by the Syriac, perhaps because the verb בָּעַל (has married) was garbled in its *Vorlage* as בָּא עַל (went at, or the like). It is also theoretically possible that the common Hellenistic era practice of mixed marriages by Jews occasioned a purposeful dampening of the meaning of the text at this point. Even more likely is that the Septuagint took the expression as a few modern commentators have (Isaksson, Kraetszchmar, O'Brien, Torrey) to refer to goddess worship (e.g., Hvidberg, *Weeping and Laughter*, p. 121: "A 'daughter of a god' is a goddess"). This is not a tenable interpretation of the Hebrew, however. Like its masculine parallel בֵּן (son, son of), בַּת (daughter, daughter of) can mean "one who identifies with, participates in, represents" (see Gen. 6:2, 4; 27:46; 1 Sam. 1:16; Isa. 1:8; 22:4). Additionally, the full term נֵכֶר בַּתאֵל would represent unnatural Hebrew for "goddess" (as Hugenberger, *Marriage as a Covenant*, pp. 34–

36, has shown). At any rate, the Masoretic Text is surely sound.

12. יַכְרֵת ... מֵאָהֳלֵי (may [Yahweh] cut off ... from the tents of): Similar expressions occur in Job 18:14 and Psalm 52:7 [5] (using "tent") and the specific punishment of being "cut off" (כרת) from the community is widely attested (Lev. 17:10; 20:3–6; Amos 1:5–8; Nah. 2:14 [13]; Zeph. 1:3; etc.). On אֹהָלִים (tents) as an Old Testament metonymy for "the nation, the place where the people live," see, for example, Numbers 24:5; Deuteronomy 5:27 [30]; 2 Samuel 20:1; Psalm 78:55; Jeremiah 30:18; Hosea 4:20; Zechariah 12:7. יַעֲקֹב (Jacob): The name is commonly used throughout the Old Testament, including the prophets, as a parallel or alternative for יִשְׂרָאֵל (Israel). Its presence here echoes 1:2. It does not particularly connote "the worshiping or cultic community" as opposed to the nation in general

---

3) returned to an impoverished land, a thoroughly destroyed capital (Lam. 1–5), hostility from neighbor states (Ezra 4–5; Neh. 4, 6), exploitation by unscrupulous Judeans who had not been taken into exile (Neh. 5), and an economy that was considerably under the control of foreigners (Neh. 13:6–22). Who had the wealth? Who would it be prudent to ally oneself with via marriage if one wanted to get ahead? To the west were the Philistines, and to the east were the Ammonites and Moabites (Neh. 13:23). Other nationalities were surely involved, but these were the prominent ones.

Sex was probably less often the dominant motive than money, but must also have played a role, especially in those cases where a man had become tired of his first wife (vv. 14–16). Pagan practices allowed for women to be treated as sex objects in contrast to what biblical law enjoined (Num. 25; Hos. 4:6–14; Amos 2:7–8; etc.), and many Israelite men must have found it easier to marry outside their people and faith, into pagan families who would not insist on monitoring their daughter's welfare in the home of her husband as Israelite families would. Pagan families would also tolerate marriages after divorce—marriages based on physical attraction rather than on arrangement while one was still in childhood—more easily than their Israelite counterparts.

12. The penalty for violating the holy people ("Yahweh's sanctuary," v. 11) is the same as it is in Leviticus 19:8—the sinner must be cut off from his people. Some sins are so heinous that they require elimination of the sinner from the com-

munity of faith. A considerable number of pentateuchal laws specify being "cut off" (*kārat*, hiphil) as the requisite punishment if they are violated. Scholars have long debated whether "cut off" means death or banishment. In fact, it probably means either, depending on the particulars of the offense and the best judgment of the judges who tried the case. It is a penalty somewhat less explicit than the death penalty (normally expressed by the Hebrew *môt yāmût*, "he must die") but nevertheless clear in its implication that the one punished cannot remain within the confines of Israel.

However, when the Pentateuch describes a sin's penalty using the hiphil of *kārat* as Malachi uses it here, it speaks of Yahweh as the one who will do the cutting off (Lev. 17:10; 20:3, 5, 6). Malachi is thus employing an imprecation, a prayer wish that the covenant violators be exterminated by divine action from Israel. This fits squarely within curse type 24, the curse of death and destruction (Deut. 4:26, "you will quickly perish from the land . . . will certainly be destroyed;" see also Deut. 28:20–22, 44, 48, 51, 61, etc.).

In the final clause of the verse Malachi introduces a subtheme, that of pagan-style worship. It is important to understand that most ancient peoples thought that sacrifices were guaranteed to work. Central to the idea of idolatry—practiced by all ancient peoples, including the heterodox among the Israelites—was the notion that an idol captured the presence of a god or goddess and thus guaranteed that a worshiper would have his or her altar gift noticed and credited by the god being

(contra some commentators). לְאִישׁ (the person): This is the direct object of the verb יַכְרֵת (cut off) and not an indirect object or prepositional phrase. The *lamed* is here used as commonly in Aramaic but only rarely in Hebrew to introduce the direct object (GKC §177n; see e.g., Num. 10:25; 2 Sam. 3:30; 1 Chron. 29:22; Ezra 8:16; Ps. 69:6; Isa. 11:9; Jer. 40:2). עֵר וְעֹנֶה (every single one, lit., witness and testifier, perhaps idiomatically the equivalent of "one who says this and one who says that"): As the Septuagint (ἕως, = Heb. עַד) and at least one medieval Hebrew manuscript as well as 4Q12a attest, the *reš* is a copy error for *dalet*, *reš-dalet* confusion being the most common copying error involving letters. Thus עֵר must be corrected to עֵד (witness). ענה is another standard term for witness (see its use in the ninth commandment, Exod. 20:16). But what exactly does this pair of words, found only here in the Old Testament, mean? It is almost surely an idiomatic expression for totality ("every single one") via the citation of two instances in a category. Hebrew has many similar expressions, virtually identical in format, including שֹׁרֶשׁ וְעָנָף (root and branch, Mal. 3:19 [4:1], etc.), עָצוּר וְעָזוּב (slave and free, 1 Kings 14:10, etc.), רֹאשׁ וְזָנָב (head and tail, Isa. 9:13 [14]), מוֹצָאֲךָ וּמֹבָאֶךָ (your

coming and your going, 2 Sam. 3:25, etc.), and the famous טוֹב וָרָע (good and evil, Gen. 3:5, etc.). Glazier-McDonald's elaborate case (*Malachi*, pp. 94–99) for retaining the Masoretic Text and understanding it to refer to sexual practices connected with the Canaanite fertility cult ("the aroused one and the lover") is interesting mainly for the inventive way it stretches Hebrew root meanings. Why did Malachi choose this particular term for "every single one" from among the many available to him? Surely because its covenantal-legal overtones were so appropriate for an oracle that emphasizes the responsibilities of covenant (see also the Exposition of v. 14). וּמַגִּישׁ (even if he brings): This translation, taking the final clause as dependent and adverbial, is the most contextually sensible of the various possibilities.

13. שֵׁנִית (another thing, lit., a second [thing]): The Septuagint missed this perfectly normal adjective/adverb/noun (it is used all three ways) found often in the prophets to introduce further revelation (Isa. 11:1; Jer. 1:13; Ezek. 4:6; Jon. 3:1; Hag. 2:20; Zech. 4:12; etc.) and guessed that the word was a first-person common singular perfect from שׂנא (hate), supplied a relative pronoun for sense, and translated ἃ ἐμίσουν (which I

worshiped. Moreover, idolatry involved a quid pro quo sort of theology. It was believed that the gods, no matter how powerful, lacked one important skill. They could not feed themselves. That is where the humans "had" the gods. If humans fed them, the gods were *obliged* to benefit them. In this view, sacrifice was seen as purchasing favor. This is, of course, diametrically different from the New Testament metaphorical statement that Christ's sacrifice "purchased" the church (Acts 20:28; cf. 1 Cor. 6:20; 7:23).

It was widely believed that a god could not turn away a worshiper, no matter how personally evil or even criminal that worshiper was, since a god would thus be starving himself or herself. Regardless of personal morality, if you sacrificed to a god, that god owed you something and had to accept you. This was not the revealed biblical view, however. Biblically, sacrifice is an obligation of gratitude to God, not a means of controlling God's behavior (Amos 5:21–27; Mic. 6:6–8; Mal. 2:13). Thus Malachi concludes verse 12 with the words "even if he brings offerings to Yahweh of the Armies"—not because such offerings would change the outcome of God's curse, but to remind his audience that Yahweh did not relate to offerings as the false gods were presumed to do. This

is, in other words, the language of rejection of the cult (curse type 2). The attack on pagan worship styles is continued immediately in verse 13.

13. This verse makes two points: (1) the Israelites are practicing pagan-style worship, and (2) God rejects it (curse type 2, rejection of the cult; cf. Lev. 26:31, "I will take no delight in the aroma of your sacrifices"). Pagans assumed that the gods could be influenced by loud displays of emotion, intended to demonstrate the earnestness of the worshiper's appeal. Since the laity could not actually approach the altar (see the Exposition of vv. 1–14) it was presumably the priests, acting on their behalf, who did the actual weeping at the altar itself, caricatured by Malachi as "flooding Yahweh's altar with tears, with weeping and groaning." The fact that he uses two different words for crying and one for groaning, in a spaced, repetitive fashion, leaves no doubt that he wanted his audience to focus on the nature of the action itself. His use of the term *groaning* (ʾănāqâ) demonstrates that temple worship in the 460s B.C. went far beyond a simple (and acceptable) attitude of contrition. It was pagan worship, emphasizing manipulative mourning and misery (Hos. 7:14).

hate). כַּסּוֹת (covering/you cover): This piel infinitive, probably used in place of a finite verb (see the Exegesis of 2:16) takes one object (Yahweh's altar) and three adverbial accusatives (with tears, with weeping, and with groaning) in a complex but regular grammatical construction. מֵאֵין עוֹד (without there being any longer; most translations: "because he no longer . . ." or the like): Contrary to the normal meaning of מֵאֵין (without, from מִן + אֵין) Glazier-McDonald trans-lates as if the second half of the verse were an independent sentence of prediction ("There will no longer be a turning to the offering, nor a taking"). She rightly recognizes, however, that מֵאֵין is not a verbal reference to Yahweh's action but more neutrally to the lack of effect of the pagan worship style, and that it governs both infinitives that follow it (פְּנוֹת, "to turn," and לָקַחַת, "to take."). רָצוֹן is employed adverbially: "with favor."

In worship among pagans, self-inflicted pain was sometimes added as a means of showing that one was truly sincere and not frivolous. First Kings 18:26–30 provides an example of altar worship by Baal-Asherah prophets:

> they called on the name of Baal from morning until noon crying "Baal, answer us!" . . . They limped around the altar . . . they cried aloud and as was their custom they cut themselves with swords and lances until the blood gushed out over them. . . . As midday passed they raved on until the time of the evening sacrifice. . . .

Ezekiel also scorns the emotionalistic excess of pagan worship, which, like that Malachi described, took place at the Jerusalem temple:

> Then he brought me to the entrance to the north gate of the house of the LORD, and I saw women sitting there, weeping for Tammuz [Babylonian dying and rising fertility god]. He said to me, "Do you see this, son of man? You will see things that are even more detestable than this." (Ezek. 8:15)

Isaiah describes the pagan style of Moabite worship-mourning:

> Dibon goes up to its temple, to its high places to weep . . . they all wail, prostrate with weeping. (Isa. 15:2–3)

It is not weeping per se that is wrong. Mourning for sin was desirable (Num. 25:6; Ezra 3:13; 10:1). But weeping/tears/groaning as a style of worship was improper in its motive, an attempt to move the gods to compassion. To the extent that such emotionalism has continued or resurfaced in modern-day Christian worship, that worship also smacks of a pagan misunderstanding of what the true God desires (Neh. 8:9; Eph. 5:19–20; Col. 3:16–17).

And, of course, it doesn't work. It is rejected by the true God. That is the import of Malachi 2:13b. Why should God honor pagan, manipulative worship? He will not "regard" (pānâ ʾel) or "accept with favor" (lāqaḥ rāṣôn) the people's gifts (minḥâ). The pagan gods were thought to accept offerings as long as they were accompanied by fervor, even if given by evil people. Personal morality was irrelevant in pagan worship.

But not Yahweh. There was nothing the Israelites could do by way of intensity of worship that would cover over the fact that they were violating the ancient divine covenant against religious intermarriage, and thus the first commandment. They could not get Yahweh's blessing through worship while yet sinning. As Jesus taught,

> So if you are offering your gift at the altar, if you remember that your brother or sister has something against you, leave your gift there in front of the altar and go. First be reconciled to your brother or sister, and then come and offer your gift. (Matt. 5:23–24)

III. Third Disputation (2:10–16)
B. The Lord Will Not Accept Their Offerings because He Must Enforce the Covenant (2:14)

STUART

¹⁴You say, "Why?"

Because the LORD is witness to the covenant between you and your childhood wife, to whom you have been unfaithful, though she is your companion and your covenant wife.

NRSV

¹⁴You ask, "Why does he not?" Because the LORD was a witness between you and the wife of your youth, to whom you have been faithless, though she is your companion and your wife by covenant.

14. עַל־מֶה (Why?) is a common expression in Old Testament Hebrew, and the alliteratively corresponding conjunction עַל כִּי (because) occurs five times in the Old Testament, with no doubt as to meaning. הֵעִיד (is a witness) is a term with major covenantal overtones (see the Exposition). אֵשֶׁת נְעוּרֶיךָ (your childhood wife, often rendered, "the wife of your youth"): The construct pattern is standard in this expression, as in Isaiah 54:6, Proverbs 2:15, and Malachi 2:15. Since "childhood" is abstract, the masculine plural form of

the noun, which is the common form for abstracts in Hebrew, is used. וְהִיא (though she is): The syntax is disjunctive, and "though" or "in spite of the fact that" is the appropriate translation for וְ here. בֵּינְךָ וּבֵין (between you and . . .): This covenant terminology identifies the primary two parties to the covenant (see Gen. 31:37; 32:16; etc.). אֵשֶׁת בְּרִיתֶךָ (your covenant wife) is a hapaxlegomenon as a term, but analogical in form to אֵשֶׁת נְעוּרֶיךָ (your childhood wife). See the Exposition.

---

14. Here begins the attack on aversion divorce. In this third disputation the assertion (the first of the four disputation elements) is quite long (vv. 10–13) and the objection (just "why?") is quite short. The response ("Because Yahweh . . .") occupies the rest of the verse. The final part, the implication, comprises verses 15 and 16.

Note the second-person masculine singulars in the response portion of the verse (e.g., between *you* and *your* childhood wife, etc.). This reminds one of pentateuchal legal style, where the second-person masculine singular is the appropriate vehicle for commandments, since it is individual action that is normally in focus. Pentateuchal laws, of course, apply to women as well as men, the masculine gender being nothing more than the accepted citation form. But here the fact that men are divorcing their wives, and almost certainly not the other way around, makes the masculine singular citation form doubly appropriate. Malachi is reminding his audience of a legal obligation, not merely a moral opportunity.

Though Malachi has not yet mentioned the term *covenant (bĕrît)* in connection with what he is going to say in this part of the dispute (assuming that the mention of covenant in v. 10 applies to the issue of intermarriage), his audience would know instantly that something covenantal was now to be discussed because *hēʿîd* (to be a witness) is a strictly covenantal term in Old Testament Hebrew. Indeed, the fuller expression, "to be a witness between *x* and *y*" (here in v. 14, "between you and your childhood wife") is a description of a standard aspect of covenant making and enforcing. Covenants always had witnesses. Pagan covenants named various gods and goddesses as witnesses. Orthodox Israelite covenants, whether between individuals (Gen. 21; 26; 31), nations (1 Kings 5; 15), kings and their subjects (2 Sam. 5; 2 Kings 11), or husband and wife (Prov. 2:17; Ezek. 16), had God as their witness, either implicitly or explicitly. Compare Genesis

31:44–54, where God is the "witness" (v. 50) and a stone-heap is also called symbolically a "witness" in the sense of a reminder thereof.

But what did a witness do? He or she surely did much more than watch the covenant being made. Rather, the job of the witness was actually that of enforcer or guarantor. Thus a covenant witness is not the same as a court witness, who simply gives testimony in a trial. A covenant witness was the third party who could and did make sure that the direct parties to the covenant kept its terms. There may have been many human covenants in the ancient world that were enforced by kings and other powerful figures or groups functioning as third-party witness-enforcers, but these are not extant. What we have from extrabiblical materials that have survived and from the Bible itself is a group of covenants that assign the role of witness-enforcer to a divine figure. Some biblical covenants add the mention of "heaven and earth" as witness-enforcers, not in contrast to but in addition to God's role, since the divine control of nature was a vehicle for the punishment of covenant breakers (Deut. 4:26; 30:19; 31:28; and note the many natural disasters that function as covenant punishments or blessings in Deut. 28–33).

Does this mean that a marriage was viewed in Old Testament times as a legal contract? Undoubtedly. Hugenberger has systematically and convincingly demonstrated that "covenant" (*bĕrît*) here in Malachi 2:14 refers to marriage (*Marriage as a Covenant*, pp. 27–45), that polygyny was tolerated in the Old Testament and therefore there was no covenantal excuse for divorcing one's first wife on the basis of aversion (pp. 84–120), that marriage covenants were almost surely solemnized by formal vows (pp. 234–93), and that marriage is considered covenantal in other contexts outside Malachi (e.g., Hos. 2:18–22 [16–20]; Prov. 2:17; Ezek. 16:8, 59–60, 62; 1 Sam. 18–20; etc.; pp. 296–355). De Vaux had earlier argued that the practice of providing written bills of divorce in ancient Israel (Deut. 24:1–3; Isa. 50:1; Jer. 3:8) implies that there must have also been written contracts of marriage (*Ancient Israel*, p. 33). In other words, cohabitation without contractual vows was not marriage, and neither premarital nor extramarital sex could be condoned as "biblical."

"Your childhood wife" (*ʾēšet něʿûrêykā*, often rendered "the wife of your youth") reminds us that marriages in Bible times (and still in many parts of the world) were arranged. Sometimes before children were born, almost always before they reached puberty, very rarely when they were grown (Judg. 14:1–10), their parents would make a contract with the parents of an appropriate mate in anticipation of the time that the two would be married ("given in marriage"—language carefully chosen). Prior to the marriage they were betrothed, a legal status. Upon marriage, contracted probably in writing, solemnized by vows, witnessed by ceremony and celebration, and enforced as a covenant by God himself, they certainly were legally obligated to one another. Since nearly all marriages were arranged during the childhood of both parties, the term "wife of your childhood," here translated more naturally "your childhood wife," made sense. Men could marry other wives later, but these could never be called "your childhood wife." They could be called *pîlegeš* (concubine, non-inheriting wife) as in Judges 19:1, or "other wife" as in Genesis 4:19; Deuteronomy 21:15; 1 Samuel 1:2. Marrying a second or subsequent wife (polygamy was never outlawed in Scripture) was never an excuse for divorcing a first one.

One's childhood spouse, even though chosen for him or her, was nevertheless supposed to be the special spouse, even in a multiple-spouse marriage. Language about "wives of childhood" reflects this (e.g., Joel 1:8). The expectation of romantic love in marriage is a modern, Western notion. It is not prohibited by the Bible, but neither is it encouraged. Romance had to be the main reason behind the intermarriages Malachi described in 2:10, and aversion—lack of romance and more—was certainly the reason for the divorces he now condemns. A man's first wife, the one his parents arranged for him in his childhood, was his wife for life under God's law. Though the children of an additional marriage could share in his inheritance (Ruth 4:6), they could not displace the children of the first. Though a second wife could be loved, she must not be treated to the disadvantage of the first (1 Sam. 1:2, 6–8).

The marriage covenant, properly understood, was nothing more than a subcovenant within the broad scope of the pentateuchal covenant. To violate it was to violate one of the many stipulations that make up the entire covenant (Exod. 19–Deut. 33) and thus to incur any of the curses that Yahweh, the witness-enforcer of that covenant, too, would choose to unleash (see the Introduction). To break the marriage covenant was to be "unfaithful" (*bgd*) to one's "companion" (*ḥăbērâ*).

The importance of this latter term must not be understated. A *ḥābēr* (masc.) or *ḥăbērâ* (fem.) was a companion in the sense of a friend or partner. Malachi is using the language of equality here, as the Bible so often does with marriage even though it was written in a culture that decidedly regarded women as inferior to men. Indeed, though some covenants were given by a superior to an inferior (Mal 2:4), the marriage covenant, as one negotiated by parents of equal stature from the point of view of the assumptions behind covenants, was surely a covenant of equals (often called "parity covenant"). Malachi uses "your companion" and "your covenant wife" appositionally, as essentially synonymous terms. His audience was being challenged, indeed warned, indeed threatened, to realize that they hadn't the slightest right to divorce their covenant partner. In the marriage covenant they were only equals, not superiors. Under this covenant that a faithful God would enforce, their aversion-divorce decrees were pure "unfaithfulness." This divorce that they were practicing was just as much "unfaithfulness" as if they were committing adultery.

And did not Jesus say just this about aversion divorce? His words are entirely consistent with the view of marriage enunciated in Malachi's third disputation: "Whoever divorces his wife, except for unchastity, and marries another commits adultery" (Matt. 19:9).

III. Third Disputation (2:10–16)

C. The People Must Preserve Their Spirit and Not Be
Unfaithful (2:15–16)

STUART

¹⁵Was it not one he made, with a remnant of spirit? And what is the one seeking? Godly seed. So watch out for your lives and do not be unfaithful to your childhood wife. ¹⁶If one hates and divorces (Yahweh, Israel's God, said), he covers his clothes with crime (Yahweh of the Armies said). So watch out for your lives and do not be unfaithful.

NRSV

¹⁵Did not one God make her? Both flesh and spirit are his. And what does the one God desire? Godly offspring. So look to yourselves, and do not let anyone be faithless to the wife of his youth. ¹⁶For I hate divorce, says the LORD, the God of Israel, and covering one's garment with violence, says the LORD of hosts. So take heed to yourselves and do not be faithless.

15. The Hebrew of verse 15 is extremely terse and often odd. It reads—at best—like some of the more laconic proverbs, or even a cryptic puzzle. It is linguistically elliptical, that is, it contains fewer words than are necessary to perceive its meaning upon first reading; and it is logically asyndetic, that is, it doesn't contain the sorts of conjunctions and modifiers that would tell the reader unambiguously how its component parts relate to one another. Torrey called the text of Malachi 2:15 and 16 "hopelessly corrupt" ("Prophecy of 'Malachi,'" pp. 16–20). Hvidberg said it was "completely unintelligible" (*Weeping and Laughter*, p. 123). Though it surely made sense in its original form, it does not clearly make sense in the form in which it has been transmitted to us. We must therefore admit that our understanding of the various statements in the verse has no confidence attached to it (except for the final clause; see below) . The text is highly questionable at several points. At the beginning of the verse, following Targum Jonathan, the Syriac, and the Vulgate, many commentators change וְלֹא (and no/and not) to the interrogative הֲלֹא (did [he/one] not?). The Septuagint reads ἄλλος or ἄλλο (other/another) or some (presumably inner-Greek) corruption of it (such as καλὸν, "good," or καλῶς, "well") in both places where אֶחָד (one) occurs in the Masoretic Text. This almost surely came from a Septuagint *Vorlage* containing אַחֵר (other) for the Masoretic Text's אֶחָד (one), reflecting the common *reš-dalet* confusion. There is no automatic way to tell which is the more original. Most Septuagint manuscripts add εἴπατε (you said) without any representation thereof in the Masoretic Text, so that the middle of the verse reads, "And you said, 'What other than seed is God seeking?'" This, if not merely a rendering out of desperation on the part of the Septuagint translator, would imply haplography in the Masoretic Text of an original וַהֲאֹמְרוּ (and you said). Finally, the last word in the verse is reflected in most of the ancient versions and several medieval Hebrew manuscripts as the second-person singular form of the verb, אַל־תִּבְגֹּד (do not be unfaithful), rather than the Masoretic Text's third-person masculine singular אַל־יִבְגֹּד (let him not be unfaithful). In this latter instance, there can be little doubt that the Masoretic Text is less than original. The text issues are minor, however, in comparison to the grammatical-semantic issues. Considering only the outset of the verse, the following questions are among

---

15. Because of the difficulty of the Hebrew wording of this verse, particularly the first half, it has been interpreted in a great many ways. Indeed, van der Woude wrote: "Mal. 2:15 is one of the most difficult passages of the whole Old Testament. It would be a hopeless task to record all the attempts that have been made to explain this verse" ("Malachi's Struggle"). Some scholars have even suggested that Hebrew scribes altered the text, and in the process obscured it, in reaction to its perceived teaching (e.g., Baldwin, Tosato).

What are we to do? Most commentators sort through the options, pick one, and then attempt to justify it. This is meritorious in its motive, but ultimately fruitless. My approach is somewhat different. I would advise the reader that since nobody really understands what point verse 15a is making, the worst thing that could be done would be to assume that it *can* be understood.

The difficulty of trying to understand verse 15 may be expressed in one paragraph by listing some of the major possibilities for interpretation. It may say something about God's being one, thus echoing verse 10, but it may also be using the term *one* in purposeful contrast with God. It may implicitly say something about the way Adam and Eve were created (made, '*āśâ*) as one (flesh?), thus echoing the parity language of the prior verse in reference to a man and his wife, but it may simply be saying something about what "one" (or "another" if we follow the LXX) did (*'āśâ*), thus echoing the "every single one" language of verse 12. It may also be saying that nobody (*lō'-'eḥād*) did something. It may be asking one or more questions or it may be making one or more declarations. It may say something about a "remnant of the spirit" (*še'ār rûaḥ*), but that need not be taken to refer in some way to the Holy Spirit. Conversely, many commentators have concluded that *še'ār* (remnant) is probably a slight corruption of *še'ēr* (flesh) so that the verse is actually saying something about humanity being created "flesh and spirit," the focus being the bipartite completeness of humans. It may be talking about God's desire for continuation of the "godly seed" (*zera' 'ĕlōhîm*)—whatever that is—via proper, lifelong marriage, or it may be saying that Israelites who divorced and remarried were (vainly) seeking "godly offspring." Wendland's observation ("Linear and Concentric Patterns," p. 117) that there is a concentric pattern to the divine names in the passage [v. 10, God/ v. 11, Yahweh/ v. 12, Yahweh/ v. 13, Yahweh/ v. 14, Yahweh/ v. 15, God / v. 16 (combining) Yahweh God] at least suggests that the expression "godly

those that have been raised: Is אֶחָד (one), or its alternative, אַחֵר (other), the subject of עָשָׂה (made) or its object? Does רוּחַ (spirit) belong as the fifth word in the Hebrew of the verse, or should it be emended (e.g., to "her" as RSV/NRSV)? Does אֶחָד (one) refer to Abraham in either or both places it occurs in the Masoretic Text? Is אֶחָד (one) adjectival rather than substantival? And so on. Hugenberger (*Marriage as a Covenant*, pp. 125–72) offers a complete coverage of the salient options, far too extensive to replicate or even summarize here. Our best judgment is that the Masoretic Text is probably to be followed (why not? the other ancient versions aren't any clearer) except for the need to read the second-person masculine singular in the last word, and that there are two major options in attempting to translate the verse: (1) "And not one has done it who has a remnant of the spirit. And what was the one seeking? Godly offspring? So preserve your spirit, and do not be unfaithful to your childhood wife." (2) "Did he not make [humanity] one, with a remnant of the spirit belonging to it? And what was the one seeking? A godly seed. So watch out for your lives and do not be unfaithful to your childhood wife." The first of these options is fairly similar to the translation proposed by Glazier-McDonald (*Malachi*, p. 82) and the second is fairly similar to that proposed by Hugenberger (*Marriage as a Covenant*, pp. 172, 186). Note that only the last clause ("do not be unfaithful to your childhood wife") is largely certain. All that comes before it in the verse is to one degree or another in dispute, and ultimately suspect because it simply does not read like normal Hebrew, and combines terms and concepts that are not otherwise found together in Scripture. In other words, it is not at all clear what point(s) three-fourths of verse 15 is making.

16. כִּי (for): Most manuscripts of the Septuagint, Targum, and Vulgate take this as the condi-

---

offspring" is not secondary, but that does not mean that we know how to understand it. The passage may be urging the preservation of the spirit or Spirit (lit., "and guard yourselves in your spirit," *wĕnišmartem bĕrûḥăkem*) among the Israelites, or it may be warning "watch out for your lives!" Fortunately, this latter imperative seems to me to be at least roughly understandable. The way that it is stated in this verse and repeated in the next would suggest that it is some kind of idiomatic call to action. It has also been interpreted as a challenge to avoid diminishing part of one's essential being (the spiritual part) or the remnant of the Holy Spirit that still indwells one. Both of these latter options for understanding *wĕnišmartem bĕrûḥăkem*, though advocated by some commentators, fail on the ground that they are not compatible with what the Old Testament elsewhere says about anthropology and the presence of the God's Spirit. It would be difficult indeed to prove that Malachi or any other part of Scripture advocates the possibility of losing one's spirit while remaining alive physically, or that each Israelite had a bit of the Holy Spirit in him or her that might be lost via sin. Those individuals who had the Spirit could lose the Spirit (1 Sam. 16:14; Hag. 2:5)—while most never had it in the first place (Num. 11:29)—but Israelites did not all have a bit of it (a' la the old "divine spark" concept).

Happily, there is one thing we know that the verse *does* say, and that comes at the very end: "Don't be unfaithful to your childhood wife," that is, you have no right to divorce on the basis of aversion. Whatever the meaning of the words that precede this command, the desired outcome is clear. It is highly likely that verse 15a originally stated something or some things that would serve as a logical reason for this command to faithfulness. It may well have been something about the way God had intended men and women to be related in marriage, based on the way he had made them in the first place. It may have included something about how that was not being done by the Judeans of Malachi's day. Whatever it was, the action it was intended to undergird was the discontinuation of aversion divorce. We know, then, with regard to the content of this verse, what Malachi was inspired to demand of his people, even if we don't understand what argumentation he gave them in support thereof.

16. Hugenberger (*Marriage as a Covenant*, p. 51) notes that there are "nine major interpretive approaches to Malachi 2:16 which, for convenience, may be divided into four categories." Those four categories may be summarized as follows: (1) Malachi 2:16 says nothing about divorce, but rather concerns pagan worship. (2) Malachi 2:16 requires, or at least permits, divorce. (3) Malachi 2:16 prohibits all divorce, of whatever kind. (4) Malachi 2:16 prohibits aversion-based divorce but is not concerned with divorce for other reasons.

In favor of the first option would be the assumption that "wife of your youth" and other terms in the passage that seem to speak of mar-

tional, "If" ("If a man hates . . ." or "If you hate . . ."), thus "If you hate her . . . divorce her." Some witnesses, however (LXX ℵ, A, B, Q, V) keep the conditional force but interpret very differently: ἐάν μισήσας . . . καὶ καλύψει (If you hate and divorce, then . . .). For the entire verse the Old Greek probably had the equivalent of "If you hate and divorce, says the Lord the God of Israel, then ungodliness [ἀσέβεια] will cover your thoughts [ἐνθυμήματά σου], says the Lord Almighty. So watch your spirit and do not be unfaithful." The Greek tradition is undoubtedly interpretive, as almost any English translation is forced to be in light of the ambiguities of the Hebrew, but at the same time it witnesses sufficiently to the consonantal text, which may then be regarded as original. שָׂנֵא שַׁלַּח: Does this combination mean "he hates divorce," as it is pointed, or is Yahweh the speaker ("I hate divorce") as some modern translations have construed it, both of these options interpreting שׂנא as a participial verb form? Could haplography have eliminated an original yod preformative on שׂנא, the original having been "Indeed he should hate . . ." ? Could שָׂנֵא שַׁלַּח be a compound meaning, in effect, "aversion divorce," since these two Hebrew roots are used with just the same meanings (aversion, divorce) in Deuteronomy 24:3? One can follow the arguments for all these options via Hugenberger (*Marriage as a Covenant*, pp. 52–83). Fortunately a convincing solution, one that follows the Masoretic Text, is at

---

riage are used metaphorically to speak of idolatry. There can be no doubt that the prophets—Hosea and Ezekiel notably—sometimes liken apostasy from Yahwism to marital infidelity, but this option requires redefining language that straightforwardly speaks of husbands and wives in the present passage.

The second option is less likely grammatically, requiring a translation for the first three words ("If he hates, let him divorce!" or "If you hate, divorce!") that is both syntactically awkward in the overall context and inconsistent with the predominant message of the passage.

The third option runs counter to what is taught in Deuteronomy 24:1–4 and Ezra 9, and grammatically requires the assumption that Yahweh is the unannounced subject of the second word, "hate" (*śānē'*), inconsistent with the third-person forms in the latter part of the verse.

The fourth option is grammatically tenable and contextually reasonable. It relies on the soundness of the translation "If he hates and divorces . . ." or its alternative, "If (it is) hateful divorce . . . ," neither of which requires emendation of the consonantal Masoretic Text and both of which allow for consistency with Deuteronomy 24 and Ezra 9. For those who think of the prophets as unrelated to the law, this consistency would be of limited interest. For those who recognize the overt dependency of the prophets on the Pentateuch and of Malachi specifically on Deuteronomy, it is entirely reasonable to expect that Malachi would be careful in the process of condemning what his contemporaries were doing—divorcing their first wives to marry pagans—not to state that all divorce was illegal. He might do this in the most semantically economical way (by the use of a single adjective ["hating"] to pin down the type of divorce under attack), but he would certainly want to do it.

Ezra required the divorce of illegal wives, married in violation of the covenant laws and seen as a serious threat to Judah's religious fidelity (see the Exposition of v. 11). Malachi also condemned such marriages and could hardly have failed to cheer Ezra's strong response to them were he still alive to witness it. Deuteronomy 24:1–4 provides a different focus, however. There the topic is the process of divorce and its legitimacy under the old covenant in certain cases:

> If a man marries a woman who becomes displeasing to him because he finds something indecent about her, and he writes her a certificate of divorce, gives it to her and divorces her from his family, and if after she leaves his family she becomes the wife of another man, and her second husband dislikes her and writes her a certificate of divorce, gives it to her and divorces her from his family, or if he dies, then her first husband, who divorced her, is not allowed to marry her again.

We note, with regard to Malachi 2:16, that this law does not permit divorce based on lack of affection. It does cede to the husband the judicial power to find his wife "indecent" (*'erwat dābār*, Deut. 24:1), a personal, subjective power that Jesus takes away in the New Covenant (Matt. 5:31–32). But under the law of Moses a man could not divorce his wife merely because he tired of her or no longer felt that he loved her. Moreover, he had to divorce her legally, with an official docu-

hand. It requires recognizing, as van Hoonacker, Glazier-McDonald, and Hugenberger have all argued convincingly, that the bulk of 2:16 is a conditional sentence with a typical "if . . . then" structure. Its first three words, כִּי שָׂנֵא שַׁלַּח, begin the protasis of the conditional sentence, and must be construed in accordance with the teaching on divorce of Deuteronomy 24:3, which they surely reflect (see the Exposition). The apodosis of the sentence is the four words וְכִסָּה חָמָס עַל־לְבוּשׁוֹ (then he covers his clothes with crime). This grammatical structure has ample parallels elsewhere. With regard to opening a conditional sentence with a participle, see Genesis 9:6; Exodus 21:12; and Psalm 75:4 (GKC §116u). With regard to commencing the apodosis of such a sentence with a finite verb, with or without ן (and), see Isaiah 14:7; 43:7; Ezekiel 22:3; Psalm 136:13–14 (GKC §116x). Smith, followed by van Hoonacker and others, including Glazier-McDonald, points שׁלח as the third-person masculine singular piel perfect, שִׁלַּח (send away, divorce; see Gen. 21:14; Deut. 22:19, 29; 24:1, 3; Jer. 3:1; Isa. 50:1; Ezra 10:44). This is not unreasonable, given the likelihood that the Masoretes would have found the verse difficult. Hugenberger retains the

---

ment, because he had married her legally and officially in the first place (see the Exposition of v. 14). We do not know if the divorce certificate (sēper kĕrîtût, Deut. 24:1) had to specify the nature of the charge of indecency or not. We can be fairly sure that most Israelites probably paid little attention to the niceties of Deuteronomy 24:1–4, just as they neglected major stipulations of the covenant for most of their history as a people (Neh. 8:17). But Malachi, an inspired prophet, was another matter. Through him came the revelation of God in consistency with all prior divine revelation, some of which regulated—but did not license—divorce. Moses and Malachi come at the issue of divorce from different angles. Moses allows it under certain conditions. Malachi condemns it except under certain conditions. But inasmuch as those conditions appear to be identical, employing even the same essential vocabulary in definition of the actions involved, their respective doctrines are compatible.

The topic is a controversial one, and we are not surprised to find Malachi employing two messenger formulas ("Yahweh, God of Israel said" and "Yahweh of the Armies said") in the same verse to bolster the authority of his condemnation of aversion divorce. This pronouncement must surely have infuriated large numbers of Judeans, in light of the long history of the practice of divorce in Israel and the frequency of the practice of second marriages (after divorce) in Judah as evidenced in the Books of Ezra and Nehemiah. And the fact that Ezra and Nehemiah had to act forcibly in this regard makes it obvious that Malachi's oracle had not convinced most people to repent. People like to be in charge of their own lives. Israelite men may not have had a role in arranging their first ("childhood") marriages, but as adults they had the power to take matters into their own hands to end those marriages via divorce and then marry other women to whom they were attracted. This was not a freedom they were likely to give up voluntarily, and Malachi's words could not have fallen pleasingly on their ears.

Aversion divorce is here called, metaphorically, "covering one's clothes with crime." What is the point? Practically every statement in the Old Testament and ancient Near Eastern literature having to do with "robes," "garments," and the like, has been scoured by commentators for an answer to that question. Some have suggested, based on tenuous Arabic parallels, that one's wife can be described as one's "garment." There is nothing of this in the Old Testament, however. Others have assumed that the idiomatic expression "to cover with one's robe" (as in Ruth 3:9; Ezek. 16:8), referring to marriage, is somehow behind the wording here, even though the wording here has nothing to do with covering someone with clothes, but is about having one's clothes themselves covered with something else. In all likelihood Glazier-McDonald has captured something of the sense of this otherwise unattested expression: "Expressed colloquially, the one who divorces his wife airs his dirty linen in full public view" (Malachi, p. 112). The term ḥāmās (crime, perhaps even serious crime) is so strong that I would go further. The point is more like the expression, "You've got blood on your hands." "Crime on your clothes" is the equivalent—connoting obvious and inescapable guilt because of the commission of a major sin.

Again the imperative appears: "Guard yourselves in your spirit." Again, we can only guess that it means at least "Watch out!" if not "Watch out for your lives!"

Finally, what constitutes the ethical teaching of this verse? Does it really prohibit God's people from "no-fault" divorces, based on "irreconcilable differences," as Jesus' teaching in Matthew 5 and

Masoretic Text pointing and takes שָׁלַח as the piel infinitive absolute functioning as a finite verb, a grammatical possibility also well attested (Waltke and O'Connor §35.5.2; Moran, "Canaanite Infinitive Absolute"). Note that already in this passage Malachi used a piel infinitive construct as a finite verb in 2:13 (כַּסּוֹת, you cover). חָמָס (crime): The word is usually mistranslated "violence," a definition that does not do justice to its actual range of meaning.

---

19 also does as the very least? The answer must be that it does. Because the prohibition is stated principially as a matter of divine law, because of its position in the prophetic books rather than in the temporal law of Moses (cf. Gal.), and because of its reinforcement in the teaching of Christ, it cannot be dismissed as no longer binding on New Covenant believers. Aversion divorce is unfaithfulness. "Don't be unfaithful!" warn the final words of the disputation.

IV. Fourth Disputation (2:17–3:5)
A. The People Doubt the Lord's Justice (2:17)

STUART

[17]You have wearied the LORD with your words.

"How have we wearied him?" you ask.

By saying, "All the evildoers please Yahweh and he likes them," or "Where is the God of justice?"

NRSV

[17]You have wearied the LORD with your words. Yet you say, "How have we wearied him?" By saying, "All who do evil are good in the sight of the LORD, and he delights in them." Or by asking, "Where is the God of justice?"

17. The verse is linguistically and textually clear. הוֹגַעְנוּ (lit., How have we wearied?): The suggestion by some commentators that this should be emended to הוֹגַעְנֻהוּ (how have we wearied him?) fails to recognize that parts of the Septuagint tradition, as well as the Syriac, Targum, and Vulgate, felt obliged to supply a pronominal object in order to translate idiomatically, just as the English versions do. That the main Septuagint tradition, translating literalistically, did not supply a pronominal object is proof enough that none was present originally. In Hebrew idiom the object (him) is implicit since Yahweh has already been mentioned.

2:17–3:5. Malachi's fourth disputation introduces a new topic: the coming of the divine messenger to cleanse God's people and restore true worship and obedience to the ethical standards of the law. If Yahweh's name was to be great among the nations (1:11), it had to be represented among them by a people and priesthood that was pure and obedient to his covenant.

The reader is introduced here for the first time in Malachi to three themes, all of which may be expressed, for convenience, as needs: the need for messianic intervention, the need for a day of judgment, and the need for social justice. Malachi also addresses here two themes that are not new: the need for reform of the priesthood, and within that broad theme, the more specific need for restoration of acceptable worship practices.

There is a substantial repetition of key vocabulary in this disputation: *yāgaʿ* (vex, 2:17), *ʾāmar* (word, say, 2:17), *mišpāṭ* (justice, 2:17; 3:5), *malʾāk* (messenger, 3:1), *hinnēh* (behold, 3:1), *yôm* (day, 3:2, 4), *mĕṣārēp* (refiner, 3:2, 3), *ṭāhēr* (cleanse, 3:3), *kesep* (silver, 3:3), *minḥâ* (offering, 3:3, 4) and *śākār* (wage/wage-earner, 3:5) are all employed twice. *bwʾ* (come, 3:1–2), certainly the key action word of the passage, appears three times. However, no repetition of compounds (two or more words) appears, and the repetition is therefore somewhat less noticeable to the hearer or reader than in the two prior disputations. Indeed, many commentators have also failed to notice it (e.g., Glazier-McDonald, *Malachi*, p. 124: "Significantly, there is little vocabulary repetition in the fourth oracle unit") even though it is actually as frequent relative to the size of the passage as anywhere else in the book.

Verse 17 is programmatic for the entire disputation. Its "response section" accuses the nation of two things under which can be grouped the several sins mentioned above: practicing evil as if it were acceptable, and practicing injustice as if God would never intervene in their affairs. This charge is made via the skillful use, also in verse 1, of two sayings placed on the lips of the people in Malachi's time that reveal popular attitudes as well as practices.

The basic structure of this disputation follows the four-part pattern of the others in the book—assertion, questioning, response, and implication. It may be outlined as follows:

2:17a	assertion by the prophet	"You have wearied the LORD with your words."
2:17b	questioning by Israel	"How have we wearied him?"
2:17c	response	Israel shows itself wearisome to God by two of its popular sayings: (1) "All who do evil are good in the sight of the LORD, and he delights in them" and (2) "Where is the God of justice?"
3:1–5	implication	The messenger will come, Yahweh will judge, worship and justice will be restored.

Wendland (117) sees in this disputation a simple, four-part concentric structure, which he describes via following outline:

a warning—the day of judgment is coming: "judgment" plus "come" plus "says Yahweh of Hosts" (2:17–3:2a)
b means—purification of the people (3:2b–3a)
b′ result—pleasing offerings (3:3b–4)
a′ warning—the day of judgment is coming: "judgment" plus "come" plus "says Yahweh of Hosts" (3:5)

This particular pattern is not a chiasm, since only the first and last elements are clearly parallel, but an *inclusio* or "sandwiching" pattern, in which the final statement complements, or, as here, echoes the initial statement. Wendland's observation is particularly helpful in settling the debate as to whether the present disputation ends at 3:5 or 3:6. The way that 3:5 echoes 2:17 leaves little doubt that the majority of scholars are right in seeing 3:5 as bringing to a conclusion the fourth disputation and 3:6 as the opening the fifth.

Perhaps most intriguing of all the issues raised by the fourth disputation is its implicit identification of the "messenger of the covenant" as Yahweh himself. No other passage in the Old Testament so clearly assigns divine prerogatives and nomenclature to the figure of the Messiah (though the term *māšîaḥ* is not itself employed by Malachi). When one examines how this disputation describes the identity and actions of the "messenger of the covenant," one can only conclude that he is divine. In the overall context of Scripture, this provides an important part of the portrait of Christ. Who else is both the sender and the sent? The messenger described in 3:1 and following is sent by Yahweh yet also does the kinds of things that only Yahweh has the power to do (3:2–5). The present disputation thus presages an aspect of trinitarian Christology: Christ is sent on his mission by God and yet is also himself God in the flesh.

In the chiastic arrangement of the book (see the Introduction) the fourth and third disputations are loosely linked by their thematic content. This linkage may be illustrated by the following table, which emphasizes vocabulary connections:

Catchword	Third Disputation	Fourth Disputation
divorce/sending (*šlḥ*)	2:16 (piel)	3:1 (qal)
seeking (*bqš*)	2:15	3:1
covenant	2:10, 14	3:1
offering (*minḥâ*)	2:12–13	3:3–4
Israel, Jerusalem, Judah	2:11	3:4
Yahweh a witness (*ʿēd*)	2:14	3:5

It should be noted that the fourth disputation also has affinities with the second, with which it shares particular interest in the corruption of the priesthood and the need for a restoration of righteousness. And it shares with all the other pericopes in the book a concern for obedience to the divinely revealed covenant, Malachi's central governing concern (see the Introduction).

The date and provenance of this fourth disputation cannot be discerned with any more certainty than is the case with the other parts of Malachi's prophecy. The lawlessness alluded to in 2:17, the corruption of the priesthood in 3:3, the inadequacy of worship in 3:4, and the corruption of personal and civil morality in 3:5 were all conditions of the mid-fifth century B.C. as the Books of Ezra

and Nehemiah demonstrate. Malachi could have preached this disputation anywhere that people gathered. It may well have been the temple, but that cannot be proved.

The authenticity of parts of the passage has been questioned, but only rarely and for good reason. The style and the content so well comport with the rest of Malachi that proving any part of 2:17–3:5 inauthentic would be difficult in the extreme.

This is the first of the Day of Yahweh passages in Malachi (the second passage being the sixth disputation, particularly the portion in 3:19 [4:1] and following). The prophets gave these passages about Yahweh's decisive intervention in history several emphases: the swiftness and suddenness of the arrival of the Day, its profound bleakness for Yahweh's enemies (who can be Israel if their sins so warrant), Yahweh's complete conquest of his foes, and his judgment, resulting in the righting of past wrongs and the reversal of sinful societal order. Each of these elements is present to one degree or another in this disputation.

17. "You have wearied Yahweh with your words" is a somewhat gentler criticism than those which began the prior two disputations. It is not as positive as the "I love you," which began the first disputation. But it certainly suggests that this fourth disputation is an attack on the people of Judah. And that is what it proves to be.

Because of the language in 3:1 about the messenger "whom you desire . . . want" the passage has sometimes been taken to be a sort of chiding, but not an excoriation. In fact, this disputation has occasionally been understood as either an oracle of encouragement, or at least an admixture of criticism and encouragement, a combination of judgment and hope. It is true that many biblical scholars are afflicted with monolithism, unable to imagine that a prophet and his audience could be concerned about more than one subject in their lifetime (e.g., a preexilic prophet could not have spoken about postexilic matters; a northern prophet could not have prophesied about Judah, etc.) or viewing all differences from an idealistic norm as "interpolations." Predictably, then, certain scholars have argued forcefully that the disputation is addressed only to the pious in Judah, intended to give them reassurance, while others have argued that the audience is the nation's reprobate, with no support or encouragement given to anyone.

But what do Malachi's words actually say? They say that the people—on balance, as a generalization—are overly pessimistic about the intervention of God in the affairs of his people (v. 17) but also that when that intervention takes place, it will not be what they expect (3:1–5). The prevailing attitude is captured by two characteristic statements, which I presume are actually the prophet's compositions intended to convey the gist of the sorts of things that people were often saying. In the same way that 1:4 "quoted" the Edomites, who surely didn't speak with a single voice, the two sayings "quoted" in 2:17 are surely summations rather than citations. It's not that Malachi couldn't have heard or overheard people say things of the sort mentioned in this verse. It's just that there is reason to assume that they were saying many kinds of things at many places and times, the sentiment of which was captured by these two statements. In other words, it is not necessary to conclude that Malachi is actually quoting popular proverbs here, as Ezekiel, for example, once did (Ezek. 18:2).

The first saying, "All the evildoers are pleasing to Yahweh and he likes them," is an expression of frustration and probably also of resignation. By these words Malachi indicates that a considerable number of his contemporaries—the exact percentage need not be specified—felt that things had degenerated seriously in their society and that God seemed to be doing nothing about it. The statement is both ironic and metaphorical. Orthodox Yahwists, however many there were, would not have actually have argued that God really liked and favored evildoers, and it is hard to imagine that other segments of society, including heterodox and outright evildoers, would have actually contended for that notion either. But as a statement of irony it makes sense. Since evil prevailed so greatly in the nation, God couldn't be very bothered by it, could he? In fact, he must love it, or else he'd do something about it! The level of sin, crime, and corruption was such that it was as if God were encouraging it.

The second saying, offered as an alternative example ("or"), is neither ironic nor metaphorical, and therefore more straightforwardly a summation of people's frustration with the level of societal and personal behavior in their day, delivered in question form: "Where is the God of justice?" We can appreciate why Malachi was inspired to put this question second, since it is the more simple and rationally addressable of the two. The first is more a venting of emotion; this is more a call for explanation, which, of course, the rest of the disputation will provide. Note that by concluding the "response" portion of the disputation with the word mišpāṭ (justice) Malachi leaves his readers/hearers with that very concept—justice—central in their thinking as he comes to the implication section of the oracle. They knew that Yahweh was supposed to be the God of justice (Deut. 4:5–8; Ps. 89:15 [14]; Isa. 30:18), and they wanted to see the sort of action that such a God should provide.

Both sayings call for an answer. Why does God allow such evil as to make it seem like he takes pleasure in the accomplishments of evildoers? And where is he, who is supposed to be the essence of and bringer of justice? These kinds of concerns were certainly not limited to Malachi's day, but were described as well by Moses (Deut. 32:5, 16–18, 28), the psalmists (Pss. 37; 49; 73), Habakkuk (1:2–4, 12–17), Paul (Rom. 1:29–32), Peter (2 Peter 3:4), and John (Rev. 6:9–10), among others.

Would the people of a nation as corrupt as Malachi has described it in the second and third disputations really be looking for justice in the fourth disputation? The answer is, absolutely! And that is because sinners are invariably inconsistent. The thief is always outraged when someone steals from him. The liar is deeply offended when someone lies to her. The cheater deeply resents finding that she has been defrauded, and the murderer wants himself and his family to live in peace. The expectations of sinners are characteristically hypocritical, as Paul so compellingly points out (Rom. 2:1–16). All people, not just the pious, want justice, at least for themselves.

IV. Fourth Disputation (2:17–3:5)

B. When the Messenger Comes, the Lord Will Display His Justice (3:1–5)

STUART

3 I will send my messenger, who will clear the way before me. Then suddenly the Lord you are seeking will come to his temple, the messenger of the covenant, whom you want. He is coming (Yahweh of the Armies said), ²but who can endure the day of his coming? Who can stand when he appears? For he will be like a refiner's fire or a launderer's lye. ³He will sit as a refiner and purifier of silver; he will purify the Levites and refine them like gold and silver so that Yahweh will have people to present offerings properly, ⁴and the offerings of Judah and Jerusalem will delight Yahweh, as in the ancient times, as in the early years. ⁵So I will come to you for judgment. I will be quick to testify against sorcerers, adulterers, and those who swear dishonestly by my name, against those who cheat on the pay of laborers, who oppress the widows and the orphans and victimize aliens and do not fear me (Yahweh of the Armies said).

NRSV

3 See, I am sending my messenger to prepare the way before me, and the Lord whom you seek will suddenly come to his temple. The messenger of the covenant in whom you delight—indeed, he is coming, says the LORD of hosts. ²But who can endure the day of his coming, and who can stand when he appears?

For he is like a refiner's fire and like fullers' soap; ³he will sit as a refiner and purifier of silver, and he will purify the descendants of Levi and refine them like gold and silver, until they present offerings to the LORD in righteousness. ⁴Then the offering of Judah and Jerusalem will be pleasing to the LORD as in the days of old and as in former years

⁵Then I will draw near to you for judgment; I will be swift to bear witness against the sorcerers, against the adulterers, against those who swear falsely, against those who oppress the hired workers in their wages, the widow and the orphan, against those who thrust aside the alien, and do not fear me, says the LORD of hosts.

3:1. הִנְנִי שֹׁלֵחַ (I am sending) is a typical *hinneh* clause, announcing commitment to future action. Contrary to some commentators, it does not necessarily mean "I am about to send," that is, that the action is very near to being undertaken (GKC §166p; Driver, *Tenses in Hebrew* §135; König §237 g). מַלְאָכִי (my messenger): The term can also be translated "my angel," but angel and messenger would not be distinguished from one another in the mind of the Hebrew speaker as they would be for the English speaker. Biblically, angels are God's messengers. וּפִנָּה-דֶרֶךְ (and he will clear the way): The typical translation, "prepare the way," does not connote the necessary sense of the piel of

---

3:1 God now answers the frustrations expressed in 2:17. The verse contains three vocabulary repetitions: come (*bwʾ*), messenger (*malʾāk*), and "behold" (*hinnēh*). The messenger is described from Yahweh's point of view (as one whom Yahweh is "sending," identified as "my messenger") and from the people's point of view (the one who is "coming," "the messenger of the covenant"). Thus God tells the people through his prophet that he is responding to them, doing something for them.

This is a promise (restoration blessing type 1, the renewal of Yahweh's favor/loyalty/presence), a prediction of positive events, as is made manifest by the two clauses that describe the messenger: "the Lord whom you are seeking" and "the messenger of the covenant whom you want." The latter clause is technically ambiguous grammatically, since the adjectival "whom you want" (*ʾăšer-ʾattem mĕbaqĕšîm*) can modify either "messenger" or "covenant" in light of the way the two nouns are conjoined in the construct state. The natural conclusion, however, must be that it is the messenger of the covenant (as a compound), rather than merely the covenant, that the people want. Nonetheless, the latter is grammatically possible. More important, they are expecting good things to happen when the messenger comes. Following the usual assumption that the Day of Yahweh would be positive for Israel (Amos 5:18–20; see v. 2 below) they wanted the divine messenger to arrive.

Four central assertions are made in the verse: (1) God is sending a *malʾāk* (messenger), who will make way for God's personal intervention. (2) The Lord will appear suddenly at the temple. (3) He (the Lord) is the messenger of the covenant. (4) He will be the one the people are hoping for. Within the overall context of the plan of redemption revealed in Scripture, and also within the prophetic corpus per se, this is unmistakably messianic doctrine. Exodus 23:20–23, or at least the theology behind it, may well stand in the background of the first few words in the verse. It describes God's angel who represents God among the people and goes ahead of them as they leave Sinai for the promised land, to prepare their way so that they will have success in conquering the promised land. There are definite verbal similarities between Malachi 3:1 and Exodus 23:20:

Exodus 23:20	Malachi 3:1
hinnēh ʾānōkî šōlēaḥ malʾāk (I am going to send an angel)	*hinnî šōlēaḥ malʾākî* (see I am sending my messenger)
lĕpānêykā lišmārĕkā baddārek (in front of you, to guard you on the way)	*ûpinnâ-derek lĕpānāy* (to prepare the way before me)

If this connection is purposeful, as I judge it must be, it suggests that Malachi 3:1 is employing well-known terminology to describe the same sort of thing that Exodus 23:20ff. describes: the coming of the predecessor to a mighty act of victory that God will achieve for his people. It should be noted that Exodus 23 concludes the part of Exodus sometimes called the "Covenant Code" (Exod. 24:7), a consideration that may also be part of the linkage between this portion of Exodus and Malachi. The Exodus passage concerns a supernatural figure, an angel, whose identity merges with that of Yahweh as the passage unfolds (vv. 23–33), in a manner typical of many angel stories in the Old Testament (e.g., Gen. 16:7–14; 21:17–21; 22:1–18; Exod. 3:2–22; Judg. 13:3–23). This history of the term *messenger* (*malʾāk*) helps clarify how the term might be used here of Yahweh himself.

Full appreciation of the meaning of the verse requires recognizing that its language is of the sort often associated with theophany, the decisive intervention of God in the affairs of human beings, and particularly with the theophanic concept of the Day of Yahweh, a major prophetic theme elsewhere in the prophets, (cf. Isa. 13:6,9; Jer. 46:10; Ezek. 13:5; 30:3; Joel 1:15; 2:1, 11, 31; 3:14; Amos 5:18–20; Obad. 15; Zeph. 1:7, 14; Zech. 14:1; Mal. 4:5). At a future point, Yahweh will appear as conquering judge to vindicate the righteous swiftly and decisively defeat the wicked, including the wicked among his people. His coming will be a day of victory against his foes, a day of cataclysmic reversal during which

פנה, that is, emptying, removing, clearing (the road of traffic so that the sovereign can proceed unhindered). הֵיכָלוֹ (temple): The term can also be translated "palace," depending on whether an English speaker chooses to envision a human messiah or a deity (a distinction unnecessary for Christians, of course). Again, this distinction was irrelevant to Hebrew speakers, who viewed the temple as Yahweh's palace. הָאָדוֹן (the Lord): Crucial to the understanding of this verse is the recognition that, grammatically, this word must be the subject of the verb יָבוֹא (he will come). While הָאָדוֹן (the Lord) can refer to a human, it more typically indicates God, and in the present context is

---

the expectations of wicked people are dashed and the hopes of righteous people suddenly rewarded, and a day that ushers in an era of blessing. In the New Testament all references to the Day of the Lord (Acts 2:20; 1 Cor. 5:5; 2 Cor. 1:14; 1 Thess. 5:2; 2 Thess. 2:2; 2 Peter 3:10) are to the second coming of Christ, which will fulfill all the expectations for the Day of the Lord found in the Old Testament prophets. Since Malachi uses the expression "the day of his coming" in 3:2 and the precise expression "the Day of Yahweh" in 4:5 means that one is surely justified in seeing the notion here in 3:1.

Who exactly are the figures mentioned in this verse? First comes "my messenger," sent to clear the way. Then, "suddenly," comes "the Lord," who is also then called "the messenger of the covenant." Is the first messenger ("my messenger") different from the second (the messenger of the covenant)? As might be imagined, this question has generated no little debate, and a host of views have been put forward. Some have assumed that "my messenger" is the prophet himself (Malachi), who sees himself as the harbinger of the Day of Yahweh on which the "messenger of the covenant" (Yahweh, or sometimes a more imprecise eschatological figure, or sometimes the angel of death) will come. Others have assumed that both messengers are the same, a human deliverer of some kind. Others opine that both messengers refer to an angel (the angel of death and the angel that gives the law), and others that both refer to God. Since, as we have seen, Malachi referred to the ideal, responsible priest as "the messenger of Yahweh of the Armies" (2:7), some have concluded that one or both of the messengers in the present verse is a priest. The weakness of this suggestion is that the contexts of 3:1 and 2:7 are so different, and the term *messenger* so potentially broad in referent, that we could never justify the idea that it always points to the same person, or kind of person, every time Malachi uses it. Yet others have thought that one part or another of the verse was not original, but an interpolation intended to take what was once a simple attack on injustice and to give it eschatological meaning.

While a full discussion of these options might be enlightening for some, in the final analysis these questions are obviated by the simple fact that the verse is overtly messianic in outlook, that it identifies the first messenger as a forerunner and the second messenger as the Lord (ha²adôn). In other words, the verse says that God is going to send someone to prepare people for the sudden arrival of the individual whom people are seeking/ wanting and that this second individual is both Lord and covenant messenger. Just who are these persons? Unless we wish arbitrarily to exclude the New Testament from our purview, the answer is not difficult: the messenger sent as forerunner is John the Baptist, and the Lord, the covenant messenger, is Christ.

Of course, the precise term "messenger of the covenant/ covenant messenger" (mal²ak habbĕrît) is not used of Jesus in the New Testament. One the other hand, he surely is identified in a variety of ways as the initiator of the New Covenant (Luke 22:20; 2 Cor 3:6; Heb. 7:22) in fulfillment of what Malachi 3:1 appears to call for. The idea that in the age to come (from the Old Testament perspective) there would be a new covenant is well known from such passages as Isaiah 55:3; 61:8; Jeremiah 31:31-34; Ezekiel 16:62; 37:26, so we should not be surprised that Malachi would also be inspired to mention it here.

That the Messiah should come suddenly (pit²ōm) fits with both the Old Testament and New Testament concept of the Day of the Lord (see esp. God's sudden intervention in Isa. 29:5; 48:3; Jer. 15:8; 18:22; Luke 12:39-40; 2 Peter 3:10; Rev. 16:15). Behind the concept is the ancient Near Eastern notion that a great sovereign can gain victory over his enemies in a single day (Stuart, "Sovereign's Day of Conquest," pp. 159-64). That the Lord should come to his temple is also a theme of both covenants (Ezek. 43:4; Zech. 6:12-15; Matt. 21:12-16; Eph. 2:21; Rev. 7:15-17), since the temple is, by definition, the palace of Yahweh, from which he rules. There was no royal palace in Judah or Samaria in Malachi's day, since both palace and temple had been destroyed by the Babylonians in 586 B.C. But the Second Temple had long

overtly messianic. Someone who would come suddenly to his temple or palace—at a time when there was no palace in Israel—is obviously no mere prophet or leader but a very special kind of king. הִנֵּה בָא (he is coming): These two words, resumptive of the promise of sending "my messenger" at the beginning of the verse, are best taken as the outset of a sentence that continues in verse 2, thus, "He is coming (said Yahweh of the Armies), but who can endure."

2. כִּי־הוּא כְּאֵשׁ מְצָרֵף (for he is like a refiner's fire): The Septuagint adds εἰσπορεύεται (will come) so that the sentence says, "For he will come like a refiner's fire." It is technically impossible to tell whether this represents a contextually influenced

attempt at clarity on the part of the Septuagint translator or whether an original בָא dropped out of the Hebrew, but the spare, parallelistic style of verse 2b suggests strongly that no Hebrew has been lost. בְּרִית מְכַבְּסִים (launderers' lye): בְּרִית means just "lye" (in spite of some modern translations, it cannot mean "soap" because soap as we know it was not available in ancient times) and some commentators have linked it to the lye used in the metal-smelting process, since several of the images in this and the following verse relate to metal smelting. Lye was indeed used in metal smelting (Isa. 1:25) because it functioned as a reagent to make metals melt faster, and lye was often one of the by-products of smelting as well.

---

been built, the very temple at which Jesus was to worship and to which he rode in triumph on the day now celebrated as Palm Sunday.

Malachi 3:1 and 3:23–24 [4:5–6] together constitute one of Malachi's special contributions to prophecy. They are the most detailed Old Testament contexts indicating that the coming of the Messiah would be preceded by a precursor who would announce the need to prepare for his coming. In this regard Malachi is even more explicit than the more famous verses from Isaiah 40:3–5 (compare Isa. 57:14; 62:10) that speak of the "voice" that announces the messianic advent. As to the identity of the forerunner, the first "messenger" in 3:1, see the Exposition of 3:23–24 and the discussion there of the second Elijah as John the Baptist (compare Matt. 11:10; Mark 1:2; Luke 1:76; 7:27).

Throughout recorded history all cultures have employed the commonsense method of sending messengers to prepare people for the arrival of an important person, or to negotiate something that an important person would wish settled in advance of his or her arrival. Christ's first and second comings are both announced in advance according to Scripture. Malachi 3:1 speaks of the heralding of his first arrival. On the announcement of Christ's second coming, via trumpet sound and angelic shout (angelos (messenger/angel) being the New Testament equivalent of malʾāk (messenger/angel) here), see 1 Thessalonians 4:16.

2. This verse contains the kind of "reversal language" that characterizes much prophetic speech about the Day of the Lord. The Israelites looked forward to the day as bringing divine deliverance from their enemies. They assumed, of course, that their enemies were God's enemies. The prophets had the task of explaining that the Israelites them-

selves were also God's enemies, by reason of their having broken his covenant. So although they might eagerly desire/want (see 3:1) the messenger of the covenant to come, in fact his coming would not be pleasant for them. Amos, also had the difficult task of announcing that the Day of the Lord would be just the opposite of what the people were naively expecting.

This does not mean that all prophetic references to the Day of the Lord portray it as a time of judgment for Israel. When the nation is righteous, the day is indeed an occasion of deliverance. When Yahweh comes to judge his enemies, it all depends on who is *at that time* in covenant with him. Those people who belong to him will be delivered and blessed. Those who do not—whether Israelites or non-Israelites—will be judged and punished. Day of Yahweh passages that emphasize its positive aspects for Israel (i.e., see it from the point of view of its deliverance of the righteous in Israel from their foes) include Isaiah 13:6–13; Jeremiah 46:10; Ezekiel 13:5; 30:3–4; Joel 3:1–5 [2:28–32]; 4:14 [3:14]; Obadiah 15; Zechariah 14:1. Those that emphasize its negative aspects for a sinful Israel include Joel 1:15; 2:1, 11; Amos 5:18–20; Zephaniah 1:7, 14–18.

Thus the Day of Yahweh is often described as a time of division—of separation (just from unjust, sheep from goats, etc.). *Who can endure . . . ? Who can stand . . . ?*: The answer to these synonymous questions for any who knew Malachi's preaching, or yahwistic prophetic preaching in general (Joel 2:11), or who were attuned to what he had been saying so far in this fourth disputation, would be obvious: only those who have faithfully kept Yahweh's covenant. And, conversely, these questions force the thoughtful listener to ask, "Who can*not* endure . . . ? Who can*not* stand?" Again the

But מְכַבְּסִים clearly means "launderers," so there can be little doubt that washing lye is the term under discussion. The term could cover any of several alkali compounds of varying quality (e.g., sodium or potassium hydroxide from ground deposits or potassium carbonate leached from wood ash), but all worked essentially the same way. Does the term בֹּרִית appear here partly because it is so close in sound to בְּרִית (covenant) in the prior verse ("messenger of the covenant")?

Possibly so. Malachi is known for his repetition of vocabulary, and this particular repetition of sounds would probably have been noticed—or at least could have been noticed—by his audience as they heard him preach these words. This is not to say that the context in some manner focuses especially on the covenant–lye sound interplay; only that such assonance was part of the verbal artistry that prophets employed routinely. In Jeremiah 2:22, the only other place in the Old Testament

---

answer is evident: Those who have violated the covenant, and who are therefore no longer under its protection (curse type 24, death/destruction). The separation theme is driven further by verse 2b, which likens Yahweh to fire and lye (not soap—it was not known in Bible times). Both "burn," both feel hot to the touch, and both were used as agents of separation.

Fire was essential for the refining of valuable metals, the first metaphorical image employed in verse 2b. The differing melting points of various metals allowed the refiner, by careful application of fire, to separate one from another. Fire made it possible to take the slag or dross out of the ore, leaving only the desired, pure end product. But the fire had to be large and hot. Impressive refining fires could be seen virtually any day of the week around Jerusalem in Malachi's day, and there would be few in his audience who would not immediately identify this image. Other prophets use the image of purifying fire as well, whether describing the process of Yahweh's anger eliminating what is undesirable (curse type 10, destruction by fire), or more positively, his purification of his people (Isa. 29:6; 30:27–30; 66:15–17; Jer. 15:14; Ezek. 22:20–21; 36:5; Joel 1:19–20; 2:3; Nah. 1:6; Zeph. 1:14–17). Perhaps the closest parallel among the prophetical references to Yahweh as being like fire is Zechariah 13:9:

A third I will bring into the fire.
I will refine them like silver and test them
  like gold.
They will call on my name and I will an-
  swer them.
I will say, "They are my people,"
And they will say, "Yahweh is our God."

This close association of fire imagery with Yahweh is yet another example of Malachi's continuity with the Pentateuch, which often speaks of Yahweh as revealing himself through or in fire. A notable example is the story of the burning bush (Exod. 3) but there are many others (Exod. 19:18; 24:16–17; Deut. 4:11–15, 33–36). As Moses reminded the Israelites: "Yahweh took you and brought you out of the iron smelting furnace" (Deut. 4:20) and "Yahweh your God is a consuming fire" (Deut. 4:24).

Lye, the second of the cleansing agents employed as a metaphorical image in verse 2b (and possibly linking v. 2 to v. 1 because of the similar sound of *bōrît* [lye] in v. 2 and *bĕrît* [covenant] in v. 1), was widely used in the process of fulling, that is, cleaning clothes by soaking them in water in which lye had been dissolved, then beating and scrubbing them, and finally rinsing them. This was a separation process as well—separating dirt from fabric. The dirt was taken away and the pure fabric remained, just as in refining the slag was taken away by the heat of the fire and the pure metal remained (compare similar imagery in Jer. 2:22). Thus fire and lye characterize Yahweh's role on his day. Like fire and lye he will separate what deserves to remain from what is not worthy of keeping.

With regard to Christology, this verse and those that follow it are important Old Testament precursors of trinitarian theology. The messenger who is sent by Yahweh in 3:1 turns out to be none other than Yahweh himself. How can God both send and be sent? This question may be asked likewise of Christ: How can he be sent by God and also be God in the flesh? The answer, to the partial extent that humans can comprehend it, is found in the doctrine of the Trinity. The Messiah is God the Son who serves the will of the Father, yet also has equality with the Father. God is both Father and Son, and both Father and Son are Spirit as well.

3. "He will sit" suggests either or both judgment and rule, sitting being the posture of judging (Exod. 18:13; Ruth 4:1–2; Dan. 7:9–10) and ruling (1 Sam. 1:9; Pss. 29:10; 132:12; Jer. 17:25) in most ancient (and modern) literature. Yahweh is now not merely likened to the fire of refining or the lye

where בֹּרִית (lye) occurs, such assonance does not appear to be present, but merely the metaphor of cleansing from sin, as here in Malachi.

3. This verse is free of textual or grammatical problems. בְּנֵי־לֵוִי (the Levites): This is the standard idiomatic term for Levites, with no different meaning from the collective singular that Malachi used in 2:4, 8. מִנְחָה בִּצְדָקָה (offerings in righteousness/right offerings): This compound is grammatically ambiguous, but probably purposely so. The prepositional phrase בִּצְדָקָה can modify either the earlier verb, מַגִּישֵׁי (bringers of) or מִנְחָה (offerings—a collective noun). It can, thus, at the same time indicate how the offerings are brought, and/or the quality of the offerings themselves. The term צְדָקָה has a wide semantic range, connoting such concepts as rightness, proper order, fairness, and justice, and thus the final clause in the verse may be translated in any of the following ways: "so that they will present offerings to Yahweh in righteousness," "until they will present proper offerings to Yahweh," "then Yahweh will have people who will bring offerings in righteousness," "so that they will be to Yahweh as those who bring offerings correctly," "so that Yahweh will have people to present offerings properly." The latter seems slightly more idiomatic in the context, but English cannot do justice to the rich ambiguity of the Hebrew.

4. This verse is best understood as concluding the sentence begun in verse 3. וְעָרְבָה (will delight): On this meaning of the qal of ערב, see Psalm

---

of fulling, but to the refiner himself, the purifier of silver. But this is merely a metaphorical way of leading in to the thrust of the verse, which is the purification of the Levites, on the analogy of the purification of gold and silver by a refiner. Among the reforms of the Day of the Lord will be the alignment of the Levites with God's will, with the result that the abuses described in disputations 2 and 3 will be brought to an end. Again, the concept is that of separation. By implication, those Levites (i.e., both priests and the rest of the Levite clan who aided in worship and religious leadership) who had broken the covenant of Levi (2:4, 8) by bringing improper offerings to God (1:8, 13) were to be eliminated, and those who would serve Yahweh faithfully would be retained and employed for his honor in proper worship.

Thus verse 3 answers two of the needs mentioned in earlier disputations: the need for offerings to be properly done, and the need for priests who did what the levitical covenant called for in general. Thus the theme of covenant remains just beneath the surface. The divine messenger to come (3:1) would make sure that his covenant was followed. From an overall biblical perspective, this does not conflict with the New Testament assertion that Christ's ultimate, once-for-all sacrifice eliminated the need for further temple food offerings (Heb. 10:1–17). Nothing in Malachi, including this verse and verse 4, implies that the Messiah's work on the Day of Yahweh would be to restore the same offering system that the Sinai covenant specified. Rather, the Day of Yahweh would usher in the practice of true worship, of a sort that was acceptable to God, just as proper Israelite tabernacle/temple worship had also once been acceptable to God when it was properly

done. In other words, this verse and verse 4 must not be interpreted as advocating that the Day of the Lord (which biblically is clearly the coming of Christ) would do nothing more than restore Old Covenant worship styles.

Nothing less than the purification of the nation as a whole is the ultimate purpose of that day (v. 4), and the emphasis on the Levites in verse 3 stems from the simple fact that the purification has to begin with them. Until such time as they would repent and conform to the covenant (which finally occurred in adequate measure during the reforms of Ezra and Nehemiah; see Neh. 13:30) the greater reform of the nation, accomplished by the work of Christ, would be forestalled. Purification of the Levites, the priests, and the rest of the nation was, in other words, a way station on the road to the pan-historical redemption of God's people in general . Malachi was inspired to call for it as well as to predict it, Ezra and Nehemiah implemented it, then in turn proper Old Covenant worship was restored, and then, eventually, God did send the Day of Yahweh, the coming of Christ, thus completing the purification process in the most effective way of all. Christ's atoning death meant that the entire sacrifice-based system could be brought to an end, its assigned purposes having been fulfilled.

4. The Day of Yahweh has as its goal the purification of the nation as a whole, not merely some portion thereof. Thus "Judah and Jerusalem," capital and country, function together to suggest the completeness of the sanctification of God's people. From the point of view of biblical hermeneutics, any subsequent people of God—including Christians in the current covenant age—can be the referent (Gal. 3:29).

104:34; Proverbs 3:24; 13:19; Jeremiah 6:20; 30:21; 31:26; Ezekiel 16:37; Hosea 9:4. It connotes the sense of something's being pleasant, delightful, entirely welcome to someone. כִּימֵי עוֹלָם וּכְשָׁנִים קַדְמֹנִיּוֹת (as in the ancient times, as in the early years): This construction employs two synonymous expressions, intended to have the effect of emphasis and thus clarity. The meaning is not analogous to the vague English "in the olden days" or (even less accurately) "in the good old days," even though it is sometimes found in contexts that look back wistfully to better times in Israel's relation to Yahweh. It refers, rather, to the time of Israel's first covenant relationship with her God, when at Sinai and thereafter, under the leadership of Moses, the people gave the kinds of offerings in the way they were supposed to, to the delight of God as offerings are supposed to function. עֹלָם (ancient [times]): The term refers to the indefinite past or future, whose end is not known. It can mean eternity/eternal but can also mean "the past far back," "an ancient era," " a time long ago" (Gen. 9:16; 49:26; Pss. 41:14 [13]; 143:3; Eccles. 1:10). Of the two expressions employed here, כִּימֵי עוֹלָם (as in the ancient times) is also used in Amos 9:11, where it refers to the power of Israel under David centuries prior, and Micah

7:14, where it refers to Israel's early days as a people inhabiting the rich pasturelands of the Transjordan, also centuries prior. For virtually the same expression, see Micah 5:1 [2], also referring back to David's time, and Isaiah 63:9, 11, which clearly refers back—longingly—all the way to the days of Moses. Malachi's words in the present context are encouraging precisely because they remind the people that it will be even better in the divinely appointed future than it was in the great days of Moses. The expression וּכְשָׁנִים קַדְמֹנִיּוֹת (as in the early years) is a hapaxlegomenon, but its meaning, especially since it is used synonymously with the prior two words, is clear; קַדְמֹנִיּוֹת (early) occurs by itself in the plural only in Isaiah 43:18, referring to "earlier times."

5. וְקָרַבְתִּי אֲלֵיכֶם (I will come to you): This expression is typically translated "I will come near to you" or the like, which is not quite idiomatic modern English for this context. Yahweh is coming in judgment right to his people, not merely "near" them, in correspondence to the use of יָבוֹא (he will come) in 3:1. The verb קרב, which connotes coming to or presenting oneself formally at a particular place, is commonly found in sacrifice contexts, referring to coming near the altar (1:8), and this is surely the reason for its ironic use

---

Malachi has been inspired to spend a good deal of time on the issue of proper sacrifice, because worship is such a basic indicator of overall faithfulness to the covenant, and here again he describes the result of the sanctification of the people of God in terms of its effect on the way worship is performed. For background, see the Exposition of 1:6–14 and 2:12.

What does Malachi mean by sacrifices that will "delight" God? What he surely does not mean is that the sacrifices themselves have to be especially large or expensive or in any other way quantitatively impressive. The notion, at home in paganism, that the more you give a god the more he blesses you in return, has no counterpart in biblical revelation. For worship to delight God, it has to have two characteristics: it has to be the right kind of offering, and it has to be offered by the right kind of person. In other words, it must be correct according to covenant specification, and it also be offered by people who are otherwise keeping the covenant. This viewpoint is reflected notably in Amos 5:21–27, also a Day of Yahweh passage, which excoriates worship that is intense and voluminous but not accompanied by covenant obedience otherwise, that is, hypocritical.

Why? Because true worship is neither its own end, nor a feeding of the gods, as in the pagan mentality. It is a response of the believer to the grace of God, offered freely and in conformity with the fact that the believer loves God and is only too happy to have the honor of giving to him that portion of the believer's wealth that already belonged to God anyway. While the text of Genesis 4:3–7 does not explicitly so state, it is evident that these elements were lacking in Cain's offering (note v. 7: "If you do what is right, won't you be accepted?"). In the new covenant, 2 Corinthians 9:7 summarizes the proper attitude toward offering by the charge "Each of you must give as you have made up your mind, not grudgingly or out of necessity, because God loves a cheerful giver." Implied by the promise of Malachi 3:4 is the fact that God has not made it all that difficult to please him via offerings. The standards are not impossible. The goal is not unreachable. The goal was once reached, in the ancient past under Moses while the Israelites were in the wilderness ("as in the ancient times, as in the early years"; compare Hos. 2). Offerings rightly given by people in right relationship to God do indeed please him.

here. While קָרַב (drawing near), the related noun, can be used in battle contexts (a drawing near to engage the enemy), so can all sorts of other "neutral" terms; war involves many kinds of motions. There is no battle imagery in the verse, but legal imagery. To draw near "for judgment" (לַמִּשְׁפָּט) is a prophetic wording attested elsewhere (Isa. 41:1). וְהָיִיתִי עֵד מְמַהֵר בְּ (I will swiftly bear witness against): On the meaning "witness against" for עֵד + בְּ, see Numbers 5:13; Deuteronomy 19:15–16; 31:26; Joshua 24:22; 1 Samuel 12:5; Proverbs 24:28; Micah 1:2. Again, the terminology of the verse is legal, and the defendants are not so much *promised* the right to a speedy trial as *warned* that they will get one whether they like it or not. The participle מְמַהֵר (here translated adverbially, "swiftly") reprises the adverb פִּתְאֹם (suddenly) in 3:1. מְכַשְּׁפִים (sorcerers): These could be women or men who purported to be able to predict the future as well as to exert a measure of control over it (Isa. 47:9–12). מְנָאֲפִים (adulterers): This term refers to any persons who were married and had sex with someone other than their spouse, or any persons who had sex with a married person. While it is true that some biblical references to adultery (Lev. 18:20; 20:10; Deut. 22:22–27; Prov. 5:15–19;

etc.) may seem to speak of married men as adulterers in language that concentrates on their offense against other men, and women as adulterers in language concentrating on their offense against their own husbands, this distinction is not principial, but an accommodation to cultural sensibilities about marriage in Bible times. Jesus' teaching on adultery and divorce does not follow this pattern, however (Matt. 5:27–28; 19:3–9). נִשְׁבָּעִים לַשֶּׁקֶר [בִּשְׁמִי] (those who swear [oaths] dishonestly [by my name], i.e., perjurers): The term can refer to those who give false testimony on the witness stand as well as those who make phony promises invoking God or a god as witness in business or other societal dealings. The Septuagint (τῷ ὀνόματί μου) and a good many Hebrew manuscripts (בִּשְׁמִי) read "[those who swear falsely] *by my name*"—sufficient evidence to suggest that they are preserving wording that has accidently fallen out of the text in parts of the Masoretic Tradition and should be restored, as in my translation. It is easy enough to see how a word group beginning with the Hebrew letter *bet* could be subject to haplography via homoioarchton, since there are so many such word groups in this particular verse. עֹשְׁקֵי (oppressors of/defrauders of): This

However, this ability to delight God cannot be attributed in the final analysis to a believer's skill in offering, but to Christ's supreme offering of which all others are mere emblems (Heb. 10). Offerings in the new covenant, therefore, are no longer a matter of atonement for sin (Heb. 10:18) but of gratitude for acceptance. It is that understanding of offering that gives sense to the prediction of Malachi 3:4 that all of God's people would one day bring offerings that delighted God (restoration blessing type 3).

5. Some commentators have tended to view Malachi as a cult prophet, whose interests were limited to ensuring proper rituals in worship, since so much of the book concentrates on such issues as sacrifices and tithing. This verse belies that notion (as do the first and sixth disputations and the epilogue, for that matter) and has thus led some scholars, most notably Rudolph (*Maleachi*), to regard it, often along with verse 4, as inauthentic, the product of a later interpolater. However, their inability to imagine that Malachi and his audience could be interested in more than one topic, while surprising because of its stubborn disregard of the evidence, is hardly convincing.

In fact, 3:5 corresponds to 2:17 and rounds out the disputation by listing some of the kinds of

behavior that caused people to say, "All the evildoers please Yahweh, and he likes them," or "Where is the God of justice?" (2:17). Seven violations of the Mosaic covenant are listed, as discussed below. They specify the reason that Yahweh will "come to you for judgment" (curse type 26, general punishment/curse/vengeance). Why these seven covenant violations? It is likely that they are chosen not because they are the seven worst or because they precisely represent the various categories of sins mentioned in the Pentateuch, or for any such programmatic reason. It is far more likely that these seven are listed—somewhat randomly—for three simple reasons: (1) seven was the ancient equivalent of modern English "half a dozen"—a rough, approximate number with no special significance. (Contrary to widely held popular notions, it is not the biblical number for perfection or completeness or anything similar. It is most often, when not literal, simply a way of saying "several.") (2) These sins were among those prominent in Malachi's day. (3) These seven were sufficient to demonstrate that the covenant was being violated, thus requiring the intervention of God.

This way of describing sins seems to be the rule, rather than the exception, among the prophets. The listing of a few sins, in any order, is con-

participle in construct governs two two-word objects, (1) the hired worker's wages and (2) widow(s) and orphan(s). The first of these two-word objects, שְׂכַר־שָׂכִיר (pay of a hired worker), is also found in Deuteronomy 15:18, obviating the suggestion of some commentators that the text be emended to reverse the word order so that the worker is being oppressed rather than his pay. This emendation is advanced on the theory that both objects of עשק ought to be either personal or impersonal, not one of each (i.e., "pay" and "orphans/widows") for the sake of consistency. In fact, עשק (abuse, suppress, oppress, wrong, rob, cheat, defraud, etc.) can certainly take "pay" as its object just as easily as "payee." On the ability of עשק to take both a nonpersonal object and a personal object in the same clause, see Micah 2:2. The problem of inconsistency exists only in the mind of the commentators. אַלְמָנָה וְיָתוֹם (orphans and widows [singulars used collectively]): This common hendiadys is utilized often in Scripture as a shorthand (synecdochic) way of denoting any persons who are needy and dependent rather than referring only to individuals who have lost husband or parents (Exod. 22:21 [22]; Deut. 24:17, 19–20, 21; 26:12; Prov. 13:21; 19:17; 22:9; Isa. 1:17; 10:2; Jer. 7:6; Lam. 5:3; Zech. 7:10; James 1:27).

מַטֵּי־גֵר (those who victimize aliens [singular of גֵר, alien, used collectively]): The hiphil of נטה (stretch, extend, bend, tilt, mislead, turn aside, pervert, etc.) has an idiomatic meaning in legal contexts that is best translated "mistreat, victimize" (Isa. 29:21; Amos 5:12, similarly, Amos 2:7). This idiomatic meaning may have derived from abbreviation of the fuller expression נטה מִשְׁפָּט (pervert justice) as in Exodus 23:6; Deuteronomy 16:19; 1 Samuel 8:3; Proverbs 17:23; 18:5. At any rate, the verb can be used by itself, as here, to indicate a denial of justice to, or the unfair treatment of someone. גֵר (alien, resident alien): The older translation "stranger" did not properly convey the definition, which indicates not someone who is unknown, but someone who is not a citizen of the place in which he or she resides, and thus is at the mercy of those who are citizens and control the political and legal system. לֹא יְרֵאוּנִי (they do not fear me): Because of modern psychological notions that it is harmful to portray God as one to be feared, it has become commonplace to translate ירא in contexts where God is the object by such softer notions as "be in awe of" or "reverence." "Fear," however, is the better translation. See the Exposition.

---

sidered more than enough evidence to convict the nation of having broken God's law. This reflects a basic aspect of the doctrine of covenant, and indeed, also of modern law. It is not necessary to break all the stipulations of a covenant to have broken that covenant. Breaking only one stipulation puts one in the position of having violated the agreement as a whole. By way of modern analogy, it requires only the breaking of a single law to become a "lawbreaker" or conviction for a single crime to be considered a "criminal." The prophets therefore felt obligated only to list a few crimes against God's law, without concern for the order of the listing or the categories involved, to make the point that Israel had broken God's covenant and deserved his punishment. The fact that Malachi lists seven (a longer list than typically found in the prophets, the average probably including no more than three) is perhaps a testimony to the degeneracy of the nation in his day, but it hardly means that these were the only sins being committed or that these were even the worst.

Day of Yahweh passages in the prophets tend to have one or more of the following emphases: the suddenness or surprising timing of the Day, its bleakness for those who are Yahweh's enemies,

its complete conquest of Yahweh's foes, and its juridical righting of past patterns of wrong. It is the juridical function of the Day that is under discussion here in v. 5.

As regards the seven sins mentioned in the verse:

1. Sorcery (kšp): The practice was an abomination to God (Deut. 18:12) borrowed from pagan religion (2 Kings 9:22) and, though widely popular in Israel (2 Chron. 33:6; Jer. 27:9), deserved the death penalty (Exod. 22:17 [18]). It counterfeited true prophecy (Deut. 18:19–22) and thus led the people who followed it to destruction rather than salvation—an outcome well worthy of capital punishment. The fact that sorcery was going on in Malachi's day is an indication of the severe level of disregard for the Mosaic covenant in Judah. The term kšp can be used to refer to almost any kind of magic and divination, and has many subcategories (necromancy, rhabdomancy, augury, hepatoscopy, etc.). On sorcery as an abomination in the New Testament, see Revelation 21:8; 22:15.

2. Adultery: Adulterers were violators of the ten commandments (Exod. 20:14; Deut. 5:17 [18]) and thus were certainly examples of moral breakdown that nullified the covenant and called for divine punishment. Adultery was also a capital crime (Deut. 22:22) like rape (Deut. 22:23–27) as opposed to "statutory rape," which was punished by lesser penalties though still a serious violation of the law (Exod. 22:15; Deut. 22:28–29). Adultery was even sometimes referred to as the "great sin" in the Bible (Gen. 20:9; 39:9) and other ancient Near Eastern literature (Moran, "Great Sin," Rabinowitz, "'Great Sin'"). On the severity of the crime in the New Covenant, see Matthew 5:27–32; Romans 2:22; 1 Corinthians 6:9; Galatians 5:19; Hebrews 13:4; James 2:11. While some commentators have suggested that Malachi's mention of adultery stems from his having the divorcers of 2:10–16 in mind, this does not seem to be a demonstrable contention. Both sorcery and adultery were routine in foreign religious practices. Isaiah calls idolaters "children of the sorceress and offspring of the adulterer" (Isa. 57:3).

3. Swearing dishonestly by Yahweh's name (perjury): The oath ("May Yahweh strike me dead if I'm not telling the truth" or "As Yahweh lives, I promise . . . ," and countless similar formulations) was intended to indicate the solemnity of the oath-taker's resolve to tell the truth. Those who lied under oath were not merely cheating their neighbors, but also dishonoring Yahweh by taking his name in vain. The offense is thus both against the community and against God. Swearing falsely is a specialized, elevated form of lying, done in a context designed to prevent lying. Yahweh's name was invoked in oaths, which were legal (Lev. 19:12; Deut. 6:13; 10:20; 1 Sam. 20:42) but swearing falsely, perjury, was a serious crime (Lev. 19:12; 20:3; compare Zech. 8:16–17). Jeremiah calls it an abomination (tôʿēbâ, Jer. 7:9–12). Its most principial condemnation is found in the Decalogue, of course, in the ninth commandment ("Do not give false testimony," which though limited by the language (ʿānâ ʿēd šeqer, speak false testimony) to legal contexts, is nevertheless a parade example of the general sin of false swearing.

4. Cheating on the pay of hired workers: While theoretically a person could oppress a hired worker by unfair working conditions, the main means was by paying less than the agreed-on wage or paying it later than the end of the day, or paying a nonliving wage to people who were so desperate for food that they would work anyway. Hired workers were not slaves, who had long-term (but voluntary!) employment (Exod. 21:2–6; Deut. 15:12–18), and they were obviously not family members, who did most of the labor in ancient societies, including Israel. They were people without land of their own for whatever reason (virtually always a violation of the covenant, which, if it had been followed, provided everyone something to farm. Lacking land of their own, they hired themselves out to others, usually as "day laborers," and were to be paid at the end of each workday since most of them lived from hand to mouth and had no savings or stored-up food that would allow them to wait for a periodic payday (Lev. 19:13; Deut. 24:14–15). They were a desperate and easy to exploit part of the population, and like the widows, orphans, and aliens mentioned immediately after them in the verse, were dependent on the fairness of others for their well-being, having no assets or societal power with which to exert influence or demand their rights.

5. Oppression of widows and orphans: Since "widows and orphans" is stereotyped language for "the needy" and Yahweh is the refuge and vindicator of the poor and afflicted, it could not have escaped the thoughtful among Malachi's audience that the nation's behavior was in clear conflict with the very nature of God, as well as with the explicit revelation of his law (Deut. 10:18: "He defends the cause of the orphan and widow") The foundational covenant curses of Deuteronomy 27, shouted by the Levites from Mount Ebal as a warning to all Israel then and thereafter, warned of the danger from God of withholding justice from the alien, orphan, and widow (Deut. 27:19).

6. Mistreating aliens: Like orphans and widows, aliens are used as examples of dependent peoples who of necessity rely on others for justice since they are not in a position to demand it, or mete it out, themselves. The alien was a reflection of the

Israelites at an earlier stage: "Do not mistreat an alien or oppress him for you were aliens in Egypt" (Exod. 22:20 [22:21]). Israel was also told: "He . . . loves the alien, giving him food and clothing. You are to love those who are aliens, for you yourselves were aliens in Egypt" (Deut. 10:18–19). Exploitation of aliens was clearly an act of covenant violation (Glazier-McDonald, *Malachi*, pp. 167–68).

7. Not fearing Yahweh: The statement that "they do not fear me" is both a sin in its own right and a kind of summary statement for the six sins mentioned prior, since it is the most general of the accusations. As a sin in its own right, see Deuteronomy 4:10 ("let them hear my words, so that they may learn to fear me . . . and that they may teach their children so") and Deuteronomy 5:29 ("Oh that they had such a mind as this always, to fear me and to keep all my commandments").

Fearing God is not a matter of being terrified of him as if he is always angry, or arbitrary and capricious in his dealings so that one should always be wary of what he might do. Rather, believers fear God's wrath if he is not obeyed. Thus "fear" functions as a shorthand for "fearing the consequences of disobeying," and often for just "not believing in or taking Yahweh seriously." Compare Jeremiah 5:22 ("Should you not fear me? says the LORD; Should you not tremble before me?") and Jeremiah 32:39 ("I will give them one heart and one way, that they may fear me for ever").

As a summary statement, the final clause of Malachi 3:5 may be understood to encompass all the various sins that the Israelites of Malachi's day are guilty of. They are not Yahwists in the true sense. They don't care about his covenant, and they do the sorts of things it forbids, because they don't fear/obey/believe in him in a way that represents a true commitment to doing his will.

Of course, to say that they don't fear him is also to say that they don't belong to him (Jer. 32:39) and thus that they are deserving of his wrath rather than his protection.

V. Fifth Disputation (3:6–12)

A. In Spite of the People's Disobedience, the Lord Does Not Change (3:6–7a)

STUART

⁶Since, I, the LORD have not changed, you, children of Jacob, are not destroyed. ⁷Ever since the days of your ancestors you have turned away from my commands and have not kept them.

NRSV

⁶For I the LORD do not change; therefore you, O children of Jacob, have not perished. ⁷Ever since the days of your ancestors you have turned aside from my statutes and have not kept them.

6. . . . יְ . . . כִּי (If . . . [so/then] . . .): This is a common, typical structure for a Hebrew conditional sentence, with the protasis introduced by כִּי (if) and the apodosis by וְ (rigidly "so"/"then," but actually not requiring a corresponding English word when translated). It is entirely unnecessary to regard כִּי as a coordinating conjunction (for, because) linking 3:6 to 2:17–3:5 (see the Exposition). לֹא שָׁנִיתִי (I have not changed): The verb is used intransitively here, and in light of the histor-

---

6–12. It has sometimes been argued that Malachi 3:6 is part of 2:17–3:5, in part because 3:6 begins with *kî*, often translated "for" or "because," and thus can be understood to relate to what precedes rather than what follows. Moreover, the first two clauses of verse 7 can also be linked with the prior disputation if one wishes to do so, since they speak of Israel's incorrigibility, a fitting theme in light of the list of sins in 3:5. But this approach is not necessary. Malachi 3:5 ends naturally and logically with a summarizing statement ("they do not fear me") and a messenger formula ("Yahweh of the Armies said"), both typical ways to bring a prophetic oracle to a conclusion (on ending with a messenger formula, see 3:12, for example). Moreover, *kî* does not always function as a coordinating conjunction. Sometimes it has an emphatic meaning, such as "indeed" or "surely" (Gen. 18:20; 1 Sam. 14:44), which could be its sense at the beginning of 3:6, and often it has the meaning "since" or "if" at the outset of conditional sentences, which I judge to be its actual semantic value in 3:6. The issues of the fifth disputation are certainly related to those of the fourth (and second and third as well), but the connection of 3:6–7 to 2:17–3:5 is a matter of topic rather than form.

The basic structure of this disputation once again follows the four-part pattern of the others in the book (i.e., assertion, objection, response, and implication). As in the second disputation (1:6–7), the assertion and objection part of the format is presented via two assertion–objection sequences rather than just one. The passage may be outlined as follows:

6–7a Assertion by Yahweh
The people that have turned away must return to Yahweh
7b Questioning by Israel ("How can we return?")
8a Assertion (more specific) by Yahweh "Should a human being rob God? You are certainly robbing me!"
Questioning by Israel ("How are we robbing you?")
8b Response ("Tithes and offerings!")

9–12 Implication
The robbery takes the form of slighting tithes. But if God receives his due he will in turn grant such abundance to Israel that they will be blessed and famous for it.

Wendland ("Linear and Concentric Patterns," pp. 118–19) sees in this disputation a seven-part concentric structure (A-B-C-D-C'-B'-A'), which he describes via the following outline:

a Introduction: a divine premise (v. 6)
b Appeal—repent:
  i) stated negatively: "you have not turned away from my statutes" (7a)
  ii) stated positively: "return to me" (7b)
c Indictment: "you have robbed me" (8)
d Verdict: CURSE! (9a)
c' Indictment: you are robbing me" (9b)
b' Promise—blessings upon those who repent:
  i) stated positively: an overflowing harvest (10)
  ii) stated negatively: protection from calamity (11)
a' Conclusion: a Messianic vision

While this analysis has some merit, in that it identifies certain of the factors that provide relative balance to the passage, it is also misleading, because it suggests an obvious, purposeful chiastic structure when none is really present. Malachi's audience would not have perceived the fifth disputation as chiastic. They would not have seen the appeal of verse 7a as symmetrically complemented by the promise of verses 10 and 11 (there is nothing particularly natural about these two elements as a poetic pair); they would not have viewed a promise of protection (v. 11) as something "stated negatively" (thus they would have missed Wendland's negative/positive/positive/negative pattern so apparently impressive in his diagram but invisible in the original); they would

ically retrospective context is best translated by the English perfect (I have not changed) rather than the present (I do not change). לֹא כְלִיתֶם (you have not been destroyed): Van Hoonacker's proposal to emend the pointing of this verb to the piel (which could mean "you do not stop") has been followed by some commentators on the theory that the idea of the verse ought to be that Israel keeps on sinning just as Yahweh keeps on being consistent. The only virtue of this proposal is that

not have considered a "divine premise" (v. 6) as brought to a conclusion by "a messianic vision" (v. 12); they would not have necessarily identified verse 12 as a messianic vision at any rate; nor would they have automatically understood verse 9 as the centerpiece of the oracle (by a better analysis, v. 9 functions as the premise to the implication section, stating the current situation of curse as a motive for seeking blessing instead). In other words, Malachi's audience would have considered the rhetorical disputation format that governs the passage the sole and sufficient overall structural device for this oracle. We must as well.

Again Malachi has employed his characteristic hallmark, vocabulary repetition for clarity as well as emphasis. The term rob (qbᶜ, vv. 8, 9) occurs four times. One term, return (šûb, v. 7) occurs three times. The following terms occur twice: you say (ʾămartem, vv. 7, 8); how? (bammeh, vv. 7, 8); curse (ʾrr, v. 9); tithe (maᶜăśēr, vv. 8, 10); house (bayît, v. 10); people (gôy, vv. 9, 12). Two other words are especially strongly represented in the passage: to/for you (ʾălēkem or lākem, six times in vv. 7, 10, 11, 12) and all (kol, vv. 9, 10, 12; cf. the partial homonym destroy/eliminate [klh] in v. 6, though whether this, too, could have been detected by the audience is uncertain). In all, this amounts to a modest degree of vocabulary repetition compared to Malachi's other disputations, but a high degree compared to Old Testament prophetic oracles in general.

At the end of the disputation, the reader is struck by a clause structure that governs the final seven clauses of the passage, from the end of verse 10 through the end of verse 12. This pattern is characterized by the following order: a verb, followed by a second-person element (lākem, or ʾelêkem, to you; ʾetkem, you; or ʾattem, you), followed by any other parts of speech necessary to conclude the clause. Thus verses 10–12 are closely linked stylistically.

There is nothing in this disputation to indicate its specific date or provenance. Mention is made of the general state of economic depression that afflicted the postexilic community (v. 9, interpreted in light of vv. 10–12) but this kind of economic distress was present as early as Haggai's prophecies (520 B.C.; Hag. 1:6; 2:16–19) and after Malachi in the days of Nehemiah (444 B.C.; Neh. 1:3; 2:3, 17; 4:2;

5:1–5; 9:36–37) as well. The concern for tithing was also a major concern of Nehemiah (444 B.C. and thereafter; e.g., Neh. 10:37–39; 12:44; 13:5, 10–13), and indeed it is one of the several factors linking Malachi to the Ezra–Nehemiah era (see the Introduction). The concern for Israel's status among the nations (v. 12) is consistent with that reflected in the first disputation (1:2–5).

In accordance with the overall chiastic structure of the Book of Malachi, in which the disputations are arranged in a loosely concentric pattern (see the Introduction), the fifth disputation is relatively closer in theme to the second disputation than to any of the others. Both call for proper offerings in obedience to the law of God. The major similarities of theme and vocabulary can be expressed as follows:

1:6–2:9	3:6–12
Inadequate offerings	Inadequate offerings
Temple (1:10)	My house (3:10)
The nations (1:11, 14)	The nations (3:12)
Cheat (1:14)	Rob (3:8, 9)
Curse (1:14; 2:1–2)	Curse (3:9)
Blessing (2:2)	Blessing (3:10, 12)
Decimation [threatened] (2:3)	Decimation [forestalled] (3:6)
Appeal to patriarchal age (2:4–6)	Appeal to patriarchal age (3:6–7)
Covenant, law (2:4–6, 9)	My decrees (3:7)

In spite of these connections, the fifth disputation is a very different oracle from the second. The second focuses on the priests; the fifth does not even mention them. The second warns of the turning of blessings into curses; the fifth promises blessing instead of curse. The second is about the inadequate quality of animal offerings; the fifth about the inadequate quantity of tithes. The second warns the priests of judgment for disobedience, the fifth invites the nation to obey and witness the generous benefits of obedience. The second is about worship; the fifth is about temple support.

Aside from parts of verses 6–8, which contain poetry, the oracle appears to be mainly prosaic in structure.

it tries to do justice to the parallelism of the verse by construing it as synonymous (see the Exposition). The disadvantage is that it does injustice to the point of the passage as a whole and at the same time ignores the fact that a conditional sentence can be just as strictly parallelistic as a standard compound sentence, and so-called synthetic parallelism just as complementary as synonymous or antithetical parallelism.

7a. לְמִימֵי (since the days of): This is a contracted compound of two prepositions plus the construct of the Hebrew word for "days" (לְ + מִן +

---

6. This verse is a fully complementary poetic couplet, with each part of speech paralleled precisely between the two lines of the couplet:

kî	ʾănî	yhwh	lōʾ	šānîtî
since	I,	Yahweh,	have not	changed,

wĕ-ʾattem	bĕnê-yaʿăqōb	lōʾ	kĕlîtem
so you,	children of Jacob,	have not	been destroyed.

Malachi's audience would surely have appreciated this as an epigrammatic way, in an otherwise largely prose oracle, of stating a thesis. This thesis is one of the basic themes of Scripture: God's faithfulness contrasted with the chronic unfaithfulness of his people. Old Testament history, as recorded by the narratives from Genesis to Nehemiah, is much dominated by the tragic fact that Israel failed to live up to the divine standards and practice in its covenant relationship with Yahweh. The fact of this contrast, however, does not mean that the parallelism of the couplet is antithetical, as if the essential statement of the second line contrasted with the essential statement of the first (though some scholars have taken it this way: e.g., "Indeed I Yahweh to not change // but you, children of Jacob . . ."). The parallelism is in fact of the sort called "synthetic," in which the first line of the couplet is only part of a sentence, which is completed by the second line. (On the utility and limitations of the classical terminology for Hebrew parallelism, see Geller, *Parallelism in Early Biblical Poetry*).

It would not be advisable to attach any special significance to the use of the term "children of Jacob" (bĕnê-yaʿăqōb) in this verse rather than the more common "children of Israel"/"Israelites" (bĕnê-yisraʾel). "Jacob" is certainly used by the prophets routinely as an alternative way of indicating "Israel" (as in Mal. 1:2), and "Jacob" and "Israel" occur together in either strict poetic parallel or prose complementation eighty times in the Old Testament. The present phrase "children

of Jacob" is found sixteen times in the Old Testament, sometimes in contexts that seem to emphasize the earliest Israelites, the patriarchs (as, e.g., in 1 Kings 18:31; 2 Kings 17:34; 1 Chron. 16:3), but at other times in contexts that employ the phrase as nothing more than a way of talking about Israel (e.g., Ps. 22:24 [23], where it is used in parallel to "children of Israel"; or Ps. 105:6, where it is used in parallel to "seed of Abraham").

What the verse does emphasize is the grace of God. Israel deserved destruction for its long history of breaking the covenant, but instead it had not been destroyed. Why? Because God hadn't changed. Obviously, something about his immutable nature, yet unstated, is the basis for his not destroying his chronically rebellious people long before this. In the remainder of the disputation the reason becomes overt: Yahweh is a blessing God, a forgiving, merciful God. This fact should have been well known to anyone in Malachi's audience who knew the Scriptures and /or the ancient confessions, since it was part of the famous confessions of Israel (Exod. 34:6; Num. 14:18; Neh. 9:17; Pss. 86:15; 103:8; 145:8; Jon. 4:2; Nah. 1:3). At this point in the disputation it leads nicely into the charge of covenant breaking (v. 7) by reminding the Israelites of the severity of what they have done. They are committers of acts that deserve the national application of the death penalty ("you are not destroyed") but it has not been applied only because God's unchanging nature allows him to forgive what deserves to be punished ("I have not changed"). The unchangeableness of God gives foundation to both the truth of Scripture and the promise of eternal life (see 1 Sam. 15:29; Ps. 110:4; Jer. 4:28; 15:6; 20:16; Lam. 3:22–23; Ezek. 24:14; Hos. 11:8–9; 13:14; Zech. 8:14; Jas. 1:17; Heb. 13:8).

7a. The theme of change of direction (turning away and returning) structures the language of this verse. The unchanging God is willing to forgive the changeable people who have broken his covenant if they will repent and return to him (restoration blessing type 1, renewal of Yahweh's favor/loyalty/presence). But their whole history as a people ("since the days of your ancestors") has been characterized by rebellion against his cove-

יְמֵי) Aside from its unusual form, it presents no difficulties in translation. וְלֹא שְׁמַרְתֶּם (and you have not kept them): The object of the verb (them) is understood rather than expressed in the Hebrew. This is a common feature of Hebrew grammar and it is by no means necessary to supply an object for the verb, such as the commonly suggested מִשְׁמַרְתִּי (my command), based on its presence in a similar expression in verse 14.

nant stipulations ("my statutes," *ḥūqqay*) from which they have departed. The charge that the present sins of the people reflect a long history of rebellion against God, and are not just problems of the current generation, is something that the prophets in general point out often (Isa. 65:7; Jer. 2:5; 3:25; 9:13 [14]; 14:20; 23:27; 34:14; 44:9; Lam. 5:7; Ezek. 2:3; Hos. 10:1–2, 9; 11:1–2; 13:4–6; etc.) and that Malachi has already been inspired to declare in various ways (2:4–10; 3:4).

V. Fifth Disputation (3:6–12)
B. The People Can Return to God by Restoring to Him Their Tithes and Offerings (3:7b–12)

STUART

Return to me, and I will return to you (Yahweh of the Armies said). But you say, "How are we to return?"

⁸Should a human rob God? Yet you are robbing me.

But you say, "How are we robbing you?"

Tithes and offerings! ⁹You have been cursed, yet it is I you are robbing—the whole nation! ¹⁰Bring the whole tithe into the storehouse, so that there may be nourishment in my house. Test me in this (Yahweh of the Armies said), and see if I will not open the windows of heaven and pour out for you a blessing that is beyond containing. ¹¹I will cut off the crop-eating insects so that they will not destroy your produce, and the vines in your fields will not fail to bear (Yahweh of the Armies said). ¹²All the nations will call you blessed, because you will be a delightful country (Yahweh of the Armies said).

NRSV

Return to me, and I will return to you, says the LORD of hosts. But you say, "How shall we return?"

⁸Will anyone rob God? Yet you are robbing me. But you say, "How are we robbing you?" In your tithes and offerings! ⁹You are cursed with a curse, for you are robbing me—the whole nation of you! ¹⁰Bring the full tithe into the storehouse, so that there may be food in my house, and thus put me to the test, says the LORD of hosts; see if I will not open the windows of heaven for you and pour down for you an overflowing blessing. ¹¹I will rebuke the locust for you, so that it will not destroy the produce of your soil; and your vine in the field shall not be barren, says the LORD of hosts. ¹²Then all nations will count you happy, for you will be a land of delight, says the LORD of hosts.

7b. The verb שׁוּב (turn, return), which occurs here three times, is a major theological term in the Old Testament (see Holladay, *Root Šûbh in the Old Testament*) that frequently means "convert" and sometimes functions as the Old Testament equivalent of New Testament μετανοέω (repent). Some commentators have suggested eliminating וַאֲמַרְתֶּם בַּמֶּה נָשׁוּב (You say, "How should we return?") as an interpolation that disrupts the flow of the passage since it is a question that does not receive an answer. In fact, it does receive an answer, which is found both in what has been said already (returning means keeping God's decrees and laws) and what is about to be said (returning means supporting the work of God via tithes).

8. הֲיִקְבַּע אָדָם אֱלֹהִים (should a human rob God?): The Septuagint has εἰ πτερνιεῖ (should . . . insult/deceive) as if the verb here and in the two other times it occurs in the verse were עקב (trick, etc.)

7b. Yahweh tells his people that if they will return to him he will return to them. Does this mean God had left them? Yes, it means precisely that. Divine rejection was one of the covenant curses (type 1; Lev. 26:28, "I will be hostile toward you"; Deut. 31:17, "I will . . . forsake them, I will hide my face from them . . . because our God is not with us"; Deut. 32:19, "Yahweh . . . rejected them"). This divine rejection is part of what verse 9 alludes to when it states that the nation is under a curse. As a covenant-breaking nation, Israel had been relegated to the miseries that people not under Yahweh's protection had to endure. He was not blessing them as their Sovereign would if they had been obedient to the statutes of his covenant. Why, then, were they not destroyed if he had abandoned them?

We must remember that within history, prior to the final judgment, God's abandonment does not mean death or destruction, the withdrawal of his common grace, or the nullification of his omnipresence. In this life God's rejection may in fact not even be noticed by people whose values and practices are sufficiently corrupted that they cannot see any difference between a world with and a world without God. Malachi's Israelite contemporaries lived under difficult conditions, but were for the most part (there were many exceptions, of course) unaware that their hardships were the result of their unfaithfulness to the Mosaic covenant. Various ones among them undoubtedly assumed that Yahweh was ineffective, or limited in his power (1:5), or distracted, or some such thing. Many compromised their religious loyalties by their own personal situations (3:5), including divorce and intermarriage (2:10–16). Others were engaged in the full-blown worship of foreign gods (2:11) or worship of Yahweh by pagan means (2:12–13). Their actions had brought upon them the curse of divine rejection, so that Yahweh had turned from them. But he was willing to turn again toward them if they would do the same to him. What would be required on their part? Repentance of all actions inconsistent with his covenant, which demanded that he be the only God (Exod. 20:3–6; Deut. 5:7–8). In other words, the inadequate worship attacked in the second disputation, the infidelities attacked in the third, the serious societal sins attacked in the fourth—all would have to change. Through Malachi, God is asking them to "turn" (*sûb*), using the term most commonly employed by the prophets in describing repentance and conversion (Jer. 3:22; 4:1; 5:3; 8:4–5; 18:7–10; Ezek. 3:17–21; 14:7; 17:21–32; Joel 2:12–14; Zeph. 2:3 and especially 2:7, 9 [9, 11]; 3:5; 5:4; 6:1; 7:10; 11:5; 12:6 [12:7]; 14:1–2 [2–3]; etc. cf. Deut. 4:30; 30:2–3, 8–10).

But they didn't know what was involved in repentance, and thus asked, "How are we to return?" Their words, yet another brief attributive verbal summary of the prevailing national attitude (1:2, 6, 7, 12, 13; 2:14, 17), suggest that they are either puzzled as to the means of repentance, or else pessimistic that it can be accomplished, or both. It is not possible from the grammar of the Hebrew text to tell, and the ambiguity may be purposeful. Perhaps the best way to indicate what is happening at this point in the disputation is to paraphrase what the people are saying as: "What are we supposed to do?" The answer comes in terms of a major, symptomatic issue—tithing—in the following verses. Tithing was not all that they needed to do, by any means, as the rest of Malachi's preaching clearly indicates, but it would serve as a parade example of what returning to Yahweh would entail. God's turning to them would bring the kinds of blessings sampled in verses 10–12.

8. This verse states that the Israelites were robbing God, and in answer to the question of how it states that that this robbery occurred in connection with tithes and offerings. It must not be forgotten that verse 8, in addition to introducing the topic of the tithe that will now dominate the following verses, is itself also an answer to the ques-

rather than קבע (rob). The Septaugint reading could reflect a different Hebrew *Vorlage,* but it could also reflect ignorance on the part of the Septuagint translator(s): they may have guessed that קבע, a relatively rare verb whose meaning they were probably unsure of, was related in meaning to עקב. Some commentators have even suggested that the verb is a purposeful artificial metathesis to avoid reading the consonants היעקב in the first word, which then might mean "Is Jacob [a man, a god]?" But this takes insufficient account of the normalcy of the verb קבע (rob; Prov. 22:23) and of the context, which is about keeping wealth from God, or robbing him. Other commentators have concluded that the original verb was עקב, intended as a paronomasia with the name of Jacob in verse 6 but garbled by miscopying at a later stage. If this were intended as a paronomasia, it is a miserable failure. For a paronomasia to work it has to be obvious to the listener. Homophones so widely separated from one another as עקב in verse 6 is split from the posited uses of עקב in verse 8 are simply not what a listener would catch aurally. With regard to the Hebrew imperfect verb form in the first word of the verse, it has several possible modal meanings and thus any of the fol-

lowing translations of the verb in this clause might be defended: will . . . rob, can . . . rob, would . . . rob, may . . . rob, might . . . rob. For אָדָם (human, i.e., human being as contrasted to God or animals) the Revised Standard Version uses "man" ("Will man rob God?") acceptably; the New International Version uses "a man" misleadingly as if any individual were involved. The New Revised Standard Version ("Will anyone rob God") is even more misleading, stemming awkwardly from the desire to be politically correct and avoid the word "human," which contains the word "man" and thus offends radical feminists. The question is not about "anyone" robbing God; the concept "anyone" would be expressed by Hebrew אִישׁ in such a case. It is about the outrageous presumption involved in the idea that *human beings* could think themselves justified in stealing from their own Creator. הַמַּעֲשֵׂר וְהַתְּרוּמָה (tithes and offerings!; lit., the tithe and the offering): Grammatically, this expression appears to be a simple exclamation. Several ancient versions (Syriac, Targum, Vulgate) add what appears to be a clarifying preposition at the beginning of this two-word phrase ("In/by tithes and offerings!"), while the Septuagint has an entire clause of explanation: ὅτι . . . μεθ-

---

tion posed in verse 7, "How are we to return?" In effect the answer may be paraphrased: "by not robbing me any more, as you have been doing, by not giving me proper tithes and offerings!"

Four questions may be asked here: (1) How is not paying a tithe a form of robbery? (2) What is the difference between a tithe (*maʿăśēr*) and an offering (*tĕrûmâ*)? (3) Was Malachi's audience really being told that tithing was central to repentance? (4) If Christians do not tithe, are they also robbing God?

The answer to the first question comes via understanding the biblical doctrine that "the earth is the Lord's and the fulness thereof" (Ps. 24:1; see also Ps. 50:12) and that, covenantally, all wealth of any kind is God's in its entirety (Exod. 19:5, "all the earth is mine"; Lev. 20:26, "all Israel is mine"; Lev. 25:23, "all the land is mine"), and that his people never own it, but only possess it (or "handle" it) temporarily (this is particularly emphasized with the firstfruits and tithes: Exod. 13:2; 34:19; Lev. 27:30, 32; Num. 8:17). On the concept that offerings are being brought to their owner rather than given by their owners, see the Exposition of 1:12–14. Thus, if God owns the tithe in the first place, and has clearly stated in his covenant law that he expects it to be given over to

him at the appropriate times of the year, withholding it is robbery. Taking something and keeping it from its owner is robbery.

The answer to the second question is somewhat less certain. There are two options. It is quite possible that Malachi 3:8 ends with two terms, *tithe* and *offering,* as a way of encompassing all gifts to the Lord, so that the general responsibility of temple and worship support will be understood as a covenant obligation. To be sure, the following verses then concentrate on the tithe per se, but all offering is meant to be included in the general principle. On the other hand, it is possible that *tĕrûmâ* (offering) is intended in a more technical sense, that of Numbers 18:16. There the Levites are told that they are the ones who receive the tithe, and that they themselves must then also tithe, that is, give a tithe of the tithe, which is called *tĕrûmat yhwh* (the Lord's offering). By this definition, "tithe and offering" (*maʿăśēr wĕhattĕrûmâ*) may be a way of saying "everything that the Levites are supposed to get." However, in light of the dozens of uses of *tĕrûmâ* throughout the Old Testament to refer to all sorts of offerings, and in the absence of any contextual indication to the contrary, it would seem likely that we ought to assume that "offerings in general" is what

ὑμῶν εἰσιν (because [the tithes and offerings] are with you). Did the Septuagint read from a Hebrew *Vorlage* that contained another word (עִמָּכֶם, "with you," or the like) that was more original than the Masoretic Text, or did the Septuagint simply make sense of a laconic Hebrew text by adding an explanatory set of words? What helps us answer that question is the presence of yet another terse exclamation in the following verse (הַגּוֹי כֻּלּוֹ, the whole nation!). That one is not textually problematic, and its existence gives credibility to the conclusion that God's words in this verse are also an unadorned exclamation in the original. I conclude that the Septuagint was at this point translating expansionistically for sense rather than for literalness, and that the Masoretic Text preserves the original wording.

9. בַּמְּאֵרָה אַתֶּם נֵאָרִים (you are cursed): The translation sometimes provided for these words, "you are cursed with a curse," is abnormal English, produced by failure to appreciate the resumptive style common to Hebrew. The Septuagint (ἀποβλέποντες ὑμεῖς ἀποβλέπτε, "you cer-

tainly look away from me") mistakenly reads the verb רָאָה (see) rather than the verb אָרַר (curse) here, probably because the niphal of אָרַר (curse) is so very rare, occurring only here in the Old Testament. וְאֹתִי אַתֶּם קֹבְעִים (yet it is I you are robbing!): The initial position of the object pronoun in the clause indicates that it is emphasized, as in my translation. The וְ is rendered "yet" according to the demands of the Hebrew parataxis in context. Continuing action (you are robbing) is suggested by the use of the present participle קֹבְעִים. הַגּוֹי כֻּלּוֹ (the whole nation!): This exclamation is taken two main ways in the Septuagint traditions: either τὸ ἔθνος συνετελέσθη (the nation is finished) or τὸ ἔτος συνετελέσθη (the year is completed). The former would appear to support the consonantal Masoretic Text, or perhaps a slight corruption thereof, that is, הַגּוֹי כָּלָה. The wording containing τὸ ἔτος (the year) is probably the result of an inner-Greek corruption. Because גּוֹי (nation) is often used in the Old Testament, mainly in the plural, to refer to "the nations" who are not under God's covenant, it has become a commonplace in Old

---

těrûmâ means, and that *maʿăśēr* means more specifically the obligation to give a tenth of one's income to Yahweh annually.

The third question must be answered affirmatively. Tithing is central to covenant obedience and without covenant obedience no conversion has occurred. On this, see further below.

The fourth question has been answered by the apostle Paul in 2 Corinthians 9:6–7. Tithing per se is not a Christian requirement, not a stipulation of the New Covenant. But financial giving positively is. And there is a connection between generosity and reward, says the apostle, just as Malachi 3:8–12 also implies. Giving is one of the five aspects of Christian worship (prayer, praise, giving, hearing the word and communion), and Christian worship is the basic, initial, and permanent response of the believer to God.

9. Three points are made here: (1) the nation is under a curse (type 26, general punishment/curse/vengeance); (2) this curse results from robbing God; (3) the robbing is a general practice, not something isolated.

The fact that God has cursed his people recalls language found in the second disputation: 1:14 ("cursed is the cheater who has a male in his flock and vows to give it, but then sacrifices a defective animal to the LORD") and 2:2 ("If you don't listen, and if you are not zealous to honor my name, [said Yahweh of the Armies] I will send a curse upon

you, and I will curse your blessing. Yes, I am cursing it, because you have not been zealous"). This emphasis on curse is, of course, one of the several linkages between the fifth and second disputations. Here it is clear, however, that not only those who cheat (1:14) or the priests who offer faulty offerings (2:2) are under a curse. Now the entire nation is indicted, via the closing exclamation of the verse ("the whole nation!").

Since this nationwide condemnation concerns tithing, whereas the more specific condemnations (cheaters and allied priests) in the second disputation concerned the offering of low-quality animals, does this indicate that a higher percentage of the people were skimping on tithes than were participating in the bad animal offering scheme? It might. We can easily imagine how hard it must have been for all Judeans, whose economic conditions were far from ideal in the mid-fifth century B.C., to bring themselves to fulfill the tithing law in its entirety. The animal quality rules pertaining to the second disputation might well have been more often obeyed than the tithe law. After all, animals brought for sacrifice were always subject to inspection, no matter how corrupt the inspection practice may have become, so one would assume that not all the animals brought were of poor quality, but only a significant percentage. By contrast, tithing was a much harder thing to enforce. An individual's

Testament scholarship to suggest that whenever one sees גוֹי used of Israel instead of the more common עַם (people, nation) it should be assumed that a critical, pejorative attitude toward the nation is indicated. This is simply not true. In fact, גוֹי is used positively of Israel in all sorts of contexts, including the patriarchal promises (Gen. 15:14; 17:20; 18:18; 21:13, 18; 46:3) as well as a large variety of miscellaneous texts (Exod. 19:6; 32:10; Num. 14:12; Deut. 9:14; 26:5; Josh. 3:17; 5:6–8; Isa. 9:2 [3]; 26:2, 15; etc.). גוֹי is an essentially neutral term, whether or not applied, as here, to Israel and its use should never be seen as signaling a condemnatory attitude.

10. הָבִיאוּ (bring): The Septuagint took this verb not as the imperative but as a perfect, and translated καὶ εἰσηνέγκατε (and you have brought), which surely does injustice to the context, but follows on the Septuagint confusion over the end of verse 9 (LXX: The year is finished [and you have brought . . .]). With the other ancient versions I read without hesitation the Masoretic Text. בֵּית הָאוֹצָר (the storehouse) is one of several terms used for the many chambers in the temple complex where food and other valuables were stored (Lev. 27:30; 1 Kings 7:51; 2 Kings 12:19 [18]; 1 Chron. 9:26; 26:2–26; 28:11; 2 Chron. 5:1; Neh. 10:39 [38]; 13:12). וִיהִי (so that there may be): The וְ plus

---

actual income was a more private matter, and certainly not one that the priests would have actual jurisdiction to determine.

Who would know, when a person brought his or her "tithes" to the temple, if they really represented a tenth of that person's income? Any fellow Israelite or honest (or dishonest) priest could tell at a glance whether a sacrificial animal was fit for the altar, and surely people looked at each other's animals as they entered the temple area and waited in line for the priestly inspection. But evaluating the degree to which one's neighbor's wagon or pack animals were actually carrying a full tenth of his or her income—that was much more difficult to determine, especially if it was not brought all at once, but in repeated trips, or brought in various portions at the various festivals throughout the year.

On the other hand, the Bible does not contain any ranking of sins, or even categorization of sins into groups such as the medieval notion of mortal and venal sins (on 1 John 5:16–17, consult the commentaries). And the covenant curses are not designated according to type or severity of sin. Moreover, if God chooses in this disputation to stress through his prophet the fact that the whole nation is under a curse, that does not mean that it is only because of the tithing problem. There can be no doubt that he demands that his entire covenant be kept, and does not consider tithing the sum total of the law. Thus we cannot conclude that disobedience in the matter of tithing brings a curse on the whole nation whereas other sins affect only individuals or special groups within the nation. In this verse failure to tithe is described as a direct sin against God himself ("it is I you are robbing"), but not because the people's other sins were less severe or did not offend God. It is simply that they needed to realize that

skimping on tithes—easy to do and difficult for others to prove—is in fact a form of stealing from God, and cannot go unpunished.

10. Six general observations are appropriate in connection with this important verse: (1) It does not constitute a promise that individual believers become prosperous if they tithe. (2) Partial tithing is a contradiction in terms. (3) God here subjects himself to testing, but not of the sort prohibited elsewhere as ungodly. (4) Malachi was not a narrow ritualist who valued preservation of the cultus over moral living. (5) The actual kind of blessing promised is a combination of abundant rain and freedom from crop pests, used as a synecdoche for restoration blessings of all sorts. (6) There is an eschatological overtone to the promise.

The verse is a combination of command and promise. It begins with imperatives and concludes with conditional imperfects describing what can happen if the command is obeyed. While it is clear from the rest of the book that God wants his entire covenant to be kept, this verse brings the focus down to one key, symptomatic stipulation: tithing. If the nation complied with the tithing laws, God would bless it abundantly. The promise is, however, corporate, not individual, as are virtually all Old Covenant promises of abundance. No person or family can assume from this oracle that they will get rich from tithing. The nation as a whole can expect, however, to have more than enough food to go around, if it will practice, as a nation, across the board, tithing.

The tithing laws (mainly found in Lev. 27:30–33; Num. 18:21–28; Deut. 12:6–17; 14:22–28; 26:12–14) were not voluntary guidelines. They constituted a compulsory system, and set forward a minimum expectation of 10 percent of one's income being paid to the temple for support of priests, Levites, temple singers and servants, and

imperfect (jussive) is best understood as introducing a result clause, for which the modal "that there may be" is the most natural English rendering. מֶרֶף (nourishment): While the more common meaning is "prey" or "carrion," the term can mean simply nourishment (Ps. 111:5; Prov. 31:15), thus obviating Brichto's notion that this verse describes a situation in which the temple ("my house") was getting putrid food while the average individual's barn (what Brichto concludes "storehouse" refers to) was getting the tithe that should have gone to the temple (*Problem of "Curse,"* p. 105). בְּבֵיתִי (in my house): The Septuagint has ἐν τῷ οἴκῳ αὐτοῦ (in its house), presumably thinking of the food in its warehouse rather than the temple. נָא: Contrary to some commentators, the

for supplies and maintenance. Israel's proper worship (in contrast to the fact that most of its worship for most of its history was improper) was centralized and required substantial financing to provide for the support of the tribe of Levi as well as the costs of the temple. The Levites constituted roughly one-twelfth of the population of the nation, and therefore required roughly 8.3 percent of the nation's income if they were to be fully supported by tithes. Adding to this the cost of operating and maintaining the temple meant that approximately 10 percent of the nation's wealth would be needed for a full worship system to prosper. Nine percent wouldn't do, nor would any other number short of the full tenth. Less than the tithe was unacceptable. By definition, a partial tithe is not a tithe at all. Contributions above the tenth (as from freewill offerings and the like) were welcome, and all to the good, but contributions short of the tenth represented a kind of a starving of the nation's worship, as well as a starving of the Levites out of employment. Deep concern for the support of proper worship is manifested also in Ezra and Nehemiah, where considerable attention is given to the restoration of the role of the Levites in the life of the postexilic nation, as well as the proper functioning of the sacerdotal subsection of the Levites, the priests (Ezra 8:24–36; Neh. 10:31–32, 38–40 [32–33, 37–39]; 12:1–26; 13:10–13).

God's command, "test me in this," has several parallels elsewhere in the Old Testament. God sometimes invited testing of his willingness to aid his people when their faith might be weak. Moses was commanded to watch his staff become a snake and his hand turn white as a sign of God's power (Exod. 4:1–9). At God's command Elijah arranged the famous contest of divine response to prayer on Mount Carmel in which the prophets of Baal were humiliated (1 Kings 18:22–39). The promise of the virgin birth was part of a sign to Ahaz urged on him by Yahweh (Isa. 7:10–17). In a similar vein, the psalmist invites, "taste and see that Yahweh is good" (Ps. 34:8), and Acts 17:11 commends the Bereans for examining the Scriptures to see whether Paul's preaching was accurate. This proper testing, in which an individual or group investigates the truth, is hardly the same as the attitude of testing that demands that God show off to prove his existence or verify his word (Judg. 6:36–40; Matt. 12:38–39; John 4:48; 6:30). Deuteronomy 6:16 warns against this sinful kind of testing: "You shall not put Yahweh your God to the test as you tested him at Massah"; 1 Corinthians 10:9 reminds: we must not put the Lord to the test as some of them did, and were destroyed by serpents. For God to invite investigation or action that will confirm his promises is a gateway to blessing; for people to demand that God prove himself true is a door to sin.

Because Malachi's prophecy here again concerns the support of the temple and its priests and Levites, some scholars have concluded that this verse reveals yet further the extent of Malachi's preoccupation with the Yahwistic cultus, rather than nobler matters of personal and corporate ethics. This criticism comes largely from the liberal Protestant view that worship is relatively unimportant and social equality is the highest goal of religion. Inasmuch as this view sharply distorts the biblical message, it cannot appreciate the significance of the role of worship in a believer's relationship to God both in this life and the life to come, and thus cannot, of course, appreciate the message of this fifth disputation as fully consistent with the emphases of the rest of scriptural revelation.

What does "I will open the windows of heaven and pour out for you a blessing" mean? Surely it refers to rain, the key to agricultural prosperity at virtually all times and places in the history of the world. Language related to the "windows of heaven" and similar concepts of atmospheric water is common in the Old Testament as a way of indicating abundant rain (Gen. 7:11–12; Isa. 24:18) or lack thereof when the sky is "shut" (1 Kings 8:35–36; 2 Chron. 6:26). Compare Hebrews 6:7, "For land which has drunk the rain that often falls upon it, and brings forth vegetation useful to those for whose sake it is cultivated, receives a blessing from God " and especially

Hebrew נָא after "test me" has no softening or gentling force. It is merely an optional imperative marker and does not mean "please" or the like. עַד־בְּלִי־דָי (that is beyond containing): Literally the Hebrew says "up to not sufficiency," which is best conveyed by the translation I have given.

11. וְגָעַרְתִּי (I will cut off): On the definition of "cut off" rather than the less likely "rebuke" for this word, see the Exegesis of 2:3. אֹכֵל (crop-eating insects, lit., eater): Since this term is never used of locusts in the Old Testament—and many terms for locusts are employed (see Joel 1:4)—it must be understood to refer more generally to crop pests (NEB, NIV) as opposed to merely "the locust" (NRSV). וְלֹא יַשְׁחִת (so that they [lit., it] will not destroy):

Here the Septuagint has the first person (and I will not destroy), possibly by reason of taking the consonants of יַשְׁחֵת as a first-person (converted) perfect form and assuming that the root (יׁשח) would have roughly the same meaning as שׁחת (cf. יֶשַׁח, dung). At any rate, the third person form of the Masoretic Text is clearly preferable in the context.

12. This verse is free of textual or grammatical problems. The two clauses of the verse complete the pattern established at the end of verse 10, and carrying through verse 11, of a verb followed by a second-person element, followed by other parts of speech, typically objects. Thus verses 10b–12 are closely linked stylistically. אֶרֶץ חֵפֶץ (delightful

---

Deuteronomy 11:13–14, "If you faithfully obey the commands I am giving you today . . . then I will send rain on your land in its season, both autumn and spring rains" (see also Joel 2:23–24; Zech. 10:1; 14:17). The promise of rain implies that Malachi and his contemporaries may have been experiencing a lack of it, which is indication of a covenant curse (type 6a; Lev. 26:19; Deut. 28:22–24).

Finally, I note the eschatological element in the promise of blessing here. Many commentators have pointed out the connection between the promise of rain in the prophets and the eventual fecundity of the promised land as measured by harvests of unprecedented bounty (Isa. 30:23–26; 44:3; Joel 2:23–27; 4:18 [3:18]; Amos 9:13; Hag. 2:18–19; Zech. 8:12; 10:1). This is restoration blessing type 5 (Lev. 26:42, "I will remember the land"; Deut. 30:9, "[you will be] prosperous . . . in the crops of your land"). In other words, what Malachi is conveying to the people is not simply that God invites them to tithe and get more rain, as if it were simply a quid pro quo arrangement for successful farming. He is inviting his covenant people to realize that if they will return to him (v. 7) and keep his covenant, he will have in store for them good things their own experience could not equal. God's words through his prophet envision something that goes beyond the limited expectations of the little Judean community to which they were first delivered.

11. The promise is continued and further specified. Abundant rain is not the sum total of what is needed for agricultural abundance (restoration blessing type 5). Absence of crop pests and crop diseases is also required. Yahweh here promises to prevent these, too, if his covenant is kept, so that his people can enjoy what their labors have been

directed toward. This kind of blessing is a reversal of the crop pest and disease curses of the Pentateuch (types 6 b–c; Deut. 28:38–39, "locusts will devour . . . worms will eat your vineyards"; Deut. 28:40, "the olives will drop off"; Deut. 28:42, "swarms of locusts will take over all your trees and the crops of your land."). It very closely parallels, in reverse, the language of Leviticus 26:20, "your soil will not yield its crops, nor will the trees of the land yield their fruit."

Agricultural abundance is such a common theme in the prophetic predictions of the new covenant age that it would be a basic mistake to miss the overtones of eschatology here. Even a word like "vine" is often used as a synecdoche for the pleasant rewards of the age to come (Mic. 4:4; Hag. 2:19; Zech. 8:12). Crop bounty is a way of signaling the favor of God and is often more symbolic than literal in the prophets (Amos 9: 13–15).

12. It must be remembered that verse 12 is part of the conditional promise of blessing that depends for its fulfillment on the obedience of Israel to the covenant. It is not an outright guarantee of blessing, no matter how the nation behaves. But if the people will indeed return to Yahweh (Mal. 3:7) in accord with the imperatives of the law (Deut. 30:1–10) then, as the law promises, he will bless them. The restoration blessings upon Israel are described in two ways in this verse: (1) it will be so impressive that the nations of the world will "call" Israel "blessed"; (2) as a country, Israel will be, to the general recognition of all, delightful. This represents a hint of restoration blessing type 1, renewal of God's favor, loyalty, and presence (Lev. 26:45; Deut. 4:31; 30:3, 9) and, clearly, type 6, restoration of general prosperity, well-being, and health (Deut. 30:3, 5, 9; 32:39). Since most restoration blessings represent at least in

country): The phrase is nonspecific as to the identity of those who would find the country delightful, and attempts by some commentators to narrow the focus are misguided. It isn't a question of whether the nations as a whole would appreciate how nice Israel would be in the eschaton, or whether Yahweh alone would do so, or whether only the Israelites and Yahweh would do so, or any such thing. The land would be delightful intrinsically, so that anyone could appreciate it.

---

part reversals of the covenant curses, it is not surprising that we find numerous references in the Old Testament to the way that the people's sin had turned their land into a place undesirable to live (fulfilling curse type 9c; Lev. 29:32–35, 43; Deut. 29:22 [23]; Jer. 12:11; Ezek. 12:19; Zech. 7:14). Now came the chance for just the opposite—righteousness producing a land that would be a joy to inhabit.

What does it mean for someone to call someone else blessed? Janzen studied the issue of the Hebrew root "to bless" (ʾšr) and concluded that it means "to magnify or extol [another] person's condition as a desirable one." Statements of blessing are almost always spoken from an inferior to a superior, or "by one who is in a less desirable situation than the one he addresses" ("Ašrê," p. 215). In other words, for the nations of the world to call Israel blessed is for them to acknowledge that God has made Israel specially favored among them and to admit, implicitly, that they wish they could be as well off as Israel. It is not just a polite, diplomatic statement that the nations are here portrayed as saying. It is an admission that Israel has become the nation to be envied. Why? Because God will have transformed Israel. The Israel of Malachi's day was a defeated little remainder state under Persian domination consisting of some of the former Judah and some of the former Benjamin, much of it still in ruins, its capital city still largely unpopulated (Neh. 11) and its people eking out a hardscrabble existence in an area of the world that no one could ever call "lush." But the future would hold for them things that they had never experienced, expressed here, as is typical in the prophets, in grand materialistic terms, though surely having their ultimate import in terms of the people's spiritual relationship to God.

At the beginning of the disputation Yahweh asserted that because of his unchangeable nature, Jacob had not been destroyed. It is God's nature to bless (Deut. 11:27; 28:8; Ps. 24:5; 2 Cor. 9:8; Eph. 1:3; Heb. 6:7) those who are obedient to him, and through Malachi the Israelites had been once again reminded of this possibility in spite of their sins.

VI. Sixth Disputation (3:13–21 [3:13–4:3])
A. The People Have Overruled God (3:13)

STUART

NRSV

[13]You have overruled me (the LORD said). You say, "What did we say against you?"

[13]You have spoken harsh words against me, says the LORD. Yet you say, "How have we spoken against you?"

13. חִזְקוּ עָלַי דִּבְרֵיכֶם (you have overruled me): Most English translations render the clause in some such manner as "you have said harsh things against me" and are thus misleading. The idiom involved (עַל + דָּבָר + חָזַק) is also found in 2 Samuel 24:4 and its parallel in 1 Chronicles 21:4, and means that the words "overcome, overpower, overrule" those to whom they are spoken, so that the opinion of the speaker(s) prevails over the opinion of the one who is spoken to. The popular English translations err in classic fashion, by translating the individual words rather than the idiomatic expression that they constitute. This opening charge (that the people have overruled God) parallels the opening charge in the prior disputation (that the people are robbing God). Of course, the people's words don't overrule God because he is weak any more than their withholding the tithe robs him because he is unable to defend himself (see the Exposition). מַה־נִּדְבַּרְנוּ (What did we say against you?): The tenor of these words is probably not neutral (i.e., not "What did we say about you?"), but the translations that render the expression "How have we criticized you?" are probably overly negative. The statement can also conceivably be translated, "What did we say

13–24. The sixth and final oracle in the Book of Malachi follows the rhetorical disputation format of the five others (see below). It combines an excoriation of the arrogance involved in ignoring the will of God with words of reassurance to the faithful among Malachi's contemporaries. The second longest of the six disputations (the longest being the second, 1:6–2:9) it addresses the nature of the coming Day of Yahweh (Day of the Lord), a feature it shares with the fourth disputation (2:17–3:5). It is important to note that the description of the Day of Yahweh here in verses 19–21 is one of the most positive in the prophets (see the Exposition of v. 19). Like the other disputations, it contains a considerable number of internal vocabulary repetitions, a feature that consistently characterizes Malachi's style and that contributes to the clarity and emphasis of the oracle. Several words occur four times: $r\check{s}^c$ (evil, wrong, wrongdoer, vv. 15, 18, 19, 21), $^c\check{s}h$ (do/make, vv. 15, 17, 19, 21), $b\check{e}n$ (son, vv. 17, 18, 24 twice), $b\bar{a}^{\text{,}}$ (come, vv. 19 twice, 23, 24), $y\hat{o}m$ (day, vv. 19 twice, 20, 23), and $yr^{\text{,}}$ (fear, vv. 16 twice, 20, 23). The following words occur three times: dbr (word/ say/ speak, vv. 13, 16), $^{\text{,}}mr$ (say, vv. 13, 14, 17, in addition to the three times it is employed in the messenger formulas), and $^{\text{,}}bd$ (do, make, vv. 17, 18 twice). The following words occur twice: $\check{s}mr$ (obey, observe, v. 14 twice), mah (what , vv. 13, 14), gam (v. 15 twice), $zed\hat{i}m$ (arrogant, vv. 15, 19), $^{\text{,}}\check{s}h$ (make, do, vv. 15, 17), $yir^{\text{,}}\check{e}$ $yhwh$ (those who fear Yahweh, v. 16), $^{\text{,}}is$ (person, man, someone, vv. 16, 17) zqr (remember, remembrance, vv. 16, 22), $\d{h}ml$ (show appreciation, spare, v. 17 twice), $\d{s}dq$ (righteous, righteousness, vv. 18, 20), swb (return, vv. 18, 24), $l\bar{e}b$ (heart, v. 24 twice), and $^{\text{,}}\check{a}b$ (father, v. 24 twice).

It is important to note that there are also a number of close vocabulary connections between this disputation and the preceding (fifth) disputation. These are summarized via the following table:

Disputation 5 (Mal. 3:6–12)	Disputation 6 (Mal. 3:13–24 [3:13–4:6])
$\check{s}mr$ (keep, obey) v. 7	$\check{s}mr$ (keep, obey) v. 14
$^{\text{,}}\check{s}r$ (call blessed) v. 12	$^{\text{,}}\check{s}r$ (call blessed) v. 15
$b\d{h}n$ (test) v. 10	$b\d{h}n$ (test) v. 15
swb (return) v. 7, three times	swb (return, do again) vv. 18, 24
$^{\text{,}}ere\d{s}$ $\d{h}\bar{e}pe\d{s}$ (delightful land) v. 12	$^{\text{,}}ere\d{s}$ . . . $\d{h}\bar{e}rem$ (land . . . destruction) v. 24

Especially significant is the way that the fifth and sixth disputations end similarly, with $^{\text{,}}ere\d{s}$ $\d{h}\bar{e}pe\d{s}$ and $^{\text{,}}ere\d{s}$ $\d{h}\bar{e}rem$ respectively. This may be one of the "catchword" connections that the structuring of the oracles was based on.

There are, moreover, vocabulary and thematic connections to most of the other oracles, notably the fourth disputation, with its similar concern for decisive divine intervention on the Day of Yahweh (2:17–3:5). These will be noted in connection with the comments on individual verses below.

The format of the sixth disputation may be outlined as follows:

3:13   Assertion by Yahweh
        ("Your words have overruled me.")
        Questioning by Israel
        ("What did we say about you? ")
14–15   Response
        Israel claims that "serving God is useless" and that "evildoers prosper."
16–24 [Eng. 3:16–4:6] Implication
        But the faithful among Malachi's contemporaries launch a covenant renewal. God promises to favor the

among ourselves against you?" emphasizing the fact that the verb is in the niphal, but this is not very idiomatic English and the addition of "among ourselves" doesn't really clarify the meaning in any useful way. Indeed, the ancient versions do not in their translation of the Hebrew include any reflex of the reciprocal "among ourselves." The point is that the people were making their decisions without considering what God wanted, as already long revealed in his covenant word and through the preaching of his prophets, and thus were overruling him. The translation "What have we said against you?" should be understood to mean something like "What have we said that you would have taken offense at?" In other words, the people are portrayed by their words as not having *consciously* set out to criticize Yahweh.

---

faithful, and the Day of Yahweh will punish the wicked and reward the righteous. If the covenant is not kept, the land will be destroyed.

The dominant speaker in this last disputation is Yahweh, as was the case with the first, second, and fifth disputations. Only the "center disputations," the third and the fourth, are characterized by a predominance of prophetic speech with God spoken about rather than doing most of the speaking. In this oracle the response section is fairly typical in its summarizing quote of the people's attitudes (vv. 14–15; cf. 2:7, 12; 2:17), a wording that we again surmise is designed to represent briefly the wide range of statements and conversations that actually would have been heard in and around Jerusalem and Judah in Malachi's time.

The implication portion of the oracle (vv. 16–24 [3:16–4:6]) begins with what appears to be a third-person narrative (perhaps the voice of the prophet) describing a movement of covenant renewal on the part of the orthodox among the people (v. 16). Nothing quite like this appears in any of the other implication sections of the various disputations, and it serves to remind us of the fact that the inspired prophet has not been straitjacketed by the format he has adhered to. The rhetorical disputation format provides the general structure for each oracle, but the content is far more important than the form and is expressed whether or not it exactly fits an idealized norm. To one extent or another this has been the case throughout the book, so that none of the oracles is a mirror image of any of the others. The "freest" part of the structure in terms of its length and the topics of its content has always been the implication section, and the final disputation is no exception.

Where does the sixth disputation end? This question has been raised repeatedly by commentators, and many have concluded that 3:22–24 [4:4–6] constitutes an epilogue of some sort, thus being distinct from any of the disputations, including the sixth. By this reasoning, those verses, containing as they do the command to obey the Mosaic law and the prediction of the coming of Elijah, are best understood as constituting an independent conclusion to the book as a whole rather than completing the sixth disputation. It is commonly argued that they are only mildly connected to the prior material, the sixth disputation, and function to summarize all of Malachi's teaching, in the command to obey the law, as well as pointing his audience toward awareness of the danger of continuing in the present course lest it bring divine judgment. For the reasons behind the contrary view, that the "epilogue" is actually the conclusion to the sixth disputation—and thereby, but not independently—to the book as a whole, see below.

Some question exists as to whether the passage contains some, or is even mostly composed in, poetry. Elliger, the editor of Malachi in the BHS, treated this disputation, and most of the book, as poetry. His arrangement of the stichometry appears almost uniformly forced, however, and in the absence of any of the classic earmarks of poetic style (clear parallelism, recognizable meter, lack of enjambment, employment of formulas, etc.), there can be no warrant for regarding this disputation as poetic. Thus the prominent modern English versions, rightly, treat the passage as prose. Glazier-McDonald presents the structure stichometrically, but her schema reveals only limited parallelism, with many occasions where any form of parallelistic concordance is missing. The most that one could reasonably argue in terms of the oracle's structure is that it is carefully worded, somewhat parallelistic prose, which that is what most prophetic prose is.

The four messenger formulas found in the passage are rather typical in number and type of those found in the other parts of the book (with the notable exception of 1:6–2:9, which is packed with messenger formulas, presumably for support in attacking the priesthood). Once ᵓāmar yhwh is employed (v. 13) and three times ᵓāmar yhwh *ṣĕbaʾôt* occurs (vv. 17, 19 [4:1] and 21 [4:3]). The fact that the final three verses lack any messenger formulas does not mean that they are to be divorced from the present disputation. Malachi 1:1–5 ends comparably, and only two of the six disputations, the fourth and fifth, actually conclude with messenger formulas (*ʾāmar yhwh ṣĕbaʾôt* in both cases). In this regard, then, as well as in others, the style of the sixth disputation is typical of the first five, reflecting the overall consistency in the book that obviates any speculation about lack of integrity or multiple authorship.

13. The assertion that the people have overruled God is remarkably parallel to the assertion of the fifth disputation that they are robbing God. Can people actually overrule God? Of course they can. God has chosen to restrain his own actual sovereignty so as to give to human beings autonomy, which they may use for or against God. If they choose to reject him, they can do so and not suffer the consequences in this life, though surely at the judgment to come. If they decide that they know better than he does (i.e., overrule him) they can act accordingly, as most of the world has always done and continues to do daily. It is not by reason of God's weakness or inability to defend himself that he can be overruled. It is by reason of his having given to humanity such an exalted status in the order of creation.

By reason of the patterns established in the prior disputations, we now expect not only a charge against the people of Judah, but a summation of what they are thinking and saying—or would say, if they could speak with one voice—in response to it. Their response, "What are we saying about/against you?" indicates that they find the charge surprising; they would not have thought of themselves as having said anything that would represent a criticism of Yahweh. This reaction, of course, sets the tone for the charges of the next verse, which characterizes the people's sense of responsibility to God as one of indifference or irrelevance. If it doesn't seem to them that their God does anything one way or the other when they ignore his law, they would naturally not understand why anything they were thinking or saying would offend him. Since they weren't talking about him at all, how could he possibly be bothered by anything they were saying?

VI. Sixth Disputation (3:13–21 [3:13–4:3])
B. The People Believe It Is Useless to Serve God (3:14–15)

STUART

¹⁴You said, "Serving God is useless. What benefit is there from Yahweh of the Armies if we keep his rules and if we go around in darkened mourning clothes? ¹⁵So now we call ungodly people blessed. Even evildoers prosper. Even when they test God they get away with it."

NRSV

¹⁴You have said, "It is vain to serve God. What do we profit by keeping his command or by going about as mourners before the LORD of hosts? ¹⁵Now we count the arrogant happy; evildoers not only prosper, but when they put God to the test they escape."

14. שָׁוְא עֲבֹד אֱלֹהִים (serving God is useless): This terse Hebrew verbless clause has the ring of a saying or proverb, as if it were something that may have been spoken often in Judah in Malachi's day, but this simply cannot be proved. The remainder of the verse is more prosaic, however. The meaning "useless" for שָׁוְא derives from its root sense of "emptiness" or "nothingness." קְדֹרַנִּית (in darkened mourning clothes; lit., darkened): The darkening of clothing to indicate mourning probably came from the dirt and ashes placed on the mourner's clothes rather than from choosing to wear black or other dark colors, but either or both may have been involved in individual cases. וּמַה־בֶּצַע . . . מִפְּנֵי יְהוָה צְבָאוֹת (What benefit is there from Yahweh of the Armies?): This clause is broken up by the two conditional clauses that intervene, but grammatically מִפְּנֵי יְהוָה צְבָאוֹת (from Yahweh of the Armies) follows on כִּי וּמַה־בֶּצַע (What benefit is there if? . . .). In other words, the meaning of the second part of the sentence is *not* "if we go around in darkened mourning clothes *before* Yahweh of the Armies," and most English translations of the clause are therefore misleading. The meaning "benefit" for בֶּצַע is a derived one, from the more literal meaning "cut" (compare English "How much is my cut?", i.e., share or profit). For similar uses of כִּי מַה־בֶּצַע, see Genesis 37:26 and Psalm 30:10 [9]. כִּי שָׁמַרְנוּ מִשְׁמַרְתּוֹ (if we keep his rules): The noun מִשְׁמַרְתּוֹ (his rules) is used here as a collective, thus translatable with the plural, as in most of the ancient versions. The terminology is essentially legal-covenantal; see its use in such contexts as Genesis 26:4–5 and Deuteronomy 11:1 in parallel to other standard legal terms for obedience to the divine command (law, instruction, statute). It often appears in contexts where the issue is fulfilling one's legal obligation, particularly in connection with priestly duties (Lev. 8:35; 18:30; 22:9; Num. 9:19, 23; 2 Chron. 13:11; Ezek. 44:1, 8, 15–16; Zech. 3:7).

---

14. Futility is the theme of this verse—and not just any futility, but the futility of faith in Yahweh! It is "useless" and of "what benefit?" to obey and worship. It is, of course, obedience and worship that are the twin pillars of true biblical religion, especially when one understands that worship is the initial evidence of faith. Mere works without faith are insufficient, and mere worship without a life that conforms to God's covenant is hypocrisy. Of course, Malachi at this point could have portrayed the people as talking more broadly about keeping the covenant and keeping the faith. Instead, he employed a technique that the prophets commonly employ in speaking of broad issues, synecdoche. The futility of obedience to Yahweh is expressed via reference to keeping his rules, a synecdoche for obeying his covenant in general. And by reference to the garb of the mourning process, Malachi touches on the topic of faith and worship. Mourning was conducted not as an end in itself, but as part of the process of appeal to God for relief from distress. In other words, mourning is a subcategory of prayer, which is itself a subcategory of worship.

No hint is given here that Malachi's contemporaries are mourning any particular thing. Rather, the futility of mourning is merely an indicator of the futility of worship. Mourning was the most abject, self-denying aspect of worship. It required going without the pleasures of life in order to call God's attention to one's plight, dressing uncomfortably, fasting, dirtying oneself, and so on. It might well be argued that if God would not notice mourning, with all its visible intensity of appeal, he would not notice anything. "Nothing makes any difference. He doesn't listen to us," is what the people are saying in effect.

We have here, then, the people's conclusion that God didn't matter in their lives, demonstrated by reference to a combination of inaction and action, somewhat similar to the concept of sins of omission and commission. If they failed to keep his covenant rules (inaction), nothing happened to them. That is, not doing what was right did not make any difference. On the other hand, mourning (action), which was a right thing to do, also did not make any difference. Nothing happened in response to an act of worship either. Thus the people's conclusion, stated at the beginning of the verse: serving God is useless.

Their conclusion was falsely based, however. It followed a line of reasoning characterized by (1) a false assumption, namely, that whatever happens to people in life is a direct result of how they behave, and (2) a false argument from silence, namely, that when God did not act in response to people's expectations, it was the result of his inability to or disinterest in doing so. The fact that these two reasoning flaws are extremely common among religious and semireligious people today gives the passage currency in spite of its antiquity. On the complaint that God did not do anything, compare the similar popular notion in Zephaniah

15. אֲנַחְנוּ מְאַשְּׁרִים (we call blessed): The subject, the people in general, has been expressed all along via suffixal pronouns, and the presence of the self-standing pronoun must not be thought to indicate that the clause is consciously disjunctive, as if the "we" represented a new or different group. The use of the self-standing pronoun with the present participle is simply an alternative to the use of an imperfect or perfect verb form containing a pronoun marker. This obviates the suggestions of commentators who have tried to argue on grammatical grounds that the separate "we" must indicate a group other than the people at large, such as the impious or the prophet's enemies. זֵדִים (ungodly people): The root meaning (zwd or zyd) may be "puffed up," "arrogant," but the usage biblically concentrates on the idea of those who are unwilling to submit themselves to God's will, thus "ungodly." Repeatedly in Scripture it is used of people who disobey God's law and practice wickedness (e.g., Pss. 19:14 [13]; 86:14; 119 [passim]; Prov. 21:24; Isa. 13:11; Jer. 43:2; Ezek. 18:27; 33:19) as the parallelism in this verse with עֹשֵׂי רִשְׁעָה (evildoers) also confirms. נִבְנוּ (prosper):

1:12, a condemnation of those "who think the Lord will do nothing, either good or bad."

15. Malachi's characterization of the people's pessimistic assessment of the usefulness of serving God continues. All three assertions in the verse make essentially the same point: God doesn't do anything when people disobey him. The first assertion (we call ungodly people blessed) can be taken either as defeatist in tone (we've resigned ourselves to admitting that ungodly people are fortunate) or even jealous (it's obvious that the ungodly are better off than we are). In either case, resentment is obvious. The people resent the fact that when they go to the trouble of keeping the covenant of God, with all its personal, social, and legal obligations, they are wasting their time. This pessimism is somewhat similar to that described in Ezekiel 13:22, which attacks the false prophets for "disheartening the righteous with your lies." Here in Malachi's time, those who ignore the covenant and live selfishly, using their money, time, energy, and intelligence for their own benefit, end up better off than those who unselfishly serve Yahweh, a dedication that leads to nothing but discouragement. At least that's the way it seems to the majority whose views the prophet is summarizing.

The second assertion (even evildoers prosper) is parallel to the first, with evildoers corresponding to ungodly and prosper corresponding to blessed. The second assertion somewhat amplifies the first in bluntly stating that doing evil is rewarded. Success is to be found not in a faithful godly life but in a life of wickedness. From the popular point of view, success attended the way of those who chose the path of evil, not the way of the righteous, the very opposite of what biblical revelation espoused (Ps. 1).

The third assertion (even when they test God they get away with it) is not so much making a new point as giving further evidence for the single general point of the verse—that people are getting away with evil. It does, however, add something to the intensity of the overall indictment, and that is the idea that people can actually go so far as to test God and suffer no consequences. Because this final clause begins with the verse's second use of "even" (gam) it is reasonable to assume that Malachi intends for this statement to indicate the most extreme behavior of all ("Why, they even go so far as to test God!").

What is the meaning of this third charge, "they test God" (bāḥănû ʾĕlōhîm), and why would such testing be regarded as even worse than the first (being ungodly) and the second (doing evil) charges? The answer comes with the realization that bḥn (test) can have, as it surely does here, the meaning "to try to provoke a reaction." In this usage, it functions much as does its synonym nsh (test), the more common verb for testing/tempting/trying God. Testing God, under this definition, means doing something with the purposeful, calculated intent to force God to respond. This meaning of bḥn is actually quite close to that of bḥn in 3:10, where God says, "test me," that is, "do something to make me respond." When God invites such testing, it is not sin. When he tests humans to see if they will respond faithfully, it is also not sin (Gen. 22:1; Exod. 15:25; 20:20; Deut. 8:2, 16; 13:4 [3]; Judg. 3:1, 4; 2 Chron. 32:31; Job 7:18; Pss. 11:5; 26:2; Zech. 13:9). When humans test God, however, out of selfish, even malicious, motives, to try to force him to react according to their wishes, it is a serious sin, cited frequently in Scripture as a parade example of rebellion against God (Exod. 17:2, 7; Num. 14:22; Deut. 6:16; 33:18; Pss. 78:18, 41; 56; 95:9; 106:14; Isa. 7:12; Matt. 4:7 par; 1 Cor. 10:9; Heb. 3:9). The opportunity to sin against God in this very manner was one of the facets of Christ's wilderness temptation (Matt. 4:1–11 and par.) because to accede to it would have meant full rebellion against the Father.

One of the abstract meanings of הנב (lit., build) is "prosper" and here the third-person masculine plural niphal is used with just that nuance ("be built up" > "prosper"). גַּם בָּחֲנוּ אֱלֹהִים (even when they test God): בחן is the same verb used in 3:10, where God invites the people to test him. Here the testing of God is obviously sinful, however. For an explanation, see the Exposition. יִמָּלֵטוּ (they get away with it): Translations such as "they escape" do not capture the perfectly obvious meaning of the verb מלט in this context.

What, in fact, were the people of Malachi's day doing so as to be described as "testing God"? One can only assume that the charge covers a variety of overt, purposeful violations of the Mosaic law done openly and repeatedly, virtually with the attitude, "let's see what God will do about *that!*"

The feeling of the people who did not themselves do such things but saw others seemingly getting away with them is what verse 15 is describing. Serving God had no effect (v. 14) and neither did sinning boldly against him (v. 15). God seemed to be absent and unresponsive in either case.

VI. Sixth Disputation (3:13–21 [3:13–4:3])
C. The Faithful People of Malachi's Day Have a Covenant Renewal Ceremony (3:16–21 [3:16–4:3])

STUART

¹⁶Then those who feared Yahweh said to each other, "Yahweh has paid attention! He has listened!" A memorial scroll was written in his presence for those who feared Yahweh and honored his name. ¹⁷They will be (Yahweh of the Armies said), in the day when I act, my personal property. I will spare them, just as someone would spare his child who serves him. ¹⁸And you will again see the difference between the righteous and the wicked, between the person who serves God and the person who does not serve him ¹⁹For the day is coming, burning like a furnace [and it will consume them]. All the arrogant and every evildoer will be stubble, and the coming day will set them on fire (Yahweh of the Armies said). Of them not a root or a branch will be left. ²⁰But for you who revere my name, the sun of righteousness will rise with healing in its wings. And you will go out and jump around like well-fed calves! ²¹Then you will tread on the wicked; they will be ashes under the soles of your feet on the day when I act (Yahweh of the Armies said).

NRSV

¹⁶Then those who revered the LORD spoke with one another. The LORD took note and listened, and a book of remembrance was written before him of those who revered the LORD and thought on his name. ¹⁷They shall be mine, says the LORD of hosts, my special possession on the day when I act, and I will spare them as parents spare their children who serve them. ¹⁸Then once more you shall see the difference between the righteous and the wicked, between one who serves God and one who does not serve him.

4 See, the day is coming, burning like an oven, when all the arrogant and all evildoers will be stubble; the day that comes shall burn them up, says the LORD of hosts, so that it will leave them neither root nor branch. ²But for you who revere my name the sun of righteousness shall rise, with healing in its wings. You shall go out leaping like calves from the stall. ³And you shall tread down the wicked, for they will be ashes under the soles of your feet, on the day when I act, says the LORD of hosts.

16. אָז (then): For this word the Septuagint reads ταῦτα ("thus," or "these things"), as if the meaning of the verse were "Thus [i.e., the statements cited in vv. 14 and 15] spoke those who feared Yahweh to one another." Many commentators have accordingly emended the Masoretic Text אָז to זֶה or זֹאת (both meaning "this") on the assumption that some such word originally stood behind the Septuagint choice of ταῦτα (thus). But the emendation must be viewed as unwarranted for several reasons. First, the well-established rhetorical disputation format makes it unlikely. In the five prior disputations, what the people say at this same relative point in the disputation sequence is wrong and needs correction—it is *not* acceptable to God as the Septuagint translation would suggest. Second, there is the force of the immediate context of this sixth disputation, which promises the pious that they will see the distinction between the righteous and the wicked (v. 18)—hardly the same thing as approving the cynicism of verses 14 and 15. Third, there is the overall theology. How could the pious (those who feared God and honored his name, v. 16) possibly say something as outrageous as "serving God is useless" (v. 14)? Finally, there is the fact that in the Septuagint of the Minor Prophets, including Malachi, the translator(s) at dozens of points produced free, interpretive, and sometimes even expansionistic translations of the Hebrew *Vorlage*. In other words, while the Septuagint remains a crucial witness to the state of the Hebrew text sometime around 200 B.C., the translators themselves were not always perfect in their syntactic and lexical knowledge and occasionally produced translations that reflect more their subjective sense of how a sentence or verse ought to read than an accurate rendering. There is, in other words, good reason to think that the translator(s) of 3:16 simply assumed that the verse was identifying those who had spoken the words quoted in 3:14–15 and translated accordingly, essentially ignoring the usual force of אָז (then). נִדְבְּרוּ יִרְאֵי יְהוָה אִישׁ אֶת־רֵעֵהוּ (those who feared Yahweh said to one another): The grammar of this clause is ambiguous, because נִדְבְּרוּ (said) can be either transitive (as above in v. 13; see also Ps. 12:3; Ezek. 33:3) or intransitive. It could mean "spoke with one another" (intransi-

---

16. In the other disputations, Yahweh's speech is quoted at various points, but he is never the only speaker. In the case of this sixth and final disputation, likewise, other speakers are quoted, including the population whose words are quoted by Yahweh himself (vv. 14–15). Now in verse 16 the pious Jews, who disagree with the prevailing view that God is ineffective and inactive, are quoted. In other words, it is the faithful among Malachi's contemporaries who provide part of the "response" portion of this particular disputation. For their faithfulness they will receive divine commendation (v. 17) and eventual rescue from judgment (vv. 18ff.), even though at the moment they stand alone against the prevailing faithlessness of their generation.

What is their point? It is that the majority are utterly wrong. They assert, contrary to popular opinion, that Yahweh *has* paid attention and *has* heard. On what basis do they make their assertion? Though that basis is not stated in the passage, it can only be their faith in the nature of God. The question is not, of course, *Can* Yahweh pay attention and hear? That he can do so is not doubted by the majority who speak in verses 14 and 15, and would have seemed obvious enough to all Israelites, including those who may have been guilty of the practices condemned in the prior disputations. The question was, *Did* Yah-

weh pay attention and hear? The question has relevance because the terms "pay attention" (*qšb*) and "hear" (*šmꜥ*) do not refer in Hebrew only to auditory perception, but routinely carry also the nuance of "respond to" (for *qšb*, see 2 Chron. 33:10; Neh. 9:34; Jer. 6:19; 8:6; Zech. 1:4; for *šmꜥ*, see Gen 39:10; Exod. 3:7; Deut. 1:43; Ps. 6:9 [8]; Isa. 1:19; Zech. 1:4; 7:13). In other words, was God going to do anything about the arrogant, the evildoers, those who test him (v. 15)? Did it make any difference when people appealed to him in prayer for help (v. 14)? The answer was surely yes, and *how* he had chosen to respond is described in the verses ahead.

Meanwhile, the pious minority also had a response of their own. In an effort to show their resolve to be loyal to Yahweh in the face of the skeptical majority's lack of faith, they prepared a "memorial scroll." Almost surely this was a scroll that contained their names as signatories to some sort of statement of their commitment to Yahweh in faith that they were disassociating themselves from the prevailing sins, that his promises were reliable, and that his covenant was to be kept. In other words, it was a covenant renewal document.

We may assume that Malachi was also a signatory and could well have been the instigator of this enrollment. There are close parallels to such an undertaking in the immediate historical set-

tive) or simply "said" (transitive). If the verb דבר (niphal) is taken as transitive, אִישׁ אֶת־רֵעֵהוּ can mean "to one another" (compare Zech. 8:16). If it is construed as intransitive, the phrase means "with one another," as most modern English translations take it. Perhaps the most determinative factor is the use in verse 13 in a transitive manner. Of course, Malachi could have chosen to employ the verb a second time intransitively, in contrast to the first, but in the absence of any hint that he has done so, it is best to regard נִדְבְּרוּ as meaning "said." What, then, was said? וַיִּקְשֵׁב יְהוָה וַיִּשְׁמָע ("Yahweh has paid attention! He has listened!"): Instead of being a summation of Yahweh's response to the God-fearers' grumbling, this compound clause is in fact probably a quote of their affirmation that the general, popular mentality cited in verses 14 and 15 is wrong—God knows what's happening, and will respond as he sees fit. There is nothing in the particular grammatical construction (converted imperfect verb forms) that mitigates against taking these three words as an assertion. סֵפֶר זִכָּרוֹן (memorial scroll): While this exact phrase is found only here in the Old Testament, the Bible contains a great many lists and documents, as do the remains of ancient Near

Eastern literature, the function of which was to make sure that arrangements, lineages, contracts, promises, and the like—and the identity of those who made them—were not forgotten.

לְיִרְאֵי יְהוָה (for those who feared Yahweh): The preposition לְ (for) has a wide range of meanings, including "concerning," "about," "belonging to," "by," and "according to." Context must assign the specific meaning, and in this verse the context seems to be shaped substantially by the following verses, which speak of protection for those who feared God and did not adopt the prevailing attitude expressed in verses 14–15. Accordingly, לְ (for) would seem to have the sense of "for the benefit of." וּלְחֹשְׁבֵי שְׁמוֹ (and valued his name; lit., and for those valuing his name): On the meaning "value/honor/esteem" for חשׁב, see Isaiah 13:17; 33:8; and rabbinic Hebrew (e.g., *Berakot* 14a). Here it functions as a reinforcing synonym for the prior phrase ("those who feared Yahweh").

17. וְהָיוּ לִי (they will be mine): This wording (verb of being, expressed or understood, plus לְ) is the standard construction for ownership or possession in biblical Hebrew.

לַיּוֹם אֲשֶׁר אֲנִי עֹשֶׂה (on the day when I act): If the verb עשׂה (make, produce, etc.) is understood to be

---

ting. Ezra 10 records the list of Israelite men who had married foreign women, but who were willing to enter into a public confession of their guilt (v. 11) and to be formally identified by name (v. 16). The list itself (vv. 18–43) is almost surely an example of a memorial scroll, intended to make sure that the matter was not forgotten and not repeated. Nehemiah's list of returning exiles (Neh. 7:6–63) is probably another memorial scroll, compiled for the purpose of legitimizing their citizenship in the Judean temple community (7:64–65). Likewise, Nehemiah 10 provides a similar list, which recorded for perpetuity the names of the legitimate priests and Levites among the restoration community. But the most obvious parallel is found in Nehemiah 9–10, where a covenant renewal document containing a review of the faithfulness of God and a commitment to eschew sin is formally signed (10:1 [9:38]) by a large representative group (10:2–28 [10:1–27]) who promise to keep the Mosaic covenant in contrast to what had been the practice beforehand (10:29–40 [10:28–39]).

It is clear that Ezra and Nehemiah were the instigators of their respective scrolls of remembrance, and it is not difficult to imagine that Mal-

achi, or someone closely allied with him, was behind the memorial scroll mentioned here.

Many commentators have attempted to link the notion of the "memorial scroll" (*sēper zikkārôn*) in this verse with the concept of the "book of life" that appears in a variety of contexts in both Old Testament and New Testament. Their tendency to do so is predicated largely on the assumption that verse 16 says that "Yahweh listened and heard and a scroll of remembrance was written," as if Yahweh were the writer, or at least commissioner of the scroll and its content were mainly the names of the faithful whom he would later spare from his wrath. This is the main feature of the "book of life" concept in Scripture, which functions to reassure the faithful that they are enrolled in the census of the "living" and will have eternal life accordingly, whereas the names of the wicked will be erased from that census (Exod. 32:32–33; Ps. 69:29 [28]; 139:16; Isa. 4:3; 65:6; Ezek. 13:9; Luke 10:20; Phil. 4:3; Rev. 13:8; 17:8; 20:12). The more likely scenario in the case of Malachi 3:16, however, is that the people who are faithful set out to enlist themselves in a written covenant to trust and obey God in spite of what the majority of their contemporaries are doing.

transitive, the meaning would be "on the day I produce a personal possession." However, if עשה is taken to be intransitive, the meaning must be something like "on the day when I act," in which case the following word would not be its object but a predicate nominative corresponding to the subject of the verb at the beginning of the verse (lit., they will be for me ... personal property). Even though עשה is less commonly intransitive in the Hebrew Bible than transitive, usually meaning "to be busy" rather than "to act" in such cases, it can be either (and the parallel usage in v. 21 certainly confirms the meaning "act" here). Moreover, since the normal expression סגלה היה ל (to be a personal possession of; Exod. 19:5; Deut. 7:6; 14:2; 26:18) is clearly recognizable here, by process of elimination there is no other meaning possible for עשה than the intransitive (Hag. 2:4).

סגלה (personal property): This word is routinely mistranslated "treasured possession" or the like because of the natural tendency to want to describe God's people in a special, even romanticized way, but in fact it simply means personal property, the emphasis being on exclusive ownership rather than priceless value (Exod. 19:5; Deut. 7:6; 14:2; 26:18; 1 Chron. 29:3; Ps. 135:4; Eccles. 2:8). וְחָמַלְתִּי עֲלֵיהֶם can be translated "I will spare them" or "I will have mercy on them." Either translation would be acceptable in the context for the idiom חמל ל (spare/have mercy). כַּאֲשֶׁר יַחְמֹל אִישׁ (as someone would spare): The focus is not on a man as opposed to a woman or child, but on "a person." The translation "would spare" is one of several modal options always potentially better suited to translating the Hebrew imperfect than the simple indicative.

---

17. Now Yahweh speaks in turn, as the common messenger formula (Yahweh of the Armies said) makes abundantly clear. His words address two concerns raised earlier: the popular notion that he does nothing (vv. 14–15), and the idea of the righteous that they must remain faithful to him (v. 16). He reassures the faithful that they belong to him as his personal property (restoration blessing type 1, renewal of Yahweh's favor/loyalty/presence), and speaks of the coming day when he will "act." When the faithful see how they are spared like loyal members of the family, their resolve to serve him, in spite of the prevailing attitudes of their contemporaries, will have been rewarded. But the skeptics, and the arrogant and evildoers and those who admired them as mentioned in verse 15, will not be spared when that day comes.

While "day" (yôm) can be used rather generally in the sense of "time" as in English, it so often functions in the prophets as a metonymy for the Day of Yahweh that one must be prepared for that nuance of meaning to be present when the word yôm appears in the prophets. And here the implication that the Day of Yahweh is intended is in fact inescapable. Not only have Malachi's prior oracles focused in part on the Day of Yahweh, but verse 19 [4:1] of the present disputation uses the language of decisive divine intervention and judgment that commonly characterizes the day. And all the more obviously, verse 23 [4:5] employs unambiguously the phrase yôm yhwh (the Day of Yahweh). Of course, if one were to regard 3:23 [4:5] as part of a separate, con-

cluding oracle as many commentators do, this last argument is mitigated.

Malachi 3:17 threatens the wicked, mainly by implication, but provides overt hope for the righteous. It is not fruitless to keep Yahweh's covenant. It is not true that he never does anything. It is not correct that the arrogant are blessed and the evil prosper and those who test God get away with it—not forever, that is. While it may seem like God does not act swiftly (2 Peter 3:4), and though remaining faithful to him may seem to offer few rewards in this world, things will be very different when he chooses to act decisively. Then the reward of the righteous will come.

Will they merely escape the worst of his wrath, or perhaps merely fare somewhat better than those who have spurned the Lord? No, they will be spared like beloved children (restoration blessing type 10, freedom/restoration from death/destruction). The son who serves his father (or, more neutrally, the child who serves a parent) is twice beloved. He enjoys the love of the father automatically because he is his child, and beyond that he has pleased the father by faithful service. The father's favor is both natural and earned, both instinctive and merited.

This, of course, is analogical speech and not some sort of hidden metaphor for the way that faith and works together earn salvation. It is merely intended to show by comparison to a father's love for a human child specially appreciated and protected, how sure the faithful from among Malachi's contemporaries could be of their favor with God when he would act decisively in judgment on his Day. Yahweh had not

18. This verse employs standard, unambiguous Hebrew grammatical constructions. Some scholars, following the Septuagint, Peshitta, and Vulgate, have considered וְשַׁבְתֶּם (and you will again . . .) to be independent from what follows, and have translated it "and you will repent/return" or the like. It can certainly have such a meaning when occurring independently, but with the following converted perfect (וּרְאִיתֶם) almost surely means, in spite of the versions, "and you will again see" (i.e., שׁוּב plus finite verb form meaning "do x again"; see esp. Holladay, *Root Šûbh in the Old Testament*, pp. 66–72; GKC

§102d). בֵּין . . . לְ (between *x* and *y*; in this case, between the righteous and the wicked, between those who serve God and those who do not serve him): In the translation the word *difference* is supplied to fit the English idiom ("see the difference between" rather than "see between" as the Hebrew would be literally translated). צַדִּיק לְרָשָׁע (the righteous and the wicked): Both the Aramaic and the Syriac have the corresponding terms in the plural, a simple interpretive translation decision not affecting the reliability of the Masoretic Text.

---

failed to notice their loyalty. He had not overlooked their written covenant (v. 16), enacted in the face of considerable opposition and perhaps even ridicule (vv. 14 and 15). He knew his own.

18. God makes a reassuring promise to his faithful. What they have seen in the past, but cannot see now, will one day be evident again. Lying behind the words of this promise ("you will again see") is the assumption that the difference between the righteous and the wicked can, at least sometimes, be seen. The complaint of the people in verse 15, that it was not evident, is thus answered directly here.

But what exactly is meant? There are at least three options. One is that the faithful will sometime in their lifetimes again see a day in which righteous people are receiving rewards in this life for their faith and good deeds, and evil people are getting in trouble for their infidelity and misdeeds. By this understanding the verse promises what is sometimes called rigid prudentialism, the false concept that people get what they deserve already in this life, not to mention the life to come. Job's comforters held this view, and it was the basis for their inaccurate accusation that Job must have sinned greatly against God, since he would not otherwise have had such terrible things happen to him.

Another option for the meaning of this promise is that the faithful will learn how to tell the difference between the righteous and the wicked, even if the righteous do not fare better than the wicked. By this interpretation, the society in which the faithful live doesn't get better, but they at least live with the reassurance that it really does make a difference whether one is righteous or wicked, and this discernment sustains their faith until the next life, as they continue to live in an unfair world.

The third option, which I judge to be the actual point of the verse, is that it promises the coming of divine judgment. This is made all the more evident by the language of the following verse (3:19 [4:1]) but is also logically discernible from verse 18 alone, against the background of biblical theology. Scripturally, the "difference between the righteous and the wicked" is not a matter of how they appear to anyone or how they are understood by anyone, but how they are treated by God.

Ezekiel 18:9 contains a related assertion: "He follows my decrees and faithfully keeps my laws. That person is righteous; he will surely live." So does Psalm 1:5–6: "Therefore the wicked will not stand in the judgment . . . for Yahweh watches over the ways of the righteous but the way of the wicked will perish." These and many other Old Testament passages provide reassurance to the righteous that they will one day see the difference that their faithfulness to God has resulted in. The theme is a common one in the Old Testament precisely because it is often so hard in this world to detect any advantage to being righteous.

The verse also defines the terms *righteous* (ṣaddîq) and *wicked* (rāšāʿ) by reason of the corresponding explanatory synonyms, "the person who serves God" (= righteous) and "the person who does not serve him" (= wicked). To serve God is both to worship him and to live under and for his authority. Serving God was the purpose of the exodus (Exod. 7:16; 7:26 [8:1], 8:16 [20]; 9:1, 13; 10:3, 7–8, 11, 24, 26; 12:31; 23:25). It is the basic responsibility of those who bind themselves to God via Israelite covenant (Deut. 10:12, 20; 11:13; 13:5 [4]; Josh. 22:5; 24:14–15 *passim*; see also Jer. 30:9; Zeph. 3:9; Luke 4:8). Behind these terms lies a major theological truth, reflected often and in various ways throughout Scripture: the sole arbiter of right and wrong is God, and proper behavior is definable as believing his Word and doing his

19 [4:1]. הִנֵּה הַיּוֹם בָּא (for the day is coming): Many commentators have argued that the grammatical construction (הִנֵּה + participle) emphasizes immanence, as if Malachi believed that the relief predicted in these words for the righteous, as over against their critics and the wicked, was just around the corner. But this cannot be demonstrated. The only thing such a construction supports is the definiteness that the relief would be coming in the *indefinite* future. It is routine for the prophets to speak of "the day that is coming" or "the coming day," using various forms of יוֹם (day) and בָּא (come/coming) in their descriptions of Yahweh's future action, without indicating any specificity as to immediacy. בֹּעֵר כַּתַּנּוּר (burning like an oven): At this point the Septuagint adds καὶ φλέξει αὐτούς (and it will consume them). Did the Hebrew original read here וְכָלָה אֹתָם (and it will consume them), a clause that was lost via haplography? I think probably so, but we cannot tell for certain. Such a clause would parallel nicely the clause וְלִהַט אֹתָם (and it will set them on fire) that follows in the second half of the verse. There is much parallelistic prose present in the context, and the idea being expounded is the sure destruction of the wicked, which the missing clause comports convincingly with. On the other hand, it is always possible that the clause in question was added, either by the translator or a copyist, or by an earlier copyist in the Hebrew tradition of the *Vorlage* used by the Septuagint translator, instinctively or accidentally (e.g., as a doublet of וְלִהַט אֹתָם; and it will set them on fire). כָּל־זֵדִים (all the arrogant): Here the Septuagint (ἀλλογένοις, "[all the] strangers") clearly read זָרִים (foreigners) rather than זֵדִים (arrogant), a typical case of *reš-dalet* confusion, the most common type of orthographic confusion in Old Testament text criticism. While there are places in the prophets where foreigners are described as prohibited or unwelcome among

---

will. Any form or rebellion against him is sin, whether it be a matter or belief or performance, and, conversely, it is insufficient to believe in him without doing his will.

19 [4:1]. Fire imagery dominates this verse, introducing the topic of the Day of Yahweh, which is covered in verses 19–21 and again in verses 23–24 [4:5–6]. Fire language is commonly used in connection with divine judgment and anger (Gen. 19:24–28; Pss. 2:12; 89:47 [46]; Isa. 30:27; Jer. 4:4; 21:12; Amos 1:4, 7, 10, 12, 14, 2:2, 5; and frequently in the New Testament) although the use of the participle "burning" (*bōʿēr*) is unique to this passage. Destruction by fire is a type of covenant curse (type 10; Deut. 28:24; 32:22). The phrase "burn like a furnace" alludes to the hottest fires people in ancient times saw, the confined fires of the large beehive-shaped metal-working furnaces that were stocked with wood, ignited, and fanned as hot as possible for the smelting process. These furnaces had holes in the top for ventilating, out of which flames shot high into the air when the furnace was burning hotly (Dan. 3; Hos. 7:7). Malachi has already referred to the "refiner's fire" (3:2) as a metaphorical comparison to the cleansing God will bring about on the day, when the wicked will be eliminated.

"All the arrogant and every evildoer" is a hendiadys, not intended to differentiate in some way between the one and the other, but intended to refer comprehensively to all those who are in rebellion against God. In the continuing metaphor of the verse these are "stubble" (*qaš*), the dry, easily ignitible grain stocks, stubble, and chaff left from harvesting grain, and the day itself is a devouring fire. It will completely consume them, "root and branch" (in plant metaphor, a merism for "totally"; cf. Job 18:16; Ps. 80:9–12 [8–11]).

Thus the coming Day of the Lord will provide what the righteous have been hoping for: vindication of their faithfulness over against those who have consistently ignored and/or violated Yahweh's covenant (v. 15) and in the process "overruled" (v. 13) Israel's God. This verse indicates the fate of the wicked: annihilation. Nothing will be left of them (Isa. 10:20–34; Mic. 5:9–14 [10–15]; 7:13). The ancients noted that when fire burned something up, nothing was left of it. Thus fire functions fittingly in Scripture to depict total elimination.

In this regard, Malachi's prophecy sees the future after the Day of Yahweh in the same manner as do all the prophets. God's people in the restoration era will be a pure nation, cleansed of all iniquity and those who are iniquitous, righteous and blameless and in fully right relationship with their God (Isa. 2:11, 17; 12:4; 17:7; 27:9; 60:21; Jer. 23:5; 33:15; Zeph. 3:9). This is, of course, what the New Testament predicts as the outcome of the judgment that ensues from the second coming of Christ, the final Day of the Lord in Scripture (1 Cor. 5:5; 2 Cor. 1:14; 1 Thess. 5: 2; 2 Thess. 2:2; 2 Peter 3:10; see also Matt. 7:23; Rom. 2:9; 1 Cor. 6:9; 2 Thess. 2:10; 2 Peter 2:9). Thus the New Testament assigns to the eternal era following the return of Christ the full measure of the expecta-

God's people in the coming age (e.g., Ezek. 44:7–9; Joel 4:17 [3:17]) the context of this wording makes it almost certain that the Masoretic Text, not the Septuagint, is to be followed. The topic at hand is the differentiation between the righteous and the wicked, not the native and the stranger. אֲשֶׁר לֹא יַעֲזֹב לָהֶם שֹׁרֶשׁ וְעָנָף (of them not a root or branch will be left): The Septuagint's passive verb ὑπολειφθῇ would suggest the niphal pointing for the verb in the Hebrew clause (i.e., יֵעָזֵב). The English translation need not be affected, and the consonantal Masoretic Text is affirmed by either reading. For שֹׁרֶשׁ וְעָנָף (root nor branch) the Targum has the equivalent of "son nor grandson," an interpretive translation that does not warrant any question about the original wording of the text.

20 [4:2]. This verse is free of text problems. לָכֶם יִרְאֵי שְׁמִי (for you who fear my name): The obvious referent of "you" is the righteous faithful of verse 16, "those who feared the Lord," even though in verse 16 they are referred to in the third person, and not the critics and doubters of verses 13 and 14, even though these are initially referred to via second-person address. שֶׁמֶשׁ צְדָקָה (sun of righteousness): The Hebrew construct pattern could also be rendered "the righteous sun," but contextually the emphasis is not on the sun but on the righteousness (see the Exposition). כְּעֶגְלֵי מַרְבֵּק (like well-fed calves; lit., like bull calves of fattening): This is a well-understood expression in the Old Testament (1 Sam. 28:24; Jer. 46:21; Amos 6:4). However, the translations most often seen in

tion of uniform righteousness indicated here. What Malachi's faithful contemporaries longed for will be the same thing, and will happen at the same time, as what believers today long for. In other words, the Old Testament prophets were inspired to include under the notion of the Day of Yahweh a number of expectations that were fulfilled at various times, such as the fall of the north and the south in 722 and 586 respectively, the restoration that began with the decree of Cyrus in 539, the first coming of Christ, his second coming, and eternal life thereafter. (On the concept and how it functions in Scripture, see Stuart, "Sovereign's Day of Conquest.)

20 [4:2]. The comparison to jumping around like well-fed calves (not "calves released from the stall"; see the Exegesis) draws on a sight that most people in an agrarian society would have witnessed personally. Young bull calves love to run and leap, as part of the process of their muscle development, and their friskiness naturally suggests exuberance to the human observer. Fattened calves are especially healthy and strong (note that they are not "fat" but "fattened," that is, purposely farmer-fed rather than simply allowed to subsist on the land) and therefore run the fastest and jump the highest.

Verses 20–21 provide a description of the Day of Yahweh that is relatively positive, in contrast to most such passages in the prophets. Because Israel so often violated the Mosaic covenant and stood so far from the sort of righteousness that would allow her to be the beneficiary of God's grace, most prophetic passages concerning the Day speak of its negative consequences for Israel. The Day of Yahweh is routinely portrayed as a

time when God intervenes in the world to set things right and to punish evildoers, to punish his enemies and reward his allies. Thus if Israel is evil, she is his enemy, not his ally. Therefore, the prophets usually speak of the day in terms of gloom, darkness, destruction, and punishment for Israel, rather than the brightness, sunshine, healing, and joy that characterize much of verses 19–21 in the present passage. The popular belief among the people was that on the Day of Yahweh Israel would be rescued from all its foes by its national God, Yahweh, and exalted among the nations into an era of great prosperity. The prophets had the unpleasant task of trying to disabuse the people of this fatally naive notion and thus regularly employed language depicting the Day as a time of wrath and misery for Israel (Isa. 2:6–22; 13:6–9; Jer. 46:10; Ezek. 30:3; Joel 1:15; 2:1–11; 3:4 [2:31]; Amos 5:18–20; Obad. 15; Zeph. 1:7, 14; Zech. 14:1; Mal. 3:2–5, 23 [4:5]).

What makes this passage different? What justifies the more positive imagery in verses 20 and 21? The answer is that Malachi's focus is salvifically eschatological, referring to an entirely new and grand era, not merely a time a few years, or generations, ahead of his own. Christ confirms this by his identification of the new Elijah predicted in 3:23 [4:5] as John the Baptist (Matt. 11:14), not some prophet of Malachi's day or shortly thereafter. In other words, Malachi was here inspired to emphasize the christological, "gospel" side of the doctrine of the Day of the Lord, with its aspect of the Savior's coming to his people, as opposed to the judgment side of the doctrine, with its aspect of the elimination of evildoers, a theme he has already dealt with in 3:2–5.

English ("like calves released from the stall," etc.) are both grammatically unjustified and logically misleading. Even if מַרְבֵּק meant "stall," which it does not, the full expression would still not mean "calves *released from* the stall."

21 [4:3]. Again, the text appears to be well preserved. וְעַסּוֹתֶם (you will trample): This is a common verb for stepping on or mashing down with the feet (Joel 4:18 [3:18]; Isa. 63:2–6, where it applies to treading grapes in a winepress) and is here used metaphorically to indicate victory and sovereignty for the righteous over the wicked in

the providence of God. אֵפֶר (ashes): The metaphor is apt in light of the burning metaphors of verse 19. בַּיּוֹם אֲשֶׁר אֲנִי עֹשֶׂה (on the day when I act): Also possible is the translation, "On the day when I do this/it." I judge, however, that the wording is not so much concerned with reference to things mentioned thus far, but to the very fact of God's acting in all the great ways he will on the Day of the Lord. The meaning is thus more likely "when I make my move" than "when I do what I have just described."

The sunshine imagery of the verse, in sharp contrast to the "gloom" and "darkness" imagery employed in most Day of Yahweh passages in the prophets (see above), suggests the warmth, brightness, happiness, and well-being that will come to God's people when he intervenes on their behalf on his great Day. It is, of course, "those who fear/revere my name" rather than all the people (most of whom surely did not revere Yahweh's name) who will be the beneficiaries of God's blessing on that Day. To "fear" God's name (i.e., revere and obey him) is a concept that has already appeared several times in Malachi's prophecies (1:6, 11, 14; 2:2, 5; 3:16). The expression "the sun of righteousness with healing in its wings" (*šemeš ṣĕdāqâ ûmarpēʾ biknāpêha*) is also metaphorical. It refers to the picture of the sun rising, that is, the Day of Yahweh beginning, in a manner that brings righteousness (the result of the purification process described in v. 19) and also producing healing/well-being. The "wings" of the sun are its rays. The Egyptians depicted the sun as a disk with wings representing its rays (see *ANEP*, figs. 351, 531, 532, 536). The language here is consistent with Old Testament usage of "wing" to connote "edge" or "fringe" (see 2 Sam. 21:11=Ps. 18:10; Ps. 104:3; Hos. 4:19; Hag. 2:12; Zech. 8:23 et al.).

The actual emphasis of the verse is not on the sun, which functions only as a metaphor, but on God's granting righteousness (*ṣĕdāqâ*) to his faithful people. The imagery is not unlike that of Psalm 37:6 ("he will make your righteousness shine like the dawn, the justice of your cause like the noonday sun") or Isaiah 58:8 ("then your light will break forth like the dawn and your healing will quickly appear; then your righteousness will go before you, and the glory of the Lord will be your rear guard"). Both examples also involve direct address to people who are being promised the reception of divinely granted righteousness, just as in Malachi 3:20. Righteousness is a major

concept in the Bible, and within its semantic field are a number of English words and terms, including rightness, innocence, justification, good behavior, acceptance with God, salvation, and the like. In the present context I judge that the essential meaning of "righteousness" is something like "justification, acceptance, and salvation given by God." The faithful can look forward to complete vindication and the ongoing favor of God, in contrast to the destruction awaiting the wicked as described in verse 19.

How does the coming day bring healing and what exactly does it mean? Here I judge that the full sense of the term would be something like "restoration, peace, comfort, and rescue from misery" (i.e., restoration blessing type 6, restoration of general prosperity/well-being/health). The faithful among Malachi's contemporaries had suffered through the hard times of the mid-fifth century B.C. (3:9–11) and the arrogance of those who had thrown off the restraints of the Mosaic covenant (3:14–15). Healing (*rpʾ*) is sometimes used in the Old Testament as a synonym for forgiveness and salvation (Jer. 17:14), sometimes as a synonym for restoration to divine favor (Isa 53:5), and yet other times as a synonym for reception of divine favor in general (Ps. 6:3 [2]). The coming day brings such healing because of the One who comes then—the same one already mentioned in 3:1, the messenger of the covenant, the Messiah.

21 [4:3]. This verse concludes the encouraging description of the Day of the Lord in verses 19–21, making two simple points followed by Malachi's typical messenger formula "Yahweh of the Armies said" (*ʾāmar yhwh ṣĕbāʾôt*). The two points are: (1) the faithful will prevail and the wicked will be eliminated; (2) this will happen when the Day of Yahweh comes ("on the day when I act"). The promise to the faithful is not that they will be the agents of annihilation of the wicked. That is, "you will trample on the wicked" is not a call for the righteous to exterminate the ungodly. Rather, God will already have accomplished this by his Day, which will have burned (in the dominant metaphor of this part of the passage) the wicked to ashes, again following the logic of curse type 10, destruction by fire (Deut. 28:24; 32:22). What the righteous will tread on is the ashes of the already dead wicked, not live persons who are to be killed by trampling. The restoration blessing type alluded to here is type 9, power over enemies/aliens. The verse employs the language of eschatological divine judgment, in which the wicked are exterminated with nothing left of them (the second death of Rev. 20–21) and the righteous are rewarded forever with the joy of the Lord.

VII. Concluding Summary (3:22–24 [4:4–6])
A. The People Are Exhorted to Remember the Law of Moses (3:22 [4:4])

STUART

22Remember the law of my servant Moses, the statutes and laws I commanded him at Horeb for all Israel.

NRSV

4Remember the teaching of my servant Moses, the statutes and ordinances that I commanded him at Horeb for all Israel.

22 [4:4]. צִוִּיתִי אוֹתוֹ . . . חֻקִּים וּמִשְׁפָּטִים (the statutes and laws I commanded him): This double accusative structure is not unusual in itself, but its use in combination with עַל (for [all Israel]) is paralleled only by 1 Chronicles 22:13. More typically, double-accusative constructions that go on to speak of something done "for" someone employ אֶל rather than עַל (as in Exod. 25:22; Lev. 27:34; Deut. 1:3). The meaning is clear in any case. כָּל־יִשְׂרָאֵל (all Israel): This term is more often than not used as a synecdoche to mean "representatives from all Israel" or "a full range of Israelites"

22–24 [4:4–6]. Many scholars have argued that verses 22–24 are not part of the sixth disputation but a late appendage (or two late appendages) to the book. One common view is that these verses reflect concerns of the Hellenistic era, when obedience to the law of Moses had once again waned after the reforms of Ezra and Nehemiah had run their course. Some have tried to demonstrate on stylistic grounds that these verses are not genuine to Malachi (lack of messenger formulas, slightly different terminology for the law than is found in 2:8–9 or 3:9); others opine that the conflict between parents and children referred to in verse 24 refers to the abandonment of Jewish traditions in the wake of Hellenistic thought and custom. These arguments are all weak and founded almost purely on speculation and tenuous inference.

In fact, the themes of these verses are entirely consistent with those of the book as a whole, as well as with the sixth disputation. For example, with regard to the description of Moses as "my servant" in verse 22, compare "servant" (ʿebed) in 1:6 and "serves" (ʿōbēd) in 3:18. And, of course, the need to keep the "law" (tôrâ) in verse 22 is already the subject of 2:6–9. The prediction "Behold, I am going to send you Elijah the prophet" (hinnēh ʾānōkî šōlēaḥ lākem ʾēt ʾēlîyâ hannābîʾ) in verse 23 is remarkably similar to the promise of 3:1, "Behold I am going to send my messenger" (hinnî šōlēaḥ malʾākî). The concept of the Day of Yahweh in verse 23 is well reflected in the book already in 3:2 and 19–21 [4:1–3]. The emphasis on its "coming" (bōʾ) here and in verse 24 [4:6] is already known from verse 19 (see also 3:1–2). The theme of parents and children in verse 24 is parallel to that in 1:6, and the theme of honoring the ways of parents to the language of 2:10. The risk of a curse (verse 24) echoes 1:5, 14; 2:2; and 3:8–12. Linguistically and theologically, 3:22–24 [4:4–6] is part and parcel of Malachi's prophecies.

Perhaps the most obvious consideration in favor of the authenticity of 3:22–24 [4:4–6] as part of the sixth disputation is its similarity to the fourth disputation (2:17–3:5). In both cases the final part of the four-element structure, the implication section, is dominant in terms of the allotment of space. In the same way that 2:17 covers the assertion, questioning, and response in the fourth disputation and the remainder of that disputation is the implication, here in the sixth disputation 3:13–15 covers the first three parts and 3:16–24 is a (comparably long) implication section. Both implication sections are concerned with what will happen to the wicked and the righteous in the future. Both predict the Day of the Lord, and see it as bringing the unrighteousness that concerns the faithful to an end, and ushering in a time of righteous faithfulness to Yahweh. Both predict the elimination of the wicked by divine action and the reward of those who have been faithful to the covenant. Both look forward to a divinely commissioned messenger who will call for repentance. And both provide an encouraging picture of the future—once the Day of Yahweh comes—for those who remain loyal to God.

Naturally, the fourth and sixth disputations are not identical and the awareness of their similarities ought not to be allowed to obscure their many distinct and individual characteristics. The point of my comparison is simply to demonstrate that there is nothing about the way that 3:13–24 [3:13–4:6] is structured, and nothing about its essential content, that should lead us to conclude that it is composite rather than a single, unified disputation of a type already present in the book. The fact that verse 22 [4:4] urges, with broad intent, the keeping of the law of Moses, or that verses 23–24 [4:5–6] call for broad-scale reconciliation to revealed truth in no way disqualify them from functioning as a proper ending for the sixth disputation. There are no convincing grounds for seeing the last three verses of the book as a separate pericope imposed either at a later date or outside of the normal disputational structure found elsewhere in Malachi's oracles.

22 [4:4]. Everything that the people and priests had been doing that displeased God and that was the subject of Malachi's excoriations earlier in the book could be summed up as refusal to honor the Mosaic covenant. Thus the command to "remember the law of Moses." What was the problem? Was the law of Moses too new for the people to have learned it? Not at all. It had been around since Sinai, since the Israelites gathered there after the exodus from Egypt in 1440 B.C. Mount

or "all the Israelite soldiers" (Josh. 7:24–25; 8:21; 1 Sam. 17:11; 28:4; 2 Sam. 10:17; 1 Kings 11:16; 21:1; etc.) but here it carries its more inclusive meaning of "everyone in the people of Israel" (Exod. 18:25; Deut. 13:12 [11]; Josh. 3:17; 1 Sam. 3:20; 2 Sam. 8:15; 1 Kings 4:1; Ezra 8:35; etc.). In Deuteronomy 29:14–15, the entire covenant people, whether or not they were physically present for the covenant-making ceremony, are called "all Israel" just as in the present verse. חֻקִּים וּמִשְׁפָּטִים (statutes and laws): This common hendiadys composed of two synonyms denotes the full corpus of the Mosaic covenant (Deut. 4:8, 44–45; Neh. 10:30 [29]; etc.). In the Septuagint tradition, verse 22 [4:4] was sometimes placed after verse 24 [4:6] so that it concluded the book. There is a strong possibility that this placement may have been original to the Septuagint, but there is no way to determine if verse 22 [4:4] was ever in the final position in the book in the Hebrew tradition. The order of the final verses may have been adjusted by a Septuagint translator or copyist in order to make the book end on a more positive note (rather than with a curse threat) or on a more comprehensive theme (that of keeping the law, a most basic notion in Judaism), but we simply cannot be sure. The wording of the verse itself is free of textual difficulty.

Horeb is simply an alternate name for Mount Sinai. Horeb means "wilderness/wasteland," emphasizing the geographical nature of the area where the mountain was located, whereas Sinai means "the one in Sin," referring to the name of the peninsula where the mountain was located. Since "Horeb" is found mostly in Deuteronomy it is often assigned by source critics to the so-called D source in the Pentateuch. However, it is also found in Exodus 3:1; 17:6; 33:6, where it is then assigned usually to the so-called E source. In fact, "Horeb" and "Sinai" are also found in a range of Old Testament poetry that is clearly old, and distinctions on the basis of source in Malachi are entirely speculative. Malachi clearly knows the entire Pentateuch, not merely the supposed D portions thereof.

The call of verse 22 [4:4] is for renewal of obedience to the covenant of God. Three synonyms are used to refer to the covenant. The first is "law" (tôrâ). It is to be "remembered" (i.e., obeyed—the problem was not that it had been lost to memory, but ignored) and thus the verb "remember" (zkr) is employed here in one of its usual meanings, "to heed, pay attention to, be mindful of."

The second and third are "statutes" (ḥuqqîm) and "commandments" (mišpāṭîm). The repetition of these terms is a means of underscoring the task at hand; there is no particular distinction among them in the context.

All Israel had agreed to obey the law at Mount Horeb. All Israel—not just some of Malachi's audience—needed to agree to obey it once again. That is the message Malachi has been preaching all along, and it is what he now once again reiterates as the sum of his message and the conclusion of his sixth disputation.

VII. Concluding Summary (3:22–24 [4:4–6])

B. The People Receive a Promise of Elijah and a Warning of Destruction (3:23–24 [4:5–6])

STUART

²³Behold, I am going to send you the prophet Elijah before the coming of the great and fearsome Day of Yahweh.

²⁴He will restore the loyalty of parents to children and the loyalty of children to their parents; or else when I come I will strike the land with destruction.

NRSV

⁵Lo, I will send you the prophet Elijah before the great and terrible Day of the Lord comes. ⁶And he will turn the hearts of parents to their children and the hearts of children to their parents, so that I will not come and strike the land with a curse.

23 [4:5]. This verse is also textually and grammatically trouble-free. הִנֵּה אָנֹכִי שֹׁלֵחַ (behold, I am sending you) is a simple way of stating the future, and is not, as some commentators have tried to suggest, a grammatical construction that implies that the event will take place soon *(futurum instans)*. הִנֵּה (behold) plus the participle *may* indicate that something is just about to happen, but does not automatically do so. The fact that the verse uses the pronoun אָנֹכִי (I) here instead of Malachi's more usual pronoun for "I" (אֲנִי) has been taken by many critics as evidence that 3:22–24 [4:4–6] is not from Malachi but from a later source. Since both אֲנִי and אָנֹכִי were used widely in biblical Hebrew for the first-person singular pronoun, it is difficult to imagine that scholars would actually attempt to differentiate literary sources on the basis of which of the two was used in any given place. Glazier-McDonald has demonstrated

the absurdity of using the pronouns as source indicators by pointing out that Hosea, Jonah, Jeremiah, Isaiah, Ezekiel, and Amos use both pronouns. (Hos. 3:3; 4:6; 5:2–3, 12, 14; 7:15; 10:11; 13:5; 14:9 [8] use אֲנִי, while Hos. 1:9; 2:4 [2], 10 [8]; 5:14; 7:13; 11:3; 12:10–11; 13:4 use אָנֹכִי). Notably, Ezekiel uses אֲנִי typically, but אָנֹכִי once (36:28), a situation virtually exactly parallel to that in Malachi. Amos does the opposite—using אָנֹכִי regularly and אֲנִי only once (4:6). Thus we see that some prophets use one of the two first-person pronouns exclusively, some use both commonly, and others use one mostly and the other rarely. Obviously, no inference about sources can be drawn from such usage patterns. אֵלִיָּה (Elijah): This is the apocopated form of the name also found in 2 Kings 1:3–4, 8, 12; 1 Chronicles 8:27; Ezra 10:21, 26. The fuller form אֵלִיָּהוּ predominates somewhat in 1 and 2 Kings. בּוֹא יוֹם יְהוָה (the coming of the [great and

---

23 [4:5]. There is no doubt who is speaking here. It is the Lord himself (see the Exegesis) speaking through his prophetic messenger. He tells the people that he will send the prophet Elijah as a predecessor to the Day of the Lord. This promise raises several questions, at least theoretically: (1) Why send Elijah, rather than, say, Moses, Abraham, David, or an unspecified prophet? (2) How is it possible to send a past prophet, long dead, to introduce a future event? Elijah lived in the early ninth century B.C. Malachi preached in the mid-fifth century B.C. The predicted Day of Yahweh would follow sometime in the indefinite future. (3) Was Elijah to appear from heaven or be resurrected? Or reincarnated? (4) Why would anyone need to be sent at all? The other prophetic predictions of the Day of Yahweh do not include such as specification. (5) Is this "prophet Elijah" the same Elijah of 1–2 Kings, or should we understand the prediction to refer to "a new Elijah" or "an Elijah-like prophet"? In other words, is "the prophet Elijah" used metaphorically or literally? All these questions were raised historically, and their answers were not obvious even to Jesus' disciples until he clearly identified John the Baptist as the referent for this prediction (Matt. 11:14).

In response to these questions, the following observations may be made. First, the function of the prophet would be to sound a warning. This is a matter of divine grace. The Day of Yahweh would represent doom to all evildoers, as 3:1–5, 19–21 [4:1–3] indicates. Therefore, advance warning would allow for repentance, so that those who turned from sin might be forgiven and spared in

the Day of the Lord's judgment. This is exactly what John the Baptist did, of course. He preached the need for repentance in order to be accepted into the kingdom of God (Matt. 3:2; see also Acts 19:4). Second, the person of Elijah provides an ideal model or paradigm for such a herald, since Elijah fearlessly proclaimed the need for repentance (1 Kings 18:37; on the vocabulary connection with the present passage, see the Exposition of v. 24 [4:6]) at a time when the vast majority of Israel was straying from true belief and practice (1 Kings 19:14–18). Third, Elijah was notorious for being stubbornly faithful in proclaiming the Word of God when all other orthodox Yahwistic prophets had gone into hiding (1 Kings 18:3–14). In this regard he was, like John the Baptist, a lone voice. Fourth, he was a person outside the power structure of his society, even to the extent of living much of the time in the wilderness (1 Kings 17:2–6). Finally, and most important, he was a covenant messenger, preaching the law of Moses to a nation (northern Israel) that had drifted far from it (1 Kings 17:24; 18:36; 19:10).

Thus, Moses and Elijah were remembered as two key figures in faithfulness to God's Word, and it is no accident that they are both mentioned here in verses 22–24 [4:4–6], just as it is no accident that they were present at Christ's transfiguration (Matt. 17:3–4). It was at the transfiguration that conversation turned to the very question of these verses from Malachi, when the disciples asked, "Why then do the teachers of the law say that Elijah must come first?" (Matt. 17:10). Jesus' reply (17:11–13) reiterates that John the Baptist

fearsome] Day of Yahweh): The proximity and contextual connection of this infinitive of בֹּא (come) and the first-person imperfect form of the same verb אָבוֹא (I will come) in verse 24 [4:6] makes it very clear that it is Yahweh himself who plans to come on the Day of Yahweh and to send the new Elijah as his precursor. See the Exposition on the implications of this for Christology. הַגָּדוֹל וְהַנּוֹרָא (great and fearsome): This adjectival hendiadys is a combination well attested in the Old Testament, referring often to God himself (Deut. 7:21; Neh. 1:5; 4:8 [14]; Ps. 89:8 [7]; Dan. 9:4) or to his deeds (Deut. 10:21; 2 Sam. 7:23; 1 Chron. 17:21) or his name (Ps. 99:3). It is not, contrary to some commentators, a specifically "deuteronomic" expression. The combination is also used to describe the wilderness of Sinai in Deuteronomy 1:19 and 8:15, and the deeds of Moses in Deuteronomy 34:12. It modifies the Day of the Lord one other time in Joel 2:31. Always the meaning is related to beings or things that are so impressive as to be overwhelming.

24 [4:6]. וְהֵשִׁיב לֵב־אָבוֹת עַל־בָּנִים (he will restore the loyalty of parents as well as children): This

expression (and its counterpart in the next clause) does not have an exact parallel in the Old Testament, but its meaning ought not to be difficult to deduce. הֵשִׁיב, the hiphil of שׁוּב (turn), routinely means "restore" or "bring back," and לֵב (heart) often has the connotation of "affection," "loyalty," "care," and the like. Thus Holladay (*Root Šûbh in the Old Testament*, p. 99) renders the idiom as "bring back someone's loyalty." What exactly is meant? The idiomatic expression is obviously somewhat elliptical, as most idiomatic expressions are, but in all probability it means not "to unite the generations in thinking and acting along the same lines," but rather "to get everyone—not just some of the people—converted back to God." On the well-attested meaning of "in addition to/as well as" for עַל, see Genesis 28:9, Deuteronomy 19:9, and Jeremiah 4:20. Implied, but not stated overtly, is that the conversion would represent restored fidelity to the will of God. See also the Exposition. פֶּן אָבוֹא וְהִכֵּתִי (or else when I come I will strike): The beginning of this final clause in Malachi is usually translated "or else I will come and strike," as if a lack of repen-

---

was the predicted metaphorical "Elijah," rather than that Elijah the Tishbite had actually come earlier in the flesh. A special contribution of the Book of Malachi, then, to the explication of redemptive history is its emphasis on a forerunner of the Day of Yahweh (the coming of Christ) in 3:1, 23 [4:5]. John the Baptist was that forerunner, who came "before the Lord, in the spirit and power of Elijah, to turn the hearts of the fathers to their children and the disobedient to the wisdom of the righteous—to make ready a people prepared for the Lord" (Luke 1:17). Since the majority of Jesus' first followers and disciples came from John's followers and disciples, John had indeed fulfilled the predictions of Malachi. He was thus "Elijah who was to come" (Matt 11:14) or as we might more typically say it in modern English "another Elijah" or "a new Elijah." John's role was part of the work of God's saving grace in the world. People were to be given a chance to repent. They were to be given time to come to their senses and become right with God.

24 [4:6]. This final verse in the book links conversion and salvation. As for conversion, this is what the words about restoring "the parents as well as children and children as well as their parents" (lit., I will bring back the hearts of parents on top of children) are concerned with. Malachi's preaching is not merely calling for some sort of

generational or family closeness, but for unified obedience to the faith on the part of everyone. Although the object of this conversion is not specified in the verse, it is quite obvious contextually that the object is faith in God. Elijah was famous for his effectiveness in the process of converting the Israelites of his day back to faith in the true God, Yahweh (1 Kings 18:37). The new Elijah would be sent by God to do the same thing in the future. Parents (*ʾābôt*) and children (*bānîm*) here function in a well-paralleled fashion as a merism meaning "everybody" (Jer. 6:12; 13:14; Ezek. 5:10; Joel 3:1 [2:28]; Matt. 10:21).

As for salvation, this is what the closing clause ("lest when I come I strike the earth with destruction") addresses. The clause provides a clear warning of destruction (a combination of curse type 24, death/destruction, with curse type 9c, desolation of the land; see Lev. 26:32, "I will lay waste the land" and Lev. 26:33, "Your land will be laid waste"; see also Lev. 26:34–35, 43; Deut. 28:51; 29:22 [23]) But because this warning is about a covenant punishment that is escapable ("lest when I come I strike") it also represents an invitation to salvation. The coming of God to his people is what produces the events associated with the Day of Yahweh, a day that brings salvation to his allies and defeat to his foes. Throughout Scripture, God's presence is a reward to the righteous and a

tance on the part of the people at the preaching of "Elijah" might mean that the Lord would not choose to come at all (if they repent, he doesn't come; if they don't repent, he comes and strikes). The construction (פֶּן + imperfect + converted perfect) is admittedly somewhat ambiguous. It can mean either "lest I come and strike" or "lest in coming I strike." In the context, however, the lat-

ter is surely the intended sense. On similar usages of פֶּן with more than one following verb, see Deuteronomy 8:11–14; 25:3; Psalm 28:1; Proverbs 25:10, 16. חֵרֶם (destruction): This Hebrew word means "destruction," "elimination," and "ban," yet has usually been translated in Malachi 2:24 [4:6] by the English word "curse," which is not actually within its semantic range.

danger to the unrighteous. "When I come" clearly speaks of the Lord, and thus the one whom the forerunner Elijah precedes is God. Whom did John the Baptist precede? Jesus of Nazareth. Does this passage by implication suggest that Jesus of Nazareth was "Yahweh," Israel's God? Yes, it does. If one believes that Malachi's Elijah announces the coming of Yahweh and that John the Baptist was that Elijah, the one whose coming he announced was, by inference, Yahweh. The ubiquitous reference to Jesus as *kyrios* (Lord) in the New Testament and the several overt New Testament confessions that "Christ is Lord" (Phil. 2:11) certainly rest upon an identification of Jesus with the Lord of the Old Testament.

The central question before Malachi's audience, and still before the modern reader of these last words of the book, is posed by Christ in Luke 18:8: "However, when the son of man comes, will he find faith on the earth?" If he finds faith (the hearts of old and young alike converted to God),

there will be no need for destruction. If he does not, destruction will be the inevitable consequence. But which coming of Christ was Malachi's prediction of the new Elijah intended to presage—the first or the second? The answer is both. The New Testament clearly views both comings as the Day of Yahweh, since they both bring about bring about the combination of salvation and judgment that the concept of the Day entails (on the Day as the first coming, see Luke 1:78; 4:21; John 8:56; Acts 2:20; on the Day as the second coming, 1 Cor. 5:5; 2 Cor. 1:14; 1 Thess. 5:2; 2 Thess. 2:2; 2 Peter 3:10).

Thus John the Baptist's work as the predicted Elijah heralded both comings of the Lord, and his message (repent for the kingdom of God is near) is just as applicable today, prior to the second coming of the Lord, as it was in the first century, prior to the first coming of the Lord. Malachi 3:24 [4:6] speaks of a basic reality that still should arouse and inspire the hearts of believers everywhere.

Scripture Index

Genesis

1:2—923
1:3—932
1:5—1041
1:7—1292
1:11—1147
1:20-31—911
1:22—976
1:26-27—982
1:28—942, 1172
1:29-30—1176
1:30—1195
1:31—922
2:5—997
2:9—1320
2:16—942
2:17—917, 1320
2:19—1100
3:5—1334
3:8—1174
3:14-19—912
3:15—1147
3:16-19—911
3:17—1030, 1121
3:17-19—937
4:2—954
4:3-7—1355
4:4—1156, 1162
4:19—1338
4:25—998
4:26—951, 1041
6:1—1127
6:2—1333
6:4—1333
6:8—1088, 1139
6:11—920, 943
6:13—911, 920, 943
6:14—928
6:17—1067
6:19—1067
7:3—1095, 1147
7:11-12—1370
7:21—1067
7:21-33—911
7:23—1053, 1144
8:15—1027
8:21—951
8:22—1147
9:2—977
9:3—1176
9:5—1132
9:6—1343
9:11—998
9:15—1183

9:16—1355
9:25—932
10:2—1171
10:5—936, 1080
10:6—936
11:1-9—951, 951
11:4—951
11:8-9—951
11:9—1095
11:31—911
12:1—1030
12:2—961, 1148
12:3—960, 1064, 1121, 1156
12:5—932
12:6—1237
12:7—953, 1172, 1184
12:8—951
12:16—1167
12:19—1112
13:12-15—932
13:14-15—932, 939
13:17—1010
15:1—1145
15:1-6—953
15:2—934
15:5—953, 1053, 1185
15:5-6—1137
15:7-10—1170
15:9-18—988
15:13—961, 1047
15:13-21—953
15:14—1369
15:17—1211
15:17-21—1044
15:18—1185
16:4—1139
16:5—943, 1139
16:6—1139
16:7-14—1350
16:11—1038, 1041
16:12—1159
16:13—1038
17:1—942
17:3—1151
17:5-6—1053
17:7—1064, 1065, 1170, 1317
17:7-8—1141, 1181
17:8—1142
17:20—1369
17:22—1151
18:3—1139
18:14—1139
18:18—1369

18:20—1361
18:21—924
18:25—911
18:28—1170
19—1001
19:2—1138
19:3—1098
19:19—1058, 1131
19:24-28—1386
19:25—951, 1078
19:29—951
19:35—1051
19:36-38—931
19:37-38—933
20:5—1132, 1156, 1162
20:9—1358
21—1337
21:1—919, 1179
21:12—1077
21:13—1369
21:14—1343
21:17-21—1350
21:18—1369
21:23—913
21:29—1036
21:31—1096
22:1—1379
22:1-18—1350
22:3—947
22:13—935
22:16—934, 1043, 1098
22:17—1053, 1058, 1170, 1174
22:17-18—953, 1121
22:18—951, 960
23:2—1127, 1214
23:6—978
23:8—997
24:11—974
24:27—1130
24:37-40—1332
24:41—1095
24:44—1074
24:48—1130
24:49—1135
24:51—1112
24:61—1034
25:19-34—1284
25:21—951
25:22—913
25:25—1221
25:29—995
25:30—1034

26—1337
26:3—1096
26:5—1073
26:18—1095
26:28—1095
27—1284
27:3—1112
27:4—997
27:28—1174
27:31—1156
27:34—1156
27:37—1174
27:44—1137
27:46—1332, 1333
28:1—1332
28:6—1332
28:9—1395
28:21—1141
29:7—974
29:20—958
29:30-33—1283
29:32—1064
29:32-35—912
29:34—1064
29:35—1041
30:3—1156
30:18—1042
30:23—960
30:28—1145
30:37—1194
31—1337
31:19—1176
31:24—921
31:30—927
31:34-35—1176
31:37—1337
31:38—1039
31:39—1308
31:40—978
31:41—1039
31:44-54—1337
31:50—1337
32:16—1337
32:22—1098
32:32—961
33:5—1088
33:8—1088
33:17—1177
34:8—1151
34:29—922
34:31—961
35:2—1176
36—1312
36:8—1285
37:3—958

37:17—1177
37:20—1100
37:22—1199
37:24—1170
37:26—1378
37:35—1044
38:7—1139
38:18—1002
38:25—1002
39:9—1358
39:10—1382
39:16—1103
40:14—1131
41:16—1027
41:35—1160
41:49—1160
41:56—1095
42:6—1221
42:16—1131
42:33—1112
42:35—1092
43:6—1148
43:7—1048
43:30—912, 1043
43:34—977
44:5—1148
44:15—1092
45:3—924
45:7—933
45:8—1035
45:11—1205
46:3—1369
46:29—1205
46:31—1144
47:8—1051, 1125
47:27—1183
47:28—1183
49:4—943
49:6—1195
49:8-10—912
49:11—1167
49:15—951, 1194
49:26—1290, 1355
49:27—948
50:5—933
50:10—1127
50:17—953

Exodus

1:7—1183
1:9—1156
1:12—1183
1:20—1183
2:6—1053